ENCYCLOPEDIA OF ASIAN THEATRE

ENCYCLOPEDIA OF ASIAN THEATRE

Volume 2: O–Z

Edited by
SAMUEL L. LEITER

GREENWOOD PRESS
Westport, Connecticut • London

Library of Congress Cataloging-in-Publication Data

Encyclopedia of Asian theatre / edited by Samuel L. Leiter.
    p. cm.
  Includes bibliographical references and index.
   ISBN 0-313-33529-X (set : alk. paper)—ISBN 0-313-33530-3 (vol 1 : alk. paper)—
ISBN 0-313-33531-1 (vol 2 : alk. paper) 1. Theater—Asia—Encyclopedias. 2. Performing arts—
Asia—Encyclopedias. 3. Oriental drama—Encyclopedias. I. Leiter, Samuel L.
PN2860.E53 2007
792.095—dc22   2006031211

British Library Cataloguing in Publication Data is available.

Library of Congress Catalog Card Number: 2006031211
ISBN: 0-313-33529-X (set)
      0-313-33530-3 (vol. 1)
      0-313-33531-1 (vol. 2)

First published in 2007

Greenwood Press, 88 Post Road West, Westport, CT 06881
An imprint of Greenwood Publishing Group, Inc.
www.greenwood.com

Printed in the United States of America

The paper used in this book complies with the
Permanent Paper Standard issued by the National
Information Standards Organization (Z39.48–1984).

10 9 8 7 6 5 4 3 2 1

The index for these volumes was compiled at the publisher's discretion.

CONTENTS

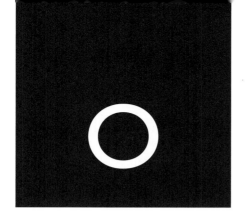

OGWANDAE. Southeast **Korean • masked • dance**-drama, with differing versions in municipalities such as Chinju, Kasan, and T'ongyŏng along the southern coast. *Ogwangdae* literally means "five performers," but some historians refer to the five directions, elements, and colors of **Chinese** cosmology.

Legend says that villagers in the town of Pammari pulled a chest of masks from the Nakdong River. Though reluctant at first to touch them, the villagers nevertheless felt called to perform a masked dance-drama. This early *Ogwangdae* soon spread, performed to ensure a plentiful harvest, bountiful fishing, and safety.

All dramas have five acts, but each version requires a different number of characters. The *ogwangdae* of Kasan uses about two dozen masks, the T'ongyŏng *ogwangdae* nine. In Kasan, the most important masks are for the five Imperial General deities that represent the five directions, each differentiated by **costume** and mask color. For example, the Imperial General of the Center wears yellow, the Imperial General of the East, blue. In variant forms, papier-maché masks are painted with symbolic colors, for example, red for the south where the sun is strongest, and black for the north.

Ogwangdae combines dance, pantomime, and satirical dialogue, all accompanied by **music**. There is a lion dance, but the most important dance is the *dotboegi-ch'um*, danced to a six-beat rhythm played by a small gong and typified by an abrupt pose after a series of vigorous movements, followed by slow steps. *Ogwangdae* remains popular, and the government has designated T'ongyŏng *ogwangdae* an Important Cultural Property.

FURTHER READING

Cho, Oh-Kon, trans. *Traditional Korean Theatre*.

Oh-Kon Cho

OHASHI YASUHIKO (1956–). Japanese **• playwright, director**, and **scenographic** designer. Although best known for his signature play, the **Kishida [Kunio]** Prize–winning *Godzilla* (Gojira, 1987), Ohashi has written more than forty plays since the early 1980s. He is a member of the fourth generation of post-1960 playwrights and has been significantly influenced by **Tsuka Kôhei**, with whose work many of his plays form "intertexts."

Ohashi came to theatre indirectly, having studied electrical engineering at Musashi Institute of Technology, which contributed to his effect-driven dramaturgy, replete with elaborate visuals. His technical background also drives Ohashi to write not from a particularly aesthetic or word-based motivation but from a desire to transform theatrical space to do what has not been done there before. This penchant for technical spectacle, bolstered by his take on popular culture, has ensured Ohashi's popularity with younger audiences.

In 1983, Ohashi, with Itô Yumiko (1959–) and others, formed the Freedom Boat Company (Gekidan Riburesen), whose name suggests the themes of both voyage and freedom, artistic and otherwise. *Godzilla* features the titular monster meeting the family of the young (human) girl he hopes to marry and the family's rejection of him as a son-in-law, an amusing satire on contemporary Japanese values. In addition to their humor and technical savvy, his works evince playfulness and innocence. Other major works include *The Red Bird Has Fled* (Akai tori nigeta, 1986), about the 1985 Japan Airlines crash that killed 520 people, and *Subjection* (Sabujekushon, 2002).

Kevin J. Wetmore, Jr.

OH T'AE-SŎK (1940–). Korean • **playwright, director, theorist**, and founder of the Raw Cotton Repertory Theatre Company (Mokhwa, 1984). Born in southern Ch'ungch'ŏng Province, he studied philosophy at Yonsei University and emerged as an **experimental theatre** artist in the 1960s, opposing the dominant, realistic *shingŭk*.

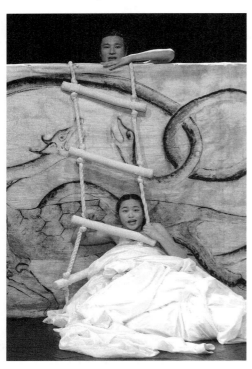

Oh T'ae-sŏk's production of *Romeo and Juliet* for the Raw Cotton (Mokhwa) Repertory Theatre, Seoul, Korea, 2005. (Photo: Courtesy of Raw Cotton Repertory Theatre)

Unrelentingly avant-garde in his sixty plays, Oh searches for what he calls "Korean-ness," combining traditional elements with **Western** dramaturgy. He frequently explores Korea's history, performing arts traditions, shaman rituals (see Religion in Theatre), and legends while embracing foreign sources, such as Grotowski and Kantor, as well as collateral media—**dance**, film, and fine art. *Lifecord* (T'ae, 1974) revisits a fifteenth-century historical event; *Ch'unp'ung's Wife* (Ch'unp'ung ŭi Ch'ŏ, 1976) mixes traditional masked dance-theatre with an old story; *By the Moonlit Paekma River* (Paekma-gang talbamae, 1993) utilizes shaman rites; *Bicycle* (Chajŏngŏ, 1983) and *DMZ, My Love* (DMZ nae sarang, 2002) address the lasting impact of the Korean War; *Why Did Shim Ch'ŏng Plunge into the Sea Twice?* (Shim-ch'ŏnginŭn wae indangsue tubŏn mom ŭl tŏnjŏt nŭnga, 1990) criticizes the loss of humanity in modern Korea.

In Oh's theatre of images, text is secondary to the overall visual representation. As a director, he treats his script like a loose map, which he constantly alters during rehearsals, performances, and even after the production is closed. Oh's theatre is extremely physical, immediate, and full of surprises.

At the center of Oh's unique directing is his theory of "Skips and Omissions," extracted from traditional culture and art. The basic idea is to show only the essential clues, allowing the "gaps" or "blank spaces" to be filled in by the audiences. Oh insists that his **actors** look directly out at the audience, breaking the "fourth wall," and ensuring the circulation of energy between performers and audience.

FURTHER READING

Kim, Ah-jeong, and R. B. Graves, trans. *The Metacultural Theatre of Oh T'ae-sŏk: Five Plays from the Korean Avant-Garde*.

Ah-Jeong Kim

OKAMOTO KIDÔ (1872–1939). Japanese • playwright, novelist, **critic**, and essayist. A student of **Chinese** and English literature, Okamoto began publishing unperformed plays in 1896. Ultimately, he completed 196 plays, mostly historical dramas. With *kabuki* • **actor** • **Ichikawa Sadanji** II, he was a key figure in establishing *shin kabuki*. While his *Before and after the Restoration* (Ishin zengo, 1908) garnered considerable success, his first great work, *The Tale of Shuzenji* (Shuzenji monogatari, 1911), a psychological depiction of a medieval **mask** maker and his daughter and their service to the shogun, was hugely popular. Other still-seen works include *The Gang Leader and the Mansion of Plates* (Banchô sarayashiki, 1916) and *Gonza and Sukejû* (Gonza to Sukejû, 1926).

In contrast to the rising genres of *shinpa* and *shingeki*, Okamoto promoted an actor-driven theatre with greater realism than *kabuki*, eliminating **dance** and **musical** accompaniment. He treated traditional subjects in contemporary terms, as in *Love Suicides at Minowa* (Minowa no shinjû, 1911), its characters evincing modern attitudes toward subjects like love suicide, and *Onoe and Idahachi* (Onoe Idahachi, 1915), portraying the repercussions of a botched love suicide. He also wrote metatheatrical dramas, such as *A History of Tenpô Drama* (Tenpô engeki-shi, 1929), ostensibly about resisting government **censorship** but self-reflexively considering backstage life.

Okamoto wrote *The American Envoy* (Amerika no tsukai, 1909) to celebrate the fiftieth anniversary of the opening of Yokohama's port. Later dramas were marked by simplicity and based on everyday life. In 1937, he became the first dramatist elected to the Japan Art Academy.

Kevin J. Wetmore, Jr.

OKINAWA. *See Kumi odori.*

ÔKURA SCHOOL. Japanese school (*ryû*) of *kyôgen* • **actors**. The other is the **Izumi school**. The Ôkura comprises various branch families, the Yamamoto and Ôkura in Tokyo, the Shigeyama Sengorô and Shigeyama Chûzaburô families in Kyoto, and the Shigeyama Zenchiku family of Osaka and Kobe. Today's Ôkura families express the historical contrasting identities of the art as a samurai ceremonial entertainment and as amusements to the imperial court and Kyoto townsmen.

Records indicate the founder as an Enryaku-ji Temple priest named Genne (1269–1350), who also wrote seventy-eight plays. Yet scholars believe that the school derived from Ômi (today's Shiga), Tanba, Uji, and Yoshino *sarugaku* players attached to the Yamato Konparu troupe, and was founded by an early "headmaster" (*iemoto*) named Zenchiku Shirôjirô, great-grandson of **Zeami Motokiyo**. Warlord Hideyoshi Toyotomi (1536–1598) favored the Ôkura school, performing in *Ear-pulling* (Mimi-hiki) in 1593 and making a gift to the actors of the **costumes**. Another warlord, Oda Nobunaga (1534–1582), gave the name "Tora" to the eleventh headmaster, Ôkura Yaemon (1531–1596). **Ôkura Yaemon Tora'akira** (1597–1662), thirteenth headmaster, compiled the first extant book of scripts, *Tora'akira's Book* (Tora'akira bon, 1642) and also wrote *Young Leaves* (Waranbe gusa, 1660), an important **theoretical** treatise on *kyôgen* history and acting. The nineteenth head, Ôkura Torahirô (1768–1792), compiled *Torahirô's Book* (Torahirô bon, 1792), containing 165 scripts in versions close to those performed today.

When the shogunate fell (1868), performers left their samurai patrons and pursued their craft in major cities. The headmaster's line was temporarily extinguished with the passing of the twenty-second, Ôkura Toratoshi, in 1881. Post–World War II meritocracy, ease of travel on bullet trains, and a plenitude of performances led to the rise of ambitious and talented individuals, regardless of school or family hierarchies. Yamamoto Tôjirô I (later Azuma, 1836–1902) shifted from service to the Bungo lord to Tokyo in 1878. The severe, martial Yamamoto style, based on early Edo (Tokyo) texts, flourished under Tôjirô III (1898–1964), an intellectual performer who disparaged the more casual Shigeyamas.

Kyoto's Shigeyama Sengorô family continues a line active since 1687. The Sengorô family, attached to the Hikone daimyo Ii Naosuke (1815–1860) only in 1837, has traditionally been nurtured by the imperial court and Kyoto amateurs. Known for its popular, even slapstick and improvisatory, style, the family appropriated a **critic**'s withering description—"tofu-ism"—as its motto: providing high-quality *kyôgen* accessible to the masses at a wide variety of temple and civic celebrations.

The Sengorô family enjoyed a remarkable postwar run of exceptional performers, including Sensaku Shigeyama III (1896–1986), designated a Living National Treasure (1976), and Shigeyama Sensaku IV (1919–), Living National Treasure–designate (1989), who gains chuckles by merely entering as the servant Tarô-kaja. Younger brother Shigeyama Sennojô (1920–) is a jack-of-all-trades whose activities include acting, writing, and **directing** traditional *kyôgen*, inter-genre **experiments**, and opera. The brothers were nearly excommunicated from *kyôgen* for their 1960s experiments but, thanks to their father's intervention and mass media support, managed to gain independence to do non-*kyôgen* projects, opening the door for others. These new traditions continue with their descendents on television, in sci-fi and contemporary-themed *kyôgen*, adaptations of Beckett, Shakespeare, and the Brothers Grimm, and collaborations with a wide variety of writers, genres, and venues.

Shigeyama Chûzaburô I (1813–1887) established a branch of the Sengorô family in Kyoto in 1826; it is currently led by Chûzaburô IV (1928–). His gentle, "artless" flavor has been praised for retaining the true Kyoto spirit. Shigeyama Yagorô (1883–1965), adopted son of Chûzaburô II (1848–1928), received the Zenchiku name from the headmaster of the Konparu *nô* school so that he could begin a branch family in 1963. Designated a Living National Treasure in 1964, a *kyôgen* first, his detailed realism won a place in Osaka and Kobe for the Zenchiku line under his four sons. His second son married the former Ôkura headmaster's great-granddaughter, reviving the dormant Ôkura headmastership in 1941 as Ôkura Yatarô (later Yaemon, 1912–2004).

Jonah Salz

ÔKURA YATARÔ [YAEMON] TORA'AKIRA (1597–1662). Japanese •

kyôgen • **actor** who compiled the first book of *kyôgen* texts, the *Kyôgen Book* (*Kyôgen no hon*, a.k.a. *Tora'akira's Book* [*Tora'akira bon*], 1642), and an important **theoretical** treatise, *Young Leaves* (Waranbe gusa, 1660).

Tora'akira was the thirteenth headmaster of the **Ôkura school**, son of Ôkura Tora-kiyo (1566–1646); his mother was a shoulder-drum (*kotsuzumi*) master's daughter. He began studying at five, debuting successfully at Nara's Kasuga Wakamiya **Festival** in 1603, establishing a name for himself and his school. He became head in 1634.

Tora'akira's Book is composed of 203 plays classified into eight categories. There are significant discrepancies in plays and dialogue with his father's *Torakiyo's Book* (Torakiyo bon, 1646); subsequent texts of the Sagi and Izumi schools demonstrate the volatile nature of early *kyôgen* as it shifted from an improvisatory to a codified art.

Young Leaves is a five-volume guide to *kyôgen* **training**, performance, and artistic context. The preface and eighty-eight sections are intended as a secret yet accessible manual, written in the *kana* syllabary in order to be read to children by their mothers. *Young Leaves* offers pithy practical hints and metaphors meant as advice to the budding professional from an old master knowledgeable in matters military and **religious**. Tora'akira suggests that actors drink water for a better voice, cultivate a forward-leaning posture, distinguish the difference between use of the **mask** and the face, and learn to analyze varieties of tears and laughter. The actor must be diligent in practice, yet relaxed on **stage**. Sincerity and correctness are vital, as it is better to be clumsy than deceitful; most *kyôgen* are auspicious pieces, and art is a tall, straight bamboo with few joints. If the stage is our body, entrances and exits on the "bridgeway" (*hashiga-kari*) are as vital as inhaling and exhaling. A recurrent theme is the importance of maintaining the Ôkura school's moderate performance style, even as rival families achieved fame with flashier methods. When *kyôgen* is too serious it becomes *nô*, he points out, yet if it is too vulgarly entertaining it becomes *kabuki*. Being interesting is more important than being funny, and peer respect is more important than popular acclaim. Despite its obviously being an attempt to elevate the status of *kyôgen* and the Ôkura school style to combat the rival Sagi (now practically extinct), *Young Leaves* is important as the longest and earliest *kyôgen* treaty extant.

Jonah Salz

ON'AMI. *See* Kanze Motoshige.

ONG KENG SEN (1963–). **Singapore**'s best-known **director**, due largely to his intercultural productions seen outside of Singapore, the best known of which are *Lear* (1997), *Desdemona* (2000), and *Continuum—Beyond the Killing Fields* (2001). As artistic director of TheatreWorks, Ong was instrumental in building a young, educated, relatively affluent, English-speaking audience for new works. His early directorial work included successful collaborations with writer Michael Chiang and composer Dick Lee on a number of Singapore-themed musicals, notably *Beauty World* (1988), *Fried Rice Paradise* (1991), and *Private Parts* (1992).

Singaporean director Ong Keng Sen's intercultural collaboration on *Lear* with Japanese playwright Rio Kishida fused disparate Asian performance traditions and toured extensively, 1997 to 1999. Chinese *jingju* star Jiang Qihu, as the eldest sister, is shown here with attendants. (Photo: Henrick Lau; courtesy of TheatreWorks)

After returning from graduate study at New York University, Ong began to combine many of the characteristic features of environmental theatre with an assertive, pan-Asian style of interculturalism. The first major work embodying this new style was *Broken Birds* (1995), a vast environmental piece that dealt with the plight of **Japanese** prostitutes during the colonial era. Two groups founded by Ong, the Flying Circus Project (1994) and Arts Network Asia (1999), have brought together practitioners of a wide range of regional traditions and contributed to the further development of his signature style. In many of Ong's "process-oriented" projects, master practitioners of traditional Asian arts share the same **stage** but remain largely sealed in their own unique aesthetic worlds, highlighting the differences rather than the similarities between individual cultures. While Ong's directorial work has toured extensively in the festival circuit, he has also worked on major projects with Berlin's House of World Cultures, Vienna's Schauspielhaus, the New York Shakespeare **Festival**, and New York's alternative space, The Kitchen.

William Peterson

ONOE BAIKÔ. Line of seven **Japanese • kabuki • actors**. The family "house name" (*yagô*) is Otowaya. The two major figures were Baikô VI and Baikô VII; earlier, Baikô had been a "poet's name" (*haimyô*) held by actors who eventually became **Onoe Kikugorô** I, II, and III, but it was briefly used as a **stage** name by Baikô IV and Kawarasaki Kunitarô II.

Baikô VI (1870–1934), adopted son of Kikugorô V (1844–1903), was Nishikawa Einosuke and Onoe Eizaburô V before becoming Baikô VI in 1903. This "female impersonator" (*onnagata*) excelled in "domestic dramas" (*sewa mono*) and "ghost plays" (*kaidan mono*), playing romantic leads against his adoptive father and the great stage lover **Ichimura Uzaemon** XV. Baikô headed the Imperial **Theatre** (Teikoku Gekijô) company when that playhouse, Japan's first in true **Western** style, opened (1911).

Baikô VII (1915–1995), adopted son of Kikugorô VI (1885–1949), was first known as Onoe Ushinosuke IV and Onoe Kikunosuke III. He became Baikô in 1947. Soon after, he cofounded the Onoe Kikugorô VI troupe. He and **Nakamura Utaemon** VI were considered the "twin gems" among postwar *onnagata*. A Living National Treasure, he was one of the great **dancers** of his time, even though he was somewhat stout for an *onnagata*. The great star Onoe Kikugorô VII (1942–) is his son.

Samuel L. Leiter

ONOE KIKUGORÔ. Seven generations of *kabuki* • **actors**. The line's "house name" (*yagô*) is Otowaya. Each Kikugorô, with the exception of Kikugorô IV, has specialized in both male and female **role types**, thus acquiring the appellation "versatile actor" (*kaneru yakusha*). The only nonstar was Kikugorô II, who died young.

Kikugorô I (1717–1783), son of a worker at Kyoto's Mandayû **Theatre** (Mandayû-za), began by playing youths and later played young **women** (*wakaonnagata*). Notable was Lady Taema in *Narukami*, opposite **Ichikawa Danjûrô** II. He later became an actor-manager (*zamoto*) in both Osaka and Edo (Tokyo). He played the multiple roles of Yuranosuke, Kampei, Hangan, and Tonase in *The Treasury of Loyal Retainers* (Kanadehon chûshingura) to acclaim.

Kikugorô III (1784–1849), adopted son of Onoe Shôroku I (1744–1815), became Kikugorô in 1815. He excelled in many types, including samurai of integrity (*jitsugoto*), and was famed in "raw domestic plays" (*kizewa mono*), especially "ghost plays" (*kaidan mono*), for which he created various chilling effects. His greatest role was Oiwa, the vengeful female ghost, in *The Ghost Stories at Yotsuya on the Tôkaidô* (Tôkaidô Yotsuya kaidan, 1825).

Kikugorô IV (1808–1860) married Kikugorô III's daughter and became his adopted son. He was often paired with Kikugorô III and was the only Kikugorô to specialize solely in "female impersonation" (*onnagata*).

Kikugorô V (1844–1903), grandson of Kikugorô III, was the last manager of the Ichimura Theatre (Ichimura-za). He became **Ichimura Uzaemon** XIII in 1851 and Kikugorô in 1868. He premiered several of the new "cropped-hair plays" (*zangiri mono*) of the Meiji period (1868–1912). He compiled the line's collection of ten famous roles, the "Collection of New and Old Theatre" (*shinko engeki jûsshû*). Danjûrô IX, **Ichikawa Sadanji** I, and Kikugorô V reigned over Meiji theatre as Dan-Kiku-Sa.

Kikugorô VI (1885–1949), son of Kikugorô V, is still referred to as "Number Six" (Rokudaime). One of the century's greatest actors, he was **trained** by Danjûrô IX. He excelled at "history plays" (*jidai mono*), "domestic plays" (*sewa mono*), *shin kabuki*, and "dance plays" (*shosagoto*). Notable roles include Gonta in *Yoshitsune and the Thousand Cherry Trees* (Yoshitsune senbon zakura) and Hanako in *Maiden of the Dôjô-ji Temple* (Musume Dôjô-ji).

Kikugorô VII (1942–), son of **Onoe Baikô VII** (1915–1995) and grandson of Kikugorô VI, is a versatile, highly acclaimed star and maintains a friendly acting rivalry with Danjûrô XII. His son, Onoe Kikunosuke V (1977–), is an expert *onnagata* and dancer.

Holly A. Blumner

ÔNO KAZUO (1906–). Japanese • *butô* master, born in Hokkaidô. Ôno saw the Spanish dancer Antonia Mercé y Luque, known as "La Argentina," perform in Tokyo in 1929 and was deeply moved. He trained with Eguchi Takaya (1900–1977), a Mary Wigman protégé, making his solo debut in 1949 with *Devil's Cry* (Kîkoku) and *First Flower of the Linden Tree* (Bodaiju no uibana ga).

In the 1950s, he worked with **Hijikata Tatsumi** to develop *butô*, their efforts culminating in Hijikata's milestone, iconoclastic adaptation of **Mishima Yukio**'s *Forbidden Colors* (Kinjiki, 1959), performed by Ôno and his son, Yoshito. A creative hiatus followed until 1977, when he danced *Eulogy for La Argentina* (Ra Aruhenchîna shô), **directed** by Hijikata. It was Ôno's homage to the great inspiration of his youth, and his performance won the Dance **Critics'** Circle Award. Although he continued to collaborate with Hijikata, Ôno's performances increasingly emphasized improvisation and a child-like innocence. He has been described as the light in contrast to Hijikata's darkness. Ôno's major works include *My Mother* (Watashi no okasan, 1981) and *Dead Sea* (Shikai, 1985).

Ôno has performed in Europe, the Americas, Australia, Asia, and in several *butô* films. He has also written several books.

FURTHER READING

Fraleigh, Sondra, and Tamah Nakamura. *Hijikata Tatsumi and Ohno Kazuo.*

Yukihiro Goto

OPERA BATAK. Itinerant **musical** theatre of the Batak people of North Sumatra (see Indonesia), now largely defunct. *Opera batak* was formed in Tapanuli in the 1920s by composer-**playwright** Tilhang Oberlin Gultom (1896–1970). The percussion-driven music accompanying **dances** and played between scenes, known generally as *uning-uningan*, was derived from pre-Christian *gondang* ceremonial **religious** music traditionally used to accompany dance, enliven weddings and funerals, and attract ancestral spirits. Dramaturgy, wing-and-drop **scenography**, and **acting** and singing styles were based on *bangsawan* and *komedi stambul*—*opera* being a term for these syncretic Malay-language theatres since the 1890s.

Opera batak was a secular theatre, and the first true Batak-language dramatic form. Touring *opera batak* troupes played on temporary **stages** erected in vacant fields to ticket-purchasing spectators for weeks at a time. Dramas were based on local legends; many new, loosely scripted plays set in traditional Batak society were also devised. At the height of *opera batak*'s popularity in the 1950s, thirty professional **theatre companies** toured North Sumatra; the theatre acted as a major engine for musical change.

Opera batak declined in popularity in the 1970s; by 2000, only two troupes were registered as existing by the provincial government of North Sumatra. Opera Batak

Tilhang Serindo, a Jakarta-based company headed by A. W. K. Samosir (1928–), survived due to media and government patronage, and the generosity of businessmen of Batak origin living in Java. *Opera batak*'s influence remains apparent in nearly all Batak music forms, and since ca. 2000 *opera batak* also has been adapted for video compact disc. A revitalization project has been underway since 2002.

Matthew Isaac Cohen

OSANAI KAORU (1881–1928). Japanese • *shingeki* • playwright, director, **critic**, teacher, translator, essayist, and **theatre company** manager. A key figure in modernizing Japanese theatre, Osanai helped adapt naturalism, expressionism, and other European styles to the Japanese **stage**. Graduating in English literature from Tokyo Imperial University, he founded the Free Theatre (Jiyû Gekijô) in 1909 with noted *kabuki* • **actor** • **Ichikawa Sadanji** II. Rejecting *shinpa* and uninterested in reforming *kabuki*, Osanai eschewed **scenographic** spectacle for psychological realism. Heavily influenced by Ibsen, his first production was *John Gabriel Borkman* (1909), heralding a stream of **Western** naturalist and modernist drama that, Osanai calculated, would challenge prevailing social conventions.

Osanai and Sadanji also wanted to create a place for re-**training** *kabuki* actors in the Stanislavski System. They sought to transform such consummate professionals into a company of amateurs. Osanai's interest in psychological acting increased after his 1912–1913 trip to Europe, where he witnessed Reinhardt's and Stanislavski's work. However, in 1919, Osanai dissolved the Free Theatre to undergo a kind of sabbatical.

In 1923, following the Great Kantô Earthquake, he and **Hijikata Yoshi** founded an ensemble at the newly built Tsukiji Little Theatre (Tsukiji Shôgekijô) that was dedicated to producing new Western plays in translation. This provoked controversy, given the many Japanese *shingeki* playwrights seeking outlets for their work. For two years, Osanai refused to produce their plays including his own, believing that Japanese playwrights had not yet been exposed to enough Western drama to be able to write naturalistic plays.

Osanai and Hijikata opened a summer acting school (1924) to educate actors in *shingeki* style. The most important training took place in rehearsals, with both Osanai and Hijikata treating the process itself as an educational forum. The two sometimes clashed, however, over style; Osanai was much more committed to Stanislavski and naturalism, while Hijikata sought to explore the European avant-garde. Nonetheless, they continued to work together, producing a blend of Western naturalist works, expressionist plays, and, eventually, new Japanese plays, until Osanai's early death.

David Jortner

ÔTA SHÔGO (1939–). Japanese • **playwright, director**, and **theorist**. Childhood memories of **China**, where he was born and lived until repatriation in 1945, have had lasting impact on Ôta's plays, with recurring images of barren land and debris. On leaving Gakushûin University in 1962, he briefly joined the *shingeki*-oriented **theatre company** Discovery Group (Hakken no Kai), then cofounded the Theatre of Transformation (Tenkei Gekijô, 1968). By 1970, he was company head, becoming a major figure in the avant-garde *shôgekijô* movement.

Ôta Shôgo's *Water Station* at the Tenkei Theatre Studio, Tokyo, Japan, April 1981, with Ōsugi Ren (left) and Satō Kazuya. (Photo: Courtesy of Waseda University Theatre Museum)

Inspired by *nô* aesthetics, existentialism, and absurdism, Ôta **experimented** extensively in playwriting and staging methods. He initially challenged traditional forms, writing "old-age" (*rôtai*) plays and staging **kabuki** in "underground" (**angura**) fashion. His approach, abundantly discussed in his theoretical works, including *The Divested Theatre* (Ragyô no gekijô, 1980) and *The Hope for Drama* (Geki no kibô, 1988), emerges from his view that the body precedes consciousness and social life. He thus regards humans as a species traveling nonchalantly, almost unconsciously, through the birth-to-death cycle; although equipped with words, humans cannot express themselves adequately. Therein lies the absurdity of the human condition. Inventing a physical grammar to give this vision form became Ôta's mission.

In 1977, Ôta's experiments coalesced into a radical performance code of divestiture in his major work, *The Tale of Komachi Told by the Wind* (Komachi fûden), based on the *nô* play *Komachi at the Gravesite* (Sotoba Komachi). Divested of words and realistic movement, Komako remains silent and moves at a *nô*-like pace throughout the play. While she cooks instant noodles, past events and lovers troop randomly through her room in a fantastical procession of memories. The play won the 1978 **Kishida [Kunio]** Prize.

By 1981, with *Water Station* (Mizu no eki), Ôta had fully developed his signature aesthetics of quiescence. The action is minimal and wordless: eighteen characters pass by a dripping water faucet in a vast wilderness, while a man inhabiting a junk pile observes them. Ôta aims to create a perspective reminiscent of the human view of life held by the dead "principal character" (*shite*; see Role Types) in a "dream" (*mugen*) *nô* play. The action is calculated to stimulate feelings of strangeness and dislocation on stepping back into normal society.

Ôta's output can be divided into silent "station" (*eki*) plays and spoken plays. The former, nonverbal, stylized, set in elemental landscapes, includes *Earth Station* (Chi no eki, 1985), *Wind Station* (Kaze no eki, 1986), *Sand Station* (Suna no eki, 1993), *Water Station 2* (Mizu no eki 2, 1995), and *Water Station 3* (Mizu no eki 3, 1998). While the early station plays portray dark scenes of sterility, devastation, and cultural collapse, those dating from 1993 are brighter, more hopeful of civilization's regeneration. His spoken plays, depicting similar concerns about human existence but with a stronger absurdist touch, include *Afternoon Light* (Gogo no hikari, 1987), *Vacant Lot* (Sarachi, 1991), and *Elements* (Eremento, 1994).

FURTHER READING

Boyd, Mari. *The Aesthetics of Quietude: Ôta Shôgo and The Theatre of Divestiture.*

Mari Boyd

OTOME BUNRAKU. *See* Puppet Theatre: Japan.

OUYANG YUQIAN (1889–1962). **Chinese** educator, **actor, director**, and **playwright**, a pioneer of modern "spoken drama" (*huaju*). In 1907, as a student in Tokyo, he performed in the Spring Willow Society (Chunliu She) production of *The Black Slave's Cry to Heaven* (Heinu yutian lu). Adapted from a Chinese rewriting of *Uncle Tom's Cabin*, it marked the beginning of China's modern theatre. Influenced by **Japanese** • *shinpa* actors, such as Kawai Takeo (1877–1942), he subsequently excelled in female roles. Back in China in 1910, he became one of the best-known actors of "civilized drama" (*wenming xi*)—*huaju*'s predecessor—in Shanghai, where he and other Spring Willow Society members reunited to form, at first, the New Drama Fellowship (Xinju Tongzhihui, 1912) and then Spring Willow Theatre (Chunliu Juchang, 1914). His 1913 *The Power of Enticement* (Yundong li) marked the beginning of his productive career writing both *huaju* and *xiqu*. Between 1914 and 1928, he also performed *jingju* in the female **role type** (*dan*) and was best known for his dramatization of the novel *Dream of the Red Mansion* (Hong lou meng). His fame rivaled **Mei Lanfang**'s.

In 1918, Ouyang created the Nantong Actors' School, the first of his several **training** endeavors. Although it only trained *xiqu* actors, his curricula emphasized general education so that his actors could take part in theatrical reform. After it failed, he joined the Shanghai Drama Society (Shanghai Xiju Xieshe) in 1922 where he and **Hong Shen** initiated mixed-gender *huaju* performances. He was also involved with **Tian Han**'s Southern China Society (Nanguo She). During the society's 1927 Fish and Dragon **Festival**, he wrote and performed *Pan Jinlian*, a *jingju* that transformed the eponymous protagonist from her traditional image of licentiousness into an individualist who lived and died for love. Between 1929 and 1931, he oversaw the Guangdong Research Institute of Drama, which included drama and **music** schools, two **theatres**, and a publishing branch that published a magazine and a weekly newspaper supplement. This marked a prolific period for his writing and translation of both plays and articles.

Ouyang worked twice in the Shanghai movie industry as an actor, writer, and director. During the Second Sino-Japanese War (1937–1945), he was known for his patriotic plays, his leadership in Guangxi opera (*guiju*) reform, and his role in organizing the 1944 Southwestern Drama Exhibition. After the war, he was the director for Shanghai's New China Drama Society (Xin Zhongguo Jushe), which toured Taiwan in 1947 and 1948.

After 1949, he served as the president of the Central Academy of Drama. He held numerous official positions, including vice-chairman of the All-China Dramatists Association.

Siyuan Liu

PADAMSEE, ALYQUE (1931–). Indian English-language **director** and **stage** and film **actor** based in Mumbai (Bombay), who has had a successful career as a top-level advertising executive. Padamsee was born into a wealthy Muslim family with strong theatre connections: his older brother, Sultan Padamsee, was a founder-member of the English-language **theatre company**, Theatre Group, which **Ebrahim Alkazi** joined and later managed (1950–1954). Alkazi married Padamsee's sister, Roshan, a well-known **costume** designer, and ceded the management of Theatre Group to his brother-in-law when he established Theatre Unit in 1954.

Padamsee is the foremost Indian director of plays written originally in English or performed in English translation. He has had a shaping influence on the careers of major English-language **playwrights**, with key productions, such as Partap Sharma's *A Touch of Brightness* (1961) and *Begam Sumroo* (1997), Gurcharan Das's *Mira* (1972), and **Mahesh Dattani**'s *Tara* (1991) and *Final Solutions* (1994). Padamsee also has written and produced a few pieces of his own, notably *Bandra Saturday Night* (1961) and *Trial Balloon* (1968). Much more extensively, he has revived the **Western** canon, ranging from Sophocles, Shakespeare, Marlowe, and Goldsmith to virtually every significant modern and contemporary Western dramatist, including Ibsen, Strindberg, Shaw, Wilde, Miller, O'Neill, Williams, Saroyan, Albee, Pinter, Shepard, Simon, Weiss, and Kopit. Padamsee has also undertaken lavish Bombay versions of Broadway musicals, such as *Cabaret* (1988) and *Evita* (1999). In a different context, his English production of **Girish Karnad**'s *Tughlaq* (1970) set the standard for the verbal and theatrical translation of Indian-language drama for the metropolitan **stage**.

Aparna Dharwadker

PAKISTAN. The Islamic Republic of Pakistan was formed out of the West **Indian** subcontinent shortly after the British ended their colonial rule in 1947; through the painful division of the region, the cultures, languages, and people were torn asunder. Originally, Partition created a West Pakistan and an East Pakistan, on either side of one thousand miles of Indian territory. After three wars, and the migration of millions of Muslims from India to Pakistan and non-Muslims to India, East Pakistan declared independence as **Bangladesh**. On the west border of Pakistan (formerly East Pakistan) is Iran, on the east is India, while Afghanistan sits to the north and northwest and **China** occupies the northwest to the northeast. There are four provinces, Punjab, Sindh, North West Frontier, and Baluchistan, each with its own language and culture.

The most populous city, Karachi, in Sindh, was the capital until 1959, when the much smaller Islamabad took over. Lahore, capital of Punjab, is Pakistan's cultural heart. The national language of this mostly Sunni Muslim nation is Urdu, despite the large population of Punjabi-speakers, because the **political** and cultural division sought to disenfranchise any common cultural traits between India and Pakistan.

Historical Background. Though the political entity of Pakistan is relatively recent, the region's cultural history reaches back to the Indus Valley civilization, which thrived between 2600 and 1700 BC and encompassed a geographic area twice as large as the concurrent civilizations in Egypt, Mesopotamia, and China. While remarkably advanced, the Indus Valley civilization remains something of an enigma due to its mysterious disappearance and only recent rediscovery. Archeologists have not yet been able to translate its unique script, making it difficult to identify specific ritual practices. Some evidence suggests a cultural link between the Indus Valley civilization and the extant traditional cultures of South India, so it is possible that certain Dravidian ritual practices may be traced back to these ancient times.

The subsequent invasions and migrations of Central Asians, Greeks, Persians, Huns, and Mongols all have influenced the region's culture. British influence began to be felt from 1600, with the establishment of a British East Asia Company, and by 1857 the British had established autonomy. But no culture was more influential than that of the Muslims, which first appeared early in the eighth century.

Bhaand Troupes. The Sunni Muslim culture that thrived in the West Indian subcontinent embraced **dance**, **music**, and **storytelling**, but **religious** beliefs forced it to look askance at dramatic productions; nonetheless, small-scale itinerant **theatre companies** have existed in rural Pakistan for centuries. Traveling jesters (*bhaand*, from the Hindi for buffoon, *bhaanda* [see *Bhaand pather*], a.k.a. *naqal*), have long plied their trade in northwestern India and functioned as minstrels as court entertainment or as popular street theatre; rural **festivals** were a major draw. As masters of disguise, the *bhaand* have an extraordinary range of both male and female characters into which they transform themselves. *Bhaand* work alone or in pairs in their largely satirical skits, which alternately praise and humiliate merchants into giving them alms. *Bhaand* performers also collaborate in larger musical productions called *swang* (or *naqal*), which have fully developed plots based on Punjab legends and folklore.

Scripted Plays. The origins of scripted Urdu plays are debated. A few private performances were first staged for and by Wajid Ali Shah (1822–1887), the last reigning Mughal monarch, who was deposed by the British. His mammoth, spectacular, musical, all-female productions in 1851 and 1853 were seen by only a select few. Far more influential was Amanat Lakhnawi's (1816–1859) spectacular *The Court of Lord Indra* (Indar sabha), first staged at Wajid Ali Shah's Lucknow court (1853), which would become the most widely performed play throughout South Asia and usher in **Parsi theatre**, an amalgam of traditional music and dance and British-inspired melodrama. The attempt to introduce social issues into Parsi theatre led to the imposition by the British of **censorship** in the form of the Dramatic Performances Control Act of 1876, which remains in effect even today. Though the Parsi theatre faded in the 1930s, it had a lasting impact on the development of popular theatre, which readily adopted its eclectic mix of music, high-pathos, romance, and comedy.

Lok. Early Punjabi-language performance found its voice in *lok*, which flourished during the early post-Partition (1947) years. This centuries-old, semi-nomadic song and dance **folk theatre**, operating out of Lahore, may still be found attached to rural market fairs at harvest time. Its audiences were almost exclusively male peasants who watched the mixed-gendered cast from behind barbed wire. The **women** performers seldom joined of their own volition and were often sold into contracts by unscrupulous male relatives. There was, however, among the various companies, one run by an actress, the popular Bali Jati (or Jutti), who owned the Shama **Theatre**. The widespread popularity of *lok* and Parsi theatre began to wane because of competition with films, which recruited the best talent and drew much of their audience.

An important early contributor to early Urdu drama and literature was Dr. Syed Imtiaz Ali Taj (1900–1970), who wrote several plays, including the popular romance, *Anarkali* (1922). Set during the reign of Shah Akbar (r. 1556–1605), it tells of Akbar's rebellious son falling in love with a poor nautch-girl. It has become a classic of star-crossed lovers that has been retold many times in various folk theatres and movies.

1940s to 1960s. The period from the 1940s to the 1960s saw widespread hardship and social upheaval. The few new plays focused on the pressing social issues of the day. The International People's Theatre Association (IPTA), founded by the Communist Party of India in 1942–1943, maintained a presence in Lahore and Karachi. Most of this early political theatre was strongly socialist and established the framework for leftist agitprop theatre, often produced in the streets. Much of this abruptly ended with Partition, when many IPTA performers, for political or religious reasons, left Pakistan. The painful division exaggerated the nations' cultural differences; a number of traditional forms that once freely borrowed Hindu themes eliminated every trace of their once mutual culture and began to import more Arab culture from the Middle East.

Robert Petersen

Modern Pakistani Theatre's Struggle. Pakistani theatre, despite a population of over 162 million people, has not thrived since Partition. Visual artists have fared better than performing artists under Pakistan's various civil and military dictatorships. Teaching positions and national awards are available for visual artists, but there is comparatively little provided to performers to provide economic support and social enhancement. Furthermore, political corruption during times of civilian governments and the repeated imposition of censorship and martial law have had a chilling effect on theatre's development. Nor has the nation's Islamist ideology proved friendly to theatre: authoritarian regimes and fundamentalism have little faith in media that can question issues and beliefs.

Still, commercial **theatres** exist in Lahore, having emerged from the *lok* tradition, but it is little more than broad, off-color farce performed in Lahore's Rabia Theatre and Tamaseel Theatre. Despite being despised by artists longing for a more meaningful art, such productions have been successful in gathering an audience.

There were several advances toward a serious theatre at mid-century, beginning with former IPTA participant Ali Ahmed starting a company called Natak whose achievements included making political statements through classic **Western** plays; the establishment by artists and writers of the Pakistan Arts Council (1948), a private institution seeking to promote the arts that became a respected producer of mostly serious theatre in Lahore in the

Talat Hussein performing in Sarmad Sehbai's *Hash*, directed by Farooq Zamir, 1974. (Photo: Mohammed Nadir Shah; courtesy of Sarmad Sehbai)

1960s; the appearance in Peshawar of a small number of amateur Islamic companies; and the work of Karachi's Drama Guild (1952), founded by **playwright** and **director** Khawaja Moenunddin. Although the banning of the Communist Party in 1950 hindered leftwing expression, this company produced a number of important productions concerning social and political issues. Their successful 1953 production (one performance played to ten thousand stadium spectators), *From the Red Fort to Laloo Khaith* (Laal Qilay se Laloo Khaith), dealt with Partition, but one year later *New Mark* (Naya nishan, 1954), concerning the contested region of Kashmir, proved too sensitive and was officially closed.

Although some socially concerned works were written in the 1960s by Major Ishaq Mohammed and Sarmad Sehbai (1945–), it was not until during General Zia-ul-Haque's martial law regime (1979–1989), which effectively killed conventional theatre for a decade, that the most progressive companies, such as Dawn of a New Day (Ajoka) and the Punjab People's Theatre (Lok Rehas), formed the "parallel theatre" protest movement. Eschewing conventional theatres, these groups—several of which performed into the 1990s—engaged in street theatre in an effort to directly reach the people on sensitive issues. A number of plays written by **Shahid Nadeem** for Dawn of a New Day have directly addressed the issues of religious intolerance and the rights of Pakistani women. People's Theatre performs exclusively in Punjabi as an extension of its protest against the Urdu-speaking government's cultural oppression. Their work often makes use of *lok* traditions. Another product of the resistance to Zia-ul-Haque is Karachi's Women's Movement (Tehrik-e-Niswan) group, founded in 1981 to help organize women textile workers; it also employs folk song and dance in its work. Other groups have appeared along the same "people's theatre" lines.

Festivals and College Groups. Despite the government's general indifference to the performing arts, and censorship's ever-present shadow, a number of international theatre and **puppetry •festivals** have taken place. Beginning in 1992, the Rafi Peer Theatre Workshop has sponsored a number of international festivals in Lahore that have furthered the dialogue between Pakistani troupes and the rest of the world. There is also ongoing theatrical activity in college groups, such as the Government College Dramatic Club, revitalized by Safdar Mir (1922–) in the 1950s. They perform in English for an educated audience, and have produced a number of important artists, such as director Fareed Ahmed (1935–1993), actor Zia Mohyuddin, or Moyeddin, (1931–), and playwright-director Shoaib Hashmi (1939–).

FURTHER READING

Afzal-Khan, Fawzia. *A Critical Stage: The Role of Secular Alternative Theatre in Pakistan*; Qureshi, M. Aslam. *Wajid Ali Shah's Theatrical Genius*.

Vibha Sharma

PANCHALI. *See* Bangladesh.

PANDAV LILA. North **Indian • religious** ritual play (*lila*) found only in the former Hindu kingdom of Garhwal, in Uttaranchal in the west central Himalayas; related oral traditions have been reported from the former kingdom of Kumaon (also part of Uttaranchal), and from neighboring Himachal Pradesh.

Performance Circumstances. It is an amateur and oral tradition concerning the five Pandava brothers, protagonists of the epic *Mahabharata*. Performances typically occur between mid-December and mid-February; reports exist of performances at other times as well. Performances range from only one to three days to several weeks, with singing, **dancing**, public processions to sacred places, visits by the main characters to people's houses, and dramatizations of particular *Mahabharata* episodes. Though frequency varies from place to place, many say that villages should perform *pandav lila* at least once in a generation.

Music is supplied by artists playing a large two-headed drum (*dhol*), and either (in eastern Garhwal) a small single-headed drum (*damaum*) or (in western Garhwal) a brass gong (*bhaina*), and occasionally the "battle-horn" (*ranasingha*). As for **costumes**, male dancers in eastern Garhwal typically wear skullcaps, trousers, and flowing skirts, all made of white cloth and colorfully embroidered, while females always wear traditional dress: black woolen robes, white cotton cummerbunds and scarves, and heavy silver jewelry. In some areas, **women** are discouraged from dancing, which is considered inappropriate; however, Kunti is always played by an elderly woman.

*Ritual Practices and Possession. Pandav lila*s are collectively organized by villages, which reap the spiritual benefits believed to flow from successful performances. Before the drama begins, the village deity is worshipped, and asked permission to perform the *lila*. A typical performance begins in a central square attached to a temple or home where drummers play while reciting the names and praises of the Pandava brothers, their ally Krishna, their mother Kunti, their common wife Draupadi, and other members of their "army," often including the "monkey-god" Hanuman. Some characters, such as Kaliya Lohar, the weapon-making blacksmith, are not in the *Mahabharata*. When thus ritually praised, the Pandavas themselves are believed to become present and to possess their dancer-performers. Draupadi is considered an incarnation of the goddess Kali, making performances, in effect, forms of Kali-worship (see also *Terukkuttu*). When dancers begin to tremble and shake, this indicates that they are possessed; sometimes this happens to onlookers as well, who, possessed by one of the characters, leap up and join the dancers.

Characters are identified by the characteristic signs or weapons with which they dance: the eldest brother, Yudhisthira, also known as King Dharma, dances with a royal staff; Bhima, the "strong man," dances with a club; Arjuna, the consummate warrior, dances with a bow and arrow; and so on. The dancers, temporary "containers" (*patra*), "beasts" (*pasva*), or "mounts" (*dungari*) of the divine characters, must remain pure throughout by avoiding sexual activity as well as the consumption of flesh and alcohol. The power of their asceticism, combined with that of the divine beings temporarily inhabiting their bodies, generates a spiritual energy ensuring good fortune, bountiful harvests, and good health. *Pandav lila* is more ritual than entertainment.

Performances involve the dramatization and/or "dancing" of *Mahabharata* vignettes, often interspersed with stylized **storytelling**. Their recitation sometimes is competitive, with local "bards" challenging each other to recall particular details from the epic. Local versions differ in certain respects from those familiar to Indian and **Western** scholars. Of central importance is the funeral ritual (*sraddha*) of the Pandavas' father, King Pandu. According to Garhwalis, this mandatory Hindu ritual was not properly completed after Pandu's death; a full-scale *pandav lila* incorporates and often culminates with an authentic funeral ritual performed by a Brahman priest. Indeed, *sraddha* and *pandav lila* are used interchangeably to refer to performances, which typically involve processions from house to house, or to neighboring villages, to collect various ritual items. Most important is a rhinoceros hide, from which a ring is made that was traditionally worn by the ritual's sponsor. According to the local version of the *Mahabharata*, Arjuna's son, Nagarjuna, possessed a mythical rhinoceros whose hide was required for the ritual. Neither Arjuna nor Nagarjuna knew they were father and son. When Arjuna killed the rhinoceros, Nagarjuna retaliated by slaying him in combat, though he was later revived. Dramatizations of this episode are powerful, often leading members of the audience to fall unconscious. Almost every *pandav lila* dramatizes a version of this episode, variations of which are also found in Rajasthan and elsewhere, suggesting the existence of a widespread, vernacular *Mahabharata* tradition.

The "rhinoceros *lila*" exemplifies the importance of local notions of descent and territory in *pandav lila*. In **Sanskrit** versions of the *Mahabharata*, a curse prevented Pandu from conceiving children; the Pandava brothers were actually borne of Kunti with divine help. In Garhwal, however, the youngest brother, Nakula, is believed to be Pandu's biological son; it is he who performs the funeral ritual for his father. Garhwali Rajputs, members of the warrior caste (*ksatriya*), believe they are Nakula's descendants, and that *pandav lila* is both a form of ancestor worship and the fulfillment of a religious duty. Nakula's dance further underscores his identification with local people, as it re-enacts the stereotypical actions of a local cowherd. The idea that local Rajputs are Pandava descendents becomes slightly more plausible when one considers that prominent local places are mentioned in Sanskrit and vernacular versions of the epic.

Martial Features. Other popular *lila* also emphasize martial aspects of the epic, thus underscoring local Rajputs' identification with the Pandavas. The *sami*-tree *lila* evokes an episode in which the Pandavas are required by the terms of a wager to leave their weapons behind before going into exile in the forest. They are unable to find anyone willing to keep their weapons until the *sami* tree, growing in the midst of a creation ground, agrees to do so on the condition that the Pandavas must worship it after they return. In the *lila*, an unblemished pine tree is uprooted (cutting it would be disrespectful) and carried to the dancing square, where it is erected and worshipped. The "circular array" (*cakravyuha*) *lila* refers to the scene in which the Pandavas' mortal enemies, the Kauravas, lure Arjuna's young son, Abhimanyu, into the middle of their circular array battle formation. The circular array takes the form of a maze constructed from wooden frames and women's saris, in which Kaurava warriors are strategically stationed. Abhimanyu battles to the maze's center, where his cousins treacherously kill him. Some local versions in the Mandakini Valley began incorporating written scripts as early as the mid-twentieth century. In the late 1990s, local scholars and **actors**, led by Prof. Data Ram Purohit of Garhwal University, successfully adapted this episode for the urban **stage**.

Performers erect a *sami* tree in the middle of the dancing square. (Photo: William S. Sax)

FURTHER READING

Sax, William S. *Dancing the Self: Personhood and Performance in the Pandav Lila of Garhwal.*

William S. Sax

PANIKKAR, KAVALAM NARAYAN (1928–). **Indian** Malayalam-language **director**, **playwright**, composer, novelist, poet, and **critic**, born in Kavalam, an agricultural village in Alppuzha District, Kerala, which he claims had a profound effect on his work. The stories from the *Mahabharata* and *Ramayana* that senior members of his family often narrated to the children made a deep impact on him early in life, inspiring him later to organize public poetry readings. He researched India's **folk** and classical arts, which served as a backdrop for his contributions. His productions of **Sanskrit** dramatist **Bhasa**, for example, have been a highlight of contemporary theatre, helping to revive interest in ancient drama.

Panikkar has a diverse academic record, including a degree in law, which he practiced from 1955 to 1961. In 1961, he was appointed secretary of Kerala's National Academy of **Music**, **Dance**, and Drama (Sangeet Natak Akademi), leading him to move to Trichur (Thrissur), Kerala's cultural capital, where his artistic and cultural interests blossomed. During his ten-year tenure, he was instrumental in organizing numerous cultural **festivals**.

Panikkar wrote over twenty plays, translated English plays into Malayalam, and directed over two dozen productions. His first play in Malayalam was *The Witness* (Sakshi, 1964–1965), which emerged from public performances of Panikkar's poetry. (He considers theatre "visual poetry" [*drishya kavya*].) It and others of his early Malayalam plays, like *The Revered God* (Daivattar, 1973) and *Tiruvazhithan* (1974), were produced by Koothambalam, an **experimental • theatre company** he founded in

Alappuzha. In 1974, he moved to the state capital, Trivandrum (Thiruvananthapuram), changing Koothambalam's name to Tiruvarang. There, G. Aravindan's production of his *One's Own Impediment* (Avanavankadamba, 1975) gained him acclaim, partly because it abandoned the proscenium for the outdoors, using real trees and audience interaction. His plays—among them *The Lone Tusker* (Ottayan, 1977), *Sacrificial Firewood* (Arani, 1989), and *Outsider* (Poranadi, 1995)—are noted for their theatricality, de-emphasis on language, and focus on the **actor**'s rhythmically expressive (sometimes athletic) nonverbal communication. In 1996, he wrote *Aramba Chekkan*, based on the Greek legend of Orpheus and Eurydice, for American director Erin Mee to stage with Sopanam, a group Panikkar formed in 1965 as the theatre wing of Bhasabharati, a Trivandrum center for performing arts research and **training**. Forms like **kathakali** and **kutiyattam** as well as the martial art of **kalarippayattu** have played an unusually significant role in his work. This places him centrally in India's "theatre of roots" movement, which calls for drawing direct inspiration from the indigenous classical and folk theatre.

Panikkar's own directorial achievements, acclaimed at national and international **festivals**, began with Bhasa's *The Middle One* (Madhyamavyayoga, 1979), performed at Ujjain (and later in New Delhi) in the original Sanskrit, *Karna's Task* (Karnabhara, 1984), *The Broken Thighs* (Urubhanga, 1988), *The Vision of Vasavadatta* (Svapna–Vasavadatta, 1993), and *The Messenger's Words* (Dutavakya, 1996). In these productions, and those of Sanskrit dramatists **Kalidasa** and Mahendravikrama Varman, he employed ideas gleaned from the ancient *Treatise on Drama* (Natyashastra; see Theory).

While working on an Indo-Greek cultural project (1981 to 1991), he combined two great epics, *The Iliad* and the **Ramayana** in a *Iliyayana*, produced by a Greek troupe.

V. Gireesan as Dasaradha in K. N. Panikkar's production of Bhasa's Sanskrit drama, *The Statue*, produced by Sopanam, India, 1999. (Photo: Courtesy of K. N. Panikkar)

During his forty-year career, Panikkar successfully revived many classical and folk traditions, especially those of Kerala, including the use of *kalarippayattu*. He emphasizes nonverbal expression through a physical movement alphabet closely tied to the other nontextual, **musical**, and visual production elements.

Panikkar has received many awards, including the National Academy of Music, Dance, and Drama (Sangeet Natak Akademi) award (1985), and a National Academy of Music, Dance, and Drama fellowship (2002).

Shashikant Barhanpurkar

PANJI. Hero in a key story source for theatre in **Indonesia**, **Malaysia**, **Thailand**, **Cambodia**, and **Burma**; also known as Malat or Inao. The Panji romance is sometimes referred to as a cycle; actually, episodes are independent of each other and form variations on a theme.

The setting is invariably eastern Java during a semilegendary age (before the arrival of Islam) dominated by small competing kingdoms, such as Daha (also Kediri), Kuripan, and Singasari. Panji, prince of Kuripan, is betrothed to Candra Kirana, princess of Daha. She disappears, and Panji leaves the court to quest for her through forest and countryside, usually accompanied by a small band of followers. Some Panji stories feature the rapacious overseas king Klana, who desires to marry Candra Kirana and threatens to destroy Daha to obtain her. Deception, disguise, and mystery are hallmarks.

The earliest Panji texts were written in Middle Javanese poetry (*kidung*) in ca. fifteenth-century Bali, where Panji is called Malat. These texts have long been enacted as *gambuh*. Panji is also a basis for *arja*, *topeng*, *wayang* (see Puppet Theatre), *liké*, and many other Southeast Asian genres. A 20,520-verse Inao adaptation for *lakon nai* attributed to Thailand's **Rama II** was published in three volumes in 1921.

FURTHER READING

Rassers, W. H. *Panji, the Culture Hero: A Structural Study of Religion in Java.*

Matthew Isaac Cohen

P'ANSORI. **Korean** narrative performing art in which a solo vocalist delivers a story through a combination of singing, stylized speech, and gesture to the rhythmic accompaniment of a single drum. Though best classed as a form of **storytelling**, *p'ansori* is theatrical in that the singer takes on the personae of different characters and may address the drummer as another character. *P'ansori* is the ancestor of two more fully theatrical genres, mixed-cast *ch'angguk* and all-female *yosong kukkuk*, in which multiple **actors** play the various characters, singing in *p'ansori* style.

The extant repertory consists of five well-known stories, though the titles and (in most cases) plot outlines of at least twelve are recorded. The stories originate in folktales and historical legends, some having cognates in other parts of Asia, and most involving animal and supernatural characters and miraculous events. All have happy endings in which virtue is rewarded and evil punished, though, until that ending is reached, the narratives tend to dwell on scenes of hardship and suffering, offset by episodes of broad humor, often bawdy or scatological.

In performance, the vocalist conventionally holds a fan and handkerchief, which serve to cool and mop the singer's brow, emphasize gestures, and occasionally represent elements of the story. For instance, when the text mentions sawing, the singer may move the fan back and forth as if it were a saw. More important than these movements (*pallim*) is singing (*ch'ang*). Most of the text, especially when describing intense emotion or rapid action, is sung, with the spoken passages (*aniri*) serving to advance the story and refresh the voice. The singing is noted for a husky or raspy timbre, deliberately cultivated through arduous **training**.

Musical accompaniment employs rhythmic patterns marked by an accompanist who plays a small barrel drum (*puk*), striking both the skin and the body of the drum to produce contrasting sounds. The drummer interjects cries of appreciation and encouragement (*ch'uimsae*), which may also be given by knowledgeable spectators. Singers, in turn, sometimes make extemporaneous remarks to the drummer or audience, speaking in their own voice, thus shifting among three types of persona: narrator, character, and performer.

First documented in 1754, *p'ansori* originated as an oral tradition among commoners in southwestern Chŏlla Province. It probably developed from shamans' narrative songs, gradually elaborated by professional itinerant performers (*kwangdae*) (see Folk Theatre). During the nineteenth century, it won widespread favor in all social strata, including the court. To make it more acceptable to elite patrons, an aficionado, Shin Chaehyo (1812–1884), prepared written texts incorporating overt Confucian morality and elegant phrases from **Chinese** poetry and ameliorating the obscenity of many passages. These modifications, however, coexist with surviving undercurrents of satire and subversion, earthy regional dialect, and Rabelaisian humor. Shin also trained the first female singer, Chin Ch'ae-sŏn (1847–?); by the mid-twentieth century, **women** singers outnumbered male, as they still do.

The nineteenth-century practice of performing a complete story over a day or more gave way to the performance of "highlights" as one item in a variety show of traditional performing arts. This remains the most common approach, though accomplished singers are sometimes expected to be able to give full-length performances lasting from two to five hours. Except for occasional spontaneous remarks and slight rhythmic variations improvised by the drummer, the performance is given from memory.

The traditional repertory is increasingly supplemented by newly composed stories. This began with "songs of martyred heroes" (*yŏlsaga*), first performed after liberation from **Japanese** rule (1945) and eulogizing heroes of resistance. From the 1970s came pieces on **religious** themes, such as the life of Jesus, and on **political** themes, such as the 1980 massacre of protestors in Kwangju. These weighty subjects left little scope for the humorous qualities of traditional *p'ansori*, but since around 2000, these enjoyable features have been rediscovered in a spate of new pieces written in contemporary language on such topical themes as business troubles, Alzheimer's disease, teenagers' university entrance anxiety, and rural men's difficulties in finding a wife.

FURTHER READING

Park, Chan E. *Voices from the Straw Mat: Toward an Ethnography of P'ansori Singing*; Pihl, Marshall R. *The Korean Singer of Tales*.

Andrew Killick

PANTOOMKOMOL, SODSAI (1934–). Thai • *lakon phut samai mhai* • **director**, play translator, and scholar. After graduate study at UCLA in the 1960s on a Fulbright, she returned home as an English professor. She staged the first Thai translation of a modern American drama, Howard's *The Silver Cord* (Luk khong mae, 1967). In 1970, Sodsai became the first chair of Chulalongkorn University's Department of Dramatic Arts, which offered Thailand's first bachelor's degree in **Western** drama and theatre.

Her translations and stagings of modern Western plays introduced the public to a wide variety of foreign **theories** and practices. Noteworthy examples include Williams's *The Glass Menagerie* (1970), Pirandello's *Six Characters in Search of an Author* (1973), Ibsen's *Hedda Gabler* (1974), Albee's *The American Dream* (1978), Brecht's *The Good Person of Setzuan* (1979), and Giraudoux's *Ondine* (1982).

Pantoomkomol wrote a widely read and referenced book on acting in modern theatre (1995). In her retirement, she continues to lecture in **acting**, playwriting, and **directing** in addition to advising **theatre companies**. In 1995, the country's first and only modern playwriting competition, the Sodsai Award, was named in her honor.

Pawit Mahasarinand

PAOLUENGTONG, RASSAMI (1952–). Thai • **director**, dramaturg, **playwright**, play translator, and screenplay writer. A graduate of Chulalongkorn University, where she studied with **Sodsai Pantoomkomol**, Paoluengtong was highly active in translating, writing, and directing social and **political** dramas during the 1970s antimilitary government protests.

In 1984, she became the first, and still only, Thai dramatist to graduate with an MFA in dramaturgy from the Yale School of Drama. A year later, she cofounded Theatre 28, a professional **theatre company** focusing on highbrow dramas with contemporary social and philosophical issues. Representative directing projects include Brecht's *Galileo* (1985), Frisch's *Biography: A Game* (1986), Dürrenmatt's *The Visit* (1989), Camus's *The Fall* (1992), and Ionesco's *Rhinoceros* (1994). Sample play translations are *Man of La Mancha* (1987) and *Kiss of the Spiderwoman* (2001).

In 1996, Paoluengtong worked with a group of upcountry non-**actor** children in creating an original children's play, *Buffaloes Don't Eat Grass* (Kwai mai kin yah). It has toured to many provinces and has been revived frequently with most of the original cast members.

In 2003 and 2005, with support from the European Commission, Paoluengtong led a team of Thai dramatists in translating contemporary Continental European plays, and organized the **Festival** of European Plays. Accompanied by discussions and lectures, drama students performed excerpted scenes for a public familiar mainly with Anglo-American plays. Later on, a few of these plays were produced full-scale.

Currently, Paoluengtong heads the theatre and motion picture program of the Ashram of Arts, an experimental tertiary institution, and guest lectures at many campuses.

Pawit Mahasarinand

PARSI THEATRE. **Indian** hybrid theatre form created and managed by the Parsis, a business community of Zoroastrians that migrated from Persia to Gujarat a millennium ago, and settled in large numbers in Bombay (Mumbai) in the nineteenth century. Founded in 1853, it was India's first modern, professional, urban, commercial theatre totally based on a ticket-buying audience's patronage. Parsi theatre, taking its cue from British touring troupes and amateurs, incorporated **Western** techniques, Hindu, Persian, and European stories, including those from **folk**, mythological, and historical sources, and **music** and **dance**. Some consider its melodies to be Parsi theatre's greatest contribution. Despite its Parsi origins, artists involved eventually included diverse ethnic groups.

Its nucleus was in Bombay, where the Parsi business community was concentrated. Early performances were in Gujurati or English, and Westerners were among the spectators. Parsi theatre had a strong influence all across India; beginning with Urdu performances in 1871, **theatre companies** eventually arose in a wide variety of languages and remained active for many years, even after the original Bombay version declined. In Maharashtra, it had a strong influence on *sangeet natak*, and was popular even in remote rural areas. In the 1930s, when sound films emerged, it began to vanish, although Calcutta's (Kolkata) Moonlight Theatre survived into the 1960s under the leadership of **actor** Fida Hussain (1899–1999), the form's last star.

The first company, premiering in 1853, was the amateur Parsee Stage Players, at the Grant Road **Theatre**. Later, there were the Victoria Theatrical Company, the Elphinstone Dramatic Club, the Zoroastrian Theatrical Club, the Alfred Theatrical Company, the new Alfred Theatrical Company, the Madan Theatres (in Calcutta), and so on, all of them commercially successful, paying salaries to **playwrights**, actors, and technicians. They performed on proscenium **stages**, using elaborate **scenography** with perspective backdrops showing the locale—usually standard ones, such as gardens, palaces, and streets—in detail. **Costumes** and **properties** were elaborate, especially for mythological and historical plays. Spectacle was a draw, and mechanical effects, including flying, were common. No previous Indian theatre had seemed so realistic. On the other hand, female impersonators played **women**'s roles and were extremely popular; actresses began performing in the 1870s, sharing the **stage** with female impersonators, as in **Japan**'s *shinpa*.

Themes ranged from the romantic to the mythological to the social. Famous plays include *The Court of Lord Indra* (Indar sabha, 1853), seen at Wajid Ali Shah's Lucknow court, *Bakkavali's Flower* (Gul Bakkavali), and *Laila and Majnu* (Laila-Majnu). Plays based on the ***Ramayana*** and ***Mahabharata*** were also popular, as were works adapted from Shakespeare, Victorian melodrama, and the *Arabian Nights*. Many plays, such as *Bakkavali's Flower*, received regional-language versions and were later filmed. Most plays, which stressed high moral values, followed a five-act, European-influenced **dramatic structure** using multiple subplots, and were highly melodramatic and emotional both in writing and performance. Among the most important writers were Agha Hashr Kashmiri (1879–1935), who made two adaptations of Shakespeare, *White Blood* (Safed khon, 1906) and *Saide Hawas* (1907); Narayan Prasad Betab (1872–1945), whose twenty-six works included the anti-British *Poisonous Snake* (Zahri sap, 1907), as well as an adaptation of *Comedy of Errors* called *Labyrinth* (Gorakhdandha, 1909); and Radheshyam Kathavachk (1890–1963), whose plays were usually based on mythological topics. *See also Bangsawan; Nurti.*

FURTHER READING

Gupt, Somnath. *The Parsi Theatre*.

B. Ananthakrishnan

PARTHASARATHI, INDIRA (1930–). Indian Tamil-language **playwright**, academic, and founder-director of the Sri Sankara Doss Swamikal School of Performing Arts, University of Pondicherry. He was born in Tamilnadu, completed his master's in Tamil, and became a university professor. In New Delhi, he was exposed to the works of **Ebrahim Alkazi** and influenced by **Western** dramatic traditions. He is among the few who opposed conventional Tamil playwriting by introducing new **dramatic structures** with a modern sensibility.

His first play, *The Rain* (Mazhai, 1972), concerns generational relationship problems in changing milieus. In *Aurangazeb* (1973), a history play, the eponymous emperor is portrayed with a human face. Other plays include *Time Machines* (Kalayanthirangal, 1977), *Legend of Nandan* (Nandan kathai, 1978), *Bodies Wrapped with Blankets* (Porvai portiya udalkal, 1978), and *Ramanujar* (1996), about the eponymous Tamil scholar and poet. Parthasarathi's works also include adaptations of Tamil classics, like *Fire in the Breast* (Konkai thee), into regional forms; he also adapted *King Lear* into Tamil.

As the director of the Pondicherry school, he developed curricula for **training** courses with emphasis on Tamil traditions. His research interests are focused on exploring **folk theatres** like *terukkuttu*. He authored several articles on theatre and also edited a literary magazine, *Kanaiyazhi*.

B. Ananthakrishnan

PASKU. Sri Lankan "passion play" dealing with Christ's death and resurrection. The earliest version of this **religious** form is said to have been produced in Pesalai on the island of Mannar, in the north. This led to its development further north in the Catholic parts of Tamil-speaking Jaffna, from whence it progressed to churches in Chilaw and Negombo on the Sinhalese-speaking western coast.

Although passion plays were possibly performed by priests on several occasions at different places during the seventeenth century, beginning with the Portuguese occupation, the records of the Oratorial Order note that the first passion play in its Sri Lankan traditional form was written and produced in Jaffna in 1706 by Father Joseph Vaz (1651–1711), who had witnessed such plays with **puppets** in Goa, **India**. The venue was a large, temporary, shed-like structure, about twenty feet high, surrounded by palm leaf walls, with the audience seated on the ground outside and looking in through a large opening. As someone in front chanted the narrative, life-size figures of the story's individuals were moved about by others hidden in palm leaf coverings, giving the effect that the figures—seen above a six-foot wall of palm leaves—were moving on their own. Behind them were painted scenes. Parts of the performance extended to nearby areas, with villagers participating, so that some might walk through the rice fields carrying a figure of Christ to reenact his path from Gethsemene to Calvary.

At Chilaw and Negombo, statues represented Jesus, the Virgin Mary, Mary Magdalene, Saint John, and Veronica, while others were portrayed by **actors**. Various priests further developed such presentations, writing new sermons and chants for their presentation, and offering them in permanent structures before it was decided to move them outdoors. Today, only Pitipana—whose biennial tradition is more than a century old—has a performance in a permanent, enclosed structure; it is situated directly across from the church. Pitipana is also interesting in that it uses elements of the *nadagam* • **folk theatre** style.

Passion plays elsewhere in Sri Lanka use a temporary pavilion (*pasku maduva*) with a **stage** around six feet high, with huts possessing their own stages on two sides, in a manner reminiscent of the Sri Lankan puppet play tradition.

K. Lawrence Perera (1890–?) established the elaborate Shridhara Boralessa passion play (1923) under the influence of Germany's Oberammagau passion play, which he adapted into Sinhalese, with songs added from native sources, Christian hymns, and his own creation. His passion play abandoned statuary—which he thought "crude"— for an all-living cast of over one hundred local villagers dressed and coiffed in the Oberammagau manner. It ran from 3 p.m. to 4 a.m. Remarkable tableaux vivants were one of its most distinguishing features. A five-stage arrangement was used, not unlike the three-stage one mentioned earlier. Despite its ever-increasing popularity, the 1939 decision to use four local **women** to play the female roles led to its being **censored** by the Archbishop of Colombo, who felt (despite the use of women in the Duwa passion play) that the mingling of the sexes was inappropriate.

The most renowned example is the play created on the island of Duwa (off the coast of Negombo) in 1937 by Fr. Marcelline Jayakody (1902–1998), a proponent of indigenous culture, who wrote the hymns and used as his text the nine sermons called the "Dukprapthi Prasangaya," written in the eighteenth century by Fr. Jacome Gonsalvez (1676–1742), successor to Joseph Vaz. He also took the revolutionary step of replacing the statues with actors, except for Christ and Mary. A boy plays Veronica.

The Duwa play, employing over 250 locals, is famous throughout Asia. It uses the three-stage arrangement of the Jaffna play and employs Christian church music played on the organ. There is now a tradition whereby Duwa's passion play is given there for two years and at St. Joseph's Church in Negombo in the third year.

The passion plays used to occupy several days of a prescribed schedule, opening on Palm Sunday with Old Testament scenes, the temptation of Christ, and Christ's entry into Jerusalem. Subsequent performances on Monday, Thursday night, Good Friday, and Easter Sunday presented scenes relevant to those days. In the Good Friday performance, which includes Christ and the two thieves bound to their crosses—Christ (a statue) in the center and the thieves (actors) on the side stages—the thieves must endure a three-hour ordeal in place before being relieved. A Saturday scene gave license to the local boys to play as devils under Lucifer's command, but their behavior grew so mischievous and led to so many scrapes that their appearance was banned.

FURTHER READING

Sarachchandra, E. R. *The Folk Drama of Ceylon.*

Samuel L. Leiter

PATEL, JABBER RAZZAK (1942–).

PATEL, JABBER RAZZAK (1942–). **Indian** Marathi-language **director**, born in Pandharpur, Solapur District, Maharashtra. He received a medical degree in 1968 from Poona (Pune) University, where he was active in theatricals. While practicing medicine in Daund, he commuted to Pune to direct plays for Bhalba Kelkar's Progressive Dramatic Association (PDA), such as **Vijay Tendulkar**'s *That's How Birds Arrive* (Ashi pakhare yeti, 1970), for which he earned awards.

His most famous PDA production was of Tendulkar's *Ghashiram Kotwal* (Ghashiram the Policeman, 1972), an allegorical attack on a threatening **political** party, but it was so controversial that he and several others left PDA to form Theatre Academy, known for its street theatre (a.k.a. "parallel theatre") activities. In *Ghashiram*, Patel combined the **folk theatre** of Konkan with modern techniques, using **music** and **dance** to create a new style of Marathi theatre, then laboring under the constraints of realism. A chorus of singers served as a **curtain** to hide and reveal the action. The production subsequently was considered a Marathi landmark, and helped guide the way for Indian theatre to find its identity. The production toured the nation and was produced in Europe, the United States, and the USSR.

Also at Theatre Academy, Patel directed a couple of politically progressive musicals, **P. L. Deshpande**'s *Three-Paisa Tamasha* (Tin-paishacha tamasha, 1978), based on Brecht's *Threepenny Opera*, and Arun Sadhu's *War Drums* (Padgham, 1984). Subsequently, Patel turned to film directing, and his theatre work slackened off.

From 2004 to 2005, Patel served as honorary executive director of the P. L. Deshpande Maharashtra Kala Academy. His other honors include the Padmashree award (1980) and the Punyabhushan from Pune (2002).

Shashikant Barhanpurkar

PHILIPPINES. The Philippines is an archipelago in Southeast Asia consisting of 7,107 islands with a total land area of 300,000 square kilometers. It has three geographical divisions: Luzon, Mindanao, and the Visayas with the first two among the country's largest islands. For **political** administration, the country is divided into seventeen regions.

The population of 89.5 million (2006) comprises more than seventy ethnolinguistic groups, the largest being Tagalog, Ilocano, Pampango, Cebuano, Ilocano, Ilonggo, Bicolano, Leyte-Samarnon, and Pangasinense. The national language is Filipino, based on Tagalog and accommodating words from indigenous and foreign languages. Both Filipino and English are considered official languages for communication and instruction. The majority of Filipinos is Catholic (80.9 percent) or Christian; Muslims constitute 5 percent and the remainder is Buddhist or unspecified.

Archaeological findings reveal the existence of flake tools from 28,500 BC and human fossils from 22,000 BC, linguistic studies show Arabic-Malay connections in the sixth century, and **Chinese** documents testify to trade relations from the tenth century. The Spaniards arrived in the sixteenth century, renamed the archipelago Felipinas, and imposed a colonial rule that lasted three centuries, ending only with the 1896 revolution and the 1898 declaration of independence. After losing the Spanish-American War, Spain ceded the Philippines to the United States, prompting a Philippine-American War (1899–1902) and American colonial rule until 1942. The Japanese occupied the Philippines from 1942 to 1945, and the Philippines regained independence in 1946.

Today, the Philippines has a presidential political system, a semifeudal and semicapitalist economic system, and, because of its colonial experience, a movement toward the promotion of national culture.

Philippine theatre encompasses all the performances mounted by the country's natives in one or more of the cultural traditions that have flourished during at least five centuries of its recorded history. To the oldest or precolonial tradition belong the mimetic performances, namely, the rituals, **dances**, and customs, still found among certain highland, interior or coastal communities that have not been substantially changed by contact with foreign or lowland Christian cultures.

Ritual Performance. **Religious** rituals are held to ensure victory in war, a bountiful harvest, recovery from illness, good fortune for the newly born or wed, or peace for the departed. In the ritual, a shaman (representing the spirit) takes the life of the sacrificial animal (representing the supplicant) so that the supplicant's life may be saved. Mimetic dances, performed during festivities for the harvest as well as for baptisms and weddings, include animal dances, such as those mimicking birds, monkeys, squirrels, ducks, and flies; and occupational dances, which may depict battle, fishing, beehive or bird hunting, and stages of rice-planting, harvesting, and winnowing. Mimetic customs are typified by courtship songs and dances between a male and a female, wedding rites where the parents of the bride and the groom exchange symbols of the dowry already agreed upon, and funeral rites that send off the dead with a supply of his/her favorite food, clothing, and weapons. As a whole, indigenous dramas reflect the common activities and concerns of the tribe as well as the natural environment that surrounds it. Collective in execution and communal in orientation, these **folk** performances answer basic tribal needs for economic and political survival as well as for social harmony.

Spanish Catholic Influences. Three hundred thirty-three years of Spanish colonization (1565–1898) introduced to lowland Christian groups, constituting more than 80 percent of the total population, semi-religious dramatic forms like ***komedya*** as well as religious didactic genres like ***sinakulo*** and the various playlets associated with the Catholic calendar's liturgy. Performed on an open-air **stage** for several evenings in honor of the town's patron saint, *komedya* dramatizes the biographies of patron saints or, more commonly, the lives and loves of princes and princesses in medieval European and Middle East kingdoms. The Christians win their battles with Moors decisively, and the Moors bow their heads for baptism rather than lose them. Staged during Lent and Holy Week, *sinakulo* is a verse play based on the *pasyon*, which narrates the history of Christian salvation, highlighting the scenes of Christ's passion and resurrection. As in *komedya*, rural folk who join *sinakulo* do so in fulfillment of religious vows.

As didactic as *sinakulo* are the playlets that dramatize an event or episode in Christ's life. The Christmas season is associated with the *panunulayan,* which enacts the search for an inn by Mary and Joseph on the first Christmas eve; the *pastores*, which has thirteen **women** and men dressed as shepherds in wide-brimmed hats, dancing and singing carols from house to house during the same season; and the *tatlong hari*, which features a procession of three men or boys dressed as the Three Kings. During Holy Week, most parishes hold the *osana*, which relives Christ's entry into Jerusalem on the first Palm Sunday; the *via crucis*, where the priest leads the faithful in a reenactment of Christ's carrying of the cross through the streets; the *paghuhugas*, which depicts Christ's washing of the feet of the twelve Apostles on Holy Thursday; the *huling hapunan*, an actual dinner served to the priest representing Christ and twelve men dressed as the Apostles at the last supper on Holy Thursday; the *siete palabras*, which, from noon to 3 p.m., relives Christ's agony on the cross with reflections on his Seven Last Words; the *salubong*, which enacts the meeting of the Virgin Mary and the Risen Christ on early Easter Sunday; and the *moriones*, which narrates the story of the Roman soldier Longhino, beheaded by Pilate's soldiers for proclaiming Christ's resurrection. For the fiesta of some towns, the *moros y cristianos*, a choreographed battle between Moors and Christians, ending with the baptism of the Moors, is sometimes performed for the patron saint.

All in all, theatre under Spanish rule presented characters and stories from a foreign culture that were discontinous with the native experience. They also propagate colonial mentality, as well as values of passivity and authoritarianism that ensured and ensures strict subservience to authority, regardless of the benefits to the people.

American Influences. American colonial rule (ca. 1900–1946) and the continuing American influence from 1946 to the present saw the rise to popularity of two forms introduced from Spain in the late nineteenth century, ***sarsuwela*** and ***drama***. Both, however, were eventually supplanted by the forms brought in by American rule, namely, ***bodabil*** and plays in English. *Sarsuwela* is a prose play with music that initially had anti-Spanish themes but eventually concentrated on exposing and reforming the social evils of gambling, corruption, and oppression of the poor by the powerful. *Drama* is a prose play revolving around a love situation that could either be comic, tragic, or allegorical. The last is also called *drama simboliko* and is exemplified by **Aurelio Tolentino**'s *Kahapon, Ngayon, and Bukas* (Kahapon, Ngayon, and Bukas, 1903), which shows three oppressors of the Filipino: the **Chinese** yesterday, the Spanish today, and the Americans tomorrow.

Dramas like *Kahapon* were brutally suppressed by the American military, so later *drama* and *sarsuwela* had to content themselves with criticizing social foibles. By the 1930s, *sarsuwela* and *drama* were already being banished from Manila **theatres** by *bodabil* (vaudeville), which, like its American antecedent, was a highly entertaining variety show of popular American (and later, Filipino) songs, dances, comedy skits, and circus acts. And while ordinary Filipinos were devouring *bodabil* numbers, students of the new American educational system were being trained in English language and literature, not only through class exercises but through the staging of major English-language plays or plays translated into English. In general, colonial rule suppressed anti-American themes, encouraged **playwrights** to choose "safe" subjects, and, more important, propagated and facilitated Americanization through the commercial **stage** and school auditorium.

Filipino Synthesis. From the 1940s to the present, the fourth tradition synthesized or transformed the many genres, elements, and styles from the first three. It accounts for (1) local translations and adaptations of foreign works, and (2) modern original plays written and produced by Filipinos.

Because they are studied in literature classes, foreign classics have been staged for the last five decades, either English or in English translation, or in Filipino translation or adaptation. Shakespeare's plays, notably, *Hamlet, Macbeth*, and the *Merchant of Venice*, have been staged and also have been performed in Filipino translation. Major works by Ibsen, Dürrenmatt, Chekhov, Williams, Miller, Brecht, Lorca, Genet, and Hwang have enjoyed several productions in Manila alone. Filipino adaptations of foreign classics, however, are fewer in number. A recent successful adaptation of *Romeo and Juliet* (1997) interpreted the star-crossed lovers as overseas Filipinos working in Japan.

Original works have used various styles to define the contemporary experience. **Western**-type realism has been adopted by local playwrights and follows two tendencies: the psychological, which dissects the problems of individuals, and the social, which relates individual issues to the larger framework of a class society. Psychological realism is exquisitely represented by Nick Joaquin's (1917–2004) *A Portrait of the*

Artist as Filipino (1955), the tragedy of two unmarried sisters who embody Hispanic gentility amidst the onslaught of prewar American-type commercialism. On the other hand, social realism is seen in Malou Jacob's (1948–) *Juan Tamban* (1987), about a social worker who gets politicized when she conducts field research for her MA thesis on a boy who reportedly eats lizards and roaches.

Recognizing that Philippine theatre has an older folk tradition, city-based theatre artists have attempted to bridge the gap between traditional and modern by revitalizing genres such as *komedya, sinakulo, sarsuwela, drama,* and *bodabil.* In 1988, Al Santos (1954–) contemporized *sinakulo* with the successful Good Friday staging of *Calvary of the Poor* (Kalbaryo ng maralitang taga-lungsod), where fourteen Christs representing fourteen poor communities in Manila carried crosses identified as anti-poor laws through the streets.

The dramatic monologue, which is inexpensive and portable, became popular after it was used in many political rallies against the Marcos dictatorship, especially in the 1980s. An outstanding example is Chris Millado's (1961–) *Moon and Gun in E Flat Major* (Buwan at baril sa eb major, 1984), whose separate episodes depict a range of very different characters engaged in the protest movement of the 1980s: a farmer and a worker, a priest and an Itawis woman, a socialite, the wife of a slain New People's Army leader, a student activist, and a police interrogator.

Music, movement, and dialogue are employed in creative ways by dance-dramas, which emerged in the 1980s to 1990s as a popular genre in urban and rural areas. At the First National Theatre **Festival** of the Cultural Center of the Philippines (1992), the epic *Hinilawod* was narrated in witty choreography by Agnes Locsin for the Dagyaw Company of Iloilo.

Producers, writers, and **directors** of musicals of the 1980s and 1990s selected elements from *sarsuwela* to *bodabil,* from radio to film, from *The Threepenny Opera* to *Les Miserables,* to structure original musicals, such as the stage adaptation of Jose Rizal's (1861–1896) *Touch Me Not* (Noli me tangere, 1995), by Bienvenido Lumbera and Ryan Cayabyab (1954–), and the ethnic musical rendition of the epic *Radia Magandiri* (1992), by Rody Vera (1960–) and the PETA music pool.

While slapstick comedies abound in television and film, social comedies or comedies of manners are few and far between in theatre. Recent comedies that break new ground are Dennis Marasigan's (1962–) *Life Is a Movie* (Ang buhay ay pelikula, 1992) and Butch Dalisay's (1954–) *Mac Malicsi, T.N.T.* (1991), about the travails of illegal migrants in the United States.

The most riveting contemporary plays, however, are those that liberally **experiment** with different styles to communicate insights into Filipino personal or social realities. Tony Perez's (1951–) *On North Diversion Road* (1988) presents ten vignettes, each showing the same **actors** in a car playing several married couples with very different reactions to the problem of the husband's infidelity. Anton Juan's (1950–) *Death in the Form of a Rose* (1991), uses chorus, **mask**, and metaphor to delineate the pain and passion in the life of Italian director Pier Paolo Pasolini.

Since independence arrived in 1946, theatre artists, like their counterparts in literature, visual arts, architecture, music, dance, and cinema, have patiently devoted their efforts to the creation of a national theatre. While that goal has not been reached, one cannot deny the fact that theatre artists have succeeded in the past two decades in moving toward a clearer definition of that theatre. This is so because the many spatial, cultural, and colonial distances that have kept artists apart for so long have, for the most part, already been bridged or minimized. For one, the cultural gap between highland communities, rural folk, and urbanized Filipinos has been reduced by the serious attempts by city-based artists not only to research forms from the ethnic, Hispanic, and American traditions, but to revitalize them so that they can be more meaningful to audiences of whatever class or sector. On the other hand, the spatial gap between artists spread out all over the archipelago has been bridged by the creation of government programs (for example, grants, festivals, outreach and exchange programs) that encourage and recognize original works coming from the regions and acknowledge the value of their work in defining the national soul from below. Finally, the colonial gap that drove a wedge between urban artists hung up on the Western theatre of New York and London and urban and rural artists who consciously rejected a theatre of slavish imitation has been partly bridged with the involvement of "legitimate" artists in original productions for all classes on the one hand, and the selective but successful use of "nationalist" artists of the latest genres and styles from the West in the portrayal of authentic Filipino experiences. With constant exposure to each other and each other's works, there is now much more openness among artists of very diverse backgrounds and origins, and much more of a willingness to experiment with whatever genre could examine and expose the Filipino experience in a truer light.

FURTHER READING

Brandon, James R. *Theatre in Southeast Asia*; Bañas, Raymundo C. *Pilipino Music and Theater*; Fernández, Doreen G. *Palabas: Essays on Philippine Theater History*; Tiongson, Nicanor G. *Dulaan: An Essay on Philippine Theater*.

Nicanor G. Tiongson (with Joi Barrios)

PILLAI, G. SANKARA (1930–1989). **Indian** Malayalam **playwright**, **director**, academic, **critic**, translator, and folklorist. He was born in Chirayinkil, Thiruvananthapuram District, and studied Malayalam at Kerala University. Pillai was a Malayalam university lecturer until 1977. During the 1950s and 1960s, he played a crucial role in building up the modern sensibility in Malayalam theatre, focusing mainly on introducing **experimental** trends in playwriting and directing.

His major plays include *Messenger of Love* (Snehadootan, 1956), *Marriages Are Made in Heaven* (Vivaham swargathil, 1958), *Prayer Room* (Puja-muri, 1966), *Crazy World* (Pae pidicha lokam, 1969), *Swansong* (Bharata vakyam, 1972), *Presentation: Lunatic Asylum* (Avataranam bhrantalayam, 1976), *Prisoner* (Bandi, 1977), *In Search of a Dark God* (Karuthadaivathe thedi, 1980), and *Hunter's Tale* (Kiratam, 1985). These works, several of which verge on social satire, represent a range of approaches; they generally seek a total theatre effect, and sometimes employ movements based on *kalarippayattu*, the martial art.

Starting with a small village group, Prasadhana Little **Theatres**, he began and led the "theatre workshop" (*nataka kalari*) movement, based on practical workshops throughout Kerala. A supporter of the "theatre of roots" philosophy, Pillai laid a strong foundation by incorporating native traditions as well as **Western** practice. *Nataka kalari* was part of a bigger radical movement, in arts and literature, that took place in Kerala in the 1960s immediately after the **political** split within India's Communist Party, a division that helped bring new ideas, directions, and cultural values unhindered by local communist surveillance (see Censorship). Plays were directed in the workshops by

In Search of a Dark God, by G. Sankara Pillai, directed by S. Ramanujam, Trivandrum, India, January 2005. (Photo: Courtesy of the Abhinaya Theatre Research Centre)

eminent directors like S. Ramanujam (1935–). Direction, **acting**, and **scenography** were taught locally for the first time in these workshops.

The School of Drama, University of Calicut, of which he became founder-director (1977), was the final outcome of the workshop movement. There he created the Calicut University Little Theatre (CULT), the first Malayalam repertory company. In 1988, he founded the School of Letters, Mahatma Gandhi University.

His essays on various aspects of practice and **theory**, both Asian and Western, are seminal. He also wrote a book on Malayalam theatre history. His many awards include the National Academy of **Music**, **Dance**, and Drama (Sangeet Natak Akademi) and Soviet Land Nehru awards. As chairman of the Kerala Sangeeta Nataka Akademi, he carried out many projects on Kerala's folklore and performance traditions.

B. Ananthakrishnan

PLAYWRIGHTS AND PLAYWRITING

Playwrights and Playwriting: Bangladesh

Calcutta (Kolkata), center of Bengali theatre after **India**'s independence (1947), was dominated by middle-class Bengali Hindus. **Pakistan**'s creation (1947) launched new **political**, economic, social, and cultural issues between both countries, eventually reflected in theatre. In **Bangladesh**, dramatic literature's popularity dates to the nation's struggle for liberation from Pakistan and its attainment of independence in 1971. West Pakistan's autocratic rule led to an increasing polarization of playwriting trends in East Pakistan: **religion**-based nationalism and language-based nationalism. The religion-based trend glorifies Islamic history in the Middle East, India, and

Bengal. Its chief playwrights are Akbaruddin (1895–1978), Ibrahim Khan (1894–1978), and Ibrahim Khalil (1916–). The language-based trend was led by a number of playwrights associated with Dhaka University productions: participating in the political unrest, courting arrest, and going to the battlefronts helped radicalize students. Theatre became a site where political and humanist issues were played out.

Raging political issues are raised in Ascar Ibn Shaikh's (1925–) *Fire Mountain* (Agnigiri, 1958), and **Muneir Chowdhury**'s "The Grave" (Kabar, 1953) and *The Blood Fields* (Raktakto prantor, 1959). Anees Chowdhury (1929–1990) wrote *Map* (Manchitra, 1963) and *Album* (1965). Playwrights responding to popular movements created a new impetus.

The language movement of 1952 set further parameters by intensifying the level of social awareness and commitment. "The Grave" was written while Chowdhury was a political prisoner in Dakha Central Jail; the inmates performed it clandestinely, using hurricane lanterns and matches for light. Its essential appeal lies in its theme of the inalienable right of one's cultural heritage in the face of officially condoned brutality. A number of **experimental** playwrights emerged subsequently, including Syed Waliullah (1922–1971) and Saeed Ahmed (1931–). Waliullah, a famous novelist, introduced political symbolism with a strong materialist emphasis far removed from the spiritualism of **Rabindranath Tagore**. His three plays include *Bahipir* (1960), *Tarangabhanga* (1964), and *Ujane Mrtyu* (1964). Saeed Ahmed introduced absurdism in *The Thing* (Kalbela, 1966), among other plays. Zia Hyder (1936–) also was among avant-garde playwrights.

Plays from the post-independence era of the mid-1970s combined both euphoria over independence and the first shock of disillusionment. Subsequently, the collapse of the well-made play and the inspiration of **folk theatre** and its conventions inspired the next generation.

Selim Al-Deen (1948–), an experimentalist, went from politically charged plays to works using folk elements, such as *Hat Hadai*, a look at the ethnic people in a remote rural area. Abdullah Al Mamun (1942–) revealed an interest in the anti-imperialist movement and issues of class struggle in plays such as *The Promise* (Sapath, 1978) and *War All Around* (Charidike Yuddha, 1983). Syed Samsul Haq (1935–) wrote the verse drama *You Can Hear the Footsteps* (Payer awaj paoa jaye, 1976), set during the War of Liberation. His landmark play *The Entire Life of Nurul Deen* (Nurul Deener sarajiban, 1982) is about a peasant revolt under British rule. Actor-**director** Mamunur Rashid (1948–) is known for his socially and politically conscious plays, including *They Are Kadam Ali* (Ora Kadam Ali, 1978) and *The Devil* (Iblish, 1982). Nurel Momen (1906–1989) wrote *Nemesis* (1984), about a famine in the 1940s, and the comic *Transformation* (Rupantar, 1948). Showkat Osman (1917–1998) attacked capitalism in *The Bureaucrat's Trial* (Amlar mamla, 1949).

FURTHER READING

Ahmed, Syed Jamil. *Acin Pakhi Infinity: Indigenous Theatre of Bangladesh.*

Bishnupriya Dutt

Playwrights and Playwriting: Cambodia

In the 1950s and 1960s, playwrights such as **Hang Tun Hak** and Peau Yuleng (1917–1981) introduced "spoken drama" (*lakhon niyey*) to **Cambodia**, which thrived until the Khmer Rouge takeover (1975). Hang Tun Hak was renowned for controversial plays about contemporary **politics** and social relations. Peau Yuleng, who was a **director** as well, also wrote plays with contemporary themes. Playwriting became established in the National Conservatory of Performing Arts and then, in the mid-1960s, in the Royal University of Fine Arts.

Between 1975 and 1979, all theatre activity, as Cambodians had known it, ceased. In the 1980s, after conditions allowed theatre's resumption, **Pich Tum Kravel** rose to prominence, combining historical references with then-current political realities. Since the end of communism and an opening to the broader international community in the 1990s, artists have had a chance to revisit older work as well as to explore evolving local and global themes.

Contemporary playwrights study and work at the Royal University of Fine Arts or the Ministry of Culture and Fine Arts' Department of Performing Arts, producing works that address themes ranging from Buddhist teachings to the legacy of the Khmer Rouge revolution, to prostitution and AIDS. Their pieces are performed at various **theatres**. Playwrights include Kim Pinun (1961–), Chen Neak (1946–), and Khem Bophavy (1964–), among others.

Catherine Filloux

Playwrights and Playwriting: China

Pre–Twentieth Century. The main pre-modern dramas the **Chinese** classify as good literature are *zaju* and *kunqu*. Other styles, notably *jingju*, are loved more as performance items than as literature. Until the twentieth century their authors were usually unknown; even today few are regarded as literary masters.

The **storyteller**'s art predates the origins of China's drama and is a major source of plots for both dramas and novels. Stories were told in the streets about the civil wars of the Three Kingdoms period (220–265) from at least as early as the Tang dynasty (618–907). Such stories were adapted into dramas and the novel *The Romance of the Three Kingdoms* (Sanguo zhi yanyi) by Luo Guanzhong (fl. fourteenth century), the novel becoming the main source of numerous popular items. These storytellers set a basic pattern followed by most Chinese dramas (and novels) until the twentieth century: they are episodic, not climactic, relating individual episodes of a long story rather than weaving a plot that rises to a climax.

The authors of the earliest dramas, ***nanxi***, are unknown. Some items probably came from "writing clubs" (*shuhui*), active in vernacular literature from about the eleventh to fifteenth centuries. The earliest group of known professional playwrights wrote *zaju*. Most important was **Guan Hanqing** (ca. 1220–ca. 1300), but there were many others. Wang Shifu (?–ca. 1320), author of *The Story of the Western Chamber* (Xixiang ji), is representative. His play is not only among history's most famous but is an archetypical representative of the romance in which a scholar wins his love against her parents' opposition and passes the official examinations.

The fourteenth century saw the re-emergence of southern drama in ***chuanqi***. Initially written in crude language, like *nanxi*, *chuanqi* were taken up by the educated elite. The language grew refined and elevated. From the beginning, themes focused on romance, the hero sometimes gaining success in the examinations. As the literati took them over, themes and ideology became more Confucianized, with emphasis on virtues like filial piety, loyalty, and service to the ruler.

The rise of *kunqu* spawned another series of great dramatists, especially **Tang Xianzu** and his contemporaries **Hong Sheng** and **Kong Shangren**. With performances of these episodic works lasting three days and nights, the practice of giving only key scenes quickly arose.

Tang Ying (1682–1756) wrote *kunqu* but also gained inspiration from regional theatre, unusual since literary figures typically despised popular mass theatre. He was among the last significant *kunqu* dramatists. From the mid-eighteenth century on, regional theatre moved to center **stage**. Most of its pre-twentieth-century authors are unknown, and at least some were probably the **actors** themselves. Playwriting was the adaptation of already existing stories drawn from earlier dramas/novels to a different regional style, not the creation of new pieces.

An important work showing the transition of creativity from *kunqu* to regional theatre is the anthology *White Furcoat of Compositions* (Zhui baiqiu), collected from the first half of the seventeenth century to 1777. It contains 438 scenes from eighty-seven *kunqu* dramas, and fifty-nine regional scenes, including *yiyang qiang* and **bangzi qiang**. Though *kunqu* are still more numerous, the fact that there are regional pieces makes the collection special, since these were usually transmitted orally and kept by actors, not written down for publication. Also significant is that the items are scenes extracted from longer dramas, which is how regional dramas were usually performed.

From early times, dramas subdivide into "civilian" (*wen*), dealing with such matters as family affairs, and "military" (*wu*), featuring battle scenes. *Jingju* represents the acme of this division, with acrobatic battle scenes. Even **role types** feature civilian and military subdivisions.

Jingju items were mostly special to one particular actor and transmitted, if at all, to disciples. Nineteenth-century examples are rarely attributable to a particular author and published collections are rare.

Traditional Forms: Republican Period. The Republican period (1911–1949) saw the rise of "new dramas" (*xinxi*), some of them concerned with social reform. Many new *jingju*, however, were jointly created by scholars and actors. Mostly adaptations of old stories, they contained reformist messages only indirectly if at all, becoming the actor's exclusive property. **Mei Lanfang, Chang Yanqiu, Shang Xiaoyun** and **Xun Huisheng**, the "four great *dan*" after their female-role (*dan*) specialty, were foremost among actors for whom these "new dramas" were created, by far the most important partnership being that between **theorist** and playwright Qi Rushan (1877–1962) and Mei. Other major collaborating playwrights included Luo Yinggong (1880–1924), who created many plays with Chang Yanqiu, and Chen Moxiang (1884–1942), who created a number of plays with Xun Huisheng, and also worked with Chang.

Playwrights were also instrumental in many regional forms. Cheng Zhaocai (1874–1929) of Hebei Province helped create the *pingju* form, writing approximately one hundred plays for it. Other important regional playwrights who both adapted traditional dramas and wrote new reformist plays include Fan Zidong (1878–1954) and Ma Jianling (1907–1965), who wrote for Shaanxi's *qinqiang* and Fan Cuiting (1905–1966), who wrote for Henan's *yuju*.

The single most important independent *xiqu* playwright of the period was **Tian Han**. He created, adapted, or translated over 120 plays, including thirty-two *xiqu* plays for Hunan's *xiangju*, Shaoxing's **yueju**, *kunqu*, and *jingju*, among the most famous being his classic *jingju* of *The White Snake* (Baishe zhuan).

Traditional Forms: People's Republic of China. Under the People's Republic, old dramas were initially revived and preserved, and the creation of two types of new dramas was encouraged: those covering traditional themes, **xinbian lishi ju**, and those on modern themes, "contemporary plays" (*xiandai xi*).

During the Cultural Revolution (1966–1976), traditionally themed items were **censored**, and "model works" (**yangban xi**) on revolutionary themes were developed by committees. Since the late 1970s, in creating new plays in *jingju* and many other forms of *xiqu*, playwrights have generally served among the main members of teams including actors, **musicians**, **directors**, and experts. About one hundred new *jingju* were thus created from 1950 to 2000.

FURTHER READING

Birch, Cyril. *Scenes for Mandarins: The Elite Theater of the Ming*; Idema, Wilt L., and Stephen West. *Chinese Theater, 1100–1450: A Source Book*; Shih, Chung-wen. *The Golden Age of Chinese Drama: Yuan Tsa-chu*; Sieber, Patricia. *Theaters of Desire. Authors, Readers, and the Reproduction of Early Chinese Song-Drama, 1300–2000;* Swatek, Catherine C. *Peony Pavilion Onstage: Four Centuries in the Career of a Chinese Drama.*

Colin Mackerras and Elizabeth Wichmann-Walczak

Modern Drama to 1949. Playwriting is conventionally considered the essence of modern "spoken drama" (*huaju*), as indicated by the term's emphasis on language. However, performances of *xinju* or *wenming xi*, antecedents to *huaju*, relied upon scenarios (*mubiao*), rather than scripts (*juben*), and incorporated improvisation, as influenced by *xiqu* and **Japan**'s **shinpa**. With **experimental theatre**'s appearance in the post-Mao period, performance has received greater emphasis, reducing the hegemony of the script in the theatrical experience.

Western playwrights and their emphasis on dialogue and well-made plots inspired *huaju*'s development. The earliest dramatists were students of foreign literature. **Hong Shen** wrote the one-act "Pear Salesman" (Mai li ren, 1915) while attending Qinghua University. Zhang Pengchun (1892–1957) began writing scripts after going to the United States to study in 1910; his "The Awakening" (Xing), originally written in English, was performed in China in 1916, as was his five-act *A Momentary Lapse* (Yi nian cha).

Intellectuals and writers of fiction and poetry began writing plays after being encouraged by the leaders of the May Fourth Movement to challenge cultural traditions. Hu Shi (1891–1962), an intellectual and educator, wrote the one-act "The Greatest Event in Life" (Zhongshen dashi, publ. 1919), inspired by Ibsen's *A Doll's House*. A farcical critique of arranged marriage and an expression of support for free love, it exemplified how plays could advocate social change; produced for friends while Hu studied in the United States, it was deemed inappropriate when a girls' school attempted to stage it in China in 1919. Chen Dabei's (1887–1944) *Ms. Youlan* (Youlan nüshi, 1921) and **Ouyang Yuqian**'s "Shrew" (Pofu, 1922) and "After Returning Home" (Huijia yihou, 1924) imitated Ibsenian dramaturgy while promoting individual emancipation. In the 1920s, playwrights also adopted satire as a form of social criticism, as represented by Ding Xilin's (1893–1974) "Wasp" (Yi zhi mafeng, 1923) and "Oppression" (Yapo, 1926).

Some playwrights, especially those who had studied abroad, began employing modernist techniques, as in Hong Shen's *Yama Chao* (Zhao Yanwang, 1922), inspired by the expressionism of O'Neill's *The Emperor Jones*. Hong incorporated **stage** directions to guide **directors**, **actors**, and **scenographic** designers; playwrights had to be knowledgeable about performance.

Influential, foreign-educated, **women** playwrights of the period include Bai Wei (1894–1987) and Yuan Changying (1894–1973). While Bai's poetic style in *Julie* (Zhuli, 1925) and *Sophie* (Sufei, 1926) drew from Maeterlinck, Strindberg, and Wilde, her acclaimed *Escape from the Haunted Pagoda* (Da chu youling ta, 1928) adopts a more natural style, attributed to Galsworthy, in its tragic portrayal of revolution, love, and censure of the "old society" that had victimized her. Yuan, a proponent of the art-for-art's-sake circle that resisted the trend toward proletarian literature, used Western techniques to write fiction, drama, and poetry on what were later labeled "bourgeois" themes. Her "Southeast Flies the Peacock" (Kongque dongnan fei, 1929), portrays a couple's suicide and a widow's emotional distress due to the traditional society's constraints.

Since *huaju*'s inception, translations/adaptations of Western dramas have played an important role. Li Jianwu (1906–1982) translated and adapted more than fifty classical and modern dramas, including works by Shakespeare, Sardou, Molière, Gorky, Chekhov, and Tolstoy.

The turn in the 1930s toward proletarian plays is exemplified by Tian Han. His early plays, such as "One Night in a Café" (Kafeidian zhi yi ye, 1920) and "The Night the Tiger Was Caught" (Huo hu zhi ye, 1922), paralleled the "amateur theatre movement" (*ameide*) and were written for students, aiming at educational and artistic, rather than commercial, purposes. Influenced by Wilde's aestheticism and a sense of romanticism, he wrote *Death of a Star* (Mingyou zhi si, 1927) and "Tragedy on the Lake" (Hushang de beiju, 1929). The year he joined the Communist Party, Tian wrote "The Alarm Bell" (Luanzhong, 1932), a leftist playwriting model.

Playwriting's maturity is associated with **Cao Yu** and Xia Yan (1900–1995), an influential leftist dramatist of the 1930s. Their tragic masterpieces critiqued capitalism. Cao Yu's *Thunderstorm* (Leiyu, 1933) roughly followed the Aristotelian unities. His *Wilderness* (Yuanye, 1937) was inspired by expressionism, while another modernist approach was used in his imagistic tragi-comedy *Peking Man* (Beijing ren, 1940). Xia Yan's *Under Shanghai Eaves* (Shanghai wuyan xia, 1937) depicts a cross-section of five poor Shanghai families, each given distinct spatial and temporal representations on stage.

Satire also took aim at social conditions. Chen Baichen's (1908–1994) *Seeking Political Promotion* (Shengguan tu, 1945), inspired by Gogol, is the most celebrated work of this type.

Post-1949 Playwriting. From 1949 to 1966, playwriting served mainly to bolster communist ideology by extolling characters who upheld party values. Socialist realism, which inherently emphasized the class struggle, and romanticized the new over the old, was adopted as the major style. Sun Yu's "Women's Representative" (Funü daibiao, 1952) challenges rural traditional values regarding women while endorsing their full participation in China's workforce. Both *Sentries under the Neon Lights* (Nihongdeng xia de shaobing, 1962) by Shen Ximeng et al. and *The Younger Generation* (Nianqing de yidai, 1963) by Chen Yun (1923–1999), which adhere to the 1962 doctrine of class struggle, exemplify contemporary ideology regarding how to carry on the "glorious revolutionary tradition." The former portrays how a group of communist soldiers, after successfully "liberating" Shanghai, defeat the class enemy's new style of attack "wrapped with sugar paste." The even more ideologically rigid latter contrasts two university graduates and their relatives, most of them offspring of the first generation of revolutionaries. It eulogizes the victory of selfless devotion to the party and socialism over selfish bourgeois values. Both were later filmed; playwrights also wrote screenplays at state studios.

"Historical dramas" (*lishi ju*) during the 1950s and 1960s once more became veiled mediums for criticizing the government. Cao Yu's *The Gall and the Sword* (Dan jian pian, 1961), set in the fifth century BC, is considered an allegory encouraging the people to lift their spirits in the wake of various disasters, including China's breakup with the USSR and the great famine of the early 1960s. Tian Han's *Guan Hanqing* (1958), named for the ancient dramatist, also used allegory to leverage artistic and intellectual expression. Guo Moruo (1892–1978), author of the historical drama *Qu Yuan* (1942), penned *Cai Wenji* (1959) and *Wu Zetian* (1962). They romanticized excoriated historical figures to extol China's revolution and construct a heightened sense of national and cultural unity.

Lao She's "slice of life" realist masterpieces *Dragon Beard Ditch* (Longxugou, 1950) and *The Teahouse* (Chaguan, 1957) established the influential Beijing playwriting style that emphasizes local vernacular, colorful characterization, and a critique of modern Chinese history. During the Cultural Revolution (1966–1976), play publication ceased, with the exception of the politically correct *yangban xi*, written to support the politics of Mao Zedong (1893–1976) and the Gang of Four.

Since 1976, social and economic reforms have helped to diversify dramatic content and form. Important women playwrights emerged, including Bai Fengxi (1934–), who wrote "First Bathed in the Moonlight" (Mingyue chu zhao ren, 1981), and Zhang Lili (1956–), writer of *Green Barracks* (Lüse yingdi, 1992). Beijing-style scripts include *The World's Top Restaurant* (Tianxia diyi lou, 1988), by female playwright He Jiping (1951–), Li Longyun's (1948–) *Small Well Hutong* (Xiaojing hutong, 1981), and Guo Shixing's (1952–) *Birdmen* (Niao ren, 1993).

Playwriting—influenced by modes such as absurdism—adopted greater formal experimentation in the 1980s and 1990s, as seen in **Gao Xingjian**'s *Bus Stop* (Chezhan, 1983), Sha Yexin's (1939–) *Jiang Qing and Her Husbands* (Jiang Qing he ta de zhangfumen, 1991), and *Jesus, Confucius, and John Lennon* (Yesu, Kongzi, pitoushi Lienong, 1989), in addition to **Wei Minglun**'s absurdist *chuanju Pan Jinlian* (1986).

Adaptations of Western dramas remained important in the 1990s, including Huang Jisu's (1955–) *Accidental Death of an Anarchist* (1998), adapted from Dario Fo. Some recent productions, especially those directed by Mou Sen (1963–) and Meng Jinghui (1965–), which emphasize theatricality and visual effect, have diffused the centrality of the written script, the spoken word, and the playwright that conventionally are *huaju*'s hallmarks.

FURTHER READING

Chen, Xiaomei. *Acting the Right Part: Political Theater and Popular Drama in Contemporary China, 1966–1996;* Li, Ruru. *Shashibiya: Staging Shakespeare in China.*

Jonathan Noble

Playwrights and Playwriting: India

Sanskrit Drama. Sanskrit emerged in **India** about 1500 BC as an elite language associated with devotion and nobility; it was augmented by a number of common dialects called Prakrits. Over the centuries, Sanskrit changed very little while the Prakrits evolved into independent literary languages. Indirect evidence of dramatic enactments appears in some of the earliest extant Sanskrit literary works. Though no names of plays or playwrights survive from then, it seems likely that Sanskrit drama thrived in parts of the South Asian subcontinent from sometime between 200 BC and 900 AD.

The *Treatise on Drama* (Natyashastra; see Theory) describes many aspects of **Sanskrit theatre** production, including playwriting instructions. Although it indicates that playwrights were commonly members of a **theatre company**, available information suggests that they were either kings or closely associated with the nobility. It seems unlikely that high-caste nobility would have worked closely with low-caste performers. The extent to which kings actually wrote plays, or were honored with the attribution of authorship, is debated. Some believe that the earliest extant play is fragments (discovered in 1911) of what they believe is a second-century work by poet and Buddhist philosopher Ashvaghosa, *The Story of Sariputra* (Sariputtaprakarana), which—dealing with conversions to Buddhism—follows the *Natyashastra*'s concerns even though its morals are Buddhist. The playwright with the greatest number of extant works—thirteen—is **Bhasa**, although there are questions about their provenance. They include the only two surviving tragedies, *The Broken Thighs* (Urubhanga) and *Karna's Burden* (Kanabhara). Bhasa is best known for *The Vision of Vasavadatta* (Svapna–Vasavadatta).

Ten different play types are described; only four are represented in the surviving works, whose most common types are the *nataka* and the *prakarana*, each typically ten acts long and dealing with a wide range of emotions and dramatic activity. The *nataka* is primarily distinguished from the *prakarana* by its story type. The *prakarana* tells an invented story based on minor nobility; the *nataka* is based on a well-known story involving kings and queens. The classic *nataka* is **Kalidasa**'s *The Recognition of Shakuntala* (Abhijnana Sakuntalam). Kalidasa elevated the story's tone so the leading lovers become caught up in a swirl of mythic events beyond their power to change. Kalidasa's poetry and sentiment has rarely been equaled. The most famous of the extant *prakarana* is *The Little Clay Cart* (Mrcchakatika) by the pseudonymous Sudraka. The first four acts are a near copy of an earlier work by Bhasa. The play is a curious mix of love interest and murder mystery possessing some of Sanskrit drama's most colorful characters.

Later notable playwrights include Visakhadatta (sixth or seventh century) and **Bhavabhuti** (early eighth century). Visakhadatta wrote only the seven-act *The Signet Ring of Rakshasa* (Mudrarakshasa), presenting a tightly wrought **political** intrigue—unique in Sanskrit drama—from the court of Chandragupta; concerned with an almost Machiavellian king's rulership, it has a rare lack of humor and romantic interest. Bhavabhuti has three surviving plays, most notably *The Latter Exploits of Rama* (Uttararama-carita), whose tragic irony and complex poetic images evoke psychological states. Afterward, Sanskrit drama declined as the plays turned more formulaic, and the language quality deteriorated as Sanskrit became increasingly removed from everyday speech. Islam's arrival and Buddhism's departure further eroded the foundations for theatre over the next several centuries.

A few Sanskrit drama innovations appeared after the first millennium; Krsnamisra's widely imitated *The Rise of the Moon of Intellect* (Prabodhacandrodaya, 1098) is an allegorical drama with some humorous parody; for the most part it functions as a didactic morality play extolling Vishnu's virtues. The gradual return of drama would be partly due to the wide popularity of Vaishnavist **religious** cults sponsoring various performances as ritual enactments of religious devotion. Unnayi Varrier (1665–1725) and Kottayam Tampuran (1675–1725) are playwrights who contributed to the growing number of devotional **dance**-dramas, such as *kathakali*. Derived partly from the *nataka*, the new works used well-known *Ramayana* or *Mahabharata* episodes and included Sanskrit quatrains but relied on a literary Dravidian-based language, Manipravalam, for dialogue (*see also* Dramatic Structure).

Nineteenth Century to 1947. Modern drama was first introduced to South Asia by way of the British colonial enterprise. London exported productions to India as early as 1770, and amateur productions of **Western** drama by British expatriates were underway for nearly twenty years before. By 1795, in Calcutta, Russian entrepreneur Herasim Lebedeff began the first Bengali-language **theatre**. The plays were translations of British farces, but they set new precedents by using proscenium **stages**, charging admission, and having men and **women** perform together.

Popular entertainment grew dramatically in the mid-nineteenth century with the rise of **Parsi theatre**. The play launching this movement was the Urdu romance, *The Court of Lord Indra* (Indar sabha, 1853) by Amanat Lakhnawi (1815–1859), first produced at Wajid Ali Shah's Lucknow court. It was South Asia's most frequently performed late-nineteenth-century play and established the paradigm for contemporary popular entertainments with spectacular **scenography** and copious **musical** numbers. Agha Hashra Kasmiri (1879–1935), Narayan Prasad Betab (1872–1945), and Radhey Shyam Kathawachack (1890–1963), among others, freely adapted Shakespeare to appeal to rising urban middle-class tastes. In 1914, Kavi Nanalal Dalpatram (1877–1946) wrote *Jaya-Jayant* in order to elevate Parsi theatre's literary quality, but despite such efforts this theatre declined after "talkies" arrived in the 1930s.

Assamese playwright Gunabhiram Barua (1837–1894) was a pioneer who attempted to bring together Sanskrit and Western theatre in *Ram and Nabami* (Ram-Nabami natak, 1857). Shortly thereafter, Bengali **Michael Madhusudan Dutt** (1824–1873), in *Sharmishtha* (1859), set the tone for many plays that would try to revive the Sanskrit aesthetic while promoting modern values. Later, similarly styled plays include *False Pride* (Mithyabhiman, 1870) by Gujurati playwright Dalpatram (1820–1898) and *The Story of Sobhadra* (Soubhadra, 1883) by Hindi playwright **Annasaheb Kirloskar**. Symbolic spiritual allegory appeared in the Sanskrit-styled work of **Girish Chanda Ghosh** and Nobel Prize–winning **Rabindranath Tagore**. Tagore represents the artistic zenith of Indian symbolist theatre. Many of his works were seen only as private productions during his lifetime but became more widely appreciated after World War II.

A more confrontational anti-colonial sentiment was expressed in **Dinabandhu Mitra**'s famous *The Indigo Mirror* (Nildarpan, publ. 1860; prod. 1872). This hard-hitting, realistic play exposed the terrible abuses of the colonial indigo planting system. It was banned by colonial authorities and the ensuing controversy led to the establishment of the Dramatic Performances Control Act of 1876.

Faced by strong **censorship**, most playwrights had to abandon direct attacks against the colonizers and instead took up composing convoluted allegories based on classical stories or pure fantasies laden with social commentary. Plays also criticized Hindu culture and exposed the abuses of Brahmanical authority, child marriage, widow burning, and excessive dowries. Two notable Telugu plays in this style are by Gurazada Venkata Appa Rao (1862–1915) with *Bride-Price* (Kanyasulkam, 1892) and Kallakuri Narayana Rao (1871–1927) with *Varavikrayamu* (1923). Hindu Nationalists embraced this style of theatre, and it was developed and promoted by **critics** and playwrights, such as **Bharatendu Harishchandra**, who advocated for greater attention to social consciousness.

While some plays written from the 1870s to the 1930s saw their way into print, most existed primarily on the stage. Dramatists were usually also known as **actors**, managers, or **directors**. Colonial-period theatre often privileged performance over literary quality.

Social realism slowly returned in the 1930s and 1940s, beginning with *A Train* (Agagdi, 1934), a Gujarati play by Chandravadan Chimanlal Mehta (1901–1991), which describes the desperate lives of the poor living and working alongside the railroad. It was followed by the Hindi *New Harvest* (Navanna, 1944) by **Bijon Bhattacharya** and in 1945 by an Oriya play, *Rice* (Bhata), by Kali Charan Patnaik (1898–1978).

Support from the Indian People's Theatre Association (IPTA, founded 1942–1943)—allowed leftist political theatre to become a dynamic force as street theatre took its causes to the people. Street theatre's socialist/minimalist agitprop style had a lasting impact on Indian drama's future and is referred to as the "parallel theatre" movement. By doing away with proscenium theatres there was a sense that the modern stage was at last becoming more uniquely Indian.

Post-1947. The end of World War II, with the subsequent civil war, arrival in 1947 of independence, partition of **Pakistan**, and assassination of Gandhi, brought about a deep despair and search for new meaning. Several different directions appeared in the plays of the 1950s and 1960s as realism gave way to **experimentation**. **Dharamavir Bharati**'s *The Blind Age* (Andha Yug, 1962) powerfully spoke to the prevailing mood by retelling the story of the end of the great war (*bharatayudha*) from the *Mahabharata*. It infused existential philosophy into the Hindu epic and staged the action in the manner of a Greek tragedy with a few Sanskrit theatre elements. Kannada playwright **Adya Rangacharya** (1904–1985) first represented this tumultuous period with his realistic *The Wheel of Sorrow* (Shokachakra, 1956), but later adopted a more minimalist, Sanskrit-like style for *Listen, O! Janamejaya* (Kelu Janamejaya, 1960).

FURTHER READING

George, K. M., trans. *Masterpieces of Indian Literature*; Keith, A. Berriedale. *The Sanskrit Drama*.

Robert Petersen

India has a spectrum of skilled playwrights across a range of styles. Most, although in many cases writing in the 1950s and 1960s, remained virtually unknown outside India for several decades. Until the 1980s, very few plays were published in English or English translation. The last two decades have seen a substantial increase, and work is now available via Oxford India, Seagull, Rupa, and other publishers. It is still difficult, however, for young writers to make a mark, even in Indian languages, let alone in a form accessible to international audiences. The same is even more true of women. There are also very few **training** opportunities for writers in any genre. The only routes to getting new writing performed are by working through established groups and/or directors, or—even more problematic—entering competitions.

Playwrights may be broken down into major stylistic areas and representative examples as follows (only selected plays published in English are cited):

"Theatre of Roots" (**folk**; traditional; rural):

> **Kavalam Narayana Pannikar** (Kerala): *The Domain of the Sun* (Suryasthan, publ. 1989), *Theyya Theyyam* (Spirit of the Spirit, 1991), *The Lone Tusker* (Ottayan, 1971), *Karimkutty* (1983).

> **Chandrasekhar Kambar** (Karnataka): *Jokumaraswami* (1972).

> **Girish Karnad** (Karnataka): *Tughlaq* (1964), *Horse-Head* (Hayavadana, publ. 1971; first prod. 1973), *Play with a Cobra* (Naga-mandala, 1988), *The Fire and the Rain* (Agni mattu male, 1994).

> **Habib Tanvir** (Chhattisgarh): *Bazaar in Agra* (Agra Bazaar, 1954), *Charandas Chor* (1975).

> **Ratan Thiyam** (Manipur): *Battle Formation* (Chakravyuha, 1984), *Hiroshima* (1994).

> **Heisnam Kanhailal** (Manipur): *Pebet* (1975), *Memoirs of Africa* (1985).

Bourgeois (urban, realist):

> **Vijay Tendulkar** (Maharashtra): *Ghashiram the Policeman* (Ghashiram Kotwal, 1972), *Silence! The Court Is in Session* (Shantata! court chalu ahe, 1967), *Sakharam the Book-Binder* (Sakharam Binder, 1972).

> **Mahesh Elkunchwar** (Maharashtra): *Party* (1976), *Flowers of Blood* (Raktapushpa, 1981), *Reflection* (Pratibimb, 1987).

> **Mahesh Dattani** (Maharashtra/Karnataka): *Tara* (1990), *Dance Like a Man* (1989), *On a Muggy Night in Mumbai* (1998).

Incorporating Aspects of Both the Above:

> **Badal Sircar** (West Bengal): *Bhoma* (1976), *Procession* (Micchil, 1974), *Stale News* (Basi khabar, 1979), *And Indrajit* (Evam Indrajit, 1963).

> **Usha Ganguli** (West Bengal): *The Mourner* (Rudali, 1992).

Historical/Political:

> **G. P. Deshpande** (Maharashtra): *Chanakya Vishnugupta* (1996), *The Ruined Sanctuary* (a.k.a. *A Man in Dark Times*; Uddhwasta dharmashala, 1974).

In making this list, of course, omissions and inadequacies appear: Mahasweta Devi draws on a variety of forms from the cinematic to the **music** hall; Karnad and Tendulkar also write overtly historical and political pieces, and so on. Most of the playwrights mentioned would claim in some way to be addressing the role and function of theatre in India from 1947, and doing so in the context of both aesthetics and politics. There are others like **Indira Parthasarathy** and Omchery (1924–). And regrettably, English versions of work by **Utpal Dutt**, **Mohan Rakesh**, and others are difficult if not impossible to access. But even this inadequate outline indicates some major trends, and reveals that only a relatively few languages (Marathi, Bengali, Kannada, Malayalam, Manipuri, Hindi/Chhattisgarhi, and English) circumscribe most of the major work published to date. Similarly, many of these writers are also directors and/or actors, and have either founded their own theatre companies (Panikkar, Dattani, Kanhailal, Thiyam, Ganguli, Sircar) or worked closely and over a long period with a single company (Tanvir, Alekar). Many enjoy the kind of "guru" status familiar in India's performance scene; although valuable in celebrating and preserving important work, it can also produce an intimidating and somewhat monolithic edifice.

"Indianness" has been presented and contended in many forms over the last sixty years, not least in the theatre. In these writers' plays, a strong awareness of the form and functions of theatre (originating in the prologues of Sanskrit drama) emerges as a conscious metatheatricality (in, for example, Karnad, Kambar, Panikkar, and Tanvir), enhanced in many cases by the "presentational" style of much folk performance that underpins contemporary work. To this are added tendencies derived from the 1950s: the use of agitprop, the encounter with Brecht (emerging as a strongly Marxist-oriented theatre for the people in the work of the IPTA), as Sircar's "Third Theatre" (Anganmancha, literally, "open-air theatre"), as protest and conflict in the work of **Safdar Hashmi**, and the processions of KSSP (Kerala Shastra Sahitya Parishad, that is, Kerala People's Science Movement) in Kerala. Although not all this was by any means scripted, it has fed into the awareness of theatre's political and social impact; so has familiarity with world theatre, encountered via experiences, for example, at England's Royal Academy of Dramatic Art (Tanvir) and Oxford (Karnad), as well as through reading and debate.

Establishment of an (exportable) cultural model—which often privileged the "theatre of roots"–based work—runs parallel to the increasing need to "write back" by evolving a richness and flexibility of forms that include an ironic awareness of their own problematics. The spectrum of writing that has emerged is rich and varied; many writers are thoroughly experienced in all aspects of performance and are known as versatile "theatre persons." They produce work that is urbane and witty (Karnad, Dattani), combative and intelligent (Tendulkar, Karnad), philosophically and politically challenging (Dutt, Sircar, Kanhailal), sensitive and intimate (Elkunchwar, Dattani), vibrant and active (Kambar, Karnad, Panikkar, Thiyam), imaginative and magical (Panikkar, Thiyam), and nearly always beautifully crafted and strongly theatrical. They position themselves within and against Indian history and the mythological inheritance, attempting to read these against the political and social issues of contemporary India, drawing on but also investigating inherited tradition and discourse. There are plays that reframe questions of sexuality, of gender roles, of power and political authority, of marginalization and oppression; plays that foreground many of the most prevalent issues—dowry, corruption and hypocrisy, generational conflicts and responses to "Westernization"; plays that reflect and examine the complexity of personal and national identity.

FURTHER READING

Dalmia, Vasudha. *Poetics, Plays, and Performances: The Poetics of Modern Indian Theatre;* Deshpande, G. P., ed. *Modern Indian Drama*; Dharwadker, Aparna Bhargava. *Theatres of Independence: Drama, Theory, and Urban Performance in India since 1947*; Jacob, Paul, ed. *Contemporary Indian Theatre: Interviews with Playwrights and Directors.*

Ralph Yarrow

Playwrights and Playwriting: Indonesia

Indonesian playwrights have from the beginning engaged with both **Western** and indigenous theatrical philosophies and genres. Western forms were introduced by European colonials in major cities in Java during the nineteenth century; by the beginning of the twentieth, playwrights had undertaken experimentation with realism and naturalism, eventually abandoning forms such as *bangsawan* in favor of the well-made play. Roestam Effendi's (1903–1978) *Essential Freedom* (Bebasari, 1926) is the first modern Indonesian play with a national theme. It turns the *Ramayana* story of Rama's rescue of Sita from the ogre, Rawana, into a parable of patriotic youth expelling the Dutch to liberate the beloved country. The play marks the beginning of Indonesia's nontraditional or modern theatre, followed by the plays of the brothers Sanusi (1905–1968) and **Armijn Pané**.

The growth of modern theatre accelerated during the **Japanese** occupation and subsequent struggle for independence (1945–1950). Playwrights of that time include Usmar Ismail (1921–1971), who also cofounded the National Academy of Theatre in 1955 with poet, playwright, and screenwriter Asrul Sani.

In 1954, **Rendra** wrote his first play, *People in the Intersection of the Road* (Orang-orang di tikungan jalan), which won a prestigious award. Rendra went on to write twenty plays, many translated into English and Dutch. Many are **political** protests against the repressive New Order government (1966–1998) led by President Suharto (1921–). Rendra's plays *The Mastodon and Condors* (Burung kondor dan mastadon, 1973) and *The Struggle of the Naga Tribe* (Kisah perjuangan suku naga, 1975) were **censored**, and Rendra was jailed several times.

Indonesia's next best-known playwright is **Nano Riantiarno**, a **director-actor** who has staged over one hundred plays, most of them his own. His plays fuse **music**, song, and local traditions with naturalism, American **musicals**, and various Brechtian devices. His early career as a journalist is visible in the emphasis on social conditions and problems in plays such as *Time Bomb* (Bom waktu, 1982) and *The Cockroach Opera* (Opera kecoa, 1985). In 1968, he cofounded the Popular **Theatre** (Teater Populer) with Teguh Karya (1937–2001). Riantiarno's works have been translated into English, Dutch, and German. As with Rendra, many of Riantiarno's plays have been considered controversial; one, *Succession* (Suksesi, 1990), was banned. (see Censorship)

Putu Wijaya's work draws from magic realism and surrealism, in a style he calls "new tradition" (*tradisi baru*), deliberately synthesizing Western conventions and devices with adaptations of traditional forms such as *wayang kulit* (see Puppet Theatre). Also experimenting in this vein were **Saini K. M.**, whose plays employ legends to make social commentary, and Jim Lim (1936–); both come out of the Bandung Theatre Study Club (Studiklub Teater Bandung).

During the late twentieth century, playwrights continued to experiment with blending Western and local forms and devices, with **experimental theatre** and performance art increasingly added to the mix. **Ikranegara** blended adapted performance art techniques to make political and social statements, while younger artists have combined elements from Indonesia's traditional theatre with contemporary, often political, themes. Azuzan J. G. (1958–), founder of the **theatre company** S'mas, uses the traditional form of *lenong* to make political statements, while **Ratna Srumpaet** has based several plays on actual incidents in order to dramatize injustices perpetrated by the New Order government.

FURTHER READING

Mohamad, Goenawan. *Modern Drama of Indonesia.*

Craig Latrell and Evan Winet

Playwrights and Playwriting: Japan

Traditional Playwrights. Many playwrights of early traditional **Japanese** theatre were also **actors**, such as **Zeami Motokiyo** and **Konparu Zenchiku**, both of whom composed numerous works of *nô*. The plays of *kyôgen* were largely improvised until the seventeenth century, although based on earlier performances. **Ichikawa Danjûrô** I, a key figure in the birth of Edo (Tokyo)–style *kabuki*, was one of many actors in seventeenth-century *kabuki* to write as well as improvise plays. In the late seventeenth century, career playwriting began with **Chikamatsu Monzaemon**, with a resident system in which plays were written for specific performers. Chikamatsu wrote for *bunraku* (see Puppet Theatre) narrators at the Takemoto Theatre (Takemoto-za) and for *kabuki*'s **Sakata Tôjûrô** I. **Kawatake Mokuami**, *kabuki*'s most prolific playwright, wrote specifically for certain stars, such as Ichikawa Kodanji IV (1812–1866), **Onoe Kikugorô** V, and **Ichikawa Danjûrô** IX.

For *bunraku* and *kabuki* career playwrights, playwriting was not a solitary occupation. **Theatres** employed up to a dozen or more writers who occupied a strict hierarchy ranging from low-level apprentices (*minarai*) through *sanmaime* and *nimaime* ranks to "head playwright" (*tate sakusha*). Starting from around the mid-eighteenth century, as the demand grew for longer and more complex plays, it became common for single *bunraku* works to be composed by playwriting teams (*gassaku*), each member assigned certain scenes according to rank and ability. The most notable team was that of **Takeda Izumo** II, Miyoshi Shôraku (1696–1772), and **Namiki Sôsuke** (also Senryû), who created the "three masterpieces" of *bunraku* and *kabuki*: *Sugawara and the Secrets of Calligraphy* (Sugawara denju tenarai kagami, 1746), *Yoshitsune and the Thousand Cherry Trees* (Yoshitsune senbon zakura, 1747), and *The Treasury of Loyal Retainers* (Kanadehon chûshingura, 1748). *Gassaku* soon became common in *kabuki* as well.

Traditional playwrights drew inspiration from a tremendous variety of source material, ranging from folktales to up-to-the-minute scandals. The fascination across all genres with Japan's great classical narratives, such as *The Tale of the Heike* (Heike monogatari), which provided many stories for the **stage**, is remarkable. In *kabuki* parlance, these narratives form "worlds" (*sekai*) of well-known events and constellations of characters into which innovative material (*shukô*) was woven, so to speak, to produce fresh plot twists and characterizations. During the Edo period (1603–1868), the inventory of available *sekai* grew with the addition of incidents and characters derived from popular "domestic plays" (*sewa mono*).

One of the best ways to get a sense of the hundreds of plays constituting the repertories of *nô*, *kyôgen*, *bunraku*, and *kabuki* is to look at the various categories and subcategories into which the genres have been divided. The categories and their labels, which may have variations in addition to the ones noted here, are generally the products of long-standing custom.

Nô. All of the approximately 240 works in the repertory can be broadly characterized as either "present-time" (*genzai*) *nô*, in which the character played by the main actor (*shite*; see Role Types) represents an actual person, or "dream" (*mugen*) *nô*, in which the *shite*'s character is a dream-apparition evoked in the mind of the character played by the supporting actor (*waki*). Composed according to aesthetic principles, such as ideal or "mysterious beauty" (*yûgen*), which shaped the form and content of the repertory, each play also belongs to one of five major groups, again classified according to the *shite*'s role: first group: "deity" (*kami*) plays; second group: "warrior-ghost" (*shura*) plays; third group: "woman" (*katsura*, literally, "wig") plays; fourth group: miscellaneous plays, including, "crazed-person" (*kyôran*), *genzai*, and "human-feeling" (*ninjô*) plays; and fifth group: demon (*kiri*, literally, "concluding") plays.

In the past, programs took an entire day, beginning with the ritual celebratory *Okina*, followed by one piece from each of the five categories. *Kyôgen* plays were given between the *nô* plays. Examples of plays and categories are *Atsumori*, a warrior-ghost play by Zeami; *The Well-Curb* (Izutsu), a woman play, also by Zeami; and *Tamakazura*, a crazed-person play by Konparu Zenchiku. Because many manuscripts do not date back further than the sixteenth century, the authorship of some works is unverifiable. All of these examples have roots in older literature: *Atsumori* is based on episodes from *The Tale of the Heike*, while *Tamakazura* is related to the eleventh-century *Tale of Genji* (Genji monogatari) and *The Well-Curb* to the tenth-century *Tales of Ise* (Ise monogatari).

Kyôgen. The size of the *kyôgen* repertory is about the same as that of *nô*, but the category divisions are not as formal. This reflects the less sophisticated, comic-relief nature of the art form. Best known are the "minor landlord" (*shômyô*) plays, like *The Delicious Poison* (Busu), which feature the servant Tarô-kaja. There are also *daimyô* plays, "demon" (*oni*) plays, "mountain priest" (*yamabushi*) plays, "sons- and mother-in-law" (*muko onna*) plays, among others. *Mushrooms* (Kusabira) is a mountain priest play, while *Two Daimyô* (Futari daimyô) belongs, as its title indicates, to the *daimyô* category. An integral part of *nô* programs, *kyôgen* also contains parodies of *nô*. Called "**dance**" (*mai*) *kyôgen*, works such as *The Cicada* (Semi) make light of warrior-ghost plays.

Bunraku. Over one thousand *bunraku* (*ningyô jôruri* before the 1870s) scripts were written and published during the Edo period for aficionados and avid amateur narrators (*tayû*), although its active repertory is now far smaller. As in *kabuki*, works are basically divided into two main categories: "historical plays" (*jidai mono*), which take their source material from pre-Edo-era narratives, and "domestic plays" (*sewa mono*) focused on contemporary townsman life. There is also a minor category of "dance plays" (*keigoto* or *keiji*). A *jidai mono* is **Chikamatsu Hanji**'s *Japan's Twenty-four Paragons of Filial Piety* (Honchô nijûshikô, 1766), which depicts the sixteenth-century conflict between military strongmen Takeda Shingen and Uesugi Kenshin. With its courtesans and chivalrous commoners, *Summer Festival: Mirror of Osaka* (Natsu matsuri Naniwa kagami, 1745), by the same team that wrote the "three masterpieces," falls into the domestic category. Because of **censorship**, historical plays are not necessarily straightforward dramatizations of stories from the distant past but are often tools used to disguise the characters and settings of Edo-era events involving the samurai class. The pre-eminent example is *The Treasury of Loyal Retainers*, which takes an actual incident from recent times and sets it centuries earlier.

Kabuki. Thousands of *kabuki* plays were written during the Edo and Meiji (1868–1912) periods. *Kabuki* scripts, considered useful only for the duration of a play's run, and subject to revision with each subsequent revival, were generally not published until modern times. Even now, it is difficult to declare a particular script authentic since actors do not necessarily adhere to fixed texts.

In addition to the basic categories of historical and domestic plays shared with *bunraku*, a substantial number of the approximately three hundred plays in the active repertory are dance plays (*shosagoto*; *keigoto* in the Osaka/Kyoto area). Among *kabuki*'s most beautiful works, popular dance plays include *The Wisteria Maiden* (Fuji musume, 1826) and *The Mirror Lion* (Kagami jishi, 1893).

Because *kabuki* by nature is a protean art, ready to adapt the works of other forms, certain categories clarify a particular play's origin. "Pure" (*jun*) *kabuki*, produced by playwrights such as Sakurada Jisuke I (1734–1806) and **Tsuruya Nanboku** IV, were originally created for *kabuki*. Subcategories of pure *kabuki* include Mokuami's "cropped-hair plays" (*zangiri mono*) and "living history plays" (*katsureki geki*). Works originally written for *bunraku* have various labels, but are generally known as *maruhon mono*, a reference to the chanters' texts. In performance, these plays retain *bunraku*'s narrator and *shamisen* **musician**. Many *kabuki* dramas were first written for puppets. Another category is dance plays closely adapted from *nô* and *kyôgen* and performed in a style resembling their originals. Dating from 1840's *The Subscription List* (Kanjinchô), these are called "pine-board plays" (*matsubame mono*) because of the pine tree painted on the backdrop. A popular *kyôgen* example is *Fishing for a Wife* (Tsuri onna, 1901). **Shin kabuki** refers to works written during the Meiji and Taishô (1912–1926) periods by playwrights such as Okamoto Kidô (1872–1939), who created *Tale of Shuzen-ji* (Shuzen–ji monogatari, 1909). The *shin kabuki* style was pioneered by **Tsubouchi Shôyô**, whose *A Leaf of Paulownia* (Kiri hitoha, 1904) is often considered the style's first.

Plays also are separated into various other categories based on style and content. "Ghost plays" (*kaidan mono*) and "raw" or "pure" domestic plays (*kizewa mono*) are categories developed by Nanboku IV. (*Kaidan mono* are actually a subcategory of *kizewa mono*.) Nanboku's *The Ghost Stories at Yotsuya on the Tôkaidô* (Tôkaidô yotsuya kaidan, 1825) represents both. Jisuke III (1802–1877) and Mokuami further developed the raw domestic play into dashing "bandit plays" (*shiranami mono*), a category including the latter's *The Three Kichisas and the New Year's First Visit to the Pleasure Quarters* (Sannin Kichisa kuruwa no hatsugai, 1860). Another theme-based category covers "samurai family dispute plays" (*oie sôdô mono*), one example being *The Precious Incense and Autumn Flowers of Sendai* (Meiboku Sendai hagi, 1778) by Nagawa Kamesuke (fl. 1764–1788). "Love-suicide plays" (*shinjû mono*) are particularly, though not exclusively, associated with Chikamatsu, whose *The Love Suicides at Sonezaki* (Sonezaki shinjû, 1703) and *The Love Suicides at Amijima* (Shinjû Ten no Amijima, 1721) were adapted from *bunraku*. Another category mainly concerning the unhappy fate of lovers is "separation plays" (*enkiri mono*), an example being *The Sword Kagotsurube and Sobering up the Brothel District* (Kagotsurube sato no eizame, 1888) by Kawatake Shinshichi III (1842–1901). Situations where one person selflessly takes the place of another are crucial to the storylines of "substitution plays" (*migawari mono*), as with "The Village School" ("Terakoya") scene from *Sugawara and the Secrets of Calligraphy*, in which one child is killed in place of another because of a parent's secret debt of obligation. "Soga brothers' plays" (*soga mono*), once a mainstay of the repertory, were inspired by the thirteenth-century epic *Tale of the Soga Brothers* (Soga monogatari), and include *Sukeroku: Flower of Edo* (Sukeroku yukari no Edo zakura, 1713) by Tsuuchi Jihei II (1679–1760).

The repertory is often analyzed in terms of its scenes. "Love scenes" (*iromoyô* for mild encounters, *nureba* for more sexually suggestive liaisons) are a predominant type, as in the secret rendezvous of Otomi and Yosaburô in *Sympathetic Chatter and the Scandalous Hair Comb* (Yowa nasake ukina no yokogushi, 1853) by Segawa Jokô III (1806–1881). At the other end of the emotional spectrum are "murder scenes" (*koroshiba*), as in *Five Great Powers That Secure Love* (Godairiki koi no fûjime, 1794) by Namiki Gohei I (1747–1808). "Extortion scenes" (*yusuriba*) are associated with the bandit plays of Mokuami in works such as *The Glorious Picture Book of Aoto's Exploits* (Aotozôshi hana no nishiki-e, 1862), a.k.a. *Benten Kozô*. *Kabuki*'s renowned "fight scenes" (*tachimawari*), often heightened by the beat of "clappers" (*tsuke*), are written into numerous works.

Selecting plays that he felt most fully represented his family's "rough style" (*aragoto*)–acting specialty, Danjûrô VII in the 1830s and 1840s created a category he boldly dubbed "Kabuki's Eighteen Favorites" (*kabuki jûhachiban*). Similar lists were created by later stars. In a sense, Danjûrô's eighteen favorites also represented Edo-style *kabuki* as a whole, in contrast to "Kyoto/Osaka area plays" (*kamigata kyôgen*), which tend to be softer, more emotional dramas acted in the "gentle style" *wagoto*. Set in the pleasure quarters, "courtesan buying" (*keisei kai*) plays, such as *Love Letter from the Licensed Quarter* (Kuruwa bunshô, adapt. 1808 from a 1712 Chikamatsu puppet play), exemplify the genre.

FURTHER READING

Gerstle, Andrew C. *Circles of Fantasy: Convention in the Plays of Chikamatsu*; Hare, Thomas Blenman. *Zeami's Style: The Noh Plays of Zeami Motokiyo*; Keene, Donald. *World within Walls: Japanese Literature of the Pre-Modern Era, 1600–1867*; Keene, Donald. *Seeds in the Heart: Japanese Literature from Earliest Times to the Late Sixteenth Century*; Takaya, Ted Terujiro. "An Inquiry into the Role of the Traditional *Kabuki* Playwright."

Barbara E. Thornbury

Moden Theatre. Can Japan be **modern** without losing national identity? Before World War II, playwrights struggled to prove equality with the **West**, seeking a "civilized" (that is, Westernized) national voice apart from traditional performance. Often embracing foreign ideologies (Marxism and Christianity) and artistic strategies (psychological realism), most prewar playwrights failed to find a distinct, national voice. The search continued postwar, influenced by the bomb and the American Occupation, often emphasizing rediscovery of traditional culture and modulated by international avant-garde trends. Shifting socio-**political** realities and the ongoing quest for personal and national identity gradually resulted in distinctive genres.

Departure from Tradition. As the Meiji era commenced, artists traveling to Europe discovered a literate drama radically different from actor-driven *kabuki* where ideas succumbed to static or episodic scenes and collaborative playwriting further diluted structural or thematic unity. In contrast, successful European playwrights were venerated. Literary value informed Chekhov's tragicomic plots and understated language,

Shakespeare's poetry and philosophy, and Ibsen's social conscience and dramatic structure.

Shinpa impresario **Kawakami Otojirô** dramatized topical events, including an attempted political assassination, and performed satirical, vulgar, front-of-**curtain** interludes like the nonsensically titled "Oppekepe." His freely adapted *Othello* and vivid accounts of the Sino-Japanese and Russo-Japanese wars glorified Japanese imperialism. Later, after touring abroad, Kawakami further departed from tradition by eliminating music, dance, "female impersonators" (*onnagata*), and the "flower path" (*hanamichi*). Such changes, displeasing many, foreshadowed *shingeki* realism.

Mainstream *shinpa,* using both *onnagata* and actresses, often dramatized popular, serialized novels or adaptations of Western works. Playwrights preferred sentimental, melodramatic, nontopical plots. The fantastic, gothic novels of **Izumi Kyôka**, whose fictional style likely derives from traditional **storytellers** (*rakugo*) and their archaic, nonnaturalistic dialogue, were often adapted.

Shingeki's Origins. To enhance theatre's respectability, intellectuals like **Tsubouchi Shôyô** and **Mori Ôgai** determined to dissociate playwriting from actors' domination. Their printed debates helped legitimize playwriting's literary qualities. Tsubouchi, in *Our Country's Historical Drama* (Wagakuni no shigeki, 1893–1894), opposed the Confucian demand for didactic drama. He translated Shakespeare and advocated realism through characterization, dialogue, and actresses. Mori, deeply influenced by modern Western theories, saw drama as universal and idealistic. His translation of Ibsen's *John Gabriel Borkman* was **Osanai Kaoru**'s first production (1909). Although staged something like *kabuki,* it is often considered *shingeki*'s first production.

Literary journals such as *New Trends in Thought* (Shinshichô) and *New Trends in Drama* (Engeki shinchô) published scripts, but new plays were seldom produced. Unfamiliar themes and styles confused audiences. In addition, productions in the 1910s were **censored** for failing to reward good and punish evil; even translations were required to change original endings to conform to Confucian values.

When Osanai and **Hijikata Yoshi** founded the Tsukiji Little Theatre (Tsukiji Shôgekijô, 1924), playwrights assumed it would produce their work. Osanai shocked them by excluding native plays for two years, implying Japanese playwriting inferiority. Osanai saw this hiatus as an opportunity to train writers and performers in European techniques.

Art versus Politics. The Tsukiji Little Theatre transformed *shingeki* playwriting. In showcasing Western thought, dramaturgy, and characters, Osanai paved the way for such alien ideologies as feminism, Marxism, psychological/social realism, and Christianity; new Japanese plays reflected the influence of European models. Tsukiji's first native-written production was Tsubouchi's *En the Ascetic* (En no gyôja, 1926), a dense play about evil and spirituality. With Osanai's death (1928), the company split along ideological lines.

Politically leftist, social-realist playwrights, including **Murayama Tomoyoshi**, **Miyoshi Jûrô**, and **Kubo Sakae**, formed the mainstream. Kubo was typical: he translated German plays and appreciated new European writing and theory but preferred social realism and believable characters to Brechtian/Marxist **experimentation**. His *Land of Volcanic Ash* (Kazanbaichi, 1937) depicted farm life in Hokkaidô. With other prominent leftists, Kubo was imprisoned in 1940.

Prewar nonpolitical playwrights included **Kubota Mantarô**, Iwata Toyoo (1893–1969), and **Kishida Kunio**, who jointly founded the Literary Theatre (Bungaku-za, 1937). Inspired by French **theorist/director** Jacques Copeau, Kishida advocated psychological realism, publishing nonpolitical scripts in his literary journal *Playwriting* (Gekisaku). Kishida's *The Two Daughters of Mr. Sawa* (Sawa-shi no futari musume, 1935) is typical, depicting a family challenged by modern social changes, hardly able to communicate. Japan's highest playwriting award, the Kishida Prize, is named in his honor.

***Postwar* Shingeki *to 1960*.** With the devastation of World War II, many Japanese comprehended that their leaders had betrayed them into embarking on a disastrous war. During the Occupation (1945–1952), playwrights, like others, turned to the United States to rebuild lives, redefine society, and rejoin the modern world. Translations of Miller and Williams were influential. Mainstream *shingeki* continued to value socialist realism, perceived as representative of American democracy and cultural values.

Christianity, long equated by *shingeki* with Western civilization, was now seen as a key American value. Although less than 1 percent of Japanese are practicing Christians, numerous *shingeki* playwrights were (or are) Christians; others demonstrate significant Christian influence, including Kishida, **Tanaka Chikao**, **Fukuda Tsuneari**, **Kinoshita Junji**, Miyoshi Jûrô, **Katô Michio**, and **Satoh Makoto**, among others.

While realism dominated through the 1960s, notable playwrights experimented with variations. Kinoshita's folkloric *Twilight Crane* (Yûzuru, 1949) offered escape into a mythical past involving universal human suffering, greed, and love. A different nostalgia permeates **Mishima Yukio**'s modern *nô* plays; poetic allegories performed realistically, these plays imply Mishima's ultra-nationalist yearnings. **Abe Kôbô** created idiosyncratic, absurdist works exploring the loss of identity. All sought a distinctive, native sensibility.

***Anti*-Shingeki *Playwriting Emerges*.** By 1960, Japan still suffered psychological and physical war scars, including the loss of national identity, exemplified by an emperor stripped of divinity; lingering horror and international stigma relating to the atomic blasts; and a sense of political, cultural, financial, and military colonization by an omnipresent and apparently omnipotent United States. The U.S.-Japan Mutual Security Treaty (Anpo) was to be renewed in 1960. Widespread protests prevented the American president's visit; the Diet secretly met to ratify the treaty at midnight. National outrage stirred playwrights, who questioned *shingeki*'s ability to change or to reflect it.

One response was **Betsuyaku Minoru**'s *The Elephant* (Zô, 1962), the first "underground" (*angura*) play. Using Beckettian dramaturgy and reflections of *nô* and *kyôgen*, *The Elephant* conflates atomic bomb victims' helplessness with that of the anti-Anpo protestors. Other playwrights abandoned **theatres**, turning to streets, tents, coffee houses, even abandoned buildings, to present antirealistic works.

In 1969, discontent over Vietnam and other issues, again including impending Anpo renewal in 1970, erupted. Protest plays were rampant. Satoh Makoto's Kishida Prize–winning *Nezumi Kozô: The Rat* (Nezumi kozô jirôkichi, 1969) is a difficult, dense, mystifying, raucous *kabuki*-esque condemnation of militarism and the status quo.

Kara Jûrô founded Situation Theatre (Jôkyô Gekijô, 1963); in 1967, he began presenting plays in a Red Tent (Aka Tento), often in defiance of the law. His comic, vulgar, terrifying scripts intentionally confuse and surprise audiences. Fragmented, apparently random plots mingle times, locations, and characters. *The Virgin's Mask* (Shôjô kamen, 1969) conflates imperialism, **Takarazuka**, and postwar angst.

Unlike political activists, **Terayama Shûji** wanted a revolution of imagination. Damning American and Japanese values and aesthetics, he angered rightists and leftists alike. His total theatre was often designed for specific staging. Audiences might be plunged into total darkness or physically assaulted; streets or bathhouses became theatres; innocent bystanders became performers. *The Hunchback of Aomori* (Aomori-ken no semushi otoko, 1967) and *Heretics* (Jashûmon, 1970) reveled in dark folklore, shamanism and incest, intentionally critiquing Kinoshita's more family-friendly folkloric vision.

***Diversity after* Angura.** After 1980, new styles emerged. **Noda Hideki** challenged *angura*'s intensity with ironic, fast-paced, large-scale, youth-oriented, popular-culture parodies. From 1993, he shifted to serious social critiques, discussing issues like terrorism, the emperor system, and cultural misunderstanding. **Kôkami Shôji, Kawamura Takeshi, Watanabe Eriko,** and **Ohashi Yasuhiko,** among others, have followed similar trajectories.

Perhaps the most distinctive recent playwriting style is "quiet theatre" (*shizuka na engeki*), a reaction to the raucous 1980s. Practitioners include **Iwamatsu Ryô, Matsuda Masataka, Miyazawa Akio,** and **Hirata Oriza**. Quiet theatre, like Hirata's *Tokyo Notes* (Tôkyô nôto, 1994) avoids obvious plot and action, emphasizing small, daily activities, overlapping dialogue, and incomplete thoughts.

Playwrights whose styles defy categorization, but who often critique contemporary society in either serious or comic ways, include **Sakate Yôji, Nagai Ai, Kaneshita Tatsuo, Inoue Hisashi, Nagai Ai,** and **Saitô Ren**.

FURTHER READING

Eckersall, Peter. *Theorizing the Angura Space;* Jortner, David, Keiko McDonald, and Kevin J. Wetmore, Jr., eds. *Modern Japanese Theatre and Performance;* Keene, Donald. *Dawn to the West: Japanese Literature in the Modern Era: Poetry, Drama, Criticism*; Powell, Brian. *Japan's Modern Theatre: A Century of Continuity and Change.*

Carol Fisher Sorgenfrei

Playwrights and Playwriting: Korea

Because of its oral tradition and the collective nature of performance preparation, **Korean** traditional theatre was not concerned with individual authorship. The concept of playwrights and playwriting evolved in the first quarter of the twentieth century, advanced by two important groups: the Dramatic Arts Society (1920) and the Dramatic Arts Research Society (1931) (see Kim U-jin; Yu Ch'i-jin). Both consisted of Koreans studying in **Japan**, and both studied **Western** plays and promoted dramatic realism, but the development of social realism was stymied by Japanese colonial **censorship** (1910–1945), and by ideological strife during the years between World War II and the Korean War (1950–1953), when many socialist playwrights fled to **North Korea**.

In the south, despite repressive **political** conditions, some playwrights wrote works of distinction. Oh Yŏng-jin's (1916–1974) artistic inspiration lay in folklore and mythological themes. His major play, *Wedding at Mr. Maeng's House* (Maengjin sa taek kyŏng sa, 1943), satirizes aristocratic class foolishness concerning traditional wedding conventions.

In the 1950s and 1960s, many a playwriting career was launched by having one's work published in a prestigious literary magazine or by winning a literary contest.

Ch'a Bŏm-sŏk (1924–) won a newspaper literary contest with *Homecoming* (Kwi hyang, 1956), and became a leading playwright with *Burning Mountain* (San bul, 1962), a realistic drama depicting the plight of female villagers trapped between communist guerrilla and nationalist forces, while Lee Kŭn-Sam (1925–2003) opened the door to antirealist and **experimental theatre** with his *Manuscript Paper Form* (Wŏnko chi, 1959), published in a literary journal.

Playwriting as a respected discipline gained ground in 1962 when Yŏ Sŏk-ki started his playwriting workshop at the Drama Center, a facility opened by **Yu Ch'i-jin** with a grant from the Rockefeller Foundation. In that same year at the Drama Center, Yu also directed the Korean Theatre Academy, predecessor of the current Seoul Institute of the Arts, offering theatre studies programs. These two ventures produced numerous dramatists, among them, Pak Jo-yŏl (1930–), who impressed the Korean theatre world with his dramaturgic style influenced by Brechtian epic theatre and Theatre of the Absurd. His plays dealing with Korean division and its innocent victims include *Sightseeing Zone* (Kwangwang chidae, 1963), and *General Oh's Toenail* (O changgun i palth'op, 1974), which was **censored** until 1988.

In the 1960s, as small professional **theatre companies** began to flourish, important playwrights became associated with them: Lee Kŭn-sam with the Minchung Theatre Company (Minchung Kŭkdan) and Kagyo Theatre Company (Kagyo Kŭkdan), Ch'a Bŏm-Sŏk with Sanha Theatre Company (Sanha Kŭkdan), and **Kim Kwang-lim** with Yŏnu Stage (Yŏnu Mudae). These and others took the lead in shaping the nation's theatre, experimenting with imports and rediscovering traditional plays in the search for a truly Korean drama.

A more mature theatre evolved in the 1970s. Ch'oe In-hun (1936–) wrote poetic, imagistic plays, such as *When Spring Comes to Hill and Dale* (Pom-i omyŏn san-e tŭl-e, 1977), based on his reinterpretation of traditional Korean folktales. **Lee Kang-baek** and **Oh T'ae-sŏk** emerged as leading writers, followed in the 1980s by **Kim Kwang-Lim** and **Lee Yun-t'aek,** both making distinctive and diverse contributions. Among many others of note, Lee Hyŏn-hwa (1943–) shocked the theatre world with *Cadenza* (K'adenja), a historical play about King Sejo's usurpation of the throne staged in Theatre of Cruelty style, and Lee Man-hŭi (1954–) made his mark with his award-winning *It Was a Small Darkness inside the Hole of a Buddhist Wood Block* (Kŭgŏsŭn mokt'ak kumŏng sok-ŭi chagŭn ŏtumiŏtsŭmnida, 1990), depicting monks suffering from their painful past.

Of younger playwrights, **Cho Kwang-hwa** indicts patriarchal values and violence in his *The Male Urge* (Namja ch'ungdong, 1996), while Pak Kun-hyŏng (1963–) unsparingly portrays family violence, directionless youth, and the power of love in *In Praise of Youth* (Ch'ŏngch'un yech'an, 2001). Kim Myŏng-hwa (1966–) is a **woman** playwright whose *Birds Don't Use a Crosswalk* (Sei-dŭl ŭn hoengdanpodo-ro kŏnnŏji annŭnda, 1998) depicts challenges faced by former student activists caught between their activist past, faded ideals, and a younger generation.

Despite artistic and financial challenges, Korean playwriting has matured in less than six decades into an art form expressing a uniquely Korean spirit, and native plays increasingly are the subject of international study. *See also Madangnori; Shinp'agŭk; Shingŭk.*

FURTHER READING

Han, Sang-chul. "Trends in Postwar Theatre"; Kim, Yun-Cheol, and Miy-Ye Kim, eds. *Contemporary Korean Theatre: Playwrights, Directors, Stage-Designers*; Korean International Theatre Institute, ed. *Korean Performing Arts: Drama, Dance and Music Theatre.*

Hyung-jin Lee

Playwrights and Playwriting: Malaysia

Birth of Scripted Theatre. Although there are numerous traditional forms in **Malaysia**, all are unscripted. Even **bangsawan** is an improvisational form based only on synopses. Scripted theatre, and with it the emergence of playwrights, started only in the early 1920s with the establishment of the Translation Bureau at the Sultan Idris Teacher **Training** College in Tanjung Malim, Perak. Students were initially introduced to translations of **Western** plays. The first published script in Malay, *Megat Terawis* (1950), was written by Teh Fatimah binti Abdul Wahab; her script revives the brave exploits of an ideal hero upheld in oral tradition. Early *sandiwara* plays were written during the period of rising Malay nationalism and focused on heroic historical and legendary characters. *Sandiwara* scripts reflect the influence of Shakespeare as well as **Indonesian** drama.

Scholars generally agree that *sandiwara* playwright **Shaharom Husain** initiated and promoted scripted drama. Although his plays were not published until 1961, Husain staged his first drama in 1930. *Dahlan, the Lawyer* (Lawyer Dahlan, 1939) was produced in 1943. His later work, *The Hunchback of Tanjong Puteri* (Si bongkok Tanjong Puteri, 1960), takes a critical view of colonial-period history.

Another noteworthy *sandiwara* playwright is Kalam Hamidi, famous for *The Promised Child of the Seven Saints* (Anak nazar tujuh keramat, 1964), which also critiques leadership. Set in an Arab locale, it concerns a feudal ruler charged with **religious** hypocrisy. A third major *sandiwara* playwright is **Usman Awang**, whose one-act, "The Death of a Warrior (Jebat)" (Matinya seorang pahlawan [Jebat], 1961) captures a new image of the rebel Jebat by justifying his actions against feudal authority.

Realistic Playwrights. The 1960s saw the emergence of realistic playwrights like **Mustapha Kamil Yassin**, a.k.a. Kala Dewata, who pioneered plays using realistic **acting**, dialogue, **costumes**, and **scenography**. Many such plays, such as Yassin's *Tiled Roof, Thatched Roof* (Atap genting atap rembia, 1963) and *Two or Three Cats A-Running* (Dua tiga kucing berlari, 1966), are set in the sitting room of the main characters' home and are produced in proscenium **theatres**. Other writers who scripted realistic plays include Usman Awang and Awang Had Salleh. Drawing on Western and Indonesian realism, the social dramas of this era deal with the challenges that nation-building and the drive for progress posed in the post-independence period. Speaking colloquial Malay, characters representing various societal sectors encounter in their daily lives recognizable issues facing the new nation. Some plays clearly contrast rural and urban lifestyles as characters reconnect with their past as a means of retrieving values that can help guide the present.

Unlike earlier realist plays, those of Bidin Subari (a.k.a. Malina Manja, 1937–2001) end not with resolutions but with discord and confusion. His *Datuk Ahmad Dadida* (1971), *The Calf Whose Mother Died* (Anak kerbau mati emak, 1972), and *The Cock and the Hen* (Ayam jantan ayam betina, 1973) present harsh scenarios loaded with sexual innuendo in unrefined, coarse language. Other plays, such as *Where the Moon Always Cracks* (Di mana bulan selalu retak, 1963) by A. Samad Said, *Visitors at Kenny Hill* (Tamu di Bukit Kenny, 1967) by Usman Awang, and *Anna* (1972) by Ahmad Kamal Abdullah (a.k.a. Kemala, 1941–), also end without a clear resolution, indicating that social problems cannot be easily remedied. They foreshadow the subsequent, more pluralistic playwriting approach.

Experimental Playwriting. The 1970s was a decade of **experimental theatre**, called "contemporary theatre" (*teater kontemporari*), during which many playwrights wrote antirealistic, often surrealistic dramas. With his landmark eclectic work, *'Tis Not the Tall Grass Blown by the Wind* (Bukan lalang ditiup angin, 1970), **Noordin Hassan** ushered in the period of angst-ridden characters searching for identity, meaning, and hope in a nation stunned by the ethnic riots of May 13, 1969.

As the decade progressed, dramatists continued to probe social issues of the day, but they also gave attention to universal views of life. Individual, more existential concerns surface as does recognition of human irrationality. Additionally, playwrights explored the nature of theatre itself and incorporated traditional elements in an effort to create a more theatricalized staging. Along with contemporary characters, historical and legendary figures are reshaped to address current issues. Dinsman (1949–), Hatta Azad Kahn (1952–), and Johan Jaaffar (1953–) are among the "third generation" (*generasi ketiga*) dramatists noted for their absurdist style, which initially captivated audiences intrigued by such innovation. Experimentalists, influenced by Western and Indonesian absurdism, gave vent to their imagination, portraying dreams, illusions, and visions, to illustrate a more layered and complex reality.

Syed Alwi, known for his earlier work in English-language theatre, sought in the aftermath of the 1969 riots to reconnect with the Malay community and entered the world of Malay-language drama. His plays reflect universal, humanistic concerns emphasized through multimedia techniques. His move was consistent with the government's new cultural policy, which gave increased support to the development of Malay culture, arts, and language. Meanwhile, English-language playwrights of the 1960s, such as Edward Dorall, Patrick Yeoh, and Lee Joo For, who had created both realistic and experimental works, distanced themselves from the Malaysian **stage**.

The 1980s: Islamic Revivalism to English-Language Drama. Toward the end of the 1970s, as plays became more obscure, audience interest in absurdism diminished. In addition, Islamic revivalism gained momentum as an offshoot of Iran's Islamic Revolution of 1979. In this atmosphere, government support for Malay theatre declined. However, even though the Malay stage was more theatrically subdued, it was not silent. Coinciding with the more **religious** times, Noordin Hassan introduced his "theatre of faith" (*teater fitrah*). In *1400* (1981), he strove to inspire a spiritual catharsis in both the individual and society.

The 1980s also saw the emergence of both new and veteran playwrights who reacted to abstract drama by writing plays harnessed to national concerns. Among these are Zakaria Ariffin's *The Opera House* (Pentas opera, 1989) and Syed Alwi's *Servant of God* (Hamba Allah, 1989), both of which feature a *bangsawan* troupe as part of the plot. At the end of the 1980s, Noordin Hassan focused on an integrated concept of nationalism in *Children of This Land* (Anak tanjung, 1989). Ethnic integration is also a major theme in Rahmah Bujang's *Puteri Li Po* (1992). Intent on revitalizing *bangsawan* for the modern stage, Bujang strives for psychological depth as she recounts the story of the **Chinese** princess who wed Sultan Mansur Shah in fifteenth-century Malacca.

Meanwhile, the 1980s witnessed a renewed interest in writing for English-language plays. Initially, some playwrights explored issues relevant to their ethnic community: K. S. Maniam (1942–) wrote of **Indian** estate life in *The Cord* (1984) and Leow Puay Tin (1957–) portrays the Chinese experience of town life in *Three Children* (1992). On

Kee Thuan Chye as a police interrogator accusing the heroine Wiran (Salleh Ben Joned) of being "a threat to national security" in Kee's *1984 Here and Now*. (Photo: Courtesy of Kee Thuan Chye)

the other hand, Kee Thuan Chye (1954–) tackled the question of integration in Malaysian society in *1984 Here and Now* (1985). Kee went on to write **political** dramas such as *The Big Purge* (1988) and *We Could **** You, Mr. Birch* (1994).

Plays also became more multilingual, such as the Five Arts Centre's productions of *Us* and *Work*, two group-devised pieces, and more experimental, such as K. S. Maniam's multiart exploration, *Skin Trilogy* (1995). Also of note, Syed Alwi returned once again to English with *I Remember . . . the Rest House* (1994).

The 1990s. In the 1990s, with government support once more operative, Malay playwrights initially wrote entertaining one-acts to woo audiences back to the theatre, such as Rahim Razali's "Class 2020." More critically, Anwar Ridhwan's (1949–) "Little People" (Orang-orang kecil, publ. 1990) and "They Who Appear and Disappear" (Yang menjelma dan menghilang, publ. 1992) delve into Malaysian politics, questioning power and its abuse.

In addition, monodramas have taken center stage in both Malay- and English-language theatre. Dinsman's *It Is Not Suicide* (Bukan bunuh diri, 1974) is an existential piece that probes the individual's search for meaning and God beyond the givens of traditional religious and secular knowledge. In Sabera Shaik's *The Other Can't* (1993), an older woman reflects on her experience as mistress to a married man and the child born of their relationship. In *A Modern Woman Called Ang Tau Mui* (1993), Leow Puay Tin depicts the frustrations faced by a cleaning woman whose dreams remain unfulfilled. Choreographer/**dancer** Ramli Ibrahim created a set of three monodramas, *In the Name of Love* (1992), including one featuring a *mak yong* performer. In *From*

Table Mountain to Teluk Intan (1999), Shahimah Idris comments on her own life journey from South Africa to Australia to Malaysia.

FURTHER READING

Ishak, Solehah. *Histrionics of Development: A Study of Three Contemporary Malay Playwrights*; Zuhra, Nur Nina (Nancy Nanney). *An Analysis of Modern Malay Drama*.

Solehah Ishak and Nancy Nanney

Playwrights and Playwriting: Nepal

Many of **Nepal**'s ancient kings augmented seasonal festivities by dramatizing stories of ancient gods and goddesses. One of the earliest was Jagajjyotir Malla (r. 1614–1637), king of Badgaun in the Kathmandu Valley. The Hindu epics ***Ramayana*** and ***Mahabharata*** provided the subjects of dramas penned by Patan kings Siddhi Narasimha Malla (r. 1618–1661) and Srinivasa Malla (r. 1661–1685), Kathmandu king Pratapa Malla (r. 1641–1674), and Bhupatindra Malla, who ruled Badgaun from 1696 to 1722. These plays attempted to adhere to **theoretical** precepts established in India's ancient *Treatise on Drama* (Natyashastra).

The first modern Nepali drama, *Atal Bahadur* (1898), by Pahalwan Singh Swar (1878–1934), was based, not on an ancient epic, but on *Macbeth*. The most eminent dramatist, Balakrishna Sama (1902–1981), wrote fifteen plays spanning a range of themes influenced by Indic scholastic traditions and Hindu mythology, as well as by **Western** literary traditions. In plays such as *Heart Ache* (Mutuko vyatha, 1926), Sama wrote in blank verse, employed **Sanskrit** meter, and focused on the poetics of relationship while writing relatively real characters. Other plays, such as *Mukunda Indira* (1937), focus on predicaments in love between high-caste leaders and lower-caste **women**, though Sama also wrote on historical events, dramatizing valor, strength, and virtue, as well as on rural and mythological subjects.

Modern dramatists influenced by European social realism and by Freud and Marx were less interested in traditional and mythological subjects and focused on conflicts between the individual and society, as well as on psychological impulses. Gopal Prasad Rimal's (1918–1973) *The Commission* (Ayog) takes up the theme of Ibsen's *A Doll's House*, and his masterpieces, *Cremation Ground* (Masan, 1946) and *This Love* (Yo prem, 1965), dramatize tensions in relationships of the urban middle class. Brothers Vijaya Malla (1928–1999) and Govinda Malla (1922–) also focus on the desire of the individual for self-expression in plays such as *Why Should Someone Be Ruined?* (Kohi kina barbadhos, 1959), although *Story of the Stones* (Pattharako katha, 1969) has a more surrealistic tone.

Theatre moved on to the streets with the pro-democracy movement of the 1980s, and plays that expressed anger at a system of economic exploitation and corruption, such as *We Are Waiting for the Spring* (Hami basanta khojir hechou, 1982), were hastily written and staged by Ashesh Malla (1950–). In the post-democracy era, Abhi Subedi's (1945–) *Dreams of Peach Blossoms* (Aaruka Fulka Sapana, 2001) attempts to regain and develop indigenous expression. Subedi embodies Nepal's identity crisis in the dilemma of his female character, Maiju. In a time of rampant **political** corruption and an increasingly violent Maoist insurgency, Subedi's *Fire in the Monastery* (Agniko

katha, 2002) and *Journey Into Thamel* (Thanmelko yaatraa, 2002) put female characters center **stage**, where their pain reflects the despair of their society and dramatizes
the prevailing disillusionment.

Carol Davis

Playwrights and Playwriting: Pakistan

Urdu playwriting originated in a versified operatic style, from Nawab Wajid Ali Shah's
(1822–1887) "theatrical gatherings" (*jalsah*s) to Amanat Lakhnawi's (1816–1859) *The
Court of Lord Indra* (Indar sabha, 1853) to Mirza Qaleej Baig's late-nineteenth-century
Laila and Majnu (Laila-Majnu). Agha Hashr Kashmiri's (1879–1935) plays blended
verse and rhymed prose, song, and **dance**, with mythology, folklore, and **Western** plot-
lines. His declamatory and poetic expression inspired Imtiaz Ali Taj (1900–1970), who
developed a more balanced dramaturgy, based on the inherent **musicality** of the spoken
word, with continued inclusion of song and dance. His most famous play is *Anarkali*
(1922), and his *My Killer* (Meera qatil, 1955) constituted the first Lahore Arts Council
production. Rafi Peer (1898–1974) placed similar emphasis on mannered speech,
deploying rhymed prose in a range of styles, from the comedy of manners *Sweet Whis-
pers* (Razo niaz, ca. 1934) to the suspense thriller *The Host of the Afterlife* (Uqba ka
meezban, ca. 1941) to serious plays like *The Mask* (Naqab, ca. 1948), about atomic war.

Despite a smattering of original plays, the early post-Partition (1947) years were
dominated by English-language productions of Molière, Gogol, Shakespeare, and
Ibsen, later translated and adapted in Urdu and regional languages. Sufie Tabassam
adapted *A Midsummer Night's Dream*, and Ali Ahmed provided a radical adaptation of
Waiting for Godot (1957), which, unlike the original, ended in hope. Shoaib Hashmi's
(1939–) adaptations include plays by Shaffer and Molnar. Khalid Ahmad provided an
acclaimed adaptation of Priestley's *An Inspector Calls* (1989), while Akram Butt's version of Molnar's *Liliom* (1964) launched the first Punjabi production on the Lahore
Arts Council's **stage**.

Khwaja Moenuddin wrote a number of original Urdu satires, including *From the Red
Fort to Laloo Khaith* (Laal Qilay se Laloo Khaith, 1953), about Partition, *Mirza Ghalib
on Bunder Road* (Mirza Ghalib Bunder Road per, 1966), and *Adult Education* (Talee-e-
Balghaan). A satire trend is apparent in Kamal Ahmed Rizwi's (1930–) *We Are All
Thieves* (Hum chor hain) and *Whose Wife, Whose Husband?* (Kis ki bivi kis ka sohar);
Sajjad Haider's Punjabi *Hai Koi Aisa* (1969); and Imran Aslam's (1951–) Urdu-English
journalistic-inspired works, such as *Cricket Breaks Down Divisions* (mid-1990s).

Najam Hussein Syed (1936–) and Sarmad Sehbai (1945–) have been significant in
reviving Punjabi language, history, and legends with contemporary socio-**political** consciousness. Najam Hussein's plays include *Throne of Lahore* (Takht Lahore), *Dulan
Bhatti, Protector of the Jungle* (Jungle da rakha, 1967), and the six-hour *Epic of Alfo,
the Storyteller* (Alfo). Sarmad Sehbai's Punjabi plays include the first Government College original Punjabi production, *Know Thyself* (Tu kaun?, 1971). His Urdu plays,
which fuse modern techniques, symbolism, and poetic vernacular, include *The Noose*
(Phandey, 1972) and *Hash* (1975).

Shahid Nadeem writes mostly for the Dawn of a New Day (Ajoka) **theatre company**
in Urdu and Punjabi, his plays including *The Acquittal* (Barri, 1986). Lakht Pasha is

resident writer for the People's Theatre (Lok Rehas) company, creating work in Punjabi on social themes, like *Path of Darkness* (Andherhay da pandh) and *Oppression* (Dhroo).

FURTHER READING

Afzal-Khan, Fawzia. *A Critical Stage: The Role of Secular Alternative Theatre in Pakistan.*

Claire Pamment

Playwrights and Playwriting: Philippines

The **Philippines**' earliest playwrights were priestesses (*babaylan*) and epic chanters (*binukot*) who followed the conventions of rites, rituals, and **storytelling** while improvising. They were followed by the **folk theatre** playwrights of the Spanish colonial period (1521–1898), who wrote *sinakulo*, *komedya*, and short plays based on biblical events and characters, metrical romances, apocryphal stories, and other popular publications. They borrowed liberally from other texts. However, their written scripts (*orihinal*) were safeguarded so as not to be used by other groups. Among *komedya*s that went beyond stereotypes and had well-written verses were Manuel Roque's *Life of Atamante* (Vida de Atamante, ca. 1887), Francisco Baltazar's (1788–1863) *Orozman and Zafira*, and Jose de la Cruz's (1746–1829) *Traitors of the Country* (Los traidores de la patria).

Similarly, *sarsuwela* writers transformed the Spanish form (*zarzuela*) and focused on Filipino domestic and social issues. While Jose Rizal's (1861–1896) *Beside the Pasig* (Junto al Pasig, 1893) and Norberto Romualdez's (1975–1941) *The Help of St. Michael* (Ang pagtabang ni San Miguel, 1899) had **religious** themes, later *sarsuwela*s such as Severino Reyes's (1861–1942) *Not Wounded* (Walang sugat, 1902) and Mena Pecson Crisologo's (1844–1927) *Noble Rivalry* (Natakneng a Panagsalisal, 1911) were love stories in the context of war and revolutions.

During the American colonial period (ca. 1900–1946), the public education system, the establishment of more universities, and the use of English resulted in original one-acts in English. Among the most important playwrights are Jesusa Araullo and Lino Castillejo, who wrote the first English play, "A Modern Filipina" (1915); teacher and **director** Wilfrido Ma. Guerrero (1917–), with "Wanted: a Chaperone" (1940); Severino Montano (1915–1980), author of "Parting at Calamba" (1955); and Alberto Florentino (1931–), who wrote "The World is an Apple" (1955).

Contemporary playwrights, such as Amelia Lapeña Bonifacio (1930–), Tony Perez (1951–), Bonifacio Ilagan (1951–), Malou Jacob (1948–), Paul Dumol (1951–), Rene Villanueva (1954–), Al Santos (1954–), Reuel Aguila (1953–), Rody Vera (1960–), and Chris Millado (1961–) have been influenced by realism, Brecht's epic theatre, Theatre of the Absurd, indigenous forms, and Asian theatre. They have explored themes such as the negotiation of relationships, corruption, patriarchy, human rights, and sovereignty.

FURTHER READING

Hernandez, Tomas C. *The Emergence of Modern Drama in the Philippines, 1898–1912*; Tiongson, Nicanor G. *Dulaan: An Essay on Philippine Theater.*

Joi Barrios

Playwrights and Playwriting: Singapore

As early as the 1960s, Lim Chor Pee (1936–) and Goh Poh Seng (1936–) sought to create a uniquely **Singaporean** theatre, though both were faulted for creating characters whose language failed to reflect the rhythms, structure, and idioms of Singaporean English. Robert Yeo's (1940–) *One Year Back Home* (1980) broke new ground by addressing contemporary **political** concerns. Stella Kon's (1944–) *Emily of Emerald Hill* (1985) delighted Singaporean audiences with the bittersweet saga of the fierce matriarch Emily, the first **stage** character whose speech accurately reflected the shifting registers of Singaporean English. By the mid-1980s, **Kuo Pao Kun** emerged as the country's pre-eminent playwright with his influential and much-revived one-act monologues "The Coffin Is Too Big for the Hole" (1984) and "No Parking on Odd Days" (1986). The most popular playwright of the late 1980s and early 1990s was Michael Chiang, who wrote the book for a number of crowd-pleasing, Singapore-themed **musicals**, including *Beauty World*, *Fried Rice Paradise*, and *Private Parts* (1992). Eleanor Wong's (1962–) *Mergers and Accusations* (1993) and *Wills and Succession*s (1995) depicted lesbian relationships honestly and sympathetically, helping to set the stage for the eventual acceptance of plays with sympathetic gay men later in the 1990s.

Of the other promising playwrights that emerged in the 1990s (including Russell Heng, Tan Tarn How, and Ovidia Yu), only Haresh Sharma (1965–) of The Necessary Stage continues to have a playwriting profile. Because of the shift away from text-based drama, playwrights' professional production opportunities have diminished significantly since the mid-1990s.

FURTHER READING

Peterson, William. *Theater and the Politics of Culture in Contemporary Singapore*; Tan Chong Kee, and Tisa Ng, eds. *Ask Not: The Necessary Stage in Singapore Theatre*.

William Peterson

The 1998 revival of the musical *Beauty World*, a paean to 1960s Cantonese melodrama, written by Michael Chiang with music by Dick Lee. (Photo: Courtesy of TheatreWorks)

Playwrights and Playwriting: Sri Lanka

Nurti. In the traditional **Sri Lankan** • **folk theatre**, represented by *kolam*, *nadagam*, and *sokari*, authorship of plays was not documented, and there were no written scripts. By the late nineteenth and twentieth centuries, as folk theatre receded to the villages, a new genre, ***nurti***, grew popular. *Nurti* plays evolved from touring **Indian** • **Parsi theatre** troupes in the 1870s; soon, Sinhalese versions—often with nationalist **political** messages—were written, and commercially run proscenium **theatres** were built to house them in Colombo. This "golden age" of Sinhala drama dwindled away in the 1930s when faced with competition from movies.

Jayamanne *Plays*. In the 1940s and 1950s, **actor** Eddie Jayamanne, the "Charlie Chaplin of Ceylon," starred in comedies identified as the *jayamanne* play, named for Jayamanne's playwright and filmmaker brother, B. A. W. Jayamanne. In *Seethala Nadiya* (1958), Jayamanne's actress-singer wife, **Rukmani Devi**, played the main role. Despite their dramaturgical weakness, these plays provide a bridge to modern Sinhalese playwriting. Unable to remove all the outmoded conventions of *nurti*, they were emotionally overdone domestic melodramas, mingling comedy and bathos, and also introducing songs; their literary language was inappropriate to the everyday people speaking it. Still, they dealt with ordinary middle- and upper-class life in Colombo and addressed such social issues as caste and the dowry system. Subplots presented the lower as a foil to the higher classes, whose lives looked confused in comparison with their less well-off fellows. Their plays were popular enough to spark the first Sinhalese films, in which their actors became Sri Lanka's original movie stars, among them Rukmani Devi and Eddie Jayamanne.

Ediriweera Sarachchandra. During this era, the growing influence of **Western** dramaturgy was evident in productions of translations of Western plays at the universities and by amateur groups, such as the Minerva Amateur Dramatic Club.

Sinhalese playwriting changed drastically with Ediriweera (E. R.) Sarachchandra (1914–1996), a university professor who had studied indigenous traditions in order to create a nonrealistic, modern theatre. His work fused Western techniques, folk forms like *kolam* and *nadagam*, and *nurti*, all of it seasoned with an effective use of **music**. In 1956, he produced the groundbreaking *Maname*, a love tragedy based on a Buddhist birth story (*jataka*) and staged in *nadagam* style. Its story is also enacted in *kolam*, although the dramatist revised the depiction of the treacherous wife to make her sympathetic. *Maname* was not solely an attempt at reviving a folk genre. With *Maname*, Sinhalese playwriting achieved some measure of poetic depth.

It was followed by *Sinhabahu* (1958), another lyrical drama, which invoked the popular myth of the Sinhala race. Sarachchandra's plays cut across social, economic, and educational boundaries and remain popular because they express a modern sensibility in a social sense. From his plays emerged a stylized, poetic **dance**-drama that became the nation's most popular theatrical expression. It bears some relation to India's "theatre of roots" movement, in which indigenous forms inspire new methods of writing and production.

The 1960s: Realism Arrives. The mid-1960s and 1970s saw a shift to realism; original plays about social issues were produced. G. K. Hathotuwegama (1942–) became the chief exponent of Sri Lankan "street theatre," introduced in the 1970s as a form of socio-political protest. It was inspired by radical activist ideologies to which many young people were drawn. In the 1980s, various groups were formed nationwide with street theatre often being occasion-oriented, taking shape on Human Rights Day or for other social or political events.

Playwriting flourished in the 1960s because of active sponsorship. The annual State Drama **Festival**, which began in the 1960s, continues to attract serious theatre, and generates great interest in the theatre community. It is a major source of theatre funding. Younger playwrights also have been encouraged by a subsequent event, the Youth Drama Festival. Many playwrights who win awards here go on to perform at the State Drama Festival.

Henry Jayasena (1931–) revolutionized Sinhalese theatre by introducing realism and breaking away from Sarachchandra's stylized form. His plays include *Window* (Janelaya, 1961), *Strikes That Entice the Mind* (Mana ranjana vada varjana, 1966), and *No Way out for Us, My Son* (Apata puthe magak nathe, 1968).

Another leading figure since the 1960s has been actress-playwright Somalatha Subasinghe (1936–). She wrote and directed *Distortions* (Vikurti, 1982), as well as several children's plays, including *Ratmalee* (an adaptation of "Little Red Riding Hood") and *Snow White and the Seven Dwarfs* (Himakumari).

Sugathapala De Silva (1928–2002) is considered "the architect of the modern Sinhala theatre." His best play is considered by many to be *Dunna Dunu Gamuwe*, written just after the nation's 1971 insurrection. He combined 1960s realism with 1970s absurdism.

Asoka Handagama (1962–), also a renowned film and television **director**, has written socially pointed plays like *Don't Kill* (Magatha, 1989), produced during the height of 1988's communistic Nationalist Freedom Party (Jatika Vimukti Peramuna [JVP]) uprising, after which there was a crackdown on civil liberties; its plot uses a traditional law as a mechanism to critique the contemporary justice system.

Other playwrights of the 1960s include Dayananda Gunawardene (1934–1993), Gunasena Galappathy (1927–1984), and K. B. Herat (1941–). Younger playwrights in today's Sinhalese theatre have moved away from politics to interweaving issues related to youth and their problems. These plays indirectly critique politics by demonstrating their effects on problems encountered by youth.

English-Language Playwriting. Playwriting in English has been limited. The most prominent playwright of the 1970s and early 1980s, Ernest MacIntyre (1934–), wrote, directed, and acted in plays such as *The Loneliness of the Short Distance Traveler* (1969), *Let's Give Them Curry* (1981), and *Rasanayagam's Last Riot* (1990), which have been performed in Sri Lanka and Australia.

Other noteworthy English-language playwrights of the 1980s were Nedra Vittachi (1954–), whose works include *Poppy* (1984) and *Knots* (1987, 1999), and transgender dramatist, actor, director, and producer Indu Dharmasena (1956–). Both produced several plays grappling with social issues, the latter in a satirical way. Dharmasena is well known for the comedy series *Tomiya* in the 1980s. Her other comedies include *It's All or Nothing* (1988) and *Colombo* (2004).

During the 1990s, more overtly political issues were brought into the English theatre. Ruana Rajapakse (1958–), Regi Siriwardena (1922–2004), Senaka Abeyratne (1952–), Ruwanthi de Chickera (1975–), and Jehan Aloysius (1977–) wrote and produced plays that marked a change in playwriting by grappling with issues related to conflict and its impact on the common person. Rajapakse's *War Story* and *All in a Day's Work* (1998) focus on the effects of war. De Chickera and Aloysius have discussed political issues in plays such as *Checkpoint* (2002), but also social issues such as poverty and tradition, which are related to the nation's war problems.

Tamil Theatre. In the Tamil theatre, a few playwrights have produced original work on issues of socio-political relevance. Kuzanthai M. Shanmugalingam (1931–) is a director-playwright who has dealt with social issues. *Hellish Heaven* and *The Conflagration Mother Set Off* deal with the torture in security camps of people from all classes. Sumathy Sivamohan produces and directs plays in which she herself acts, among them a Tamil adaptation of **Girish Raghunath Karnad**'s 1988 *Play with a Cobra* (Naga-mandala). Her work is about the power of narrative, politics, women, and land, and includes *Thin Veils: In the Shadow of the Gun and the Wicked Witch* (2003).

FURTHER READING

Obeyesekere, Ranjini. *Sri Lankan Theatre in a Time of Terror: Political Satire in a Permitted Space.*

Neluka Silva

Playwrights and Playwriting: Thailand

A major problem in modern **Thai** theatre is the shortage of professional playwrights. Students take university classes in world drama and playwriting; most then apply their education to writing for soap operas. Although **theatre companies** are constantly producing new plays, they are rarely published or revived, probably because each play is specific to the style and **direction** of each company. There are no new play development programs, staged readings, or dramaturgs.

Theatre 28, a company known for its translations of highbrow **Western** dramas, initiated The Project for Creating Thai Stage Plays in an attempt to solve this problem. It commissioned five well-known novelists to write one-act social dramas, held staged readings, and published them as *Five Thai Stage Plays* (Ha botlakon vethi Thai, 1991). Criticized for their lack of stage practicality, none has been produced, nor has this anthology been republished.

In view of this, the bilingual publication of Kamron Gunatilaka's **political** drama *The 1932 Revolutionist* (Kue phoo apiwat 2475, 1987) after many revivals by Crescent Moon Theatre (Prachan Siew Karn Lakon) is remarkable. Still, no other professional and student troupes have produced it.

Daraka Wongsiri remains Thailand's most prolific playwright, notwithstanding the criticism that she writes solely for the commercial company Dream Box. Although none of her plays has been published, photocopies are available for purchase. Students restage her dramas and comedies in **acting** and directing classes, and study them in playwriting classes.

Another noteworthy playwright is Nikorn Tang, a Thammasat University graduate who continued his advanced training at École International de Théâtre Jacques Lecoq. Representative social satires for Theatre 8×8 are *Bangkok: Lovely Madness* (Krungthep narak nachang, 2001), *Insomnia* (Non mai lhab, 2002), and *Desperation of God* (Phrachao Seng, 2005). *See also Lakon phut samai mhai.*

FURTHER READING

Rutnin, Mattani Mojdara. *Dance, Drama, and Theatre in Thailand: The Process of Development and Modernization.*

Pawit Mahasarinand

POLITICS IN THEATRE

Politics in Theatre: Bangladesh

Theatre in independent **Bangladesh** was conceived during the war of liberation (1971) and as the legacy of other political battles over language and identity. The post-independence theatre movement grew up exploring issues such as national aspirations, identity, and the euphoria of independence. A wide range of plays was produced from the early 1970s to the early 1980s reflecting politically sensitive issues related to the liberation war. These went from the Wilderness (Aranyak) **theatre company**'s production of **Muneir Chowdhury**'s "The Grave" (Kabar, 1972), dealing with issues related to the language movement, to the Citizen (Nagorik) troupe's presentation of *The Life of Nurluddin* (Nuruldeener sarajiban, 1981), in which the revolt of Rangpur (1783) is shown as a metaphor for the recent conflict. By the mid-1970s, other groups had come into being and taken on nationalist themes.

With the euphoria slowly receding during the 1980s as autocratic and dictatorial rule increased, a feeling of disillusionment gave way to a **critical** attitude that sought to explore in theatrical terms the political, philosophical, and psychological issues left shelved during the years of nationalist struggle when other problems had priority. A large number of international plays, particularly those of Brecht, were staged with close readings of the political subtext reflected in contemporary interpretations. Still, theatre remained largely restricted to expressing the concerns and issues of the urban middle class. Bureaucratic control has led to harassment of artists, particularly in regional centers and suburban towns. Political expression is often manifested in defiance of **censorship** and repression.

Bishnupriya Dutt

Politics in Theatre: Cambodia

Cambodia's *robam kbach boran* has been the object of several high-stakes political tugs of war during the past one hundred years—mainly contesting who "owns" and controls it. During the French protectorate, the **dance** troupe within the king's harem was an oasis of Khmer influence and prestige. A potent element of **religious** ceremonies, it also linked the king to the ancient Angkor empire, whose grand palaces were festooned with dancing *apsara*s.

Starting around 1905, the French became determined to wrest control of the dance, not least so that they could show it off at will. Claiming (as colonial culture minister

Georges Grolier put it) that they were saving Cambodia's patrimony from the "whims" of Cambodia's royalty, the government repeatedly moved to replace the palace troupe with an outside "state" company. These attempts failed thanks largely to the dedication and savvy of Princess (later Queen Mother, later Queen) **Sisowath Kossamak**.

In the 1980s, exiled factions alleged that the **Vietnam**-installed government was altering *robam kbach boran*, and they cited this supposed outrage as prime evidence that the foreign occupiers were destroying Cambodian culture. Meanwhile, within their refugee camps, the factions set up classical troupes, emblems of *their* claims to legitimacy.

Robam kbach boran has always been a voice for those in power. *The Blessing Dance* (Chuon por) has on occasion included waving the national flags of visiting dignitaries. After King Norodom Sihanouk (1922–) abdicated in favor of his father in 1955, the royal troupe often performed *Preah Vessandar*, about a king who abdicates in favor of his father. On Sihanouk's desperate diplomatic missions abroad during the escalating U.S.-Indochina war, he nearly always took dancers with him as goodwill ambassadors.

Cambodia's other forms have frequently contained political and social commentary and protests against those in power. Like most Southeast Asian shadow **puppetry**, *lakhon sbaek* includes clowns whose humor may be not only slapstick and crude but also topical. The small-format shadow puppet genre (*lakhon sbaek touch*) includes contemporary as well as traditional stories and has sometimes offered up ferocious satire. During the French protectorate, the small puppets bashed French corruption, physiognomy, and sexual prowess.

In the mid-1950s, **Hang Tun Hak**'s government-sponsored **theatre company** performed politically pointed "spoken drama" (***lakhon niyeay***), including comedies Hang wrote attacking corruption and social abuses. (After one show, **actors** had to waylay an enraged, gun-brandishing official to allow his impersonator to flee.) The troupe was dissolved after a year, and the performers barely escaped arrest.

Political issues have also found expression in ***lakhon bassac***, ***yiké***, and *ayay chlong chlay* (a classical male-female sung duet genre). Sometimes traditional stories are given a particular slant. Other times, new stories are created to spotlight political and social issues.

Eileen Blumenthal

Politics in Theatre: China

Pre-modern Traditional Theatre. Throughout the ages **Chinese** governments and ruling elites have used the theatre as a bulwark of their own values and policies, and exerted **censorship** against plays they thought harmful to the political or social order. Frequently, rebels against regimes have also used the theatre to promote their own causes. Both governments and their opponents saw the theatre as one way of influencing the people. It did not require literacy, and performers could spread an atmosphere favoring a particular cause or attitude.

Ming dynasty (1368–1644) imperial regimes used the theatre to bolster their Confucian politics and values. Confucianist Wang Shouren (1472–1528) advocated using drama as moral propaganda by emphasizing plays about loyal subjects and filial sons, and eliminating all lewd or subversive material. The Qing dynasty (1644–1911) was even more deliberate in politicizing and Confucianizing the theatre.

There is strong evidence that, by the nineteenth century, rebel movements were actively using popular plays to promote their causes. Notable was the use by rebels of the novel *Water Margin* (Shuihu zhuan) and the plays based on it; this focuses on rebels, showing them as essentially good people. In the mid-1850s, Cantonese *yueju* • **actor** Li Wenmao (?–1861) even led an army of **actors** against the authorities of Guangdong and Guangxi, briefly setting up an independent kingdom based in Liuzhou (Guangxi).

Modern Traditional Theatre. Although politics became much more prevalent in twentieth-century forms such as "spoken drama" (*huaju*; see Playwrights and Playwriting), it also was highly relevant in ***xiqu***. Reformist-minded ***jingju*** actor Pan Yueqiao (1869–1929) was active militarily in the capture of Shanghai (November 1911), which was crucial to the success of the monarchy's overthrow. The thinkers behind the May Fourth Movement (1919) were suspicious of *xiqu* because of its links with tradition. They demanded it be reformed to suit the modern age, and, in the case of the radical Qian Xuantong (1887–1939), advocated its total negation. During the Second Sino-**Japanese** War (1937–1945), *xiqu* actors actively used their art to stir up resistance.

In 1942, in his "Yan'an Talks on Literature and Art," Chinese Communist Party (CCP) Chairman Mao Zedong (1893–1976) declared the supremacy of political criteria over artistic concerns for any work of art; he said that all literature and art were geared to definite political lines and served the purposes of particular classes. This resulted in *jingju* dramas highlighting rebellion against the feudal ruling classes (see *Xinbian lishi ju*). One example was *Three Attacks on the Zhu Family Village* (San da Zhujia zhuang), which lauds the *Water Margin* rebels, their opposition to the feudal ruling classes, and their military strategy.

When the CCP came to power in 1949, it ensured that all drama should follow its political line. Patriotism and/or progressive values were mandatory ingredients. Plays set in the past highlighted values such as love of China or rebellion against the feudal ruling classes, while those set in the present or recent past spotlighted the virtues of the Party as China's savior. An important *jingju* is *Women Generals of the Yang Family* (Yangmen nüjiang, 1960), set in the eleventh century; it is suffused with patriotism, especially of **women**, while also lauding their military and political role.

It is doubtful if the politics-theatre relationship was ever tighter in China than during the Cultural Revolution (1966–1976). Mao's dicta were interpreted with extreme rigidity. The small selection of "model dramas" (***yangban xi***) all lauded the CCP enthusiastically, eulogizing CCP heroes and demonizing opponents and even those who sought neutrality.

Xiqu is generally expected to support the current political line, or at least not to oppose it. However, the tight link with politics Mao imposed became an object of contempt to many. Few *xiqu* deal directly with the modern world, audiences preferring to escape rather than confront politics.

Colin Mackerras

***Politics in* Huaju.** Throughout the twentieth century, the endowment of China's theatre with a political purpose has often prevented *huaju* from following its own path. With a few exceptions, changes were propelled by outsiders with a preference for ideological over artistic value, of literary merit over theatricality, and of spoon-feeding the audience with ideology while ignoring its need for entertainment and participation.

Turn-of-the-century opinion makers, like Chen Duxiu (1879–1942), denounced *xiqu*'s inability to reflect contemporary life and carry out a political agenda, and advocated for a **Western**-style theatre. Thus *huaju* was endowed with a political and ideological purpose from its infancy. Its first full-length production, the 1907 Tokyo production of *The Black Slaves' Cry to Heaven* (Heinu yutian lu), was adapted from the anti-slavery novel *Uncle Tom's Cabin*. Many actors in *wenming xi* (a form that led to *huaju*) took part in the 1911 Revolution either artistically or by joining the rebels on the battlefield. Wang Zhongsheng (1884?–1911), an enthusiastic spoken drama advocate, was executed by the Qing government. In the late 1910s, Ibsen became popular for his observation of contemporary life and advocacy of individual freedom.

Still, in the 1920s, there was a determinedly apolitical countercurrent that emphasized learning from the artistry rather than the content of Western theatre. An example was the "national theatre movement" advocated by Yu Shangyuan (1897–1970) and Xu Zhimo (1897–1931). However, these attempts failed to win popular acceptance and were denounced by leftwing artists as "art for art's sake." By the early 1930s, the looming threat of Japanese invasion, the political struggle between the communists and Nationalists, and the influence of international leftist theatrical movements moved mainstream *huaju* practitioners to the left, culminating in the creation of the League of Leftwing **Theatre Companies** in 1930 in Shanghai (a year later, it became the League of Leftwing Dramatists, a union of individuals). Apart from staging such influential productions as the Soviet *Roar! China* (1933), the League also created many touring troupes that staged motivational plays for the working class and organized dramatic activities among workers and students.

At the same time, the Nationalist government also enlisted *huaju* in its campaign to eliminate illiteracy. Sponsored by the Council for the Promotion of Education for the Ordinary People, Xiong Foxi (1900–1965) carried out a successful **experiment** in popularizing *huaju* in the villages of Ding County, Hebei Province, between 1932 and 1937. Using amateur and newly written or adapted scripts suited to his audience, his outdoor productions were welcomed by peasants and **critics** alike and were hailed as *huaju*'s future.

Mao Zedong's **theory** of the arts became the dominating principle for all theatre both in the pre-1949 communist-occupied areas and in mainland China thereafter. In 1949, following the Soviet model, the All-China Dramatists Association (originally Chinese Dramatic Workers' Association) was established as theatre's official governing body. From 1953 onward, the government made several pronouncements in an effort to regulate privately owned companies, resulting in their gradual conversion into state-owned companies with state employees. As a result, practitioners became dependent on the government for their artistic and financial survival, theatre's function became predominantly social and ideological education, and government officials became not only regulators but often controllers of the creative process from playwriting, rehearsal, and production to **criticism**. Theatre became an active "participant" in politics.

The raw political power over theatre reached unprecedented height during the Cultural Revolution, when most artists were sent to reform camps. In the post-Mao era, although overt prosecution of artists has largely diminished, political movements, such as the "anti-spiritual pollution" (1983–1984) and "anti-bourgeois liberalization" (1986–1987) campaigns, were again invoked in order to weed out plays that had veered from official ideology.

Since the late 1980s, the government has resorted to promoting politically correct productions in campaigns such as "Main Melody," which urges **theatres** to promote productions that praise socialism and the CCP. The government has also promoted two projects: the "Five Number Ones" and the more recent "Acclaimed Theatrical Works of National Distinction." The former requires local cultural authorities to promote each year one best book, play, television program, and film, and one essay that endorses "socialist spiritual civilization." The latter selects ten productions from all genres nationally each year between 2003 and 2007 as representative of contemporary theatre. Works considered by these projects gain extra state support; thus local cultural authorities always focus on award-oriented productions, neglecting the needs of worthy recipients.

FURTHER READING

Chen, Xiaomei. *Acting the Right Part: Political Theater and Popular Drama in Contemporary China*; Hay, Trevor. "China's Proletarian Myth: The Revolutionary Narrative and Model Theatre of the Cultural Revolution"; Jin, Jiang. "Women and Public Culture: Poetics and Politics of Women's Yue Opera in Republican Shanghai, 1930s–1940s."

Siyuan Liu

Politics in Theatre: Hong Kong

Compared to its counterpart on mainland **China**, the emergence of "spoken drama" (*huaju;* see Playwrights and Playwriting) in the British colony did not fulfill any social or political mission. Instead, it simply aimed to entertain British troops and European merchants present since the mid-nineteenth century. For a long time, local theatre was apolitical, noticeably so after the two big riots of 1966 and 1967 spurred by China's Cultural Revolution (1966–1976) and various socioeconomic problems. The government carefully diverted its subjects to more harmless activities, including theatre, **music**, and **dance** in parks and squares. Even in 1982, fifteen years after the government had cleared a path to social reform, and eight years after the Urban Council had attained independent statutory status, leading cultural administrator Alex Wu (Wu Shuzhi) stated in a speech on cultural and artistic policy: "Instead of producing great composers, we are only hoping to make top-rate skillful players." He also proposed that artists should "avoid interfering with politics."

However, alongside this apolitical, entertainment-oriented scene, ran an undercurrent of "relevant theatre." The Federation of Students' Drama **Festival**, inaugurated in 1966, was an early example. "**Hong Kong** consciousness" was clearly expressed in plays presented here, and these were followed by more radical **theatre companies**. Mok Chiu Yu (Mo Zhaoru), a social activist cum dramatist, founded the Hong Kong People's Theatre (Minzhong Juchang, 1979) and often organized street performances. The Asian People's Theatre Festival Society, a collaborative organization involving **India**, **Bangladesh**, the **Philippines**, and other Asian countries, became his regular platform in the early 1990s. Alternative theatre has also been offered by Zuni Icosahedron (Jinnian Ershi mian ti), founded by Danny Yung (Rong Nianzeng) in 1982. Calling itself an independent cultural collective, Zuni has been engaged in diverse activities including arts education and **criticism**, policy advocacy, multimedia, and installations. In 1985, after two years' negotiation, Zuni, through its production of

Chronicle of **Women** (Lienü zhuan), succeeded in convincing the government to rescind the **Censorship** Act issued by the Television and Entertainment Licensing Authority. Hong Kong theatre, therefore, has enjoyed much more freedom than its mainland counterpart. Zuni's dialectical theatre has recently given way to social satire, which further enhanced its popularity.

It is noteworthy that the colonial government's tolerance for demands for more artistic freedom and its spirit of compromise were closely associated with developments resulting from both the 1984 signing of the Sino-British Joint Declaration, and the subsequent "Handover." Consequently, the democracy enjoyed locally from the 1980s on gave artists more confidence in dealing with political subjects, leading to the emergence of more relevant work. Many productions focused on issues such as cultural identity, heritage, and Hong Kong's future. A good example in this category was the Sino-English (Chung Ying) Theatre Company's (Zhongying Jutuan) *I Am Hong Kong* (Wo hai Xianggangren, 1985). However, this activity was curtailed by 1989's Tiananmen Square incident.

The political scenario has changed since 1997, when Hong Kong was reunified with China, and became a Special Administrative Region (SAR) under the "One Country, Two Systems" arrangement. In 2000, the SAR government abolished two municipal councils, and their original cultural and arts responsibilities were assumed by the Leisure and Cultural Services Department (LCSD) of the Home Affairs Bureau (HAB). Lacking the previous system of checks and balances between the two councils, and with a bureau having no legitimate policy, culture and arts in Hong Kong became subject to undesirable, highly centralized, executive-led governance. In 2001, the SAR government privatized all previous Urban Council troupes. Although entertainment is still a predominant theatre goal, an increasing number of productions express concerns about social and political issues. Examples include *Yes, Chief Executive* (Haige, teshou, 2004), a satire on the weak and irresponsible SAR government, and *East Wing West Wing 2005– West Kowloon Story* (Dong gong xi gong, 2005), a political comedy dealing with the hot issue of new cultural development on the West Kowloon site, a reclamation from Victoria Harbor that boldly questions the real intentions of Hong Kong's centrally appointed leader in supporting the monopoly consortium's development proposal.

Hardy Tsoi

Politics in Theatre: India

In the nineteenth and early twentieth centuries, under colonialism, some of **Rabindranath Tagore**'s plays and those of the **Parsi theatre**, particularly in urban or "intellectual" contexts (for example, Delhi, Mumbai [Bombay], Calcutta [Kolkata]), took on **Western** production elements, such as the proscenium arch and the "well-made play"; it used them to help express (relatively politely and nonconfrontationally) a variety of Indian perspectives. At the same time, **folk theatre** forms retained elements of improvisation and audience engagement that allowed a degree of irony, including the classical fool (*vidushaka*) character.

Post-independence Theatre. After independence (1947), much urban street and site-specific theatre (including factories) in the 1950s and 1960s addressed a working-class audience in an attempt to raise its consciousness—in the manner of Brecht's "teaching plays" (*lehrstücke*)—about the economic relationship of labor and capital.

Indian history is seen as the articulation of identity in the plays of **Utpal Dutt**, **G. P. Deshpande**, and **Girish Karnad**, among others. These dramatized—and problematized—key historical moments and figures in order to encourage a "re-historicization" of Indian heritage. At the same time, while traditional or "classical" performance had always been heavily dependent on the *Mahabharata* and *Ramayana*, the conscious "return" to these sources, and to folktales or myths, by a number of highly educated (sometimes "Western-returned") **playwrights** after 1960 was seized upon by the cultural establishment (via the National Academy of **Music**, **Dance**, and Drama [Sangeet Natak Akademi]) as a recognizable—and exportable—model of cultural and political unity of "Indianness" known as the "theatre of roots."

Major events and the context against and within which theatre took place include independence, Partition, and the development of forms of nationalism; Indo-**Pakistan** relations and troubles in the Punjab; assassinations of major leaders (M. K. Gandhi, Indira Gandhi, Rajiv Gandhi); land issues, governance in northeastern states, the Naxalite (communist revolutionary groups) problem; violence in Gujarat; **religious** fundamentalism; and ethnic politics.

Theatre is a public event; as such it rarely is not political in some sense. In a country that has in the last one hundred years moved from colonialism to independence, and then to a significant position in the global economy, while also experiencing numerous assassinations and major internal and external conflicts, political concerns are at least subtextually present in much of its artistic production. An impressive history of aesthetic scholarship and artistic practice, combined with a strong and subtle intellectual and **critical** tradition, produces an awareness of theatre being a form of political and moral action. This is particularly true when, following the end of colonial rule, many writers were at the forefront of a productive and imaginative form of "writing back." Although the existence of a singular Indian theatre is as problematic as that of a single "India," there is nevertheless a consistency in how political life is manifested across the forms of theatre.

Because Indian theatre encompasses a wide range of forms, and because, rooted in the aesthetic perspective of the ancient *Treatise on Drama* (Natyashastra; see Theory), it always understood that all of them are *forms*, not unchangeable "reality," the spectator must always enter the process to interpret, rather than to "read," a simple "message." Thus nearly all Indian theatre is political, even if not overtly so; however, the most ardent exponents of agitprop or street theatre rarely ignore performance aesthetics in the process of engagement and deliberation. Moreover, the focus of many recent plays has been on a range of recurrent issues—power and corruption, land control, tradition, ethnic and religious conflict, and so on.

Street Theatre. Street theatre has drawn on traditional styles—including **music** and song, clown figures and improvisation, as well as short "naturalistic" scenes—to address concerns. In the 1940s and 1950s, the leftist Indian People's Theatre Association fused this with a confrontational "Brechtian" style; **Badal Sircar**'s "Third Theatre" (Anganmancha, literally, "open-air theatre") in Calcutta similarly attempted to attract mass audiences in public places. Celebrated productions included **Safdar Hashmi**'s *Woman* (Aurat, 1979) and *Machine* (1978), and Sircar's *Procession* (Michhil, 1974). In Kerala, the KSSP (Kerala Shastra Sahitya Parishad, that is, Kerala

People's Science Movement) organized processional events that toured the state and even beyond, promoting literacy and sometimes addressing other issues; in Karnataka, the leftwing **theatre company** Samudaya used similar methods. In Delhi, Hashmi's work led to his murder by Congress Party thugs in 1989; he has since become a martyr to street theatre workers, who celebrate his death annually with **festivals**; his company, People's Theatre Platform (Jana Natya Manch, or Janam), still promotes social justice.

The work of many similar groups overlaps to a considerable degree with that of "theatre for development" practitioners. Funding is generally even more tenuous than for more conventional forms, and the danger of excessively enthusiastic agitprop attitudes is ever-present. However, many performers move between different companies and styles, and street theatre often provides a valuable stimulus and **training**, and alerts performers—if not always receivers—to theatre's potential intervention at all levels of political life.

Theatre for Development. Following Marx and Brecht, what is also known as "theatre for social change," "interventionist theatre," and, in some places, "community theatre," now refers more explicitly to Freirian politics and Boal's "Theatre of the Oppressed." India's leading Boalian company is Sanjoy Ganguli's Jana Sanskriti, based near Kolkata but operating *ad hoc* teams of performers in rural areas throughout West Bengal, as well as in neighboring states and in Delhi, Gujarat, and Maharashtra. Ganguli has frequently given workshops to other groups; not all of them use "forum theatre"—in which Boal aims to make audiences into "spectactors" who intervene to suggest alternative courses of action in a problem-centered scenario. They often work in conjunction with government agencies or nongovernmental organizations, which may cause difficulties about goals and methods of delivery when balanced against funding.

There are now up to one hundred groups that regularly or occasionally use theatre for "development" or "outreach" purposes, engaging with a whole variety of issues: HIV/AIDS, street children, **women**'s health, communalism, land issues, aborting

Jana Sanskriti Forum theatre production at Jadavpur University, Kolkata, October 2004. (Photo: Franc Chamberlain)

female babies, gender roles, environmental concerns, community politics, literacy, alcoholism, and others. Major groups include Vidya (Ahmedabad), which focuses on the status of the girl-child in urban slums; Naz Foundation (Delhi), which works on HIV/AIDS, and the Chennai (Madras)–based women's group Voicing Silence, which initiated several Kulavai festivals (named for women's ritual ululations) in recent years.

FURTHER READING

Baskaran, S. Theodore. *The Message Bearers: Nationalist Politics and the Entertainment Media in South India 1880–1945*; Bharucha, Rustom. *Rehearsals of Revolution: The Political Theater of Bengal*; Boon, Richard, and Jane Plastow, eds. *Theatre and Empowerment: Community Drama on the World Stage*; Srampickal, Jacob. *Voice to the Voiceless: The Power of People's Theatre in India*.

Ralph Yarrow

Politics in Theatre: Indonesia

Indonesian theatre has long been used as a tool for addressing political and social problems, although until recently such critiques were expressed indirectly. Traditional forms such as *wayang* (see Puppet Theatre) have frequently been utilized as tools for political expression and communication, during both colonial and postcolonial times. *Randai* was allegedly used as a way to secretly hone self-defense skills during the **Japanese** occupation. Early modern spoken theatre (*sandiwara*), influenced by **Western** models, aligned itself with anti-colonialism. **Playwrights** have adapted techniques from political authors such as Brecht and Boal to question government policies.

Playwrights, including **Rendra** and **Nano Riantiarno**, whose plays critique government policies, have attempted (sometimes unsuccessfully) to avoid reprisal, such as **censorship** and detainment, through strategies like setting plays in fictional countries, or using historic parallels. **Theatre companies** such as Teater SAE, Grave Theatre (Teater Kubur), Black Umbrella Theatre (Teater Payung Hitam), Bali **Experimental** Teater, and Teater Re-Publik, have produced work critical of the New Order government using nontext-based forms.

Director-playwright **Ratna Sarumpaet**'s *Marsinah: Song from the Underworld* (Marsinah: nyanyian dari bawah tanah, 1993), concerning the brutal murder of a labor activist, was banned, and Ratna was arrested in 1998 and held for seventy days for participating in a pro-democracy event. More recently, working-class groups, such as Independent Women's Theatre of North Sumatra (Teater Perempuan Independen Sumatera Utara), formed to express the concerns of rural working **women**, have begun to take root. Indonesian anti-government protests since 1995 have increasingly had strong theatrical elements; in 2000, a group of students arrested for organizing a street happening wore **masks** of ex-President Soeharto (1921–) during their trial.

FURTHER READING

Brandon, James R. *Theatre in Southeast Asia*; Hellman, Jörgen. *Performing the Nation: Cultural Politics in New Order Indonesia*; Peacock, James L. *Rites of Modernization: Symbols and Social Aspects of Indonesian Proletarian Drama*.

Eka D. Sitorus

Politics in Theatre: Japan

Meiji Period through World War II. Theatre practitioners in **Japan** from the Meiji Restoration (1868) through World War II often contended with government authorities bent on nation-building. In 1872, the government co-opted theatre to purvey official philosophy and improve public morals, placing **actors** under the newly established Ministry of **Religious** Instruction and requiring them to encourage virtue, castigate vice, and avoid derogatory references to the emperor.

Tremendous social and political changes in the Meiji period (1868–1912) inevitably moved **playwrights** to socio-political expression. **Kawatake Mokuami** wrote *The Morning East Wind under the Cleared Sky of the Southeast* (Okige no kumoharau asagochi, 1878) for *kabuki*, depicting **Japan**'s 1877 civil war. Sudô Sadanori (1867–1907), charismatic Liberal Party leader, formed the Great Japan Courageous Men's Society for Reforming Theatre (1888). Sudô is credited with founding *shinpa*, a genre anchored in his group's amateurish, bluntly political sketches (*sôshi shibai*), performed to counter official conservatism. **Kawakami Otojirô** realized *shinpa*'s full potential, mounting his pioneering production, *Itagaki's Misfortunes: The True Account* (Itagaki-kun sônan jikki, 1891), about the attempted assassination of Itagaki Taisuke, the popular rights movement leader. The Sino-Japanese War (1894–1895) prompted more *shinpa* plays extolling war heroes and arousing patriotism. Similarly patriotic war plays were staged during the Russo-Japanese War (1904–1905).

The Russian Revolution in 1917 and post–World War I unrest awakened working-class self-awareness, stimulating the emergence of proletarian **theatre companies**. In 1925, the Trunk Theatre (Toranku Gekijô) arose to support the labor movement. In 1926, the Vanguard Theatre (Zen'ei-za) emerged, promoting Marxism. The two merged in 1928 as the Tokyo Leftwing Theatre (Tokyo Sayoku Gekijô), becoming in 1934 the New Cooperative Troupe (Shinkyô Gekidan). Following founder **Osanai Kaoru**'s death in 1928, the Tsukiji Little Theatre (Tsukiji Shôgekijô) split into the Japanese Proletarian Theatre Association (Nihon Puroretaria Gekijô Dômei) and the New Tsukiji Theatre (Shin Tsukiji Gekidan) in 1929. Plays staged by these troupes include Russian proletarian dramatist and **theorist** A. V. Lunacharsky's *The Liberated Don Quixote* (1921), **Miyoshi Jûrô**'s *The Much-Maimed Oaki* (Kizu darake no Oaki, 1927), **Murayama Tomoyoshi**'s *Account of a Terrorist Gang* (Bôryokudan ki, 1929), and **Kubo Sakae**'s *Land of Volcanic Ash* (Kazanbaichi, 1937–1938).

Despite these achievements, the proletarian movement was plagued by internal disputes over the relationship between politics and art and how to apply Soviet-style socialist realism. **Censorship** posed a more serious threat, promulgating the Peace Preservation Law in 1925 for "thought control." As Japan embarked on fifteen years of war (1931–1945), such control extended to theatre. In 1940, all film and theatre practitioners were required to register. The same year, the Cabinet Intelligence Bureau was established, just before the New Cooperative Troupe and the New Tsukiji Theatre were disbanded, with about one hundred arrested, including Murayama, Kubo, **Takizawa Osamu**, **Senda Koreya**, and **Akita Ujaku**.

Categorically banning "domestic dramas" (*sewa mono*) as trivial, officials encouraged "patriotic theatre" (*kokumin engeki*), like the *bunraku* (see Puppet Theatre)/*kabuki* play *A Treasury of Loyal Retainers* (Kanadehon chûshingura), presumably to boost Japanese morale. In 1941, the Japanese Touring Theatre Association was established to send patriotic theatre throughout the country. During the war, even some "art-for-art's-sake" dramatists collaborated, willingly or otherwise, as with **Kishida Kunio**'s appointment to the Imperial Rule Assistance Association and **Morimoto Kaoru**'s commission to write supporting the war.

Postwar Japan. During the Occupation, politics interfered with theatre from another direction. Under the rubrics "demilitarization" and "democratization," Occupation censorship authorities banned some two-thirds of *kabuki*'s repertoire as "feudalistic" or "militaristic." This policy was lifted in November 1947. Meanwhile, leftwing *shingeki* plays enjoyed a revival, dominating postwar theatre despite the burgeoning cold war and the 1950 "red purge" barring communists from acting. Kubo's masterpiece was among the first postwar productions, and *shingeki* companies like the Actor's Theatre (Haiyû-za), the People's Art Theatre (Mingei), and the Tokyo Art Theatre (Tôkyô Geijutsu Gekijô) resumed activities or were newly established. Even a Workers' Theatre Council was formed, linked to the Japanese Communist Party (JCP). In this context, the leftwing *kabuki* troupe Progressive Theatre (Zenshin-za) joined the JCP en masse in 1949.

Following the war's profound trauma, the revelations in 1956 of Stalinism's atrocities, and particularly the failure of nationwide demonstrations in 1960 against the U.S.–Japan Mutual Security Treaty (Anpo), many young artists felt disillusioned with old-left dogma and deemed orthodox *shingeki* realism as inadequate to capture contemporary experience. Seeking alternative dramaturgy, they turned to Japan's pre-modern imagination, rejected as "irrational" by *shingeki*. Inspired by **Hotta Kiyomi**'s *The Island* (Shima, 1955) and **Tanaka Chikao**'s *The Head of Mary* (Maria no kubi, 1958), on, respectively, the Hiroshima and Nagasaki bombs, post-*shingeki* playwrights began to deal experimentally with Japan's traumatic defeat, redemption, and imperialist legacy. Such works include **Betsuyaku Minoru**'s *The Elephant* (Zô, 1962), **Satoh Makoto**'s *Nezumi Kozô: The Rat* (Nezumi kozô jirôkichi, 1969) and *My Beatles* (Atashi no Bîtoruzu, 1967), **Fukuda Yoshiyuki**'s *Find Hakamadare!* (Hakamadare wa doko da, 1964), and **Akimoto Matsuyo**'s *Kaison the Priest of Hitachi* (Hitachibō Kaison, 1965). Nor was mainstream *shingeki* immune to the post-1960 ferment, as when the Literary Theatre (Bungaku-za) split for political reasons or **Kinoshita Junji**'s plays, like *A Japanese Called Ottô* (Ottô to yobareru nihonjin, 1962), pitted the individual against history's momentum.

The late 1960s into the early 1990s witnessed unprecedented economic growth, tempered by earthshaking events like the Red Army's shocking crimes and accompanied by antithetical trends: shedding old ideologies while seeking individual and national existential purpose. This environment stimulated the socio-political concerns characterizing many 1970s plays, including **Kara Jûrô**'s *John Silver: The Beggar of Love* (Jon Shirubâ: ai no kojiki, 1970), broaching possibilities of salvation through Japanese imperialism and from contemporary life's emptiness; Betsuyaku's parody, *Legend of Noon* (Shôgo no densetsu, 1973), exposing the imperial system's underlying psychology; **Suzuki Tadashi**'s transcultural adaptation, *The Trojan Women* (Toroia no onna, 1974), attacking both Japanese militarism and the American bombings; and **Tsuka Kôhei**'s *Kanbara Michiko* (Hiryûden, 1979), on the anti-Anpo student demonstrators.

As Japan's economic miracle continued into the 1980s, many dramatists saw through the economic bubble's superficial comforts to society's pervasive emptiness and nuclear-age uncertainties. Such plays include **Kitamura Sô**'s *Ode to Joy* (Hogiuta, 1979) and **Kokami Shôji**'s *The Angels with Closed Eyes* (Tenshi wa hitomi wo tojite, 1988), both depicting a postnuclear-war world; **Kawamura Takeshi**'s *Nippon Wars* (Nippon Uoâzu, 1984) with its apocalyptic vision; and **Noda Hideki**'s *A Fake Piece: Beneath* *the Cherry Forest in Full Bloom* (Gansaku sakura no mori no mankai no shita, 1989), irreverently plumbing state-power origins.

Political concerns were rarely dominant in post-1960s theatre. However, as the national—and international—discourse heatedly continues on Japan's peace-constitution revision and on historical views radically different from Asian neighbors, Japan's imperial past has re-emerged periodically as a key theme, seen at twentieth-century's end in plays like **Hirata Oriza**'s *Citizens of Seoul* (Sôru shimin, 1989) and **Kaneshita Tatsuo**'s *Ice Blossoms* (Kanka, 1997), both treating Japanese-**Korean** mutual regard; **Inoue Hisashi**'s *Hotel Sakura at Kamiyachô* (Kamiyachô sakura hoteru, 1997), on the state-to-theatre relationship; and **Makino Nozomi**'s *Tokyo Atomic Klub* (Tôkyô genshi-kaku kurabu, 1997) on Japan's possible complicity in creating the bomb. Such socio-political themes likely will continue in the twenty-first century, as demonstrated in the 2005 revival of a **musical** trilogy (1991, 2001, and 2004) by the apolitical Four Seasons Company (Gekidan Shiki), tracing Japan's tragic Shôwa period (1926–1989) history to commemorate the sixtieth anniversary of the war's end.

FURTHER READING

Jortner, David, Keiko McDonald, and Kevin J. Wetmore, Jr., eds. *Modern Japanese Theatre and Performance;* Powell, Brian. "Left-wing Theatre in Japan, Its Development and Activity to 1934"; Powell, Brian. *Japan's Modern Theatre: A Century of Continuity and Change.*

Guohe Zheng

Politics in Theatre: Korea

Since the first quarter of the twentieth century, **Korean** theatre has reflected the country's tumultuous politics. Most especially during the 1960s and 1970s, theatre often was a political weapon opposing ruling military regimes. However, even **masked** • **dance** drama, **puppet theatre**, and *madanggŭk* (open-air entertainments) of the seventeenth and eighteenth centuries reflected in some ways an underprivileged people's struggle against the hegemony imposed by a rigid Confucian hereditary class system.

During the **Japanese** annexation of Korea (1910–1945), colonial authorities suppressed traditional theatrical activities as well as nascent nationalistic movements in the modern theatre. Instead, *shinp'agŭk*, a sentimental, emotionally exaggerated dramatic form imported from Japan, was used to manipulate the public's political and national consciousness. While some artists such as **Kim U-jin** tried to focus on socio-political issues important to farmers and urban laborers, artistic resistance in the theatre never became a substantial voice for political action. Under the repressive colonial circumstances, which included **censorship**, such a voice could not resonate with the general public. Rather, propagandistic plays favoring the colonial government proliferated, promoted mostly through government awards; for instance, the 1942 Theatre Award went to **Yu Ch'i-jin**'s *Jujube Tree* (Taech'u namu), which defended a colonial policy that forcibly relocated Koreans to Manchuria.

After the country's liberation (1945) and the Korean War (1950–1953), theatre suffered from ideological conflict between nationalists and socialist/communists. The U.S.-backed regime of President Yi Sŭngman (Syngman Rhee, 1875–1965) imposed rightist, draconian measures supporting anti-communist propaganda plays but stifling dissent in dramatic literature or theatre performance.

Perhaps the April 19, 1960, student uprising that led to Yi's exile signaled a change in the dynamic between politics and theatre, for the mainstream theatre of the 1960s and 1970s is characterized by its critique of colonial history, the aftermath of the Korean War, and changing social conditions seen as negative products of a developing industrial economy. However, theatre was subject to strict scrutiny by government authorities for its potentially subversive and antigovernment implications. Park Jo-yŏl (1930–) struggled to dramatize his personal desire for the country's reunification—a politically taboo subject—in an objective and critical way that immediately brought strict censorship of his plays, among them *General Oh's Toenail* (O changgun ŭi palth'op, 1974). Ch'oe In-hun's (1936–) *When Spring Comes to Hill and Dale* (Pom i omyŏn san-e tŭl-e, 1980) uses fantasy to question socio-political conditions, and playwrights such as Oh Yŏng-jin (1916–1974), Lee Kŭn-sam (1925–2003), and **Lee Kang-baek** resorted to **criticism** through satire, symbol, fable, and myths that often transformed into a powerful political force despite censorship.

In the 1970s and early 1980s, the *madanggŭk* movement emerged around college campuses and factories, recharging the national consciousness and spirit. Combining traditional **folk** burlesque forms, street, and agitprop theatres, *madanggŭk* was a powerful voice calling for Korea's reunification; it united students and laborers in the struggle against social injustices, including human rights abuse and the Kwangju massacre of civilians in 1980. However, as the nation prospered, and labor unrest abated and politics grew increasingly democratic in the 1990s, *madanggŭk* became popularized. Mainstream South Korean theatre now manifests little serious interest in political affairs.

FURTHER READING

Kim, Moon-hwan. "Ideology and Historical Influences in Modern Drama," in *Korean Cultural Heritage: Performing Arts*; Suh, Yon-Ho. "Status and Prospects of Korean Political Drama." *Korea Journal*. 28 (August, 1989): 19–30.

Hyung-jin Lee

Politics in Theatre: Malaysia

Malaysian • playwrights are notably social-minded. In particular, during the independence era, and especially just after independence (late 1950s through early 1960s), Malay playwrights used drama (*sandiwara*) to reflect on the country's past with an eye to developing a more progressive future. Prior to independence (1957), *sandiwara* dramatists contributed to the nationalist cause by portraying the heroism of historic figures connected with the royal courts. The British had resumed control after World War II. Thus these plays were meant to contrast the periods of British colonialism with an earlier, sovereign era in Malay history. Dramatists wanted audiences to feel pride in their heritage.

Post-independence *sandiwara* playwrights looked more critically at the country's feudal past. Plays such as **Shaharom Husain**'s *The Hunchback of Tanjong Puteri* (Si bongkok Tanjong Puteri, 1960) critique Malay leaders as well as the colonizers in an effort to deconstruct the feudal structure and envision a more democratic future. **Usman Awang**'s "Death of a Warrior (Jebat)" (Matinya seorang pahlawan [Jebat], 1961) also upholds the ideal of a free people, **women** as well as men, shirking a past that upheld feudal loyalty at the cost of justice. Writers of this era were committed to "art for society." Independence themes went hand in hand with a concern for social justice and national prosperity.

During the 1960s, plays depicted contemporary life as ordinary citizens dealt with the nuts and bolts of nation-building. Rather than a concern with political matters per se, plays dealt with issues such as how to bridge the gap between rural and urban values and ensure progress for all. During the 1970s, playwrights shifted directions as they responded to the sudden challenges posed by the tragedy of May 13, 1969, when ethnic riots shattered the illusion of a harmonious state. The government attributed the underlying cause to economic disparity, and took steps to overcome poverty, especially within the Malay community. Playwrights also began to reflect more deeply about the nature of poverty and how to change engrained attitudes; at the same time, they attempted to build a Malay cultural identity on the modern **stage** by, in part, incorporating adapted traditional elements in their work.

The first play to pursue this quest for new directions was *'Tis Not the Tall Grass Blown by the Wind* (Bukan lalang ditiup angin, 1970) by **Noordin Hassan**. An allegory of May 13th, it concludes with a Malay man thinking reflectively of past and future events; it is for the audience to decide whether he is a common person or, more provocatively, a political leader.

In the 1980s, some plays recalled the period of rising nationalism. These include Hassan's *Children of This Land* (Anak tanjung, 1989) and Zakaria Ariffin's (1952–) *Opera Stage* (*Pentas opera*, 1989).

Among English-language playwrights, Kee Thuan Chye (1954–) is notably political. His *1984 Here and Now* (1985), an adaptation of Orwell's novel, challenges post–May 13th policies; Kee exposes the tensions evident in Malaysia's multiethnic society and seeks to surmount them through appeals for a free, just, and equal society. *The Big Purge* (1988), not staged in Malaysia, was written in response to Operation Lalang (1987) during which more than one hundred Malaysians were arrested under the Internal Security Act. *We Could **** You, Mr. Birch* (1994) re-tells the story of J. W. W. Birch, Malaya's first British resident. Its relevance to contemporary times and the politics of power are evident.

Although in many cases playwrights include innuendos, allusions, and allegorical material with political relevance, theatre artists, for the most part, have not created an overtly political theatre. Partly, this is because of the inherent constraints incurred in publishing or producing controversial material, requiring permits before a play can be produced (see Censorship). Exceptions include Kuala Lumpur's Instant Café Theatre, which performs cabaret-style political satire. Political issues also surface in the plays of Huzir Sulaiman (1973–), founder in 1996 of the Straits **Theatre Company**. His satirical piece, *Atomic jaya* [sic] (1998) spoofs political ambitions by postulating that some want Malaysia to become a nuclear power. In *The Smell of Language* (1998), Sulaiman draws upon a case involving the chief minister of Malacca, charged with raping a teenager.

The arrest in 1998 of former deputy prime minister Anwar Ibrahim generated a pro-democracy (*reformasi*) movement, some effects of which could be seen on stage. In 2000, Amir Muhammad's *The Malaysian Decameron* was performed in the Actor's

"History is fiction," declares Mano Maniam (playing Sultan Abdullah) to a bewildered Ahmad Yatim (as Datuk Sagor) in *We Could **** You, Mr. Birch.* (Photo: Kee Thuan Che)

Studio Theatre under Kuala Lumpur's Freedom Square (Dataran Merdeka), where *reformasi* demonstrators previously had gathered. Inspired by Boccaccio, it introduces four characters taking shelter from the aboveground demonstrations. Two plays by the Alternative Stage were written in response to the Anwar Ibrahim case: *Nurse* (Misi, 2000) and an adaptation of *Julius Caesar* that satirizes political relationships. Also, in the wake of *reformasi*, new groups formed, such as ARTicle 19 and Rep 21. ARTicle 19 produced *Chaos* (Kecoh, 2000) but did not remain active. Akshen, under the Five Arts Centre, presented *More Chaos* (Lebih kecoh, 2001) and *Stadium* (2002). Rep 21 (2000) staged Miller's *The Crucible* (2001), with allusions to Ibrahim's trial.

FURTHER READING

Lo, Jacqueline. *Staging Nation: English Language Theatre in Malaysia and Singapore.*

Nancy Nanney

Politics in Theatre: Nepal

Traditional theatre in **Nepal** was decidedly nonpolitical but, during the pro-democracy People's Movement of the 1980s, contemporary theatre emerged as a persuasive medium for influencing society about important issues.

With "street theatre plays" (*saadak naatak*) such as *We Are Searching for the Spring* (Hami basanta kojir hechou, 1982), **playwright-director** Asesh Malla (1950–) led university students in dramatizing injustices under the partyless system of government advocated by King Birendra Shah (r. 1972–2001). With the coming of democracy

(1989), activist artists focused on human rights, **women**'s rights, and police brutality, and looked to international nongovernmental organizations for support of productions about children and AIDS. Led by **actors** previously associated with Malla's Representing Everyone (Sarwanam) **theatre company**, the 1990s saw the emergence of small troupes using agitprop to battle local problems; eventually, they were silenced by larger national issues. Despair over elected politicians' corruption of democracy gave way to a Maoist insurgency that began in 1996 and has claimed over seven thousand lives. Today, few rural troupes dare to advocate for either side of the violent Maoist-government debate.

In Kathmandu only has contemporary theatre returned to its political roots, and Malla is again at the forefront with plays such as *Who Is Declaring War?* (2001) and *Death Festival* (2003), in which he portrays the plight and trauma of the common people caught between corrupt politicians and brutal rebels.

Carol Davis

Politics in Theatre: Pakistan

Against the dominant colonial trend of English drawing-room comedies and adaptations, there emerged in the 1950s the political satire of Khwaja Moenuddin, which attacked the lack of social change in the new **Pakistan**. He spurred a trend of political satires from Kamal Ahmed Rizwi (1930–) to Imran Aslam (1951–).

The first military dictatorship (1958–1969) of President Ayub Khan (1907–1974) prompted a symbolic play of power hierarchies in literature and theatre through original and radical adaptations, like Ali Ahmed's revolutionized version of Beckett's *Waiting for Godot* (1957) and Najam Hussain Syed's (1936–) *Protector of the Jungle* (Jungle da rakha, 1967), adapted from Bengali to Punjabi.

With popular movements for democracy from the late 1960s under the leadership from 1971 to 1978 of Zulfikar Ali Bhutto (1928–1979), the Arts Council was taken over by the government. There was a boom in original **playwriting** in Urdu and Punjabi by Sarmad Sehbai (1945–) and Najam Hussain Syed, who reinterpreted **folk** legends and history from a contemporary socio-political point of view. Marxist Ishaq Mohammed's *The Untouchables* (Mussali) had many performances in lower-class neighborhoods across the Punjab, some by the sweepers themselves.

In 1979, when Bhutto was ousted and Zia-ul-Haq (1924–1988) seized the country, the performing arts were **censored**. State funding was cut, and new government-sponsored **theatres** were rented to commercial producers who created popular comedies for the mercantile class, with satirical jibes at moral and political hierarchy. A leftist "parallel theatre" evolved, involving many artist-activists drawn primarily from universities. Because government auditoriums were closed to them, they performed mostly in clandestine locations: foreign cultural institutions, private homes, and the streets, producing work attacking the establishment. Brecht, **Badal Sircar**, and **Safdar Hashmi** became inspirations. In Karachi, the politically inclined **theatre companies** the Knock (Dastak), Grips Theatre, and **Women**'s Movement (Tehrik-e-Niswan) were formed. In Lahore, Dawn of a New Day (Ajoka) began by staging Sircar's *Procession* (Jaloos, 1984).

Following the Soviet Union's collapse, international funding poured into Pakistan, which saw the rise of nongovernmental organizations (NGOs). With little state support, groups like Dawn of a New Day, Women's Movement, and People's Theatre (Lok

Discussing the Unheeded performed by Women's Movement (Tehrik-e-Niswan). Sheema Kermani in center. (Photo: Courtesy of Tehrik-e-Niswan)

Rehas) became NGOs along with the formation of a host of new NGO companies, like Creative Anger, Katha, Insan Natik, and Interactive Resource Centre. International donors, and, increasingly, the government, have supported them to serve their developmental agendas. Their work has tended toward social issues rather than exploring broader historical and political contexts and is often performed in urban areas for invitees only, with occasional rural performances. On the other hand, a liberal alternative has been fashioned in partnerships between the government and multinationals in sponsoring English-language plays, often adaptations of blockbuster **Western** films.

The self-financing and popular commercial **stage**, mainly in Lahore, is generally snubbed by the intelligentsia and government for its bawdy repartee. Nonetheless, it draws upon popular forms of **music** and **dance**, clowns (*bhaands*), and "comic repartee" (*jhugaat*), with deeply satirical content, pulling jibes at official morality and socio-political order.

FURTHER READING

Afzal-Khan, Fawzia. *A Critical Stage: The Role of Secular Alternative Theatre in Pakistan.*

Claire Pamment

Politics in Theatre: Philippines

Politics has always informed **Philippine** theatre; Filipino artists have participated in discourses on colonialism, globalization, gender, and militarization, and have aligned themselves with groups that seek to initiate change in society.

Amidst the Philippine-American War (1899–1903), **theatre companies** staged symbolic dramas (*drama simboliko*) such as **Aurelio Tolentino**'s *Yesterday, Today, and Tomorrow* (Kahapon ngayon, at bukas, 1903), Juan Abad's (1872–1939) *Chains of Gold* (Tanikalang ginto, 1902), and Juan Matapang Cruz's *I Am Not Dead* (Hindi aco patay, 1903). While the narratives seemed to be about love, the names of characters such as Karangalan (Honor) and Tanggulan (Defender), as well as **stage** conventions (**costumes** using flag colors; a miniature flag used as a handkerchief, and so on), enabled allegorical readings.

During the **Japanese** occupation, (1942–1945), vaudeville **actors** used satire (imitating soldiers), and popular songs like "I Shall Return" (Babalik ka rin), which referred to General MacArthur's promise to return to the Philippines, while the native army (Hukbalahap) staged plays featuring a weeping Mother Country encouraging her children to join the guerillas.

From the turbulent years of the First Quarter Storm (late 1960s to early 1970s), throughout the days of martial law (1972–1981) imposed by President Marcos (1917–1989), and up to the present, artists have staged plays in **theatres**, in the streets, and in the countryside. Among the most popular are Bonifacio Ilagan's (1951–) *People's Worship* (Pagsambang bayan, 1977), using the form of the Catholic mass; Malou Jacob's (1948–) *Juan Tamban*, focusing on poverty; Al Santos's (1954–) *21st of May* (Mayo beinte-uno), addressing a peasant uprising; Chris Millado's (1961–) *Moon and Gun in E Flat Major* (Buwan at baril sa eb major, 1984), on the events of 1984; and Reuel Aguila's (1953–) *Turmoil* (Ligalig, 1987), on the 1986 uprising. Influenced by Brecht, Boal, and the **Chinese** revolution, street theatre—performed by groups such as Peryante, PETA (Philippine Educational Theatre Company), and the Negros Theatre League—has used a variety of forms and styles, such as the poem-play (*dula-tula*),

People's Worship by Bonifacio Ilagan, directed by Behn Cervantes for the UP Repertory Company at the Wilfrido Ma. Guerrero Theater, Manila, Philippines, 1977. (Photo: Courtesy of Madeleine Nicolas)

improvisational theatre, effigy theatre, radio dramas, vaudeville, pantomime, and movement pieces.

In the past few decades, a significant development has been the organization of cultural groups among workers, the urban poor, teachers, and health workers, and in various regions such as Mindanao and the Cordillera, thus responding to the need to articulate specialized and regional issues through theatre.

FURTHER READING

Erven, Eugène van. *Stages of People Power: The Philippines Educational Theatre Association.*

Joi Barrios

Politics in Theatre: Singapore

The most important single force shaping the **Singaporean** theatre scene is the National Arts Council (NAC), the organization that runs the annual Singapore Arts **Festival**, the largest event showcasing theatre from both Singapore and overseas. The NAC's plan for developing the arts was clearly articulated in a 1988 report that established the role of the arts in the country's development strategy by arguing that "strategizing for a potentially vibrant performing arts environment in Singapore is no different from the strategies successfully applied to Singapore's high-tech economic activities."

The systematic way in which **theatre** spaces have been developed, arts districts created, and individual companies, artists, and projects funded suggests that this technocratic spirit has been applied to the performing arts. Many established **theatre companies** now have their own permanent homes in designated arts districts, while one of the country's most important structures, the old Parliament House, has been turned over entirely to the arts and features a gallery and performance spaces. While financial support has tended to favor companies with significant track records, it has also been responsible for creating the conditions under which a larger number of individuals can make a living in theatre. Even though the government provides strong support for theatre, overt political **criticism** of Singapore's ruling People's Action Party remains unacceptable.

FURTHER READING

Lo, Jacqueline. *Staging Nation: English Language Theatre in Malaysia and Singapore*; Peterson, William. *Theater and the Politics of Culture in Contemporary Singapore.*

William Peterson

Politics in Theatre: Sri Lanka

The history of **Sri Lankan** theatre reveals that socio-political critique has always been one of theatre's thematic discourses. As Ranjini Obeyeskere notes: "In times of political crisis, whether of tyrannical kings, colonial powers or modern day authoritarian rulers, the satiric subtext of performances becomes ever more important providing a powerful critique of the political realities of the age.

The Theravada Buddhist tradition of critical skepticism may have facilitated this tradition. While satirical innuendo has always constituted a part of traditional drama, in the post-independence (1948) period, especially since the 1980s, theatre has become a vehicle for lashing out against repression. In the southern part of the island, urban audiences turned to secular theatre for protest. Plays such as *Black and White* (Sudu saha kalu) by Simon Navagathegama (1939–), *White Terror* (Dhawala bhishana) by Dharmasiri Bandaranayake, and *Magatha* by Asoka Handagama (1962–) notably depicted the contemporary political climate.

In the 1990s, the trend of protest theatre continued, and **directors** like Somalatha Subasinghe (1936–) staged plays like *Dedan Kimathi* (an adaptation of Ngugi's *The Trial of Dedan Kimathi*, 1994), *Antigone* (1995), and *Mother Courage* (1998). These foregrounded the sufferings of the people in conflict situations. Adaptations of *Lysistrata*, *The Trojan Women*, and translations of Dorfman's *Widows* (1998, 2003) and *Death and the Maiden* (2000) were also produced. But the theatre also started dealing with other issues, such as historical plays with social themes, for example, K. B. Heart's *Dona Katherina*, *Yasodhara* and *Death by the Moon* (Sandalanga maranaya) in 2004, the latter an adaptation of Lorca's *Blood Wedding*.

Youth-related problems, such as love relationships and sex and gender power relations, were produced by younger **playwrights** like Dhananjaya Karunaratne, Rajitha Dissanayake, and Piyal Kariyawasam. These reflect a shift in concern from narrow, overt commentary to more subtextual concerns with issues that emerged from Sri Lanka's prolonged ethnic conflict and stalled peace process.

In Tamil-language theatre, too, with the rise in military activity during the 1980s, there was a looking back to traditional forms, such as ritual, as a means to express collective rage and open a discursive space for coping with grief created by political machinations. Jeyshankar, at Eastern University, who has used the *kuttu* form to perform in temples and other innovative spaces, has engaged with social and political issues through theatre.

The post-independence English-language theatre has been criticized for eschewing the dominant social and political concerns faced by the nation's majority. English theatre in the 1980s, unlike its Sinhala counterpart, did not engage with the nation's socio-political vicissitudes, but was mostly confined to drawing-room comedies. There was very little original work in this period, other than the plays of Indu Dharmasena (1956–).

Beginning in the early 1990s, English theatre underwent a change, the first example being Ernest MacIntyre's (1934–) *Rasanayagam's Last Riot* (1993). A new generation of playwrights began to deal with contemporary reality. Examples include Senaka Abeyratne's (1952–) *Por La Libertad* (1994), Ruana Rajapakse's (1958–) *All in a Day's Work* (1998), Michael de Zoysa's *Ropes of Sand* (1998), and Delon Weerasinghe's *Thicker than Blood* (2003). Ruwanthi de Chickera (1975–) and Jehan Aloysius (1977–) also challenged the status quo with their focus on social issues. These playwrights questioned assumptions of the **Westernized** middle classes and their relationship to contemporary politics, thereby changing the trajectory of English theatre in Sri Lanka.

FURTHER READING

Obeyesekere, Ranjini. *Sri Lankan Theatre in a Time of Terror: Political Satire in a Permitted Space.*

Neluka Silva

Politics in Theatre: Taiwan

Taiwan's tumultuous modern history and politics have fashioned modern Taiwanese theatre in significant ways. The **Japanese** colonization period (1895–1945) saw the formation of a modern consciousness in theatre. Japanese influence could be found in many homegrown performances. The colonial policy encouraged assimilation and banned artistic activities that invoked **Chinese** cultural elements. The Japanization campaign, a.k.a. *kominka* (or *huangminhua yundon*, 1937–1945), had a widespread effect on the content (dramatization of Japanese militarism and the incorporation of Taiwan into the Japanese empire) and form (imitation of *shingeki*) of Taiwanese theatre.

Ironically, with the Japanese departure (1945) and the Chinese Nationalists' takeover (1949), Taiwanese society did not enjoy the freedom it anticipated for artistic creation. Theatre continued to be subordinated to politics. On February 28, 1947, an island-wide uprising erupted, starting with a demonstration in Taipei against the police's brutal beating of a peddler. This was followed by a series of massacres of Taiwanese intellectuals by government troops. Martial law was declared in 1949, and for four decades, theatre was molded by Nationalist Party cultural policies designed to counter the Japanese legacy, foster anti-communist sentiments, and preserve Chinese traditions. To eradicate Japan's influence, a campaign to speak Mandarin was initiated, and theatre and the mass media were used as tools to achieve that goal. It took an artist like **Lee Man-kuei**, with connections to the policymakers, to rescue theatre from the peril of politicization.

The 1980s witnessed drastic changes at all social levels. A large number of artists returned from foreign residency. The pro-nativist Democratic Progressive Party (DPP) was founded in 1986; the next year, martial law was lifted, creating more space and incentives for innovation. Democracy was introduced and new political ideas appeared. What once was politically correct and mainstream became obsolete, and nativism emerged as a new mode of expression; a significant number of artists subscribed to nativist politics, believing that it was time to mold authentic Taiwanese voices.

Ever-present are tensions between mainland Chinese immigrants who followed Chiang Kai-shek (1887–1975) to Taiwan as refugees in 1949 and those who claim to be bonafide Taiwanese, between Mandarin- or Taiwanese-speaking bourgeois urban residents and ethnic minorities (the aboriginals) residing in the mountains, and—since the 1990s—between the pro-unification-with-China Kuomintang followers and pro-independence DPP followers. The extended period of colonization and the Kuomintang's long rule complicated the political and cultural landscape. From the 1990s, ideologies continued to exist, but the dominant ideology faded. In the process of diversification, polyphonic Taiwanese theatres—both commercial and **experimental**—stage conflicting ideologies, allowing them to play off against one another.

FURTHER READING

Guy, Nancy. *Peking Opera and Politics in Taiwan*.

Alexander C. Y. Huang

Politics in Theatre: Thailand

Since the inception of "spoken drama" (*lakon phut*) in early 1900s, **Thai • playwrights** have made use of this new genre to voice political ideas. For example, patriotism is evident in King **Rama VI**'s *A Warrior's Heart* (Huachai nakrob, 1914) as well as **Luang Wichitwathakarn** post–World War II history plays.

Likewise, *lakon phut samai mhai* ("new spoken theatre"), as *lakon phut* came to be known from the late 1960s, serves political purposes as effectively. During the anti-military government demonstrations of 1973 and 1976, novelists wrote political plays based on **Western** absurdist and existentialist models. Meanwhile, student troupes satirized such issues as the exploitation of rural people, the invasion of American imperialism, and capitalism. Founded in 1973 was the political **theatre company** Crescent Moon Theatre (Prachan Siew Karn Lakon), whose signature work is *The 1932 Revolutionist* (Kue phoo apiwat 2475, 1987). Influenced by Brecht's epic theatre and Grotowski's poor theatre, Kamron Gunatilaka's play chronicles the political achievements and struggles of Pridi Banomyong (statesman and founder of Thammasat University) before, during, and after the 1932 change from absolute monarchy to democracy.

The government's recent shift toward democracy has meant a decrease in political theatre. Nevertheless, to celebrate the centenary of Bhanomyong's birth in 1999, *The 1932 Revolutionist* was successfully revived, toured nationally and internationally, and the script was published in both Thai and English. Moreover, Thammasat University students continue to stage political satires, not as *lakon phut*, but as *ngew*, traditional **Chinese** theatre (*xiqu*). A 2006 version was produced during a demonstration against Prime Minister Thaksin Shinawatra, a business tycoon.

Pawit Mahasarinand

Politics in Theatre: Vietnam

Politics has long been an element in **Vietnamese** theatre. The **folk theatre • *cheo*** acquired a social protest element, the clown (*he*) often wittily denouncing social ills and corruption, or **women** making accusations against evil power holders. The authorities used ***tuong*** as a means of promoting Confucian values. The Trung sisters, popular in the Vietnamese patriotic imagination for rebelling against **Chinese** rule (40 AD), have featured in *tuong*, ***mua roi nuoc***, and other theatrical forms.

The various modern colonial and revolutionary regimes have regarded theatre as a propaganda weapon for their own values and policies. The French wanted through theatre to spread their modern values and oppose Confucianism. During the Franco-Vietnamese war (1946–1954), which ended French colonialism, theatre was a vehicle for Vietnamese patriotism. Both the pro-American and the pro-communist regimes and forces in the south from 1954 to 1975 used theatre to push their own political viewpoints and to attack each other.

Among patriotic and propaganda theatres, the most developed is the communist. To a 1951 suggestion that he was trying to politicize the arts, President Ho Chi Minh (1890–1969) responded proudly: "nothing is more true." He regarded politics and art as inseparable and wanted theatre with socialist and patriotic content. Although the inseparability of politics and theatre has persisted, it has dwindled in importance, especially since the reform period began in 1986. *See also* Censorship.

Colin Mackerras

PRASAD, JAISHANKAR (1890–1937). Indian • **playwright,** poet, novelist, and short story writer, born in Benares (Varanasi), Uttar Pradesh. He lost his parents and elder brother at sixteen and became responsible for the family business. Fluent in **Sanskrit,** Hindi, Urdu, Bengali, and English, he took a special interest in history and archeology, which is clearly reflected in his works.

Considered among the top figures of the romantic (*chhayavadi*) age of Hindi poetry during the 1920s and 1930s, Prasad sought to reflect the consonance of human feelings with nature, and with the Indian psyche and lifestyle. His epic poem *Kamayani* (1935) remains one of the greatest modern contributions to native literature. Prasad was a staunch nationalist and idealist, attitudes prominent in his writing. Influences on him run from Sanskrit through Bengali and **Parsi theatre** plays; on the one hand, he rejected the excesses of Parsi theatre while, on the other, he borrowed some of its conventions. Dwijendra Lal Roy's (1863–1913) historical plays had a particularly strong impact, as did **Western** dramaturgy, but his idealism rejected Ibsen's realism, whose plays he found too fatalistic.

Prasad's thirteen plays, which deal with mythological, historical, and social themes, reflect an enormous amount of historical and literary research into the glories of past Hindu power. All are related to the major issues confronting society when they were written. They include *Noble* (Sajjan, 1911), *Rajyasri* (1915), *Vishakh* (1921), *Ajatsatru* (1922), *Desire* (Kamna, 1923), *Janmejaya's Nag Sacrifice* (Janmejaya ka nagyajna, 1926), *Skandgupta* (1928), *Chandragupta* (1931), and *Dhruvaswamini* (1932). One of their chief characteristics is the presence of powerful **women** who abandon convention to attain their ends.

Prasad was essentially a closet dramatist whose plays—with their grandiose style, densely poetic language, seriousness, and complex characters and plots—proved too challenging for either the amateurs or professionals of his day. Nevertheless, they became popular after his death, as Hindu nationalism became a potent **political** force. Among the leading **directors** taking up the gauntlet and demonstrating their viability were **B. V. Karanth, Shanta Gandhi,** and **Ram Gopal Bajaj.**

Shashikant Barhanpurkar

PRASANNA (1951–). Indian Kannada-language **playwright,** poet, **director,** and social worker. He abandoned his chemistry studies to attend the National School of Drama (NSD), and then **trained** himself as a designer in various crafts. A major figure in the **political** theatre movement of the mid-1970s, he founded Karnataka's leftwing Community (Samudaya) **theatre company** in 1975; it was behind the statewide *jatha* (literally, "processions") that took street theatre to the countryside. Although he has written original plays, Prasanna, who works in both Kannada and Hindi, is best known as a director, staging plays for the NSD and other institutions. Major productions have been of plays such as *A Folk Tale* (Ek lok katha, 1979), *Tughlaq* (1982), *The Illusory Market* (Maya bazar, 1982), *The Story of Rama* (Uttararamacharita), *Gandhi*, and various **Western** classics, including *Hamlet* and several Brecht works, *Galileo*, *Mother Courage*, and a masterful version of *Mother*. He also has directed in English, beginning with Fugard's *Road to Mecca*.

Prasanna's philosophical drama, *Beyond the Border* (Seema paar), which he also directed, is based on the life of **Bharatendu Harishchandra**, the nineteenth-century Hindi playwright and devotional (*bhakti*) poet; it reveals his artistic integrity and the power of his creative vision.

Prasanna collaborates with composers and **scenographic** and **costume** designers to materialize his conceptions, which are complex combinations of ideas, action, verbal **music**, rhythm, and color. His productions are mainly realistic but often make room for theatricalist effects; this was particularly true of *Galileo*, considered revolutionary in Karnataka's theatre. He demands a high level of discipline, but allows room for creativity. Prasanna's bold, socially activist views on theatre often incur the displeasure of the cultural establishment. His work was recognized with a National Academy of **Music**, **Dance**, and Drama (Sangeet Natak Akademi) award (2001).

Debjani Ray Moulik

PROPERTIES

Properties: China

In **China**, the traditional concept closest to that of "properties" is *qimo*, encompassing not only the small and large hand properties employed by *xiqu* • **actors**, but also all of the simple **scenography** used in their staging. *Qimo*, literally, "laid [as in bricks] tips/nonessentials," clearly indicates the secondary, supporting nature of these objects relative to the actors' own performance.

Early Examples. Early mentions of *qimo* include ca. 100 BC references to weapons in court **dances**, and ca. 760 descriptions of bamboo tablets of office employed in performances related to *canjun xi*. Descriptions and murals of Jin (1115–1234) and Yuan (1280–1368) dynasty performances including *zaju* indicate weapons and tablets of office as well as fans, traveling bags, cangues, fly whisks, dolls (representing babies), cooking utensils and tableware, and bamboo "hobbyhorses" attached to performers' bodies, a practice believed to have originated in **folk** dance. More elaborate *qimo* developed during the Ming dynasty (1368–1644), and quite realistic *qimo* were occasionally employed during Ming and especially late Qing (1644–1911). Overall, through long usage and the conventionalization of **experimental** practice, *qimo* have developed as simplified, stylized actor's tools. They are generally light and portable, and well adapted to the enhancement of dance, combat, and acrobatics.

From Weapons to Plot Devices. Weapons (*wuqi*), also called "sword and spear handles" (*dao qiang bazi*), constitute the most straightforward category. "Knives" (*dao*) are broad, curved, single-edged blades, especially prevalent being the "great knife" (*dadao*), similar to a saber or scimitar. "Spears" (*qiang*) may be single or double headed, the latter usually employed by the "martial young female" (*wudan*) and "martial young male" (*wuxiaosheng*) **role types**. The *jian*, a straight double-edged sword, is worn at the waist in a decorated scabbard. Other weapons include "axes" (*fu*), "staves" (*bian*), "cudgels" (*bang*), and "rods" (*gun*). All are made of lightweight, often flexible, materials, usually wood or cane.

Transportation props indicate the travel mode and facilitate the actors' performance of it. The "hobbyhorse" has evolved into the "horse whip" (*mabian*), a flexible, tassel-decorated rod with a thong at one end that can be wrapped around the fingers; its color indicates that of the horse, and its use conveys walking the horse, mounting, riding, dismounting, tethering, and so on. Similarly, a boat and its progress are represented by an oar and its manipulation. A carriage or chariot is established by two actors moving together, one holding a flag with wheels on both sides (*che qi*) in each hand, and the other "riding" in the vehicle by remaining between the flags. The same tandem movement conveys the progress of a sedan chair when the "driver" carries two poles from which are suspended a narrow "small **curtain**" (*xiaozhang*).

Most utensils for daily life are simplified versions of the actual objects, often made of wood and painted a single color. These include ink sticks and grinding stones, gold or silver candlesticks, tea and wine sets, as well as imperial arrows of command. Lanterns are made of red paper or cloth, and suspended from poles for travel. Some of these *qimo*, including official mandates and correspondence, are larger than in real life for visual focus. Others, like firewood on carrying poles, water buckets, baggage, and other packages, are smaller for ease in handling. Chopsticks, bowls, brushes, fans, and handkerchiefs are essentially the real things.

Articles for manifesting locale and atmosphere are the most unique and characteristic *qimo*. Larger examples can be considered **scenographic** elements. Smaller examples include a wide variety of military and imperial banners, flags, standards, pennons, and fans, mounted on poles and highly decorative, and items that establish individual status: the "ivory tablet of office" (*yahu*), representing the vertical strip of ivory, jade, or bamboo carried by ministers at court; the "cloud broom" (*yunzhou*) or "fly whisk" (*yingchen*), a horse-tail whisk carried by **religious** and supernatural figures as well as eunuchs and maids; and the "fish cangue" (*yujia*), fish-shaped and worn by criminals. Amorphous or invisible forces are represented by black "wind flags" (*fengqi*), red "fire flags" (*huoqi*), and white or blue "water flags" (*shuiqi*), which sweep across the **stage**, over and under tumbling performers. Two-dimensional "cloud shapes" (*yunpian*) are carried before immortals, indicating that they are riding on harnessed clouds.

Qimo required as plot devices in specific plays are often conventionalized representations of the necessary items. A rolled cloth on a tray can represent a fish, and in a boot, a severed leg. A small round bundle wrapped in red cloth can stand for a severed head; a small square in yellow cloth, an official seal. Real items are introduced only for comic effect—in other contexts, they would be considered in bad taste. This general aesthetic is applied even in **xinbian lishi ju** and "contemporary plays" (*xiandai xi*), where properties are easily recognizable as what they represent, but are essentialized and beautified, in keeping with *xiqu*'s governing aesthetics.

FURTHER READING

Kalvodova-Sis-Vanis. *Chinese Theatre*; Scott, A. C. *The Classical Theatre of China*.

Elizabeth Wichmann-Walczak

Properties: Japan

Properties are used imaginatively and strategically in **Japan**'s *nô*, *kyôgen*, *bunraku* (see Puppet Theatre), and *kabuki*, organized and decorated according to each genre's particular aesthetic balance of realism and theatricalism, minimalism and spectacle.

Nô *and* Kyôgen. Since there is neither painted **scenography** nor special lighting on the traditional *nô* **stage**, carefully considered properties serve as powerful symbols in the bare mise-en-scéne. Because of their simplicity of form, properties can shift meanings within the same play to create a web of related symbols: the rain hat hiding the hunter in *Cormorant* (Utô) becomes in turn a bird's nest, a net, and finally a stupa. The same skeletal frame of bamboo and cloth (*tsukuri mono*) can be a hut, cave, or shrine, depending on its decorations. Small wooden platforms (*ichijôdai*) serve as beds, mountains, bridges, or palaces. Properties specific to particular plays include a wheeled salt-car in *Pining Wind* (Matsukaze); three candles glowing in an iron crown worn by a jealous wife in *Iron Crown* (Kanawa); a spinning-wheel in the crone's hut in *Adachigahara* (a.k.a. *Kurozuka*). Other specialty props create potent effects, such as the unfurled threads entangling warriors in *The Earth Spider* (Tsuchigumo), or the giant bell of *Dôjô-ji Temple* (Dôjô-ji) that drops dramatically over the jealous **dancer**, later raised to reveal a transformed demon (the difficult **mask** and **costume** change is done inside the bell).

Hand properties reflect *nô*'s ritual origins, when fans or branches were used as channeling instruments for shamanic dances. Today, beautifully decorated fans are featured in virtually all plays, utilitarian extensions of hand gestures to point and scoop, or to indicate rain, moon, or waves. Other crucial hand props include halberds, umbrellas, fishing poles, mallets, and rosary beads.

The fan is *kyôgen*'s indispensable tool: closed it is a pipe, oar, ladle, sword, saw, brush, or hobbyhorse. Open it becomes a sake flask or cup, tray, sliding door, or even a fan. The *kazuraoke* (literally, "wig-box") is a lacquered cask that serves as a stool, trees, a molasses barrel, sake keg (with the lid a cup), or tea box. A few elaborate properties are employed for specific plays: a miniature castle with flags and drawbridge in *Beard-Fortress* (Higeyagura) is worn like a beard and attacked by housewives bearing scissors-halberds, and giant tweezers; a fox-trap is set in *Fox Catching* (Tsurigitsune).

Bunraku *and* Kabuki. Properties in *kabuki* and *bunraku* are larger, more numerous, colorful, and realistic than in *nô* and *kyôgen*, reflecting these genres' popular origins, quotidian themes, and bigger stages. *Bunraku* props, scaled to the size of the puppets, resemble *kabuki*'s, but there are fewer of them, since they require stage assistants' constant manipulation. Props in both genres are either large, scenic ones (*ôdôgu*) or hand props (*kodôgu*).

Fans, pipes, umbrellas, hand towels, mirrors, and weapons are manipulated for erotic, heroic, comic, and tragic effect. Larger props include trays, shelves, screens, palanquins, and oxcarts. Many are actual objects employed in the Edo period (1603–1868), or larger and more colorful replicas. Heroes of *kabuki*'s exaggerated "rough style" (*aragoto*) bear super-sized swords, arrows, and axes. Stage assistants (*kurogo*) in black (making them conventionally invisible), white, or blue (to match snow or water scenes) place and remove props to create an appropriate appearance for each moment of a scene, as well as to manipulate props for spectacular effect: a seething ocean materializes in a rippled blue cloth; butterflies flutter on long, bamboo rods (*sashigane*); a freed dragon flies up a waterfall. There are also many unusual props designed to create trick effects, like a stone water basin that splits in two when struck by a sword, or another one that allows a picture to appear on the side opposite that on which it is painted.

FURTHER READING

Leiter, Samuel L. *Historical Dictionary of Japanese Traditional Japanese Theatre.*

Jonah Salz

PUPPET THEATRE

Puppet Theatre: Burma (Myanmar)

Yokthe pwe. Burmese (Myanmar) string puppet theatre also called *yokeson thabin*. Marionette theatre was patronized by the nineteenth-century court, though it is not popular today. The repertoire consists of Buddha's birth stories (*jataka*) as well as local folklore and legends. Troupes have up to forty members, including singers, manipulators, and musicians. **Music** is supplied by the *saing waing* orchestra, seated between the **stage** and the audience; singers, all male, sit at the back of the stage; and puppeteers work behind a waist-high screen. Voices of the dancing royal characters are performed by the singers, while the monk's topical dialogue and the clown's **political** satire are spoken by the puppeteers. A proper troupe has a minimum of twenty-eight wooden puppets, each about two feet tall.

In precolonial Myanmar, puppetry had a high place among the arts. Traditionally, only puppets could enact the sacred *jataka*. Until the end of the nineteenth century, puppets could perform on stages, but human **dancers** could perform only on the ground, since **women** dancers could not stand above men in the audience. Puppets had the freedom to advise the king on state and family affairs that needed attention, a privilege denied to all others at court. Dancers also learned classical choreography from marionettes; it said that actors must dance like puppets and puppets dance as if they were human. For rural people, *yokthe pwe* was a means of hearing the latest political news and scandals of the capital and appreciating literature during a time when palm leaf manuscripts were scarce.

Each puppet represents a **role type** with a distinct function. The "medium" (*nat kadaw*) opens each show with a dance of supplication to the spirits (see

The *nat kadaw* puppet that appears at the beginning of a Burmese *yokthe pwe* puppet play, and moves like one possessed. Although she may be married to a mortal, she is also the bride of a spirit (*nat*) who uses her as his medium for prophesy. She is always dressed in red, with a red band across her brow. (Photo: Ma Thanegi)

Religion in Theatre). The lavishly attired "prince" (*mintha*) and "princess" (*minthamee*), adorned with real human hair, are the romantic heroes. Bodaw, the monk, dispenses wisdom. Thagyar Min, King of the Celestials, is the savior. The sparkling Sama-deva is a good celestial who points out right from wrong. An evil celestial, Nat Pyet, symbolizes temptation. The two jesters bring comic relief. The king and four ministers inform the audience of state affairs while the two prince regents teach general knowledge. Minor characters include the handmaiden, pageboy, Brahman astrologer, Zawgyi the magician, city and jungle ogres, the *naga* dragon, the *galon* bird, the white horse, the monkey, the elephant, and the tiger. Some sets include old man, old woman, parrot, stork, and crocodile puppets. Evil characters have pink faces, and the rest have white. Puppets are treated reverently, and roles that are natural enemies, such as the two ogres or the tiger and elephant, are never stored in the same trunk.

The Burmese monarchy's destruction under British colonial rule and competition from other forms of entertainment contributed to *yokthe pwe*'s decline. Today it is performed for tourists, taught at the University of Culture, and occasionally tours overseas.

FURTHER READING

Singer, Noel F. *Burmese Puppets*; Thanegi, Ma. *The Illusion of Life: Burmese Marionettes*.

Ma Thanegi

Puppet Theatre: Cambodia

Lakhon sbaek. Cambodian shadow puppet theatre, a.k.a. *nang sbaek*. It includes two main forms: "large format" (*lakhon sbaek thom*) and "small format" (*lakhon sbaek touch*), a.k.a. *ayang*. Both use opaque figures carved from tanned buffalohide or cowhide (*sbaek*) either unpainted or colored in shades of orange and black. Both formats are accompanied by the *pin peat* **musical** ensemble of bamboo or metal xylophones (*roneat*), brass gongs (*kong*), drums (*skor*), and a quadruple-reed flute (*sralay*).

Lakhon sbaek thom. *Lakhon sbaek thom*, traditionally performed during **religious** ceremonies (including *buong suong* blessings and royal cremations), now is mainly presented for general entertainment. Its stories come mainly from the *Reamker*, the Khmer version of the **Ramayana**. Like **Thai** *nang yai* puppet theatre and some **Indian** shadow theatre, *lakhon sbaek thom* is more picture-**storytelling** than puppetry per se. Performers manipulate a sequence of panels, up to six feet tall and five feet wide, illustrating action being narrated by two chanters. Each unarticulated leather figure shows a scene with one or more characters surrounded by decorative motifs and, sometimes, **scenographic** elements, usually enclosed within a frame. Thus when Reap (Ravana) approaches Neang Séda (Sita) to abduct her, each is at first in a separate panel, including the respective settings. When he grabs her, those two panels disappear, replaced by a single one showing both characters.

In a *lakhon sbaek thom* performance, a dozen or more male (or *mostly* male) players **dance** holding the leather panels overhead via support sticks. They perform both behind and in front of a cloth screen twenty-five to thirty-five feet wide and nearly fifteen feet high, in either case appearing essentially as silhouettes due to the backlighting by torches or electric lights. The screen's lower portion may be a dark color, making the dancers' shadows much more subtle than those of the puppets. Performances take place after dark. Traditionally, ceremonial performances used to last seven nights. Nowadays, they rarely last more than a couple of hours.

Lakhon sbaek touch. *Lakhon sbaek touch* is more like southern Thai *nang talung* and Malay and Javanese *wayang kulit* in form than like *lakhon sbaek thom*. Its individual-character puppets may have movable arms, legs, jaws, or other parts. Separate carved leather figures represent **scenographic** elements. The wide-ranging subject matter comprises stories from the life of Buddha as well as contemporary **politics**, and it typically includes comedy, even slapstick. Unlike *lakhon sbaek thom*, whose panels are passed down essentially unchanged through generations, *lakhon sbaek touch* continually adds new figures, such as big-nosed **Westerners**, motorbikes, and army tanks. Until the introduction of European-style plays in the 1950s, *lakhon sbaek touch* was Cambodia's only spoken (rather than chanted or sung) theatre.

Both types of *lakhon sbaek* were devastated by the Khmer Rouge's genocide of the late 1970s, with only a handful of performers surviving, but both have been revived. A third form of leather-figure theatre, *lakhon sbaek poar* (*poar* meaning "colored"), rare even before the Khmer Rouge period, has been lost. Apparently performed in daylight, it was a picture-storytelling theatre featuring leather panels painted in the style of Angkor Wat bas-reliefs.

FURTHER READING

Kravel, Pech Tum. *Sbek Thom: Khmer Shadow Theater*.

Eileen Blumenthal

Puppet Theatre: China

Puppetry is extremely ancient in **China**, the idea of a life-size marionette being known by the Han dynasty (206 BC–220 AD) and puppets manipulated by strings from above being popular by the Tang (618–907).

By the Song (960–1279), with its highly developed urban culture, puppetry was popular throughout society, including the imperial court. By that time, puppets were of various kinds, including water puppets (like **Vietnam**'s *mua roi nuoc*), rod puppets manipulated from below, and string puppets. Puppeteers used their art for **storytelling**.

An extant regional form in Putian and Xianyou, near the coast of central Fujian, is "Puxian drama" (*puxian xi*), which, among current styles, shows the strongest traces of Song-dynasty *nanxi*. Some *puxian xi* gestures exhibit strong resemblance to local marionettes, suggesting that puppetry may have been an important influence in the formation of *nanxi* and hence in the origins of Chinese drama as a whole.

Puppetry reached its acme in the Qing dynasty (1644–1911), by which time the four main puppetry types were marionette, glove, rod, and shadow. Puppetry became closely associated with regional theatre, with **musical** and various other performance features of the main regional styles being adapted to puppetry, including *jingju*, *chuanju*, and various *bangzi qiang* styles. One genre had the puppeteer standing in the open air, a mini-**stage** on his shoulders. A screen on the mini-stage concealed his head from the audience, while he manipulated a puppet on stage.

Chinese puppet theatre experienced little change after the fall of the Qing, the four main traditional types being still widely performed. Private troupes continued to tour with their traditional mainly *xiqu*-derived repertoire. There were also a few adaptations from "civilized drama" (*wenming xi*), an early form of modern drama. In the 1930s, a group of Shanghai intellectuals introduced **Western** techniques, such as **scenography** and lighting, into puppet performances. They also introduced the roles of **playwright**, **director**, and designer within a troupe. Examples include the Wooden Man Theatre Troupe (Muren Jushe) in the 1930s and the Shanghai Amateur Puppet Troupe (Shanghai Yeyu Muou Jushe) in the 1940s.

Under the People's Republic, the state established professional puppet **theatre companies**. A series of financial and organizational supports helped elevate the **folk** pastime to a professional art. In the early 1950s, most performers were organized into government-subsidized companies, with only a few remaining private. In 1955, the China National Puppet Art Company (Zhongguo Muou Yishu Jutuan) was founded in Beijing under the direct administration of the Ministry of Culture. In 1955, the first National Showcase of Puppet and Shadow Puppet Performances opened in Beijing, with subsequent showcases in 1960, 1975, and 1981. The Quanzhou International Puppet **Festival** has attracted international attention since its inception (1986). These events highlighted a significant expansion of the traditional repertoire, with material from folklore, myths, children's tales, adaptations from other theatrical and literary genres, and **Western** dramatists, including Shakespeare and Gogol. Puppet performances also expanded from traditional operatic style to include modern "spoken drama" (*huaju*), dance-drama, and song-drama.

Although outdoor shows are still popular in the countryside, most performances have been moved from makeshift outdoor stages into professional **theatres** utilizing modern techniques. In the 1970s, large-scale performances involving complex scenery emerged, such as *The Flaming Mountains* (Huoyanshan, 1978). Innovations in production have also freed directors from conventions. In some cases, different puppetry

Shanghai Puppet Theatre production of *New Monkey Subdues the White-bone Demon*, with live actors performing together with puppets. (Photo: Courtesy of Shanghai Puppet Theatre)

styles are fused into one performance, and in others the puppeteers themselves are made part of the spectacle. Puppet performances are still given at festivals or at major functions like large-scale banquets or family occasions like weddings.

FURTHER READING

Chen, Fan Pen Li. *Visions for the Masses: Chinese Shadow Plays from Shaanxi and Shanxi*; Obrotsov, Sergei V. *The Chinese Puppet Theatre*; Ruisendaal, Robin. *Marionette Theatre in Quanxhou*; Stalberg, Roberta Helmer. *China's Puppets*.

Nan Zhang and Colin Mackerras

Puppet Theatre: India

Ancient Examples and Ritual Practices. The first historical evidence of **Indian** puppet theatre dates back to the Indus Valley civilization; it takes the form of a terracotta bull with a detachable head that can be manipulated by a string, and a terracotta monkey manipulated with a stick. From a spiritual standpoint, humans were stringed marionettes in God's hands. The **Sanskrit** *Treaty on Lovemaking* (Kamasutra) considers puppetry an important tool for attracting young girls. It also elucidates how to make puppets—including mechanical ones—from different materials, such as flour, clay, elephant tusk, and animal horns. Further, the ancient *Treatise on Drama* (Natyashastra; see Theory) gives the name "string holder" (*sutradhara*) to the **director**-producer.

Indian puppetry, which formerly received royal patronage, and whose popularity increased with the breakdown in the classical tradition after the tenth century, is strongly rooted in **religious** practices. Almost all puppeteers place great importance on pre-performance rituals, such as invoking the elephant-headed deity Ganesha, followed by the enactment of a dedicatory ritual prologue (*purvaranga*). The performance itself is deemed an act to purify the locality of evil and to bring peace and prosperity to all spectators. Performances are still often associated with rituals and temple **festivals** and celebrations. They are commonly sponsored by those fulfilling vows, or they may be given to celebrate marriages or births, or to bring well-being to the community or appease the gods.

Performance Practices. The traditional puppet theatre has a sung or read narrative text based mainly on the **Ramayana** and **Mahabharata** (mainly the former), myths, and Puranic literature; both the narrator and singers are hidden from the audience. They normally memorize the script and never write it down. Traditional characters are generally identified by conventional vocal, **makeup**, and **costume** elements. Comic characters are present in all traditional plays. Traditionally, **women** were not allowed to be puppeteers, although nowadays female voices are preferred for female characters.

Performance methods are inherited by practitioners. **Training** is informal and learned on the job, sometimes starting at age four or five. Only shadow puppeteers make their own puppets; others make only the costumes. **Directors** do not exist, nor are there formal rehearsals. Most shows are presented on a makeshift **stage**, often using a **curtain**. Kerala's shadow puppeteers, however, still use oil lamps, which are necessary to retain their special light and shade effects. **Music** and **dance**, mostly inspired by regional **folk theatres**, but also employing classical motifs, are very important.

Traditional puppetry varies from one part of the country to another. Its major environment has been in rural villages, where it often was the people's chief entertainment. Many forms have a close relation to theatre using **actors**, often being a puppet version of the genre, such as *kathakali* or *yakshagana*. The actors in certain forms are skillful manipulators of their counterparts, and the musicians may perform for either the puppets or actors, since the music and even the **dramatic structure** are the same.

The four major forms, each of which has many variations, are glove, rod, string, and shadow puppetry; some composite forms exist as well. Sadly, India's traditional puppet theatres must struggle to survive and their future is uncertain. Modern Indian puppet theatre suffers similar neglect.

Glove Puppets. Here, the puppet is worn like a glove, and the head is manipulated with the forefinger and the arms with the thumb and middle finger. Puppets are normally between one and a half to two feet high and made of wood, paper, or terracotta. The puppeteers normally squat or stand in full view. Representative genres include the now rare *pava kathakali* (or *pava koothu*) of northern Kerala, based on *kathakali* plays rich in action like *The Wedding of Princess Uttara* (Uttara Swayamvaram); three to four puppeteers manipulate puppets designed to resemble elaborately costumed and made-up *kathakali* actors. *Kundhei nach* of Orissa tells the story of Krishna and Radha; two puppeteers perform, one controlling Radha, the other Krishna. One also sings and beats one side of a drum with his free hand, and may also strike the other side with the puppet hand. Other glove puppet types include *baner putli* of West Bengal, largely based on social events and belonging to the Kahar caste, and *putul nach*, also of West Bengal, which has better-known rod and string variations.

Rod Puppets. Rod puppets, popular in the northern states of West Bengal, Orissa, and Jharkhand, have a main rod connected through a frame attached to the puppet's rounded torso to support its head, with two subsidiary rods attached to its wrists. The puppet is held over a screen from below. *Putul nach* of West Bengal, with its four-and-a-half-foot-tall puppets, is closely associated with *jatra*, whose scripts and costumes it usually adapts. Smaller puppets belong to Orissa's *kathi-kundhei nach*, which are from twelve to eighteen inches tall.

Puppets are generally made of wood and clay and are painted in oil colors. As in a number of other forms, a single body can be used with several heads, so that replacing the head and costume can change the character instantly. Plays are excerpts from the *Ramayana* or from local legends; song and dance sequences are often changed nowadays to suggest popular film or theatre stars. However, rod puppetry is facing extinction and, because of its low earning potential, children are discouraged from learning it.

String Puppets. String puppets or marionettes, India's oldest and most popular puppets, are seen in such states as Rajasthan (*kathputli*), Karnataka (*gombeyata*), West Bengal (*putul nach*), Assam (*putla nach*), Orissa (*sakhi kundhei nata*), Maharashtra (*kalsutri bahulya*), Tamilnadu (*bommalattam*), Tripura (*putul nach*), Andhra Pradesh (*keelu bommalatta*), and Kerala (*nool pavakuthu*).

String puppets provide the most detailed movement of all forms. Shows generally last from forty-five minutes to an hour and the puppets are made of wood, varying in height from one to three feet. Themes vary from the epics to Bollywood films though

Rajasthan's *kathputli* doesn't have any particular theme and the emphasis is on dance. The epics remain the most favored subject matter.

Rajasthan's *kathputli* (literally, "wooden doll") puppets, about one and a half feet high, with their mango wood heads and limbs stuffed with cotton, have a uniquely large number of movements even though no wooden control is used. Most have only two strings; one is attached to the top of the head and runs over the manipulator's fingers and returns to the puppet's waist, which allows for bodily movement. The second operates the hands. (The dancer [*rasdhari*] puppet, however, has nine strings.) Simple as it sounds, these puppets are capable of a wonderful variety of activities, from combat to delicate dancing. Individuality is expressed more through movements and gestures than facial appearance. Manipulation of their long skirts makes the legless puppets seem to have legs. Puppets requiring special skill include a horse and rider, and a snake and snake charmer. The gesture language of Rajasthani puppets can be more expressive than words. The principal Rajasthani puppet play is *Amar Singh Rathore*, about a brave Mughal chieftan. Troupes are small, consisting of a husband and wife; the man is the puppeteer and the wife is the drummer-singer. The puppeteer speaks in a high-pitched voice created by the use of a split-bamboo reed.

Orissa's *sakhi kundhai nata* (literally, "companion doll dance"), which tells the story of Krishna and Radha and borrows costume styles and stories from *jatra*, shares certain similarities with *kathputli*, such as the lack of legs and the use of long skirts to hide this absence. These puppets are handled with five to seven strings attached to a triangular control piece.

Karnataka's *gombeyata* (or *gombe atta*; literally, "dance of the puppets") takes its stories from the epics and Puranas, and closely resembles *yakshagana*; the person conducting the show is the *bhagavatar*. These puppets are often drawn on carts during festivals. The puppets are three-dimensional, with jointed limbs, hips, and shoulders, and have a minimum of five strings each; rods are sometimes used instead for increased control.

Tamilnadu's *bommalatta* (literally, "puppet dance") marionettes, on the verge of extinction, are presented by troupes of five to seven in tents at temple festivals or in villages, where the folk believe it will bring prosperity and ward off evil. There are two types: *tanjavour* and *kumbakonam*. Performances often continue from 10 p.m. to 4 a.m. and may last for a week or more. These three-dimensionally rounded puppets, some as tall as four and a half feet, which wear elaborate costumes and headdresses, are controlled with two rods for the hands and the other joints by strings. Their raised stage is built with a front that allows only the three-foot, ornately costumed puppets to be seen against a black backdrop through a twelve-feet-high opening. Religious stories drawn from the epics and Puranas are now supplemented with socially conscious plays on subjects like family planning. A clown puppet plays a major part. A shadow puppet form (see below) in southern Tamilnadu is called "leather puppet dance" (*tolu bommalatta*). It uses puppets manipulated by rods behind a backlit white cloth, but the expenses of this dying art have forced the sole remaining artist to use cardboard.

Tripura's *putul nach* is linked with local tribal traditions. The troupes announce the shows and even use banners depicting the troupe's characters, including one for popular Hindi film star Vaijayantimala drawn on a larger scale than the rest. The company contains ten members and performs about sixty shows annually, attracting many spectators.

Maharashtra's increasingly rare string puppet form (only one rural troupe remains) is *kalsutri bahulya* (literally, "threadskill dolls"), which uses small, legless dolls with strings attached to their heads and hands. Musicalized and narrated episodes from the *Ramayana* constitute most performances.

Shadow Puppets. Shadow puppeteers strictly observe their religious customs; puppets representing gods and goddesses are stored separately from demons. *Mahabharata*, *Ramayana*, and Purana stories are vital. Shadow puppets, whose history predates string puppets, are made of buffalo or goat hide. This kind of puppetry is reflected in five South Indian forms and one from the north. The former are Andhra Pradesh (*tholu* [or *tolu*] *bommalata*), Karnataka (*togalu gombeyata*), Kerala (*thol pavaikkuthu*), Tamilnadu (*thol pavakuthu*), and Maharashtra (*chamadyache bahulya*); in the north, only Orissa (*ravanacchaya*) still has such puppets.

Shows are presented by itinerant artists on elevated stages fronted by a white curtain, on which shadows are cast by a kerosene lamp, and generally last from seven to twenty-one nights, performances running all night long. The performers behind the curtain both move the puppets and speak and sing their words. Puppets are ornately painted and delicately perforated to allow light to shine through and to highlight decorative features. The characters, seen in profile, have bamboo rods attached to the limbs.

Tholu bommalatta (literally, "leather puppet dance") of Andhra Pradesh are the largest shadow puppets, even reaching human size in the case of Hanuman and Ravana. Unlike most other puppet theatres, they enact *Mahabharata* stories. Music and singing are performed by specialists standing behind the puppeteers. The *togalu gombeyata* of Karnataka resembles this form, but has both medium and small versions. Whereas these puppets are translucent and colorful, Kerala's "leather doll dance" (*thol pavaikkuthu*) uses opaque puppets that create black and white shadows. Their material is mostly derived from a Tamil version of the *Ramayana*, but it is performed for Malayali-speaking audiences by Marathi-speaking performers.

Orissa's highly stylized shadow puppets are quite small, only six to eight inches, and lacking joints. They are striking nonetheless, especially the ten-headed, twenty-armed Ravana.

Depending on the genre, puppets are shown in profile or three-quarter face, standing or sitting, and with or without jointed limbs and heads. Plays based on the epics typically require 150 puppets. Some puppets are restricted to a single role, others are used for multiple characters. There also is a tableau puppet, found in Karnataka and Andhra Pradesh, where a group effect is created by carving multiple characters—such as Hanuman and his monkey soldiers—into a single puppet figure.

Composite Puppets. Most composite puppets are combinations of rod and string puppetry. An important example is *bommalatta* (or *pavakkuttu*), which uses rods attached to the puppet's hands and operated from above (most rod puppets are operated from below). Strings connected to the puppet's head are manipulated by being attached to a wire worn on the puppeteer's head. Strongly influenced by *yakshagana* (which name they may also use), they are popular at religious festivals in Tanjore and Mysore, Tamilnadu, and are believed to have auspicious powers. Audiences sit through the night viewing plays inspiring faith and teaching morality (always leavened by humor), the epics being the main source; the classical musical accompaniment is highly admired. The three-feet-high puppets are renowned for their realistic mimicry.

FURTHER READING

Blackburn, Stuart. *Inside the Drama House: Rama Stories and Shadow Puppets in the Drama House*; Contractor, Meher R. *Puppets of India*; Tilakasiri, J. *The Puppet Theatre of Asia.*

Arya Madhavan

Puppet Theatre: Indonesia

Wayang. *Wayang* is the **Indonesian** and **Malaysian** term encompassing traditional puppet, scroll, and human theatre enacting puppet plays. *Wayang* can refer to an artistic genre and the object of performance. Thus, *wayang kulit* means both "shadow puppet theatre" as well as "shadow puppet." *Wayang*, in fact, refers to a wide variety of forms and related entertainments. Professional female social dancers accompanied by a mixed ensemble of *gamelan* and **Chinese** • **musical** instruments in the Jakarta area are known as *wayang cokek*. Dramatic forms of *topeng* • **masked** • **dance**-theatre are *wayang topeng*. Traditional Chinese theatre in the Malay world was also called Macao *wayang* (*wayang makao*), or *wayang* for short; and **Singapore**'s traditional Chinese small-scale street performances are still called *wayang*. Chinese glove puppetry is sometimes called *wayang titi* (or *po te hi*). Indian **Parsi theatre** and its offspring *bangsawan* were likewise known when introduced to Malaysia in the 1870s and 1880s as *wayang parsi*. **Actors** in *bangsawan*, *tonil*, *sandiwara*, and other forms of human theatre are "children of the *wayang*" (*anak wayang*). **Western** drama in nineteenth-century Malaysia and Singapore was "white people's *wayang*" (*wayang orang puteh*). Early cinematic exhibitions in Malaysia were referred to as "mute *wayang*" (*wayang bisu*) and later as "picture shows" (*wayang gambar*) or "dark *wayang*" (*wayang gelap*). The dominant usage of *wayang* today, however, is for traditional Indonesian shadow and rod puppetry, Malaysia's *wayang* traditions having receded in popularity since independence.

The remainder of this entry has subsections on *wayang*'s minor (*wayang beber*, *wayang gung*, and *wayang krucil*) and major forms (*wayang golek and wayang kulit*) in that order.

Wayang beber. An Indonesian scroll theatre represented today by a single troupe in Pacitan, East Java. A solo narrator (*dalang*) unrolls a series of illuminated scrolls on wood batons and expresses them through narration, dialogue, and "mood songs" (*sulukan*) derived from classical literature, to the accompaniment of a small *gamelan* ensemble made up of spiked fiddle (*rebab*) and percussion. The surviving troupe owns only one set of scrolls narrating a **Panji** story; presumably, past troupes owned many more. *Wayang beber* was hired a century ago for alleviating children's ailments, but today is sponsored mostly for official purposes.

Wayang gung. "Grand" *wayang*, also *wayang gong*, a *wayang* genre performed among the Banjar people of southern Kalimantan, Indonesia. It employs an arena **stage**, using only a table, chairs, or benches. The actors' hide headdresses bear *wayang kulit* puppet heads illustrating the characters depicted. A trio of **costumed** narrators debates the meaning and ascribes significance to the story. Only a few troupes survive.

Wayang krucil. A rare form of puppetry found primarily in East Java, Indonesia, a.k.a. *wayang klitik*. Its puppets have the same basic shape as *wayang kulit*'s but are made of flat wood, except for their arms, usually fashioned from hide. The core repertoire corresponds to stories from the middle section of the nineteenth-century *Book of Kings* (Pustakaraja); favorites are Damarwulan and Panji episodes. *Wayang krucil* can also perform *The Origin of Kala* (Murwakala) for the ritual purpose of "disempowerment" (*ruwatan*); this might be the most common cause for sponsoring *wayang krucil* in East Java today.

Wayang golek. A rod puppet theatre that emerged in Java during the last two hundred to five hundred years. As rod puppetry is found in China, **Thailand**, and other parts of Asia, some believe this form originally was a cultural import adapted by Javanese artists to their own needs. The puppets are manipulated from below by a plain wooden rod that runs through a carved-out wooden torso and attaches to a delicately carved head. The head can swivel from side to side and the torso can move up and down to create the appearance of breath. Jointed arms are attached to the torso and manipulated by means of secondary control rods, as in *wayang kulit*. The puppet is **costumed** in cloth, sometimes richly embroidered. Most puppets lack feet; the bottom part of the central control rod is covered by a skirt to conceal the puppeteer's hand.

Dramaturgically, *wayang golek* is derivative of *wayang kulit*, with a *dalang* reciting all dialogue and narration, singing "mood songs" (*sulukan*) derived from classical literature, and conducting a *gamelan*. A full set typically contains about one hundred wooden puppets; these are rounded out by **properties** and hide scenic pieces, including a "tree of life" (*kayon*) puppet, a leaf-shaped cosmic symbol that starts and ends performances, divides plays into scenes, and functions as an all-purpose prop and set piece.

Wayang golek was originally associated largely with Islamic stories, such as the Amir Hamzah cycle; Islamic tales still dominate the repertoires of rod puppet theatres in the Kebumen area, Central Java, and on Java's north coast. Kebumen's type, sometimes called *wayang golek menak*, is nearing extinction. The more abundant north coast puppeteers perform *wayang golek cepak* or *wayang golek pepak*. Communities there occasionally sponsor *wayang golek* depicting tales of the **religious** proselytizers (*wali*) and the early history of Islam in Java in conjunction with ancestral commemoration rites in cemeteries. **Enthus Susmono** is a major innovator in north coast puppetry.

Wayang golek's main center is in West Java's Sundanese region. Rod puppetry was introduced to Sunda in the nineteenth century and was embraced by landed elites and ordinary villagers. It took over *wayang kulit*'s repertoire; hence rod puppetry here is sometimes called *wayang golek purwa*. *Wayang golek* became so popular in Sunda that few traces of Sundanese *wayang kulit* remain.

Increasingly, Sundanese rod puppetry is less a sacred form than a light entertainment starring the buck-toothed clown-servant Cepot. Sundanese *wayang golek*'s iconography originally was closely based on *wayang kulit* prototypes. However, carvers and painters have increasingly employed greater realism. **Asep Sunandar Sunarya** introduced a large stock of new ogres, some with effects like exploding heads. Purists decry such innovations, but these are well suited for the television productions to which puppeteers aspire.

A fight scene in a London *wayang golek* performance by Sundanese puppeteer Asep Sunandar Sunarya from West Java, Indonesia, 2002. (Photo: Matthew Isaac Cohen)

Wayang kulit. This Indonesian and Malaysian shadow puppet theatre, known in High Javanese as *ringgit wacucal*, is one of the world's oldest and most dramaturgically sophisticated continuing theatre traditions. Various forms of shadow puppet theatre, in which painted and filigreed figures cut from animal hide (*kulit*) cast shadows on a white cotton screen by being interposed between screen and a light, are believed to have existed in ancient China and **India**, and possibly the Mediterranean world. Scholars generally believe that shadow puppetry was brought to Java from India in the first millennium AD. Some believe that *wayang* is derived from *hyang* ("god" or "goddess"), and that Java's shadow puppet theatre was originally a devotional form used to commune with ancestors or invisible spirits.

Historical Background. A paucity of early sources prevents precise determinations of *wayang kulit*'s origins. It is clear, however, that shadow puppetry developed into a complex, independent form used to present *Mahabharata* and *Ramayana* episodes, and then spread to other Indonesian islands, as well as the Malay peninsula. *Wayang kulit* weathered the introduction of Islam, though numerous modifications were made, later attributed to the proselytes (*wali*). Javanese Muslim exegetes read *wayang kulit* symbolically, interpreting the relation between puppet and puppeteer as a metaphor for man and God.

Primarily an oral form, its manuals and scripts were written under the auspices of royal sponsors starting in the nineteenth century. Between 1850 and 1900, Surakarta court poet Raden Ngabehi Ranggawarsita (1802–1873) and his followers arranged the major story summaries enacted in the *The Book of Kings* (Pustakaraja), one of the longest literary works ever composed. Courses and later puppetry schools were opened in Java starting in 1923, providing **training** for amateurs not from puppeteer dynasties. Under Dutch colonialism, Javanese migrant laborers brought *wayang kulit* to Surinam and New Caledonia. Today, puppeteers around the world use *wayang kulit* to tell their own tales or versions of the traditional repertoire.

Puppets. Puppets are made from buffalo skin or cowhide painted on both sides. A central control rod (sometimes of buffalo horn) runs down the puppet's middle. Most puppets also have two ancillary rods attached to their hands. Puppets are jointed at the shoulders and elbows. When not in use, puppet sets are stored in chests.

A full Javanese set numbers between 150 and 250; sets of more than four hundred are owned by courts and wealthy patrons. A set contains numerous **role types**: Hindu gods and demigods, knightly heroes and villains, Brahmanic sages, queens, and princesses, grotesquely disfigured clown-servants, maids in waiting, ordinary rank-and-file foot soldiers, ogres, spooks and apparitions, animals, and tools and weapons. Many are essentially stock figures that can be assigned different names in different plays, but some depict specific characters, such as Kresna (Krishna), Bima, or Semar. For these, there are often different variants (*wanda*) that can be selected depending on the scene. A *wanda* of Gathotkaca deployed in a battle scene, for example, will have a more upturned head than one used for a court audience scene. A central nonfigurative, all-purpose puppet is the leaf-shaped "tree of life" (*kayon*, a.k.a. *gunungan*, *babat*, or *pohon beringin*).

Joko Susilo (*dalang*) manipulating Cakil in a "flower battle" (*perang kembang*), the centerpiece of traditional Central Javanese *wayang kulit*. (Photo: Aviva Kartiningsih Cohen)

Dalang *of* Wayang kulit. The principal performer is the solo puppeteer (*dalang* or *dhalang*), who is highly respected in traditional societies for his knowledge of stories, control of language, and magical abilities to bring fortune to individuals or a community and appease spirits through his performances. A Javanese puppeteer manipulates all the puppets, sings "mood songs" (*sulukan*) derived from classical literature, intones dramatic narration, speaks all the character voices, and provides sound effects by knocking with a wooden mallet (*cempala*) against the puppet chest to his left or banging, with his foot, metal plates (*keprak* or *kepyak*) strung up on the chest. Dialogue in traditional *wayang kulit* is extemporized, but the puppeteer draws on a rich stock of formulaic exchanges, aphorisms, and stock commentary.

The puppeteer sits cross-legged in front of the screen (*kelir*), which is stretched taut inside a wooden frame and attached at the bottom to a banana tree log. This log, and usually a smaller one adjacent to it at a lower height, also serves as the stage; during scenes, the puppeteer plants puppets by their central rod into one of the logs. A dozen or more puppets can thus contribute to a single scene. Higher status characters are placed in the upper log, lower status characters in the lower. The light, nowadays an electric bulb, is situated above the puppeteer's head so that shadows extend downward, hiding his hand.

Music. Puppeteers often begin as musicians under a senior puppeteer before becoming puppeteers themselves. Music varies according to time and geography. Javanese *wayang kulit* is inseparable from *gamelan*, a primarily percussion ensemble consisting typically of twelve to twenty-five musicians, under the direction of a drummer. A five-toned *gamelan* known as *gamelan slendro* in Central and East Java and *gamelan prawa* in Cirebon was the mainstay of *wayang kulit* through the twentieth century. Today, many ensembles also use a seven-toned *gamelan pelog*. Balinese *wayang kulit* is usually accompanied by a pair or quartet of xylophones (*gender wayang*), but can be accompanied by a larger *gamelan* on special occasions. In traditional Kelantan, a complete ensemble was made up of a reed instrument called a *serunai*, drums, gongs, and hand cymbals. Lombok's *wayang kulit* is accompanied by a small ensemble of flute, drum, gong, and cymbals. Puppeteers can start and stop music and control its pulse and dynamics through rhythmic knocking and singing. The music tends to be cyclical, rather than through-composed, allowing for indefinite numbers of repetitions to accompany the extemporized action.

Plays. *Wayang kulit* in most of Indonesia and Malaysia enacts plays (*lakon, lampahan*) based on the *Ramayana* and *Mahabharata*. Many Southeast Asians do not recognize these as foreign, feeling that these epics took place in their own lands. The courtly characters present models for proper behavior. New stories based on old motifs, known as "branch stories" (*lakon carangan* in Java; *cerita ranting* in Kelantan), allow performances to address emergent societal concerns. Many centralize the clown-servants (*punakawan, panakawan,* or *penasar*), who function primarily for comic relief.

The Indic repertoire is sometimes referred to as *wayang kulit purwa* or "ancient" *wayang kulit*. This classification harkens to Ranggawarsita's encyclopedia, which is divided into two prologue volumes—*Versed in Letters* (Jitapsara) and *The Highest Yoga* (Paramayoga)—both of which concern the deeds of Hindu-Javanese gods; *The Ancient Book of Kings* (Pustakaraja purwa), which redacts Javanese versions of the *Ramayana* and *Mahabharata*; *The Middle Book of Kings* (Pustakaraja madya), dealing with the period after the Great War; and *The Final Book of Kings* (Pustakaraja wusana), narrating the period around the arrival of Islam in Java.

Middle plays can be enacted by the same ensemble and puppets presenting "ancient" plays, but there are also two nearly extinct shadow puppet genres that developed in Java around the "middle" repertoire. *Wayang kulit gedog*, a genre predating Ranggawarsita's encyclopedia, presents Panji stories with specialized puppets and *gamelan pelog* accompaniment. *Wayang kulit madya* was created in 1870 by Mangkunagara IV (r. 1857–1881) to present Ranggawarsita's "middle" tales. Some 422 new puppets, one hundred summaries, and many new musical pieces for *gamelan* (*gending*) were fashioned for this purpose. The form enjoyed little currency outside court circles.

Few traces remain of *wayang kulit wusana*, which presented Islamic tales based on the encyclopedia; this does not mean that *wayang kulit* is hostile to Islam. *Wayang kulit* among the Sasak people of Lombok enacts stories featuring Amir Hamzah, uncle of the Prophet Muhammad, and related Islamic figures; these are also known as *menak* stories. Ranggawarsita also included stories merging Hinduism and Islam, including one in the *Paramayoga* pitting Bathara Guru (Shiva to South Asians) against Jesus. This tradition of integrating Islam and Hinduism has been continued by puppeteers such as **Abyor Dayagung**.

Performance. Performances tend to be communal, not ticketed, affairs, sponsored in conjunction with rites of passage and communal celebrations. Spectators are invited by the host, or are locals drawn by a show's sound and bustle. Most performances take place during the cool hours of the night, and might run all night long. Daytime performances (*wayang lemah* in Bali and *wayang awan* in Java) exist, often performed without a screen. Kelantan and Lombok performers work in temporary booths constructed by the sponsor. Cirebonese puppeteers perform on temporary stages about four feet high; invited guests sit in chairs or on mats watching the shadows while the uninvited masses stand around to watch the puppeteer and musicians from the screen's opposite side, or sit in food stalls and listen at a distance. The medial section of a classical Central Javanese mansion's pavilion is literally "place of the puppets" (*paringgitan*), where the screen is to be erected. In ordinary Central Javanese houses, the house's front wall is removed and replaced by a screen. The invited audience sits in the house watching the shadows, while the rabble watch from the other side. Few stay for an entire performance and attention is selective.

Ritual Aspects. Most performances are secular and intended primarily for entertainment; there are also ritual dramas intended to effect changes on people and communities. "Disempowerment" (*ruwatan*) ritual dramas are sponsored in Java by the families of a person afflicted with perennially bad luck. The puppeteer enacts the myth of *The Origin of Kala* (Murwakala) concerning the demonic son of Bathara Guru who is granted leave by his father to eat humans who have violated certain taboos. Guru realizes that Kala's entitlements are too broad, and through metatheatrical machinations he and the other gods trick Kala into forgoing the eating of a child, who is given the same name as the real-life ritual subject. The puppeteer presents offerings and incantations to appease Kala and other malevolent spirits, and thereby drain their power and influence over the ritual subject. Related plays are shown in Bali and were presented in the past in Malaysia at "feasting the spirits" (*berjamu*) rites. There are also ritual dramas combining dramatic narratives with ritual gestures to avert epidemics, bring rain, bless a rice crop, honor ancestors, or ensure a good fishing season.

Modern **Wayang kulit.** Many modern forms, often short-lived, were created during the last century. The rarely performed "mouse deer *wayang*" (*wayang kancil*), created by Bo Lim in 1925, presents simple animal fables for children. Various forms called "illuminating *wayang*" (*wayang suluh*), "revolutionary *wayang*" (*wayang revolusi*), and "five-pillar *wayang*" (*wayang pancasila*; Pancasila is Indonesia's state ideology) were created for **political** propaganda purposes around the time of the national revolution (1945–1949); all are today essentially museum pieces. "Divine revelation *wayang*" (*wayang wahyu*), a Catholic form created in 1960, enacts biblical episodes, and is normally produced around Christmas, Easter, or Pentecost.

There have been various projects to adjust *wayang kulit* to the pace of modern life and tailor it for recordings and radio. A "condensed" version (*pakeliran padat*) was fashioned in the 1970s. Lasting from ten minutes to two hours, plays tend to ignore normal chronology, relying on flashbacks and dream scenes. Musical pieces begin and end abruptly and do not follow standard **dramatic structure**. *Pakeliran padat* tends also to focus more intensely on character psychology than classical *wayang kulit*. Initially academic in ethos, the form was adopted in the late 1980s by "superstar" puppeteers who used it for prologues to all-night performances; it appeared on television in the 1990s.

Other forms remain more **experimental**. "*Wayang* in Indonesian" (*wayang sandosa*) uses multiple puppeteers and light sources and Indonesian, rather than Javanese, narration and dialogue. The long rehearsal process, complex lighting, and extensive personnel have prevented it from being widely adopted outside the academy. "Measured *wayang*" (*wayang ukur*), developed by Yogyakarta artist Sukasman (1936–), uses two puppeteers situated on both sides of the screen, translucent puppets, and classical dancers. "Legendary *wayang*" (*wayang legenda*) is a 1988 creation of Yogyakarta's Heri Dono (1960–). Initially, it presented legends from outside Java, but it has taken a postmodern turn. "Electric *wayang*" (*wayang listrik*), created by **I Wayan Wija** and American Larry Reed, has been succeeded in Bali by I Made Sidia's *wayang kontemporer* and *wayang skateboard*, in which multiple puppeteers shuttle back and forth in front of the screen on skateboards. Projections and video are also used. Indonesian *wayang kulit* has often figured in transnational collaborations, and its stories and dramaturgy have provided fodder for modern **playwrights** such as **Rendra** and **Nano Riantiarno**.

Dwindling audiences for Malaysian traditional *wayang kulit* have contributed to the emergence of many academic and pop variants telling nontraditional stories in attempts to regenerate the tradition and reach new audiences. For example, Kelantan puppeteer Dollah Baju Merah (1938–) collaborated with British novelist Edward Carey in 2005 to produce the Malay adaptation, *Macbeth in the Shadows*. *See also Wayang wong*.

FURTHER READING

Brandon, James R., ed. *On Thrones of Gold: Three Javanese Shadow Plays*; Buurman, Peter. *Wayang Golek: The Entrancing World of Classical Javanese Puppet Theatre*; Herbert, Mimi, with Nur S. Rahardjo. *Voices of the Puppet Masters*; Hobart, Angela. *Dancing Shadows of Bali: Theatre and Myth*; Irvine, David. *Leather Gods and Wooden Heroes: Java's Classical Wayang*; Keeler, Ward. *Javanese Shadow Plays, Javanese Selves*; Long, Roger. *Javanese Shadow Theatre: Movement and Characterization in Ngayogyakarta Wayang Kulit*; Mangkunagara VII. *On the Wayang Kulit (Purwa) and its Symbolic and Mystical Elements*; Ness, Edward C. van, and Shita Prawirohardjo. *Javanese Wayang Kulit: An Introduction*; Weintraub, Andrew. *Power Plays: Wayang Golek Puppet Theater of West Java*; Zurbuchen, Mary Sabina. *The Language of Balinese Shadow Theater*.

Matthew Isaac Cohen

Puppet Theatre: Japan

Ko-jôruri. *Ko-jôruri* (literally, "old *jôruri*") refers to **Japan**'s seventeenth-century puppet theatre prior to the start of the collaboration between **playwright • Chikamatsu Monzaemon** and chanter (*tayû*) **Takemoto Gidayû**. Chikamatsu's *The Soga Heir* (Yotsugi Soga, 1683), written by Chikamatsu for chanter Uji Kaga no jô (1635–1711), and *Kagekiyo Victorious* (Shusse Kagekiyo, 1685), composed for Gidayû, are regarded as transitional, marking the end of *ko-jôruri* and the start of the newly sophisticated *jôruri* (see *Bunraku*) shaped and defined by Chikamatsu's texts. Whereas Chikamatsu's plays have highly developed plots and complex characters, with stories drawn from both contemporary and historical sources, *ko-jôruri* works tend to be relatively simple narratives based on familiar legends and tales.

Jôruri is a term taken from Lady Jôruri, a lover of Minamoto Yoshitune, a heroic, twelfth-century personage. By the early sixteenth century *The Tale of Lady Jôruri in Twelve Episodes* (Jôruri jûnidan sôshi) was a staple performed by lute (*biwa*)–playing narrators. *Ko-jôruri* grew out of performances by chanters who initially recited tales from the fourteenth-century *Tale of the Heike* (Heike monogatari; see Storytelling). By the 1590s, the *jôruri* legend formed the centerpiece of a newly emerging genre in which puppets enacted dramatic situations as narrators told the story to the **musical** accompaniment of the *shamisen*, a three-stringed instrument that had recently arrived in Japan by way of the Ryûkyû islands, and that quickly surpassed the *biwa* in popularity to become associated with both the puppets and **kabuki**.

The *Storybook in Twelve Sections* (Jûnidan-zôshi), about Lady Jôruri, is *ko-jôruri*'s principal text. Other works—all from the late-sixteenth and early-seventeenth centuries—include *Round the Capital* (Miyako meguri), *Amida's Riven Breast* (Amida no munewari), *Lady Goô* (Goô no hime), and *The Story of Ushiwakamaru in Twelve Parts* (Ushiwakamaru jûnidan). In addition, several *nô* plays, including *Takasago*, were adapted for *ko-jôruri*.

Ko-jôruri flourished in Kyoto and Osaka as well as in Edo (Tokyo), where Kyoto-trained chanters such as Satsuma Jôun (?–1669) established theatres by the 1620s or even earlier. *Kinpira jôruri*, puppet plays based on the exploits of the legendary warrior Kinpira, particularly attracted Edo (Tokyo) audiences with their scenes of violence and spectacle. Such was the general popularity of puppet theatre that a number of musical narrative styles (*bushi*) developed. These include *sekkyô bushi*, which flourished in the late seventeenth and early eighteenth centuries and focused on subdued, Buddhist-related **religious** themes.

Throughout the *ko-jôruri* period puppets tended to be of relatively simple construction and manipulated by one person—in contrast to the sophisticated puppets later originated in *bunraku* for three puppeteers. Still, early- to mid-seventeenth century texts of the *ko-jôruri Amida's Riven Breast* indicate that puppetry was secondary to musical performance, which remained true of *bunraku* as well.

FURTHER READING

Dunn, C. J. *The Early Japanese Puppet Drama.*

Barbara E. Thornbury

Bunraku. *Bunraku* is Japan's traditional puppet theatre, created in the late fifteenth century when three preexisting arts came together to form what is now called *bunraku* but which grew out of *ko-jôruri* and was formerly known as *ningyô shibai* ("puppet theatre") and *ningyô jôruri* ("puppet *jôruri*"). These arts were puppet manipulation (*ayatsuri*), **storytelling** (*katari mono*), and *shamisen*.

Early Historical Development. Japan's puppet shows go back at least to the eighth century. Early practices included performances by concealed operators of handheld puppets or stick puppets operated on miniature portable **stages**. Indigenous practices most likely mixed with imported continental entertainments to form the earliest presentations. Itinerant, part-time puppeteers often performed as part of shrine or temple **festivals** or rituals. Mechanical puppets were most likely imported early on from **China**

and again in the fifteenth century; Christian missionaries may also have brought mechanical puppets in the mid-sixteenth century. Still, other than the eventual use of internal strings to manipulate facial features and hands, the Japanese generally preferred handheld, nonmechanical, puppets.

The puppets known today developed their lasting qualities from the late 1600s to the mid-1730s. Limbs were added in the 1690s, and techniques to manipulate facial features (eyes, mouths, eyebrows, and so on) were created in the late 1720s and 1730s. The first instance of a manipulator coming into full view of the audience (although behind a translucent screen) was when Takamatsu Hachirobei did so in 1703; in 1705, Hachirobei formalized the method, eliminating the screen. Three-man puppeteering (*sannin zukai*) with larger puppets (nearly two-thirds life size) was introduced in 1734. After that, only minor roles had one handler (using crude, smaller puppets). Two causes led to these developments: first was the late seventeenth century competition between Osaka's chief puppet **theatres**, the Toyotake Theatre (Toyotake-za) and Takemoto Theatre (Takemoto-za); second was the need to depict increasingly realistic characters whose stories were based on real events.

While *bunraku* became an urban entertainment in the Edo period (1603–1868), countryside performances always had been popular in wintertime months where specialists were local farmers made idle by the requirements of the agricultural cycle. Awaji island holds a special place in countryside traditions for creating what was to become *bunraku*. Unlike the developed art of *bunraku*, puppeteers—rather than chanters (*tayû*)—usually spoke the dialogue for their puppets in rural performances. In the late sixteenth century, Shinto legends and Buddhist texts and sermons were being delivered via puppetry by shrine and temple specialists. Wandering storytellers, with their tales of historical events and personages, together with temple and shrine traditions, offered the genesis and backbone of *bunraku* art. The combination of puppetry and chanted text is *bunraku*'s central feature, where (in most cases) a single chanter delivers all the dialogue as well as description and commentary.

When, as noted above, *The Tale of Lady Jôruri in Twelve Episodes* was picked up in the sixteenth century as the earliest plot material for the newly formed puppet-narrative-*shamisen* entertainments, the term *jôruri* was born. The old form, *ko-jôruri*, flourished for much of the seventeenth century, as chanter-**playwrights** like Uji Kaganojô developed individual styles of narration. Uji effected the move from violent plays about the superhero Kinpira (*kinpira jôruri*) to stories depicting real human emotions, and altered the **dramatic structure** of plays to the five-act method governed by the rhythmic principle of *jô-ha-kyû* (literally, "introduction, break, fast" but usually rendered as "introduction, development, conclusion").

Chikamatsu Monzaemon and Takemoto Gidayû. In 1686, a transition occurred in which *ko-jôruri* was supplanted by "new *jôruri*" (*shin jôruri*) when playwright Chikamatsu Monzaemon and chanter Takemoto Gidayû became a team at the Takemoto Theatre, beginning with *Kagekiyo Victorious* (Shusse Kagekiyo). Both men had been given their start by Uji Kaganojô, and when Gidayû's narrative style—*gidayû bushi*—and Chikamatsu's linguistically rich and dramatically polished plays combined, the art's full possibilities were launched. Henceforth, playwriting and chanting were separate occupations, with chanters depending on playwrights for new material, and playwrights writing for specific chanters.

Gidayû and Chikamatsu's collaboration created masterpieces in the major play genres of *bunraku* and *kabuki*, "history plays" (*jidai mono*) and "domestic plays" (*sewa mono*). *Kagekiyo Victorious* is a *jidai mono*, while *Love Suicides at Sonezaki* (Sonezaki shinjû, 1703), was both the first *bunraku* domestic play and the first "double suicide play" (*shinjû mono*). Unlike the fantastical actions of Kinpira-type plays, these were often inspired by tragic occurrences of recent memory (sometimes only days earlier) or by actual historical events.

Along with the Gidayû-Chikamatsu collaboration, the competing Takemoto and Toyotake Theatres (the latter founded in 1703 by **Toyotake Wakatayû**) brought the arts of chanting and puppeteering to their first significant highpoint. After Gidayû's death in 1714, Chikamatsu primarily wrote for Gidayû's successor, Takemoto Masatayû (Gidayû II), whose weak voice he offset with the highly developed language of his final period. Highlights of these years included *Love Suicides at Amijima* (Shinjû Ten no Amijima, 1720) and *The Battles of Coxinga* (Kokusenya kassen, 1715).

Post-Chikamatsu Years. The greatest plays were created during the mid-eighteenth century, when puppet plays were written collaboratively (*gassaku*), with acts and scenes divided up among a team of playwrights organized under a "head playwright" (*tate sakusha*). Many plays were so successful that, beginning with a 1717 adaptation of *The Battles of Coxinga*, much of *kabuki*'s repertoire was adapted from *bunraku*, including the so-called "three masterpieces," *Sugawara and the Secrets of Calligraphy* (Sugawara denju tenarai kagami, 1746), *Yoshitsune and the Thousand Cherry Trees* (Yoshitsune senbon zakura, 1747), and *The Treasury of Loyal Retainers* (Kanadehon chûshingura, 1748), by **Takeda Izumo II**, Miyoshi Shôraku (1696–1772?), and **Namiki Sôsuke** (or Senryû). They were followed by others, **Chikamatsu Hanji** being *jôruri*'s last great author. These playwrights dramatized the emotional turmoil of characters embroiled in impossible historical conflicts or burdened by unbearable social obligations; the classic conflict was between duty (*giri*) and emotion (*ninjô*) created under the constraints of Confucian-inspired morality.

Performance. The sophisticated three-man puppets, which debuted after Chikamatsu's death, allowed for greater possibilities of portrayal. An increasing number of head types also developed over the years as new characters and **role types** (designated by puppet head types) entered the repertory.

Over time, a specially adapted **stage** was developed. **Scenographic** effects, while attractive, are less intricate, and **properties** less numerous than in *kabuki*; this restraint makes sense when one considers the crowd of puppeteers and puppets often clogging the stage. The stage is divided into three discrete horizontal sections, set off from one another by low railings the tops of which serve to represent the ground or floor.

The chief puppeteer (*omo zukai*) wears high clogs to allow better manipulation of the right hand, head, and torso, which are his responsibility. While the left arm operator (*hidari zukai*) and leg operator (*ashi zukai*) **costume** is typically a black robe and hood, the *omo zukai*, depending on the play, may wear a formal kimono (generally, white or black) with divided skirt-trousers (*hakama*), sometimes supplemented with an embroidered *kataginu* vest, which has stiff, wing-like shoulders. Usually, his face is exposed.

The chanter, seated before his lacquered reading stand on a special stage-left platform, wears the formal *kataginu* and *hakama* attire called *kamishimo*, as does his

Scene from the *bunraku* play *The Precious Incense and Autumn Flowers of Sendai*. The chanter and shamisen player are at the right. (Photo: Courtesy of Waseda University Theatre Museum)

musician partner, at his left. In performance, a great chanter's skill—alternating between dialogue and the lyrical chanting of descriptive, poetic passages—shares attention with the focus of the puppeteers. Years of **training** have developed their skills of timing and coordination, and of the depiction of movements based on common human actions (*furi*) balanced with striking poses.

Later History. *Kabuki* and *bunraku* became closely interrelated during the eighteenth century, when they shared subject matter, techniques, and audiences. An intense rivalry evolved and, while *bunraku* was on top for much of the mid-eighteenth century, by the 1760s, Osaka's *bunraku* theatres were forced to close down in the face of *kabuki*'s increased popularity. The late eighteenth century, however, did witness a brief efflorescence of puppet theatre in Edo. The puppets barely held on until a man from Awaji, Uemura Bunrakuken (1737–1810), revived the art in Osaka at the turn of the nineteenth century. His descendants continued his work through the nineteenth century, even though they usually were restricted to performances on temple and shrine grounds. His name inspired the term *bunraku*, which became common after the establishment of Osaka's Bunraku Theatre (Bunraku-za, 1872). Subsequently, *jôruri* frequently came to designate the scripts specifically.

Soon after the Bunraku Theatre opened, it was rivaled by the Hikoroku Theatre (Hikoroku-za), briefly recalling the glory days of the Takemoto and Toyotake Theatre competition; the Hikoroku, however, closed down in 1893 (although revived under other names for several years). In 1909, Shôchiku, a rising entertainment conglomerate, took over the Bunraku Theatre's management. In 1926, fire destroyed the theatre and many of its treasured effects, and it was not until 1929 that a new theatre opened. However, due to dwindling audiences, *bunraku* faced extinction, and was saved only by a Diet bill (1933) granting it a government subsidy. The government encouraged *bunraku* as well during the war, when it introduced several propaganda plays.

Postwar **Bunraku.** The difficult times resumed in the postwar period. In 1945, when air raids again destroyed *bunraku*'s theatre, the old puppet heads and properties were lost. Further, the company split into two warring factions in 1948, the pro-Shôchiku Chinami-Kai and the pro-union Mitsuwa-Kai, with largely younger practitioners challenging their tradition-bound seniors. In 1956, when the players moved, united, to a new theatre in Osaka's Dôtonbori entertainment district, the traditional *bunraku* area, the art resumed on a more secure footing.

The Bunraku Association was founded in 1963, as a foundation of performers and government representatives dedicated to maintaining the art. Its effect, together with the 1966 opening of the National Theatre (Kokuritsu Gekijô) in Tokyo (with its smaller theatre intended for *bunraku*) and the 1984 opening of the National Bunraku Theatre (Kokuritsu Bunraku Gekijô) in Osaka, a few blocks from Dôtonbori, led to the end of precarious times and the continuation of a once-again flourishing art.

Tours abroad have been a postwar feature, garnering admiration and a worldwide audience. New plays, some based on **Western** classics like *Madame Butterfly* and *Hamlet*, were attempted in the 1950s but had no lasting influence. A training program was started in the 1970s to ensure *bunraku*'s longevity. The designation of certain top puppeteers, chanters, and *shamisen* players as Living National Treasures also ensured renewed interest and increased respect.

FURTHER READING

Keene, Donald. *Bunraku: The Art of the Japanese Puppet Theatre*; Scott, A. C. *The Puppet Theatre of Japan*.

Katherine Saltzman-Li

Other Japanese Puppet Theatres. Dramas enacted by puppets and recited by *shamisen*-accompanied chanters are not restricted to *bunraku*. Although broadly categorized as **folk theatre**, many such troupes are well trained and highly skilled. Some are also recognized beyond their local communities, receiving invitations to perform at **festivals** and other national and international events. The forms cited here have been designated as "nationally important folk performing arts."

Evidence suggests that puppets have been part of Japanese culture at least since the tenth century, but it was not until the sixteenth that their use became relatively widespread and prominent. As noted, before the 1734 invention of three-man puppeteering, puppets were simpler and worked by a single puppeteer. On Sado Island, off Japan's west coast, one can still see pre-*bunraku* puppet theatre. Unsophisticated puppets handled by one person appear in plays performed to the accompaniment of *bun'ya bushi* narration, popular in Osaka in the late seventeenth century. In time, *bun'ya bushi* was supplanted by *gidayû bushi*, which became the professional standard.

Some varieties of puppet theatre employ festival floats or other types of festival stages where manipulators hidden from view control mechanical puppets (*karakuri ningyô*) with strings and wire. Such puppets can be traced back 350 years to the founding of a successful *karakuri ningyô* theatre in Osaka by Takeda Ômi (?–1704).

Mechanical puppets are now associated with events such as the Hitachi Furyû Mono festival in Hitachi, Ibaraki Prefecture. The floats employed at first appear to be enormous castles—that is, until the wings of the structures open up to reveal multilevel stages. Puppets appear on these, their handlers inside the floats. Hitachi Furyû Mono presentations are famous for their finales, in which the puppeteers simultaneously tug on strings in order to instantaneously transform warriors fresh from battle scenes into beautiful ladies ready to bring the show to a close with festive music and **dance**.

Another example is the "lantern puppet" (*tôrô ningyô*) festival of Yamefukushima, Fukuoka Prefecture. The mechanical puppets are positioned above bridgelike structures running the length of a specially built stage framed by glowing lanterns. Puppeteers hidden below use strings to move the limbs and heads of the puppets while other handlers, in the wings, use long poles to move and turn them.

Bunraku-style puppets are common in the folk arts. The Hachioji Kuruma puppet theatre (a.k.a. *otome bunraku*) of Tokyo, which appeared in the 1860s, is unusual in that it features puppeteers who work singly and within the stage's open space rather than behind a fixed set. Each manipulator handles a puppet with two hands while crouched on a movable, yet unobtrusive, wheeled seat (*kuruma*) that allows free movement around the stage. The accompaniment is *shinnaibushi*.

Said to be the immediate precursor of *bunraku*, *awaji ningyô jôruri*, the above noted puppet theatre of Awaji, had developed hugely popular puppet theatre by the early eighteenth century. *Awaji* puppet theatre features *bunraku*-style puppets manipulated by three people. However, since around 1880, the Awaji puppets are larger in size than those used in Osaka's professional theatre.

As many as forty active troupes once worked in Awaji, performing both as festival offerings and for their entertainment. The one surviving *awaji ningyô jôruri* troupe is based in a permanent visitor's center and theatre in the town of Fukura. Tourists regularly arrive to learn about the history of Awaji puppet theatre and to catch a brief demonstration. Members of the troupe also travel abroad as popular representatives of Japan's traditional performing arts.

FURTHER READING

Adachi, Barbara. *The Voices and Hands of Bunraku*; Ando, Tsuruo. *Bunraku: The Puppet Theatre*; Dunn, Charles J. *The Early Japanese Puppet Drama*; Gerstle, Inobe, Kiyoshi Inobe, and William P. Malm. *Theater as Music: The Bunraku Play "Mt. Imo and Mt. Se: An Exemplary Tale of Womanly Virtue"*; Keene, Donald. *Bunraku: The Art of the Japanese Puppet Theatre*; Law, Jane Marie. *Puppets of Nostalgia: The Life, Death, and Rebirth of the Japanese Awaji Ningyô Tradition*; Scott, A. C. *The Puppet Theatre of Japan*.

Barbara E. Thornbury

Puppet Theatre: Korea

Until the last quarter of the twentieth century, puppets were an important, popular aspect of traditional **Korean** culture, used for amusement and in Buddhist **religious** practices, shamanistic rites, and various ceremonies.

Kkoktu kakshi. The earthy, humorous *kkoktu kakshi* is perhaps the best known of the traditional puppet forms. Of unknown origin, it was introduced to Korea by wandering players from western Asia before the Koryŏ dynasty (918–1389). Never sanctioned by the government, it was performed and preserved by members of a low social class, itinerant players called "nomadic song-and-dance people" (*namsadang-p'ae*), troupes of which could be found as late as the 1920s. Plays were orally transmitted from generation to generation until transcribed in the 1930s.

Needing only puppets, **musical instruments**, and a three-sided collapsible enclosure for a **stage**, the troupe set up in marketplaces, temple courtyards, or village squares, generally performing by torchlight at night in the warmer months. A **theatre company** usually was comprised of five or six puppeteers who also spoke the dialogue, one narrator-commentator who chatted with puppets during the performance, and five or six musicians (often called upon to manipulate puppets). The number of puppets ranged between twelve and fifteen, varying from troupe to troupe.

Kkotu kakshi **dramatic structure** and content have much in common with **masked •** **dance** plays, including shamanistic remnants, a parody of apostate monks, a husband-wife-concubine triangle, and a satire of the landed nobility (*yangban*). The main character of the latter is an old *yangban* named Pak Chŏmji (the homonym for Pak means "gourd"), whose misadventures link the play's ten to twelve scenes. Another important character is a lower-echelon official, the red-painted Hong Dongji, naked and with oversize genitals, much given to horseplay, and the only puppet with legs. Satire of higher officials is delivered through the Governor, whose fancy **costumes** suggest moral turpitude.

Kkoktu kakshi puppets are unique, combining aspects of hand puppets, rod puppets, and marionette features. Held in the hand, the body rod is wedged into the head, made of dried gourd; arms are manipulated from below by strings running under the costume. Puppet size varies from fifteen to twenty-four inches tall, depending on the

Kkoktu kakshi performance given by the Korean Traditional Puppet Theatre Company, at Michigan State University, 1974. Pyo, the local gentry (center), tries to persuade his concubine, Tolmori (left), to stay with him when both she and his wife (Kkoktu Kakshi, right) decide to abandon him, finding he has another lover. (Photo: Oh-Kon Cho)

character. All puppets have caricatured features, some grotesquely so. For example, the "jilted wife" (*tolmŏri*) has many bluish spots and a severely skewed mouth. Beside human puppets, there is a pheasant puppet and a serpent puppet that terrorizes villagers in the play.

Kkoktu kakshi is no longer widely popular, but occasional performances are offered at the Folk Village in Suwon or Korea House in Seoul.

Monk Mansŏk Play. The dialogue-less Monk Mansŏk play (*mansŏkjung-nori*) is another early puppet show. Its genesis is unclear; however, anecdotal information suggests it developed during the Koryŏ dynasty to ridicule a venal Buddhist monk named Mansŏk. The performance requires several puppets of different sizes, both human and animal, including a deer, a carp, and dragon. The Mansŏk puppet's arms, which often bang its chest, are manipulated by strings looped through holes in its back. A dried gourd is used for the head and wood for its body. Animal puppets are made with paper.

Baltal. *Baltal* ("foot mask") is designated an Important Intangible Cultural Property by the Korean government. Neither strictly puppet theatre nor masked dance-drama, *baltal* has characteristics of both. The solo puppeteer, whose legs project through a **curtain**, has eight- to ten-inch-high masks attached to his feet. These "heads" are moved by the action of the puppeteer's feet and legs, while the puppet's arms are moved by strings or rods. The puppeteer, sitting or reclining in a three-sided enclosure, speaks all dialogue and sings, accompanied by musicians. His performance, satirizing the corrupt upper classes and depicting the masses' hard life, is laced with witty exchanges with the musicians or the narrator and dancer, who are on the audience side of the enclosure.

Puppetry Revival. Puppet theatre popularity waned decades ago, but attempts to revive it began in the early 1980s. Lee Kyŏng-hi (1932–) was the first to try with marionettes, adapting a Yangju ***pyŏlsandae*** masked dance-drama. For some twenty years, Ahn Chŏng-ui (1939–) and his Puppet Theatre Ch'oranyi ("ch'oranyi" may be a dialect word meaning something like "naughty children") has used a converted bus to tour plays with strong moral messages for children. Some contemporary forms, such as the open-air *madanggŭk*, have **experimented** with puppets, as have **playwrights** such as **Lee Yun-t'aek**, whose *The Dummy Bride* (Pabo Kakshi, 1993) uses *baltal* as a central artistic device in his disquieting parable about contemporary life.

FURTHER READING

Cho, Oh-kon. *Korean Puppet Theatre*: *Kkoktu Kakshi*; Cho, Oh-kon, trans. *Traditional Korean Theatre*.

Oh-Kon Cho

Puppet Theatre: Sri Lanka

Sri Lanka's traditional puppets (*rukada*, which originally meant any figure carved of wood or stone) owe a debt to their **Indian** predecessors, particularly the stringed examples of Rajasthan. Mention of human and animal puppets is found in ancient Sinhalese literary accounts, which record things such as colorful "mechanical figures" of the gods, horses, and elephants being manipulated at **religious** ceremonies in the king's presence. Leather figures manipulated by Tamil **dancers** and singers at court are cited during the twelfth century, suggesting shadow puppets; still, there is little other evidence on behalf of shadow puppetry.

Early puppet history is shrouded in mystery; at some point, puppeteers began performing in public, including fairs and **festivals**, receiving audience donations. Subject matter was either Buddha's birth stories (*jataka*), probably for proselytizing reasons, or historical tales, for patriotic ones.

The main inspiration for puppetry came from the once popular ***nadagam*** • **folk theatre,** whose **musical** instruments, texts (based largely on the ***Ramayana*** and ***Mahabharata***), **costumes**, and narrative-dialogue methods it closely imitates, although the music has largely been replaced by Hindustani tunes. The only *nadagam* role types to appear, however, are the clown and the "dancing girl." The puppeteers were themselves *nadagam* **actors** and singers, which benefited them during *nadagam*'s decline. The puppets survived *nadagam*, now vestigial, and retained some semblance of their former popularity. Some say the puppets survived when various human theatre forms waned because society's more respectable elements found the puppets more seemly than the sometimes improper actors. Moreover, puppetry was deemed appropriate as a means of stimulating religious faith.

The puppets are stringed and from three to four feet tall, with the leading characters, such as kings and princes, even taller. Such aristocrats, elaborately costumed, move very little, usually being seated. The strings are connected to one horizontal bar or two attached crossways, which the handler uses to control the movements. The puppets appear to derive from those of South India, which, however, are more sophisticated in carving and manipulation technique.

Troupes have up to two hundred puppets broken down into **role types**, such as clown, village official cum announcer, "boy-player," and "dancing girl," all of whom dance; the latter's presence is a centerpiece, although she is not originally from *nadagam*. Shows, lasting around three hours, are given on a crude, temporary, raised **stage** supplied with a low proscenium (of about four feet in height) and a central performance area—the king's audience chamber, with its throne; extending at an angle toward the audience from either side are two side stages. Dark **curtains** and roll drops dress the stage. At the base of a circular railing at the rear, about six feet high, is a ledge, a foot off the stage floor, on which the manipulators stand, hands and strings hidden by the low proscenium. Seated before and facing the stage are the musicians. A backstage chorus sings as certain puppets dance. Programming only the most popular scenes, rather than continuous plays, with comic interludes has proved successful. Audiences are mainly poor rural villagers.

Although once prevalent in southern coastal towns (the low country), and even near Colombo, the few remaining troupes have their stronghold in Ambalangoda, southern Sri Lanka; each has eight to ten manipulators, musicians, and singers. Despite the notable lack of puppetry in the central uplands, a troupe was active in Kandy in the recent past, using a style much like that of Ambalangoda, but its puppets were inferior to those of the low country. In the Tamil north, *bommalattam* puppets like those of India's Tamilnadu are known in Jaffna, where temple **festivals** were their common venue before the art petered out.

Sri Lankan puppetry is an insular world that, because of a reluctance to accept suggestions from outsiders or to open the circle to new artists, has been endangered for some years. Government support for **training** new artists began in the late 1950s, with various other innovations designed for simplification of the form put in place. A number of later developments have helped puppetry survive, including festivals that began in 1975 and that have introduced a wide variety of styles.

FURTHER READING

Tilakasiri, J. *The Puppet Theatre of Asia*; Tilakasiri, J. *Puppetry in Sri Lanka*.

Samuel L. Leiter

Puppet Theatre: Taiwan

Taiwanese puppetry includes Hakka-dialect "marionettes" (*qianxian muou*) and "shadow-puppet theatre" (*piying xi*). The most popular, however, is "glove-puppet theatre" (*budai xi*). Marionette and shadow puppet theatres are limited to particular audiences in specific regions within defined **religious** contexts. Glove puppets' venues, however, evolved from pre-1960s open-air, marketplace **theatres** to a variety of locales, including ornate **festival • stages** and television performances with puppets as tall as one foot.

Glove puppets originated on the mainland in Fujian Province's Zhangzhou area. Introduced in the early nineteenth century, they were, along with "song opera" (*gezai xi*), given in Taiwanese dialect and were the dominant forms of pre-1960s public entertainment.

The glove puppet repertoire, **role types**, style, and **music** are adapted from *xiqu*. However, the twentieth century witnessed many changes. Not only have the puppets become larger, but the venue has been expanded to include both outdoor stages and television studios. Elaborate settings and complex battle scenes are employed. The puppeteers no longer perform sitting but stand instead. The puppeteers maintain the presence of some twenty characters through narration and effects like dry ice and neon lights. Popular music generally replaces that of *xiqu*. As the puppet theatre migrated from open-air village settings to cities and television, its audience evolved from peasants and fishermen to all classes. Its repertoire now even includes Shakespeare's *Henry IV* (2002).

Alexander C. Y. Huang

Taiwanese puppet theatre performed in front of Taipei's Chiang Kai-shek Memorial by Little Western Garden Puppet Theatre, founded 1913. (Photo: Ho-yi Lin)

Puppet Theatre: Thailand

Hun. *Hun* covers a variety of **Thai** • puppet theatre forms, some of which nearly disappeared until their recent restoration or revitalization as part of the general promotion of Thailand's traditional arts. Puppets and performances are highly stylized, imitating classical **dance**-drama (*lakon;* see *Lakon ram*) rather than ordinary life; whatever their size, they wear *lakon* or **khon** • **costumes,** and are accompanied by classical **music** ensembles (*piphat*) and choruses, just like humans.

Varieties of **Hun.** "Royal puppets" (*hun luang*) or "big puppets" (*hun yai*) are old ones from the royal court that are found only in the National Museum. The figures are around three feet tall, full-bodied, and complete with body joints and limbs strung together through the body's central part; strings are manipulated from below for movement. Complex movements are possible; the eyes and neck, for example, can be manipulated to resemble those of human dancers.

"Small puppets" (*hun lek*) were created under the influence of **Chinese** rod puppets by Crown Prince Krom Prarajwangbaworn Wichaichan (1838–1885) in the reign of Rama V (r. 1868–1910). The crown prince made two sets of small puppets, one Thai (*hun thai*) and one Chinese (*hun chin*), both of them one foot tall with features like those of *hun luang* puppets. The 137 remaining *hun chin* puppets in the National Museum show their faces painted like Chinese theatre characters; they performed scenes from the Thai version of China's *The Romance of the Three Kingdoms* (Sanguo zhi yanyi).

Hun thai puppets represent characters from the *Ramakien* (Thailand's version of the

Sida (Sita), the wife of Ram (Rama), in Thailand's *hun krabok* puppet theatre. (Photo: Brad Clark)

Ramayana), whose episodes are performed with music and narrators. The puppets use the same techniques as *hun luang,* with strings connected to all important joints and limbs and then threading down through the center rod where they are hidden under a cloth bag, and manipulated from below.

"Small puppet dance-drama" (*hun lakon lek*) or "small dance-drama" (*lakon lek*) was begun in 1901 by combining two types of classical puppets. Smaller and less complicated than *hun luang* puppets, they are manipulated by three people visible throughout—one for the head and right arm, one for the feet, and one for the left arm, as in Japan's *bunraku*—and can dance as well as humans. An offstage ensemble and singers accompany the action. *Lakon lek,* revived, continues to be performed by the Joe Louis Company, where it is led by Khru Sakorn Youngkeawsod. *Lakon lek* performs parts of the *Ramakien,* the fantasy *Pra Apaimanee,* and **folk** stories. Its future remains doubtful.

Bamboo "rod puppets" (*hun krabok*), influenced by Chinese examples and older Thai forms, such as *nang yai* (see below), perform in classical Thai dance (*lakon thai*) style. They emerged in 1893, under Rama V. The richly costumed puppets, whose wooden, lacquered heads—resembling *lakon* dancers and adorned with tall, ornate crowns—have a central body rod held in the left hand, and two long, narrow sticks, held in the right, for manipulating the gracefully carved hands. The puppets, in colorful bag-like costumes, appear against a decorative background equipped with passages at either side for exits and entrances. The dialogue is delivered by the singing and dancing pup-peteer, while offstage music and a singer accompany the action.

After declining in the 1960s, it was revived in the 1970s, especially after portrait artist Chakraphan Posayakrit began restoring and making puppets, as well as perform-ing with them.

Nang. *Nang* is shadow (or silhouette) puppet theatre, the two chief types being based on the size of the "cowhide" (*nang*) puppets: the large puppets are *nang yai* and the small ones are *nang talung*. The former are used in narrative performances known from the late fifteenth century, when they were essential to celebrations glorifying the king. The shadows of characters from the *Ramakien* were reflected on a lit-up screen as poetry and dialogue were recited and an orchestra performed in the background. Although programs began with miscellaneous pieces, the main story derived from the *Ramakien*. Eventually, scripts were based on other classical sources as well.

Nang yai. The puppets are between three and six feet tall and are made of hide pan-els mounted on two bamboo rods, manipulated by male puppeteers with dance-like movements both in front of and behind a huge screen. For performances in the dark, the screen is lit from behind, but it can also be lit in the front. When the performer manipu-lates the puppet, he tilts, sways, pauses, and shakes it to give it life, dancing and moving his feet according to the musical rhythm as he handles the figure both behind and in front of the screen. **Theatre companies** have around ten manipulators, at least two nar-rators, and musicians. Daytime shows use brightly colored puppets; black is used at nighttime. Daytime performances stress dancing and do not relate the whole story. Both puppet types are arrayed with rows of aesthetically designed holes and small gaps to allow light to shine through and to further define the characters' features. Designs and forms on the panels are based on classical paintings, murals, and bas reliefs.

The **stage** sits about a yard off the ground, surrounded below by a colorful cloth skirt to decorate it. Atop the stage is a translucent screen measuring about nine by five yards, winged on each side by opaque white screens, both measuring four by four yards; the screen's frame is red. Behind the screen is a semicircular area covered by a woven reed mat.

The similarities between *nang yai* and *khon* have led some to suggest that shadow puppets were a source of **masked** dance. Both forms use similar verse and dialogue recited by male narrators, which sometimes allow for lively improvisation. Manipulators and dancers learn the same basic stamping and movements according to similar music and rhythms. Both forms are structured for dance-patterns set to the accompanying music; *pleng naphat* provides the main tunes to accompany *nang* movements, while the old-style orchestra (*wong piphat*) accompanies the performances as a whole. The musi-cians and two narrators sit in front of the screen, facing it, backs to the spectators.

The *pleng naphat* music expresses either what the character had done or would do, like flying, displaying his or her magical powers, and so on. *Pleng naphat* selections are divided into the sacred and the secular, that is, those for divine characters and those for ordinary ones. Both *nang yai* and old forms of *khon* share the same

storytelling style, using reciters and being accompanied by *pleng naphat* music. In a sense, *khon* is a three-dimensional form of these puppets.

In the early nineteenth century, *nang yai* and *khon* were performed together in a form called *khon na jor* (a.k.a. *khon na chor*, literally, "masked dance play before a screen"). Since the puppets were losing popularity, this form used them to tell the story, or parts of it, while the big combat scenes employed costumed and masked actors. Later, when shadow puppets lost audiences to films and television, *nang* came to be used for "screen," and, more generally, for movies, television, and computers. Films, therefore, are called *nang* in Thai.

There are six types of puppets, ranging from single figures in one or another type of pose, including flying, conversing, or wooing; those depicted in specific settings, such as palaces; those of multiple characters engaged in battle; and a miscellaneous group showing a variety of poses.

In the mid-1990s, as part of the celebration of the fiftieth year of Rama IX's reign, a large project began to revitalize the dying *nang yai*. Two temples, Wat Khanon in Rajburee Province and Wat Sawang Arom in Singhburee Province, have been working to conserve *nang yai* figures and to continue performances. Schoolchildren and local youths are taught to perform for interested audiences.

Nang talung. The other main form of shadow puppetry, southern Thailand's *nang talung*, likely emerged from the interaction between **Indonesian** and Malay shadow puppetry (*wayang kulit*) and *nang yai*. Probably created in the seventeenth century, it was familiar to Bangkok audiences from the reign of Rama V. It presents episodes from the *Ramakien* and **folk** as well as popular stories from other sources, including television. The puppets have been known for mocking the rich and famous and also for state propaganda. Still popular, this form includes **religious** ritual elements, such as opening prayers and offerings.

Each troupe consists of ten performers, led by a head narrator and puppeteer (*nai nang*, literally "boss-man of the hides"), with various assistants and musicians who play cymbals, a gong, an oboe, and drum. The *nai nang* creates the story, narrates the performances in southern dialects, manipulates all puppets, recites and sings the verses, and improvises the dialogue. Performances are accompanied by traditional percussion music. Stories from the *Ramakien* are often localized and woven into local folktales. Recently, modern stories and percussion have been used as well.

Still popular in Pattalung Province (*talung* is from Pattalung), where it has deep roots, *nang talung* has also remained active in southern Thailand and northern **Malaysia** (where it is *wayang siam*). It is best known for its use of contemporary references and its sharp wit that takes aim at **political** figures and current events. Performances are given at various ritual celebrations, on holidays, or at **festivals**. Nighttime performances, ending around midnight, are more common than daytime ones and, as in *nang yai* daytime shows, the shadows are less important than the brightly colored puppets.

The puppets are made of thin, translucent calfskin and painted with bright colors, and vary in size from one to two feet. Unlike *nang yai*'s frequent use of multiple-figure puppets, these always depict single figures. They are drawn from *Ramakien* characters, are cut in full face or profile form, and adopt traditional designs; important figures are well dressed with elaborate jewelry. Each has a stick placed in its center, and at least one limb can be manipulated with another, smaller stick. Forty or fifty puppets, out of two hundred or so, typically appear, and are divided into four main categories: *roop* puppets depict high-ranking figures (mostly gods, hermits, kings, and queens), who speak in Central Thai dialect; main characters, who speak in a southern dialect, are divided into male or female demons; comic character groupings; and miscellaneous characters.

The six-and-a-half-foot raised stage is enclosed within a thatch-roofed hut with a white screen measuring approximately six and a half by ten feet placed in front of it. Spectators stand to watch the screen shadows. One or more electric bulbs are hung behind the screen, and the puppets are positioned in a banana trunk and placed in front of the lamp to cast shadows onto the screen.

FURTHER READING

Tilakasiri, J. *The Puppet Theatre of Asia.*

Pornrat Damrhung

Nang pramo thai. A shadow puppet theatre associated with Isan, Thailand's northeast region, inhabited primarily by people of **Lao** ethnicity. It was created ca. 1925 by rice farmers and is still performed primarily part-time by farmers and their extended families, though a few puppeteers earn their living by performing. Puppets are generally twenty-two to twenty-seven inches tall. Stories include not only the *Ramakien*, but also Lao folktales, particularly *Sinsai*. Clowns speak the local dialect and reflect local traits, situations, and in-jokes. A kickboxing scene is characteristic: the region is famous for Thailand's best kickboxers.

Nang pramo thai uses an open-air screen set on stakes several feet high, behind which performers stand. The total number of puppeteers, singers, and musicians ranges from six to twenty. A head puppeteer is assisted by two or three male puppeteers, and at least one **woman** who animates the females. Up to four puppeteers might perform at once, some manipulating two puppets simultaneously. The basic ensemble comprises mouth organ (*khaen*), lute (*phin*), hand drums, and hand cymbals (*ching*). Some groups also add the two-stringed fiddle (*saw*), wooden xylophone (*ranad*), snare drums, keyboard, or electric guitars. In general, *nang pramo thai* resembles **mawlam**, with much singing by both male and female puppeteers.

Performances are held during the dry season (late December through March), most often at temples, and in connection with Buddhist activities, such as merit-making occasions, ordinations, and temple festivals. They are always at night, begin at 9 p.m., and last up to six hours.

FURTHER READING

Broman, Sven. *Shadows of Life: Nang Talung, Thai Popular Shadow Theatre*; Hemmet, Christine. *Nang Talung: The Shadow Theatre of South Thailand*; Yupho, Dhanit. *Classical Siamese Theatre.*

Bonnie Brereton

Puppet Theatre: Vietnam

Mua roi nuoc. **Vietnamese** water puppets, literally "puppets that **dance** on water," documented since the twelfth century. It flourished as a village entertainment in the

Red River area in the nineteenth and twentieth centuries, and since 1984 has been promoted as an icon of the socialist nation. The earliest reference, an 1121 inscription from Doi Pagoda that speaks of the king's birthday, mentions a swimming tortoise and fairy dancers (characters seen today). Performances were regularly held for temple **festivals** on ponds where permanent water puppet **stages**—like one at Thay Pagoda in Thai Binh from the Le period (1533–1703)—face the sanctuary. Older wooden figures about one and a half feet tall from the late eighteenth or early nineteenth century can be seen at Keo Pagoda in Thai Binh.

By the colonial period, the art was confined to the Red River delta and controlled by village guilds (*phuong*). All-male troupes pledged secrecy concerning mechanics and repertoire. Heading the groups were a troupe leader (*ong trum*) and mechanism expert (*truong tro*). *Phuong* performed for local festivals in ponds masked by a staging house using pole and rudder or track mechanisms while viewers sat on the shore. By the 1930s, a few groups toured with portable pools. Village performances featured short scenes showing village activities (farming, fishing, athletic contests) or abbreviated mythical, historical, or contemporary episodes. Fairies seduced mortals, and Vietnamese heroes fought off **Chinese** (or French) oppressors, in scenes borrowed from **folk theatre** (*cheo*), opera (*hat boi* or *tuong*), or current affairs. Performances began with clown commentators.

In the 1970s, President Ho Chi Minh (1890–1969), impressed by the use of puppetry to promote revolutionary **political** messages in Eastern Europe, supported the development of the Central (Puppet) Theatre (Nha Hat Mua Roi Trung Uong) in Hanoi. Vietnamese artists who studied in Prague in the 1970s first performed "land" puppets, but some of these artists began **training** with *phuong* artists. By 1984, contemporary Vietnamese water puppetry was established.

Performances are generally given by both male and female professionals in permanent indoor **theatres** using fine figures sculpted by academy-trained artists like Dang

Teu, the clown of Vietnam's *mua roi nuoc*, appears in front of the staging house that masks the puppet manipulators in a performance by the Thang Long Company, Hanoi. (Photo: Kathy Foley)

Van Thiet. **Music** is provided by professionals. Artists train formally, at the Hanoi Institute for Theatre and Film or at the Central Theatre, in multiyear programs. The Central Theatre and the Thang Long Puppet Troupe (Nha Hat Mua Roi Thang Long), led by Le Van Ngo, in Hanoi are the top **theatre companies**. Offshoots in Saigon perform at the national museum or in temporary venues at tourist sites.

Performances build from idyllic scenes of village life to stories of heroes who save the country from outside attack, and climax with mythical creatures who represent prosperity. Local urban viewers and foreign tourists witness images of nostalgia for the rural past and resolve for a self-determined future to represent modern Vietnam in a globalized world.

Kathy Foley

PUTUL NACH. *See* Puppet Theatre: India.

PUTU WIJAYA (1944–). Balinese-born **actor**, **director**, and **playwright**, one of the pioneers of Indonesia's post-1968 "new tradition" (*tradisi baru*) movement. Before founding Independent Theatre (Teater Mandiri, 1972) in Jakarta, he acted with **Rendra** and **Arifin C. Noer**. In his earlier plays, including *Ouch* (Aduh, 1973), *Crazy* (Edan, 1976), and *Roar* (Aum, 1982), Putu wrote about people failing to act decisively in times of adversity. Since 1991, with productions such as *Yell* (Yel, 1991), "The Coffin Is Too Big for the Hole" (2000, based on a one-act by **Singapore**'s **Kuo Pao Kun**), and *War* (2004), he has explored modernization's pains and frustrations.

His work has become increasingly visual, using actors, objects, slides, and unusual light sources to create a shadow **puppet**–like theatre resembling, for example, *wayang kulit*, using a huge screen to cover the proscenium. By mixing **Western** and indigenous aesthetics and conventions, his theatre strives to provoke "mental terror" in its audience through a sensory bombardment of jarring images, energetic movement, deafening **music**, and vivid color. Since 1986, Putu's group has toured internationally, and he has given lectures and workshops across the globe.

FURTHER READING

Rafferty, Ellen, ed. *Putu Wijaya in Performance: A Script and Study of Indonesian Theatre.*

Cobina Gillitt

PYŎLSANDAE. Korean • **masked** • **dance** offshoot of an earlier, now extinct, court-originated form (*ponsandae*). Yangju and Songp'a varieties of *pyŏlsandae* date back about two hundred years. It is performed in Seoul and areas north on Buddha's birthday, Ch'usŏk (the harvest moon **festival**), and other occasions; Yangju and Songp'a *pyŏlsandae* were and remain identical, with only minor variations. Preceded by offerings of food and drink to the spirits for protection from evil spirits and diseases, the performance usually lasted from night to dawn; today, shorter versions are more common (see Religion in Theatre).

Pyŏlsandae's main elements are dancing, pantomime, singing, and witty dialogue accompanied by **music** (bamboo oboe, transverse flute, two-stringed fiddle, drums).

Folk ballads and shaman songs are sung and dialogue is interspersed, with songs often unfinished. *Pyŏlsandae* dance, perhaps because of its earlier connection to the court, is considered to be more refined, elegant, and graceful than that of *t'alch'um*.

There are approximately thirty roles, but only twenty-two masks are used, requiring double use of some. Certain characters, such as the Young **Woman** and Blinker (Earth Spirit), have no lines; they only dance. Boil (a monk with a boil on his face) and Prodigal deliver witty dialogue while Elder Monk performs the most impressive pantomime.

Among *pyŏlsandae*'s subjects and themes are conflicts among monks, mockery of apostate monks, the ineffectual upper class, life and death, and problematic family relationships. The Yangju *pyŏlsandae* is officially designated Important Intangible Cultural Property No. 2. The Songp'a version is No. 49.

FURTHER READING

Cho, Oh-Kon, trans. *Traditional Korean Theatre*.

Oh-Kon Cho

PYŎLSHIN-GUT. *See* Hahoe pyŏlshin-gut.

RAINA, MAHARAJ KRISHNA (1948–). Indian Hindi-language **actor** and **director** of **stage** and screen, born in Srinagar, Kashmir. He studied at New Delhi's National School of Drama, earning the school's best actor award at his 1970 graduation. In 1972, he became a freelance director, and subsequently acted in over one hundred plays and staged over 150, presented in both urban and rural venues. He heads his own **theatre company**, Prayog, which **experiments** with various traditional and rural forms, uses creatively simple **scenography**, and has performed in over a dozen languages and toured to several South Asian countries, as well as to the United States, Europe and the USSR. Raina also gives workshops all over India.

A **political** activist—he does not deny the label "radical"—Raina believes that theatre is as necessary as hospitals. His strong commitment to social justice—he is especially upset by India's communalistic movement, in which **religion** is used for political purposes—is reflected in his play choices. He was considered an "angry young man" because of his intense, earthy acting in plays like Gorky's *Lower Depths* (1973); *Kabir Stands in the Bazaar* (Kabira khada bazar mai, 1981), an adaptation of Kipphardt's *In the Matter of J. Robert Oppenheimer* (1983); and Asghar Wajahat's *Hero's End* (Virgati, 1987). Before audiences could view the Oppenheimer play, they had to spend a half an hour at a huge arms bazaar because Raina wanted them to feel repugnance at the notion of military armament.

Other important productions include **Dharamvir Bharati**'s *Blind Age* (Andha yug, 1986), Kashmirilal Zakir's *Fortune* **Woman** (Karmanwali, 1991), *Compensation* (Muavze, 1992), **Shanta Gandhi**'s *Jasma Odan* (1996, presented at the University of Hawaii), and a Punjabi adaptation of Brecht's *Caucasian Chalk Circle* called *Another's Womb* (Parai kukh, 1988). This nearly landed him in jail when the Punjab government, which had hired him to launch the Punjab Drama Company (it lasted only two years), considered it inflammatory (see Censorship).

His multifaceted career includes using theatre as therapy for Kashmir's strife-torn children. He brings Muslim and Hindu children together to learn mutual respect. Raina's many awards include the Sahitya Kala Parishad, West Bengal (1983), the best director award from the Punjabi Akademi (1987), and the National Academy of **Music**, **Dance**, and Drama (Sangeet Natak Akademi) award (1996). In 1996, the government of Jammu and Kashmir gave him the Swarna Padak for his theatrical contributions.

Shashikant Barhanpurkar

RAKESH, MOHAN (1925–1972). Indian Hindi-language **playwright**, poet, and fiction writer, born in Amritsar, Punjab. His postgraduate work was in **Sanskrit** and Hindi. He began writing short stories while in school, and later edited the literary periodical *Sarika*. After a brief teaching stint, he turned to full-time writing, becoming an influential post-independence dramatist despite—in addition to the short "seed" plays he wrote in preparation for his full-length works—having completed only three plays; they are, however, among the most produced of all Hindi plays: *A Day in Early Autumn* (Ashadh ka ek din, publ. 1958; first prod. 1960), *The Royal Swans on the Waves* (Lahron ke rajhans, 1963), and *Halfway House* (Adeh-adhure, 1969). His untimely death prevented him from finishing *Ground beneath the Feet* (Pair tale ki zamin).

Rakesh, despite his lack of prolificacy, gave a new dimension to realism. His plays chiefly concern the relations and conflicts between men and **women**, a theme that dominates *A Day in Early Autumn*, based on an imagined artistic crisis in the life of the **Sanskrit** dramatist **Kalidasa**, who is torn between his provincial background and the demands of his metropolitan patronage. *The Royal Swans on the Waves* tells of Buddha's younger brother in an effort to capture the conflict between materialism and spirituality, and *Halfway House*—considered the first important socially relevant Hindi play—reveals a modern urban family facing collapse because of changing middle-class values. These plays have been translated into many languages.

Despite his association with realism, Rakesh ran an **experimental** workshop in New Delhi that sought ways of producing nonrealistic plays, privileging the actors' physicality over words. A vigorous literary pioneer who tried new approaches in poetry and fiction as well as drama, he used the **stage** to express himself not just with words, but with sounds, pauses, images, and fragmented verbal expression. He collaborated closely with **directors** (especially **Shyamanand Jalan**, Om Shivpuri, and **Rajinder Nath**) and **actors** to achieve his final effects, leading to multiple interpretations of his work.

Shashikant Barhanpurkar

RAMA II (1768–1824). King of Siam (**Thailand**; r. 1809–1824), a.k.a. King Nangklao, credited with creating what we know today as Thai classical **dance**-drama (*lakon;* see *Lakon ram*). Rama II reigned over a peaceful and stable Thailand, devoting much time to aesthetic pursuits. He oversaw a team of scholar-poets who reworked episodes of the *Ramayana* and **Panji** cycle (Thailand's *Ramakien* and *Inao*) as scripts for *lakon nai*. These are renowned for their beautiful verse, ingenious rhymes, and lively pacing. Spirited new **music** and choreography that complemented the scripts were also devised by artists supervised by Rama II. Under his patronage, six famous scripts for a classicized form of *lakon nok* were produced, and *khon* and *lakon* were developed to a high degree.

Rama II initiated the **training** of young girls in *lakon*. Classical and classicized popular dramas from his court remain ensconced in Thailand's performance and literary canons, read and studied as models of poetic composition.

Pornrat Damrhung

RAMA IV (1804–1868). King of Siam (**Thailand**; r. 1851–1868), a.k.a. King Phra Chomklao Chaoyuhua and Mongkut, who acceded to the monarchy at forty-seven after nearly three decades as a monk. He was fluent in many languages and studied

Western learning, including astronomy and law. He improved Siam's international standing and forestalled colonization by meeting British and French demands for the extraterritoriality of European subjects and the removal of Siamese trade barriers. He promoted foreign trade and contacts with the West, promoted modern science, medicine, and technology in the state, and established rights for Siam's citizens. Rama IV was immortalized in Broadway's *The King and I*, which dramatizes the memoirs of English governess Anna Leonowens. However, her writing and its subsequent **stage** and film manifestations are deemed inaccurate and disrespectful in Thailand.

Rama IV promoted his national culture, hoping that his refined drama and **musical** events would create, in the minds of foreign envoys, the image of a respectable, rich, and peaceful civilization. His plans to modernize Thailand included many arts departments to oversee royal entertainments. The re-established Court **Dance** Troupe **trained** young dancers to serve the court and perform the ceremonies required by protocol. Two decrees (1853 and 1861) transformed the national performance landscape. They ended the forcible recruitment of young children for *lakon* (see *Lakon ram*) training in the court, limited the use of the *Ramakien* (Thailand's version of the **Ramayana**), *Inao* (the **Panji** cycle), and *Unarut* to the royal *lakon* troupe alone, and then only for royal occasions. On the other hand, the decrees allowed female court dancers to perform outside the court, let noble houses and private homes hire female *lakon*, and taxed *lakon* and other entertainments. Finally, Rama IV formalized the homage ceremony to performing arts master(s) (*wai khru*).

The decrees reorganized Thai theatre, and led to a mixing and merging of court styles with other, common, theatre types, which led to new hybrid performances. They also added new meaning to dance and theatre as commercial, professional, private troupes under patronage connected to the royal family. Seen together, the new stories and plots, the mixing of *lakon*, and the formalization of rules helped to clarify the status of performers and their creations in modern Thailand.

Pornrat Damrhung

RAMA VI (1881–1925). Thai • **playwright**, **actor**, **director**, and monarch, also known as King Vajiravudh (r. 1910–1925). The son of Rama V (r. 1868–1910), he was educated in Bangkok and England's top schools. After becoming king, he promoted **Western** dress and hairstyles, nationalist patriotism, and compulsory education, among other ideas. He and his aides also made major diplomatic advances with the West and **Japan**, giving the nation more judicial and financial autonomy.

Vajiravudh, who debuted as a child actor in 1892, was a renowned dramatist who promoted classical and modern Thai theatre as an educational mode to communicate new ideas, such as democracy, although always in the context of an enlightened monarchy. His reign was "the golden age of Thai drama." He also did theatre scholarship and translated many plays—mainly comic—by writers like Molière, Shakespeare, and Sheridan. He supported and wrote—both prose and verse—for the new "spoken drama" (**lakon phut samai mhai**). Writing scripts based on the *Ramakien* (Thailand's version of the **Ramayana**), he created new **dance**-dramas in traditional style, introducing in them social and **political** ideas supportive of loyalty to the monarchy. His work sometimes was a hybrid of Thai forms, Western opera, and spoken theatre. Because of his pioneering efforts on behalf of *lakon phut* and traditional dance-drama, he was considered the father of modern Thai drama and of modern classical dance-drama (see *Lakon ram*). He authored around 180 plays, thirty-seven in English, making him Thailand's most prolific dramatist.

In 1904, he established the Increasing Wisdom Club to foster the dramatic, artistic, and literary arts, mostly among Western-educated noblemen; new plays were staged in its small **theatre**. His original plays for the club, written between 1904 and 1910, included *For His Child* (Hen kae luk), *Victory of Goodness* (Khwam di mi chai), *The Earl of Claverhouse* (Noi Inthasen), and *The Shield* (Ha lo). He staged and acted in many of his own plays, and also was responsible for many Western-inspired performance innovations. He maintained private theatres at his various residences.

Pornrat Damrhung

RAMANUJAM, S. (1935–). **Indian** Tamil-language **director**, academic, and **playwright**. A graduate of New Delhi's National School of Drama, he actively participated in theatre initiatives in Tamilnadu and Kerala, aiming to develop a new awareness of theatre as a meaningful art. His academic career was associated with several universities, where he sought to revive nearly extinct traditional forms.

Sankara Pillai inspired him to participate in Kerala's "theatre workshop" (*nataka kalari*) movement. He introduced a systematic directorial approach to Kerala's practice by conducting statewide workshops. He has directed in Kerala since 1967, his over forty productions including *Crime 27 of 1128* (1975), *Golden Sita* (Kanchana Sita, 1969), *The Goddess of Lanka* (Lanka Lakshmi, 2000), and *Saketham* (1982). He also directed Pillai's *In Search of the Black God* (Karutta daivatte tedi, 1983), considered both his and Pillai's masterwork; it was performed throughout India.

In Tamil, he directed **Indira Parthasarathi**'s *Time Machines* (Kalayanthirangal, 1990) and **Natesan Muthuswamy**'s *Chair Possessor* (Narkalikkarar, 1989). He also has written and directed several of his own plays, prominent examples being *Silent Voice* (Mouna-k-kural, 1994), using **folk** idioms to contrast the sensual femininity of a gypsy woman with more tradition-bound **women**, and *Possession* (Veriyattam, 1987), an antiwar play based on *The Trojan Women*.

B. Ananthakrishnan

RAMAYANA. With the *Mahabharata*, one of **India**'s two great **Sanskrit** epic poems, containing some fifty thousand lines, and describing the life of the hero Rama. Attributed to Brahman sage Valmiki, it has been transmitted orally and in written form, in South and Southeast Asian regional languages as well as Sanskrit, and has been enacted in a variety of theatrical modes for many centuries. Precisely when it was composed is controversial, but some two thousand years ago is a reasonable estimate. The text has seven sections, or books, and while the first and last seem to have less coherence and poetic merit than the others, and were perhaps composed by others, the bulk is widely regarded as having many brilliant passages of the highest quality. The text is regarded by Hindus as **religiously** significant, and Rama is understood as an incarnation of God in human form to reestablish order in the world.

The story hinges on the abduction of Rama's wife, Sita, by Ravana, king of the demons. Ravana, whose magical powers resulted from his long practice of asceticism, takes her to his kingdom of Lanka, an island off South India's coast, and tries to persuade her to forget Rama and marry him. Meanwhile, Rama gathers allies among the forest-dwelling "monkeys" and prepares to confront Ravana and his army. At the climactic battle, Rama kills Ravana and is reunited with Sita. The gods vouch for her fidelity to Rama throughout her captivity, and Rama returns to Ayodhya to rule. The story thus has a quality of good versus evil in which the divine forces overcome the demonic forces of chaos and order is reestablished on earth.

Among the many Sanskrit dramas based on the *Ramayana* are *The Wondrous Crest-Jewel* (Ashcharya-chudamani) by Shaktibhadra, and a pair of plays sometimes attributed to **Bhasa** entitled *The Statue* (Pratima) and *The Coronation* (Abhisheka). These three dramas were traditionally performed in a series for the coronation of the king of Travancore (a.k.a. Thiruvithaamkoor) in Kerala, emphasizing the parallel with the installation of Rama as king of Ayodhya in the dramas. A very different type of performance is *ramlila*, in which thousands of people constitute the cast as well as audience. The *Ramayana* remains relevant to modern Hindus, in both its religious and performative aspects.

FURTHER READING

Valmiki. *The Ramayana.*

Bruce M. Sullivan

RAMLILA. North **Indian** ritual-based Hindi **folk theatre** derived from the **Ramayana**. In scale and complexity, *ramlila* ("Rama's play") performances vary widely. Some rely on only a few performers and simple production requirements, while others involve hundreds of artists, technicians, and managers, and push the bounds of conventional staging concepts. Some are solemn while others are raucous, and in still others the solemn and raucous combine. Some are based on the public recitation of **religious** literature, and others dispense with recitation altogether in favor of dramatic invention. All varieties, however, have a distinctively devotional objective: to celebrate the divinity of Rama (Ram) and to facilitate service to him.

Rama. The premise of all performances is the story of Rama, an ideal warrior-hero at once both divine and human. Rama embodies all that is right and true, and represents the pinnacle of every virtue and skill. He is pre-eminently and unwaveringly honest and obedient, the standard by which all goodness is measured; the theatre that dramatizes his story explicitly reinforces his ideal character. Temples and shrines throughout India are devoted to Rama. *Ramlila* provides another means through which devotees can worship; many consider *ramlila* to be a direct encounter with divinity. Rama is regarded as an incarnation of Vishnu, and the **actor** playing him a literal manifestation (*svarup*) of Rama. Rama's wife, Sita, an ideal **woman**, is similarly divine, as is his brother, Lakshman. Traditionally, the actors playing these parts do not touch the ground, but are carried to the **stage** spaces on devotees' shoulders.

The Story. More directly linked to *ramlila* than the actual *Ramayana* is Tulsidas's (1532?–1623?) retelling of it in his Hindi poem *Wondrous Lake of Rama's Life* (Ramcaritmanas). This version's significance lies partly in its rendering of the story in widely accessible language, which is why *ramlila*s that rely on recitation use Tulsidas as their text. *Ramlila* is popular partly because of the increased comprehensibility it lends to a story essential to popular worship. Performances bring the sacred characters and episodes to tangible life as living illustrations for the literate and illiterate alike.

The *ramlila* story includes multiple episodes, each related to Rama's search for Sita. Regional styles include and emphasize different episodes, but the core action includes Rama's voluntary exile from his father's kingdom, the subsequent kidnapping of Sita by the demonic Ravana, Rama's search for Sita, and the monumental battle between Rama and Ravana once Sita is discovered in Ravana's island palace. Ultimately, Rama triumphs, slays Ravana, and returns home with Sita and Lakshman to assume his place on his father's throne.

Performance Elements. Performances are annual events, occurring in late fall and coinciding with the Dashehra **festival**. A typical presentation consists of ten nightly performances, the final one on Dashehra itself. This last includes two important, highly theatrical events: the death of Ravana and Rama's triumphant homecoming. The first features the burning of Ravana in effigy. The effigy can be fifty or sixty feet high; its burning occasions a celebratory atmosphere. Patrons sometimes throw stones at it. Rama's triumphant homecoming marks a special devotional moment, and patrons take advantage of the tableau emerging from Rama's resumption of his throne to worship him in the form of the actor playing the part.

Men and boys, mainly devotees whose participation is a religious service, play all parts. In some forms the boys playing Rama, Lakshman, and Sita are between eight and fourteen, chosen for their purity. Rama and Lakshman may be played by older actors elsewhere. Brahman actors are preferred, especially for the central characters. They wear elaborate **makeup** consisting mainly of sandalwood paste adorned with shiny metallic pieces requiring hours to apply. Although there is no orthodox interpretation of the makeup's symbolism, some markings identify the actors with Vishnu, and patrons read their own meanings into the rest. These three characters also wear ornate crowns, especially important to *ramlila*'s ritual character. The crown is tied to the head with ritual activity and the chanting of **Sanskrit** verses; once it is in place the actor is considered divine. Ravana, as a king, also wears a crown but his includes images of extra heads. Often, his crown is wide enough to allow two additional "heads" to hang from its brim. Each head is double-faced, front and back; another face hangs like a **mask** on the back of the actor's head, indicating ten heads altogether. Others wear lesser degrees of makeup, while some, like Hanuman and his monkey compatriots, wear masks. Hanuman removes his mask to speak.

*Ramlila*s are typically performed outdoors. Some regional forms utilize temporary **stages**: platforms with metal and bamboo scaffolding set up in proscenium style; urban productions in proscenium **theatres** also are known. Grander presentations, like those at Delhi and Allahabad, erect stages in the center of large fields, and perform in the round to huge crowds. These performances often expand to incorporate processions of floats, camel-carts, decorated elephants, and masses of devotees. Allahabad has a float-decorating competition. **Musicians** as well as narrators sit to one side of the action. Performances generally begin in the evening and continue after dark, requiring electric lighting. Amplification is common, but not universal, despite auditory difficulties.

Early nineteenth-century **Western** sources depict *ramlila* performances resembling today's. Tradition attributes the form's origin to a disciple of Tulsidas named Megha

Bhagat around 1625, who based it on his master's poem. Some sources suggest that earlier *Ramayana*-based performances may have preceded this. A *ramlila* tradition resembling **raslila** may have existed prior to Tulsidas, with his poem's popularity being linked to the established tradition.

Ramnagar. The *ramlila* at Ramnagar deserves special mention. At least since 1833, when British sources described it, this tiny town has hosted an annual *ramlila* of stunning size and scope. Under the financial patronage of the maharaja of Benares (Varanasi), Uttar Pradesh, it exceeds all others in almost every aspect. It occupies over thirty days, allowing for a more extensive dramatization of the story, and for inclusion of auxiliary episodes. It incorporates the town's entire geography, mapping the events of Rama's story onto its streets, buildings, and fields. The performance requires the enormous crowd to move from place to place to follow Rama's journey. The maharaja himself is conspicuous, arriving each evening in an antique car or on an elephant.

Ramnagar sits in a rural area across the Ganges from Varanasi, whose Hindu spiritual significance attracts hordes of pilgrims and tourists. The crowds must make the long trip across the Ganges by bridge or boat. Getting to the performance can be a pilgrimage of its own. The crowds contribute to the event's grandeur, but make it difficult to see or hear. Still, for many, the often chaotic atmosphere is primary, and simply being present is sufficient.

Ramnagar's performances are overseen by two religious authorities, *vyasa*s. Carrying large prompt books, these **director** cum stage managers coordinate the action with the chanting of Tulsidas's epic. During some episodes, the *vyasa*s must synchronize chanting and action over great distances, as the chanters may not be anywhere near the actors. One *vyasa* is responsible for the chief actors, assuring that they are in their proper places, and that they are properly respected.

FURTHER READING

Kapur, Anuradha. *Actors, Pilgrims, Kings and Gods: The Ramlila at Ramnagar;* Richmond, Farley, Darius L. Swann, and Phillip B. Zarrilli, eds. *Indian Theatre: Traditions of Performance.*

David V. Mason

RANDAI. **Folk theatre** of the Minangkabau people of West Sumatra, **Indonesia**, a dynamic mixture of martial arts, **dance**, **music**, and **acting**. Originally, *randai* was all male with female impersonators. In the early 1960s, female performers became integrated, first as singers, musicians, and actors, and, more recently, as dancers as well. **Theatre companies** are community-based, often drawing performers from youths active in martial arts schools. Several hundred, mainly amateur, troupes are active. A few have semiprofessional status and tour the province and beyond.

Randai's four key features are martial arts–based circular dances (*galombang*), song and flute accompaniment (*saluang jo dendang*), pants-slapping percussion (*tapuak*), and improvised, rhymed dialogue. Performances typically last three to four hours and are episodic and loosely structured through alternating scenes and songs that advance the story equally. In scenes, actor-combatants square off within the circular arena formed by the ring of seated dancers. Most scenes feature only two or three actors and

Galombang dance circle in West Sumatran *randai*. The performers are getting into position to slap their pants for the percussive patterns that conclude each verse of a song. (Photo: Kirstin Pauka)

concentrate on one event. Songs, accompanied by dances reflecting their mood, act as scene bridges. Melodies are drawn from a large, traditional repertoire; lyrics are created anew for each play. Depending on the mood, songs are accompanied by flute only, or by bronze kettles, drums, and different types of flutes.

The literary base consists of traditional folktales and some Arabic tales. Troupes often perform just one story, after which they are named. More professional groups have up to five stories. Performances are nonetheless varied because of the emphasis on improvisation. A lasting attraction is *randai*'s allowance for quick adjustments and commentary on contemporary events and people.

FURTHER READING

Nor, M. A. *Randai Dance of Minangkabau Sumatra with Labanotation Scores;* Pauka, Kirstin. *Theater and Martial Arts in West Sumatra: Randai and Silek of the Minangkabau.*

Kirstin Pauka

RANGACHARYA, ADYA (1904–1984). **Indian** Kannada-language **playwright, actor, director,** novelist, and academic, known as Sriranga. Born in North Karnataka, he studied **Sanskrit** at the University of London.

He began directing plays for amateur **theatre companies** in the 1930s and developed into a prolific dramatist of both full-length plays and one-acts. His socially pointed, even **political,** themes, satirical approaches, and verbosity earned him the label of the George Bernard Shaw of Karnataka. He stressed ideas over style and was accused of writing stereotypical mouthpieces instead of full-blown characters in organically developed plots. Sriranga's scholarly work included a translation into both Kannada and English of the ancient *Treatise on Drama* (Natyashastra; see Theory). His *Listen, Janmejaya* (Kelu Janmejaya, 1960) uses the **Mahabharata** as the inspiration for an allegorical treatment of nation-building.

His best-known plays—which touch on subjects like Mahatma Gandhi's ideology, the untouchable caste, independence, unemployment, adultery, and **religious** hypocrisy—include *Renunciation as Livelihood* (Udara vairagya, 1930), *Doctor-Raja* (Vaidyaraja, 1932), *Narayana of the Poor* (Daridra Narayana, 1933), *Tear the Sacred Thread* (Hari janwara, 1934), *Wheel of Sorrow* (Shokachakra, 1952), *Dark-Light* (Kattale-belaku, 1959), *Which Way to Heaven?* (Dari yavudayya vaikunthake?, 1965), *Total Churning* (Samagra manthana, 1976), and *Fire-Witness* (Agnisakshi, 1985). He staged many of these plays himself and was very strict about directors who failed to follow his precise requirements.

Samuel L. Leiter

RASLILA. Indian • **folk theatre** that dramatizes the stories of the Hindu god Krishna's childhood in Vrindavan, in North India. *Ras* indicates a circular shape important to the content and form of the performance; *lila* means "play," including, like its English counterpart, the connotations of theatre and the activity of children. As with other Indian traditional forms, *raslila* integrates **music, dance**, and drama, and is regarded as a means of worship. Because of its principal subject, and because of its historical relationship with devotional worship, *raslila* is particularly regional. It is rooted deeply in the Vrindavan area, relying on the patronage of **religious** tourists, and contributing to Vrindavan's spiritual character.

Krishna. Raslila's main character is the child Krishna, who entered popular worship around the fourth century, inspired medieval **Sanskrit** literature, and rose to prominence as the object of the devotional modes of worship that developed in Bengal and Rajasthan in the sixteenth century. Krishna purportedly was born to royalty in Mathura, about one hundred miles south of New Delhi; because of familial rivalry, he spent his youth as the child of cowherds in the forests and pastures of nearby Vrindavan. Krishna's local mythology involves the various attempts his evil uncle makes on his life to prevent him from growing up to inherit the throne. Krishna foils all of these attempts in miraculous and humorous ways.

These stories also conjure an emotional affinity by lauding Krishna's childishness. He is known for stealing and lying, teasing the village girls, disobeying his parents, getting into trouble, and generally making a nuisance of himself. *Raslila* stories delight in this impish behavior.

The mythology also celebrates the adolescent Krishna's association with the young village **women** who, hearing his flute, drop all their domestic responsibilities to dance with him at night in the forest. Among them, Radha has a religious significance similar to Krishna's. She is his foremost companion, the girl he most energetically seeks. Vrindavan temple imagery rarely pictures Krishna without Radha. *Raslila* stories of Krishna's childhood glorify his bucolic environment and celebrate his childishness, also extolling his relationship with Radha, evident in their mutual teasing, trickery, and play. Between one hundred and two hundred such stories provide the performance material.

Spiritual leader Srivatsa Gotswami worships at the feet of the actors playing Krishna and Radha in this *raslila* performance. (Photo: David Mason)

Stories with topics ancillary to the worship of Krishna also appear in *raslila*, often cleverly mixed in with stories from the standard repertoire. These ancillary plots derive from the lives of saints, poets, and other historically important devotees, and typically chronicle the difficulties they underwent for the sake of their faith, and the miracles Krishna provided on their behalf. New stories are always developing.

Actors. The importance of Krishna's childhood to devotional worship accounts for one of *raslila*'s special peculiarities. The leading **actors** are themselves children, generally between eight and fourteen, but often as young as four. They embody the principles of gaiety and play that devotion values. Typically, young actors forget their lines, confuse their choreography, lose **costume** parts, giggle, and otherwise behave like children, all of which only reinforces the event's spirituality, since this disregard for **stage** propriety corresponds with Krishna's own mischievousness. Actors are all boys, even though the main supporting characters are girls. These girls figure prominently in every performance by dancing with Krishna and appearing in nearly every story. The boys wear bright saris and headdresses, with long, black tresses clipped to their hair. When particular stories call for them, adult women such as Krishna's mother are played by men dressed in traditional women's clothes draped over their heads to hide their faces. Other males, including Krishna's childhood friends, cowherds, mythical sages, deities, demons, and kings, are played by males of almost any age.

The children most often—but not always—come from Brahman families. Those selected (via auditions) typically leave home and family to live in common quarters with a troupe in Vrindavan; their time is occupied with **training** and performing, only occasionally visiting their families. Some, when they grow older, take up other adult roles. Because these are limited, many cease acting. Some participate as musicians and crew; they may even try to establish their own companies.

Performance. Each troupe operates under the direction of a *rasdhari*, who serves as troupe bookkeeper and artistic **director**, choosing and editing scripts, arranging music, training actors, choreographing scenes, and designing sets and costumes. He may also be a chief performer. The musicians sit onstage to the side of the action, providing an almost continuous accompaniment. Sitting with them, the *rasdhari* commonly leads the singing, narrates the story as it plays out, and comments on its symbolism and spirituality.

The earliest venues may well have been outdoors, in the round, which facilitated ad hoc performances for pilgrims, who began traveling to Vrindavan in large numbers in the sixteenth century. Traditionally, the staging emulated the story in which Krishna dances with the village girls in a circle, privileging each of them equally. While that element is still essential, *raslila* aesthetics have evolved; today, the most affluent troupes commonly perform on proscenium stages, complete with modern **curtains**, lighting, and sound. These **stages**, nevertheless, are mobile. Scaffolding, **scenographic** elements, costumes, electronics, and instruments travel in trucks and can be assembled in a couple of hours. Less opulent troupes perform in three-quarter thrust arrangements, especially when utilizing temple spaces, as still happens in Vrindavan.

Troupes normally reside in Vrindavan, and perform there, seasonally. In the two weeks leading up to spring's Holi celebrations most **theatre companies** are engaged in performances somewhere in the Braj region, which includes Vrindavan, Mathura, and smaller nearby villages. Troupes are also highly active in Braj during the fall Janmashthamî **festival** celebrating Krishna's birth. Typically, festival performances consist of a series of performances, offering a different story each night leading to the holiday advent. Performances, which must end by midnight, take about two and a half hours.

Although each troupe has its own style, and each performance differs from others in some respects, certain consistent elements persist. A dramatic story is framed by dance and song, and also by ritual practice. Preliminary rites, lasting an hour or more, are essential. Ritual activity also interrupts and concludes performances. At appropriate moments, and at the conclusion of each performance, Krishna, in the body of the leading actor, is venerated. This includes admission of the audience into the performance space to engage in its own ritual worship (*puja*) by way of bowing, prostration, foot touching, financial donation, and even feeding the actor—regarded as Krishna incarnate—sweets.

After the rites have concluded, performance proceeds with the *ras* dance, in which Krishna and the girls dance in the forest. This dance, instigated either by Krishna's call or by the girls' entreaties, operates in circular formations and often concludes with the peacock dance, which finds Krishna, caparisoned in an extravagant peacock feather mantle, whirling around on his knees and toes, while musicians add peacock cries. At this transcendent moment, audiences applaud and shout praise for deities and performers.

A sermon generally follows the forest dance. Besides its spiritual function, it gives the actors time to change costumes and to prepare for playing a story. The sermon usually is delivered by the *rasdhari*, but Krishna himself may deliver it. At its conclusion, the audience may be allowed to approach to worship Krishna and Radha, seated on a dais. The drama then proceeds, accompanied by bursts of song in which spectators join; finally, spectators are invited to worship at Krishna's feet.

Pre-modern Developments. This form of *raslila* dates from the mid-sixteenth century. Certainly, Krishna dramas were performed earlier in Vrindavan, but some important things happened at this time to establish still operative conventions. Most important, attendance became a component of a devotee's Vrindavan pilgrimage, so that seeing the dramas became a devotional for pilgrims increasingly drawn to Braj from Bengal and Rajasthan. This may also have been when boys first took up the principal roles. Women may have been banned from performing as a concession to the puritanism of Bengali pilgrim followers of the saint Caitanya, who avoided associations with women. Others suggest the convention arose as a concession to prejudicial gender attitudes among Mughal rulers.

A miracle story with some sectarian variations ascribes *raslila*'s origins around 1610 to the combined efforts of two figures, Vallabhacarya and Ghamandev, a revered holy man and a devotee with a background in theatre, respectively. On a festival day at a Mathura riverside site, a crown miraculously appeared out of the sky. Vallabhacarya then chose eight Brahman boys as actors, commissioned Ghamandev to lead them, and sent them to Vrindavan to promote Krishna theatre. Despite questions about the story's veracity, these figures, along with Swami Haridas, are reasonable icons for the sixteenth-century innovation that sought to reinforce the connection between theatre and pilgrimage. Performances are still a pilgrimage activity. For devotees, these performances not only bring to life the mythology of Krishna, but make literally manifest and present Krishna's always ongoing play. *See also Ankiya nat*; *Krishnattam.*

FURTHER READING

Hawley, John Stratton, and Shrivatsa Goswami. *At Play with Krishna: Pilgrimage Dramas from Vrindaban*; Hein, Norvin. *The Miracle Plays of Mathura.*

David V. Mason

RAVANACCHAYA. *See* Puppet Theatre: India.

RELIGION IN THEATRE

Religion in Theatre: Burma (Myanmar)

Burma's primary religion is Theravada (Hinayana, a.k.a. "Lesser Vehicle") Buddhism, but also prevalent is an indigenous animist **folk** religion, notable in the belief in countless spirits called *nat*, of which thirty-seven (derived from humans and deities) are particularly significant. Most theatre artists believe in these, as well as in supernatural powers called *weitzar*.

Theravada Buddhism regards the performing arts as sensual attachments that prevent entry into Nirvana; many performers eventually gave up their art or forbade their children from entering the profession. Accordingly, performers were once considered inferior in social status.

Most theatre arts are influenced by Buddha's birth stories (*jataka*), from which *zat* ("play") is derived. Before performing, a **theatre company** offers an homage of a green coconut and three hands of bananas to the patron spirit of performing arts, the *lamaing nat*, and to other spirits who rule the local region. Most plays and **dances** incorporate religious ideas in order to appeal to audiences' belief systems.

Spirit worship is reflected in the still widespread, shamanistic spirit **festivals** (*nat pwe*), where possessed, transvestite, male (mainly) and female "mediums" (*nat kadaw*) dance and sing to vibrant **music** to propitiate the potentially dangerous spirits. The medium dances and sings about the *nat*, whom he then channels as he goes into a trance. A helper interprets the medium's prophecies. *Nat pwe*'s unique leaping and winding movements, and other elements of its presentation, are said to have influenced later forms of Burmese theatre. Most traditional forms begin with a *nat* ritual; the dancers are often polished professionals, and not real mediums.

Also emerging from trance performances was the ***anyein pwe*** dance-drama, which developed into popular entertainment after Britain's 1886 annexation of Burma. *See also Nibhatkin*; *Puppet Theatre*).

Ma Thanegi

Religion in Theatre: Cambodia

Cambodia has been a predominantly Theravada Buddhist country since about the fourteenth century, yet its strong heritage of animistic and Brahmanic traditions remains integral in numerous aspects of life, including the arts. Many performance genres have a spiritual component; some have a powerful ritual function as well. ***Robam kbach boran***, ***lakhon khol***, ***lakhon sbaek***, ***lakhon bassac***, and ***yiké*** are all preceded by a salutation to spirits and heavenly beings. Such practices—which include (depending on genre) sacred melodies, invocations of mythic and actual teachers of the arts and Brahmanic deities, elaborate offerings, and/or select **dance** or movement sequences—are meant to ensure success by asking for protection and guidance from above. *Jataka* tales—stories of the Buddha's lives—are in the *robam kbach boran*, *lakhon bassac*, and *yiké* repertoires.

The most sacrosanct *robam kbach boran* dances and dance-dramas are staged under royal auspices as part of the annual *buong suong* ceremony that asks the heavens for benevolence on behalf of the entire populace—rain in times of drought, peace in times of war.

In specific regions, local traditions serve as a kind of prayer, endeavoring to ensure balance within nature's cycle. In Svay Andet Village, Kandal Province, annual *lakhon khol* performances lasting several nights enact a liberation of water meant to call forth rain. In Siem Reap, the *trot* **folk theatre** begins at a Buddhist temple (with which that troupe is associated) and, acknowledging ancestral and village spirits along the way, enacts a deer hunt symbolizing the taming of elements that might upset nature's equilibrium.

FURTHER READING

Brandon, James R. *Theatre in Southeast Asia.*

Toni Shapiro-Phim

Religion in Theatre: China

Shamanism and shamanistic rituals have played a role in **Chinese** theatre history since ancient times. Since at least the Song period (960–1279), theatre was associated with both religion and ritual. It formed part of traditional life occasions, both domestic and communal, such as funerals, temple **festivals**, and communal exorcisms, and was part of rituals for the great clans at family ceremonies like funerals and weddings. Dramas were performed for the masses at popular festivals, usually religious in origin and intent if not in practice. The drama's content was not necessarily religious, whatever the nature of the occasion. Confucian values infuse many plays, even if not deliberately.

Some *xiqu* venues are religious. Temple **stages** were once major sites of traditional drama, and, though no longer used, still exist.

A few dramas have religious themes. By far, the most important are plays relating the story of Mulian, the longest being a court drama by Zhang Zhao (1691–1745). Many dramas, including a *zaju* and a **jingju**, were titled *Mulian Saves His Mother* (Mulian jiumu). In the Ming (1368–1644) and Qing (1644–1911) dynasties, there were **theatre companies** in many southern and northern provinces dedicated to Mulian plays.

These dramas, based on the Buddhist *Avalambana Sutra* (Yulanpeng jing), tell how Mulian's mother has been condemned to hell for destroying Buddhist sutras in fury at her husband and son's piety. Mulian undergoes perils to descend to hell to rescue her; in the end she repents and is saved. A subplot has become a short item called "Longing for the World" (Sifan) in many regional styles. It concerns a nun who escapes from her convent bent on worldly pleasure. She meets a monk with similar intent, and the two elope.

There are also Taoist plays, including some small-scale **folk theatre** styles in Shanxi and Shaanxi Provinces called *Daoqing* (literally, "Taoist songs"). These styles probably originated from Ming and Qing Taoist ballad forms, which then used temple stages for more complex presentations of Taoist stories. Mulian stories have been absorbed into Taoist funeral and other rituals.

Several ethnic minorities, especially the **Tibetans**, are not only dedicated to religion but have rich theatrical traditions.

FURTHER READING

Johnson, David, ed. *Ritual Opera, Operatic Ritual, "Mu-lien Rescues His Mother" in Chinese Popular Culture.*

Colin Mackerras

Religion in Theatre: India

Religion is essential to most forms of South Asian traditional theatre. Even the classical **Sanskrit theatre**, often regarded as relatively "secular," contained important religious elements and rituals. Ancient and contemporary forms of regional and **folk theatre** focus on explicitly religious themes, or are regarded as rituals. Theatre and drama have also been important metaphors in tantric and aesthetic philosophy.

Classical Concepts. A central classical concept is *nritya* ("**dance**"). This word, or one of the many derived from it, has long been used to denote both classical and folk theatre and dance, along with related forms. For example, the great god Shiva, in his destructive form, is known as "king of the dance" (*nata raja*), while the classical source for dramatic **theory** is the ancient *Treatise on Drama* (Natyashastra). Classical dance contains numerous dramatic elements, including **acting** (*abhinaya*), gestures,

costumes, and so on, that lead the spectator toward experiencing a particular emotion (*rasa*).

Another central concept is *lila*, meaning "play," both the play of a child and a play on **stage**. It suggests that God, being complete, did not make the world out of any particular desire, but only in a spirit of playfulness, like a child. Moreover, God's periodic earthly sojourns should be understood as "playful" manifestations of the divine, and are themselves often represented as plays (*lila*) for performance.

The most sophisticated expression of these ideas was set down by Abhinavagupta (ca. 975–1025), recognized as both a great tantric philosopher and a towering aesthetic philosopher. In his aesthetic system, as in nearly all other such classical Hindu systems, drama is considered fundamental because of its effectiveness in generating the emotions (*rasa*) that are the objects of aesthetic theory and the goal of aesthetic experience. But in Abhinavagupta's theory, drama is much more than this. Indeed, the world itself is believed literally to be a cosmic drama, and spiritual practice is the realization of the self's identity with the play's cosmic author, Shiva. As Abhinavagupta writes, "**Actor**, **playwright**, and audience have but one experience."

Drama and theology's interpenetration are also illustrated by the traditions of ***ramlila*** and ***krishnalila***, the "plays" of Rama and Krishna, the seventh and tenth incarnations (*avatara*s, literally, "descents") of Vishnu. According to Vaishnavist theology, Lord Vishnu appears on earth whenever cosmic order (*dharma*) is threatened. The best known and most popular of such "descents" were those of Rama and Krishna, who rid the world of demonic and tyrannical rulers. Theologically, these earthly sojourns are Vishnu's "games," "sports," or "plays." Dramaturgically, they are performed every year at thousands of locations, when all kinds of ensembles, from amateur village groups to hereditary performers, enact them. These ideas were developed most fully by the Bengali Vaishnavists, who developed a theology in which the cosmic *lila* of the divine lovers Krishna and Radha represented the highest reality, and the goal of spiritual practice was to realize one's role in this *lila*, typically as a servant or companion of one of the lovers. In this tradition, acting is, as scholar David Haberman has put it, a mode of religious realization.

The Hindu Epics. Away from the often rarefied world of Hindu theology, one still finds that many traditional theatre forms are closely connected to religious themes through the **Ramayana** and **Mahabharata**. *Ramlila*, a dramatization of the *Ramayana*, is perhaps the most widespread and popular theatrical form in North India. The numerous *Ramayana*s and *Mahabharata*s of literary history—ancient, medieval, and modern— have provided materials for sophisticated plays performed in Sanskrit and other courtly languages, as well as for rural and folk traditions incorporating ritual possession. Contemporary research suggests that many regional epics are "owned" by certain communities or ethnic groups, who perform them on a regular basis and who may regard them as a kind of ancestor-worship or ethnic marker. More recently, certain traditional forms of performative worship have been transformed into "tourist art," so that much of their earlier religious significance has been transformed or lost. These include Kerala's **kathakali**, **Sri Lanka**'s healing ceremonies (*bali-tovil*), the ***chhao*** dance-dramas of East **India**, and ***ache lhamo***, performed by immigrant **Tibetan** groups.

When one compares traditional Indian with traditional European theatre, one of the most striking differences is that many Indian forms are regarded as somehow efficacious. More than edifying and inspiring, as per Europe's "passion plays," they are seen as making the crops grow, healing the sick, and even leading to spiritual enlightenment.

FURTHER READING

Choondal, Chummar. *Christian Theatre in India*; Haberman, David. *Acting as a Way of Salvation: A Study of Raganuga Bhakti Sadhana;* Hawley, John Stratton, and Shrivatsa Goswami. *At Play with Krishna: Pilgrimage Dramas from Vrindaban*; Lidova, Natalia. *Drama and Ritual of Early Hinduism*; Sax, William S., ed. *The Gods at Play: Lila in South Asia*; Varadpande, M. L. *Religion and Theatre*.

William S. Sax

Religion in Theatre: Indonesia

Indonesia's earliest record of theatrical performance, a 907 AD Central Javanese inscription, describes *wayang* (see Puppet Theatre) being performed "for the gods" and the welfare of the people. Since then, theatre often (but not always) has been more than secular entertainment, related to both official religious systems endorsed by the state, as well as local tutelary and ancestral spirits.

Traditional theatre often is performed in conjunction with religious **festivals** and typically involves offerings and incantations. Performances shield against malevolent spirits and ensure health, fertility, and prosperity for sponsoring families and communities. Certain plays have exorcistic qualities. *Calon Arang* (enacted with **barong • masks**) traditionally was sponsored in Bali to ward off plague. *The Origin of Kala* (Murwakala, enacted as a **puppet** drama in Java) guards Javanese against personal misfortune.

To ensure a successful harvest, agrarian communities annually sponsor *wayang* plays concerning the Javanese rice goddess Sri. There are also *wayang* plays to summon rain and appease spirits of the sea. Instruments of performance, including puppets and masks, are also believed to be sacred; the powerful *barong* and Rangda masks of Bali, for example, are housed in temples and require blessings by a priest before use. Because they traffic with unseen forces, traditional performers often have offstage reputations as shamans and healers.

Plays frequently have religious content. The **Ramayana** and **Mahabharata** were introduced to Indonesia in the first millennium AD, and, while Indonesia today is predominately Muslim, these Hindu epics remain well known. Islam also brought its own repertoire of stories, such as the tales of Amir Hamzah, Muhammad's uncle. Performances are an opportunity for conveying religious tenets and values. Many *wayang*, *randai*, **kethoprak**, and **sandiwara** plays center on a young man (occasionally **woman**) undertaking a quest for mystical enlightenment; plays feature dramatic dialogues in which learned sages offer religious guidance. It is incumbent on performers to possess religious knowledge. Balinese puppeteers and mask artists, for example, spend long hours studying sacred texts. Many Javanese believe that the *wali*, the semi-legendary saints who brought Islam in the fifteenth century, used *wayang kulit* and other arts to spread Islam, performing and sponsoring performances at which the admission fee was to declare the Islamic statement of belief. Since 1957, the Catholic Church has used *wayang kulit* to preach the Gospels.

The nineteenth-century rise of doctrinal Islam opposed the residual Hindu-Buddhist beliefs and animistic practices that underpin much traditional theatre. Bans on theatre were imposed in devoutly Muslim communities. Muslim Theatre (Teater Muslim), a 1960 initiative launched in Yogyakarta by **Arifin C. Noer** and others to present modernist Islamic alternatives to the socialist realism pushed by socialist and communist parties, continues today in Muslim student theatre and multimedia stadium spectacles such as **Rendra**'s *Cantata to Piety* (Kantata taqwa, 1990).

FURTHER READING

Rassers, W. H. *Panji, the Culture Hero: A Structural Study of Religion in Java.*

Matthew Isaac Cohen

Religion in Theatre: Japan

Before the Meiji period (1868–1912), it would have been impossible to disaggregate theatre from religion just as it would have been erroneous to separate Buddhism from Shinto in that discussion. Buddhism, which arrived in **Japan** from the continent in the mid-sixth century, identified existence with suffering but offered teachings to escape suffering. Shinto is the rubric for the worship of Japan's native deities (*kami*). The cohesion that developed between Buddhism and Shinto is illustrated by the notion that Buddhist figures were seen as manifesting Shinto deities and vice-versa. A discussion of religion in pre-modern Japan can also be extended to include the **Chinese** philosophies of Daoism and Confucianism. Daoism sought to harmonize the individual with nature, and **actors** might take its principles into account in choosing the appropriate play for an occasion. Confucianism offered moral precepts for individual behavior and guidelines for benevolent government; its assumptions often underlie the conflict in *bunraku* (see Puppet Theatre) and *kabuki* plays between a character's personal feelings (*ninjô*) and the sense of duty to authority (*giri*). Prior to the Edo period (1603–1868), Buddhism dominated intellectual discourse, including theatre, but in the Edo era, Confucianism became more prominent but did not displace Buddhism or Shinto.

Nô, *kabuki*, and other pre-modern Japanese performing arts functioned within and perpetuated religion in three important ways. First, performances often occurred at religious settings. Second, content usually expressed religious themes. Finally, the performers themselves might act "religiously" on occasion to accrue greater profundity for their art and social legitimacy for themselves.

Shrines and temples served as important performance sites for a variety of forms, including *gigaku*, *dengaku*, *nô*, *bunraku*, and *kabuki*. In these contexts performances served both to fete the deities and to entertain human audiences. The patronage of religious institutions proved especially important in *nô*'s development in the fourteenth century. For example, the Yamato troupes (associated with **Zeami** and **Kan'ami**) long served Nara's Kôfuku-ji Temple and Kasuga Shrine. Shrine and temple **festivals** remain a mainstay of performances of **folk theatre** as well as occasionally for professional actors, such as for the annual Wakamiya Festival at Nara's Kasuga Shrine in December attended by *nô* actors. There were also numerous performances of *kabuki* and *bunraku* at shrines and temples (these were the main sites for *bunraku* through much of the nineteenth century), but the main venue for these arts came to be secular theaters in urban centers. The frequent background scene for many *kabuki* and *bunraku* plays is a temple or shrine.

It would be impossible to consider the themes of most *nô*, *kabuki*, and *bunraku* plays without taking into account how these engage religious ideas. In the case of *nô*, the supporting actor (*waki*; see Role Types) in many plays is a Buddhist priest, although of unclear denomination. In deity plays (*kami nô*), the *waki* encounters a person who he later discovers is a *kami* in disguise. In warrior plays (*shura nô*), the *waki* confronts a famous warrior's ghost, who asks for prayers for his salvation from the warrior's hell (*shuradô*). Such plays reveal the operation of Buddhist ideas including the existence of other realms of incarnation, the effects of past negative and positive actions on present circumstances, and the possibility for transcending suffering through spiritual attainment. Some *nô* plays suggest that even plants can become enlightened.

Ko-jôruri plays were often religiously inclined. Buddha or another deity commonly substituted for a living person, thus creating the "substitution play" (*migawari mono*) subgenre. Shinto animist beliefs surface in various plays, such as those about foxes that take human form to aid human beings. *Kabuki* adapted several such plays.

Religion may have provided support for pre-modern theatre but it was not above satirical criticism, as exemplified by the bumbling priests who appear in *kyôgen*. *Hooting Mountain Priest* (*Fukurô yamabushi*) portrays an ascetic's attempts to dispel the malevolent spirits plaguing someone's younger brother. The priest's prayers backfire, and not only are things made worse for the younger brother, but both the other brother and the priest himself succumb to the spell's power, leaving everyone hooting like owls.

Finally, performers act "religiously" on the stage and off to express piety and as a means to gain authority for themselves and their traditions. The ceremonial dance of *Okina* is now interpreted as an act of temporary possession or apotheosis when the leading actor dons the Okina **mask** on stage. This ritual allows actors a point of reference to delineate the core principles of *nô*, its antiquity, and their authority to perform it. *Kabuki* was originated by the shrine dancer **Izumo no Okuni**, who performed Buddhist **dances**, and who gave performances featuring the ghostly return of her late lover. *Kabuki* actor **Ichikawa Danjûrô** I attributed the Buddhist avatar Fudô for his success, and glorified him in his plays. He sponsored public pilgrimages to the Narita Fudô temple, with which his descendants still have a close association. Danjûrô demonstrated a sophisticated knowledge of esoteric Buddhism, reminiscent of the secret *nô* treatises of **Zeami** and **Konparu Zenchiku**, who incorporated complex religious concepts regarding the nature of the mind and the universe to explicate their **theories**.

FURTHER READING

Blacker, Carmen. *The Catalpa Bow: A Study of Shamanism Practices in Japan*; Dunn, Charles, J. "Religion and Japanese Drama"; Horie-Webber, Akemi. "The Essence of *Kabuki*: A Study of Folk Religious Ritual Elements in the Early *Kabuki* Theatre"; Ôchi, Reiko. "Buddhism and Poetic Theory: An Analysis of Zeami's *Higaki* and *Takasago*"; Thornhill, Arthur, III. *Six Circles, One Dewdrop: The Religio-Aesthetic World of Komparu Zenchiku*.

Eric C. Rath

Religion in Theatre: Korea

Shamanism, Buddhism, Confucianism, and even Taoism, shaped **Korea**'s early cultural development, joined by Christianity in the late nineteenth century. Various early unions of religion or moral philosophy and theatre are found in ***p'ansori*** (shamanism and Confucianism), ***t'alch'um*** (shamanism and **folk** religious observances), and **puppet theatre** (shamanism and Buddhism).

An example of the linkage between Buddhism and puppet theatre is visible in the Monk Mansŏk shadow puppet play (*Mansŏkjung-nori*) performed at temples during the Koryŏ dynasty (918–1392) to celebrate Buddha's birthday. The play, propagating Buddhism's philosophy that life is transient, disappeared in the early twentieth century. In 1983, Shim Woo-sung (1934–) and his **theatre company** Shrine of a Tutelary Deity (Sŏnangdang) resurrected shadow puppet theatre after extensive research, staging the Monk Mansŏk play four times in Korea and **Japan** between 1983 and 1989.

Buddhist themes also appear in modern plays, among them Ham Se-dŏk's (1915–1950) *Boy Monk* (Tongsŭng, 1939), Lee Man-hŭi's (1954–) *It Was a Small Darkness Inside the Hole of a Buddhist Wood Block* (Kŭgŏsŭn mokt'ak kumŏng sok-ŭi chagŭn ŏtumiŏtsŭmnida, 1990) and **Lee Kang-baek**'s *Feeling, Like Nirvana* (Nŭggim, kŭgnak kat'ŭn, 1998).

About 25 percent of Koreans are Christian. Many Protestant churches stage dramatizations of biblical stories around Christmas season, and "holy drama" (*sŏnggŭk*, new plays with religious themes) is produced regularly, but its artistic merit remains to be proven.

Shamanism. Shamanism has been the most influential religion in contemporary theatre. The ancient word *kut* simultaneously denotes shaman ritual, theatre, and a communal gathering for discussion. In the first half of the twentieth century, shamanism was marginalized because of widespread social prejudice arising out of Japanese repression of Korean culture during the colonial period (1910–1945) and the South Korean modernization drive of the 1950s. However, in the late 1960s, when **Western**-style *shingŭk* came to an artistic dead end and artists sought inspiration from indigenous sources, shaman rituals were resurrected, providing a crucial outlet for the post-*shingŭk* **experimental theatre**.

In the 1970s and 1980s—decades of military oppression and social injustices—Shim Woo-sung and others borrowed from shaman rituals to create performance art with overt **political** themes. Elements of shaman rituals also were evident in the sociopolitical *madanggŭk* (or *madangkut*), a populist form uniting students and workers, providing the underprivileged a forum for communal discussion and action (see *Madangnori*).

Two other patterns of shaman ritual applications emerged. The first pattern entails presentation of stories, legends, and myths of traditional shaman rituals in an essentially Western-style form. Representative is **Lee Yun-t'aek**'s revision of a traditional funeral ritual, *O-Gu: Ceremony of Death* (O-Gu: chukŭm ŭi hyŏngshik, 1990). Hŏ Kyu first explored this pattern of thematic borrowing in the 1970s in extensive research into ancient shaman traditions, where they were preserved. His efforts resulted in acclaimed productions of *The Curve of Water* (Muldoridong, 1977) and *Tashiragi* (a shamanistic rite unique to Chindo Island, 1979). Under the banner of "Creative Reception of Tradition," Hŏ developed a uniquely national theatre form (*minjokgŭk*), using shaman rituals along with other folk traditions. Today, Hŏ's legacy is carried out by disciples, such as **Sohn Jin-Chaek**.

The other pattern involves post-Artaudian ritualistic theatre that served as a stylistic antithesis to *shingŭk*'s realism. In 1973, Yu Tŏk-hyŏng (1938–) **directed** *Grass Tomb*

(Ch'obun), **Oh T'ae-sŏk's** surrealist play based on traditional funeral rites. Rejecting *shingŭk*'s **storytelling** realism, Yu employed nonlinguistic elements, such as light, sound, and movement, to minimize the importance of dialogue. He merged Eastern philosophy and folk rites to portray archetypal human existence and conflicts. This kind of ritualistic theatre inspired by Western models continues to be favored by many artists pursuing nonrealism.

Shaman rituals are now fully accepted as a rich tradition, some artists seeing them as an ideal form of theatre. For instance, Oh T'ae-sŏk views himself as a shaman/ theatre artist and his plays as *kut* or *nori* (as in "a game" or "to play"). Theatre artists generally have viewed shaman rituals as a part of Korea's cultural heritage, borrowing and adapting elements of shaman rituals according to their present theatrical needs rather than preserving the original forms in performance.

FURTHER READING

Soh Yon-Ho. "Ritual Reborn in Modern Theatre."

Ah-Jeong Kim

Religion in Theatre: Malaysia

Traditional **Malaysian** theatre reflects the beliefs of local communities and participants; for example, one can find animistic, Buddhist, Hindu, and Islamic beliefs embedded in various performance traditions. A tradition, such as *wayang kulit* (see Puppet Theatre), may draw upon multiple belief systems due to various influences affecting the art over time. *Bangsawan* provided a platform for stories from various sources: Arab, Persian, Indian, Malay, **Chinese**, and **Western**. Although *bangsawan* opened with a ritualistic ceremony, the art was essentially secular.

Secularism in Modern Drama: 1950s through 1970s. The first three phases of the modern drama movement, from the 1950s through the 1970s, remained largely secular. Overall, modern Malay theatre, during these formative decades, explored social values and traditions in relation to the challenges of contemporary life, in both the personal and public sphere; thus, except for several exceptions, religion per se was not a dominant concern. The exceptions include Kalam Hamidi's (1936–) *sandiwara* play, *The Child of Vows of Seven Sacred Places* (Anak nazar tujuh keramat, 1964), concerning a ruler who hesitates to apply strict Islamic law when the accused is his own daughter; his partiality is challenged as religious hypocrisy. Certain realistic plays, like **Mustapha Kamil Yassin's** *Two Three Cats A-Running* (Dua tiga kucing berlari, 1963), touch on interethnic relationships and suggest that a shared religion, specifically Islam, could create a common bond. In **Noordin Hassan's** **experimental** *Five Pillars Stand Shining Upright* (Tiang seri tegak berlima, 1973), a Chinese Muslim convert, who is a local shopkeeper, offers assistance to a poor Malay villager, demonstrating that people of different ethnicities can be cooperative; of course, the fact they are both Muslims is not incidental. The title alludes to the five pillars of Islam and to the Rukunegara, the five principles of national life proclaimed after the ethnic riots of May 13, 1969. Thus Noordin demonstrates how religion and state can be mutually supportive. Another example is Dinsman's (1949–) experimentalist monodrama, *It Is Not Suicide* (Bukan bunuh diri, 1974), about the dilemma of a young man contemplating suicide in his search for meaning and God; he stands amidst a pile of books representing the insufficiency of all his religious and secular knowledge.

The Islamic Revival of the 1980s. In the 1980s, the effects of Islamic revivalism, sparked by the 1979 Islamic Revolution in Iran, were felt in Malaysia's theatre world. Critics took the previous decade's absurdist-oriented, Western-influenced experimentalism to task for its nihilism, and plays like *It Is Not Suicide* were disapproved of for their anti-Islamic focus on suicide. A corrupt politician's offstage suicide in Kemala's (1941–) *Emptiness* (Kelongsong, 1988) was revised so that the character repented instead.

In 1981, the government sponsored a **playwriting** competition featuring Islamic drama. Islamic themes continued to surface, but in a generally moderate manner since writers may have been wary of being thought simplistic or didactic.

Noordin Hassan's "Theatre of Faith." Meanwhile, however, Noordin was shaping a more definitively religious theatre. During his "theatre of faith" (*teater fitrah*) phase, he attempted an Islamic form with religiously relevant content. In *Don't Kill the Butterflies* (Bukan bunuh rama-*rama*, 1979), the central character, Nur Atma ("Light of the Soul"), symbolizes the soul's journey toward discovery of its pure nature. In *1400* (1981), whose title marks the new Islamic century, Dolah finds life's "straight path" after being led astray by a harmful jinn. These moments of enlightenment, when characters experience a state of *fitrah*, a return to an original pure consciousness, assume a mystical or Sufi quality. Less mystical and more pragmatic content occurs in *Children of This Land* (Anak tanjung, 1988), in which an Islamic extremist is arrested; it emphasizes that Muslims must be just and conscious that others are observing their actions..   However, not all creative artists were as convinced as Hassan that there was no disjuncture between religious practice and art. Indeed, as a result of revivalism, many Malay artists began to question the relationship between Islam and art, especially in terms of theatre. Some left the scene; others reduced their participation. Also, for a period, national sponsorship for theatre competitions and **festivals** ceased. In certain states, particularly Kelantan, where **political** power was in the hands of the Islamic party, traditional forms were **censored** or restricted for religious reasons. *Wayang kulit,* **manohra**, and **mak yong** fell under suspicion since they were linked to other belief systems and thereby deemed incompatible with Muslim society. In some cases, an attempt was made to "Islamize" a form such as *wayang kulit* by removing allusions to pre-Islamic traditions and providing an Islam-related story; whether such changes unduly diluted Malay culture was also at issue.

By the 1990s, there was a renewed commitment to theatre on the part of the government and local groups. Cultural programs once again received sponsorship. New short plays, often comic, were staged regularly at Kuala Lumpur's Malaysian Tourist Information Complex; in 2000, the state-of-the-art National **Theatre** (a.k.a. Istana Budaya or Palace of Culture) opened to large-scale **musical** productions. Theatre, and other arts, became allied to tourism and economic interests.

FURTHER READING

Nur Nina Zuhra (Nancy Nanney). *An Analysis of Modern Malay Drama.*

Nancy Nanney

Religion in Theatre: Philippines

Religion—Catholicism in particular—has played a role in **Philippines** drama since the Spanish colonial period (1521–1898), and continues to do so in the contemporary theatre. Scholar Nicanor Tiongson underlines the influence on the nation's drama of seasons such as Christmas and Lent, and the celebration of Catholic saints' feast days. Among the most popular short plays in this tradition are "Search for an Inn Play" (Panunuluyan), in which **actors** playing Mary and Joseph reenact their search for an inn; the "Shepherd Play" (Pastores), which depicts shepherds searching for the child Jesus; the "Solitude" play (Soledad), which presents the Virgin Mary in mourning and singers comforting her during Black Saturday; and the "Meeting of the Virgin and the Risen Christ" (Salubong), which features angels, flying birds, **dances**, and poems.

The *sinakulo* passion play, performed out of doors during Lent, reenacts the life, teachings, and death of Christ using octosyllabic quintilla verses. Although it draws largely from the narrative of the passion (*pasyon*), its script, **music**, and **costumes** have been influenced by novels, magazines, and religion-oriented Hollywood movies. Its actors and **stage** crew are community members who see their participation as a vow (*panata*) reaffirming their faith.

Komedya may have descended from the Spanish *comedia*, but has two principal types in the Philippines: the "*komedya* of saints" (*komedya de santo*), drawn from lives or miracles of saints, and the secular *komedya* (a.k.a. *moro-moro* or *linambay*), centering on the enemy Christian and Moorish kingdoms of medieval Europe.

Contemporary plays have used religious forms and symbols to draw attention to socio-**political** issues. Among them are Bonifacio Ilagan's (1951–) *People's Worship* (Pagsambang bayan, 1977), whose structure is based on the Catholic mass; Al Santos's (1954–) *Calvary of the Poor* (Kalbaryo ng maralitang taga-lungsod, 1988), on issues of the urban poor, and Chris Millado's (1961–) street play, *Meeting in Mendiola* (Salubong sa Mendiola, 1984).

FURTHER READING

Tiongson, Nicanor G. *Sinakulo*.

Joi Barrios

Religion in Theatre: Sri Lanka

Sri Lanka has a long tradition of village rituals designed to propitiate the gods in order to prevent or dispel evil, to improve the welfare of the community, and to cure illness and induce fertility in barren **women**. These rituals include protodramatic elements, and, in a good number of cases, provide full-blown dramatic episodes. Although Sri Lanka is predominantly Buddhist, Sinhalese rituals represent a syncretic blend of Buddhist and indigenous animistic and ancestor-worshipping cults, in which religion serves the practical needs of the community rather than the spiritual needs of individuals.

Folk theatre and religion are intimately intertwined. Village rituals make much use of **dance**, **music**, rhythm, **masks**, dialogue, **costumes**, and even humor, although dance predominates. Verse narrative mingles with chanting and incantations to express stories about the deities that appear. Presentations are given in the **stage**-like "performance arena" (*ranga mandala*). The dramatic interludes often inserted into the proceedings are more likely to be concerned with providing entertainment than with furthering ritual purposes, although they are typically concluded with a priest's ritualistic observance that whatever evil influences accrued during the performance have been dispelled. These interludes are considered the bridge between ritual and the more formalized folk theatre genres of **kolam**, **sokari**, and **nadagam**.

The principal religion of Sri Lanka is Theravada Buddhism, formerly known as the "Lesser Vehicle" but now referred to as the Southern Buddhism, in contrast to Mahayana Buddhism, the "Greater Vehicle," now Northern Buddhism. As in other cultures, Buddhism here took root by absorbing many native cults. Thus, many of Buddhism's original features, such as its nonritualistic and noncongregational practices, and its emphasis on individual salvation, were altered in order to serve the need for a religion that served daily and communal needs. Practices that involved worship and propitiation of non-Buddhist gods and demons evolved to meet these needs, thus fusing local spiritual entities with bodhisattvas. The priesthood changed from individuals seeking their own salvation to those who exerted authority over the laity by virtue of special powers ascribed to them, as physicians, astrologers, and the like.

Theravada Buddhism was slower than Mahayana Buddhism in patronizing dramatic art or dance, fostering instead the noncongregational, decorative, contemplative, and less emotionally aggressive arts of painting, sculpture, and architecture. Nevertheless, religiously oriented theatrical expression eventually emerged under Buddhist patronage in the villages, in the form of processionals, **festivals**, and ritualistic activities, although never with the Buddhist hierarchy's full encouragement. The kind of ecstatic relationship between folk theatricals and dancing and Hinduism known in **India** did not arise in Sri Lanka, where the sensual aspects of representation were disparaged by a religion aiming to set mankind free of its passions.

Religious practices in which theatrical elements were present include sermons preached in dialogue style in a question and answer format, or two priests preaching from separate pulpits, with one reading the Pali text and the other commenting in Sinhalese. More significant were the village rituals in which native theatre, so to speak, appears to have been born. Their purpose was to eliminate harmful influences (*vas*) from people.

All-night ceremonies aim at propitiating gods, demons, and *rakusu*, an in-between category combining demon and god. The exorcists in charge wear unusual costumes representing specific entities, with wooden masks that can be rather frightening with their protruding features, ogre-like teeth, wild hair, and beards. Each entity has its own unique but recognizable attributes, carefully detailed in its appearance. Animals, sometimes played by children, wear simple costumes and headgear to suggest buffalo, boars, or elephants, with the actors leaning forward on sticks to simulate forelegs. Since only men perform these rituals, female impersonation—which often provokes laughter through bawdy humor—allows for dressing up as women, including coconut shells to shape the bosom.

Hinduism and Catholicism also play a role in traditional theatre. The former is represented by the *kamankoothu* genre performed by the Tamils of central Sri Lanka. These lengthy presentations, which can go on for a month in a festival-like atmosphere, celebrate Lord Kama, Hindu god of love, with professional actors sharing the **stage** with villagers, whose participation is intended to fulfill a vow of some sort. Catholicism, on the other hand, is represented by the annual performance of "passion plays" (*pasku*), which originated in Tamil-speaking Jaffna and eventually moved to the Sinhalese-speaking west coast.

FURTHER READING

Sarachchandra, E. R. *The Folk Drama of Ceylon.*

Samuel L. Leiter

Religion in Theatre: Vietnam

Although traditional performances occur at Buddhist temple **festivals** or funeral rites, **Vietnamese** theatre is more associated with entertainment than religious rituals per se. Still, spirit mediums do sword **dances** in Buddhist temples, and mediums' songs involve trance performance to extol beneficent deities. *Hat tho*'s dignified chanting differs from *hat len rong*'s incantations and psychic dancing to communicate with occult powers. Tay and Nung minority groups' religious epics (*hat then*) still depict paths to paradise and request help from the Jade Emperor. The Cham practiced ritual Brahmanism (today, 85 percent are Muslim), and performers are displayed in statuary at Danang's Cham museum.

Traditional performances were part of ritual secular offerings. For example, **stages** for water **puppets** (*mua roi nuoc*) were built with the structure facing the sanctuary so the Buddha image could watch along with the festival audience. Many episodes—wrestling, boat racing, lion dances, and events concerning beneficent figures like the phoenix—relate to village traditions that link games and fertility or exorcism. The drum connotes thunder; even pre-twentieth-century palace *tuong* was performed as part of rainmaking rituals. Though plays have Buddhist themes of suffering, few performances are clearly exorcistic or have the elaborate opening ceremonies of **Indianized** Southeast Asia.

Vietnamese patterns are closer to **Chinese**, where performance is somewhat distanced from religion, especially among the elite. Confucian teachings viewed theatre as valuable for entertainment or propaganda, but, before the twentieth century, also relegated professional performers to low status—an anomaly in non-Sinified areas of Southeast Asia. Under French influence, Catholicism encouraged extravagant performances, like *Jesus Suffered for the Sake of Mankind* (1921) of the Hot Nam thanh Giao (Southern Church), but discouraged secular drama.

Kathy Foley and Lorelle Browning

RENDRA (1935–). Javanese-born poet, **playwright**, **actor**, and **director**, **Indonesia**'s most influential literary and artistic figure. With the formation of his communal **theatre company** Workshop **Theatre** (Bengkel Teater) in 1967, Rendra (formerly W. S. Rendra) pioneered a revolutionary approach to actor **training** based on indigenous techniques, improvisation, and intellectual and ethical enrichment rather than a Stanislavski text-based approach. His "mini word" (*minikata*) plays ("Bip Bop," "Rambate," "Rate Rata," and "Piiipppp," 1968), developed from improvisatory exercises called Beautiful Movements, protested repressive social conditions under President Suharto (1921–) and conventional theatre practice based on **Western** models.

During the 1970s, his adaptations of Western plays, including *Oedipus Rex, Waiting for Godot, Macbeth, Hamlet,* and *Lysistrata,* covertly criticized the government (see Politics in Theatre). His *The Mastodon and Condors* (Burung kondor dan mastadon, 1973) and *The Struggle of the Naga Tribe* (Kisah perjuangan suku Naga, 1975) were **censored**, yet he was awarded a prestigious award for lifetime artistic achievement by the Jakarta Arts Institute in 1975.

In 1978, after participating in a reading of protest poetry, Rendra was banned from performing anywhere until 1986, when he staged his spectacular seven-hour *Prince Reso* (Panembahan Reso) to eight thousand nightly spectators in Jakarta's Senayan Stadium. Since then he has continued to head Workshop Theatre, in Depok, West Java. Although the majority of his productions have been restagings of works from the 1970s, in 2005 he directed *Sobrat* by Arthur S. Nalan, winner of the 2004 Jakarta Arts Council prize for best play.

Cobina Gillitt

REOG. Masquerade and processional form of Central and East Java (see Indonesia) featuring **dance, masks,** hobbyhorses, acrobatics, **music,** dramatic fragments, clowning, and, sometimes, trance. *Reog*'s (also spelled *reyog*) age and origins are unknown, though numerous legends exist. *Reog* is a hybrid—a spectacular *barong* mask with a tiger head and a crown of peacock feathers (*dhadhakmerak*); *klana,* a *topeng* mask depicting a character from the **Panji** cycle, and various comic masks also derived from *topeng*; hobbyhorses (*jathilan*) from a trance-dance genre found in much of Indonesia and **Malaysia**; and all accompanied by a small *gamelan* of drums, gongs, *angklung* rattles, and a raucous shawm.

No clear narrative is enacted, but a standard backstory has it that the complex assemblage of figures depicts a legendary fight between Klana Sewandana and the tiger king of the jungle known as Singabarong and his peacock companion. Klana is at first defeated by the tiger and peacock, but triumphs through the use of music, comedy, an army of horsemen, and a magical whip.

Troupes always feature a whip-wielding, bare-chested, bearded, or mustachioed *warok,* often the troupe leader, dressed in black and bearing magical talismans. The hypermasculine *warok* is traditionally in a homosexual relation with one or more of the effeminate hobbyhorse riders (*gemblak*); it is believed that avoiding sexual congress with **women** grants a *warok* great potency. *Reog* has thus functioned as an important Javanese form of institutionalized homosexuality.

Performances are typically sponsored to enliven processions and public festivities; a major celebration will have two or more troupes that can act out mock combats. Much interest comes from the clowning and comic dancing of Bujangganong, an ogre-like masked character with fangs and wild hair, and other clowns in half-masks; the acrobatics of the *barong*; and the contagiously high spirits of troupes. A climactic point comes when one of the *gemblak* rides astride the *barong*'s shoulders, already weighted by a mask weighing fifty kilograms or more.

Enactments once varied widely across Java, but the form has become increasingly standardized due to competitions, publications, mass media, and education. *Reog* is frequently called *reog ponorogo,* after the East Javanese district where it is most popular, and it is promoted as a symbol of East Javanese and, particularly, Ponorogo, identity.

Performance by *reog* troupe Wijoyo Kurdo Mojosongo, 1989. (Photo: Matthew Isaac Cohen)

Reog is also the name of an unrelated, largely defunct form of West Javanese **folk theatre** that is similar to ***longser***.

FURTHER READING

Yousof, Ghulam Sarwar. *Dictionary of Traditional South-East Asian Theatre.*

Matthew Isaac Cohen

REYES, SEVERINO (1861–1942). Filipino **playwright**, **director**, fiction writer, and, under the pen name Grandmother Basyang (Lola Basyang), a popular children's literature writer. Reyes, who wrote ***sarsuwela***s and ***drama***s during the **Philippines'** early American colonial period (ca. 1900–1946), was famous for his attacks on ***komedya***. Reyes was also among the first playwrights to use historical events and veiled messages as **political** strategies to articulate anti-colonial sentiments.

Among Reyes's greatest works are the *sarsuwela*s *Not Wounded* (Walang sugat, 1902, written with Fulgencio Tolentino), set during the Philippine revolution against Spain and concerning a revolutionary who fools a Spanish priest into marrying him to his girlfriend by saying he is dying; *Philippines for the Filipinos* (Filipinas para los Filipinos, 1905); and *R.I.P.* (1902), a controversial play that satirized *komedya*. Aside from reviving memories of the revolution, Reyes's *sarsuwela*s subverted American **censorship** prohibitions against references to revolutionaries (Katipunan) and their ideals. Other works included the Spanish play *The Fatal Cablegram* (El cablegrama fatal, 1915), an indictment of national hero Jose Rizal's trial, and *Philippine-American Conflict 1898* (Sigalot ng mga Filipino at Americano 1898, 1915), a *drama*.

Reyes was instrumental in the development of Philippine theatre and literature. In 1902, he organized the Grand Tagalog Sarsuwela Company (Gran Compañia de la

Sarsuwela Tagala), which performed in Manila and nearby regions. He also was the first editor of the still important Tagalog literary magazine *Liwayway*, and served as president of a leading writers' organization.

Two of Reyes's plays have been filmed (*Not Wounded* [1939 and 1957] and *Minda Mora* [1929]) and restaged through concerted efforts to revive *sarsuwela*. In 1994, the Cultural Center of the Philippines published the libretto of *Not Wounded* with accompanying **music** cassette tapes.

Joi Barrios

RIANTIARNO, NANO (1949−). Indonesian • **actor, playwright**, and **director**, artistic founder-director of Comma Theatre (Teater Koma, 1977). With well over one hundred productions during Comma Theatre's first twenty-eight years, Riantiarno's work is notable for its intelligent and humorous **political** relevance as well as its variety, ranging from adaptations of **Western** plays and novels (by Brecht, Orwell, Shakespeare, Molière, and Miller) to original plays dealing with poverty, social injustice, and political corruption.

Born and raised in Cirebon, West Java, Riantiarno moved to Jakarta in 1967 and studied at the Indonesian Theatre Academy. In 1968, he cofounded the Popular Theatre (Teater Populer) with Teguh Karya (1937–2001), where he was hailed as a great Stanislavski System actor. However, with the founding of Comma Theatre, Riantiarno's directing and playwriting became eclectic, fusing local traditions, such as *masres* (a.k.a. *sandiwara*) and *lenong*, with **Western** naturalism, American **musicals**, and *bangsawan*. His best-known plays, *Time Bomb* (Bom waktu, 1982) and *The Cockroach Opera* (Opera kecoa, 1985), highlight issues of social inequality and political corruption through a humorous, yet tragic, story about Jakarta's sex workers. Riantiarno's criticism of Suharto's (1921–) repressive New Order government (1966–1998) led the Department of Tourism and Education to **censor** a production of *Sampek Entay* (1989) in Medan, and in 1990 the Jakarta police shut down performances of *Succession* (Suksesi, 1990) and *The Cockroach Opera*, claiming they would incite social unrest—which never materialized. Until 1998, Riantiarno had to request special permission to perform above and beyond permits required by other groups. More recent plays include *Semar Accuses* (Semar gugat, 1995), *The Constipated Opera* (Opera sembelit, 1998), and *Bagong Republic* (Republik Bagong, 2000).

Cobina Gillitt

RIBOET, MISS (1900?−1965). Indonesian • **actress**, famous on **stage**, radio, and gramophone in the 1920s and 1930s. Miss Riboet was the prima donna of Miss Riboet's Orion, a *tonil* • **theatre company**, formed in 1925 by Riboet's husband, Tio Tek Djien (1895–1975), as the resident troupe in an amusement park Tio owned in Central Java. The park closed, but the company toured Southeast Asia, with Miss Riboet as headliner.

Orion's initial repertoire consisted of "extravaganzas" influenced by Hollywood films. Riboet's reputation was made as the eponymous swashbuckling bandit of *Juanita de Vega*. Original plays written for Riboet by Tio, Njoo Cheong Seng (1902–1962), and other company **playwrights**, such as *Singapore after Midnight* and *The Crow of Solo* (Gagak Solo) followed. These vehicles were interspersed with comic sketches and "modern" song and **dance** numbers (for example, the Charleston) accompanied by a jazz band.

Orion's success inspired imitators, most notably the Dardanella company. Riboet as comedienne has been likened to Mae West, and she was famed for her vocal range. Her gramophone recordings, prized by collectors, demonstrate her switching effortlessly from Tin Pan Alley songs to Indonesian **folk** and classical styles. Her popularity led to lucrative recording contracts and merchandise, including Miss Riboet brand pocket watches and facial powder. She was screen-tested in the 1930s but was considered unphotogenic. Orion disbanded with **Japan**'s 1942 occupation. An attempt in the 1950s to rebrand Riboet as dance impresario failed.

Matthew Isaac Cohen

RICHARDS, NORAH (1876–1971). Irish-born **director**, **actress**, and **playwright**, who moved to the Punjab, **India**, with her minister husband, Philip Ernest Richards, in 1911, and became an English professor at Dyal Singh College, Lahore. A veteran of the British Shakespearean companies run by Ben Greet and F. R. Benson, and a graduate of Oxford University, where she had **acted**, she began her Indian theatre work by staging *A Midsummer Night's Dream* with her students, after which she taught acting and playwriting. Unhappy with the low quality of local theatricals, mostly in the **Parsi theatre** vein, she set about introducing high-quality Irish drama from the Abbey Theatre to her students in 1912, but also including plays she wrote herself (these later were translated into Punjabi) in the vein of Lady Gregory's one-acts about village life. These included "Sati," "Valmiki," "Gautama," and "Mother Earth."

She was recognized as the founder of modern Punjabi theatre when she began organizing annual one-act competitions in 1912. She also wrote a number of brief treatises on theatre craft. In 1915, she founded the Saraswati Stage Society. Following her husband's death in 1920, she returned to England, but, in 1924, went back to Lahore. In 1935, the government of the Kangra district (in what later became Himachal Pradesh) gave her a fifteen-acre site in Andretta, which she made her home following Partition (1947). There she instituted an artists' center and a **training** program equipped with its own amphitheatre.

In 1970, the ninety-four-year-old Richards was made an honorary doctor of literature by Punjabi University.

Samuel L. Leiter

ROBAM KBACH BORAN. **Cambodian** classical **dance** genre (a.k.a. *lakhon kbach boran* and *robam boran*), traditionally considered sacred and associated with royalty. Cambodians trace this highly refined form, meaning "theatre using ancient gestures," to the Angkor empire (ninth through early fifteenth centuries). Angkor's monumental temples were festooned with tens of thousands of bas-reliefs of "celestial dancers" (*apsara*s). Live dancers were associated with—and apparently belonged to—the kings and temples. In modern times, dancers were part of the king's harem until 1941.

Robam kbach boran embodies legato, almost otherworldly grace. Movements incorporate extreme angles at hips, knees, ankles, elbows, and wrists, a gently arched torso, hyper-curved fingers, and hyper-extended elbows. "Gestures" (*kbach*) derive from the *chha banchos*, an hour-long movement sequence, which also forms the basis for **training**. *Kbach* sometimes represent specific actions, generally when a sung narration accompanies the dance. When there is no narration, the same *kbach*—even within the same dance—may be abstract. Dances with a prominent storyline are *roeung*.

Traditionally performed entirely by **women**, *robam kbach boran* has four distinct **role types**—female, male, ogre, and monkey—each with its own versions of the *kbach*. Normally, a dancer will play only one of these roles for the whole of her career, though a few have played both males and ogres, which have similar *kbach*, and a very few have played both females and males. Since the 1940s, the monkey role (*sva*) has been played by boys or men. Men may also play comic characters in dance-dramas.

Lavish **costumes**, based on coronation attire, are sewn from rich brocades and velvets spangled with sequins and bugle beads in dense, geometric designs. Each role type has its distinctive costume, though individual characters or dances use variations of these.

Traditionally considered sacred, *robam kbach boran* has been used to facilitate communication between earthly beings and the supernatural world. Until the overthrow of Cambodia's monarchy in 1970, this royal form figured in key **religious** events, such as the annual Boat Race **Festival** (Bon Om Tuk), a.k.a. the Water Festival, in which ceremonies predict the land's fertility for the next harvest. Important royal receptions invariably feature *robam kbach boran*.

The traditional repertory was based in religion, drawn largely from the *Reamker*, (the Khmer ***Ramayana***), and from legends of Theravada Buddhism, such as the story of the ascetic Preah Vessandar. In the 1950s, Queen Mother **Sisowath Kossamak**, influenced perhaps by **Western** ballet, had masters choreograph group dances, including the *Apsara Dance* and *Tep Monorom*, with more emphasis on abstract movement.

Given its ties to royalty, Cambodia's traditional dance was a particular target of the Khmer Rouge. The great majority of the dancers perished, and costumes and other materials were destroyed. After the Khmer Rouge's defeat in 1979, rebuilding the dance became a priority, with the few remaining masters, such as **Chea Samy**, working to **train** a new generation. Several major **theatre companies** now perform, including one based at the Royal University of Fine Arts, a "National" company, which performs for tourists and other public events, and a third company near Angkor. Smaller companies perform around the country.

The *robam kbach boran* group dance *Tep Monorom*, performed here at the royal palace, 1989. Huy Srey Phousita (in front) and the two dancers to the left are performing the female role. The woman on the right, in the epaulettes, is dancing a male role. (Photo: Eileen Blumenthal)

FURTHER READING

Phim, Toni Samantha, and Ashley Thompson. *Dance in Cambodia*.

Eileen Blumenthal

ROLE TYPES

Role Types: Cambodia

The characters of **Cambodia**'s **dance**-drama genres *robam kbach boran* and *lakhon khol* are divided into four main types, each with its own **costume** and movement style. "Females" (*neang*) have the most delicate gestures (*kbach*) and are played by the most beautiful, round-faced dancers. "Males" (*nearong*) use a wider stance and slightly broader gestures and are played by taller performers. "Giants" and "ogres" (*yeak*) have the most expansive *kbach*, and are played by the tallest, largest-boned dancers. Finally, the "monkeys" (*sva*) use more acrobatic, comic *kbach*, including somersaults and scratching.

In the 1940s, Queen Mother (later, Queen) **Sisowath Kossamak** began casting male dancers as *sva* in *robam kbach boran*, something that would have been impossible before 1941 because the royal troupe, which set the standard, was part of the royal harem. She brought in *sva* from *lakhon khol*, whose gestures were similar but more robust.

Comic characters—hermits or elderly people—also sometimes appear. These are typically played by older ex-dancers using gestures partway between natural movement and formal dance *kbach*.

Lakhon bassac, *yiké*, and *lakhon sbaek* include basic role types resembling those of *robam kbach boran*—but clowns are a requisite part of the cast. With their physical comedy and license for verbal irreverence, they often are popular favorites. In *lakhon bassac*, the types also reflect those of **Chinese •** *xiju* and **Vietnamese •** *cai luong*, including prime ministers and generals as well as royals. *Lakhon bassac* ogres and other supernatural or superstrong characters wear boldly colored and patterned **makeup**, like *xiju* "painted face" (*hualian*) characters, rather than wearing **masks** as *robam kbach boran* ogres do.

In *lakhon sbaek* shadow **puppet** plays, male characters appear in profile and females full face; *yeak* are similar in size to the royal heroes, unlike Javanese and Balinese (*see* Indonesia) ogres, who dwarf the refined characters.

See also Role Types: Southeast Asia.

Eileen Blumenthal

Role Types: China

Origins for the *xiqu* practice of classifying **actors** and dramatic characters according to role types (*hangdang*) can be seen as early as the Tang dynasty (618–907), in the "adjutant" (*canjun*) or "butt" and "gray hawk" (*canggu*) or "knave" of **canjun xi**. In the Song dynasty (960–1279), these roles developed respectively into the *fujing* and *fumo* of Song **zaju**, and were supported by functionaries and stock characters, such as the "impersonated female-role" (*zhuangdan*) and the "impersonated official" (*zhuanggu*).

The leading comic roles of these early forms were supplanted by a leading male and female role with the rise of fully synthesized *xiqu*: the "male" (*sheng*) and "female" (*dan*) of **nanxi**, and the *zhengmo* and *zhengdan* of Yuan dynasty (1280–1368) *zaju*. The earlier leading roles developed into the often comic supporting roles of these new forms: the *jing* of Yuan *zaju*, and the *jing* and "clown" (*chou*) of *nanxi*. These four basic categories remain the most fundamental today:

> *sheng*: male characters drawn closely from life;
>
> *dan*: female characters;
>
> *jing*: larger-than-life male characters, often called "painted faces" (*hualian*); and
>
> *chou*: comic or despicable characters, usually male.

During the Ming (1368–1644) and Qing (1644–1911) dynasties, many individual types developed within these categories in each of the growing number of *xiqu* forms; role types that are essentially the same may have different names, and some are unique to specific forms.

Each type indicates age, gender, and, often, social status, position, personality, and/or temperament. The performance of each requires a particular balance of song, speech, **dance**-acting, and, sometimes, combat skills; each type has its own version of these skills, stylization patterns, and conventions that make it immediately recognizable. Rigorous **training** is required, with actors generally performing one type only. However, since the early twentieth century actors have combined and expanded traditional types in creating new plays.

Kunqu *Role Types*. *Kunqu* roles evolved from those for *nanxi* and **chuanqi**. As Qing *kunqu* troupes competed with those of regional theatre, roles proliferated within each major category to showcase actors' talents. With the success of *chuanqi*'s *The Lute* (Pipa ji), *sheng* actors were restricted to sympathetic males. In Ming *kunqu*, *sheng* played dignified males either in leading (*zhengsheng*) or supporting "young male" (*xiaosheng*) roles. By mid-Qing, age distinctions were evident: *sheng* (or *zhengsheng*) played older males, *xiaosheng* young romantic males, and bearded, high-status "older men" (*laosheng*). By late-Qing, *xiaosheng* had evolved from secondary to principal male role and branched into subtypes called "official" (*guansheng*), "turbaned" (*jinsheng*), "down-at-heel" (*xiepi sheng*), and "pheasant-tailed" (*zhiwei sheng*).

The *dan*'s evolution followed that of the *sheng*. Starting with *The Lute*, it was limited to dignified female characters, and in *kunqu* was differentiated into highborn females, beautiful and typically young (*zhengdan*), vivacious females younger than the *zhengdan* character and often paired with her and "older females" (*laodan*). In Qing, the role splintered further. *Zhengdan* came to portray middle-aged or young chaste women and to possess large voices of high range, while specialized *dan* included "boudoir *dan*" (*guimen dan*), "wind and moon *dan*" (*fengyue dan*), and *laodan*; in late Qing, a "martial *dan*" (*wudan*) was added.

In *nanxi* and early *chuanqi*, *jing* portray villainous or comic characters of any status. By mid-Ming, the role was increasingly limited to characters too large or rough-hewn for the more genteel male roles (*sheng*, and the *wai* and *mo* roles inherited from *nanxi*). Thus arose specialized types dubbed "young *jing*" (*zhengjing*; later, *damian*), "villain *jing*" (*fujing*; later, *baimian* and *lata baimian*).

The *chou*, like the *sheng*, originated in *nanxi*. In *kunqu*, *chou* portray humorous commoners or secondary villains. The humorous *chou* wears short garments and white **makeup**

"Military female" (*wudan*) character and another figure in the *jingju* military scene "Gift of the Sword" from *Phoenix Mountain*. (Photo: Yuan Shuo; Courtesy of Jiangsu Provincial Kunqu Troupe)

covering half the eyes, has comedic skills, and speaks in dialect. The villainous *chou* wears a long gown and white makeup extending beyond the eyebrows, and combines acting skills from a variety of other roles. Each type plays both military and civil characters.

Jingju *Role Types.* *Jingju* types, like *kunqu*'s, are firmly based in the four main *sheng*, *dan*, *jing*, and *chou* categories. *Sheng* are classified within three major role types. *Laosheng*, generally over thirty and wearing three-part beards, and "martial older *sheng*" (*wu laosheng*). "Martial males" (*wusheng*) also over thirty, are not bearded; subtypes are the "long armor" (*changkao*), high-ranking warriors who specialize in weapons' combat, and the "short fighting" (*duanda*), lower-ranking warriors, bandits, and spirits, who fight with weapons and acrobatics.

"Young males" (*xiaosheng*) are unmarried, under thirty, and beardless; subtypes include the "civil young male" (*wen xiaosheng*), for young lovers and scholars, and the "martial young male" (*wu xiaosheng*), for high-ranking young warriors.

Jingju females have four major types. *Laodan* are dignified matriarchs of great age. "Blue garments" (*qingyi*) are demure, often impoverished, characters of great inherent dignity. "Boudoir *dan*" (*guimen dan*) are livelier, youthful *qingyi*, usually of high social status. They are sometimes classified under "flower female" (*huadan*), vivacious and frequently comedic young women, often of lower social status.

Wudan are generally more dignified than *huadan*; combat with weapons is the featured skill. A subtype is the "sword and horse *dan*" (*daoma dan*). The "flower shirt" (*huashan*) combines qualities of the *qingyi*, *huadan*, and *wudan*; it was developed by **Mei Lanfang** and others to portray more multifaceted roles.

Jing characters in *jingju* possess extraordinary strength, including great heroes, gods, and spirits. Most wear broad, solid beards; all have colorful makeup. They use a booming "natural" voice and are classified in three major role types: the "great painted face" (*da hualian*), the "second painted face" (*er hualian*), and the "martial painted face" (*wu hualian*).

Chou, a.k.a. "little painted face" (*xiao hualian*), though not necessarily comic, may improvise and directly address the audience. Generally less dignified than *sheng*, they employ a natural voice, usually have a patch of white makeup around their nose and eyes, and are classified as "civil *chou*" (*wenchou*), encompassing numerous subtypes representing scholars, officials, aristocratic youth, working commoners, comic old men, and comic female impersonation roles (*choudan*), and "martial *chou*" (*wuchou*), requiring combat with weapons and acrobatics.

Group characters, such as attendants and soldiers, are represented by the "dragon set" (*longtao*), once a separate type but now generally an ensemble function. *Longtao* usually enter in sets of four, and often stand motionless upstage, creating atmosphere for imperial and law courts.

FURTHER READING

Mackerras, Colin, ed. *Chinese Theatre from Its Origins to the Present Day*; Scott, A. C. *The Classical Theatre of China*; Yihe, Zhang, ed. *Chinese Theatre*.

Elizabeth Wichmann-Walczak and Catherine Swatek

Role Types: India

In many traditional **Indian** theatre forms, **actors** in **masks**, or just **costumes** and **makeup**, perform as gods, heroes, heroines, and villains, and audiences—based on their faith in and memory of the Hindu epics—accept them as standing in for the real deity or legendary figure. The actors, praised for their skill in embodying the character's ideal form, do not become the character as much as animate it in minute detail. Sometimes, actors will call down the character's spirit and enter a trance, becoming possessed by the spirit and allowing it to control their actions. With or without trance, through performance, characters become dynamic spiritual forces, blessing the audience with their living presence.

Natyashastra *Classifications.* The earliest attempt to delineate role types comes from the **Sanskrit** dramaturgical *Treatise on Drama* (Natyashastra; see Theory), which divides the moral temper of characters into three basic types, "superior" (*uttama*), "middling" (*madhyama*), and "inferior" (*adhama*). Superior characters are wise, benevolent, and artistically skilled. Though morally upright, they are not ascetic and are chiefly distinguished from middling characters by their virtuosity. Inferior characters have vulgar personalities and incline toward crime and treachery. Expanding on this three-part division are "mixed" characters, those of unstable temperament or uncertain gender.

The *Natyashastra* advises that actors of a particular build and personality are best suited for playing similar kinds of characters, implying that actors may have been role-type specialists. But elsewhere this source allows for much latitude in who may perform which roles; only the clown (*vidushaka*) is distinguished as a unique role requiring a specialist; this may be because clowns often had a physical deformity that kept them from performing other roles. Furthermore, the *Natyashastra* allows men and **women** to perform roles of different genders according to their ability. Indeed, it seems all-female casts were commonly employed in both secular and **religious** contexts. One of the few specific casting prohibitions concerns older actors playing younger roles and younger actors playing older roles, echoing the *Natyashastra*'s persistent concern for beauty and proportion.

An important role was the *sutradhara*, something of a lead actor, **stage** manager, and **director** for the **theatre company**. While not exactly a role type, the *sutradhara* appeared in each production to introduce the play with a brief scene that was neither entirely outside the play nor directly a part of its narrative. His function has metamorphosed in many traditional forms, such as the *naik* in **bhavai** and the *adhikari* in **jatra**, performers who act both as troupe leader and scene introducer.

Comic Characters. The *Natyashastra* states that the *vidushaka* should be the hero's companion and be expert in conversation, but does not elaborate. The many clowns in extant plays usually are high-caste Brahmans who speak only in common Prakrit rather than elite Sanskrit. These lazy, cowardly, and gluttonous fools provide the useful function of bringing the otherwise lofty language and sentiments down to earth.

Traditional forms of South Asian theatre almost universally use a *vidushaka*-like character. In **kutiyattam**, the closest surviving ancestor to Sanskrit theatre, the *vidushaka* has another important function, speaking in the regional language of Malayalam to translate the inscrutable Sanskrit and forming an important bridge between past and present. Even religious dramas deem humor essential. Mansukha, the clown in **raslila**, plays an idiot friend of Krishna, enlivening the performance with his antics. The clown may also double as a master of ceremonies, as in the *songadhya* role in **tamasha** and the *kattiyankaran* in **terukkuttu**, where the character may stand outside the action and comment on it. The comic character is not always represented as an idiot; he may be someone with a different perspective, as in **nautanki** where Munshiji acts as the household accountant and comically interjects mundane and incongruous financial issues into otherwise serious romantic narratives.

Morality as a Classifier. The distinction of types based on morality has parallels in many traditional South Asian performing arts. Indeed, role types are much more clearly delineated and elaborated on in many **folk theatre** forms than in the *Natyashastra*. **Kathakali**'s character classification is similar to other forms in how it distinguishes between many different types depending on moral character and heroic stature, aspects readily reflected in their makeup. The most refined and heroic characters are green-faced (*pacca*), like Rama, avatar of Vishnu and hero of the **Ramayana**. Krishna is the exception, being depicted, uniquely, in blue. Brahmans and females have more naturalistic makeup and are classified as "shining characters" (*minukku*). Their level of virtue is similar to the *pacca*, but they are not engaged in heroic actions. Villains are called "knife" (*katti*) and their makeup base is bright red. *Katti* wear costumes and crowns similar to the *pacca*, indicating that, though they lack virtue, they are still noble and possess heroic stature. Less refined characters are included in the "bearded" (*tadi*) class, subdivided into three beard colors: white, red, and black. Virtuous, though less refined, are the white-beards, whereas red-beards are more vulgar equivalents of the *katti*; black-beards represent the most savage of creatures, lacking all civility and representing the bestial cruelty found in forest-dwelling demons (*raksasha*).

Several other traditional forms, such as *kuttiyattam*, *raslila*, **ramlila**, *terukkuttu*, **yakshagana**, and the various **chhau** styles, also represent a range of characters using a color scheme. Of course, each tradition has developed its own symbols and elaborate patterns, but all possess a three-part division with refined and noble characters, a distinct class of nonheroic characters who are neither good nor evil, and a demonic class possessing the universe's uncivilized and chthonic powers.

Demons. Demons have a special place in many forms, being both feared and revered for their terrible power. Demons are not just to be vanquished by heroes; in many cases they are worshipped and act as guardian spirits, as in the "Visages of Glory" demon heads (*kirimukhas*) adorning temple gateways. Possession has long been a means to exorcise the hold demons have over the living. This process is most strikingly seen in **Sri Lanka**'s *sanni yakuma* (a.k.a. *bali-tovil* or *thovil*) "devil dance" where eighteen sickness-causing demons are brought forth to be propitiated and duped into letting go of their victim. The point is not to destroy these demons but to put them in their proper place through the use of ritual and laughter.

FURTHER READING

Richmond, Farley, Darius L. Swann, and Phillip B. Zarrilli, eds. *Indian Theatre: Traditions of Performance*.

Robert Petersen

Role Types: Japan

Nô. Roles in **nô** are categorized as either *shite*, *waki*, *tsure*, *kokata*, or **kyôgen**-*kata*. Technically, these are not really "role types." Principally, the *shite* ("doers") are characters on whom the play focuses, the *waki* ("side characters") are those who facilitate and observe the action of the *shite*, the *tsure* ("companion") are lesser characters, the *kokata* ("child characters") are played by children, and the *kyôgen-kata* (or *ai-kyôgen*) are the lower-class characters, played by *kyôgen* **actors**, who perform the spoken, explanatory interludes between the two acts of a play, and sometimes appear in certain secondary roles. Many plays have only the *shite*, *waki*, and *kyôgen-kata*, and actors **train** to play one of these three. In fact, *shite*, *waki*, and *kyôgen-kata* are terms also used to refer to the actors who specialize in these roles; they never cross over and play one of the others.

Shite are frequently ghosts who have returned to the world of the living in search of spiritual solace. In such cases, the *waki* is a priest who enables the *shite*'s quest. *Shite* can also be crazed, living characters, similarly in search of spiritual solace and aided in some way by the *waki*. In both cases, the *shite*'s torment arises from anguish generated by tragedy: typically, violent or premature death in the first case (often male characters), or the loss of a child, for example, in the second (female characters). *Shite*, of course, are often living characters, and their stories are not necessarily tragic.

Kyôgen. In *kyôgen*, *nô*'s comedic companion form, the roles presumably corresponding to *nô*'s *shite* and *waki* are called *shite* (or *omo*) and *ado*; despite this correspondence, they often have more or less equal importance in the action of the play. There are also companion roles in *kyôgen*. Common character types in *kyôgen* are paired lords and servants. Lords can be found as either *shite* or *ado*, depending on the play's focus. Family members—for example, husbands and wives—are also paired. Priests and animals are often *shite*. Unlike the *waki* priests of *nô*, *kyôgen* priests are usually *shite* who are mocked for their abilities and powers. With both paired adversaries and the priest and animal characters, the foibles of men and the serious tone of *nô* are directly exposed and made available for consideration.

Bunraku. In *bunraku*, roles are categorized according to **puppet** head types. Heads have been carved according to three considerations: gender, age, and degree of good or evil. Static heads often forced **playwrights** to create characters with consistently good or bad natures, although heads that could transform through the puppeteer's manipulation of changeable parts allowed for complex characters. Heads are typically called by the name of the first character to make the type significant (for example, *kiichi*, old man of good nature; *danshichi*, middle-aged man of bad nature; both named for specific characters but used in plays with similar types) or by the type of character; thus "young man" (*wakaotoko*); "young woman" (*musume*); or "courtesan" (*keisei*). There are also heads for children and minor characters, such as maids or samurai footmen. These might be considered equivalent to the companion roles in *nô* and *kyôgen*.

Kabuki. The role types (*yakugara*) of *kabuki* began with *nô* categories. In early *kabuki* there were female leads (*shite*), male characters to act opposite the *shite* (*waki*), and any others (*tsure*), together with a *kyôgen*-like comic category, *saruwaka*. After actresses were banned in 1629, actors were required to act either "male roles" (*otokogata*) or "female roles" (*onnagata*). With the passage of time and the increasing complexity of plays, new types developed according to gender, age, and nature. By the last quarter of the seventeenth century, eight types clearly emerged: from the *shite* came the "young female" (*wakaonnagata*) and the "young male" (*wakashugata*); from the *waki* came the "leading man" (*tachiyaku*) and the "villain" (*katakiyaku*); from *saruwaka* came the "comic roles" (*dôkegata* or *sanmaime*, literally, "third board" because of the position of their billboard outside of **theatres**); and from the *tsure* came the "elderly **woman**" (*kashagata*), "elderly man" (*oyajikata*), and "child's role" (*koyaku*).

Gradually, subtypes proliferated, so that there were eventually up to forty. For example, out of the *wakaonnagata* type came the young "daughter" (*musume*), "red princess" (*akahime*, a term inspired by her [usually] red kimono), and "courtesan" (*oiran* or *keisei*, literally, "castle-destroyer"). *Tachiyaku* included weak, youthful, romantic heroes acted in the "gentle style" (*wagotoshi*); less petulant, dashing young lovers (*nimaime*, literally, "second board" because of their billboard's position); mature heroes who handle tragic situations with intelligence and distinction (*jitsugotoshi*); and subtypes of the latter, including "men of judgment" (*sabakiyaku*) and "men of patience" (*shinbôyaku*). Specific villains are "red faces" (*akkatsura*, named for the color of their **makeup**), "evil women" (*akuba*), "poison women" (*dokufu*, women who commit heinous crimes), and "comic villains" (*handôgataki*).

At first, most actors specialized in a type. After general **training**, a specialization was usually chosen by the mentor in the teenage years, based on physical characteristics, talent, and the family traditions. However, in the nineteenth century, the system began to break down, as more actors played multiple types—male and female, young and old, hero and villain—and gained renown as "versatile actors" (*kaneru yakusha*).

As with **Western** theatre's "lines of business," plays were created for specific actors and their types. Playwrights were required to prepare plays that gave each important company member the chance to shine, meaning that they had to write characters whose movements, voice patterns, and internal and external characteristics were of the type that the actor was trained to portray.

FURTHER READING

Leiter, Samuel L. *New Kabuki Encyclopedia: A Revised Adaptation of Kabuki Jiten.*

Katherine Saltzman-Li

Role Types: Korea

Role types are not as important in traditional **Korean** theatre as they are in other Asian forms, where **actors** are rigorously **trained** to perform a limited range of types. On the other hand, types have been important in the development of *t'alch'um* and other traditional forms. *T'alch'um* never was closed off from the common people and was never the property of specialists; a performer thus may perform a variety of types during his performance life: the young nobleman, coquette, butcher, apostate monk, jealous wife, and so on.

Masks designate the given character or type. Between fifteen and twenty are required (one form requires twenty-nine), the total number divided among a limited number of types. An actor may play one character more than others, but it is understood that he may be called upon to perform almost any character within his regional *t'alch'um.*

P'ansori, by its very nature, obviates any artistic need to specialize in one type of role, for the sole singer-narrator must perform *all* the roles, recite the text's narration, and ad-lib with the audience and sole drummer. *P'ansori* performers must be highly proficient in a daunting range of roles crossing gender, age, and social station. However, *p'ansori* aficionados know that a given singer-narrator may render some types within the five classical texts better than others.

Richard Nichols

Role Types: Southeast Asia

Role types in much traditional Southeast Asian **dance**, drama, and **puppetry** are defined in terms of level of refinement and emotional control coupled with the status of characters portrayed. In Java, male characters are classified as refined and controlled (*alus*) or coarse and quick to anger (*kasar*); in Bali a similar classification of characters into delicate (*manis*) and tough (*keras*) prevails. Females are predominantly refined, but sometimes feature a stronger type as well, such as the *condong* in Balinese *gambuh*.

In mainland Southeast Asia, characters are similarly divided into refined male, refined female, and vigorous or coarse male, the latter used mainly for ogre or demon characters. In addition, monkey characters are prominently featured with their own unique style of movement and dance. In **Thai** dance-drama these categories are known as "refined male" (*phra*), "refined female" (*nang*), vigorous male and demon (*yak*), and "monkey" (*ling*).

Refined male and female characters are typically more restrained in their movement and slower in tempo than strong types. Male and female refined styles are fairly close to each other in these respects, with females moving slower and with more restrained gestures than refined males. In some genres, refined male and female role types can be performed by either men or **women**.

Clowns move with more freedom and often can improvise text as well as dance movement. Their low status allows them many liberties, including the ability to comment on current events. Clowns are marked by deformities such as pox and hunchbacks, and often wear ragged versions of peasant dress. In plays set in the pre-modern era, clowns portray servants, respecting their masters but behaving rudely in their own company.

Dancers and **actors** usually portray only one sort of role type throughout their performing careers. A *sandiwara* actor specializing in *alus* kings will play these parts exclusively and never be cast as an ogre or hot-headed villain. There are exceptions to this: solo *topeng* dancers, for example, need to portray a variety of role types in a single performance. *See also* Role Types: Cambodia.

Kirstin Pauka

RUTNIN, MATTANI MOJDARA (1937–). Thai • *lakon phut samai mhai* • **director**, translator of **Western** drama, and scholar. A Royal Thai Government Scholarship student, she received her PhD from the University of London's School of Oriental and African Studies. After staging Thai translations of Miller's *Death of a Salesman* (1971), Williams's *A Streetcar Named Desire* (1972), and O'Neill's *Ah, Wilderness* (1973), she became the first chairperson of Thammasat University's Department of Drama in 1978.

Most of her works are Thai adaptations of classic and modern **Western** dramas. Examples are Anouilh's *Antigone* (1976), Wilde's *The Importance of Being Earnest* (1981), Shakespeare's *Macbeth* (1982), Brecht's *The Threepenny Opera* (1983), Euripides' *The Trojan Women* (1986), and Simon's *Plaza Suite* (1990). In 2003, her translation of David Henry Hwang's *M. Butterfly* was staged by Bangkok University's Department of Performing Arts at the Bangkok Playhouse. Trained in classical Thai **dance** since childhood, she adapted King **Rama II**'s *Inao* and Rama I's *Ramakien* (*Ramayana*) into *lakon khanob niyom mhai* (literally, "new traditional dance-drama") reinterpretations of traditional drama in modern contexts and **experimental** styles drawn from both traditional and modern practices—versions of *Busba and Nakan* (Busba-Unakan, 1994) and *Rama and Sida* (Rama-Sida [Sita], 1996).

Her writings include *Dance, Drama, and Theatre in Thailand: The Process of Development and Modernization* (1996), the most comprehensive book on Thai theatre history in English.

Pawit Mahasarinand

SAINI K. M. (1938–). Indonesian • **playwright**, poet, and **critic**, born into an artistic family at Sumedang, West Java. He learned to play traditional **music** as a child and studied English literature in Bandung, subsequently developing an interest in poetry and drama. The latter led him to establish the theatre program at the Indonesian **Dance** Academy, Bandung, where he later became director and advanced the school to its current position as the Indonesian Institute of the Arts while continuing to pursue artistic activities, particularly as a dramatist.

From the beginning, Saini's work has combined modern and traditional elements. A member of the influential Bandung Theatre Study Club (Studiklub Teater Bandung), Saini's early script *Prince Geusan Ulun* (Pengeran Geusan Ulun, 1963) was directed by fellow member **director** and **actor** Jim Lim (1936–), incorporating *wayang kulit* and Sundanese traditional music. In plays such as *Panji Koming* (1984), *Ken Arok* (1985), and *Prince Sunten Jaya* (Pangeran Sunten Jaya, 1973), Saini uses legendary figures to illuminate and subtly comment on contemporary **politics** and society. *Prince Sunten Jaya* reworks a Sundanese **folk** story about Prince Munding Laya of the Pajajaran kingdom, who is to be executed by his stepbrother, Sunten Jaya. *Ken Arok* concerns the legendary ruler of the Javanese Singhasari kingdom, a popular children's tale, while *Panji Koming* is based on the character of a Javanese court servant, a version of which had became a popular cartoon character during the 1980s.

Saini's other plays include *Ben Go Tun* (1977), *Egon* (1978), *Dog Restaurant* (Restoran anjing, 1978), and *World of the Dead People* (Dunia orang-orang mati, 1986). Two children's plays, *Kingdom of Birds* (1980) and *Kalpataru* (1981), won an award from the Indonesian Department of Education and Culture.

From 1995 to 1999, he served as director of arts for the Directorate General of Culture in the Indonesian Department of Education and Culture. In 2001, he won the Southeast Asian Writers' Award. Saini also has authored a number of critical books on theatre.

Craig Latrell

SAITÔ REN (1940–). Japanese • *shingeki* • **playwright**. Born in Pyongyang, **Korea**, in 1940, Saitô attended Waseda University, but soon dropped out to join the **Actor**'s Theatre (Haiyû-za) **Training** School. He helped found the **theatre company** Free Theatre (Jiyû Gekijô) in 1966, later merging with **Satoh Makoto**'s **Theatre** Center 68/71. Saitô's first play, *Red Eyes* (Akame, 1967), was produced by Free Theatre and, despite its intricate structure, foreshadows his later preference for the well-made play. Based on a well-known comic book (*manga*), *Red Eyes* moves between past and present, history and fantasy, aesthetically linking live performance and television to frame a tale of village uprisings in the Edo period (1603–1868).

Saitô won the 1980 **Kishida [Kunio]** Prize for *Shanghai 'Vance King* (Shanhai bansukingu, 1979), a play heralding his penchant for historically detailed and popularly accessible works that also accommodate his characteristic social commentary. A unique style of musical—the actors all play live onstage—*Shanghai* captures the experience of Japanese jazz **musicians** who find in 1930s Shanghai a too-brief escape from prewar Japan's growing militarism.

Saitô continued to explore the period surrounding World War II with other historically grounded plays, such as *Grey Christmas* (Gurei Kurisumasu, 1983) and the biography *Red Dawn over Manhattan* (Asayake no Manhattan, 1993). A more recent play, *First Love: Hôgetsu and Sumako* (Hatsukoi: Hôgetsu to Sumako, 1995), chronicles the tragic relationship between pioneer **director** • **Shimamura Hôgetsu** and actress **Matsui Sumako**.

Michael W. Cassidy

SAKATA TŪJŪRŌ. Line of **Japanese** • *kabuki* • **actors** from the Osaka-Kyoto area, the first of whom was the most famous. Tôjûrô I (1647–1709), from Kyoto, was, along with Edo's (Tokyo) Nakamura Shichisaburô I (1662–1708), renowned for creating the complex "gentle style" (*wagoto*) incorporating comic eroticism, physical humor, and situational wit that became familiar in *kabuki* "domestic dramas" (*sewa mono*).

Though not strong in Genroku era (1688–1704) acting styles such as samurai acting (*budôgoto*) or **dance** plays (*shosagoto*), Tôjûrô rose to fame by developing *wagoto* to play the handsome young lover, Fujiya Izaemon, in *Yûgiri's Final New Year* (Yûgiri Nagori no Shôgatsu, 1679), a role so popular that he played it eighteen times. Tôjûrô's characters usually interacted with a courtesan or engaged in a courtesan-buying scene (*keiseikai*). His skills, recorded in contemporary **criticism**, included comedy (*okashimi*); appearing in disguise (*yatsushi*); love scenes (*nuregoto*); flirtation; sexual banter; or shows of anger toward a courtesan. He had at least one long comic monologue in each play.

Tôjûrô's gifts at reciting dialogue, as well as his eloquence during long speeches, were popular and were continuously incorporated into plays written by his **playwriting** collaborators, **Chikamatsu Monzaemon** and Kaneko Kichizaemon. His best-known roles include Umenaga Bunzô in *The Courtesan on the Buddha Plain* (Keisei Hotoke no Hara, 1699) and Takatô Tamiya in *The Courtesan and the Great Buddhist Service at Mibu Temple* (Keisei Mibu dainenbutsu, 1702).

Tôjûrô I had two unremarkable successors, and the name was no longer used after 1739. **Nakamura Ganjirô** III revived it in 2005 and became Tôjûrô IV.

FURTHER READING

Kominz, Laurence R. *The Stars Who Created Kabuki: Their Lives, Loves and Legacy*.

Holly A. Blumner

SAKATE YÔJI (1962–). Japanese • **playwright** and **director**. Influenced by **Yamazaki Tetsu**, whose mentor was **Kara Jûrô**, Sakate adopted Yamazaki's journalistic approach, dramatizing actual incidents, and Kara's **actor**-centered style. Establishing his own **theatre company**, Phosphorescence Troupe (Rinkô-gun), in 1983, he compellingly dramatizes injustices and suffering perpetrated by an oppressive society.

Legal-system injustices inform *Tokyo Trial* (Tôkyô saiban, 1988), inspired by a Korean Airlines bombing, and *A Dangerous Story* (Kiken na hanashi, 1988), on arson at Liberal-Democratic Party headquarters. A lesbian's sexual awakening propels *Coming Out* (Kamu auto, 1989). Sakate combines Tokyo garbage disposal and Aum Shinrikyô (the cult that released toxic gas in the Tokyo subway in 1995) in his 1991 **Kishida [Kunio]** Prize–winning *Breathless* (Buresuresu). Other touchy topics include Japanese whaling, in *Epitaph for the Whales* (Kujira no bohyô, 1993); the Okinawa-based American military, in *Demise of the Okinawa Milk Plant* (Okinawa mirukupuranto no saigo, 1998); and the emperor system, in *Emperor and Kiss* (Tennô to seppun, 1999), given the Yomiuri Drama Award for Best Director.

Sakate frequently experiments with structure and space, facilitating his activist intentions and provoking questions about what theatre is, one's socio-**political** assumptions, and the sense of self. Several plays borrow *nô* techniques, as in the haunting *Epitaph*'s dream structure. Action in *The Attic* (Yaneura, 2002), also awarded the Yomiuri Drama Best Director prize and toured to the United States, concerns social shut-ins and occurs entirely in a constricting four-meter-wide set. Sakate's work, including his collaborations with local actors, has been produced in fifteen cities across eight countries.

John D. Swain

SAKHI KUNDHAI NATA. *See* Puppet Theatre: India.

SAKURAMA BANMA (1835–1917). Japanese • **actor** who, along with **Umewaka Minoru** I and **Hôshô Kurô** XVI, became one of the three *nô* stars of the Meiji period (1868–1912). Banma was the seventeenth-generation descendant of the Sakurama *nô* family in the service of the Hosokawa warrior house in Kumamoto. Recognized as a child prodigy, he traveled, at the order of the Hosokawa, to Edo (Tokyo) to study *nô* chant (*utai*) with a Konparu school teacher. Banma divided his time between Kumamoto and Tokyo before finally settling in the latter in 1879. In 1881, he **danced** the lead in *Kamo* at the opening performance of Tokyo's first public *nô* stage, in Shiba. His energetic performances of *Kantan* in 1882 and *Dôjô-ji Temple* (Dôjô-ji) in 1883 secured his national fame, and he performed on that **stage** at least one hundred times. Banma was especially noted for his acting ability and energy. He again took on the highly demanding lead role in *Dôjô-ji Temple* at age seventy, and he continued performing until his death. Banma passed on his art to his son, Sakurama Kyûsen (1889–1957), who became a leading Konparu figure during the twentieth century.

Eric C. Rath

SAMARTH, ALAKNANDA (1941–). Indian actress, director, and educator, born in Pune, Maharashtra, who has worked with internationally renowned directors and acted in several major productions at home and abroad. She **trained** at Brandeis University in the United States and the Royal Academy of Dramatic Art in London. Her career began when **Ebrahim Alkazi** directed her in *Miss Julie* (1959).

Her acclaimed solo work includes *Kunti and the Human Voice* (1987), based on the writings of **G. Sankara Pillai** and Jean Cocteau. She is one of the key interpreters of Heiner Müller in India and Britain. Her major roles include *Yerma*, directed by Steve Hotchner (Boston, 1961); *The House of Bernarda Alba*, directed by Amal Allana (New Delhi, 1980); *A Song of Death*, at the Black Theatre Festival in London (1988); and *Prakriya*, directed by Rustom Bharucha (Pune and Imphal, 1989). In 1975, Samarth was the first Indian actress to play a major classical role at London's National **Theatre**, starring in John Dexter's production of *Phaedra Britannica*. Her directing includes Brecht's *Coriolanus* (1984) and Bond's *The Bundle* (1986), both at the Trichur School of Drama.

Samarth is a respected teacher of acting who has taught at the Royal Shakespeare Company, Stratford-upon-Avon, and the National School of Drama of New Delhi. She is an Associate Member of the Royal Academy of Dramatic Art.

Sreenath K. Nair

SAMSA (1898–1939). Pen name of **Indian** Kannada-language **playwright, director**, novelist, and poet Sami Venkatadri Iyer, who traveled widely through India, Southeast Asia, South Africa, and Fiji before settling in Mysore, Karnataka, in 1915.

He set about on the ambitious project of writing twenty-three plays, mainly on the Mysore dynasty monarchs, using the archaic Kannada language. Although his diary shows that he wrote a number of other plays, only six survive, all on the Mysore kings. He and a small number of contemporaries were interested in writing plays that exalted India's history; his focused only on Mysore while theirs covered a broader spectrum. The six plays—said to have grown out of Samsa's persecution complex—are grouped under the umbrella title of *Cycle of Samsa's Dramas* (Samsa nataka chatra). These closely researched dramas, influenced by Shakespeare, examine the Wodeyar family kings from 1550 to 1650, describing their best and worst features, while idealizing King Ranadhira Kanthirava (r. 1638–1659). The play's titles are *Virtuous and Serious One* (Saguna gambhira, 1918–1919), *Bettada Arasi* (1936; publ. 1953), *Vikramaraya the Wicked* (Vigada Vikramaraya, 1925), *Vijaya Narasimha* (1926), *Master of Titleholders* (Birudantembara ganda, 1937), and *Mantra Power* (Mantrasakti, 1938).

Despite several amateur presentations of the plays in the 1920s under Samsa's guidance, they were ignored until 1985, when they were revived by the Ninasam Tirugata company.

Samuel L. Leiter

SANDIWARA. "Spoken drama" in **Indonesia, Malaysia**, and **Brunei**. The term was coined in Indonesia in late 1942 when *tonil* and other Dutch-derived words were banned because of the anti-European-language **censorship** policy of the **Japanese** occupation (1942–1945). *Sandiwara* is a compound of *sandi* ("secret") and *wara* ("make known/public"); thus it is a dramatic forum for communicating hidden intentions, that is, a propaganda medium. The Japanese used *sandiwara* as a means to disseminate information to the public, encourage contributions to the war effort, and stoke anti-imperial sentiments. Most of the large-scale *tonil* **theatre companies** in pre-1942 Java were dissolved and *sandiwara* companies under the direction of the centralized Javanese Sandiwara Union were established. The Union was responsible for writing new scripts in Indonesian and translating Japanese plays. Many Japanese-era *sandiwara* scripts were jingoistic tales about brave soldiers and solidarity among Asians, but more complex psychological dramas by **Armijn Pané** and other **playwrights** also were written and performed. All major *sandiwara* companies were required to perform scripts authorized by the Union; variation was forbidden. Extra turns between acts continued in the same fashion as *tonil*, plus the occasional inclusion of Japanese songs and **dances**. During the occupation, there was little in competition from movies or other sorts of mass culture, and itinerant troupes such as Bintang Surabaya and Pancawarna attracted large urban audiences. Smaller-scale companies formed in imitation in rural areas.

The term *sandiwara* in Indonesia continued to be used after the end of the postoccupation era to refer both to commercial touring groups as well as to plays and theatrical activity among the elite. Scripts by Indonesians were exported to Malaysia and, in 1947, the term started to be used there to refer to theatre using written scripts. Many of those involved in Malaysia were students or graduates of teacher **training** colleges, where European drama, in English and translation, was studied. The influence of **Western** drama meant that Malaysian *sandiwara* plays tended to be less stylized than earlier Malay-language dramatic forms, such as *bangsawan*. However, heroic subjects from Malaysia's glorious feudal past, items also performed in *bangsawan*, tended to dominate. Many of the plays written in the 1950s were set in the glory days of the precolonial Malacca sultanate, but were implicitly anti-imperial allegories for contemporary concerns, such as the conflict between individual liberties and communal responsibilities. There is little humor and much ethnic/national flag waving.

Plays lasted under two hours, and usually had four or five acts. Scripts were not always written down in full, and while there were no "extra turns" à la *bangsawan*, plays such as **Shaharom Husain**'s ever-popular *The Hunchback of Tanjung Puteri* (Si bongkok Tanjung Puteri, 1960) feature dance and *pantun* poetry of the same sort found in residual popular theatre.

The term *sandiwara* lost favor in Malaysia in the 1960s. It was replaced by the Anglophonic *drama moden* ("modern drama") pioneered by **Mustapha Kamil Yassin** (a.k.a. Kala Dewata), which stressed realism. *Sandiwara* plays set in pre-modern times are still occasionally staged, but tend to be referred to as *purbawara* (*purb*, literally, "ancient"; *wara*, literally, "make known/public").

In Indonesia, *sandiwara* continues to be used to refer to various sorts of text-based theatre performed in schools, arts centers, and public **theatres**. Major post-independence playwrights who call their plays *sandiwara* include **Arifin C. Noer**, **Putu Wijaya**, **Nano Riantiarno**, Wisran Hadi, Saini K. N., Utuy T. Sontani, and Sitor Situmorang. Non-Indonesian plays, such as those of Ibsen, also are called *sandiwara*. Radio serials (*sandiwara radio*), often with supernatural themes, in Indonesian, Javanese, and other languages, attract massive listening audiences.

Sandiwara also has been used in western Java since ca. 1950 to refer to a sort of popular theatre with extemporized dialogue that developed out of *kethoprak*, *tonil*, and

The clown Gendut doing a monologue for the *sandiwara* troupe Yudha Putra, Indramayu, West Java, 1999. (Photo: Matthew Isaac Cohen)

local traditions. Currently, only one major Sundanese-language *sandiwara* company is active, Sandiwara Sunda Miss Tjitjih (installed in a permanent theatre in Jakarta), but there are more than one hundred active Javanese-language groups in Cirebon, Indramayu, Subang, and adjacent north coast regions. These groups are hired to perform at communal and familial celebrations on temporary proscenium **stages**.

Cirebonese *sandiwara* (sometimes called *masres* by outsiders) is today essentially an historical **costume** drama accompanied by *gamelan* **music**. Performances begin at 8 p.m. with a **musical** overture (*gagalan*), followed by a solo female dance (*srimpi*), and then a play (*lakhon*) that continues until 2 a.m. Condensed daytime performances are also sometimes offered. Most plays are set in Java's feudal past and feature martial arts, comedy, song, pyrotechnics, dry ice effects, and ghostly apparitions lit by ultraviolet light.

FURTHER READING

Cohen, Matthew Isaac, ed. *The Lontar Anthology of Indonesia Drama, 1*; Nur Nina Zuhra (Nancy Nanney). *An Analysis of Modern Malay Drama.*

Matthew Isaac Cohen

SANGEET NATAK. Indian commercial "**musical** theatre" genre of Maharashtra, dated to the late nineteenth century when **Annasaheb Kirloskar** created *Shakuntala* (partial, 1875; complete, 1880), based on **Kalidasa**'s **Sanskrit** classic. This Marathi-language form (also spelled *sangitnatak*), which enjoyed its golden age through 1925, integrated **acting** and singing, using multiple musical elements drawn from classical, semi-classical, and **folk** backgrounds. There could be nearly two hundred songs (*pada*s) in a show, and these were enormously popular, providing best-selling records for a string of famous actor-singers, none more renowned, perhaps, than the female impersonator **Bal Gandharva**. The form began as an all-male one, but once it became popular **women** joined the **theatre companies**, and there even were all-women troupes.

Although some have traced the seed back to a musical theatre piece of 1690, its true origins are more recent, dating to a work produced by all-round theatre artist Vishnudas Bhave (1819/24–1901) in 1843; it was, however, Kirloskar's ventures several decades later that established the truest expression of the genre. *Sangeet natak* came along at a time when middle-class audiences, influenced by imported cultural standards associated with the British *raj*, were losing interest in the more vulgar forms of indigenous culture (such as *tamasha*) and wished for more respectable forms.

Kirloskar, in creating *Shakuntala*, took advantage of Bhave's innovations and those of other contemporary artists, the advances being made in the popular **Parsi theatre**, and the methods of English romantic and ancient Sanskrit drama. Instead of relying on the **stage** manager-**director** (*sutradhara*) to sing (with a chorus) all the songs while the actors improvised, he reduced the *sutradhara*'s role to early in the performance, and allowed the actors to sing their own songs in a well-structured framework within which the songs helped to move the story forward rather than being sung for their own extrinsic values. The old orchestra had sat in the wings; now they were placed in a proscenium theatre's pit.

A number of later dramatist-composers made important advances in the form. Among them were Govind Ballal Deval (1855–1916), famous for *Sharada* (1899); S. K. Kolhatkar (1871–1934), whose works included *Hero's Son* (Viratanaya, 1896); B. V. Warerkar (1883–1964), known for *Wanderer in Gardens* (Kunjavihari, 1908); and Ram Ganesh Gadkari (1885–1919), author of *Force of Virtue* (Punyapravhav, 1916).

Sangeet natak's heyday arrived with two troupes, the Gandharva Drama Company (Gandharva Natak Mandali), run by Bal Gandharva, and the Lalit Kaladarsha Drama Company (Lalit Kaladarsha Natak Mandali) of Keshavrao Bhonsle (1890–1921). Their music incorporated popular recorded tunes of the day and made other alterations to the typical score and instrumentation.

The golden age had passed by the 1930s, and the form was unable to adapt to the changing social and dramaturgical needs of the times. The music went one way, the narrative another, and dramatic qualities took a back seat as shows became more like recitals than musical plays. Performers like Bal Gandharva increasingly privileged their vocal talents over their histrionic ones, in shows that lasted up to six hours. Moreover, film offered practically insurmountable competition to the declining form, although some directors and playwrights struggled to revive it. There were a number of attempts at revival in the post-independence period, with various artists trying **experimental** methods at resuscitating the form, or to create more contemporary equivalents, but— apart from occasional revivals of still popular old plays like *Musical of Saubhadra* (Sangeet Saubhadra, 1882) or from the work of various amateur companies— traditional *sangeet natak* has vanished.

FURTHER READING

Ranade, Ashok D. *Stage Music of Maharashtra.*

Samuel L. Leiter

SANNATA. **Indian** form of North Karnataka. *Sannata*'s name (literally, "small play") distinguishes it from another regional form, ***doddata*** ("big play"). *Sannata* is also called *dappinata* because its initial **musical** accompaniment was only the *dappu*, a tambourine-like drum. In some recent performances the *tabla-dagga* percussion combination replaces the *dappu* and harmonium and fiddle also accompany.

Early (ca. 1880–1920) *sannata* texts included only songs of a devotional and social nature; dialogue was improvised. Later texts usually include written dialogue and are more philosophical.

The **stage** is a simple wooden platform. **Costumes** are traditional everyday wear; a turban can represent a king's crown. **Makeup** is generally realistic. A small chorus sings the songs in Hindustani (North Indian) style and *lavani*, a local regional **folk** style. Dialogue is colloquial, straightforward, clever, and sometimes racy. All plays begin with a song in praise of a deity.

The most popular plays are some of the earliest. In one entertaining plot dealing with Krishna's teasing of a milkmaid and her servant about the milk tax, the milkmaid says she will pay the tax and marry Krishna when all of them are reborn as different characters. The social plays most often deal with the relationships of men and **women**, love, lust, deceit, betrayal, and eventual murder and/or suicide. In spite of the seriousness of these plays, the maidservant provides some humor.

Martha Ashton-Sikora

SANSKRIT THEATRE. India's classical dramatic tradition is known from some two dozen complete plays (and a few fragmentary ones) and other works about drama, all of them composed in Sanskrit, an Indo-European language spoken and written in ancient India. One of our best sources of information is the ancient *Treatise on Drama* (Natyashastra), a scholarly text on the **theory** and performance of drama, along with its associated performing arts of **music** and **dance**. From this text, the dramas themselves, and the works of literary **criticism** that analyze drama, we can conclude that Sanskrit theatre was a sophisticated tradition in which plays with complex plots were enacted by performers for audiences throughout India for over one thousand years. The tradition was less well supported after about 1200 AD with the advent of Muslim-ruled kingdoms in North India. In Kerala, South India, however, a tradition of Sanskrit performance known as ***kutiyattam*** has continued without interruption to the present day, and it preserves many features of the classical tradition.

Religious and Political Purposes of Performance. The *Natyashastra* and later critics describe as one purpose of enacting a drama the appreciation by spectators of the aesthetic experience called *rasa* (literally, "flavor"; see below). Noteworthy also are statements in the *Natyashastra* that for a ruler the merit of sponsoring a performance is equal to that of sponsoring a Vedic sacrifice, which indicates that **religious** and **political** motives were also relevant for patrons. Since Vedic sacrifice rituals were performed by Brahman priests, and sponsored by the ruling elite, as a means of pleasing the gods, securing worldly benefits for the society, and affirming social order (and the authority of rulers and Brahmans), it is interesting to see the *Natyashastra* assert a similar purpose and outcome for theatre. Additional religious significance can be seen in the text's attribution of theatre's origin to the god Brahma, and its insistence that rituals be performed for the gods, who are conceived as protecting the performance. The text also prescribes extensive rituals that are to be performed to consecrate a **theatre** and prior to each performance. Performance occasions include the coronation of a king, victory in battle, religious **festivals**, and other celebrations, the drama becoming part of the festivities and a means of staging an auspicious spectacle.

The *Natyashastra* describes **theatres** and their **stages**, giving as the reason for construction of such buildings the need for protection from disruption, such as when the mythic first performance was interrupted by demons who did not appreciate how they were depicted. While playhouses of various sizes and shapes are described, most of the text is devoted to the rectangular structure of medium size, half of its interior space for the audience, the other half for the stage and backstage.

The Dramas. Sanskrit plays have many common features. The text of each begins with a verse spoken as a benediction in which the drama is dedicated to a deity; for example, each of **Kalidasa**'s three dramas is dedicated to the god Shiva. Next there is a prologue, in which typically there is a dialogue between two or three figures who will not appear later; they refer to the drama's title and **playwright**'s name, along with the general theme. The benediction and prologue serve to mark off the drama from the preliminary ritual activities, and from the real world itself.

The *Natyashastra* lists ten different dramatic types, but describes only two in detail: the *nataka* and the *prakarana*. The *nataka* is to be based on a well-known story with a royal hero, and to have as its dominant emotional mood (*rasa*) either love or heroism. Extant examples range from five to seven acts. The *prakarana* is to tell a story of the playwright's own invention, in five to ten acts, with a hero who is a Brahman, a merchant, or a king's minister, and to have love as its *rasa*. Other types are known as well. The one-act "Drunken Farce" (Mattavilasa), attributed to King Mahendravikrama Varman (ca. seventh century), is a good example of the comic *prahasana* ("farce") category, while "The Middle One" (Madhyama) is an example of a one-act heroic play of the *vyayoga* (literally, "intense or manifold action") type sometimes attributed to **Bhasa**.

V. Gireesan as Duryodhana and Manju as Durjaya in Bhasa's Sanskrit play, *The Broken Thighs,* directed by K. N. Panikkar for Sopanam, Trivandrum, India, 2004. (Photo: Courtesy of K. N. Panikkar)

Languages and Modes of Expression. It may be somewhat misleading to describe India's classical drama tradition as "Sanskrit theatre," since Sanskrit is not the sole language used. Only high-status characters such as (especially male) members of the royal and Brahman classes speak Sanskrit. Others, including almost all **women** and members of lower-status groups, speak a dialect of Prakrit, a group of vernacular languages once heard throughout North and central India. Such an arrangement mirrored reality, since Sanskrit was the language of the elite, and most people spoke related but simpler languages. A character's status is indicated through his language.

An exception to the principle that Brahmans speak Sanskrit is the *vidushaka* (literally, "disrupter") character, a Brahman who speaks only Prakrit and is often regarded as a clown. He is the hero's friend but is poorly educated, and his interests focus primarily on food and comfort. As a comic foil to the (usually royal) hero, he often provides complications for the hero to overcome.

Usually, the plot's actions are carried forward by prose dialogue between characters utilizing both Sanskrit and Prakrit, as appropriate, with interspersed verses that convey the speaker's emotional state. These verses are almost always spoken by the hero, since the drama is focused on his struggle to attain his objective, and they typically conform to Sanskrit poetic ideals. What distinguishes poetry from prose is that poetry is metrical. With some six hundred possible metrical patterns recognized by literary **critics**, the poet had many choices in composing a verse.

In addition, all the dramas seem to have had musical accompaniment. The *Natyashastra* describes an upstage musicians' space, and some dramas refer to certain verses being sung. Music was provided by drums and other percussion instruments, flutes, stringed instruments, and voices. Whether accompaniment was almost continuous (as in *kutiyattam*) or only occasional remains disputed.

Gesture seems to have had a significant role in communication. The *Natyashastra* describes an extensive set of gestures and gaits that were understood as conveying meanings. For example, chapter 13 is devoted to the gaits employed by various types of characters, depending on their status and the emotional mood. Pantomime indicated certain actions, such as the rapid movement of a chariot or a celestial nymph flying into the sky. By convention, certain postures and movements indicated particular meanings; thus the king would demonstrate that he was in his chariot by making the motion of gripping the chariot pole with one hand while holding a bow in his other as his chariot-driver pantomimed the use of reins and whip. The chariot and its team of horses would not be on stage; instead, the characters would refer to the chariot and its motion, pantomime the actions, and move in a chariot-driving fashion. The *Natyashastra* also provides details on the gaits for depicting various animals, which suggests that the chariot's horses might be represented by **masked** performers moving in such a way that audiences would recognize them as horses.

Costume and Makeup. The *Natyashastra* devotes considerable attention to costumes and **makeup**. Brahmans and royal ministers wear white, and members of the royalty wear multicolored garments and extensive ornamentation (such as rings, crowns, and necklaces). Drunk or insane characters wear dirty clothes to indicate their mental state. Sages and Buddhist clergy wear orange-hued robes, while forest-dwelling ascetics wear tattered garments made of tree bark, strips of cloth, and skins. Makeup seems to have been elaborate, as there are long descriptions of how to make a wide array of cosmetic colors, but details are lacking. Mask-making is also described so there was apparently some scope for the use of masks though stage directions provide no evidence.

The Audience. Dramas rarely refer to the audience directly; an exception is the prologue to Act One of *The Recognition of Shakuntala* (Abhijnana Shakuntalam), where the *sutradhara* says that the actress's song has so enchanted the audience that they are as motionless as a painting—an indication of the "divine success" considered the highest theatrical achievement. Ideally, a spectator should be knowledgeable and experienced, so as to be capable of grasping the subtle meanings of the play's poetic expressions, as well as appreciating the emotional states exhibited by the characters in their situations. Only such a person would be capable of having the intended *rasa* experience. The text also refers to the presence of female spectators, who, presumably, were thought capable of attaining *rasa*.

Tradition. Sanskrit theatre emphasized compliance with traditional aesthetic and formal expectations over innovation and novelty. The criteria that enabled critics to evaluate the dramatic works and performance may have seemed restrictive to some artists.

The patron's important role is highlighted by Sanskrit theatre's decline having coincided with the rise of Muslim political authority in South Asia, and the resulting reduction of royal support for companies of performers and theatre maintenance. That manuscripts of dramas and literary criticism survived and were transmitted for centuries is a testament to the dedication of some to the tradition of Sanskrit theatre.

FURTHER READING

Baumer, Rachel Van M., and James R. Brandon, eds. *Sanskrit Drama in Performance*; Byrski, Christopher. *Concept of Ancient Indian Theatre*; Keith, A. Berriedale. *The Sanskrit Drama*; Kuiper, F. B. J. *Varuna and Vidushaka: On the Origin of Sanskrit Drama.*

Bruce M. Sullivan

SARDONO W. KUSOMO (1945–). **Indonesian** choreographer. Drawing from his **training** in formal Javanese **dance** and extensive work with foreign artists, Sardono has explored a wide range of issues facing Indonesian cultures and natural ecologies in national and global economies. During the years that President Suharto (1921–) ruled Indonesia (1966–1998), he was in the forefront of efforts to bridge the national modern arts culture with local traditional practices and social contexts.

As a youth in Surakarta, Sardono studied traditional *gamelan* **music** and dance. He danced for the Indonesian pavilion at the 1964 New York World's Fair, and studied under choreographer-dancer Jean Erdman. From then on he often performed internationally, choreographing a *Ramayana* project in **India** (1966) and coordinating the Indonesian exhibit at another world exposition in **Japan** (1970). In 1968, he became the youngest member of the Jakarta Arts Council, and in 1970, joined the faculty of the Jakarta Arts Institute.

One of Sardono's most famous works was *Rina's Kecak Dance* (Cak tarian Rina, 1976). In this piece, Sardono placed the entire Balinese village of Teges onstage. It toured the world, and in 1992 was made into the film, *The Dirah Sorceress* (Dongeng dari Dirah). Other works, such as *Meta-ecology* (Metaekologi, 1979) and *Plastic Forest* (Hutan plastik, 1983), are about the restoration of human balance with nature. In 1998, Sardono renovated an old Surakarta residence for artists of the sultan's court (*keraton*) into the Sono Seni arts complex, now a center for Indonesian modern dance.

Evan Winet

SARSUWELA. **Philippines** • **musical** comedy genre (a.k.a. *zarzuela*) revolving around the romantic love between typical Filipinos. Love complications and crises are played out against the backdrop of a contemporary social problem, such as card game gambling or cockfights, prostitution, loan sharking, vote-buying, "loosening" morality under American influence, landlord-peasant conflicts, or the clash between Hispanic and American concepts of womanhood.

Beginnings. Although this genre had already been introduced by Spanish troupes around 1879, the native *sarsuwela* flourished only during the American colonial period (ca. 1900–1946). It was launched with a bang with the staging of **Severino Reyes**'s

No Wounds (Walang sugat, 1902) in Manila. This was followed by many others written by notable Tagalog writers like Hermogenes Ilagan (1873–1943), Servando de los Angeles (1885–1972), Patricio Mariano (1878–1935), and Julian Cruz Balmaceda (1885–1947). After its debut, *sarsuwela* spread to the provinces and was staged in Ilocano, Pangasinan, Pampango, Bicol, Cebuano, Hiligaynon, and Waray.

Performance Elements. In the twentieth century's first decades, *sarsuwela* was either staged in Manila **theatres** or on makeshift *entablado* in the provinces, by professional **theatre companies** like the Samahang Ilagan. Later, local **playwright-directors** wrote and produced their own *sarsuwela* using their regional vernaculars as part of the celebration for the local town fiesta. In Manila and the provinces, the **stage** always had wings and borders, a front curtain, and **scenography** consisting of painted backdrops hung in sequence from front to back. The designs usually showed the interior of a rich man's house, the interior of a poor man's house, the façade of a mansion, the façade of a nipa hut, or a neutral outdoor scene. **Properties** and furniture complemented each backdrop.

Usually accompanied by a ten-piece orchestra, *sarsuwela* **actors** sang, with their natural voices, the traditional *kundiman*, *balitaw*, and *danza*, as well as the American-introduced foxtrot and, later, the tango and the cha-cha. Whether performed by professionals or amateurs, however, the same conventions were followed. **Costumes** served to distinguish the "heroes" (*bida*) from the "villains" (*kontrabida*), with the *bida* wearing more traditional costumes and the *kontrabida* more "daring" modern American fashions. Acting underscored the same dichotomy, with one set of gestures, attitudes, and movements reserved for shy or gentle *bidas* and another for their aggressive and brassy opponents.

Although *sarsuwela* succeeded in presenting recognizable Filipinos for the first time (as opposed to **komedya** and **sinakulo**, which showed characters from European culture), it nevertheless had to essentialize these characters into Good and Evil because the genre's traditional worldview demanded that events be manipulated so that they would conclude by endorsing established morality and the present order. At its transformative best, *sarsuwela* worked for social reforms but, like *komedya* and *sinakulo*, it never called for a radical restructuring of **political** power. With the advent of ***bodabil*** in the 1920s and of talking pictures in 1933, *sarsuwela* slowly disappeared from Manila, although it continued to live in the provinces until the 1960s and in movies from the 1930s to the 1970s.

FURTHER READING

Brandon, James R. *Theatre in Southeast Asia*; Chua Soo Pong, ed. *Traditional Theatre in Southeast Asia*; Fernández, Doreen G. *The Iloilo Zarzuela, 1903–1930*.

Nicanor G. Tiongson

SARUGAKU. *See Nô.*

SATOH MAKOTO (1943–). Japanese • **playwright** and **director**. A Waseda University dropout, Satoh became progenitor of the Black Tent Theatre (Kokushoku Tento a.k.a. Kuro Tento and BTT 68/71) and prominent in the Little Theatre (*shôgekijô*) movement in the 1960s and 1970s. Tent performances enabled Satoh's rejection of what **critic** Tsuno Kaitarô called the "trinity of the modern theatre"—the doctrine of universal humanism, tragic form, and the relationship between **actor** and audience dictated by the proscenium **stage**. Satoh sought rather to close the gap separating the individual's inner life from the processes of history, to encourage spectators to escape the "tragic weight" of history through a new understanding of time, tragedy, and theatrical space.

His first play, *Ismene*, produced by the Free Theatre (Jiyû Gekijô) in 1966, and directed by *nô* • **actor** • **Kanze Hideo**, demonstrates Satoh's characteristic **political** concerns and nontraditional dramaturgy. Part of a trilogy, *Hello Hero! Three Episodes in the Unending Ending* (Harô hiiro! Owaranai owari ni tsuite no sanshô), *Ismene* freely adapts Sophocles' *Antigone* and explores the relationship between tragedy, history, and inaction. Unlike her sister Antigone, Ismene cannot manufacture her own destiny; she only reacts to events, unable either to change history or participate in the tragedy, and is left alone.

With *My Beatles, or the Funeral* (Atashi no biitoruzu aruiwa sôshiki, 1967), produced by Waseda Little Theatre (Waseda Shôgekijô), directed by **Suzuki Tadashi**, Satoh reflects on Japan's long discrimination against **Koreans**. Inspired by the 1958 killing of a Japanese **woman** by a Korean man, it opens with two characters, the male Chong and female Katsura, rehearsing a play based on the incident. They are interrupted by someone called The Japanese and by the Beatles, who claim to be movers— they are also Japanese spirit figures (*marebito*)—and linger to watch. In a twist, we learn that Chong is actually Japanese and Katsura Korean. After Chong mimes raping Katsura, he is killed on a darkened stage—probably by The Japanese. The Beatles leave, despite Katsura's pleas to be spirited away to the "Emerald Peninsula" (Korea). Satoh thus crystallizes tragedy's failure to achieve meaningful resolution and Japanese cultural history's contribution to Japan's imperialist legacy.

In *The Dance of Angels Who Burn Their Own Wings* (Tsubasa o moyasu tenshi-tachi no butô), cowritten in 1970 with Yamamoto Kiyokazu (1939–), Katô Tadashi (1942–), and **Saitô Ren**, and based loosely on Weiss's *Marat/Sade*, Satoh develops further his ideas of multidimensional dramaturgy to question the efficacy of revolution and the nature of political freedom. His irreverent approach continued with *The Comic World of Shôwa* (Kigeki shôwa no sekai, 1975, 1976, 1979), a trilogy reflecting on Japan's pre– World War II imperialism.

In the 1980s, Satoh primarily served as director for the Black Tent Theatre, which toured throughout Asia. Recently, he has returned to playwriting, such as *The Last Airplane* (Zettai hikôki, 2003), an exploration of the final images occurring in terrorist Mohammed Atta's mind on September 11, 2001.

David Jortner

SAWADA SHŌJIRŌ (1892–1929). Japanese • **actor**, founder of *shinkokugeki*. As a Waseda University student, Sawada joined **Tsubouchi Shôyô**'s pioneering modern **theatre company**, Literary Arts Society (Bungei Kyôkai), making his first **stage** appearance in *The Merchant of Venice* (1911). Ambitious and with obvious potential, he soon appeared opposite **Matsui Sumako** in Art Theatre (Geijutsu-za) productions, like Maeterlinck's *Monna Vanna* (1913) and Wilde's *Salomé* (1913). By 1915, Sawada gained commercial popularity in a Modern Drama Society (Kindaigeki Kyôkai) production, playing the double role of **kabuki** actor Tamagawa Hikoshirô and Jocanaan in Ihara Seiseien's (1870–1941) popular *The Actor's Wife* (Yakusha no tsuma) and its play-within-a-play *Salomé*.

In 1917, Sawada formed the *shinkokugeki* genre, initially failing in Tokyo and Kyoto, then succeeding in Osaka, after honing his signature, film-inspired style— energetic sword fights and speedy action. This provided context for his famous "half-a-step-ism" (*hanposhugi*) theory: giving audiences "half-a-step" of the excitement they expected, while simultaneously guiding them "half-a-step" to better theatre. He catalyzed his personal popularity, appearing in two plays in 1919 by Yukitomo Rifû (1888–1959) as a late–Edo period (1603–1868) loyalist samurai, Tsukikage Hanheita, and a Robin Hood–like gambler and thief, Kunisada Chûji, and as characters in translated plays, like Raskolnikov in Laurence Irving's dramatization of Dostoevsky's *Crime and Punishment* (1920).

Returning to Tokyo with *Great Buddha Pass* (Daibosatsu tôge, 1921–1922), Sawada played Tsukue Ryûnosuke, a blind man whose "soundless stance" (*otonashi-no-kamae*) sword-fighting style triggered the sword-drama boom. Sawada acted in 169 plays in a nineteen-year career.

Yoshiko Fukushima

SCENOGRAPHY

Scenography: China

Traditional Methods. **China**'s traditional *xiqu* • **stage** is almost bare, with environment created primarily by the **actors**' performance. Certainly since the Yuan dynasty (1280–1368), the most important scenographic devices have been one or more tables and benches or chairs, used both as furniture and to represent larger man-made and natural objects. Other major aspects of traditional staging include a flat **curtain** across the rear of the stage and, by the Ming dynasty (1368–1644), a carpet, often red. While complex techniques were used for spectacular effect in a few exceptional Ming and Qing (1644–1911) performances, not until the twentieth century did elaborate scenography become widespread; it is still rarely employed for traditional performances.

Considered large **properties** (*qimo*), the one or more wooden tables and chairs, usually red, used in most traditional *xiqu* plays are conventionally known as "one table and two chairs" (*yi zhuo er yi*). Through the use of different placements and decorated coverings, this can portray specific rooms in courts, inns, prisons, cottages, and palaces; it can also be used to indicate a wide range of other circumstances, including a steep slope or precipice, a city gate tower, a ship, a well, a loom, and a bed. Other large *qimo* used to establish environment and atmosphere for traditional plays are the "cloth city wall" (*bu cheng*), a long, tall cloth painted to resemble a brick wall that is held up on poles to represent a city wall or gate, and the "door" (*men*) or "large" (*da*) "canopy-curtain" (*zhang*), an embroidered curtain attached with poles to the backs of two chairs facing one another to create between them a curtained bed, a boudoir, or a tent.

The traditional "door flag-curtain [and] stage canopy-curtain" (*menlian taizhang*) consisted of two narrow curtains that covered the upstage right entranceway and the upstage left exit, and a third, wider curtain that hung between the two, screening the backstage area from view. In the Qing dynasty and early twentieth century, these were heavily embroidered satin, often with distinctive designs unique to **actors** such as **Mei Lanfang, Chang Yanqiu**, and **Ma Lianliang**. With the move to proscenium stages and theatre reforms of the early 1950s, traditional plays have been performed with flat, rear "accent curtains" (*chen mu*) that similarly do not depict a realistic scene, but are generally a solid color with a central design feature and no upstage doors—actors enter and exit from the wings instead.

Traditionally the table and chairs were covered and arranged by one or more stage assistants (*jianchang*, literally, "inspect [the] stage") who worked à vista and wore the long street gown (*changpao*) rather than stage dress. *Jianchang* also handed props to actors, helped them with onstage **costume** changes, and raised and lowered the door flag curtains for entrances and exits. *Jianchang* left with the reforms of the 1950s. Furniture is now changed behind an inner curtain hung partway upstage; actors move downstage to continue performing while it is closed.

Probably the most outstanding traditional effect is "fire color" (*huocai*), *xiqu* techniques for creating flame and smoke that probably originated with knife swallowing and fire spitting in the Han dynasty (206 BC–220 AD). *Huocai* were used in Tang (618–907) and Song (960–1279) dynasty ghost and spirit **dance**, and since Ming for both supernatural and martial activity. *Huocai* techniques performed by actors include one in which one actor sprays flammable material such as rosin powder onto a torch held by another; in another, a performer gently blows fine particles of burning straw paper from a fire tube held in the mouth.

Spectacular lighting and scenic effects, called "lantern colors" (*dengcai*), were employed in private **theatre companies** in late Ming. For instance, the depiction of Tang emperor Xuanzong's (or Minghuang; r. 712–756) travel to the moon involved sudden darkness, thunder, a round moon glowing internally with flames the color of early dawn, and five-colored clouds and mists. In Qing, the most spectacular *dengcai* were created for palace productions. On multilevel court stages, spirits and gods descended from above, and ghosts rose from below; golden lotuses emerged from wells, opening as they ascended, and an enormous fish spewed water drawn up from below out of its mouth. In late Qing, *dengcai* plays made their way to the commercial theatre with performances of *Mulian Saves His Mother* (Mulian jiumu).

Spectacular effects were taken further with the adoption of "machine-operated stage scenery" (*jiguan bujing*) by Shanghai's New Stage (Xin Wutai) proscenium **theatre** in 1908. *Jiguan bujing* used mechanical means, including revolves and traps, to rapidly move and change props and scenery, creating effects like landslides, earthquakes, the earth splitting open, and palaces burning and collapsing. Employed mostly for plays concerning detectives, martial chivalry, and spirits and demons, *jiguan bujing* drew large audiences and was later **criticized** as crass and commercial. But it served as a precedent for realistic *xiqu* scenery, paving the way for the extensive scenery and technology in the model revolutionary *jingju* plays (**yangban xi**) of the Cultural Revolution (1966–1976), and the **xinbian lishi ju** genre born in the late twentieth century. The latter has involved soaring swaths of cloth, fog and smoke, laser and other lighting effects, raked and revolving stages, and extensive realistic scenery composed of both two- and three-dimensional flats, curtains, scrims, and screens.

Elizabeth Wichmann-Walczak

Huaju *Scenography.* Modern Chinese scenography can be divided into three stages: early twentieth century to 1949, 1949 to the end of the Cultural Revolution (1966–1976), and post–Cultural Revolution era to today.

Except in a few instances, little attention was paid to scenography in "spoken drama" (*huaju*; see Playwrights and Playwriting) prior to 1949, mainly owing to financial and material restraints. Productions at the New Stage (Xin Wutai) in Shanghai were among the first to introduce scenery, mainly realistic. Most **directors** assumed responsibility for set designing.

In the 1920s, a few enthusiasts advocated total acceptance of the **Western** theatre against *xiqu*. Thus various productions aimed at producing Western classics with realistic scenery and props. Wang Youyou's (1888–1937) staging of Shaw's *Mrs. Warren's Profession* (1920) at Shanghai's New Stage had an extravagant set using custom-made Western furniture against a painted backdrop.

Around the same period, a number of Western-trained practitioners introduced new techniques. **Hong Shen** joined the Shanghai Drama Society (Shanghai Xiju Xieshe) in 1923 after returning from abroad. In 1924, he wrote and directed *The Young Mistress's Fan* (Shaonainai de shanzi), adapted from *Lady Windermere's Fan*. It was the first in China to use three-dimensional units, such as real doors and windows, instead of painted backdrops. Hong also experimented with shifting the intensity of light to suggest scenic and atmospheric changes.

Also significant before 1949 was He Mengfu (1911–1945), a member of several companies like the Shanghai Amateur Dramatist Association (Shanghai Yeyujurea Xiehu), and dean of research at the National Theatre School, where he taught scenographic techniques. Besides writing, translating, and directing for stage and screen, He wrote on lighting design and was known for his simple but atmospheric sets, examples being *Othello*, *Jintian Village* (Jintian cun), and *Peach Blossom Fan* (Taohua shan).

After the establishment of the People's Republic of China in 1949, the government organized troupes into state-subsidized companies. Improved financial circumstances led to more sophisticated designs. Professional **training** institutions, such as Beijing's Central Academy of Drama (CAD, 1952) and the Shanghai Theatre Academy (STA, 1956), provided standardized programs. In general, the period was marked by strong Soviet influence. Illusionism dominated design. However, symbolic and expressionistic elements, sometimes inspired by *xiqu*, were occasionally seen.

When CAD and STA were established, Liu Lu (1911–1979) and Sun Haoran (1910–1995) became founding chairs of their design departments, respectively. Liu directed and designed over ten productions. He wrote extensively on the **theory** and practice of scenography, producing important texts. His earlier designs were characterized by an innovative use of light. Most of his post-1950 designs were characterized by their meticulous representation of reality.

Sun Haoran returned to Shanghai in 1940 after studying in the United States. His designs, most notably ***Guan Hanqing*** (1958), distinguished themselves by their integration of *xiqu* aesthetics with a modern vocabulary.

Other innovatively designed productions of the time include *Cai Wenji* (1959), designed by Chen Yongxiang (1925–), and *Debunking the Paper Tiger* (Zhilaohu Xianxingji, 1958), designed by Zhang Zhengyu (1904–1976).

After the Cultural Revolution, the reform policy facilitated the introduction of contemporary Western theatre. Technological advances provided unprecedented freedom for visual imagination. The emergence and popularity of **experimental theatre** and small theatre productions challenged conventions, encouraging diversity and innovation.

As design became indispensable, respect for the profession grew. A number of designers have become well known, among them Xue Dianjie (1937–), Hu Miaosheng (1936–), Liu Yuansheng (1942–), Liu Xinglin (1953–), and, more recently, Yi Liming (1963–), Zeng Li (1961–), and Huang Haiwei (1959–), among others. Innovative designs were in *The Field of Life and Death* (Shengsi chang, 1999), designed by Xue Dianjie, *Exercises of Emotions* (Qinggan caolian, 1993), designed by Liu Xinglin, *Shangyang* (1996), designed by Huang Haiwei, and *The Tea House* (Chaguan, 2000), designed by Yi Liming. Sound and lighting design have advanced with scenography.

Most contemporary designers are affiliated with particular companies or institutions but are flexible enough to freelance. Many designers cross over to other media.

From December 20, 1980, to January 9, 1981, the All-China Dramatists Association and the Ministry of Culture hosted a "Seminar on **Theories** of Scenic Design" in Beijing. Participating were 113 designers from all over China, sharing ideas and discussing problems. The China Scenic Art Association (CSAA) was established during the seminar. In 1982, the CSAA organized the National Scenic Art Exhibition, the first national Chinese scenic design exhibit, with over one thousand designs displayed. The CSAA has organized numerous seminars and workshops, and has published various research materials since its inauguration.

FURTHER READING

Mackerras, Colin, ed. *Chinese Theatre from Its Origins to the Present Day*; Scott, A. C. *The Classical Theatre of China.*

Nan Zhang

Scenography: India

Pre-modern Approaches. Locales and their shift from one place to another were depicted in traditional **Indian** theatre through **acting** conventions, not through scenic design, which provided only a bare minimum of details. There was a small stool, half-**curtains** used for entrances and exits, and painted cloths. Spectacle relied on beautiful **costumes** that enlarged the size of the actor's body while providing him with vivid colors, as seen in ***kathakali***, ***terukkuttu***, and ***yakshagana***. **Makeup** or **masks** worked similarly for the face.

Characters were classified according to a **role-type** system reflected in the colors and outline of the costuming, masks, and makeup whose striking appearance was set against the simplest of backgrounds. The **Sanskrit theatre** broke the **stage** area down into zones whose conventional uses were set by tradition. By this means, scenes taking place in differing locales could transpire simultaneously according to the actors' placement. Scene changes were effected by the simple practice of having the actor walk around the stage in a circle or ellipse. Variations of such practices continue to exist in various traditional forms.

Modern Developments. Modern stagecraft and scenography arrived with the importation of **Western** traditions and the construction of proscenium **theatres**. Major advances were made by the **Parsi theatres** of Bombay (Mumbai) during the late nineteenth century, when Victorian-era influences led to the use of two-dimensional, painted, perspective backdrops of exotic scenes combined with spectacular three-dimensional scenery, velvet curtains, and special effects. The touring **theatre companies** quickly spread such usages across the country. These productions were able instantly to change locales by replacing one backdrop with another, making the rapid alteration of scenes a major attraction and providing a new sense of reality for audiences. Regional variations in Parsi design evolved under the ministrations of local artists, whose cultural backgrounds influenced the way in which locales were depicted. Shakespearean plays, but also those from native traditions, such as the *Ramayana* and *Mahabharata*, history, legend, and myth, needed elaborate scenography to capture their worlds.

Late-nineteenth-century theatricals in Calcutta (Kolkata) and Bombay saw the introduction of sets influenced by Indianized versions of Italian Renaissance styles. In Calcutta, English scenic artist David Garrick (not to be confused with similarly named actor) painted and installed four sets at the Great National Theatre indicating a court, garden, forest, and an interior for the fairy tale *Desirable Garden* (Kamyakanan, 1873). He influenced the first known native scene painter, Nagendranath Bannerjee (1852–1910), whose scenery was painted on canvas roll-drops.

Scene painting evolved from the use of four to six separate curtains used to depict as many scenes to the "cut scenery" technique of creating three-dimensional depth by the clever placement of multiple drops cut in different shapes but kept firmly in place with scrim extensions, a method enhanced by careful lighting.

Believable special effects were developed, such as airplanes landing, train wrecks, fairies flying through the air, and combat explosions. Such scenes came to be associated with troupes such as the Surabhi Theatres in Andhra Pradesh, the Kalanilayam Drama Company in Kerala, and so forth. Even now the Surabhi Theatres remain popular for their use of such methods. **Rabindranath Tagore** deplored such literalism and called for more impressionistic, symbolic décor for his own plays, which were often staged outdoors.

Ornately painted sets dominated the modern stage until the 1930s, and are still found in some commercial companies. As realism made itself felt, there was a shift in the 1930s to box sets using flats and varying levels to create natural-looking interiors, including actual furnishings. Western devices like revolving stages and wagon stages were introduced to aid in rapid changes.

In 1933, Marathi theatre took a pioneering step when Bombay's new company, Theatre of a Changing Age (Natyamanwantar Ltd.), produced S. V. Vartak's social realist drama *School for the Blind* (Andhalayanchi shala), conceiving of theatre as a composite art amalgamating text, sets, lighting, costumes, and all other components. This represented a new understanding of Western techniques as artists, questing for a new theatre, became aware of the art's creative and intellectual seriousness. Among those helping to move scenography forward were Satu Sen (1902–1978), Charu Roy, Ramen Chaterjee, Tapas Sen (1924–), and Manindranath Das. The movement became even more productive after independence (1947).

In the 1950s, imaginative designs using abstraction, symbolism, and selective realism were introduced. Major designers included Dattatraya Ganesh Godse (1914–1992), Damu Kenkre (1928–), and Khaled Choudhury (1919–). **Utpal Dutt**'s *Coal* (Angar, 1959) and *Waves* (Kallol, 1965), designed by Tapas Sen, were pathbreaking in their integration of design elements, especially lighting, which, under Sen's inspiration, began to take giant steps forward.

The National School of Drama (NSD, 1959), long headed by **director**-designer **Ebrahim Alkazi**, emphasized the relevance of design at all production levels and helped **train** many who disseminated design's importance nationwide. NSD's productions revealed the possibilities of stage imagery in bringing out a play's spirit. Some plays were produced in spectacular natural settings, such as ruins and forts.

By the 1970s, all regional-language theatres were feeling the new influences. The work of Gaibi Nath Dasgupta (1936–2001), V. Ramamurthy (1935–), Kanishka Sen (1938–), Bansi Kaul (1949–), M. S. Sathyu (1930–), and others gave new direction to contemporary scenography.

The emergence of the "theatre of the roots" movement, based on the use of indigenous forms to inspire production, created a new spectacle culture in post-independence India. Directors used traditional torchlight, bare stages, costumes made of coconut leaves, and the like to create exotic visual effects appropriate to content. The director himself functioned as a designer in such work. Many contemporary directors also design their productions, some of which now feature the use of computer-generated projections.

B. Ananthakrishnan

Scenography: Indonesia

Since the opening of the Dutch neoclassical *schouwburg* **theatre** in colonial Batavia (Jakarta) in 1821, the proscenium **theatre** has been regarded as state of the art in **Indonesia**. Regional arts centers constructed since the 1960s typically house proscenium theatres, and most contemporary productions either take place in such spaces or in small independent galleries. When the Schouwburg Weltevreden reopened as the Jakarta Arthouse (Gedung Kesenian Jakarta) in 1987, it became the preferred venue for projects with high production values. The predominance of proscenium **stages** has been conducive to scenographic work.

Champions of realism, such as directors Teguh Karye (1937–2001) and Suyatna Anirun (1936–2002), frequently staged plays by Chekhov, Ibsen, and Williams with real (as opposed to painted) scenic elements, such as trees, or in box sets based on original European and American productions. Gigo Budisatiaraksa (1935–1986), one of the founders of the Bandung Theatre Study Club (Studiklub Teater Bandung), has gained national recognition for his realistic designs. Nevertheless, Indonesian scenography has not attained the illusionistic complexity typically associated with **Western** realism.

In most modern Indonesian theatre, the use of spectacle tends to be symbolic and presentational rather than realistic and representational. The stage directions in Roestam Effendi's *Essential Freedom* (Bebasari, 1926), the first modern Indonesian play, call for the symbolic use of footlights and color light washes against a background scrim. Lighting colors indicate chaotic demonic power (red) or mystical spiritual energy (green). A grandfather clock dominated the 1968 staging of **Arifin C. Noer**'s *Bottomless Well* (Sumur tanpa dasar, 1963) as an icon of man's existential predicament in relation to time. Suyatna Anirun enveloped the action of *The Cherry Orchard*

(1990) in a beautiful *wayang*-like (see Puppet Theatre) silhouette of a forest. In **Rendra**'s staging of *Struggles of the Naga Tribe* (Kisah perjuangan suku Naga, 1975), a real palm tree in one corner of the stage was juxtaposed to an upturned thatch broom in another, framing the action with symbols of nature and man's dependence on it. Rudjito, a prominent designer working in abstract styles, has created sets for productions by Rendra, Noer, **Putu Wijaya**, and **Nano Riantiarno**.

Rendra revolutionized approaches to spectacle through his "mini word" (*minikata*) exercises in the late 1960s. His Workshop Theatre (Bengkel Teater) created abstract works out of improvisations in which a sense of place and situation was generated by choral movement and vocalization rather than through design. Since the 1970s, Wijaya has created bold and often terrifying imagery by combining multimedia (including deafening soundtracks and handheld slide and film projectors) with choreography employing large choruses in abstract spectacular massings. In the 1990s, groups such as Black Umbrella Theatre (Teater Payung Hitam) and Open Space Theatre (Teater Ruang) brought the **actor**-centered aesthetic to new minimalist extremes, inspired by the international physical theatre movement and *butô*. In Z (2004), Open Space Theatre dispensed with scenery, and nearly did away with lighting and **costumes** as well. Spectators strained to follow the shadowy movements of loincloth-clad actors on an empty stage in nearly pitch darkness.

Evan Winet

Scenography: Japan

Japanese theatre is said to have begun when a goddess danced on an overturned tub, but as the nation's genres evolved, far more sophisticated means of embodying scenic needs evolved. Traditional theatre relies on environments varying from the Spartan *nô* and *kyôgen* theatre to the physical abundance of *bunraku* (see Puppet Theatre) and *kabuki*.

Nô *and* Kyôgen. *Nô*, a somber, Zen Buddhist–influenced **dance**-drama, is performed on a sculpturally exquisite square **stage** with four pillars and a roof. The stage's own beauty attracts the eye with no recourse to scenery per se; it offers a highly polished wood floor and walls; runway (*hashigakari*); striped, five-color *hashigakari* **curtain**; and spreading pine tree painted on the back wall. Its minimalist aesthetic is enhanced by the presence of the gorgeously **costumed • actors** and formally dressed chorus and **musicians**. **Properties** and set pieces are kept to a bare minimum; they represent rather than replicate objects. The actors use **masks, costumes,** and an occasional hand prop in addition to fans (the most versatile of props because they can symbolize many things). Set pieces are simple constructions of branches, bamboo, or cloth assembled by the actors themselves for a single performance and taken apart afterward. Large set props might include a straw hut, a giant rock, or a temple bell. Carriages, palanquins, or boats also appear in *nô*, always in lightweight, skeletal constructions (*tsukuri mono*). Audience members use their imaginations in visualizing the dramatic locale, contributing toward the sense of "mysterious beauty" (*yûgen*; see Theory) that illuminates the performance. *Kyôgen* uses the *nô* stage and has a similar visual aesthetic, although it makes less use of set pieces. Casts in both *nô* and *kyôgen* are generally small, but in a few plays there are a considerable number of actors on stage, providing an unusual image that always retains a sense of formal beauty regardless of how crowded things are.

Bunraku *and* Kabuki. In contrast to *nô* and *kyôgen*'s minimalism, *bunraku* and *kabuki* tend toward the elaborate. Although the following focuses on *kabuki*, a number of the same effects pertain to *bunraku*. Among such effects are the appearance of the performance space itself, including the auditorium "flower path" (*hanamichi*), revolving stage (*mawari butai*), elevator traps (*seri*), elaborate **curtains**, and extremely wide yet low stage opening. Further elaboration derives from the lavish costumes and wigs.

In pre-modern times, lighting was provided by opening and closing shutters high overhead at either side of the auditorium, or by candles set in holders along the front of the stage or *hanamichi*. Gaslight was introduced in the Meiji period (1868–1912), followed by electric lighting in the 1880s. Still, as a reminder of the old days, *kabuki* is generally produced with the house lights on (although dimmed somewhat), but for plays set at night or in gloomy circumstances, modern lighting is employed, including a follow spot. When an actor enters the *hanamichi* a bank of lights embedded along one side light up and then subside as he moves to the stage proper.

The *kabuki* stage (*butai*) itself captures the audience's attention at once with its billowing, tricolored, striped act curtain (*hiki maku* or *jôshiki maku*), opened and closed sideways to the sound of rhythmically timed cracks of wooden clappers (*tsuke*). Other curtains are used for a variety of different effects, often startling the audience by the brilliantly colored scenery their removal suddenly reveals.

Scenery itself usually consists of painted flats with interiors and exteriors bordering on the representational. Scenographic design ranges from the abstract, as seen in certain dance plays, to the relatively literal, on view in plays set in poor farmers' houses, brothels, or golden palaces. Both interiors and exteriors are shown, some interiors filling the entire stage and being considered to extend down the *hanamichi*, as when straw matting resembling *tatami* is placed on the runway. But many residences are shown by having the home occupy most of the central and stage left parts of the stage, their downstage walls removed, with the exterior shown at stage right and downstage. Characters may enter on the *hanamichi* or from stage right, come to a door or gateway outside the house, and then step in (or up) to enter the interior. Interiors may have walls painted to resemble a state of poverty, or they may be gorgeously adorned with gold leaf designs, suggesting opulence and wealth. The interior may be level with the stage floor or raised somewhat, requiring a step unit to allow the actors to descend to a downstage area, such as a garden. Upstage walls generally have either sliding doors or a hanging, split curtain (*noren*) for access to and from the room's interior. A number of window shapes may be placed on the set. There are also many interiors that have a small room situated at stage left, with translucent *shôji*-screen walls.

Exteriors are typically set at riversides, beachfronts, streetscapes, and outside temples or shrines. Floorcloths provide additional assistance in literalizing locales, as when cloths painted with wavelets are used to represent water or when white cloths indicate snow. Such cloths also extend down the *hanamichi*. Overhead border décor plays an important role, including hanging floral effects or slanted lines resembling rain.

Despite the variety of decorative approaches, however, the units from which sets are constructed follow standard practices and can be found in multiple examples. And sets can always be identified with specific plays, even if minor changes are introduced in different productions.

Scenery tends to have a flat, two-dimensionality to it, but can be highly detailed and elaborate, as witnessed by the huge temple settings found in a number of plays; on occasion, these large structures rise into view through the large elevator trap, sometimes with actors in place on them. A spectacular effect occurs when a scene begins on a temple roof only for the roof to be raised by wires so that it moves backward, allowing the temple beneath it to rise into view.

Perspective is present in a number of scenic designs, both as generalized views of distant landscapes beyond the downstage environment, as well as in palace interiors where sliding doors may be opened to reveal the apparent depth of a formal hall. Or a scene may begin downstage with full-sized actors and then, when the action moves upstage in the distance, replace the actors with similarly dressed children to make them seem far away. A boat may first appear in miniature at the rear of the stage, sailing the ocean blue, and then slide on at one side of the stage in its imposing actual size.

The revolving stage allows an actor to use it as a treadmill as he walks in one direction while the scenery moves in the other, or allows the action to progress from one locale to another in full view. And the entire auditorium can become part of the scenography, as in "Nozaki Village" (Nozaki mura, 1780), when a boat sails down the *hanamichi* on the audience's left with the female lead, while, on the secondary *hanamichi* on audience right, her lover simultaneously makes his exit carried off in a palanquin by two bearers.

Actor-**director** • **Ichikawa Ennosuke** III has created a modernized form called "super" (*supaa*) *kabuki* that emphasizes spectacle in its dazzling costumes and brilliant scenic and lighting effects.

FURTHER READING

Ernst, Earle. *The Kabuki Theatre*; Komparu, Kunio. *The Noh Theatre: Principles and Perspectives*.

Holly A. Blumner

Scenography: Korea

Korean traditional theatre developed without the complex scenic techniques and spectacle identified with Japan's *kabuki* and *bunraku* (see Puppet Theatre), among other forms. The first permanent **theatre** building, the Hyŏmnylusa, was built in 1902. Even after the introduction of **Western**-style realism early in the twentieth century, **masked** • **dance**-dramas, **puppet theatre,** *p'ansori*, and shamanistic ritual-performances (see Religion in Theatre) remained dominant entertainments, none requiring spectacle or even a playhouse.

After the Korean War, not a single theatre stood in which scenographic techniques could develop, nor did the dominant realism call for spectacle. Moreover, the socio-**political** climate of the 1960s and 1970s fostered the establishment of many small **theatre companies** whose agendas and finances did not stress visual effects. Productions moved into inexpensive, cramped, underground spaces in Seoul's Taehangno district, and to this day generally are staged in incommodious venues. Scenic designers, such as **Lee Byŏng-boc**, Pak Dong-u**, Shin Sŭn-hi**, Son Ho-sŭn, Sŏ In-sŏ, and Yun Jŭng-sŏp, are internationally recognized, but limited financing, restrictive access to the few large theatres, a paucity of **trained** technicians, and other factors retarded the development of spectacle, hindering free expression of the designer's imagination, even after large complexes were built in the 1980s. With few exceptions, **costumes** were the major source of spectacle well into the 1990s.

Musical theatre—*ch'angguk*, contemporary Korean musicals, and Western imports—may be the dominant commercial theatre form today. In order to thrive, they must increase the use and quality of scenography identified with musicals elsewhere.

FURTHER READING

Kim, Yun-Cheol, and Miy-Ye Kim, eds. *Contemporary Korean Theatre: Playwrights, Directors, Stage-Designers.*

Richard Nichols

Scenography: Malaysia

Typically, traditional **Malay** theatre was staged simply. Performances were held outdoors; lighting was basic, and there was no scenographic design. Originally lit by an oil lamp, the *wayang kulit* (see Puppet Theatre) shadow screen was later lit by a lightbulb. Nowadays, if performed outdoors, forms such as *mak yong* and *manohra* have the benefit of electric lighting; **costumes** resemble traditional styles.

Bangsawan was originally performed outdoors on a proscenium-style **stage**. With painted backdrops, wings, and borders, six standard sets were featured in a production: action could take place in a royal palace, a street, a jungle, a garden, a poor person's home, and a natural landscape. A performance, which was based on improvisation, also included interludes between scenes, providing songs, **dances**, pantomimes, comic skits, and other special acts. Performances were enhanced with special effects and elaborate costumes.

When modern groups attempt to stage *bangsawan* as originally performed, they may focus on these aspects of spectacle. In staging a modernized *bangsawan* production, the typical settings may not be used, as with Rahmah Bujang's (1947–) *Puteri Li Po* (1992). Bujang's script is based on the story of the **Chinese** princess who wed Sultan Manshor Shah in fifteenth-century Malacca, the marriage having been arranged by her father, the emperor of China, to enhance relations between the Malay kingdom and China. Bujang wrote and **directed** with an eye toward modern blocking and scenography. She used no interludes or improvisation; **music**, song, and dance were integrated into the drama.

The historical *sandiwara* plays of the 1950s engendered a realistic approach to setting and court manners. Costumes were reminiscent of earlier eras. During the 1960s, when realism dominated, sets were constructed to depict an indoor sitting room scene. Furnishings signified the characters' social and economic level. Certain pieces might also have had symbolic value, as when a deer's head, displayed on the sitting room wall in **Mustapha Kamil Yassin**'s *Behind the Curtain of Hope* (Di balik tabir harapan, 1960), represented the dichotomy (eventually resolved) in the main character's life: his severed connection with his rural community contrasted with his present immersion in the urban "wilderness." Costumes reflected what people wore in their daily life.

During the **experimental** period of the 1970s, more abstract, symbolic sets were created, utilizing elements adapted from traditional theatre as well as surrealistic imagery. Some **playwright**-directors staged multimedia productions, with slides, shadows, and film. Once playwrights shifted to neorealism in the 1980s, design flexibility appeared.

There also has been a return to large-scale productions. For example, in 2000, the first major professional production staged in the new National **Theatre** (Istana Budaya or Palace of Culture) was the musical *The Princess's Keris* (Keris sang puteri), with a cast of over sixty. Large-scale shows continue to be staged there.

Innovation has contributed to the growth of a revitalized English-language theatre since the mid-1980s. A striking example is the 1995 multiart staging of K. S. Maniam's (1942–) *Skin Trilogy*. Shifting among multiple spaces and perspectives in the National Art Gallery, audiences viewed avant-garde dance, music, art, and drama that sought to reveal the multiplicity within the individual.

FURTHER READING

Nur Nina Zuhra (Nancy Nanney). *An Analysis of Modern Malay Drama.*

Nancy Nanney

Scenography: Philippines

Scenography in the **Philippines** ranges from traditional backdrops to the innovative sets of **Western**-trained artists incorporating Filipino identity in their work. There are two types of backdrops used in *sinakulo* and *komedya*: those indicating **stage** space, such as the "permanent backdrop" (*telon de fondo*), the "front **curtain**" (*telon de boca*), and the "rear curtain" (*telon de fondo*), which separates the **acting** area from the backstage dressing area; and those indicating settings, such as the "street curtain" (*telon calle*), the "tropical landscape curtain" (*telon natural*), the "mountain scene curtain" (*telon bundok*), and the "palace curtain" (*telon palacio*). The scenery is created by community members using water-based paints on canvas. In *komedya*, facades representing castles are painted with colors indicating Christian or Muslim kingdoms. Among special effects are descending angels (also used in the meeting of Mary and Christ [*salubong*] on Easter Sunday), rolling boulders and fireworks for the Resurrection, ascensions using pulleys, birds flying, and unfolding flowers revealing actors.

The early *sarsuwela*s had simple sets with indoor environments—"living rooms of the rich" [*sala rica*] and "living rooms of the poor" [*sala pobre*]—defined by borrowed furniture indicating social status. In recent *sarsuwela* revivals, the scenography has included three-dimensional structures, huge staircases, and giant wedding cakes.

Among the most memorable effects have been the inexpensive and portable arena/theatre-in-round ones of Severino Montano (1915–1980) in the 1950s, the ruins of the walled city Intramuros as a backdrop for the open-air staging of *A Portrait of the Artist as Filipino* (1955), the army jeep with collapsible walls in Ray Albano's (1947–1985) design for *Bombita* (1981), the sparse set created with a guava tree and truckloads of soil by Rolando Tinio (1937–1997) for *Waiting for Godot* (1984), Salvador Bernal's coconut trunk sandboxes for *Francisco Maniago* (1988), and Mel Bernardo's recreation of a Cordillera village and rice terraces in *Macli-ing* (1988). Other leading set designers are Amiel Leonardia (1939–), Brenda Fajardo (1940–), Eric Cruz, and Lu Decenteceo (1951–).

FURTHER READING

Tiongson, Nicanor G. *Sinakulo*; Tiongson, Nicanor G. *Komedya.*

Joi Barrios

Scenography: Singapore

During the 1990s, scenography increasingly overtook text as the single most important element in **Singaporean** theatre. This increased reliance on spectacle, and the use of visual elements to communicate with audiences coincided with the development of a strong "house style" by TheatreWorks, a **theatre company** that has become identified with an aggressively intercultural aesthetic where seams among different artistic disciplines and Asian traditions are presented in ways highlighting their separateness rather than their underlying unity.

Driving this trend has been TheatreWorks' artistic **director • Ong Keng Sen** and his numerous collaborations with designer Justin Hill. **Trained** as an architect, Hill's designs often provide a series of neutral, flexible acting areas on which a range of diverse movement and **acting** traditions can be presented, providing a unit set that supports a show's visual landscape. In much Singaporean design from the mid-1990s on, concrete visual metaphors meant to anchor the production thematically are added to these open **stages**. Elaborate **costuming**—sometimes fanciful reinterpretations of historical clothing in a range of Asian contexts—is then layered onto this neutral environment, often providing the strongest visual element.

William Peterson

Scenography: Thailand

Modern **Thai** scenic techniques are highly influenced by **Western** practices. They vary according to each production's style, with selective realism being most common.

Krissara Warissarapiricha (1954–), the most prolific scenographer, often double-tasks as technical **director** for theatre, ballet, and opera. He is the author of the only Thai-language work in the field, and writing the first Thai book on lighting design. Other notable designers include Dream Box's Chalardlerd Tungkamanee, Chulalongkorn University's Ritirong Jiwakanon, and Yodchai Sukansil, who works for many companies.

Since Thailand is one of the world's most popular tourist destinations, intercultural spectacles have been created for evening itineraries. Started in 1999 and currently running nightly on the southern resort island of Phuket, *Phuket FantaSea* showcases *nang yai* **puppetry,** *khon*, Thai **folk** dances, aerial acrobatics, transvestite cabaret shows, pyrotechnics, and so on. In this Las Vegas–style, grand-scale, loosely plotted spectacle, more than one hundred **actors** share the stage with exotic animals, including water buffalos and elephants.

To celebrate the auspicious occasion of King Rama IX's Sixth Cycle birthday (1999), the *son et lumiere* spectacle *Chao Phraya: The River of Kings*, was produced on four temporary **stages** at historic sites along the banks of Bangkok's main river. From hired boats and dinner cruises, audiences watch recreations of a royal barge procession, historical war scenes, traditional ceremonies, celebrations, and **dances**. The event continued annually on a smaller scale until the tsunami tragedy of 2004. Another production in this genre is *Siam Niramit: Journey to the Enchanted Kingdom of Siam*, which began in late 2005 at the Grand Ratchada **Theatre**, equipped with a twelve-meter-high proscenium and spectacular water works.

FURTHER READING

Rutnin, Mattani Mojdara. *Dance, Drama, and Theatre in Thailand: The Process of Development and Modernization.*

Pawit Mahasarinand

SEGAL, ZOHRA (1912–). Indian • **actress** and **dancer**, born in Saharanpur, Uttar Pradesh. A Muslim by birth, she rebelled against traditional constraints and, after graduating from Queen Mary's College, Lahore, in 1929, traveled with an uncle overland by car to Germany in 1931 to study eurhythmics with Mary Wigman. This was highly unconventional for a young Muslim woman. Back in India, she became a principal dancer in Uday Shankar's (1900–1977) company in 1935, touring with it worldwide until 1943. From 1943 to 1945, she and her dancer husband, Kameshwar Segal (who eventually committed suicide), ran their own Zoresh Dance Institute in Bombay (Mumbai).

Although she joined Prithvi **Theatres** as a dance director, she quickly became a leading actress, remaining until 1959, and gaining acclaim in plays like *Wall* (Diwar, 1945), *Pathan* (1945), and *Traitor* (Gaddar, 1948). Her sister, Uzra Butt (1917–), another distinguished actress, also was in this **theatre company**. It toured all over India, playing towns small and large. Segal's range was wide, covering both comedy and tragedy. Meanwhile, she became an officer of the communist-led Indian People's Theatre Association and the head of a New Delhi theatre school. In the 1960s, she began working in London and Europe, doing theatre (including for the Old Vic and the British Drama League), films, television, and radio.

Back in India, she resumed her **stage** career, one of her great successes being in **Ebrahim Elkazi**'s adaptation of Lorca's *The House of Bernarda Alba* (1992). Even as late as 2003, at ninety-one, she was still acting on stage, appearing that year in three productions, *The Diary of Anne Frank* in Delhi, *Ek Thi Nani* with Dawn of a New Day (Ajoka) Theatre, **Pakistan**, and *Riceboy*, in Canada, and giving poetry readings. Her many awards include the National Academy of Music, Dance, and Drama (Sangeet Natak Akademi) award (1963) and the Padmashree (1998). She also holds the title Legend of India.

Samuel L. Leiter

SENDA KOREYA (1904–1994). Japanese • *shingeki* • **actor** and **director**. After beginning his career with the Tsukiji Little Theatre (Tsukiji Shôgekijô), Senda started acting in proletarian plays in 1924 and became a committed socialist. He spent four years in Germany in the late 1920s, where he picked up key techniques of agitprop theatre from the like-minded Brecht and Piscator.

Returning to Japan in 1931, Senda found **censorship** pervasive—**theatres** were enjoined from advocating communism—and, though not a Communist Party member, he was jailed for his **political** beliefs. Perpetually afoul of the militarist authorities, Senda was forced to recant his positions and was banned from directing as conditions for his third release from prison, in 1942. Still, he defied the government by doing a secret production and, with actors he was **training**, founded the Actor's Theatre (Haiyû-za) in 1944. This **theatre company** became an enduring postwar presence, producing mostly *shingeki* and translated **Western** plays. Senda directed Shakespeare,

Chekhov, Brecht, and **Abe Kôbô**; he became Japan's leading Brecht interpreter, translating and directing the original Japanese productions of Brecht's plays. He also directed most of Abe's plays from 1955 to 1965.

The Actor's Theatre was part of the leftwing coalition opposing renewal of the U.S.-Japan Mutual Security Treaty (Anpo) in 1960, but by then the younger members were rejecting *shingeki* as establishment theatre. Some left the company in 1971, but Senda remained its guiding light, a giant of modern theatre.

John D. Swain

SENDRATARI. Indonesian • **dance**-drama created in 1961, its name an acronym of *seni* ("art"), *drama*, and *tari* ("dance") coined by **Andjar Asmara**. *Sendratari* was from its start a nationalist project designed to appeal to international visitors while maintaining traditional aesthetic values. Its first incarnation was the so-called ***Ramayana** Ballet*, created in 1961 by an all-star team of classically trained Javanese dancers and **musicians** against the backdrop of the Central Javanese world heritage site of Prambanan, which features numerous *Ramayana* reliefs. **Costumes** and choreography were based on courtly *wayang wong*, but dialogue was jettisoned and replaced by pantomime, improvisation was curtailed, and action greatly condensed. Much attention was given to the army of acrobatic monkeys, which included **Sardono W. Kusumo** as Hanuman. Its success (staged annually to the present) led to numerous imitators, starting with a 1961 production of *Jayaprana* at Bali's performing arts high school. Specially constructed **stages**, such as the Sunyaragi Open Stage adjacent to the ruins of the Sunyaragi pleasure garden in Cirebon, West Java, accommodate these massive productions.

Sendratari is characterized by big budgets, large stages and casts, flashy costumes and music, polished choreography and floor patterns, and minimal humor and improvisation. Dialogue is sparse and tends to be spoken by offstage narrators, sung by vocalists, or prerecorded by **actors**. *Sendratari* is often staged for state occasions before visiting dignitaries and functions to celebrate local identity within national and international contexts. **Critics** see *sendratari* as a conservative art that emphasizes spectacle over substance, but it is actively embraced as a repository for diverse local traditions of dance, music, and folklore throughout Indonesia.

Matthew Isaac Cohen

Backstage at a performance of *The Sound of Seven Calls to Prayer*, a *sendratari* produced by the Sunyaragi Cultural Foundation in Cirebon, West Java, 1995. Director Y. Handoyo (seated) also plays the role of the poison-bearing Megananda. (Photo: Aviva Kartiningsih Cohen)

SENGUPTA, RUDRAPRASAD (1936–). Indian Bengali-language **actor** and **director**, who started his career as a teacher at Calcutta's (Kolkata) Rabindra Bharati University after completing his MA in English from Calcutta University. In 1961, he joined the **theatre company** Nandikar, for which he both acted and adapted major **Western** plays, one of which, Pirandello's *Six Characters in Search of an Author* (1961), became a big hit. **Playwrights** he adapted into Bengali included Euripides, Brecht, Miller, and Wesker. Sengupta also became an outstanding actor, specializing in antiheroic roles or villains.

He and his second wife, actress **Swatilekha Sengupta**, ran Nandikar from 1977. In 1980, Sengupta, along with **Sombhu Mitra** and other top actors formed the Calcutta Repertory Theatre, but it soon failed, although it produced Brecht's *Life of Galileo* (1980). His major productions include *Football* (1978), an adaptation of Peter Terson's *Zigger Zagger*; *The Caucasian Chalk Circle* (1978); and *Antigone* (1979). He founded the Nandikar Theatre **Festival** in 1983, and saw it become a major theatre event, with troupes coming not only from across the country but also from **Pakistan, Nepal**, and **Bangladesh**. Nandikar also offers educational workshops to schoolchildren, including those from slum environments.

Sengupta received the National Academy of **Music, Dance**, and Drama (Sangeet Natak Akademi) award in 1980. He also wrote a book on modern Western drama (1977).

Debjani Ray Moulik

SENGUPTA, SWATILEKHA (1950–). Indian Bengali-language **actress**, **director**, translator, **scenographic** designer, and **musician** (piano, flute, and violin) who grew up in Allahabad, and holds an MA in English. She began acting at seven, in Manmatha Ray's *Karagar* (1957), and by 1971, when she married and moved to Calcutta (Kolkata), had performed in Hindi, Bengali, and English. **Rudraprasad Sengupta** saw her performing in *Kolkatar Electra* (1971) and invited her to perform for his Nandikar **theatre company**, which she ultimately joined in 1977. She divorced her husband and became Sengupta's second wife.

The multitalented Swatilekha has performed under the direction of Sengupta, Buddhadeb Bose, Fritz Bennewitz, and others. Her most famous role is Bimala, the heroine of Satyajit Ray's film *The Home and the World* (Ghare baire, 1984). She was equally adept at portraying Grusha in *The Caucasian Chalk Circle* (1978), the tragic heroine in *Antigone* (1979), and the daughter of a nonconformist in *Galileo*. In 1998, Swatilekha Sengupta captured Calcutta's heart in the one-woman play *Shanu Roy Chowdhury*, adapted from Willy Russell's *Shirley Valentine*, and combining a series of Bengali monologues punctuated with effortless English, portraying the title character's search for identity as a **woman**.

Debjani Ray Moulik

SHAHAROM HUSAIN (1919–). Malaysian • **playwright** and fiction writer whose first play, *Dahlan, the Lawyer* (Lawyer Dahlan, 1939), is about a village boy who travels abroad to train as a lawyer. He returns home a "**Westernized** Malayan" who, together with his wife, lives a life devoid of Eastern values, such as filial piety. The play ends with the lawyer rediscovering his lost roots.

Despite the play's realistic nature, Shaharom has never been considered a realist, nor was he credited with pioneering the realistic mold. Rather, he is known as the *sandiwara* playwright *par excellence*, whose name is synonymous with his much-produced *The Hunchback of Tanjung Puteri* (Si bongkok Tanjung Puteri, 1960), which concerns the physically and morally deformed hunchback and his good, handsome, brother, the White Warrior. The play posits the bad and ugly, who fights for personal freedom and liberty, against the attractive hero, loyal to king and country. For Shaharom, the true warrior is the hunchback.

Shaharom believes that *sandiwara* plays are written to be performed, and that *sandiwara* stories interpret a life whose unfolding can be graphically plotted with a beginning, a climax or crisis, an anti-crisis, a falling action, and a summation. His plays follow this **dramatic structure** with slight variations.

Shaharom's plays are important in the history and development of Malaysian drama. Based on history, facts, and reality, they highlight a style and form of playwriting that was considered new. Written in poetic language, and sometimes completely in verse, the plays are not hampered by complications that would interfere with concentration.

A former teacher, the well-traveled Shaharom Husain was much influenced by Shakespeare and Shaw, not only in playwriting but in his efforts at preserving his own literary heritage. Supported by the Johore state government, Shaharom has single-handedly collected, documented, and preserved native literature in his small museum, located in his house.

Solehah Ishak

SHANG XIAOYUN (1900–1976). Chinese • **actor** of the female **role type** (*dan*) and one of "the four great *dan*" of twentieth-century *jingju* (with **Mei Lanfang**, **Chang Yanqiu**, and **Xun Huisheng**). During the Republican period (1912–1949), he came to define the *dan* as a leading rather than supporting role and was a famous exponent of a *dan* subtype called *qingyi* (literally, "blue garments").

Shang was born into a poor family in Nangong, Hebei Province, and **trained** first in the "martial male" (*wusheng*) role, but came to be famous in his own Shang school (*shang pai*). He was extremely skilled in both acrobatics and **dance**, and in playing heroines and swordswomen, as well as in the subtle development of the *qingyi*. A celebrated exponent of both "civil" or "scholarly" (*wen*) and "military" (*wu*) roles, he also was renowned for his mastery of the "water sleeves" (*shuixiu*) **costume** technique and for his posture and movement when conveying emotional states and physical conditions. For instance, when playing Meng Yuehua in *Pavilion of the Imperial Tablet* (Yubei ting), Shang introduced a special gait to indicate a young woman hurrying home in the rain along a slippery path.

Shang performed in numerous "new dramas" (*xinxi*) during the Republican period. These were essentially rather limited adaptations of old items, not to be confused with the far-reaching reforms that occurred later during the 1960s and 1970s. In 1964, he drew mention in the press for his endorsement of the revolution in *jingju*, despite which he was persecuted in 1968 for his role in performing traditional theatre.

Trevor Hay

SHI HUI (1915–1957). Chinese • actor of modern "spoken drama" (*huaju*; see Playwrights and Playwriting) and film. Born to a poor Tianjin family, he was raised in Beijing. Dire poverty made him leave school very young, after which he worked in a railway station, a hospital, canteens, and shops. Like most actors of his generation, his career arose from involvement in student dramatic clubs; he had no professional **training** before joining the theatre in Shanghai in 1940. The hardship he experienced helped him understand more profoundly the characters he created on **stage**. He played a wide range of different roles in both foreign and Chinese plays, including humble lower-class menials, upper-class masters, historical figures, a *jingju* performer, and a magician.

In 1942, he was praised as "king of *huaju*" by the Shanghai newspapers. His work with **Huang Zuolin** introduced him to cinema. He was so successful playing a foolish but cunning barber in a 1947 movie that he became "public enemy" of all the local barbers, making it impossible to visit a barbershop for almost a year. In 1957, he was labeled a rightist and committed suicide.

Ruru Li

SHIMAMURA HŌGETSU (1871–1918). Japanese • *shingeki* • director, **playwright**, translator of **Western** drama, troupe manager, and scholar. A graduate of **Tsubouchi Shōyō**'s literature department at Waseda University, Shimamura wrote plays in his youth. Yet, his fame emerges from his activities as director and translator for two pioneer modern **theatre companies**.

Envisioning an academic career, Shimamura spent 1902–1905 in Berlin and Oxford studying drama, literature, and aesthetics. At his insistence, the Literary Arts Society (Bungei Kyōkai), founded by Tsubouchi as an extracurricular study society in 1906, was transformed into an active troupe in 1909. Shimamura translated and directed two famous naturalist dramas for the Literary Arts Society, Ibsen's *A Doll's House* (1911) and Sudermann's *Heimat* (1912). They caused sensations, demonstrating *shingeki*'s capacity to stimulate debate about social issues.

After the Literary Arts Society disbanded in 1913 over tensions caused by Shimamura's affair with its leading actress, **Matsui Sumako**, Shimamura and Matsui founded the Art **Theatre** (Geijutsu-za). Shimamura ensured financial viability by extensive tours, showcasing Matsui and certain popularizing elements, such as "Katusha's Song"— Japan's first pop hit—in the company's adaptation of Tolstoy's *Resurrection*. He also introduced Maeterlinck's symbolist plays, encouraged playwrights, like Nakamura Kichizō (1877–1941), and brought *shingeki* to its widest audience ever. Shimamura's directing was known for imposing strict textual adherence and requiring from his **actors** exact memorization of words and gestures. He died in the 1918 influenza pandemic.

Brian Powell

SHIMIZU KUNIO (1936–). Japanese • *shingeki* • **playwright**, **director**, and screenwriter. Born in Niigata, Shimizu attended Waseda University, where he got involved with a student troupe and began writing plays. Soon after graduating, he was caught up in the era's seminal **political** movement: the nationwide protests against renewal of the U.S.-Japan Mutual Security Treaty (Anpo) in 1960. Shimizu saw the socio-political ferment as reflecting the confusion and ambivalence of young people, and his plays explore, with lyrical dialogue and evocative imagery (reminiscent of Tennessee Williams), issues of identity, homeland, and memory.

Those Days: A Lyrical Hypothesis on Time and Forgetting (Ano hitachi, 1967) focuses on the difficulty of determining identity by exploring the plight of coal miners suffering amnesia. Even when their spouses and friends attempt to affirm their identities, the miners remain unsettled. Whose account of the past, which version of their respective identities, are they to believe?

This kind of existential challenge is a major theme informing other Shimizu plays and is often rendered through ambivalent, confused characters confronted by history as in *Hearty but Flippant* (Shinjô afururu keihakusa, 1969), which marked the beginning of Shimizu's long collaboration with director **Ninagawa Yukio** and the Contemporary People's **Theatre** (Gendaijin Gekijô). Other examples are *Ten Thousand Years of Memories about Japan* (Nippon ichimannen, 1970) and *When We Go down that Heartless River* (Bokura ga hijô no taiga o kudaru toki, 1972), a metaphorical play that explored the purges of the United Red Army and was awarded the **Kishida [Kunio]** Prize.

Shimizu felt that the **stage • actor**'s shifting nature was ideal for exploring identity. *The Dressing Room* (Gakuya, 1977), a huge success, involves four Chekhovian actresses (two are ghosts as the play opens) desperately seeking the elusive roles that can berth them in their dressing room—a metaphor for a welcoming homeland, that is, Japan. *An Older Sister Burning Like a Flame* (Hi ni yô ni samishii ane ga ite, 1978) and *Tango at the End of Winter* (Tango fuyu no owari ni, 1984) also feature actors as primary characters. In both, aging actors return to their hometowns and confront problems of memory, family, identity, and place; they continually lose themselves in their ever-shifting memories. Similar elements also interface in *Dreams Departed, Orpheus* (Yume sarite, Orufe, 1986), in which the characters assume the roles of their parents and play out their parental memories to explore Japan's desolate prewar socio-political landscape. These last three plays share the unreliable nature of memory, conflated with a flawed sense of place and the failure of the family unit; through these themes, Shimizu comments on the impoverishment of postwar society.

Shimizu premiered *Loving People* (Koisuru hitobito) in 2000. He has taught at Tama Art University and served as executive director of the Japan Playwright's Association.

David Jortner

SHINGEKI. *Late Meiji through Taishô.* **Japan**'s "new theatre," that is, the modernist theatre arising during the late Meiji period (1868–1912) and after. *Shingeki* began with small **theatre companies**, often connected to universities, seeking to explore new ways of performance similar to those in contemporary Europe, in order to modernize Japan's theatre and present "real life" on **stage** through **Western** realistic **acting** and **playwriting**. The pioneer was the Literary Arts Society (Bungei Kyôkai, 1906), founded at Waseda University by **Tsubouchi Shôyô**. The troupe espoused two goals, developing actors and promoting plays, including Western classics—such as scenes from Shakespeare and Japan's first production of Ibsen's *A Doll's House* (1911)—and new Japanese works. Another early *shingeki* company, the Free Theatre (Jiyû Gekijô), formed in 1909 by **Osanai Kaoru** and **Ichikawa Sadanji** II, is generally credited with the first *shingeki* production, Ibsen's *John Gabriel Borkman* (1909).

Shingeki's popularity grew throughout the Taishô period (1912–1926), enhanced by the Tsukiji Little Theatre (Tsukiji Shôgekijô), formed in 1924 by Osanai and **Hijikata Yoshi**. Amidst the rubble left in Tokyo by the Great Kantô Earthquake of 1923, Hijikata and Osanai built the first theatre specifically designed for *shingeki*. The company primarily produced translated Western plays, focusing much of its energy on **training** actors in the realistic *shingeki* style. The company also explored avant-garde European trends, including expressionism, and became **politically** involved, producing leftist-oriented plays.

Early Shôwa. The early Shôwa period (1926–1989) witnessed a *shingeki* split between political and artistic camps. The former, influenced by Marxism, communism, labor unrest, trade unionism, and Japanese militarism, sought to harness socio-political messages and promoted emerging playwrights. This approach is perhaps best crystallized in **Kubo Sakae**'s *Land of Volcanic Ash* (Kazanbaichi, 1937–1938), concerning agricultural challenges in the potassium-poor soil of Hokkaidô. Kubo presents a broad societal cross-section of characters and demonstrates how preparations for war and Japan's capitalist system destroy their livelihoods. While *Land of Volcanic Ash* was successful, many other leftist works were hardly more than propaganda pieces. As militarist leaders consolidated their power, they imprisoned many leftwing *shingeki* figures.

The artistic camp, by contrast, used theatre to explore psychology and domestic life through imagery and poetic language. In 1932, a group of playwrights, including **Kishida Kunio, Kubota Mantarô**, and **Tanaka Chikao**, formed the Tsukiji Theatre (Tsukiji-za), dedicated to staging original *shingeki* works. Kishida's best-known play, the *Two Daughters of Mr. Sawa* (Sawa-shi no futari musume, 1935), explores the interpersonal relations and disintegration of the family, which results from the father's absence. In 1937, Kishida, Kubota, and Iwata Toyoo (1893–1969) formed the Literary Theatre (Bungaku-za), a company dedicated to developing talented, nonpolitical playwrights. It was the only major *shingeki* company allowed to perform throughout the war.

Postwar. The postwar Occupation of Japan was a tremendous boost to *shingeki*, with authorities initially inclined toward heavy **censorship** of the feudalistic, nationalistic themes characteristic of *bunraku* (see Puppet Theatre) and *kabuki*. *Shingeki* figures imprisoned by the militarists were freed, and the authorities encouraged plays promoting democracy.

The unfettered atmosphere yielded tremendous growth throughout the 1950s, and several of the current leading companies were founded at this time, including the Actor's Theatre (Haiyû-za, 1944) and the People's Art Theatre (Gekidan Mingei, 1950). In addition, the 1950s saw some of Japan's best-known playwrights, like **Mishima Yukio** and **Abe Kôbô**, emerge. While most playwrights continued to write in the realist/modernist form, there was some **experimentation** with classicism (as in Mishima's modern *nô* plays) and with surrealism (as in Abe's works). Mishima employs *shingeki* stylistic tropes through his glib, evocative language and psychologically complex characters. His *Deer Cry Pavilion* (Rokumeikan, 1956) features realistic dialogue and settings to explore the personal and political intrigue of the Meiji court. Abe uses *shingeki* realism to highlight the absurdity of society, as in *Friends* (Tomodachi, 1967), where an unknown family abruptly descends upon an anonymous urban apartment dweller to become his "friends," to "help" him.

Although *shingeki* was challenged in the 1960s by the rise of **shôgekijô** and **angura**, it retained its hold as Japan's most popular modern theatre. Recently, *shingeki* has seen a rebirth in playwrights like **Hirata Oriza**, whose "quiet theatre" (*shizuka na engeki*), a style also associated with several other dramatists, features realistic acting and the rhythms of everyday speech.

FURTHER READING

Allyn, John. "The Tsukiji Little Theatre and the Beginning of Modern Theatre in Japan"; Powell, Brian. *Japan's Modern Theatre: A Century of Continuity and Change;* Rimer, J. Thomas. *Toward a Modern Japanese Theatre: Kishida Kunio;* Rolf, Robert T., and John K. Gillespie, eds. *Alternative Japanese Drama: Ten Plays.*

David Jortner

SHINGŬK. Korean • **Western-influenced** genre of "new theatre" developed during the early twentieth century. The term includes translated Western dramas as well as Korean plays written in diverse Western styles. Distinct from the **Japanese**-inspired *shinp'agŭk*, *shingŭk* was founded on misconceptions about Western drama. During the Japanese occupation of Korea (1910–1945), Western influences reached Korea via Japan. All foreign-language plays were translated into Japanese, then into Korean. Ibsen's *A Doll's House*, for example, was translated from Norwegian into German, then into Japanese, and finally into Korean. Errors in translation and misinterpretations were inevitable. Naively applying the term "new theatre" to all Western forms only confused matters. The turbulent **political** situation during colonial rule, and the devastation of World War II and the Korean War (1950–1953) further fettered development (see Censorship).

The 1930s is considered *shingŭk*'s heyday. Leaders such as **Yu Ch'i-jin** endeavored to establish a legitimate Western-style theatre to raise national awareness and social consciousness while educating audiences accustomed to traditional theatre. *Shingŭk* came to be characterized by translated dramas (including Shakespeare's), Korean dramas modeled after Ibsen, Chekhov, Shaw, and others, proscenium **theatres**, and a pseudo-Stanislavskian **acting** style.

Although realism was prevalent, an interest in diverse methods is exemplified by **Kim U-jin**'s autobiographical *Shipwreck* (Nanp'a, 1926), which deals with a poet's (Kim himself) inner struggle. The German subtitle, meaning "An Expressionistic Story in Three Acts," clearly indicates Kim's intent to **experiment** with expressionism, in this case in the manner of Strindberg. Unfortunately, Kim's suicide abruptly interrupted early *shingŭk* explorations.

In the 1930s, Yu Ch'i-jin and Ham Se-dŏk (1915–1950) were deeply inspired by Irish writers Synge and O'Casey, among others. Yu's *The Mud Hut* (Tomak, 1931) imitates O'Casey's *Juno and the Paycock* and borrows elements from Synge's "Riders to the Sea." Depicting the plight of a poverty-stricken family in rural Korea, *The Mud Hut* became a model for new **playwrights** into the following decade. Ham Se-dŏk penned *A Winding Path in the Mountain* (Sonhŏguri, 1936) in close study and imitation of "Riders to the Sea." His *A Trip to Muŭi Island* (Muŭido kihaeng, 1940) is one of the few *shingŭk* plays that rose above imitation to become a modern classic.

Many new *shingŭk* playwrights in the 1950s imitated plays by Americans like O'Neill, Williams, and Miller, frequently altering the original by adding local themes and characters to appeal to native tastes, but their plays failed to capture the Korean character. To establish a Western-style theatre in a chaotic half-century was a formidable task, and a body of enduring realistic dramas never arose. By the late 1960s, *shingŭk* based on Western realism was passé. Various experiments with nonrealistic drama in the 1970s were a direct response to *shingŭk*'s shortcomings through the previous decades.

FURTHER READING

Jang, Won-Jae. *Irish Influences on Korean Theatre during the 1920s and 1930s.*

Ah-Jeong Kim

SHIN KABUKI. "New (or neo) *kabuki*," a modern outgrowth of **Japan**'s *kabuki* theatre. The term was first coined in 1919 by Kusuyama Masao (1884–1950) and later defined by Kagayama Naozô (1909–1978) as *kabuki* plays written under **Western influence**, with literary as well as dramatic merit. As used today, however, *shin kabuki* refers to works written since the late Meiji period (1868–1912) by scholars and writers who, unlike Edo period (1603–1868) **playwrights**, were not formally attached to *kabuki*. These works, tinged with modern European dramatic standards, were staged with *kabuki*'s apparatus, though they generally avoid such traditional **acting** and staging conventions as climactic poses (*mie*), special effects (*keren*), stylized **makeup**, and quick **costume** changes. Offstage **music** is used sparingly, and only when justified by the context. With these plays, *kabuki* came to be divided into "classical" (*koten*) and "new" (*shin*) periods.

Meiji-Period Origins. Following the Meiji Restoration (1868), some dignitaries and intellectuals began to criticize *kabuki* as illogical, fantastic, vulgar, virtually bereft of aesthetic value, and an inappropriate form of art to reflect modern Japan (see Theory); this led to calls for reform. *Shin kabuki*'s origins can be traced to the late-nineteenth-century reforms instituted by **Ichikawa Danjûrô** IX with his "living history plays" (*katsureki geki*), and their historical realism. This trend included the "cropped-hair plays" (*zangiri mono*), which reflected everyday life in a rapidly changing, Western-influenced Japan. After **Kawatake Mokuami** died in 1893, there was no dramatist of comparable caliber to replace him. This gap, coupled with Western theatre's growing influence and the era's great social changes, facilitated a transition from the old playwriting system, represented in the work of figures like Fukuchi Ôchi (1841–1906), with plays like *A Chivalrous Commoner's Spring Rain Hat* (Kyôkaku harusame gasa, 1897).

Tsubouchi Shôyô's *A Paulownia Leaf* (Kiri hitoha), published in 1894 but not staged until 1904 because of conservative objections, is considered the first *shin kabuki* play. The positive response to its premiere inspired others outside the official *kabuki* sphere, such as **Mori Ôgai**, Matsui Shôô (1870–1933), Takayasu Gekkô (1869–1944), Yamazaki Shikô (1875–1939), Oka Onitarô (1872–1943), and **Okamoto Kidô**, to try their hand at the new genre.

These works sought to bring to *kabuki* a modern, psychologically true dimension, which remained standard thereafter. The leading actor was **Ichikawa Sadanji** II, who took over the Meiji Theatre (Meiji-za) and sought to produce new plays reflective of notions like psychological egotism, art for art's sake, and love for love's sake. These included Yamazaki's *A Tale of Kabuki* (Kabuki monogatari, 1908) and Okamoto's

The "Second Messenger" act of Mayama Seika's monumental *shin kabuki* play *Genroku-Period Treasury of Loyal Retainers*, Tokyo Theatre (Tôkyô Gekijô), Tokyo, January 1935. Ichikawa Sadanji II (left) played Oishi Kuronosuke and Ichikawa Ennosuke (later, En'o) was Onodera Junai. (Photo: Courtesy Waseda Theatre Museum)

A Tale of Shuzen–ji (Shuzen–ji monogatari, 1909), which established *shin kabuki*'s value. Soon, all the major stars—especially **Onoe Kikugorô VI, Nakamura Ganjirô I, Ichimura Uzaemon** XV, **Ichikawa Ennosuke** II, **Morita Kanya** XIII, and **Nakamura Kichiemon** I—began to have plays written to suit them. New prewar playwrights—many famous as novelists—joining the scene included **Yamamoto Yûzô, Kikuchi Kan, Tanizaki Jun'ichirô, Mayama Seika**, Ikeda Daigo (1885–1942), Okamura Shikô (1881–1925), and **Uno Nobuo**. For a time, while *shingeki* was still testing its wings, *shin kabuki* was Japan's most advanced theatre.

Postwar Developments. After the war, playwrights were encouraged by Occupation authorities to counteract the feudalism of classical *kabuki* by writing nonfeudalistic plays. A consequent tendency to dramatize novels adversely affected *shin kabuki*'s creativity. Major examples included *The Tale of Genji* (Genji monogatari, 1951) by Funahashi Seiichi (1904–1976) and *Nayotake* (1946) by **Katô Michio**. Such plays are normally classed as *shin kabuki*, but their style does not closely resemble that of earlier *shin kabuki*. New *kabuki* plays continued to be written after the Occupation, as with **Mishima Yukio**'s *The Fishmonger's Net of Love* (Iwashi uri koi no hikiami, 1954), but such pieces are called "newly created *kabuki*" (*shinsaku kabuki*).

A post-1994 innovation is Cocoon Kabuki (Kokûn Kabuki), started by Nakamura Kankurô V (later, **Nakamura Kanzaburô** XVIII). Named after Tokyo's Theatre Cocoon (Shiataa Kokûn), this group renders, in completely new ways, classical pieces, such as *The Ghost Stories of Yotsuya* (Yotsuya kaidan) and *The Scarlet Princess of Edo* (Sakura-hime azuma bunshô). While Cocoon Kabuki utilizes simple settings and faithfully reproduces the atmosphere of Edo-period **theatres**, it also presents a clearly modern sensitivity, partly due to the participation of veteran *shingeki* practitioners, such as director Kushida Kazuyoshi (1943–) and actor Sasano Takashi (1948–).

FURTHER READING

Leiter, Samuel L. *New Kabuki Encyclopedia: A Revised Adaptation of Kabuki Jiten*; Powell, Brian. *Kabuki in Modern Japan: Mayama Seika and His Plays.*

Guohe Zheng

SHINKOKUGEKI.

SHINKOKUGEKI. "New national theatre," a **Japanese** modern **theatre company** and genre, led by **actor • Sawada Shôjirô**, formerly with the Art Theatre (Geijutsu-za) troupe. Its opening productions in Tokyo (1917) were commercial failures, forcing Sawada to decamp to Kyoto, then Osaka, for retrenchment. His new look featured realistic sword fights (not stylized as in *kabuki*), and these quickly became *shinkokugeki*'s trademark, giving it status as a separate genre.

By 1920, Sawada had developed *shinkokugeki*'s "half-a-step-ism" (*hanposhugi*) policy: half-a-step giving the audience what it wanted, half-a-step guiding it toward better drama. Through this policy, alongside the sword fights, the company performed important works by several contemporary **playwrights**, especially **Mayama Seika**, who wrote his best plays in the 1920s for Sawada and *shinkokugeki*.

Productions regularly filled the biggest Tokyo **theatres** from 1922 until Sawada's death. After brief uncertainty, *shinkokugeki* revived in the 1930s with the maturation of two worthy successors, Tatsumi Ryûtarô (1905–1989) and Shimada Shôgo (1905–2004). During the war, the ethos behind *shinkokugeki*'s sword-fight plays naturally endeared its productions to the militarists; but in the early postwar years the same ethos just as naturally fell afoul of Occupation **censors**. During the 1950s, *shinkokugeki* regained some popularity with plays featuring lone swordsmen who protected the weak, but the frequency of productions gradually declined, and *shinkokugeki* (genre and company) officially ended in 1987.

FURTHER READING

Powell, Brian. *Japan's Modern Theatre: A Century of Continuity and Change.*

Brian Powell

SHINPA.

SHINPA. Genre of modern **Japanese** theatre. During the 1880s, outsiders challenged the virtual monopoly held by *kabuki*, and by the 1890s this "new school" (with *kabuki* regarded as "old school" [*kyûha*]) drama had acquired conventions and characteristics that identified it as a new form. Influenced by *kabuki* **acting**, *shinpa* had its own "female impersonators" (*onnagata*), but from 1890, when **women** were allowed on **stage**, also employed actresses and mounted the first mixed-cast production in Tokyo in 1891. Indeed, a woman, **Mizutani Yaeko**, became the most famous star.

Shinpa generally favored stories of contemporary life, often involving the geisha world, over historical dramas. Its plays were often structured around the conflict between inescapable duties and the strong emotion (usually love) incompatible with them.

Growing out of **politically** pointed plays (*sôshi shibai*) by activists, *shinpa* gained fame in 1891 when actor-manager **Kawakami Otojirô** dramatized a political assassination to packed houses at Tokyo's Kabuki **Theatre** (Kabuki-za). During the 1890s, *shinpa* evinced two trends: in Kawakami's hands, it effectively became Japan's modern theatre with a repertory including Shakespeare and other **Western** drama, while other *shinpa* practitioners, led by actor Ii Yôhô (1871–1932), concentrated on domestic dramas of the evolving middle-class life of the time. Dramatizations of novels serialized in newspapers were an important commercial element of the repertoire.

In the early 1900s, *shinpa* almost eclipsed *kabuki*, having enriched its repertory by dramatizations of the arcane stories of the highly popular novelist **Izumi Kyôka**. *Shinpa* enthusiastically embraced the new medium of film in the mid-1910s and developed the short-lived but immensely popular "linked drama" (*rensageki*) form, part live theatre, part film shot on location. From 1917, *shinpa* enjoyed a new boom as it entered the "era of the three leaders," Ii, Kawai Takeo (1877–1942), and Kitamura Rokurô (1871–1961), all actors with large fan followings. The *shinpa* plays of **Mayama Seika**, vivid in language and trenchant in character portrayal, were prominent.

The 1930s was a time of continual success, and at the end of the decade Tokyo had four active **theatre companies**. Much of this success was due to two **playwrights**, Seto Eiichi (1892–1934) and Kawaguchi Matsutarô (1899–1985). In the early 1930s, Seto wrote eight plays depicting the different lives of three geisha and fully exploiting the acting style of *shinpa*'s leading *onnagata*, Hanayagi Shôtarô (1894–1965).

Some of this vitality was lost after World War II, when much of *shinpa*'s cultural underpinning was destroyed. The enormous popular followings of Hanayagi and Mizutani and *shinpa*'s frequent collaborations with other commercial genres ensured a continuation of financial viability in the 1950s, but with few new actors emerging in the 1960s *shinpa* experienced a steady decline. While it vigorously celebrated its own centenary in 1987 under the leadership of Mizutani's daughter—the popular Mizutani Yoshie (1939–), who took the name Yaeko in 1995—by the end of the century *shinpa* was represented only by sporadic performances. *See also Shin Kabuki; Shinkokugeki.*

FURTHER READING

Powell, Brian. *Japan's Modern Theatre: A Century of Continuity and Change.*

Brian Powell

SHINP'AGŬK. **Korean** theatre genre born in 1911. Its heyday lasted for a decade, but performances continued until the late 1920s. *Shinp'agŭk* ("new school drama") was shaped by popular **Japanese** culture, thus imitating *shinpa* in form and content in its early years; as it developed, plays based on Korean novels and popular **Western** novels appeared. Titles of plays such as *Dream of Lasting Resentment* (Changhanmong, 1913) and *Bitterness of a Faithful Wife* (Chŏngbuwŏn, 1916) suggest the melodramatic themes of painful family relationships and tragic romance at the core of *shinp'agŭk*'s popularity.

The first *shinp'agŭk*, Im Sŏng-gu's (1887–1921) *Divine Punishment for Lack of Filial Piety* (Purhyo ch'ŏnbŏl, 1911), staged by the Revolutionary Troupe (Hyŏkshindan), met with little success, but subsequent productions by the group and two other theatre companies found receptive audiences. *Shinp'agŭk* and its tragic romances soon competed with traditional entertainments. Im Sŏng-gu's death brought the end of the Revolutionary Troupe and signaled the decline of *shinp'agŭk*, though the professional group, Galaxy of Stars Theatre Company (Ch'wisŏngja Kŭktan), had *shinp'aguk* plays in its 1929 repertoire.

Though the 1920s and 1930s brought occasional *shinp'agŭk* attempting to deal with contemporary social problems, artistic advances were minimal. *Shinp'agŭk* seemed fettered by its early and continuing commercial reliance on melodrama and waned. In the 1930s, *shingŭk*, based on **Western** realistic drama and pioneered by **Yu Ch'i-jin**, would become the dominant form.

FURTHER READING

Korean International Theatre Institute, ed. *Korean Performing Arts: Drama, Dance and Music Theatre.*

Richard Nichols

SHIN SŎN-HI (1945–). Korean • **scenographer** and, since 1998, president and artistic **director** of the prestigious Seoul Performing Arts Company (Seoul Yesultan). Shin received her MFA in scene design from the University of Hawaii (1971). Teaching briefly in Korea, she returned to the United States (1975–1980) to study with designer Lester Polakov, leading the way for female Korean set and **costume** designers who would study abroad in the 1980s, among them Kim Hyŭn-suk (1954–), costume designer for the internationally acclaimed *The Last Empress* (Myŏngsŏng hwangho, 1995).

Following three years of freelance designing in the United States, Shin returned to Korea and its **director**-dominated theatre in which designers often were regarded more as skilled laborers than artists. She strove to remedy that situation through her teaching and artistry. Her design for **Oh T'ae-sŏk**'s *Bicycle* (Chajŏngŏ, 1983) received the Baek Sang Award and the Korean Drama **Festival** Award for best scenography, establishing her credentials. Over the next fifteen years, she created more than fifty designs for **dance**, theatre for youth, and drama. Her work is an important catalyst in the transformation of Korean scene design into a respected art.

Shin was a moving force in the establishment of the Academy of Scenography (1992), where she taught until assuming her current post at the Seoul Performing Arts Company. She continues to design, collaborating with major directors, such as **Lee Yun-t'aek**, recently focusing on **musical** versions of Shakespeare.

Richard Nichols

SHIRAISHI KAYOKO (1941–). Japanese • **actress** who joined **Suzuki Tadashi**'s Waseda Little **Theatre** (Waseda **Shôgekijô**) in 1967. Suzuki was developing his acting theory, and within two years he had built his intricate vision around her. Shiraishi's uncanny sense of movement and timing and ability to express nuanced emotions were integral to Suzuki's success. Her skills were on striking display as a madwoman in Suzuki's *On the Dramatic Passions II* (Gekiteki naru mono o megutte II, 1970), which brought her national and international fame.

Shiraishi has been compared to **Izumi no Okuni**, *kabuki*'s legendary progenitor. This pre-modern link doubtless helped Suzuki validate his acting **theory**, based on plumbing the Japanese psyche and utilizing the Japanese physique in his rigorous **training** program for the lower part of the body. Their intense collaboration continued for over twenty years, producing acclaimed works like *The Trojan Women* (Toroia no onna, 1974) and *Clytemnestra* (Ôhi Kuritemunesutora, 1983).

Shiraishi left Suzuki in 1989 to work freelance, regularly appearing in **Ninagawa Yukio**'s Shakespeare productions. One of Shiraishi's most recent works is her one-woman tour de force *100 Stories* (Hyaku monogatari, 1999), a series of plays drawing inspiration from Japanese folklore and contemporary literature. For this work, she earned the Minister of Education Arts Award in 2001. Shiraishi works frequently in television and film.

Yukihiro Goto

Shiraishi Kayoko in Suzuki Tadashi's production of *The Trojan Women*. (Photo: Courtesy of Waseda Theatre Museum)

SHÔGEKIJÔ. **Japan**'s "little **theatre** movement," a term first used in the 1920s by **Osanai Kaoru** with regard to the Tsukiji Little Theatre (Tsukiji Shôgekijô) to protest *kabuki*'s size and commercialism. Other **theatre companies**, notably the Actor's Little Theatre (Haiyû-za Shôgekijô), subsequently used the term, embracing Osanai's noncommercialism.

The term is now primarily used for the movement emerging from Tokyo-area universities in response to the 1960 renewal of the U.S.-Japan Mutual Security Treaty (Anpo). The youth counterculture rejected not only the treaty but old-left **politically** oriented *shingeki*, regarding it as too literary, too **Westernized**, and ultimately ineffective. *Shôgekijô* practitioners also attacked commercialism and the hierarchy of **director**, **playwright**, and **actor**, valuing collective contributions and the actor over any single individual (though, eventually, leading figures reasserted the primacy of director and playwright over performer). They borrowed, bought, or rented small spaces around Tokyo for performances. Some companies, like Situation Theatre (Jôkyô Gekijô, 1963), began performing under tents or on city streets to further challenge the notion of theatrical space and bring theatre to areas lacking established venues. New **stages** unconnected to the traditional *shingeki* world were created, including the Art Theatre Shinjuku Bunka (1963) and Kinokuniya Hall (1964).

Critic Senda Akihiko has specified four *shôgekijô* generations: the first, including **Akimoto Matsuyo**, **Betsuyaku Minoru**, **Kara Jûrô**, **Ninagawa Yukio**, **Ôta Shôgo**, **Saitô Ren**, **Satoh Makoto**, **Shimizu Kunio**, **Suzuki Tadashi**, and **Terayama Shûji**, developed alternative theatre in response to 1960s politics; the second, including **Kitamura Sô**, **Komatsu Mikio**, Okabe Kôdai (1945), Ryûzanji Shô (1948–), **Takeuchi Jûichirô**, **Tsuka Kôhei**, and **Yamazaki Tetsu**, came of age in the 1970s as heirs to the first generation, while struggling against it, adding ironic laughter to committed politics; the third, including **Furuhashi Teiji**, **Kawamura Takeshi**, **Kisaragi Koharu**, **Kôkami Shôji** (also in the fourth generation), **Noda Hideki**, and **Watanabe Eriko**, developed in the 1980s; and the fourth, including **Chong Wishin**, **Hirata Oriza**,

Iwamatsu Ryô, **Kaneshita Tatsuo**, Koike Hiroshi (1956–), **Makino Nozomi**, **Matsuda Masataka**, **Miyazawa Akio**, Nagai Ai, Ôhashi Yasuhiko, Sakate Yôji, **Suzue Toshirô**, Takahashi Isao (1961–), and **Yokouchi Kensuke**, came of age in the 1990s. Those born in the late 1960s and early 1970s now form an emergent fifth generation with little of the collective approach common in generations one and two, mostly forming instead around a specific individual artist, as in generations three and four. Included are Chiba Masako (1962), Kida Tsuyoshi (1969–), Matsumura Takeshi (1970–), Murakami Hiroki (1973–), and Nagatsuka Keishi (1975–).

Shôgekijô is sometimes conflated with *angura*. The movements are indeed related, but *angura,* rooted in 1960s politics, died out in the late 1970s and early 1980s, while *shôgekijô* remains vibrant today. Indeed, the *shôgekijô* of the 1960s and 1970s, considered as alternative theatre, slowly morphed during the 1980s "bubble economy" into a more commercial, popular, and less political form that continues today.

The differences between contemporary *shingeki* and *shôgekijô* are less clearly defined, and many now refer to both by the term "contemporary theatre" (*gendai geki*).

FURTHER READING

Powell, Brian. *Japan's Modern Theatre: A Century of Continuity and Change*; Rolf, Robert, and John K. Gillespie, trans. and ed. *Alternative Japanese Drama: Ten Plays.*

Kevin J. Wetmore, Jr.

SHUMANG LILA. Indian • **folk theatre** from Manipur. Its name (coined in 1976) comes from "courtyard" and "play." Other names are *jatra* or *jatrawali*. Some claim it developed from two early twentieth-century forms, *kabul pala* and *fadibee pala*, themselves outgrowths of a late-nineteenth-century farce form, *phagi* (also *fagee* or *phagee*) *lila*, fostered by Maharaja Chandrakirti (1850–1886). The earlier clowns mocked the nobility and pointed up various social problems while the newer versions communicated anti-British subtexts. This subtext later was replaced by other socio-**political** concerns of the Manipuri people, from family issues to the state government to unemployment to insurgency, and so on. The breadth of issues adopted is mirrored in a play about 9/11.

The first play to regularize *shumang lila*'s dramaturgical methods and to tell a straightforward story was *King Harishchandra* (Raja Harishchandra, 1918), about the travails of a pious Hindu monarch. In the 1950s, *shumang lila* evolved from a significantly improvisatory form to a scripted one, an important step in the development of Manipuri literature. Moreover, the **director**'s role as maestro in charge of all elements became significant.

Despite several female troupes (*nupi shumang lila*), most of the approximately twenty **theatre companies** are entirely male (*nupa shumang lila*), depending on high-level, extremely popular "female impersonators" (*nupi shabi*). They command high salaries and may move from one troupe to another to earn more money. Also very important is the "clown" (*phagi puba*), originally a freewheeling commentator but later integrated into the story, depriving him of his comical power. Ten to thirteen performers belong to these touring companies, which are invited by localities to perform.

The show is held in any outdoor space—from the courtyards that give it its name to a riverbank—occupying about thirteen by thirteen feet, and surrounded on three sides by spectators (divided by gender), with a single passageway through them to and from the **acting** area. Staging elements are minimal, with no raised **stage**, **curtain**, **scenography**, or the like; a table and two chairs at one side are the principal props. Lights and microphones dangle from a wire overhead. However, large-scale competition **festivals** erect substantial pavilions, including raised stages. The **actor**'s vocal and physical means take prominence. Dialogue is delivered in natural tones; prerecorded singing permits lip-syncing of the songs.

This otherwise secular form is increasingly being used in **religious** ritual contexts for marriage and death ceremonies.

Samuel L. Leiter

SHU XIUWEN (1915–1969). Chinese • **actress** in modern "spoken drama" (*huaju*; see Playwrights and Playwriting) and film, renowned for her versatility and intensity. Brought up in Beijing, she moved to Shanghai in 1931, where she dubbed the first Chinese sound film, *Sing-Song Girl Red Peony* (Genü hongmudan, 1931), and worked with **playwright** • **Tian Han**, performing in one-acts including "Comrades" (Zhanyou) and "S.O.S." before joining Yihua Film Studio in 1932.

Between 1934 and 1937, Shu acted in more than twenty films. On **stage**, Shu gained recognition by her acute portrayals of compassionate and complex roles, including Xiao Chunlan in *Mei Luoxiang* and Jinzi in **Cao Yu**'s *The Wilderness* (Yuanye, 1937).

During the Second Sino-Japanese War (1937–1945), Shu joined the mass migration inland and blossomed on stage in the wartime capital, Chongqing. Considered one of the four best *huaju* actresses, she provided rich and varied characterizations, notably the outspoken Hong Xuanjiao in *Spring and Autumn in the Heavenly Kingdom* (Tianguo chunqiu), the self-sacrificing Doctor Ding in *Metamorphosis* (Tuibian), and the cunning Empress Dowager in *Secret History of the Qing Court* (Qing gong mishi). After the war, she returned to Shanghai's stage and screen, winning Best Actress of the Year (1947). In the 1950s, Shu joined the Beijing People's Art Theater (Beijing Renmin Yishu Juyuan) and graced numerous roles with subtlety, precision, and passion, being most highly regarded for her colorful portrayal of Huniu in **Lao She**'s *Rickshaw* (Luotuo xiangzi).

Weihong Bao

SHWE MAN TIN MAUNG (1918–1969). Burmese • **actor** and **dancer**, second only to **Po Sein**. Born to poor parents without an arts background, he began **training** and working for a famous female dancer at twelve; by the time he was fifteen he was a professional, becoming famous all over Burma (Myanmar).

He brought traditional *zat pwe* to its final peak in the post–World War II years. A true showman, he improved **stage** settings, used elaborate **costumes**, and introduced modern lighting. He created the **musical** drama form *aw-pai-ya* ("opera") in 1939. He added many new plays by having obscure Buddha birth stories (*jataka*) rewritten. He was best known for changing from pure dialogue to song and back again without missing a word or a beat.

Ma Thanegi

SINAKULO. The **Philippines** "passion play," also spelled *cenaculo*, written in octo-syllabic *quintillas*, which dramatizes the whole history of Christian salvation from the creation of the world to the coronation of the Virgin Mary in heaven, with major emphasis on the public life, passion, and resurrection of Jesus Christ.

All traditional *sinakulo* derive their sequence and typology of scenes, their principal characters, and much of their dialogue from the *pasyon*, a much older verse narrative on the Christ story that was chanted in public during Lent. In time, various apocrypha on biblical characters (for example, Dimas, Magdalene, and Barrabas) were borrowed from popular novels, metrical romances, and even magazines and movies to "perk up" this somber narrative.

Performed during Lent but most especially during Holy Week (Palm Sunday to Easter Sunday), the *sinakulo* unfolds like a Catholic catechism class, on a **stage** with many **scenographic** backdrops, for audiences of town and country. As a didactic **religious** piece, it draws a sharp line between the forces of what it considers good and evil. Held up for emulation are the "holy people" (*banal*), such as Christ, the Virgin, and the Apostles, who chant in lamenting fashion, enter and exit to a funeral march, and move about like gentle lambs. Evil are the *hudyo* (literally, "Jews," but also including the Roman officials and soldiers), who use a crisp chant, march to a sprightly *pasodoble* beat, and gesticulate and strut with cocky demeanor.

In the late nineteenth century and during the American colonial period (ca. 1900–1946), *sinakulo*, like the *pasyon*, depicted Christ as a willing victim of every oppression, a god-man who was "obedient unto death." By encouraging all Catholics to be like the suffering Christ, *sinakulo* inculcated values of unquestioning obedience to de facto authority, and discouraged subalterns from questioning the basis or validity of such authority. In this way, *sinakulo* broke the **political** will of natives colonized by Spain and America, inhibiting or even eliminating dissent.

In the Catholic Philippines today, the Christ story continues to be popular among the masses, so attempts to revitalize it for a contemporary audience have not been wanting. In this spirit, some groups have introduced more sophisticated lights and sounds, more "historical" **costumes** and scenography, and more impressive artifices, but their interpretation of the story remains unchanged. However, some politicized sectors have reinterpreted the story more radically to make it responsive to the needs of the masses and the times. In these radical *sinakulo*, Christ is portrayed either as a factory worker, a peasant, or a leader of the urban poor, all of whom are punished for threatening the status quo. Through such adaptations, the Christ story has truly been indigenized by Filipino artists for Filipino audiences of our time.

FURTHER READING

Tiongson, Nicanor G. *Sinakulo*.

Nicanor G. Tiongson

SINGAPORE. Situated just north of the equator in the heart of Southeast Asia, the tiny island-nation of Singapore—population 4,475,000 (2005)—has been an important entrepot for goods traveling from Asia to the rest of the world from its early days as a British colony. In support of its mercantile ambitions, the British imported laborers to what had been a sparsely populated collection of Malay fishing villages from southern **China, India**, and nearby peninsular **Malaysia**, creating the ethnic mix that still prevails. Singapore is a wealthy multicultural country with a diverse economy and serves as the regional headquarters for numerous multinational corporations. The People's Action Party (PAP) has ruled Singapore since independence and provides the arts with significant financial support through its National Arts Council (NAC) in the hopes of establishing the country as an important regional center for creative industries. With PAP's focus on building a significant arts infrastructure through the creation of venues and the support of **theatre companies**, theatre is viewed as a creative industry in need of economic development. Thus theatre reflects both the the country's highly pragmatic and technocratic spirit, and the cultural diversity of its largest ethnic groups (Chinese, Malay, and Indian) and principal religions (Buddhist [42.5 percent] and Muslim [14.9 percent]) and languages (Mandarin [35 percent], English [23 percent], and Malay [14.1 percent]).

English-Language Theatre. Singaporean English-language drama first emerged in the 1960s through the pioneering efforts of **playwrights** Lim Chor Pee (1936–) and Goh Poh Seng (1936–), both of whom wrote naturalistic plays in a Singaporean context while following essentially British models of **dramatic structure**. Writing in a similar vein was Robert Yeo (1940–), whose *One Year Back Home* (1980) was groundbreaking for the bold manner in which it dealt with contemporary **political** and social issues. Stella Kon's (1944–) *Emily of Emerald Hill* (1985) brought to the Singaporean **stage** perhaps its most enduring character, Emily, the proud and stern matriarch. Playwright, **director**, and teacher **Kuo Pao Kun**, the "Father of Singaporean theatre," is best known for his one-acts, "The Coffin Is Too Big for the Hole" (1984) and "No Parking on Odd Days" (1986), as well as his later works, notably *Lao Jiu* (1990) and *Descendents of the Eunuch Admiral* (1995).

The vast majority of Singaporean theatre is now in English, the language of business, finance, and education that effectively functions as a national language. Because of language policies that have favored English, as well as an extensive arts education program in the schools, audiences tend to be young, and theatregoing is culturally marked as a "hip" activity.

Ethnic Theatres. Until the mid-1980s, most Singaporeans were comfortable with the traditional forms associated with their individual cultural and linguistic backgrounds. Thus older Chinese Singaporeans traditionally provided the audience for Chinese theatre in the southern dialects of Hokkien, Teochew, and Cantonese, while Malays patronized ***bangsawan***, hugely popular before the advent of mass media. As Mandarin has increasingly replaced the various southern dialects among Singapore's majority Chinese population (77 percent), traditional regional forms have struggled, while the younger bilingual generation of ethnic Chinese Singaporeans has been drawn increasingly to the glamour of English-language theatre.

The 1980s saw the creation of a number of companies that made significant contributions and appealed to this emerging younger audience, including TheatreWorks, The Necessary Stage, and The Theatre Practice. Important Malay troupes include One Vision (Teater Ekamatra), Our **Theatre** (Teater Kami), Artistic Theatre (Teater Artistik), and Sriwana; South Indian companies include Theatre of Fire (Agni Koothu), Kairalee Kala Nilayam, and the Ravindran Drama Group; and Mandarin is spoken by Page to Stage Studio and Toy Factory Ensemble.

During the 1990s, theatre clearly shifted from its early playwright-centered focus to a concentration on new and company-created work, often driven by the director and scenographer's ideas. In part because of the influential house style of **Ong Keng Sen** at TheatreWorks, the relative youth and affluence of Singapore's audience, and the tightly controlled political climate, plays about prosaic and daily concerns of the country's multiethnic populace have been increasingly replaced by intercultural works drawing upon a range of Asian and **Western** sources. At times, these works have presented Asian traditions side by side in slick and beautiful productions without seeking cultural or theatrical fusion. Thus company-created theatre is more likely to present a fresh approach to the divas of Chinese theatre or to stage a deconstructed version of *Othello* from the viewpoint of Desdemona's fractured psyche than to deal with hard-hitting social realities.

Focus on Musicals. While theatre has become increasingly dominated by the director, one constant from the late 1980s has been the endeavor to develop a Singaporean or Asian-themed **musical** that can meet with financial and artistic success abroad. TheatreWorks broke this ground with a series of successful musicals (*Beauty World*, *Fried Rice Paradise*, *Private Parts*) by lyricist Michael Chiang and composer Dick Lee that fused Broadway style with Singaporean content. Significant support from private corporations and the NAC has resulted in numerous Asian-themed musicals since the early 1990s; some have had long runs locally or on overseas tours. Among the more notable are Action Theatre's *Chang and Eng* (1997) as well as Singapore Repertory Theatre's *Sing to the Dawn* (1996) and *Forbidden City* (2002). In 2005, records were broken when S$3 million was spent on *Phua Chu Kong,* a musical based on the popular local sitcom of the same name featuring many of the **actors** in their television roles.

Challenges. Singapore's rigorous **censorship** restrictions were relaxed during the 1990s, and plays dealing with once-taboo topics such as gay and lesbian relationships can now be staged, though plays deemed to threaten domestic or **religious** harmony or that challenge the country's "core moral values" are still prohibited. In terms of infrastructure, Singapore boasts impressive performance spaces, including four indoor **theatres** housed inside the massive Esplanade-Theatres on the Bay complex (2002). In addition, many established companies have their own dedicated spaces and there are numerous rental venues. The government has made much of the need to establish the "hardware" so that artists could then provide the "heartware" that makes the arts come alive. Singapore's focus on meeting external standards of excellence may make it difficult for a vibrant theatre scene to develop organically, though there has been an impressive surge in audience support for performing arts events since the early 1990s. One such component is the annual Singapore Arts Festival, which commissions new Singaporean theatre and **dance** by established local companies while also programming foreign works, including those by world-class artists such as Robert Wilson and Robet LePage. Still, it remains to be seen whether excellence in the arts can be created primarily by wealth and meticulous attention to infrastructure.

FURTHER READING

Lo, Jacqueline. *Staging Nation: English Language Theatre in Malaysia and Singapore;* Peterson, William. *Theater and the Politics of Culture in Contemporary Singapore*; Tan Chong Kee, and Tisa Ng, eds. *Ask Not: The Necessary Stage in Singapore Theatre*; Vente, Ines, and Lim Geok Eng. *Wayang: Chinese Street Opera in Singapore.*

William Peterson

SIRCAR, BADAL (1925–). Indian Bengali-language **playwright**, **director**, **theo-rist**, and **actor**, active in Calcutta (Kolkata). Sircar (also spelled Sarkar) was a civil engineer in India and elsewhere until 1975. His affiliation with Marxist ideology and exposure to Grotowski's "poor theatre," Schechner's environmental theatre, Beck and Malina's Living Theatre, and contemporary movements in Russia and Czechoslovakia, gave rise to his "Third Theatre" (*anganmanch*, literally, "open-air theatre"). It was cre-ated as an alternative to the conventional proscenium style, although he also produced plays indoors. Audience and actors intermingle, with spectators on benches rather than specific seats. In 1972, he turned to arena-style production with *Spartacus*, adapted from Howard Fast's novel. From 1976, he began to present Saturday afternoon productions in Curzon Park (later, Surendranath Park) given gratis (or for voluntary contributions) in open-air public spaces, where audiences and actors could interact. These technically spare performances—which relied on improvisation, privileged physical expression over text, and employed audience participation—were also offered in villages.

Sircar's work addresses the urban-rural conflict and the complex relationships among individuals, society, and power in the context of postcolonial **political** transitions and their harmful intellectual effects, especially on young people. His first play, *And Indra-jith* (Evam Indrajith, 1965), was dark and absurdist, concerned with life's emptiness. He also became well known for witty comedies. In 1967, he started the Satabdi **theatre company**; it closed but reopened in 1969, becoming the icon of Indian alterna-tive theatre. His best-known plays include *The Rest of History* (Baki itihas, 1965), *Delirium* (Pralap, 1966), *Thirtieth Century* (Tringsha shatabdi, 1966), *Mad Horse* (Pagla ghora, 1967), *There's No End* (Shesh nei, 1969), *Procession* (Michhil, 1974), *Bhoma* (1976), and *Stale News* (Bhasi khabar, 1979).

FURTHER READING

Sircar, Badal. *The Third Theatre*.

B. Ananthakrishnan

SOHN JIN-CHAEK (1947–). Korean • **director**, a founding member of the Minye **Theatre Company** (Minye Kŭkdan). He studied under **Hŏ Kyu**, whose mentor-ship was influential in the development of Sohn's theatrical vision. He parted from Minye in 1986, founding his own troupe, Beauty and Ugliness Company (Kŭkdan Michoo), along with others who had gained recognition from their work in *madangnori*.

Beauty and Ugliness's fundamental goal is to revitalize traditional elements in the modern theatre; however, in his directing, play selection, and contributions to the **stage**, Sohn Jin-Chaek's approach may be described as didactic. He has been persistent in stag-ing *ch'anggŭk* and plays about myths or legends. He also tackled **politically** sensitive plays, such as Dorfman's *Death and the Maiden* and Pak Jo-yŏl's *General Oh's Toenail* (Oh Changgun ui palt'op), written in 1972, but banned until 1989, when Sohn directed it.

His didacticism led to the start of the Beauty and Ugliness Orchestra and the Beauty and Ugliness School of Drama, which, following the Minye tradition, place an empha-sis on **training** • **actors** to become versed in the traditions of **music** and **dance**. He largely is responsible for the development of *madangnori* into its present form and for the continuation of its popularity. He directed the opening ceremony for the 2002 World Cup and has directed many multinational and multicultural projects, including his 2006 staging of Dorfman's *The Other Side* for **Japan's** New National **Theatre** (Shin Kokuritsu Gekijô).

Alyssa S. Kim

SOKARI. Sri Lankan • **folk theatre** of the central hill country of Kandy, combining **religious** and secular elements. This Sinhalese form is produced in honor of the goddess Pattini; the connection between its story and the goddess seems to be related to its fertility rite subtext, which is enhanced by suggestive actions and language. The company is all male, the words are in verse, the action is accompanied by a chorus and drum (Kandy's *gata bere* drum or, in the Vanni area, the *davula*), and the performance goes on all night. The venue is a village's circular threshing floor (*sokari* is performed at harvest time), with a nearby altar to Pattini. Invocations to her precede the play. The clownish servant character wears a **mask**.

The usual story, which has different versions, dates from the seventeenth or eighteenth centuries, and contains references to the close connections then between Sri Lanka and South **India**. Guru Hami, an Indian ritual specialist, his beautiful but barren young wife, Sokari, and the servant Paraya (or Pachamira, meaning "foreigner") make a pilgrimage to Sri Lanka by ship to pray for a child; they end up there after being shipwrecked. Language difficulties lead to humorous encounters. They, like various others who appear—a Brahman, a headman, a village virago, a ritual specialist—are satirized. In Sri Lanka, a doctor treats the snake-bitten husband. Sokari either elopes with or is seduced by him, or has a fling with the clown, but one day this unfaithful wife returns and has her husband's baby (the childbirth is enacted). She may even take a baby from the audience and sing it a lullaby.

The performance uses sophisticated mime, but a less developed form of **dance**, to present the preparations for the journey to the trip itself and its aftermath. The story is enacted as the players move around the circular space, stopping to present an episode before moving on to the next position and stopping. Improvisation mingles with set language. Performers, devotees of the goddess, may go into trance, as may spectators. All concludes with the troupe bowing before the goddess, begging forgiveness for missteps. Several troupes still perform *sokari*, sometimes introducing new touches, such as pop tunes.

FURTHER READING

Sarachchandra, E. R. *The Folk Drama of Ceylon.*

Samuel L. Leiter

SPESHAL NATAKAM. **Indian** dramatic form of southern Tamilnadu, centered mainly in Madurai and nearby cities, and barely known in Chennai (Madras). Called "special drama" in English, it is a Tamil-language commercial genre whose seeds were sown in the 1890s and now has about 1,500 **actors** and musicians, male and female, including children. The largest associations (*sangam*) of artists are in Madurai, Pudukkottai, and Dindigal. The Anglo-Tamil hybrid name *speshal natakam* by which it eventually was known has various implications, including the idea that each performer is hired "specially" for each performance, so that each performance is "special."

Speshal natakam began as an urban form produced by both adult and boys' **theatre companies** (although the latter sometimes included girls) during the early twentieth century. It was strongly influenced by **Parsi theatre**, including the introduction of actresses. Gradually, the companies gave way to a freelance, noncompany system; its name came into use when the company system still existed but—unable to fight the growing popularity of movies—was disintegrating. By the late 1940s, that system was practically moribund. Performances are now held in villages and "rurban" cities like Madurai, hybrids with both rural and urban characteristics.

Speshal natakam is given mainly in connection with **religious • festivals** and presented in all-night performances. Performances are aimed both at humans and deities (Hindu or Christian), the latter present in the form of statues situated on decorated chariots. Whereas tickets used to be sold, performances are now sponsored by individuals or groups, often in fulfillment of a vow (but sometimes to show off the sponsor's wealth). Audiences are segregated by sex, although men predominate. Religious rituals precede each performance, despite the form's secularism.

Performances use makeshift **stages** (with floors of dirt, wood, or concrete) set up in open areas, and with a proscenium orientation, including **scenographic** backdrops and ceiling, back, and side walls of braided palm leaves. The actors wear fairly heavy **makeup** (the men especially) and vivid **costumes** of lamé, glitter, and sequins. Crossdressing is occasionally practiced by both sexes, but men do so only for comic purposes while the few cross-dressing actresses do so to play heroes. Subject matter comes largely from the ***Ramayana*** and the ***Mahabharata***. The principal **playwright**, whose work constitutes almost the entire repertory, was T. T. Sankaradas Swamigal (1867–1922), a performer and teacher; considered the form's founder, he left over fifty scripts in sung verse and spoken prose covering many topics (including Christian ones and versions of Shakespeare). Most frequently performed is the romantic comedy *Valli's Wedding* (Valli tirumanam), about the marriage of the deity Lord Murugan, god of youth and beauty, to his Dravidian wife, Valli. Some plays deal with reformist ideals in their treatment of the issues of chastity, child marriage, and polygamy.

All performances begin with two hours of comedy, mingling bawdy humor, **dance**, singing, and improvisational acting, and featuring a male clown (the "buffoon") and a female dancer, supposed to be sixteen. This is followed by the play proper, lasting six hours, and, unlike the comedy with its lower-class characters, employs barely any movement as the performers, playing elites, stand relatively still at microphones to speak and sing. Much of this, while based on a script, is expanded through improvisation; perhaps three of the six hours are from the script proper. Comic scenes may be interspersed throughout the night.

Casts usually require around six actors and four musicians. **Music** is supplied by traditional drums and a harmonium. Since the artists are hired individually for the performance, they may never have performed with any of the others before. The highly conventionalized form, however, with its stock **role types** and familiar repertory, allows them to work smoothly despite the lack of rehearsals.

Actors come from a broad variety of backgrounds (including castes and religions), some being born into troupes, others joining later in life. However, members of the profession, who are mostly poor, are widely denigrated; **women** performers in particular are socially stigmatized.

FURTHER READING

Seizer, Susan. *Stigmas of the Tamil Stage: An Ethnography of Special Drama Artists in South India.*

Samuel L. Leiter

SRI LANKA. Sri Lanka, known by its shape and location as "India's teardrop," is a large island nineteen miles off the southeastern tip of **India**. It was settled in the late sixth century BC when an Indian prince arrived and married a Sinhalese princess, thereby establishing a native dynasty; Buddhism arrived in the mid-third century BC. A Tamil kingdom was created during the fourteenth by a South Indian dynasty. The island was occupied by the Portuguese in the sixteenth century and the Dutch in 1658, but, in 1814, was taken over by the British, who opposed Buddhism in favor of the Church of England. Independence (as a member of the British Commonwealth) was achieved in 1948, and it became completely independent as Sri Lanka in 1972, having been known as Ceylon since colonial times.

From 1983, the country has suffered ethnic tensions initially sparked by separatist ambitions by the Tamil minority under the leadership of the Tamil Liberation Front, founded in 1976; the conflict was complicated over the years by a variety of **political** factors, but many thousands died and over 200,000 Tamils have fled to escape the conflict; the issues still seethe and conflict still erupts, despite a 2002 cease-fire between the government and the Liberation Tigers of Tamil Eelam.

Sri Lanka's eight provinces contain slightly over 20 million people; the capital is Colombo. The ethnic breakdown is 73.8 percent Sinhalese, 7.2 percent Sri Lankan Moors, 4.8 percent Indian Tamils, 3.9 percent Sri Lankan Tamils, and the rest unspecified. According to the 2001 census, its **religious** distribution is Buddhist (69.1 percent), Muslim (7.6 percent), Hindu (7.1 percent), and Christian (6.2 percent), with the remainder unspecified. Though culturally and physically close to India, it has managed to keep alive Sinhala, a language distinct from any spoken in the subcontinent. Sinhala is the national and official language, spoken by 74 percent of the people, while Tamil is spoken by 18 percent. English, understood by 10 percent of the population, is the principal language of government. The modern theatre is divided into Sinhalese, Tamil, and English categories; each has been influenced by the traditions of India and the colonial past.

Early Theatre. Sri Lanka lacks a pre-modern literary tradition, partly because classical Sinhalese writers preferred prose and poetry to drama, but possibly also because Buddhist monks considered it taboo. There are, however, are a number of highly theatrical all-night ritual performances, such as "devil dances" (bali-*tovil* or *thovil*) and *kohomba kankariya*, representing a fusion of Theravada Buddhist belief with native indigenous cults. Exorcists typically act to drive illness-causing demons away from an afflicted person. Although the dramatic interludes found in some of these ceremonials are highly theatrical, using **costumes, masks**, dialogue, mimesis, **dance**, song, **music**, characterization, and even humor, the interludes did not expand into truly dramatic forms of expression. They represented a bridgeway to the more developed **folk theatre** traditions of ***kolam***, ***sokari***, and ***nadagam***. Thus Sri Lanka's theatre derives not from the educated classes, but from the culture of rural villagers. There is also a **puppet theatre** tradition, and one involving a Roman Catholic "passion play" (***pasku***). In the late nineteenth century, while such practices were prevalent in the villages, a modern theatre began to appear.

Modern Theatre. The modern, urban Sinhalese theatre came into being with the 1877 arrival in Colombo of a **Parsi theatre** troupe from Bombay. Its spectacular gas-lit production of *The Court of Lord Indra* (Indar sabha), replete with special effects and **women** performers, had a resounding effect and quickly led to the establishment of a native version. This musical—even operatic—theatre, known as ***nurti***, fused

European and Indian dramaturgic and performative modes; it imbibed the influence of *nadagam*, which it replaced in popularity. *Nurti* was produced on a proscenium **stage** in an enclosed **theatre**; the fantastical plays (in which even flowers could speak) were based on stories from myth and legend. Despite its great popularity, *nurti* faded in the 1930s when faced with the advent of movies and with its inability to keep pace with modern concerns.

During World War II, a drama with a more immediate social base and a tighter structure was developed. Called *jayamanne* (after playwright B. A. W. Jayamanne, although his brother, Eddie, was the star), it still depended on a large infusion of song, but its contemporary themes—such as caste and dowries—were appealing.

Sinhalese theatre as a commercial, urban medium ended its first phase with the arrival of local filmmaking in 1947, when the popular Minerva Amateur Dramatic Club, from which star **Rukmani Devi** emerged, morphed into Sri Lanka's first film studio, and produced the first Sinhalese movie (1947). Film quickly outpaced theatre in popularity.

Modern Sinhalese drama was born under other, more literary auspices. For example, at the University of Ceylon (later the University of Sri Lanka), Sinhalese translations and adaptations of modern classics were annually presented, especially through the extraordinary efforts of E. F. C. Ludowyk (1906–1985), a transplanted English professor who, from the 1930s through the 1950s, **directed** numerous **Western** classic and modern plays for the University of Ceylon Drama Society (a.k.a. Dramsoc). These mainly English-language productions (he did his first Sinhalese production in 1945) helped in forging a language free from the ornate rhetoric of *nurti*. They also trained generations of new Sri Lankan artists. Other university-based groups followed suit, an important alumni company being Stage and Set, which produced major Western works.

Throughout the 1940s and early 1950s, various **experiments** in playwriting and production were undertaken. Though some were successful, the plays lacked polish. Important contributors were Lucian de Zoysa, whose The Thespians followed a Shakespeare series with plays by European modernists and those on native historical themes. The first significant breakthrough, however, came in 1956 with Ediriweera (E. R.) Sarachchandra's (1914–1996) pathbreaking *Maname*, telling a Buddha birth story (*jataka*) via *nadagam* techniques combined with Western dramaturgy.

Sri Lankan drama was boosted by the foundation of the Arts Council of Sri Lanka (1952), which, from 1959, began to sponsor Sinhalese theatre, and which later diversified to encompass Tamil- and English-language theatre as well as other types of performance. From 1967, annual State Drama **Festivals** were held to award the best new Sinhalese and Tamil plays, and other festival offshoots supporting theatre sprang up as well. Plays ranged from the conventional to the experimental, and some were considered important contributions. A number of these plays, the Sinhalese ones in particular, found productions not only in Colombo, but in other Sri Lankan cities, thus making theatre more widely known. In the 1990s, support for drama was offered by the Tower Hall Theatre Foundation and, until it was abolished, the National Theatre Trust, although it remained impossible for most theatre artists to make a living purely by working in this field. Nevertheless, at least one hundred shows a year are seen in Colombo, and provincial tours are common.

During the late 1970s and 1980s, theatre became a site for the expression of popular dissatisfaction with prevailing socio-**political** conditions. Whether offering adaptations of European plays, like *Dhawala Bishana* (based on Sartre's *Men without*

Shadows) or originals like *The Talipot Flower Has Blossomed* (Thala mala pipila), theatre became a form of subversion; using traditional and modern techniques, it provided an outlet for discussing serious problems. Recent years have seen youth-related problems, such as unemployment, love, and gender relationships, become significant. The political satires of Simon Navagathegama (1939–2000) were among the more popular pieces of the 1990s. Interestingly, as Obeyesekere points out, while Sri Lankan officials were apt to **censor** provocative topics expressed in other media, theatre, by and large, was "a permitted space" where few instances of formal suppression were known. Given such problems as the nation's heated ethnic conflict, this was remarkable.

Tamil Theatre. In Tamil theatre, two forms are considered "traditional": *kuttu* and the Tamil counterpart of *nurti*. South Indian ***terukkuttu*** was produced in Tamil in Jaffna and in the eastern provinces, mainly in Batticaloa and neighboring villages. Subsequently known as *nattu kuttu*, it is performed in a circular area. Themes are largely taken from episodes in the ***Ramayana*** and ***Mahabharata***, from Tamil legend, and sometimes from historical tales. The narrative is shown through dance. Since the 1960s, there has been a movement to rediscover *nattu kuttu*, starting with Vithianadan (1921–1984), who polished the existing form. One of the men who performed it during this time, Mauneguru, later became a producer and, in 2004, revived *Ravaneshan*, originally produced by Vithianadan (1963).

Also popular in the late nineteenth and early twentieth centuries was a Tamil form of *nurti* performed on a constructed stage covered on three sides. During the days before movies were available, a Parsi tradition of "special theatre" was enacted in both town and villages (see *Speshal natakam*). V. V. Vyramuthu produced and acted in these plays in the 1960s and 1970s.

Modern Tamil theatre comprises translations of Sinhalese theatre and many European plays. Several groups produce original work or continue the *nattu kuttu* tradition. The Theatre Action Group, led by Sithambaranathan, uses theatre as psycho-social therapy. The Performing Arts Group, in Jaffna, uses *nattu kuttu*, mime, and so on, to tackle social issues. Jeyshankar, a lecturer at Eastern University, has acted with Mauneguru's troupe and uses *nattu kuttu* for innovative theatre.

English-Language Theatre. English, introduced as an official language during the colonial period, soon became the language of upper-class citizens. English and European plays were performed from the late nineteenth century for small audiences. From the early 1930s to 1956, the work of E. F. C. Ludowyk, cited above, played a major role in introducing first-class English-language theatre. After independence (1948), English theatre continued to appeal to middle-class, urban audiences. **Theatre companies** of this type drew upon the theatrical skills of members such as Australian émigré Ernest MacIntyre (1943–), Karen Breckenridge (1936–), Shelagh Gunawardene (1935–), and Andrew David (1930–).

Plays of the 1970s and 1980s were largely adaptations or productions of European comedies or musicals, with limited original work. Serious original work was produced by MacIntyre, who, after arriving in 1974, staged a large number of plays dealing with contemporary issues. Few original plays were created in the 1980s and, during the communistic National Freedom Party insurrection of 1988, English theatre was sustained almost entirely by Indu Dharmasena (1956–). Her drawing-room comedies satirizing Colombo's middle and upper classes, often adaptations of Georgette Heyer romances, have drawn large audiences for two decades.

From the 1990s on, additional attempts have been made to engage with issues relating to the national ethnic conflict between Tamils and Sinhalese, and to social issues such as poverty, drug abuse, prostitution, and youth's frustrations. Some younger playwright-directors who have tackled these issues include Ruana Rajapakse (1958–), Senaka Abeyratne (1952–), Jehan Aloysius (1977–), Ruwanthi de Chickera (1975–), and Delon Weerasinghe. Directors such as Feroze Kamardeen (1972–) and Tracy Holsinger (1973–) have produced a number of provocative plays, bringing new concerns to the stage.

FURTHER READING

Obeyesekere, Ranjini, and C. Fernando, eds. *An Anthology of Modern Writing from Sri Lanka*; Obeyesekere, Ranjini. *Sri Lankan Theater in a Time of Terror: Political Satire in a Permitted Space*; Sarachchandra, E. R. *The Folk Drama of Ceylon*.

Neluka Silva (K. Sivathamby assisted with the Tamil material)

SRIRANGA. *See* Rangacharya, Ada.

SRUMPAET, RATNA (1949–). Indonesian • **playwright** and **director**, originally from North Sumatra. She began her theatrical career in 1969 studying with **Rendra**'s Workshop Theatre. In 1974, with the establishment of her **theatre company**, One Red Stage (Satu Merah Panngung), Ratna directed Batak (a Sumatran ethnic group) and Balinese versions of Shakespeare.

Her first original play, *Marsinah: Song from the Underworld* (Marsinah: nanyian dari bawah tanah, 1993), about the rape and murder of a young East Javanese factory worker who fought for workers' rights, marked the beginning of a series of **politically** critical plays based on actual events that **criticized** the New Order (1966–1998) government. *Marsinah Accuses* (Marsinah menggugat, 1997), written in reaction to the government's decision to end the investigation into Marsinah's death, was barred from production in two major cities by armed troops and military tanks (see Censorship). In reaction, Ratna became coordinator of SIAGA, a coalition of pro-democracy groups instrumental in President Suharto's (1921–) resignation and the end of his government. After an SIAGA-organized rally, Ratna was arrested in 1998 and imprisoned for seventy days. During this time, multiple performances of *Marsinah: Song from the Underworld* were staged around the world to protest her captivity.

Other plays include *Alia, The Wound of Aceh* (Alia, luka serambi mekah, 2000), *Children of Darkness* (Anak-anak kegelapan, 2003), and *The Prostitute and the President* (Sang pelacur dan president, 2005). Ratna has been honored several times by PEN International, as well as the Asia Foundation for Human Rights, **Women**'s Playwrights International, and Amnesty International. She has served as executive director of the Jakarta Arts Council since 2002.

Cobina Gillitt

STAGES

Stages: Cambodia

For centuries, performances of **robam kbach boran** took place on temple grounds, the **dancers**' feet tracing patterns atop the earth or stone, or more recently, carpets brought in for the occasion. In the Royal Palace compound (the capital and palace moved to Phnom Penh in the nineteenth century), dancers have performed in the Phocheny Pavilion, which includes a small raised stage, and in the Chanchhaya Pavilion. The latter provides a second-story space with river views in which the royal dancers would practice and perform on a floor of patterned tiles, or on special carpet. Here, royalty would be seated at one end of (and slightly above) the rectangular performance area, which is open on three sides. Outside of temple and court settings, *robam kbach boran* is most often performed on a proscenium stage.

Proscenium stages for **lakhon bassac** shows were built within small urban **theatres** in the first half of the twentieth century. A magnificent theatre that hosted frequent **music**, dance, and drama, the Bassac was erected in the late 1960s along the river in Phnom Penh, and burned beyond use in 1994. Outdoor *lakhon bassac* and **yiké** might take place on temporary wooden or bamboo stages, or even the back of a flatbed truck. *Lakhon sbaek* (see Puppet Theatre), held at night, and usually with no raised stage, often creates its own sacred and performance spaces by the hanging of a cloth (attached to poles placed in the soil) upon which the shadows will appear and by the calling of gods and spirits through offerings and **religious** invocations proffered on the ground in front of the "screen." **Lakhon khol**, when performed in a village, is danced on long mats laid on the ground within an open structure of wooden poles and railings. Performers emerge from behind cloths hung from these poles at one end of the space. The other three sides remain open.

FURTHER READING

Phim, Toni Samantha, and Ashley Thompson. *Dance in Cambodia.*

Toni Shapiro-Phim

Stages: China

Traditional **Chinese** stages were raised platforms, nearly or exactly square. It was normal for them to be temporary, built especially for one or a series of performances. The earliest fixed stages were of brick or stone, but uncovered and open to the vagaries of the weather. From the Song period (960–1279) we find large numbers of raised stages, square or almost square, open on all four sides and with four wooden or stone poles supporting a traditional-style tiled roof, with eaves tilted at the four corners and rising to a ridge having decorative figures at both ends.

Yuan-Period Stages. Yuan (1280–1368) *zaju* promoted the development of stages that had a wall at the back, with a greenroom behind and two openings, one upstage right for entrances and one upstage left for exits. The audience stood or sat on three sides. There were simple **properties**, but very little **scenography**.

Stage Locations. The Yuan patterns prevailed until the advent of the proscenium stage early in the late Qing (1644–1911). However, there was diversity in the location of stages. **Actors** could put up covered temporary stages more or less anywhere, including in streets or marketplaces.

Among recorded and surviving fixed traditional stages, by far the commonest location is in or outside temples. Indeed, from the Song period on, the stage was a normal part of the temple structure, whether Buddhist, Daoist, or **folk • religion**, for two main reasons. One was that temples needed ritual sites, the other that, for permanent structures, temples were the readiest site for public gatherings. Other possible sites were guild halls, mansions, palaces, teahouses, and, of course, **theatres**.

Most stages had one tier only, with a few having two. Only those for the highest status audiences had three; surviving examples being in the Summer Palace and the Imperial Palace in Beijing. The latter also has a small stage for private performances put on especially for Empress Dowager Cixi (1835–1908).

Proscenium Stages. Proscenium stages arrived with **Western** theatre. In 1866, the Lyceum Theatre (Lanxin da Juyuan) was built by the Amateur Dramatic Club of Shanghai, consisting exclusively of foreign residents. Rebuilt several times, it is still in use.

The first modern-style proscenium stage where both ***xiqu*** and *wenming xi* (a form that led to "spoken drama" [*huaju*]; see Playwrights and Playwriting) were performed and open to Chinese was located in Shanghai's New Stage (Xin Wutai, 1908). It had a slightly rounded downstage lip, but was not a thrust like traditional stages. The audience faced the proscenium, rather than sitting around tables as in traditional contexts. The stage accommodated complex scenery and was a model for later ones. With the founding of the Republic (1912), the proscenium spread rapidly throughout China. Beijing's first was built in 1914.

Besides allowing for extensive scenic and lighting effects and the use of downstage **curtains** to cover set changes, the move from a thrust to a proscenium arrangement led to a fundamental change in the use of the space. The **actors**' overall movements had previously been from entrance upstage right to performance at downstage center to exit at upstage left—a circular movement toward and then away from the audience. With entrances moved to the stage right wings and exits to stage left, the circular pattern became shallower and less connected—actors pass by the audience on their way from one disparate area to another rather than seeming to appear from and then return to the same distant place.

With the establishment of the People's Republic of China (1949) and the resultant boom in new proscenium theatres, further changes in *xiqu* occurred. Based on the Soviet model, these new theatres tended to be huge. Whereas actors traditionally had appeared as relatively large figures on fairly small, square stages surmounted by relatively low roofs, they now became small figures on large, rectangular stages with vast empty expanses between their heads and the soaring arch. Because little attention was paid to acoustics, sound systems were installed; most *xiqu* performances even today rely on amplification rather than vocal strength. It also became more difficult to comprehend the language being spoken and sung. As a result, side titles (*zimu*)—now computerized—have been posted at both sides of proscenium stages since the 1950s.

Most theatres have proscenium stages today. Among the best equipped are the Poly Theatre (Baoli Juyuan) in Beijing (1991) and the Shanghai Grand Theatre (Shanghai da Juyuan, 1998). Both present all types of performances, including *huaju*, **geju**, and *wuju*.

Black Box Stages. Black box theatres became popular with the emergence of the **experimental theatre** in the 1980s. Among the most active are the Experimental Theatre of the Central Academy of Drama (Zhongyang Xiju Xueyuan Shiyan Juchang), the TNT Theatre (TNT Juchang) at the Nine Theatre Complex (Jiuge Juchang), the two additions to the Capital Theatre (Shoudu Juchang) of the Beijing People's Art Theatre (Beijing Renmin Yishu Juyuan or BPAT), the BPAT Small Theatre (Beijing Renyi Xiao Juchang), and the BPAT Experimental Theatre (Beijing Renyi Shiyan Juchang).

The Northern Theatre (Bei Juchang), formerly the Small Theatre of the China Youth Art Theatre (Zhongguo Qingnian Yishu Juyuan Xiao Juchang), and the theatre belonging to the China National Puppet Theatre (Zhongguo Guojia Muou Juyuan) are among the few with thrust stages. Guangzhou Cultural Park Arena Stage (Guangzhou Wenhua Gongyuan Zhongxin Tai), an outdoor venue, used to be an arena but was converted to a proscenium during its 2000 renovation.

FURTHER READING

Mackerras, Colin. *The Rise of the Peking Opera, 1770–1870, Social Aspects of the Theatre in Manchu China*; Mackerras, Colin. *Chinese Theatre from its Origins to the Present Day.*

Colin Mackerras, Elizabeth Wichmann-Walczak, and Nan Zhang

Stages: India

Traditional **Indian** theatre takes place on a wide variety of stages in diverse spatial environments, sacred and profane. Performances can be held in fields, town squares, streets, parks and gardens, and inside and outside temples, depending on the needs of the event, the genre, or the audience.

Sanskrit Stages. Three different-sized and -shaped **Sanskrit theatres** are described in Bharata's *Treatise on Drama* (Natyashastra; see Theory): oblong, square, and triangular, each available in large, medium, and small sizes; the rectangular, medium-sized one of sixty-four by thirty-two cubits (*hasta*s) was considered ideal. The space was partitioned into two halves, an auditorium and a "stage pavilion." The latter was further subdivided into a stage and backstage area, each part separated from the other by a brick wall, while the stage itself was divided into equally sized upstage and downstage areas. The stage had a central acting area and two side areas with a pillar at each of four corners. At the rear was a "stage top" and orchestra platform. **Actors** entered from and exited to the backstage area through doorways, one at either side of the orchestra platform. **Curtains** (*pati* or *apati*) hanging in the doorways were manipulated to suggest the emotion of the entering actor. Pre–performance **religious** rituals were hidden behind a curtain (*yavanika*) placed at the stage's midpoint, while yet another curtain could be used to reveal a character "discovered."

The stage may have had a two-storied structure, which would have been useful in staging scenes suggesting simultaneous locales. Furthermore, the acting area was divided into separate zones, each representative of a specific place, such as a garden or street. A circular movement allowed the actor to move from one locale to another without leaving the stage. The descriptive dialogue also helped to establish place, as did various pronouncements by the characters as to where they were going and where they were at.

The only existing stages essentially built according to the *Natyashastra*'s description are the *kuttampalam*s, rectangular, elevated, gabled structures built in enclosed temple spaces in Kerala for **kuttiyattam**. The audience squats on three sides of the stage, and the raised, square stage itself is situated so that it faces the god, with roof-supporting pillars at each corner. The largest example is at the Vatakkunnathan Temple, Trichur (Thrissur). It is about seventy-eight feet long by fifty-five feet wide, with tree pillars at each stage corner. An ornate ceiling has complex mytho-religious carvings on it. The stage wall contains a door for exits and one for entrances from the dressing room. At the front edge of the performance space is a standing sacred lamp.

Ritually Charged Stages. Ritual performances, like **teyyam**, occur in the space before village temples, while temple grounds also serve for forms like *terukkuttu* and **yakshagana**. Certain religiously oriented performances require the construction of temporary shrines to serve as the staging area, after which the shrine is abandoned and its deity immersed in a river, accompanied by processional activity. Processions through streets and fields are a regular feature of many such events, and can be very colorful and elaborate, with singing, **dancing**, palanquins, and elephants.

There are numerous performance spaces within and without temples, each with its unique features, including porch halls (*mandapa*) with open sides or enclosed by walls. Special structures also may be provided outside the temple proper. (See also *Ankiya nat*.)

Some forms, like **kathakali**, specialize in giving ground-level performances, in which the spatial arrangement is replete with symbolic values. *Kathakali*'s standing lamp, used as a focus even in electrically lit performances, allows the actor to determine his movements and positions in relation to it within the confined acting area. For certain fight scenes, though, the actor may actually move into the audience itself, thereby extending the stage space beyond traditional boundaries. The space is scenically neutral, dependent on the singers' words for specificity of locale, as in *yakshagana* and similar forms, where the **makeup** and **costume**, as well as symbolic gestures, help create a powerful sense of place.

Spectacular outdoor venues used for ritually enhanced performances are found in **ramlila** and **raslila**, the former devoted to Rama and the latter to Krishna. Staging can be on the ground, on platforms, in temple environments, in public locations, and in relation to locales associated with the actual places in which the action is thought to have occurred. The spaces are ritually endowed with divine qualities by the rites performed there. The action—along with the spectators—moves from place to place throughout the city, sometimes taking place in multiple locations at the same time. Action transpires on platforms as well as at ground level. Often one cannot tell the actors from the spectators. Smaller versions of *ramlila* are found throughout North India's villages and towns, while urban open-air locations used at other times for different kinds of performances are made holy for *ramlila* presentations; pageants and tableaux floats (*jhanki*) depicting the story and characters take part in vivid processions as part of the event, stopping at fixed points for local audiences to inspect them and share in ritual ceremonies.

Similarly unusual large-scale presentations are associated with the *jatra* form called *braj jatra*, which combines the elements of a pilgrimage with theatre; much of it is done at night along a processional route associated with Krishna, and replete with features of the natural topography.

Proscenium Stages. The wide variety of outdoor stages used by ritual and folk forms is epitomized in *terukkuttu*, whose name means "street theatre," and which greatly predates the **political** street theatre of modern times, described below. Among the various types of outdoor performance are those of the **khyal, bhaand pather**, and **swang** genres. These approaches were abandoned when India began to see the construction of proscenium theatres in Calcutta (Kolkata) and Bombay (Mumbai) during the 1860s, a development that separated audiences from actors and seriously altered the nature of the experience, ignoring the multiangled perspective previously available, which included the possibility of audience movement, in favor of a single, fixed viewpoint from an immovable auditorium seat.

Samuel L. Leiter

Modern Stages. The rigorous theatre activism that emerged after independence (1947) inculcated the seminal idea that each genre has its own language and grammar based on its particular objectives and functions. Many **directors** started exploring the possibilities of new actor-audience relationships as per their expressed visions.

Street Theatre. After independence, street theatre gained significance, with its intimate audience-actor relationship, in which the space was sometimes shared by both entities. Street theatre, ultimately associated with outdoor venues ranging from street corners to factory yards, has a long tradition since, as noted, most folk forms take place in open venues, like marketplaces. The people's movements, especially the leftwing ones that arose following the founding of the Indian People's Theatre Association (IPTA) in 1942–1943, used street theatre to gain the people's involvement in serious social issues.

Early examples arose in the 1940s, especially in villages, inspiring the work of artists like **Utpal Dutt**, who called his politically charged activities "poster theatre." The movement became a force in the late 1960s, growing popular across the country in the 1970s. Street theatre allowed the issues to be brought directly to the people, without having to lure them to a conventional playhouse. Even the government began to use it to propagandize about issues like family planning, health education, and literacy.

Open-Air Stages. Theatre-in-the-round and in outdoor venues like amphitheatres also served the needs of various political movements dissatisfied with the proscenium stage's confines. Ideological reasons inspired **Badal Sircar** to abandon the proscenium in 1972 and to develop his "Third Theatre" (*anganmancha*, literally, "open-air theatre"). Even when working indoors, in public halls, he redefined the space for each production, hoping to stir his audience to think about particular issues.

Ebrahim Alkazi's productions in the backyard of New Delhi's National School of Drama, in ancient ruins, and at an old fort introduced site-specific outdoor performances to India, with the ambience contributing powerfully to the performance's effect.

As noted, theatre still maintains the environmental nature of its presentations, with audience and actors situated in a variety of interesting ways. Many **experimental** productions have employed similar arrangements to explore a variety of actor-audience relationships. **Kavalam Narayana Panikkar**, **B. V. Karanth**, and **S. Ramanujam** are among those who have explored environmental staging. Despite the presumed influence on them of traditional practices, though, equally strong has been the influence of **Western** pioneers such as Artaud, Brecht, and Schechner.

Among reasons for abandoning the proscenium were the need to create a more dynamic live experience, to make the play happen in the here and now, to express political objectives, to produce on a minimal budget, and to establish new artistic ideologies. Toward this purpose many directors chose open-air, site-specific, street, environmental, three-quarters-round, and other kinds of stages to realize their objectives.

FURTHER READING

Awasthi, Suresh. *Drama, The Gift of Gods: Culture, Performance and Communication in India*; Gargi, Balwant. *Folk Theater of India*; Panchal, Goverdhan. *Kuttampalam and Kutiyattam*; Gargi, Balwant. *The Theatres of Bharata and Some Aspects of Sanskrit Play Production.*

B. Ananthakrishnan

Stages: Indonesia

Traditional **Indonesian** stages are generally in the round, outdoors, and impermanent. In most cases, village squares or temple courtyards are temporarily transformed into performance spaces through decoration, **music**, and, above all, the presence of **actors** and spectators. Some performances, especially those associated with courts, may take place indoors or in some sort of open pavilion. Nevertheless, raised platforms, **scenographic** elements, lighting, and permanent **theatres** are generally unknown outside the modern theatre or in recently constructed facilities.

French **theatre companies** in eighteenth-century Batavia (Jakarta) apparently performed in dedicated theatres. A "bamboo theatre" built by the occupying British army in 1814 was destroyed by the Dutch in 1816, only to be rebuilt as the white-columned Weltevreden Theatre (Schouwburg Weltevreden) in 1821. This neoclassical proscenium theatre, refurbished as the Jakarta Arthouse (Gedung Kesenian Jakarta, 1987), is today a leading modern venue.

Beginning in the late 1960s, the government constructed art centers in provincial capitals, of which Jakarta's Ismail Marzuki Center (Taman Ismail Marzuki) is probably the most significant for modern theatre. When built in 1968, it was the first such public arts complex in Southeast Asia and included large and small proscenium stages, an arena stage, and an amphitheatre.

Since the 1990s, an increasingly large proportion of Jakarta's modern theatre is staged in smaller exhibition spaces, many of which are located in foreign cultural centers. This development accompanies a shift toward the aesthetics of performance and installation art in much contemporary theatre.

Evan Winet

Stages: Japan

Japan's first stage, described in the *Records of Ancient Matters* (Kojiki, 712), was an upturned tub upon which goddess Ame no Uzume no Mikoto danced "naked" to placate the angry sun goddess. Until medieval times, temporary stages utilizing open floor or ground space, halls, or temporary platforms on shrine and temple grounds, or in the imperial court, were typical. The permanent stages employed for traditional theatre today are specific to the genre.

Nô *and* Kyôgen. The three main elements of a roofed stage, dressing room, and "bridgeway" (*hashigakari*) between the two, came into existence in *sarugaku*, predecessor of *nô* and *kyôgen*, between the end of the fourteenth and middle of the fifteenth centuries. Square and round stages with a *hashigakari* adjoining from the rear, at various angles from right or left, or at both sides—to allow competing troupes to enter from different dressing rooms—were all used. The oldest extant *nô* stage (1581), at Kyoto's Nishi Hongan-ji Temple, is considered the prototype.

Made of polished Japanese cypress (*hinoki*), the central stage area (*hon butai*) is ideally approximately eighteen square feet. Four named pillars, important stage locators for **masked • actors**, support a gabled, shingled roof. A veranda-like attachment at stage left, the "chorus seat" (*jiutai-za*) is for the chorus (*jiutai*), while the rear stage (*ato-za*) is for the **musicians**. The *hashigakari* runs from right side of the *ato-za* at an oblique angle to the "mirror room" (*kagami no ma*), and a five-colored, vertically striped, lift **curtain** (*agemaku*) separates the two. Stage size and *hashigakari* length and angle vary slightly in each case. Upstage left is a small sliding door (*kiridoguchi*) used by the chorus and stage assistants (*kôken*). A large pine tree painted on the back wall or "mirror board" (*kagami ita*) provides the principal **scenography**. In the hollow space under the stage are large ceramic jars that aid sound reverberation, as when **actors** stamp, the number and location depending on each stage's acoustical needs. Seating is to the front and left of the stage, although outdoor stages formerly allowed seating to the right as well. Three live pines are placed along the *hashigakari*, and the entire stage is surrounded by white rocks or sand to reflect natural light onto the playing area. Indoor *nô* stages (*nôgakudô*), the first of which was built in Tokyo in 1881, enclose the entire stage (including the roof) and seating area.

Bunraku. Early seventeenth-century stages for *ningyô jôruri* (later, *bunraku*) were designed for one-person **puppets** operated from below. A curtain, stretched between pillars at the ends of a rectangular building and fronted by a sloping apron, hid the puppeteers and musicians performing behind. By the late seventeenth century, the sloped apron disappeared, and low curtains (now flats) stretched between side poles created two and three levels of performance space, a convention still in use.

The *bunraku* stage, developed to suit the large three-person puppets first used in 1734, has three essential parts: (1) two levels for action on the main stage, (2) an auxiliary platform (*yuka*) at stage left for the chanter (*tayû*) and *shamisen* player, and (3) two second floor screened areas above the side entrances—stage right for offstage (*geza*) music, and left for younger musicians accompanying minor scenes.

Osaka's National Bunraku Theatre (Kokuritsu Bunraku Gekijô) is Japan's only dedicated *bunraku* theatre, with a stage approximately thirty-nine feet wide by fifteen feet deep. The stage is divided into three parts by railings or borders (*tesuri*): between the approximately ten-inch-high downstage railing (*san no te*) and the approximately nineteen-inch-high middle railing (*ni no te*) is space for the traveler curtain and footlights. Behind the second railing is the main acting area, the "ship's bottom" (*funazoko*), recessed fourteen inches below stage level, about seven feet from front to rear, and extending the stage's full width into the wings. At its rear is the "first railing" (*ichi no te*) or "true railing" (*honte*), approximately thirty-three inches high. The puppets are manipulated in the *funazoko*, often representing an exterior space, and on the higher level behind the third railing, often representing an interior space. The faces of the first and second railings hide the puppeteers' lower torsos, while their top edges serve as "ground level" for the puppets, which are manipulated in mid-air. Black curtains with large white crests, used for entrances, are set at a forty-five-degree angle from the footlights at both ends of the *funazoko*. The *yuka* contains a small revolve (*bon*) that enables quick changes of the chanter and *shamisen* player between scenes.

Kabuki. Women's (*onna*) **kabuki** in the early seventeenth century used temporary *nô*-stagelike structures, including right-angled *hashigakari*. Audiences sat either in the unroofed "earthen pit" (*doma*) at the front or side of the stage, or in the more expensive raised roofed "galleries" (*sajiki*) to the right and left that eventually were built. Frequent fires, especially in Edo (Tokyo), provided ample opportunity for architectural experimentation. Consequently, developments were not uniform, compounded by regional variances between Edo theatres and those of Kamigata (Kyoto/Osaka).

Stages normally faced south, taking advantage of natural light for the all-day performances. The first major modification to the *nô* footprint began in the 1660s, when the advent of multiact plays brought the traveler curtain (*hiki maku* or *jôshiki maku*) into use. Throughout the Genroku era (1688–1704), the *hashigakari* grew shorter and nearly as wide as the main stage, and by the 1730s an unroofed forestage was added in front of the roofed main stage. This became the major acting area by 1745, placing action at the end of a thrust, with spectators surrounding the edge on three sides.

Other features facilitated an intimate audience-actor relationship. The "flower path" (*hanamichi*) from the stage through the house at audience left was used for individual productions as early as 1670, but was not permanent until the 1730s. (*Bunraku* also once used a *hanamichi*, with *tesuri*-like side panels, but it is rare now.) Edo *hanamichi* were angled, while Kamigata examples were straight. A narrower "eastern" (*higashi*) *hanamichi* through house right became a permanent feature in the 1770s. A "central walkway" (*naka no ayumi*), used largely by spectators and vendors, joined the two *hanamichi* across the rear of the auditorium. Today's theatres set up the "eastern" or "temporary" (*kari*) *hanamichi* as needed, though loss of income from the seats that must be removed results in increasingly infrequent use.

Other eighteenth-century features, which did not became permanent, included a "name-saying platform" (*nanoridai*) built off the *hanamichi*. Kamigata theatres often incorporated a small, square, well-like pit (*karaido*) at the stage left side of the junction of stage and *hanamichi*, which could hold water or mud, and had multipurpose uses.

Mid-eighteenth-century advances significantly transformed stage usage, enabling elaborate scenic changes. While a temporary "revolving stage" (*mawari butai*) built atop the stage was introduced between 1715 and 1735, a permanent revolve cut directly into the stage floor, and turned by workers pushing an axle around under the stage, was introduced in Osaka (1758), and soon became permanent. A nineteenth-century innovation was the "snake-eye revolve" (*janome mawashi*), a revolve within a revolve. Lifts (*seri*) for actors and scenic elements appeared in 1727 and 1753 respectively, and a *hanamichi* lift, the "snapping turtle" (*suppon*), usually used for characters with supernatural powers, appeared (1759). *Nô*'s residual gabled roof and four supporting pillars stage disappeared in the late 1790s in Edo, and earlier in Kamigata.

In both *bunraku* and *kabuki*, stage right is "lower hand" (*shimote*), and stage left "upper hand" (*kamite*). Since the 1850s, offstage musicians have been located in the "lower hand seat" (*geza*), a.k.a. "black curtain" (*kuromisu*), at stage right. Prior to that, musicians sat offstage left in Edo theatres, and at either side in Kamigata. When *bunraku* music (*gidayû*, a.k.a. *takemoto*) is used, *bunraku*'s *yuka* platform is set up either downstage left, or above the stage left entrance. Upstage right during the Edo period (1603–1868) was a two-tiered seating area, the upper called *yoshino* after Mount Yoshino, the lower called *rakandai* after images of Buddha's five hundred avatars (*rakan*).

Western influence brought dramatic changes during the Meiji period (1868–1912). After a fire, the Shintomi Theatre (Shintomi-za) reopened in 1878 with no forestage (eliminated in early-nineteenth-century Kamigata), no onstage seating, and a stage width of over sixty-six feet, transforming the intimate thrust into a wide picture frame stage (*gakubuchi*).

Kabuki stages remain wide in proportion to auditorium depth. Tokyo's Kabuki Theatre (Kabuki-za) opened in 1889 with a stage width of seventy-two feet and is ninety feet today.

FURTHER READING

Ernst, Earle. *The Kabuki Theatre*; Keene, Donald. *Bunraku: The Art of the Japanese Puppet Theatre*; Komparu, Kunio. *The Noh Theatre: Principles and Perspectives;* Leiter, Samuel L. *Historical Dictionary of Japanese Traditional Theatre*.

Julie A. Iezzi

Modern Stages. Japanese stages have historically occupied myriad spaces, from rudimentary riverbeds to cedar-lined court chambers. Stages today, reflecting Japan's cutting-edge technologies alongside vestiges of its straw-sandaled agrarian past, run the gamut from ur-traditional to ultra-innovative.

Practitioners since 1960, when nationwide demonstrations against renewal of the U.S.-Japan Mutual Security Treaty (Anpo) engulfed Japan, have sought authenticity by devising new spaces and new ways of developing audiences. Consider the "poster-story man" (*kami shibai*), ubiquitous in postwar Japan's pretelevision era, who circulated among neighborhoods, regaling children with folktales vivified by sliding illustrations from a wooden frame "proscenium" set up on his bicycle's backseat.

This idea of bringing performance to spectators was appropriated anew by ***angura***. Many early-1960s **playwrights** and **directors** got started at the iconic alternative space Shinjuku Bunka, a movie theatre with nonstop counterculture traffic, permitting performances on its minuscule stage at around 9:30 p.m., after film screenings ended. **Kara Jûrô** and his **theatre company**, Situation Theatre (Jôkyô Gekijô), enticed crowds by performing in unusual spaces like public toilets, railway stations, and vacant lots; he first pitched his signature Red Tent (Aka Tento, 1967) on the grounds of Shinjuku's Hanazono Shrine, red symbolizing the environment's bloody destruction. In 1970, the *angura* group Black Tent Theatre (Kokusho Tento a.k.a. Kuro Tento and BTT 68/71) also started using a tent. Similarly, **Terayama Shûji** and his Peanut Gallery (Tenjô Sajiki) made the city their stage, organizing street theatre, happenings, and often menacing chance encounters. Appropriating such venues, *angura* shared the radical *zeitgeist* of itinerant American artist-activists Julian Beck and Judith Malina and their Living Theatre, performing in steel mills, prisons, schools, and streets.

In part, these figures sought authenticity by reviving continuity with those settings—caves, copses, waterways—linked to the myth-enshrouded stories of sun goddess Amaterasu and theatre's origins—primal conflict, dark urges, erotic **dance**, and raucous laughter. They were seeking to hold their spectators, as in *kami shibai,* with space-defined performances so compelling that there could be no turning away. **Ôno Kazuo** and **Hijikata Tatsumi**, reenacting those primal urges in *butô*, also took performances to alternative stages like alleys, streets, fields, even gardens. Their approach continues with *butô* artists such as Maro Akaji (1943–) with his company Great Camel Battleship (Dairakudakan); Tanaka Min (1945–) and Body Weather Farm (Shintai Kishô Kenkyûjô), where performers explore dance's primal origins in open fields among plants and animals; the nature installations of Eiko and Koma; and the Mountain-Ocean School's (Sankai Juku) ritualistic, upside-down rope descents from theatre roofs. (Of course, *butô* is also performed indoors.)

Other modern figures have drawn from traditional structures. **Noda Hideki** modified the *hanamichi* in *Red Demon* (Aka oni, 1997). **Inoue Hisashi**'s *The Great Doctor Yabuhara* (Yabuhara kengyô, 1973) has *kabuki*-like two-dimensional boat flats, suggesting water voyage, and red cloths, signaling the gory final beheading. **Sakate Yôji** adapts *nô*'s minimalist stage in the haunting *Epitaph for the Whales* (Kujira no bohyô, 1993). **Ninagawa Yukio** has borrowed from the *nô* stage for his contemporary East/West **experiments** at Saitama Arts Center, using side ramps, roofed stage, and **masks** for *King Lear* (1999).

Unprecedented wealth in the 1970s and 1980s supported new stage construction throughout Japan, including Seibu Department Store's Parco Theatre (1973), Wacoal Lingerie's unique multi-layered Spiral Hall (1985), and Tôkyû Corporation's Culture Village (Bunkamura, 1989), all modern corporate-sponsored venues with stages flexibly configurable for straight or avant-garde productions. **Suzuki Tadashi**'s Toga Village stages, designed in 1982 by Isozaki Arata (1931–), include an open-air, Greek-style amphitheatre and a low-slung, indoor-outdoor stage recalling traditional farmhouses. Other new stages include the Suzuki-led, Isozaki-designed *nô*-Shakespearean ACM Theatre thrust stage of Art Tower Mito (1989) and Tokyo's elegant six-hundred-seat Setagaya Public Theatre (1997), including Theatre Tram, a two-hundred-seat, studiolike, multipurpose theatre with rollback chairs and movable floors supported by pillars, venues since 2001 for Nomura Mansai (of the Nomura *kyôgen* family; see Izumi School) and his inspired East-West fusions.

The price of such technical wonders forces mainstream companies to draw sell-out crowds with mass-appeal works on flashy, multilayered stages with movable sections, like the multi-screened techno-wonders of the Four Seasons Company's (Gekidan Shiki) popular **musical** extravaganzas.

In opposition to such methods, *angura* playwrights and directors, their *shôgekijô* heirs, and their impecunious young audiences, gravitate to marginal urban spaces. Indeed, new theatre is probably best experienced in the hodgepodge narrow streets of bohemian districts like Tokyo's Shimo-kitazawa. At venues like Za Suzunari, spectators sit shoulder-to-shoulder, often on straw mats, before a tiny stage. Such intimate interaction between actors and audience encourages asides, ad-libs, and trans-proscenium complicity, allowing actors and audience to share dynamic moments of creation, never to be duplicated.

Hamilton Armstrong

Stages: Korea

Korean stages generally are of three types: circular arenas used by traditional, **folk theatre** forms such as *t'alch'um* and modern forms such as *madangnori*; **Western**-style proscenium stages, and underground stages.

The age-old arena space appears throughout Korea: improvised in a riverside grove, in soccer stadiums, in specially erected *madangnori* tents with stages as big as a basketball court, or in permanent outdoor **theatres**, like that at the Seoul Performing Arts Center.

Compact new university theatres are an exception, but Western-style stages generally are equipped with lifts and turntables, and are large enough to accommodate opera or *ch'angguk*. Larger stages are not "flexible stages" accommodating a variety of configurations. Rather, theatre complexes house a smaller "black box" venue that permits three-quarters or "thrust" configurations, a configuration not widely used, though there is an impressive permanent thrust on the former campus of the Seoul Performing Arts Institute. A purpose-built arena theatre for modern plays does not exist, and theatre-in-the-round is rarely used in contemporary productions.

The vast majority of Seoul's stages are in basements—or on top floors—and are shaped by the space's architecture. Their various configurations defy classification but, with some exceptions, they offer only a cramped **acting** area, often no more than twenty-five feet wide by fifteen feet deep, with neither wings nor machinery. Such limited and limiting stages remain major challenges to enhanced production standards.

Richard Nichols

Stages: Malaysia

When traditional **Malay** theatre is presented outdoors, performers may use a simple stage, such as a temporary wooden platform installed especially for the occasion. The audience can sit on mats placed on the ground. However, viewers may also stand by the side of the stage or sit on it, along the back, to get a closer view of the performance. In rural villages, these stages may be set up in fields. Permanent outdoor stages are also available for traditional performances, such as those constructed for the Central Market and the MATIC (Malaysian Tourist Information Complex) amphitheatre in Kuala Lumpur.

Traditional **Chinese** theatre performances are also held outdoors, mostly on temporary stages of bamboo and wood erected in public spaces or temple courtyards. The structures are covered with colorful backdrops; a banner designating the name of the troupe is displayed above the stage. In addition, permanent stages may be found in many Chinese temples. Performances may continue throughout the day even though in the morning and around noon there may be no viewers; this is because the performances are meant for deities or ancestor spirits. Traditional Chinese troupes mainly perform for clan and temple groups during their **religious** festivities, such as the **Festival** of Hungry Ghosts.

Kuala Lumpur is especially well-equipped with up-to-date indoor venues, which can accommodate complex lighting and sound effects along with full stage sets. Large **theatres** are owned and operated by government bodies or agencies. These have either proscenium stages or flexible staging arrangements so that works can be mounted, for example, on a thrust stage or as theatre-in-the-round. Malaysia's showcase facility is the National Theatre (Palace of Culture or Istana Budaya), designed to feature large-scale local productions as well as touring companies from abroad. Some international organizations, such as the British Council and the Goethe Institute, may also have a performance venue on their premises, often a proscenium-style theatre. One local performing arts company, the Actors' Studio, operates two venues, one in Kuala Lumpur and the other in Penang. Some small stages may be found in office buildings. Art galleries and shopping malls can provide additional, less conventional performance spaces.

Major towns and cities have halls and auditoriums that theatre groups can use for performances. These spaces are usually suitable for proscenium or flexible/thrust staging. Universities also have large assembly halls that can be used for staging productions.

In addition, universities may have special **experimental** or formal theatres for staging plays; these may be identified as studio theatres or black box spaces.

FURTHER READING

Ishak, Solehah, and Nur Nina Zuhra (Nancy Nanney). "Malaysia."

Nancy Nanney

Stages: Singapore

Singaporean theatre utilizes a wide range of performance spaces, from the traditional, temporary, raised outdoor stage that appears in the streets during the eighth lunar month, when the ethnic **Chinese** population stages traditional works to propitiate the spirits of the dead, to the modern stages contained in the Esplanade-Theatres on the Bay complex. Many of Singapore's established **theatre companies** now have permanent homes with flexible black box spaces, though they occasionally rent larger proscenium **theatres** when necessary. Singapore's oldest proscenium theatres, such as the Victoria Theatre, date back to British colonial rule, and are still important for presenting **musical**s and other large-scale productions.

With few exceptions, productions tend to be staged either in large proscenium theatres, or in one of the many fine smaller, flexible spaces. The 1990s witnessed an explosion of theme-based original works, many of which were staged environmentally in locations such as old shop houses, abandoned warehouses, and the atmospheric Fort Canning Park. Companies most identified with the use of such "found spaces" in the 1990s were TheatreWorks and the Asia-in-Theatre Research Center. Since that time urban redevelopment has reduced the number of found spaces available, while the practice of using such spaces has generally fallen out of fashion, in part because so many companies now have permanent homes.

William Peterson

Stages: Thailand

Most **theatres** in **Thailand** are not specifically designed for theatre productions, but are multipurpose auditoriums with proscenium stages to accommodate dance, ballet, opera, concert, film, and lectures. There are neither permanent thrust nor arena theatres.

However, **theatre companies • experiment** with these auditoriums, some of which have no fixed seats. For example, when "physical theatre" company B-Floor presented *Crying Century* (2002) at the Pridi Baanomyong Institute Auditorium, the main action was not on the stage but the space in front of it where rows of chairs are usually placed. Earlier, at the same venue, Dream Masks converted an adjacent vacant office space into a highly realistic replica of a student union for their **political** satire *Hamburger Mob* (2001). In Patravadi Theatre's *Raai Phra Tri Pidok 4* (2003), the audience stood downstage watching one scene take place amidst rows of theatre seats while another proceeded upstage.

More flexible spaces, such as Thailand Cultural Center's Small Hall, Saeng Arun Cultural Center, Chulalongkorn University's Art Theatre, and Bangkok University's Black Box Theatre, are in fact variations of black box theatre and have provided increased artistic freedom. Although the end-stage configuration is most commonly used in these spaces, the arena, thrust, and traverse stages are also frequently seen. Two major art galleries, Tadu Contemporary Art and About Studio, also occasionally serve this purpose.

In addition, Bangkok Theatre **Festival**, the fringe-style annual showcase during which Dream Masks' *Afterdogs* (2003) was staged as a soccer match in a parking lot, further promotes the use of unconventional spaces with affordable rental costs.

FURTHER READING

Rutnin, Mattani Mojdara. *Dance, Drama, and Theatre in Thailand: The Process of Development and Modernization.*

Pawit Mahasarinand

STORYTELLING

Storytelling: China

Chinese storytelling—*shuochang* (literally, "speaking and singing") or *quyi* ("song arts")—is a **folk** art dating at least from the seventh century. Although narrative texts used for performance exist from Tang (618–907) times, storytelling is mainly an oral literature, transmitted from generation to generation and varied to suit time and place. From earliest times, sources of stories included the characters of the Three Kingdoms (220–265) or other war stories, love or domestic matters, the Monkey King, rebels or social outcasts, or law cases righting injustices.

Storytelling is small in scale. Many performances feature one **actor** only, who narrates in speech or song, usually rhythmically, accompanying himself with a clapper in each hand. There may be up to four performers, who sit, stand, or occasionally **dance**. One actor may play several roles, but a more usual pattern is to narrate in the third person.

A famous spoken form is *xiangsheng*, often translated as "cross-talk," which is generally a kind of comic dialogue. Arising in Beijing in the mid-nineteenth century, it is now popular all over. Another spoken form found in various places is *pinghua* (literally, "comment words").

Where **music** occurs, it is originally based on folk songs, with both melodies and accompanying instrumentation being highly regionalized. Storytelling music has contributed greatly to the various styles of *xiqu*, and in turn been much influenced by them. Speech or lyrics use local dialect. A 1982 investigation found 341 different local storytelling forms.

Among the most famous styles of musical storytelling is *nanyin* ("southern sounds"), also known as *nanguan* ("southern pipes"). Originating in Quanzhou in southern Fujian, this is one of several of the regions that are probably among China's most ancient. Accompanying instruments are wind and string.

Of Ming (1368–1644) origin are storytelling forms termed *tanci* (literally, "pluck words") because the main instrument is something like the four-string, pear-shaped lute (*pipa*), which is plucked. Up to four seated performers narrate in song or speech and play instruments. A well-known form is that of Yangzhou, in Jiangsu, which is of late-Ming origin.

Balladry is prominent among ethnic minorities, including among those lacking theatrical traditions. Ballads sung, chanted, or spoken as storytelling have for centuries been popular among such groups as the **Tibetans**, Bai, Dai, and Zhuang. In storytelling, minorities emphasize their own style, stories, and language.

Storytelling has always functioned as part of social occasions, such as weddings, funerals, or **religious** ceremonies. One or two performers can tell a story in virtually any public space, but **stages**, teahouses, or even **theatres** are preferred locations for complex forms.

FURTHER READING

Bender, Mark. *Plum and Bamboo: China's Suzhou Chantefable Tradition*; Bordahl, Vibeke, and Jette Ross. *Chinese Storytellers: Life and Art in the Yangzhou Tradition*; McLaren, Anne E. *Chinese Popular Cultural and Ming Chantefable.*

Colin Mackerras

Storytelling: India

Indian storytelling has as many forms as storytellers, some more theatrical than others. A few representative examples suggest their infinite variety. Sometimes, storytellers improvise plots and impersonate characters around popular social themes as entertainment and social critique. Other times, stories are recited and sung as **religious** service, without any particularly mimetic devices. Still other forms do not necessarily have names, but exist as recognized functions of social and ritual interaction. And **dance** forms, such as *bharata natyam*, include narrative components. There is a strong tendency to regard the varieties of storytelling (and story-hearing) as spiritually profitable.

Some of the earliest documented stories are distinctly theatrical. The Vedas are ancient religious texts (second millennium BC) consisting largely of stories that apparently provided the content of complex rituals. For ages these stories were transmitted orally. Many such stories are dialogues reflecting theatrical qualities. The oldest Veda, the *Rig Veda*, includes many such dialogue rituals.

The connection between storytelling and ritual continues. A representative form is *katha*. *Katha* ("story") refers to a Vaishnavist service in which stories of God and his incarnations—especially Krishna—from medieval Purana texts are recited by a religious figure, who embellishes the stories with theological commentary and songs. The congregation frequently joins in, singing the popular **music**. Hearing about God through this medium gives religious merit to storytellers and hearers alike. Thus *katha* functions as ritual.

In other cases, storytelling may be less formally connected with ritual. *Kirtan*s, congregational worship involving singing, **dancing**, and sermons, often include improvised storytelling. Informally organized groups also commonly tell stories as epilogues to recently completed rituals, celebrations, and fasts, with which their stories share narrative elements. Friends may gather, for example, to relate a story about Tulsi as an ornament to observing the annual ritual marriage of Tulsi and Vishnu. Devotees regard this kind of storytelling as meritorious, understanding that it explains and justifies their ritual activity.

Many secular entertainments can be classified as storytelling. In North India, *bahurupiya*s are itinerant performers, skilled in improvisation and imitation, who act out stories in spontaneous venues or at events such as weddings. Relying on clever **costuming**, quick wit, and good will, *bahurupiya*s tell jokes and play a repertoire of routines **criticizing** the upper class, the government, religious authorities, and other banes of civic life. Since turning away or treating badly a *bahurupiya* is considered inauspicious, even these secular performances are regarded as spiritually potent.

The wide variety of storytelling forms may be best illustrated by the *pat* tradition of West Bengal, descended from Hindu and Muslim traditions and related to similar forms across North India, Pakistan, and into Iran. A storyteller uses a long scroll, painted with sequential frames, which he unrolls frame by frame to illustrate his recitation.

Modern scholarship has focused on the storytelling activity of Indian **women**. Often excluded from assuming leadership roles in religious and civic life, women rely on storytelling as a means of asserting a public identity, and as a medium of community.

FURTHER READING

Narayan, Kirin. *Storytellers, Saints, and Scoundrels: Folk Narrative in Hindu Religious Teaching.*

David V. Mason

Storytelling: Japan

Japan's early narrative traditions include epic recitations and stories. One of the earliest examples is *heikyoku* or *heike biwa*, a narrative form originating in the thirteenth century. Blind Buddhist priests recited installments from the eleventh and twelfth century epic *Tale of the Heike* (Heike monogatari), accompanied by the Japanese lute (*biwa*). This was later replaced in the Edo period (1603–1868) by *jôruri* singing with *shamisen* accompaniment (see *Ko-jôruri*).

Epic recitation to music (*katari mono*) is a long-standing tradition in *bunraku* (see Puppet Theatre) and **kabuki**. In *bunraku*, story narration and the dialogue for the characters have been sung in *jôruri* style (*gidayû bushi*) since the early sixteenth century. *Kabuki* adapted *bunraku*'s stories, narration, and **music** in the eighteenth century.

Two important storytelling forms (*hanashi mono*) not accompanied by music include *rakugo* and *manzai*. *Rakugo* began as short stories developed to teach Buddhism in the sixth and seventh centuries. Today, its comic stories are told in a small variety theatre (*yose*). The narrator (*hanashi-ka*) sits on a pillow in traditional dress and illustrates his story with a fan. Tales include puns or wordplay. Characters range from the merchants of old Osaka to ghosts and foxes. There are "classic" (*koten*) *rakugo* (pre-1900) and "newly written" (*shinsaku*) *rakugo*.

Manzai dates to the eighth century when two representatives of a Shinto shrine went door-to-door during the New Year festivities. *Manzai* has undergone several metamorphoses; today it is a humorous dialogue or banter between two people. Themes focus on **politics** and contemporary life.

Other nonmusical narrations include story reading (*yomi mono* or *kôdan*), in which a performer sits behind a small desk and reads or recites a story. The storyteller uses a wooden clapper and a fan wrapped in white paper (*hari-sen*) to punctuate his moral tale.

FURTHER READING

Hoff, Frank. *Song, Dance, Storytelling: Aspects of the Performing Arts in Japan*; Morioka, Heinz, and Miyoko Sasaki. *Rakugo: The Popular Narrative Art of Japan*.

Holly A. Blumner

SUBBANNA, K. V. (1932–2005). Indian Kannada-language **director**, cultural impresario, and cofounder of Ninasam (Nilakanteshwara Natya Seva Sangh, 1949), India's premier modern **theatre company** with a rural rather than urban base. Born in the village of Kuntagodu in Shimoga District, Karnataka, and educated at Mysore University, Subbanna located his organization in the hamlet of Heggodu, near Sagar, because his goal was to make the best of world art, literature, and culture available to rural audiences. Ninasam now includes a traveling film society (1973), an institute of formal theatre **training** (1980), an annual multidisciplinary "culture course" (1989), and a repertory company that has taken four plays on an annual statewide tour since its inception (1985), reaching more than 1.5 million by 2001. Subbanna's pioneering activity was supported by two grants from the Ford Foundation, and in 1991 he received the Ramon Magsaysay award for creative communication in the arts.

As a director of Indian plays, Subbanna worked with important modern and contemporary **playwrights** such as D. L. Roy (1953), **Chandrashekhar Kambar** (1974), and **Vijay Tendulkar** (1976), but his contribution was even more distinctive in two other respects. He translated classical **Sanskrit** plays such as **Kalidasa**'s *Shakuntala* (Abhijnana Shakuntalam, 1985), Vishakhadatta's *The Signet Ring of Rakshasa* (Mudrarakshasa, 1988), and Mahendravikrama Varman's "The Ascetic and the Courtesan" (Bhagavadajjukam, 2000) into Kannada for productions by other Ninasam directors,

Sugimura Haruko in *A Woman's Life*. (Photo: Haruuchi Yorikazu)

especially C. R. Jambe and Akshara K. V. He also adapted (and selectively directed) major **Western** plays, notably Shakespeare's *Hamlet* (1984) and *Timon of Athens* (1993), Molière's *The Bourgeois Gentleman* (1995), Gogol's *The Inspector General* (1983, 1989), and Brecht's *The Threepenny Opera* (1986) and *The Good Person of Setzuan* (1989). Subbanna's outstanding intercultural production was an adaptation of Chinua Achebe's novel *Things Fall Apart* (1983), casting members of East Africa's Sidi tribe, which has a significant diaspora in north Karnataka.

Aparna Dharwadker

SUGIMURA HARUKO (1906?/1909?– 1997). Japanese • *shingeki, shinpa*, and film **actress**. Adopted, she was raised near Hiroshima's pleasure quarters with early exposure to theatre. After unsuccessfully attempting to enroll in a Tokyo **music** school, then briefly teaching music, she joined the Tsukiji Little Theatre (Tsukiji Shôgekijô) in 1927, starting an uninterrupted seventy-year acting career. She starred in approximately ninety films, but is best known as an accomplished *shingeki* actress, distinctive for portrayals of strong women in family conflicts.

Such roles included Blanche DuBois in Williams's *A Streetcar Named Desire* (1953); Asako in **Mishima Yukio**'s *Deer Cry Pavilion* (Rokumeikan, 1956), a play of love, deceit and assassination; and the mother-in-law Otsugi in Ariyoshi Sawako's *Hanaoka Seishû's Wife* (Hanaoka Seishû no tsuma, 1970), concerning love, jealousy, sacrifice, and devotion. But her most popular role was undoubtedly Nunobiki Kei in **Morimoto Kaoru**'s *A Woman's Life* (Onna no isshô, 1945), whom she played for fifty-one years, including a 1960 **China** tour.

She was a founding member of the Literary Theatre (Bungaku-za) in 1937 and played a central role leading the company through many crises, including one in 1963 when she refused to act in Mishima's *The Harp of Joy* (Yorokobi no koto) because of its **political** stance. This led to the resignation of Mishima himself, **Fukuda Tsuneari**, and other key company members.

Guohe Zheng

SUNDARI, JAISHANKAR BHUDARDAS BHOJAK (1889–1975). Indian Gujarati-language **actor** and **director**, one of the two most famous female impersonators of his day (the other being **Bal Gandharva**). Born in Visnagar, Mahesana District, he was trained by his grandfather, a singer, and a distant relative, the **musician**

Pandi Vadilal Nayak. He became a member of a professional **theatre company** in Calcutta (Kolkata) at nine. At eleven, with a Bombay (Mumbai) company, he gained fame performing a role based on Desdemona in a play adapted from *Othello*; the character was Sundari ("Beauty"), which he adapted as his **stage** name. As with the female impersonators of **Japan**'s *kabuki*, **women** were likely to ape his **costumes, makeup**, and behavior.

He sang beautifully, was a fine actor (including in Urdu and Hindi), and was attractive. He and Bapulal Nayak (1879–1947) were a popular stage couple for some time. His taste for good literature led to the adaptation of novels by well-respected writers, as well as to the staging of high-quality drama. Sundari abandoned performing for some time after 1932. In 1948, he returned to star in the centenary production of *Mustard-seed to Mountain* (Raino parvat, 1913). Afterward, he and others formed **Theatre** Space (Natmandal, 1949), a theatre school and troupe, whose productions revealed his **experimental** ideas, as when he staged a play using elements of both *bhavai* and classical **Chinese** theatre. Sundari was considered largely responsible for the focus put on the director in Gujarati theatre during the 1950s.

Samuel L. Leiter

SUNIL POKHAREL (1955–). Nepalese • **director, actor**, and leader of Nepal's **political** action theatre movement. He took part in street theatre in his youth and founded his **theatre company** To Climb (Aarohan) in 1982. From 1984 to 1987, he trained at **India**'s National School of Drama. To Climb, which used a regular **stage** at first, began doing street theatre in 1988. Its mission is to create activist theatre with aesthetic merit. It also trains local activists to do such theatre on their own. In Nepal's first general election, To Climb, by performing in the streets plays about the struggle for democracy, encouraged citizens to vote. Other plays have dealt with issues of sanitation, HIV/AIDS, environment, and family planning.

After Nepal achieved democracy, Pokharel worked with and for Kathmandu's deaf and disabled, street children, and AIDS victims. Throughout the 1980s, he directed Nepali translations from the world canon. In 2000, he staged Abhi Subedi's (1945–) *Dreams of Peach Blossoms* (Aaruka fulka sapana), dramatizing the commercial exploitation of traditional ideas and icons, in which Pokharel brought together Nepal's greatest artists: Kiran Manadhar painted his response to the play as it was performed; Aavaas composed the original **music**; and poet Manjul played the role of a poet. In 2001, Pokharel founded Gurukill, Nepal's most serious **training** program, and, in 2004, led To Climb on an artistic exchange tour, presenting Subedi's *Fire in the Monastery* and Ibsen's *A Doll's House* in Denmark and Russia. Pokharel has won many official awards for his contributions.

Carol Davis

SUPAA KABUKI. "Super" *kabuki*, a modernized style of **Japan**'s *kabuki* developed by **Ichikawa Ennosuke** III and performed by his **theatre company**, which aims at reviving the energy and excitement of Edo-period (1603–1868) *kabuki* and making it appealing to contemporary audiences. Ennosuke III's motto of "story, speed, and spectacle" infuses *supaa kabuki* at every level. These newly commissioned plays, based on well-known myths, legends, and literature, feature tighter plots than traditional *kabuki* and faster paced line delivery employing modern Japanese. Productions use high-tech special effects, dynamic lighting, a range of traditional and contemporary **music**, elaborate sets, and stunning **costumes** reminiscent of spectacular revues. Plays maintain the use of "female impersonators" (*onnagata*), though Ennosuke's progressive casting policy has resulted in the creation of some stars not from major acting families, such as Ichikawa Emiya (1959–) and Ichikawa Ukon (1963–).

The 1986 runaway success *Yamato Takeru* was the first of nine *supaa kabuki* plays to date. *The Dragon King* (Ryu ô, 1989) was a collaborative, international, cross-cultural **experiment** combining *kabuki* and **Chinese** • *jingju*. Ennosuke's collaborators include **scenographer** • **Asakura Setsu** and **playwright** Yokouchi Kensuke, author of five *supaa* plays, including *The Eight Dog Chronicles* (Hakkenden, 1993), *The New Tale of the Shining Princes and the Bamboo Cutter* (Kaguya shintaketori monogatari, 1996), and *The New Legend of the Three Kingdoms I, II, and III* (Shin Sangokushi I, 1999; II, 2002; and III, 2003).

Despite its clearly having nurtured new audiences, some purists view *supaa kabuki* as a desecration, while supporters praise Ennosuke's creative innovations.

FURTHER READING

Leiter, Samuel L. *New Kabuki Encyclopedia: A Revised Adaptation of Kabuki Jiten.*

Julie A. Iezzi

SUPER *KABUKI*. *See* Supaa kabuki.

SUZUE TOSHIRÔ (1963–). Japanese • playwright, director, and actor. Victimized by school bullying in Osaka, his hometown, Suzue subsumed the lingering psychological effects in theatre work. After graduating from Kyoto University, he established the Kyoto-based Eight-thirty Troupe (Gekidan Hachiji-han, 1993).

Suzue's early **political** fervor infuses *Crescent Moon on the Heel of the Shoe* (Kutsu no kakato no tsuki, 1992), where he rails against the emperor's wartime role. To connect with disaffected, introverted Japanese youth, however, he soon appropriated the "quiet theatre" (*shizuka na engeki*) style and won the 1996 Theatre Cocoon Drama Award with *Falling Fruit* (Koboreru kajitsu, 1995), directed in separate, well-received productions by **Ninagawa Yukio** and **Satoh Makoto**.

Suzue's signature work *Fireflies* (Kami wo kakiageru, 1995), awarded the 1996 **Kishida [Kunio]** Prize, features communication-challenged couples, adrift in vacuity and loneliness. The Japanese title—"sweeping her hair back"—dovetails with the firefly imagery, nostalgically recalling a simpler, rural past. Suzue poignantly juxtaposes this with the imagery's urban diminishment: smokers forced onto apartment balconies at night as the "firefly tribe" (*hotaru-zoku*). Just as they flash lit cigarettes at other distant smokers, so the play's characters wave words at each other without connecting.

Related situations structure other plays, including *Like a Spark* (Hibana mitai ni, 2002), about directionless young people, burned out from dead-end, part-time jobs.

Suzue won the 2003 Arts Festival Award for *Space Trip, Cicadas Singing* (Uchû no tabi, semi ga naite). Since 1994, he has co-edited the drama journal *LEAF* with **Matsuda Masataka** and Tsuchida Hideo (1967–).

John K. Gillespie

SUZUKI TADASHI (1939–). Japanese • director, theorist, and acting teacher. With former Waseda University classmates, including **playwright • Betsuyaku Minoru** and actor Ono Seki, he established the Free **Stage** (Jiyû Butai) in 1962, forerunner of the Waseda Little **Theatre** (Waseda **Shôgekijô,** 1966). A proponent of *angura*, Suzuki directed early works by Betsuyaku, **Satoh Makoto, Kara Jûrô,** and others. In 1968, Betsuyaku left the company, believing that Suzuki did not sufficiently respect playwrights' scripts. Thereafter, Suzuki began devising or adapting texts himself. His focus shifted to exploring the performing body through rigorous **training.**

Suzuki's search for "authentic" Japanese acting meant rejecting **Western** models in favor of pre-modern performance. He became convinced that Japanese performance originated in rituals and **dance** emphasizing feet pounding the earth. Accordingly, his training approach—the Suzuki Method (not to be confused with the violin-training system)—focuses on developing strength and flexibility in the lower half of the body. The Suzuki Method has gained worldwide appeal, especially in the United States.

Suzuki began developing his theory after encountering **Shiraishi Kayoko,** a remarkable, previously untrained actress, who joined him in 1967. Within three years, Suzuki had created a series called *On the Dramatic Passions* (Gekiteki naru mono o megutte, 1967–1970), designed to showcase Shiraishi's extraordinary talent.

In 1972, French director Jean-Louis Barrault invited Suzuki and Shiraishi to Paris, where Suzuki began to realize the possibilities of *nô* for contemporary training. Barrault's influence is also evident in Suzuki's determination to create a permanent theatre. Convinced that urbanization destroys theatrical creativity, Suzuki moved his company in 1976 to Toga village, Toyama Prefecture, where it continues to thrive. He soon began writing about and publishing his theories. In 1986, a collection of his writings from 1980 to 1983 (including his script *Clytemnestra*) was translated as *The Way of Acting: The Theatre Writings of Tadashi Suzuki.* In 1982, Suzuki initiated annual international summer theatre **festivals** in Toga. In 1984, the company became SCOT (Suzuki Company of Toga). After Shiraishi left in 1989, Suzuki continued to work with others (Japanese and foreign) trained in his signature style. Nevertheless, many longtime viewers felt that without Shiraishi, Suzuki's work lacked distinction. Such critics maintain that the productions' power was due more to her acting than to Suzuki's adaptations or directing.

Suzuki's international appeal rests on the stunning theatricality and universality of his style. His Greek and Shakespearean adaptations, while not overtly **political,** express horror at imperialism, militarism, nuclear holocaust, and the ravages of war on **women** and men. Several productions featured Americans and Japanese speaking their own languages but performing in the Suzuki style. Key works include *The Trojan Women* (Toroia no onna, 1974), *The Bacchae* (Bakkosu no shinjo, 1978; bilingual, 1981), and *Clytemnestra* (Ôhi Kuritemunesutora, 1983).

FURTHER READING

Allain, Paul. *The Art of Stillness: The Theater Practice of Tadashi Suzuki;* Carruthers, Ian, and Takahashi Yasunari. *The Theatre of Suzuki Tadashi.*

Carol Fisher Sorgenfrei

SWANG. **Indian** Punjabi or Haryanvi Hindi-language **folk theatre** of Punjab and Haryana, also popular in Himachal Pradesh and Madhya Pradesh. *Swang* (or *svang*) also refers to ***nautanki*** and is associated with ***naqal***. The theatrical use of the term, meaning "disguise," has been dated to the early sixteenth century, but the form itself probably began in the mid-eighteenth century. It is secular, emphasizing comedy, but may have **religious** overtones. During the colonial period, *swang* often served as an outlet for subversive humor at the expense of the authorities; social satire is still evident. As with other folk forms, it has been used to educate the populace about urgent social issues. There is a wide variety of *swang* forms, including primarily religiously oriented examples, such as one in the Kinnaur region involving the ritual killing of demons and the recitation of prayers seeking divine benediction. A major form is *haranya swang*, described here.

Although there have been some all-**women** troupes, most troupes are all-male, consisting of up to thirty **actors** and **musicians**. Female impersonators are popular, usually playing shrewish spouses; their heavy **makeup**, false breasts, wigs, and provocative behavior suggest the excesses of **Western** drag. The actors, skilled at singing, **dancing**, and improvisation, are led by the *guru*, who produces structurally chaotic plays composed of ingredients ranging from the tragic to the hilarious, mingling numerous songs and dances from a variety of folk and popular sources in a nonrealistic presentation filled with absurdist actions.

The **stage** is a simple, curtainless platform, about ten feet wide and ten feet deep. **Scenography** is minimalist, using the simplest **properties**, such as two sticks to suggest a military camp or a raised cloth to represent an imposing gateway. Actors sit on stage, out of character, when not involved in the action.

Swang is performed outdoors at wedding celebrations, fairs, and **festivals** (such as Holi), on tours to rural villages, and sometimes in urban locales. Performances may last up to five or six hours. They begin after an hour or so of atmosphere-creating music followed by a satirical invocation to the elephant-headed god Ganesha. The play itself is drawn from Punjabi folklore, popular ballads, historical and semi-historical subjects, mythology, and so on. A central feature is a lengthy question and answer section between two characters. The dramatic quality and characters are thinly developed. Familiar titles are *Sohni and Mahiwal* (Sohni-Mahiwal), *Puran Bhagat, Heer and Ranjha* (Heer-Ranjha), and *Sassi and Punnu* (Sassi-Punnu). Other plays are based on lyrical narratives (*gathas*).

FURTHER READING

Richmond, Farley, Darius L. Swann, and Phillip B. Zarrilli, eds. *Indian Theatre: Traditions of Performance*; Varadpande, M. L. *History of Indian Theatre: Loka Ranga; Panorama of Indian Folk Theatre*; Vatsyayan, Kapila. *Traditional Indian Theatre: Multiple Streams.*

Samuel L. Leiter

SYED ALWI (1930–). Malaysian • **playwright**, **actor**, and **director** who was educated in the United States, where he first wrote plays in English: *The More We Get Together*, *The Day of Efil*, and *Going North*. He was also involved with the then-named Malayan Arts Theatre Group (MATG, 1950). At that time, MATG produced almost exclusively English-language theatre, and hardly any Malaysian, let alone Malay, theatre. In 1967, Syed became MATG's chairman, stressing that it aimed to develop a truly Malaysian theatre, as well as to provide actor **training**.

Syed's involvement in English-language theatre is understandable given his participation in the now-defunct MATG. It was the race riots of May 13, 1969, that persuaded him to write in Malay as a means to encourage, develop, and empower Malay theatre. His *Alang of the Thousand Steps* (Alang rentak seribu, 1973) won the Malay Literary Award. Alang is an exuberant, excitable character who always finds a solution to help the film crew that has descended on his village. *Tok Perak* (1974), another Malay Literary Award winner, is about a medicine man. Other notable plays include *The Happy Village* (Desaria), a scathing futuristic play centered on an election process, and *Z:00-M1984*, the final part of the *Alang Trilogy*, consisting of *Alang of the Thousand Steps*, *The Happy Village*, and *Z:00-M1984*, Syed's attempt to impart his Orwellian vision of Malaysian society.

Syed's theatre was described as "multimedia" long before the term became popular and overused. He uses shadows, screen projections, and montage techniques to make his theatre distinctive. His ***bangsawan*** experience as a young boy is used, as is his involvement in radio and film.

Syed's playwriting has gone through several distinct phases: in the pre-1969 era, he wrote English-language plays; in the post-1969 era, he wrote in Malay, and, in the 1990s, he reverted to English again, producing plays like *I Remember the Resthouse*, *Members of the Club*, and *The Governor's Mansion*.

Syed was honored with the country's highest award for performance artists, the Anugerah Seni Negara (2002).

Solehah Ishak

TAGORE, RABINDRANATH (1861–1941). Indian Bengali-language **playwright**, **actor**, **director**, composer, painter, choreographer, educator, poet, author, **theorist**, and cultural ambassador. Though poetry dominates his literary reputation, he also wrote novels, essays, short stories, travelogues, and drama. Born into an affluent family that resounded with **musical**, literary, and theatrical activities, Rabindranath (also spelled Rabindra Nath) rejected conventional education in favor of home study under several teachers who taught him **Sanskrit**, English literature, physics, mathematics, history, geography, natural science, and so on. He also studied drawing, music, and gymnastics. Tagore made his acting debut at sixteen in the Jorasanko **Theatre**, built in his family's courtyard. The play was his elder brother Jyotirindranath's adaptation of Molière's *The Bourgeois Gentleman* (1877). The next year, he went to England to study.

Tagore's own playwriting—he wrote over sixty plays—began under his brother's influence. He believed drama was a medium for expressing his feelings and ideas. Thinking songs would be best suited for this, his first plays lean heavily on music. Mingling **Western** and Eastern influences, **experimenting** continuously with diverse tunes, and blending them in new ways with his exquisite lyrics, he created his own unique form of music theatre, richly imbued with his own spirit. Among his musical plays are *Valmiki's Genius* (Balmiki pratibha, 1881), with Tagore's score influenced by the Irish melodies of Thomas Moore, and staged—with Tagore in the lead—as *gitabhinay*, a then popular Calcutta (Kolkata) genre combining indigenous *jatra* and opera. Other musical plays are *The Fatal Hunt* (Kalmrigaya, 1880) and *The Game of Maya* (Mayar khela, 1888), in which all the roles were played by Tagore family **women**.

He wrote a number of verse dramas, ranging from one-scene pieces to five-act Shakespearean tragedies. These include the short "Nature's Revenge" (Prakritir pratishodh, 1884), about the love of a religious ascetic for an orphaned girl, and the full-length *King and Queen* (Raja o rani, 1889), *Immersion* (Bisarjan, 1890), *Chitrangada* (1892), and *Malini* (1896). These are vehicles for Tagore's deeply felt ideas, such as his opposition to idol worship (*Immersion*) or his appreciation of Buddhism (*Malini*). Other plays of this period include *Error at the Outset* (Goray galad, 1892), *Sacrifice* (Visargan, 1890), and *Baikuntha's Notebook* (Baikunthar khata, 1897); the first and third are farces satirizing social themes.

In 1901, Tagore founded an experimental boys' school in the village of Santiniketan, Bengal, that later became Visva-Bharati University. His subsequent plays were for his students; often they were produced out of doors amidst nature's beauty, although later produced in Calcutta. He used considerable symbolism in *Autumn Festival* (Sharadotsab, 1908); *The King of the Dark Chamber* (Raja, 1910); *The Immovable Institution*

"Post Office," written and directed by Rabindranath Tagore, Shantiniketan, India, 1917. (Photo: Courtesy of Natya Shodh Sansthan)

(Achalayatan, 1911); the internationally well-known "Post Office" (Dakghar, 1912), about a child's death, which premiered at Dublin's Abbey Theatre (1913); *The Cycle of Spring* (Phalguni, 1915); *The Waterfall* (Muktadhara, 1922); *Red Oleander* (Raktakarabi, 1924); and *Land of Cards* (Taser desh, 1933). *Red Oleander* and *The Waterfall* opposed environmentally dangerous practices of mining and river damming, respectively. Prose mingled with songs became Tagore's primary means of communication during these years.

Tagore's social plays include *Penance* (Prayashchitta, 1909), whose chief character advocates a Gandhi-like philosophy of passive resistance, *The Court Dancer* (Natir puja, 1926), an all-female play comparing Hindu with more egalitarian Buddhist practices, *Chandalika* (1938), and others. A number, such as *The Autumn Festival* and *The Cycle of Spring*, were inspired by the seasons, where both humans and nature are the dramatis personae. He also composed **dance**-dramas like *Chitrangada* (1936), *Shyama* (1939), and *Removal of Curse* (Shapmochan, 1931) that borrowed Southeast Asian methods and used an onstage chorus to sing the lyrics to the music he composed. Tagore also dramatized his novels, short stories, and poems. He often changed the words during rehearsals. Sometimes these changes were so substantial that the pieces in question required new titles. *King and Queen* became *Tapati* in 1929 and *The King of the Dark Chamber* became *Formless Jewel* in 1935.

Tagore acted in, produced, and directed his plays. His direction was marked by originality, imagination, and alertness. His dramatic thinking was always creative, never complacent. In 1891, he praised Western acting, but by 1911 he found British star Henry Irving's interpretation of Hamlet highly exaggerated. Tagore preferred that the actor use expressive body language. For him the logical culmination of theatre was a dance-drama in which dialogue meant an amalgam of verbal expression and rhythmic body movement. After seeing theatre in **Japan**, he realized how important a role dance rhythm could play in eliminating exaggeration. Tagore was one of the first Indian directors to support women appearing on stage at a time when many thought theatre an immoral profession.

According to his treatise "The **Stage**" (1911), he believed in a minimum of **properties**. He opposed excessive reliance on proscenium-stage realism, believing the audience should use its imagination to visualize the **scenographic** background, much as it did in Sanskrit theatre. Also, he felt it inappropriate for poverty-stricken India to rely on expensive trappings. Tagore was so displeased with a film he directed of *The Court Dancer* (1932) that he never made another.

Tagore received the Nobel Prize for literature (1913), primarily for his poetry, becoming the first non-European to win the prize. In 1919, in protest against a massacre in which British troops slaughtered four hundred Punjabi protestors, he repudiated the knighthood conferred on him by the British Crown (1915).

Debjani Ray Moulik

TAIWAN. Taiwan is a mountainous island off the southeast coast of mainland **China** on the western edge of the Pacific Ocean. Throughout its modern history, the ocean surrounding it has simultaneously confined Taiwan and opened it to endless opportunities for cross-cultural exchanges. Taiwan was colonized by the Dutch (1624–1662), governed by the Chinese Ming-period (1368–1644) loyalist Zheng Chenggong (1662–1683), and ruled by the Qing imperial government (1683–1895). After China's defeat in the Sino-Japanese War (1895), Taiwan was ceded to **Japan**, but when Japan was itself defeated in 1945, Taiwan reverted to China. Since 1949, when the Chinese Communist Party (CCP) gained control of the mainland and established the People's Republic of China, the Republic of China moved to Taiwan, both sides of the Taiwan Strait claiming sovereignty over the other. At present, three forces exist: the Taiwanese independence movement seeking to establish a Taiwanese republic; those seeking unification with the People's Republic of China; and those favoring maintenance of the status quo. Taiwan's 23 million residents consist of Han Chinese, Taiwanese, and nine different aboriginal groups. Mandarin is the official language, but Taiwanese and Hakka dialects are widely spoken. Taiwan's history is reflected in its languages and theatre. Influences from Holland, Japan, and mainland China are visible in Taiwanese culture, a vibrant mosaic of Chinese, indigenous, and **Western** traditions.

Both traditional *xiqu* and modern "spoken drama" (*huaju*; see Playwrights and Playwriting) are present. Since the 1980s, *huaju* has often been referred to as "**stage drama**" (*wutai ju*), shunning the emphasis on verbal expression indicated by the older term, coined by mainland practitioners. Inflected by the same language and culture, modern Chinese and Taiwanese theatres share a few similarities; however, they developed differently. Modern Taiwanese theatre is characterized by its hybridity and its unique combination of cultural and theatrical traditions from Japan, Taiwan, mainland China, the Chinese diaspora, and various forms of the "West."

Traditional Theatre. *Xiqu* encompassed an eclectic mix of mainland forms, especially from 1796 to 1820 (Taiwan's aborigines having song and **dance** but no theatre). These forms shared techniques; what set them apart were **music**, language, and repertoire. Only in modern times did a distinctly Taiwanese *xiqu* emerge (see below). However, the regional forms imported from the mainland have commingled and taken on local characteristics.

A recent essay collection discusses sixteen distinct types; those brought from Fujian and Guangdong Provinces are featured here. The earliest plays introduced into Taiwan were those performed to *nanguan* ("southern pipes"), a music indigenous to southeastern Fujian. Described as a "living fossil," *nanguan* is said to preserve quietly elegant music favored by literati of the Tang (618–907) and Song (960–1279) dynasties, including many songs used in **nanxi**. Also called *xuanguan* ("strings and pipes") after its lead instruments, *nanguan* music can be purely instrumental, but it also accompanied plays. Among these, *liyuan xi* ("pear garden plays") were typically performed by boy **actors**, whose movements imitated those of **puppets**. First confined to private households, *liyuan xi* later moved to outdoor stages erected for temple **festivals**. Especially popular was *Chan San and [Huang] Wuniang* (Chen San Wuniang), which features dialect banter between the Fujianese hero and Cantonese heroine. More salacious were performances of *gaojia xi* ("high armor plays"), whose music combined *nanguan* tunes and Fujianese **folk** songs. Its performers also were gaudily made-up boys, who solicited patrons with "piercing glances." Cruder still were *nanguan* skits featuring dialect banter between actors of the "female" (*dan*) and "clown" (*chou*) **role types**.

Beiguan ("northern pipes") music was introduced in the eighteenth century by Fujianese settlers in central and northern Taiwan. It is a boisterous blend of folk songs, **kunqu** fixed tunes, and rhythm-based music similar to that used for **jingju**. Plays belonging to the *beiguan* system are performed in Mandarin; their repertoires favor plays with historical, supernatural, and martial themes. *Beiguan* ensembles accompany **religious** plays, performed either separately or to begin a performance of secular plays. *Beiguan* plays include *luantan xi* ("miscellaneous theatre"), "*jingju*'s rural cousin" from Fujian, and *siping xi* ("four-level plays"), popular with Hakkas into the 1960s but now defunct. *Siping xi* used verses rapidly recited in dialect to explicate singing in Mandarin. By the late 1800s, *beiguan* music was popular island-wide and, in the early 1900s, *beiguan* troupes began performing in dialect to hold on to their audiences; only ritual plays and instrumental music are still performed.

In Hakka villages, "tea-picking plays" (*caicha xi*) were popular; the Hakkas were the only people who created a musical culture around tea. Full-scale plays (*caicha daxi*) developed only in the early 1900s under colonial rule. The popular short skits of the nineteenth century were simple stories typically performed by three actors (two *dan* and one *chou*). They combined mountain songs and off-color dialogue in dialect and featured playful tossing of gifts (in baskets) between performers and spectators. Most rural communities performed on festive and ritual occasions. Other examples are *chegu xi* brought from Fujian and the *nanguan* skits mentioned above.

Of Fujianese puppet theatres—"shadow-puppet theatre" (*piying xi*), "marionette theatre" (*kuilei xi*), and "glove-puppet theatre" (*budai xi*)—only *budai xi* moved beyond the narrow context of ritual to develop an ever-expanding secular form. Puppet theatre enjoys greater prestige than human theatre because of its antiquity and refinement; it is deeply rooted in southeast China and Taiwan. Today, high-tech videos of *budai xi* that feature action heroes overshadow the old style of live performances.

Gezai xi ("song opera"), Taiwan's only indigenous *xiqu* form, emerged in the early twentieth century by borrowing liberally from other *xiqu*, adapting Japanese reforms (indoor performances, recorded music, **scenography**, contemporary **costumes**, Western music and instruments), and actresses. Highly improvisational, it supplanted many of the older forms spread to the mainland, and did the same there. Since the 1980s, *gezai xi* enjoys special status with *nanguan xi* and *beiguan xi* as "indigenous Taiwanese arts."

Modern Taiwanese Theatre: Four Periods. Modern Taiwanese theatre's development can be divided into four distinct periods: (1) Japanese colonization, (2) postwar, (3) surging Western influence, and (4) diversification of styles.

Japanese Colonization (1895–1945). Taiwan's first indoor theatre, Waves Theatre (Langhua Zuo, 1897), was in Taipei, its name reflecting Japanese influence. However, modern theatre was not born until 1911, when Japanese ***shingeki*** companies toured Taiwan. *Shingeki*'s illusionism quickly gained popularity. In the following decades, modern **theatre companies** were formed with actors who were often homeless or gangsters; it therefore was dubbed "gangster theatre" (*liumang ju* or *langren ju*). Encouraged by colonial cultural policy, a group of young people were sent to Japan to study theatre in the 1920s and early 1930s. Returning, they established drama societies and companies performing "new theatre" (*xinju*), an earlier form of *huaju*. Established in contrast to *xiqu* stylization, realism was an alternative that could compete with forms such as *gezai xi*, *nanguan*, and puppet theatre.

Although more than sixty mainland *xiqu* and modern companies toured Taiwan from 1895 to 1937, Taiwan's modern theatre was much more deeply influenced and controlled by the extensive Japanese rule, which gave it a hybridity marked by both advantages and disadvantages. Artists and native elites were subordinated to state orchestrated "De-Sinicization and Japanization" campaigns (1937–1945). Taiwan, therefore, occupied a peripheral position relative to China within the Japanese empire. Theatre was an important part of Japan's state-endorsed modernization program. With the advent of Japanese militarism in the 1930s came **censorship** and tighter control. The state-controlled Taiwanese Drama Society was founded in 1942 to censor all theatre activities. This coincided with the Japanization movement, and more than ten state-directed companies were established to perform pro-Japanese propaganda plays. Their contents were predictable and dull, but a significant number of troupes capitalized on theatre's allegorical capacity and used it for **political** subversion. In 1944, Taiwanese writer Yang Kuei (pen-named Yang Gui [1905–1985]) adapted and staged Tretyakov's Soviet play *Roar! China* in a way that allowed censure of European powers invading China to be perceived as **criticism** of Japan's colonization of Taiwan.

Postwar (1946–1959). Colonization ended in 1945, and Japanese-language performances and pro-Japan plays declined. For a brief period, from 1945 to 1949, theatres in Mandarin and the Taiwanese dialects flourished under encouragement offered by visits of mainland companies. For example, in December 1946, **Ouyang Yuqian** and his New China Theatre Society (Xin Zhongguo Jushe) performed *Zheng Chenggong*, about the Ming general who, with the Taiwanese people, fought and ended Dutch colonization of the island. It marked the first professional *huaju* performance in Mandarin since colonization's end.

Ironically, local theatre was not able to freely develop following the Japanese departure. Although a number of prominent mainland *huaju* playwrights, **directors**, and actors followed the Nationalists in moving to Taiwan, their talents were suppressed by Chiang Kai-shek's (Jiang Jieshi, 1887–1975) anti-communist policies. Theatre was strictly controlled. Like the mainland communists, Chiang's Kuomintang (KMT) government knew very well that live performance could influence a greater audience than literary works. *Huaju* also was a tool to eradicate undesirable Japanese influence and promote Mandarin.

In the 1950s, all professional companies were either affiliated with the entertainment units of the armed forces or with government offices or universities; they included the Army's Glory Theatre Company (Luguang Huaju Dui), the Air Force's Blue Sky Spoken Drama Company (Lantian Huaju Dui), the Ministry of Education's Chinese **Experimental Theatr**e (Jiaoyu bu Zhonghua Shiyan Jutuan), and the National Taiwan University Theatre Society (Taida Jushe).

However, no plays fit conveniently into the anti-communist ideologies. Adaptations and revisions became necessary. Several Chinese plays written in the 1940s dramatizing the Chinese resistance to the Japanese invasion were reframed to portray the Taiwanese resistance to Chinese communism. Plays written in China satirizing the KMT were adapted into plays critiquing the CCP and staged without acknowledgement of their original authors, who were leftists or CCP members. In 1950, the Chinese Literature and Arts Award Committee was established to promote locally written and produced anti-communist plays. **Lee Man-kuei**, a mainlander who moved to Taiwan in 1949, wrote *Heaven and Earth* (Huangtian houtu, 1950), dramatizing the KMT's agony on being forced to retreat to Taiwan. It was followed by a number of plays that suited the anti-communist model. These plays, however, were not popular. State-orchestrated plot lines and lack of character development made them into propaganda lectures rather than theatre works. Further, Mandarin theatre, in contrast to the banned but popular Taiwanese *huaju*, was restricted to small audiences, as the majority of Taiwanese spoke only Taiwanese. Modern theatre almost came to a halt by the end of the 1950s for lack of autonomous artistic creativity and voluntary participation. Drastic changes took place over the next decades, when directors returning from the West and immigrant Chinese playwrights took the initiative to revive *huaju* with refreshed theatricality and performing styles.

Surging Western Influence (1960–1979). Playwright-director **Ma Sen** argues that there are two waves of "Western tides" shaping the landscape of modern Chinese theatre: (1) European realism, which arrived in the early twentieth century (and which Taiwan missed), and (2) modernism and postmodernism, which arrived in the 1960s. When Chinese theatre engaged in feverish "modernization" (a.k.a. "Westernization" for its promoters) during the first tide, Taiwanese theatre was under the control of the Japanese and was thereby sealed off from Western influence. However, between the 1960s and 1970s, when China engaged in the inward-looking Cultural Revolution (1966–1976) and sealed itself off from the West, Taiwan became the Chinese-speaking world's main site for engaging in productive dialogue with Western conventions. Works by prominent playwrights and directors, such as Ma Sen, Lee Man-kuei, **Lai Sheng-chuan**, and **Liu Ching-min**, coincided with the arrival of the second tide. These practitioners' cross-cultural experience and **training** in the West determined the hybrid nature of modern Taiwanese theatre.

Lee Man-kuei played an important role in the transition from political and state-directed theatre to artistically innovative commercial theatre. Being well connected with policymakers and opinion leaders, and holding various positions in the public sector, she was able to initiate the transformation of Taiwanese theatre not as a dissident but as an active participant in the formation of cultural policies. Propaganda plays gradually disappeared and plays dealing with a wide range of topics began to appear. Some playwrights, especially **Yao I-wei** and Ma Sen, wrote plays that broke away from illusionist representations and realism. Yao's *The Red Nose* (Hong bizi, 1969) used a Greek tragedy–like chorus. His *A Box* (Yikou xiangzi, 1973) was influenced by Theatre of the Absurd. Ma Sen's *Flower and Sword* (Hua yu jian, 1976), which did not assign the characters gender identities, explored their subconscious and the question of representation.

This new generation came from a great variety of backgrounds and received no formal training. Some had studied or lived in the West. Their theatre works were informed by their cross-cultural experiences. Their pioneering work in liberating modern theatre from colonial and political incarceration set the scene for a determined new theatre in the following decades.

Diversification of Styles (1980s–Present). While the 1970s saw bold yet premature experiments, the 1980s is often regarded as the golden age of modern Taiwanese theatre. Earlier experiments, successful or not, enriched the scene. The KMT government loosened its control while simultaneously reducing funding for theatre companies. This meant opportunity, autonomy, and challenge for practitioners. Today's major companies were either founded or flourished in the 1980s. These artistically innovative and commercially successful groups include Performance Workshop (Biaoyan Gongzuofang), Pingfeng Performance Troupe (Pingfeng Biaoyan Ban), and Godot Theatre (Guotuo Jutuan). Even those companies that later disbanded, such as Lanling Theatre Workshop (Lanling Jufang, 1976–1990), left clear marks on modern theatre's growth.

Post-1980s productions and approaches are characterized by their uniform interest in a wide spectrum of plays and genres as well as hybrid forms of representation. They incorporated *xiqu*, *huaju*, and Western styles, scenography, and music. There was a significant number of collaborative productions, as in the work of Lai Sheng-chuan and **Lee Kuo-hsiu**. Lai's seven-hour *A Dream Like a Dream* (Rumeng zhimeng, 2003) is representative of the Taiwanese theatre's latest achievements. The 1980s also marked the beginning of a new generation of U.S.-trained artists. However, Europe has always been an integral part of Taiwanese theatre's modern identity. Yao I-wei and others appropriate Brechtian, Artaudian, and many other European methods. Most Taiwanese companies have more extensive experience touring Europe than the United States.

Since the 1980s, there has not been a clear-cut distinction between *xiqu* and *huaju*. This is especially evident in the work of the Contemporary Legend Theatre (Dangdai Chuanqi Juchang, 1986). The company, led by Wu Hsing-kuo (Wu Xingguo; 1953–) and his wife, Lin Hsiu-wei (Lin Xiuwei; 1956–), experimented with ***jingju*** idioms, Western and Chinese music, and semi-illusionist sets. It is best known for its adaptations of Western classics, many of which have toured internationally and become new classics. Lee Kuo-hisu's semiautobiographical *Jingju Revelation* (Jingxi qishilu, 1996) used the metatheatrical mode to comment on the convolutions of *jingju* and *huaju*. Other *huaju* artists also are influenced by *xiqu* to various extents and, in turn, influenced *xiqu*.

FURTHER READING

Cheung, Martha, and Jane Lai, eds. *An Oxford Anthology of Contemporary Chinese Drama*; Guy, Nancy. *Peking Opera and Politics in Taiwan*.

Catherine Swatek and Alexander C. Y. Huang

TAKARAZUKA. **Japanese** entertainment conglomerate primarily offering musicals and revues performed exclusively by unmarried **women**, founded by Kobayashi Ichizô (1873–1957) soon after his Hankyû Railway was completed (1912). To entice more riders to Takarazuka City, a spa town in western Japan, Kobayashi established the Takarazuka Chorus (Takarazuka Shôtakai, 1913), consisting of sixteen teenaged girls. The following year, this became the Takarazuka Girls Opera **Training** Society (Takarazuka Shôjo-kageki Yôsei-kai). Kobayashi hoped his company would evolve into a uniquely Japanese popular opera providing affordable, morally uplifting, wholesome, family entertainment. He established the Takarazuka motto—"Purely. Beautifully. Correctly."—and began writing the company's scripts.

In 1918, the company began performing in Tokyo, becoming known in 1919 as Takarazuka Music Opera School (Takarazuka Ongaku Kageki Gakkô). Strongly influenced by French theatre, Takarazuka staged the landmark revue *Mon Paris* in 1927; the performers even called themselves "Takarasiennes." In 1924, the Grand **Theatre** (Dai Gekijô) was built in Takarazuka, followed in 1934 by the Tokyo Takarazuka Theatre. In the 1940s, the troupe's name was changed again, to Takarazuka Opera Company (Takarazuka Kagekidan).

During wartime, Takarazuka entertained troops, even traveling to Manchuria, but Occupation authorities took over the Tokyo theatre building after the war; it reopened in 1955. The company flourished in the postwar period with hits like *The Beautiful Gu* (Gubijin, 1951). It had a blockbuster in 1974, *The Rose of Versailles* (Berusaiyu no bara), often revived, based on a comic book and set in eighteenth-century France. New productions were adapted from novels, dramas, and tales, both Japanese and **Western**, including *Gone with the Wind* (1977), *The New Tale of Genji* (Shin-Genji monogatari, 1981), *War and Peace* (1988), *The Great Gatsby* (1991), and *The Treasury of Loyal Retainers* (Chûshingura, 1991). In the 1980s, Takarazuka introduced Broadway **musicals** like *Guys and Dolls* (1984), *Me and My Girl* (1987), and *Kiss Me, Kate* (1988).

Currently, the company consists of the Takarazuka Music School, where all performers are trained, the Grand Theatre in Takarazuka (2,527 seats), Tokyo Takarazuka Theatre (2,500 seats), and Bow Hall (500 seats). Over four hundred **actresses** perform in five troupes: Flower Troupe (Hanagumi), Moon Troupe (Tsukigumi), Snow Troupe (Yukigumi), Star Troupe (Hoshigumi), and Cosmos Troupe (Soragumi). At the Music School, each actress is assigned a gender **role type** based on ability, body type, and personality. Female-role specialists are "young woman roles" *(musumeyaku)*, male-role specialists—the fan favorites—are "male roles" *(otokoyaku)*. *Otokoyaku* often appear in public in their gender persona. The roles have their respective techniques for **makeup**, hairstyle, dress, speaking, singing, **dancing**, and acting. Productions are generally in two parts: musical play with narrative and "finale" with kick lines, big dance numbers, songs, and spectacular routines. Most Takarazuka fans are female teenagers; many remain lifelong fans.

Some regard Takarazuka as a site to explore gender, sexuality, colonization, and nationalism (see Politics in Theatre), exposing Japan's often contradictory, ambiguous gender and identity constructions and empowering women within a strongly patriarchal culture. Others see Takarazuka as anachronistic, offering ahistorical melodramas neither questioning nor addressing present realities or past misdeeds; the organization remains firmly patriarchal, only superficially empowering women—its instructors and **directors** mostly male and the best roles reserved for *otokoyaku*.

Fans continue to make Takarazuka among Japan's most popular theatres. Even during the post-bubble 1990s recession, it was among the few theatres maintaining full houses. Its stars go on to other show business careers in television, film, and theatre. Famous Takarazuka performers (whose birth years the company keeps secret) include *otokoyaku* Anju Mira, Anna Jun, Asaji Saki, Asami Rei, Daichi Mao (the "Japanese James Dean"), Haruna Yuri, Ichiro Maki, Kasugano Yachiyo, Shion Yû, and *musumeyaku* Fuzuki Miyo, Hanafusa Mari, Izumo Aya, Konno Mahiro, Kuroki Hitomi, Murasaki Tomo, Risa Junna, Shiraki Ayaka, and Yashiro Mari.

FURTHER READING

Berlin, Zeke. "Takarazuka: A History and Descriptive Analysis of the All-Female Performance Company"; Robertson, Jennifer. *Takarazuka: Sexual Politics and Popular Culture in Modern Japan.*

Kevin J. Wetmore, Jr.

TAKECHI TETSUJI (1912–1988). **Japanese** producer, **director**, educator, and **critic**. Son of a prominent Osaka industrialist, Takechi committed his personal wealth to innovative postwar theatre, leading movements to reform *kabuki* and create new works for *nô* and *kyôgen*.

At a time when virtuoso **acting** and formal beauty were *kabuki*'s primary goals, Takechi urged reforming **training** methods and play interpretation, with character and conflict as central. He taught his students **Western** breathing techniques and invited teachers of *nô, gidayû* **music**, and other arts, previously thought unnecessary for *kabuki* training, to coach vocalization and movement. Takechi's ideas proved effective and popular. His twenty-five productions between 1949 and 1953 established a repertory and style known as "Takechi Kabuki" and launched the careers of Nakamura Senjaku (later, **Nakamura Ganjirô III/Sakata Tôjûrô** IV) and Bandô Tsurunosuke (later, Nakamura Tomijûrô V, 1929–).

Takechi also inspired young *nô* and *kyôgen* actors to collaborate in **experimental** productions with performers of other genres and schools, activity traditionally forbidden. His productions, like Iwata Toyoo's (1893–1969) *East Is East* (Higashi wa higashi, 1954), **Kinoshita Junji**'s *Twilight Crane* (Yûzuru, 1955) and *The Story of Hikoichi* (Hikoichi banashi, 1955), and **Mishima Yukio**'s *The Damask Drum* (Aya no tsuzumi, 1955), brought together actors from *nô, kyôgen, kabuki*, *shingeki*, even **Takarazuka**. Takechi's experiments helped stimulate the revival of *nô* and *kyôgen* and the cross-fertilization among traditional and contemporary performing arts that continues today. From the late 1950s, Takechi focused on opera, then film, where he pioneered "soft porn" (pink) films.

Laurence Richard Kominz

TAKEDA IZUMO. Two **Japanese** • *bunraku* **playwrights** and **theatre** managers. Izumo I (?–1747) helped bring the **puppet theatre** to the height of its popularity by introducing spectacular innovations in the staging of plays. Becoming manager of the Takemoto Theatre (Takemoto-za) in 1705 (allegedly while still in his teens), he oversaw the administrative details of presenting **Chikamatsu Monzaemon**'s plays and eventually went on to compose his own works. His first play seems to have been a collaboration with **Matsuda Bunkôdô** (1722). Izumo I's name is associated with mechanical puppets (*karakuri*) as well as much more elaborate **costumes** and **scenography** than previously seen. Puppets also became increasingly sophisticated during his career, with more articulated features. In 1734, he wrote the first play featuring three manipulators per puppet, which typifies *bunraku* today.

His son, Izumo II (1691–1756), became one of the most celebrated *bunraku* playwrights after Chikamatsu. Like Izumo I, he worked for the Takemoto Theatre, which enjoyed its greatest prosperity during his tenure. Playwriting had become a team project (*gassaku*), and he coauthored some thirty works. Several are among the best-known pieces in the *bunraku* and *kabuki* repertoires, among them *Sugawara's Secrets of Calligraphy* (Sugawara denju tenarai kagami, 1746), *The Treasury of Loyal Retainers* (Kanadehon chûshingura, 1748), *Yoshitsune and the Thousand Cherry Trees* (Yoshitsune senbon zakura, 1747), and *Summer Festival: Mirror of Osaka* (Natsu matsuri naniwa kagami, 1745). Izumo I, Miyoshi Shôraku (1696–1772), and **Namiki Sôsuke** (a.k.a. Senryû) were among his collaborators.

Barbara E. Thornbury

TAKEMOTO GIDAYÛ. Line of two **Japanese** chanters (*tayû*) in *bunraku* (see Puppet Theatre). Gidayû I (1651–1714) originated the narrative **musical** style named for him (*gidayû bushi*) and heard in *bunraku* and *kabuki*. A farmer's son from Tennoji Village, Osaka, he apprenticed to chanter Kiyomizu Rihei and began accompanying *ko-jôruri* performances around 1676. In 1677, as Kiyomizu Gorôbei, he was performing in Kyoto with the great chanter Uji Kaga no jô (1635–1711). By the end of 1677, he became Kiyomizu Ridayû and founded his first Osaka **theatre**, which soon failed. He spent the next six years on the road, adopting the name Takemoto Gidayû around 1680.

In 1684, he established the Takemoto Theatre (Takemoto-za) in Dôtonbori, Osaka. The following year he lured **playwright** • **Chikamatsu Monzaemon** away from Kaga no jô, who had set up a competing theatre next door, without success. In his first anthology, *Collection for a Thousand Years* (Chihiro shû, 1686), he claimed to have established a new style of narrative singing, learning from courtiers reciting poetry and street peddlers alike, demonstrating that art develops from diligent **training**, and that chanting should consider both traditional melodies and contemporary songs as vital sources. In 1701, the title of Takemoto Chiku no jô was conferred upon him, reflecting his artistic status.

In 1703, Gidayû's disciple, **Toyotake Wakatayû** I (1681–1784), broke away to establish the rival Toyotake Theatre (Toyotake-za). Though still considered *gidayû bushi*, Wakatayû I's "eastern style" (*higashi fu*) was more flamboyant and made greater use of the major scale than did Gidayû's "western style" (*nishi fu*), which was more reserved, powerful, and disposed to use of the minor scale.

Takemoto Masatayû (1691–1744), Gidayû's head disciple, became Gidayû II upon taking over the Takemoto Theatre upon his master's death. He later received the title Harima no shojô. He did not have the rich, powerful voice of his predecessor, but his great dexterity expressed well characters' psychological subtleties. Chikamatsu began writing to highlight his voice, and many of these later plays are considered among the playwright's best.

Julie A. Iezzi

TAKEUCHI JÛICHIRÔ (1947–). Japanese • **playwright** and scenarist. His studies at Waseda University interrupted by the late-1960s student unrest, Takeuchi apprenticed himself to independent filmmaker Yamatoya Atsushi and devoted himself to screenwriting. His first play, *Young Giants* (Shônen kyojin, 1976), was commissioned by Sunset **Theatre** (Gekidan Shakôsha), a company he helped establish. His work reveals diverse influences: *Lemon* (1976) by a Kajii Motojirô short story; *Z* (1979) by Beckett's *Waiting for Godot*; *The Cruel War* (Hisan na sensô, 1980) by Ionesco's *Frenzy for Two*; and *Once Upon a Time: Cinema Sustenance* (Ima wa mukashi: eiyô eigakan, 1983) by Ionesco's *The Chairs*.

Surrealism has been an even stronger influence on Takeuchi than the absurd. *The Raven, Even* (Ano ôgarasu sae mo, 1980), awarded the **Kishida [Kunio]** Prize, references in both title and subject matter Marcel Duchamp's voyeuristic installation, "The Bride Stripped Bare by her Bachelors, Even." Arcanum O (Hihô Reibankan), a **theatre company** Takeuchi founded (its name a nod to André Breton's *Arcanum 17*), premiered it. Takeuchi's *Claire de Lune* (Tsuki no hikari, 1995), a surrealist murder mystery set in Prague during World War I, which revealed the influence of Kafka, won the Yomiuri Literature Prize: Drama Category.

Takeuchi continues to write plays, while also pursuing an active screenwriting career. Since 2000, he has taught at Kinki University.

M. Cody Poulton

TAKIZAWA OSAMU (1906–2000). Japanese • *shingeki* • **actor**, and **director**. **Trained** at the Tsukiji Little Theatre (Tsukiji **Shôgekijô**) from 1924, he made successful appearances with **Murayama Tomoyoshi**'s Leftwing Theatre (Sayoku Gekijô), affiliated with the Japanese Proletarian Theatre League (Nihon Puroretaria Engeki Dômei, a.k.a. Purotto), in 1930. By 1934, with the New Cooperative Company (Shinkyô Gekidan), he was recognized as an exceptionally promising actor in roles such as Aoyama Hanzô in Murayama's adaptation of Shimazaki Tôson's novel *Before the Dawn* (Yoake mae, 1934) and Amamiya Satoshi in **Kubo Sakae**'s *Land of Volcanic Ash* (Kazanbaichi, 1937–1938). Suspected of proletarian **political** tendencies, he was jailed in 1940. After the war, he, Kubo, and others founded the **theatre company** Tokyo Art Theatre (Tokyo Geijutsu Gekijô) in December 1945, and, with Shimizu Masao (1908–1975), Uno Jûkichi (1914–1988), and others, formed the People's Art Theatre (Minshû Geijutsu Gekijô, later Mingei) in 1947.

Takizawa anchored his distinctive style in Stanislavski's psychological realism and scrupulous reading of scripts to elicit his characters' physical and emotional personalities and socio-historical contexts. His most memorable roles include Van Gogh in **Miyoshi Jurô**'s *The Man of the Flame* (Hono'o no hito, 1951) and Willy Loman in Miller's *Death of a Salesman* (1954). Takizawa won the Education Ministry Fine Arts Prize (Geijutsu Senshô) for Shigenori in **Kinoshita Junji**'s *Requiem on the Great Meridian* (Shigosen no matsuri, 1978) and for directing the People's hugely successful *The Diary of Anne Frank* (1979).

Yoshiko Fukushima

TALAMADDALE. Indian theatre form of Karnataka, including only **music** and speech; a temple inscription dates its popularity to 1556. *Tala* means both "rhythm" and the two "two-inch diameter metal cymbals" that keep rhythm; *maddale* is a barrel-shaped drum. There are no **costumes**, **makeup**, or **dance**. It is related to *yakshagana* in that its literary sources, drumming patterns, and method of delivering speech are the same.

The setting is generally someone's home, a temple, or a cultural association program. Performances most often take place during the monsoon season (June through November) when outdoor **theatre companies** cannot perform. Duration can be for several hours or all night.

Performers include a singer, two drummers (for *maddale* and *chande* [a cylindrical stick drum]), a *sruti* box (wooden bellows instrument) player, who keeps a drone sound, and several people who speak as the characters, *arthadhari*s (literally, "those who possess the meaning").

All performers sit: the singer and drummers at center back and the *arthadhari*s on either side facing each other. A performance begins with a song in praise of the elephant-faced god, Ganesha, followed by the introduction of the characters. The singer sings the first song of the story, then the *arthadhari*s speak extemporaneously based on the contents of that song. The performance continues in this manner: song then speech.

In the highest quality performance, *arthadhari*s knowledgeable in ancient Indian texts cleverly discuss and debate with both seriousness and humor. They reveal the finest details of the story, often including a character's past lives. This kind of dialogue makes a *talamaddale* performance completely unpredictable and continually intriguing.

FURTHER READING

Varadpande, M. L. *History of Indian Theatre: Loka Ranga; Panorama of Indian Folk Theatre.*

Martha Ashton-Sikora (M. Prabhakara Joshy assisted with this essay)

T'ALCH'UM. Korean • **masked** • **dance**-drama derived from the Chosŏn dynasty (1392–1910) court masked dance-drama (*sandae*), developed some two hundred years ago in Hwanghae Province, now in **North Korea**. There are two representative styles, the coastal version, such as that originating around Kangryong, and the farmers' version, originating inland near Pongsan. The Ŭnyul *t'alch'um* blends the two. The North Korean government banned Pongsan *t'alch'um*, deeming it inappropriate for revolutionary purposes, but it and other variants were preserved by **actors** who fled south during the Korean War (1950–1953); *t'alch'um*, designated an Important Intangible Cultural Property, remains popular with South Koreans.

T'alch'um was performed to repulse evil spirits and pray for abundant crops and peace, and was presented on Buddha's birthday, at the important midsummer **festival**, Tano, or to celebrate a magistrate's birthday or the arrival of a new emissary. Themes common in *sandae* also appear in *t'alch'um*: satires on debauched monks and corrupt nobility, love triangles, and the hard life of the common people.

In the early nineteenth century, An Ch'o-mok, a lower-rank official, replaced the original wooden masks with paper ones. Following this innovation, local civil servants began to perform and dancing improved, enhancing the artistry of the Pongsan *t'alch'um*, which gradually became the emblematic version.

In 1915, the form moved to Sariwon, a neighboring commercial center with a railway station. With that relocation, the performance space changed from a flat riverside arrangement to a temporary skeletal **theatre**. Except for space designated for **musicians**, the standing audience encircled the open, circular **stage** area, which was covered with a straw mat. A horseshoe-shaped structure, divided into two-story compartments rented out to local restaurateurs, surrounded the audience. Food was prepared on the lower level, and patrons could watch from upstairs.

Early Pongsan *t'alch'um* included a prelude in which players and audiences danced ecstatically through town. Today, there is no prelude; the **dramatic structure** is as follows:

Act I	Four Nuns Dance
Act II	Eight Monks Dance
Act III	Dancing Girl
Act IV	Venal Old Monk Dance
	Scene I: The Shoe-Seller
	Scene II: The Prodigal
Act V	Lion Dance
Act VI	Nobleman Dance
Act VIII	Dance of the Old Woman

Pongsan *t'alch'um* uses twenty-six paper masks for thirty-four roles. The masks, thought to be bewitched and nicknamed "demonic masks" for their bright colors, are smaller than those used for most other forms. In earlier times, they were burned after performances in a purification rite, but today they are preserved for subsequent use. **Costumes** are loose-fitting with garishly contrasting colors. Long sleeves extending well beyond the hands are twirled to accentuate the vivacious dancing.

Kangryong *t'alch'um*, a younger but prominent version, originated at the beginning of the twentieth century. Its performance requires a costume parade and offerings and prayers to the masks. Though the Kangryong version uses fifteen masks for twenty-one roles and a ten-act structure, its overall contents differ little from Pongsan *t'alch'um*.

FURTHER READING

Cho, Oh-Kon, trans. *Traditional Korean Theatre*.

Oh-Kon Cho

TAMASHA. Northwest **Indian** • **folk theatre** that originated in Maharashtra, and flourished there especially during the reign of Bajirao II (r. 1795–1818). Originally, it was performed by all sections of society; over time, performing it became the right of two low-caste, untouchable communities, the *mahars* and the *mangs*, who continued performing it until recently. During the seventeenth century, another low caste, the *kolhati*, accepted the responsibility of entertaining the Moghul and Maratha military.

Lavani. Though scholars dispute *tamasha*'s origins, it is popularly argued that its origins could be traced to the tradition of Maharashtra singing in question and answer dialogue known as *lavani* (also *gondhal* or *gondhak*), a type of **religious** discourse associated with the worship of the Hindu gods Shiva and Ganesha, and the goddess Shakti. A *lavani* troupe consists of two **actor**-singers and two **musicians** who play the stringed *tuntune* and the *sambala* drum. There are two popular *lavani* categories, the first a "congregational devotional singing" and the other the dramatic representation of a popular myth. Dramatic elements were inserted in the form of dialogues between the singers. *Lavani* could also be based on mundane themes or romantic dialogue between two historical characters. The ballad singing tradition (*pavada*) and the poet-singer tradition (*shahir*) of Maharashtra are worth mentioning: during the seventeenth century, the acclaimed poet-singers were the leaders of *tamasha* troupes.

Performance Circumstances. *Tamasha*, which sometimes last up to six hours, can be held in a village square, residential courtyard, or on a proscenium **stage**. Large audiences often attend these commercially run presentations, which are shown by perhaps seven hundred **theatre companies** employing up to two thousand performers. Modern *tamasha* consists of two distinct varieties. One is the "song troupe" (*sangeet bari*) consisting of up to six female dancers, singers, and several musicians; the other, more theatrical and enriched by music and **dance**, is the **folk theatre** variety called *dholki bari*, named for the *dholki* drum, and consisting of a leading male actor, up to eight additional male actors, female dancer-singers, and several instrumentalists.

The latter's performance begins with the entry of two musicians, one playing the *dholki*, which provides the basic rhythm, and the other playing the *daf*, a large, one-sided leather drum beaten with the hand or tiny sticks, providing sharp accents. A smaller version is the *halgi*. They are soon joined by the cymbal and *tuntune* players. The singer's entry comes last; he takes up his position at the front of the instrumentalists when they perform *avahana*, the ritualistic singing of an invocatory song in dialogue form by the main singer, who also acts as stage manager-**director** (*sutradhara*). The song, in praise of a deity, is in a style similar to *lavani*. Meanwhile, the clown (*songadya*) enters and joins the singers.

Invocatory songs are followed by an actress entering as a milkmaid (*gaulana/ gavalana*) with her back to the audience. She takes part in a dialogue with the *sutradhara*, the tip of her sari held across her head by both outstretched arms throughout, providing momentary suspense and excitement for those eager to see her bejeweled face. The clown impersonates Krishna, engaging in witty and erotic exchanges with the milkmaid, with the musicians' participating. The story of Krishna trying to steal milk from the milkmaids is presented in an earthy manner, with the god treated as an ordinary human. This sequence is followed by a deep philosophical dialogue in *lavani* style between the clown and his assistant (*paindia*), usually a deformed character. This section is also known as the "quarrel" (*jhagada*) or "question-answer" (*sawal jabab*);

it intends to introduce a moral message. Despite vestigial religious elements, *tamasha* is secular.

The "literature" (*vag*) is the play proper, which draws on mythological or legendary stories as well as historical themes and issues of social injustice. The actors improvise prose dialogue while the narrative sections are sung by the *sutradhara* and the *lavani*s by the musicians. A *lavani* by the main singer introduces the main character and a summary of the play. The next *lavani* moves the play along, the two *lavani*s being connected with the heroine's dance showing the other **women** characters, who are dancers. They employ an erect upper body emphasizing toe and heel movements following the pattern of movements based on rhythmic syllables (*bol*). The female dancers, the clown, and others also use acrobatic movements. However, the movements of the *sutradhara* and other actors are only minimally dance-like, although they sometimes take stylized walks. The play always concludes on a moral note.

Tamasha is characterized by the intimate involvement between actors and spectators actualized through the exchange of teasing banter. There is also a convention for male spectators to give money to female performers in return for requested dances or songs. The actresses are called *nautchi*, suggesting "prostitute," and their performances are often bawdy, which keeps respectable women from performances.

As with any other caste-based performance traditions, *tamasha* is passed from generation to generation. **Training** is not systematized; children learn mainly by watching their parents performing. Music follows the Hindustani style and also blends many Maharashtra folk forms. **Costumes** resemble everyday dress. The musicians wear the *dhoti*, a long piece of cotton cloth, about one and a half meters wide, a long tunic (*kurta*), a waistcoat, and a turban. Women wear an eight- or nine-yard Maharashtra-style sari and normal **makeup**.

Today, there are more than 450 professional troupes. It serves as an effective and popular medium of communication to reach large numbers of commoners, particularly in educational projects. *Tamasha* has also influenced modern theatre and film. A recent example is the *tamasha*-influenced staging of the Marathi version of Brecht's *The Caucasian Chalk Circle* by **Vijaya Mehta**. Another type of *tamasha* is the "people's theatre" (*loknatya*), a refined and sophisticated form, designed for the urban upper-middle class.

FURTHER READING

Gargi, Balwant. *Folk Theater of India*; Richmond, Farley, Darius L. Swann, and Phillip B. Zarrilli, eds. *Indian Theatre: Traditions of Performance*; Vatsyayan, Kapila. *Traditional Indian Theatre: Multiple Streams*.

Arya Madhavan

TANAKA CHIKAO (1905–1995). Japanese • *shingeki* • playwright, director, **theorist**, educator, and **critic**. His first play, *Mother* (Ofukuro, 1933), signaled his preoccupation with language. It demonstrated skill with natural, realistic speech, and was a critical and popular success. He subsequently wrote for the magazine *Playwriting* (Gekisaku), joining **Kishida Kunio**'s Literary **Theatre** (Bungaku-za) in 1938, where, under Kishida's influence, he studied French theatre and the work of Vildrac, O'Neill, Pirandello, and Lorca. His Roman Catholicism also influenced his work, though he was never baptized; many of his plays feature characters struggling between belief and unbelief.

He wrote widely on stagecraft and directed several productions, mainly for the Literary Theatre. But it was not until the postwar period, with *The Edge of the Clouds* (Kumo no hatate, 1947), considered the earliest example of Japanese existentialism, that Tanaka matured as a dramatist by moving away from realism. Indeed, Tanaka sought to create a metaphysical theatre within a specifically Japanese idiom, and his plays, departing from *shingeki* orthodoxy, grew less naturalistic and more lyrical.

He joined **Senda Koreya**'s Actor's Theatre (Haiyû-za) in 1951, serving as acting coach, director, and dramaturg, and his plays written there are generally regarded as his best. *Education* (Kyôiku, 1953), written for his students, won the Yomiuri Literary Prize, and marked the beginning of what he called "misogynistic plays"—dramas in which a belief in God is challenged by **women** driven by strong, unnatural desires. The best example is Tanaka's most successful play, *The Head of Mary* (Maria no kubi, 1959), in which a nurse and a prostitute lead a group of Catholics to reassemble a statue of Mary after the Nagasaki bombing. The work demonstrated Tanaka's literary power. *Plover* (Chidori, 1959), similarly powerful in its lyricism, enhanced Tanaka's reputation as perhaps Japan's outstanding literary playwright of the era.

Tanaka explained his theories in, among other works, *Drama as Literature* (Geki bungaku, 1959), which sees the theatre as a means to express literary ideals, and *An Introduction to an Appreciation of Shingeki* (Shingeki kanshô nyûmon, 1963). Named a member of the Japan Arts Academy (1981), Tanaka was one of the most significant and successful postwar dramatists.

Kevin J. Wetmore, Jr.

TANG XIANZU (1550–1616). Chinese • *chuanqi* • playwright, whose four complete plays, collectively known as *Four Dreams of [Tang] Linchuan* (Linchuan simeng) since dreams figure in each, epitomize the brilliant style of late Ming (1368–1644) *chuanqi*. Tang's playwriting combined elegant literary and earthy colloquial Chinese in a manner widely admired but seldom imitated. Among the most difficult of playwrights to read, his plays nonetheless were widely performed in his lifetime and remain popular.

He was from a prosperous lineage in Linchuan, Jiangxi Province, and received an excellent but unorthodox education that stressed spontaneous learning over rote memorization. Tang was groomed for a public career, received the highest national degree (*jinshi*) in 1583, and held various posts from 1584 to 1598. But his experience of officialdom soured his ambition. As early as 1585, he declined a promotion from a patron, expressing a desire to distinguish himself instead with "impetuously brilliant" writing. An outspoken memorial (1591), indirectly attacking a grand secretary and the emperor, effectively ended his career.

To the dismay of his teachers, Tang began writing plays. Declaring that he preferred discussing "emotions" (*qing*) with **actors** to debating "principle" (*li*) with teachers, he felt he could reach more people in **theatres** than in lecture halls. All of his plays address the role of *qing* in human life, a central preoccupation in late Ming thought.

The Purple Flute (Zixiao ji), begun in 1577, retells a Tang-dynasty (618–907) romance between courtesan Huo Xiaoyu and ambitious young scholar Li Yi, but was never finished owing to its thinly disguised **political** references. Rewritten as *The*

Purple Hairpin (Zichai ji, 53 scenes, 1595), Tang's first complete play concludes happily as conventionally required, but the love story is darkened by satire, focused on a malicious official who comes between the lovers. Immobilized by the official's naked abuse of power, Li Yi is the first of Tang's less-than-impressive leading men. Huo Xiaoyu, love-obsessed and ever true, anticipates the heroine of Tang's next play.

Peony Pavilion (Mudan ting, 55 scenes, 1598) is generally regarded as the greatest of Ming *chuanqi*. It is also the first Tang play in which dreams become a crucial element, especially those of heroine Du Liniang. Her inner

Clown (*chou*) character in "Searching for the Road" scene, *The Peony Pavilion* (Mudan ting). (Photo: Zhou Tong; courtesy of Jiangsu Provincial Kunqu Troupe)

life, experienced in dreams and captured in language fusing subjective feelings and objective images, awakens Liniang to the suffocating conditions of her waking life and empowers her to free herself from them. The cloistered daughter of parents stubbornly blind to her awakening sexuality, Liniang first experiences love in a dream (scene 10), relives it in her imagination (12), conveys messages to her dream lover by means of a self-portrait (14, 24, and 26), dies of lovesickness (20), rejoins her lover while a ghost (28–32), and persuades him to resurrect her corpse (36). Having tasted freedom as dreamer and ghost, once restored to life she defies her father and persuades the emperor to sanction her unorthodox marriage to her lover, Liu Mengmei (55). Many scenes became popular, extracted and performed separately.

Peony Pavilion is the most lighthearted of Tang's plays, probably because it was largely written while Tang served as a district magistrate far from the world of Ming politics. In his last two plays, written after resigning and returning to Linchuan, political exposé takes center **stage**, now encapsulated *within* a dream-world where most of the action is set. Both Chunyu Fen, the protagonist of *The Story of Nanke* (Nanke ji, 44 scenes, 1600), and Lu Sheng, the central figure of *The Story of Handan* (Handan ji, 30 scenes, 1601), are men gripped by powerful desires and ambitions. What distinguishes them from Li Yi and Liu Mengmei is the corrosive effect of their *qing*.

Response to Tang's plays was electric, but success brought aggravation as others adapted them, notably for **kunqu** performance This entailed rewriting lyrics and distorting Tang's ideas, beginning a process by which the staged versions of his plays have diverged markedly from the originals.

FURTHER READING

Lu, Tina. *Persons, Roles, and Minds: Identity in Peony Pavilion and Peach Blossom Fan.*

Catherine Swatek

TANIZAKI JUN'ICHIRÔ (1886–1965). Japanese novelist and **playwright** whose plays, written between 1910 and 1933, were staged by **actors** in a variety of genres, including *kabuki*, *shin kabuki*, and *shinpa*. As with *The Tale of Hôjô-ji* (Hôjôji monogatari, 1915) and *Age of Terror* (Kyôfu jidai, 1916), they feature exquisite dialogue, historic settings, and a modern spirit that ridiculed conventional morality through characters bent on realizing private fantasies whatever the cost to others. Indeed, in their fascination with crime, extreme emotions, irrational acts, and illicit love, several plays, including *The Age to Learn of Love* (Koi o shiru koro, 1913) and *The Eternal Idol* (Eien no guzô, 1922), ran afoul of **censors**. His best such plays are *Because I Love Her* (Ai sureba koso, 1921) and *Okuni and Gohei* (Okuni to Gohei, 1922).

Although he derided *shingeki*'s slavish allegiance to naturalism, he nevertheless called **Osanai Kaoru** his mentor and was happy to have his plays performed in any style. *Night Tales of Honmoku* (Honmoku yawa, 1922), generally performed as *shingeki*, and the fable-like *White Fox Spa* (Byakko no yu, 1923) lampoon modern Japan's infatuation with **Westerners**, anticipating his novel *Naomi* (Chijin no ai, 1924). He wrote some of the first modern Japanese dramas to be translated into Western languages. Tanizaki tends to be long-winded—Osanai radically cut *Age of Terror* for its staging at the Tsukiji Little **Theatre** (Tsukiji Shôgekijô)—and his characters wooden, but writing drama proved excellent **training** for the clever dialogue and dramatic high jinks that endear readers to his novels.

M. Cody Poulton

TANVIR, HABIB (1923–). Indian Hindi-, Chhattisgarhi-, and Urdu-language **playwright**, **actor**, and **director**, born in Raipur, Chhattisgarh. After college, he worked in a Bombay (Mumbai) ammunitions factory (1945–1954). He also joined the leftist Indian People's Theatre Association (IPTA, founded 1942–1943), writing and directing a street play, *Laborer: Messenger of Peace* (Shantidut kamgar, 1948), followed by his adaptation of a Munshi Premchand story, *Chess Pieces* (Shatranj ke mohare, 1951). Leaving IPTA and moving to Delhi in 1954, he directed his play *Bazaar in Agra* (Agra bazar), about the Urdu poet Nazir Akbarabadi, with university students and villagers in a then unconventional nonproscenium staging. In later years, he restaged it with Chhattisgarh performers.

In 1955, Tanvir received a fellowship to **train** at the Royal Academy of Dramatic Art and to observe **Western** productions. His travels took him to East Germany's Berliner Ensemble, where he saw and was influenced by Brecht's work. Back in India, he and Begum Qudsia Zaidi co-founded the Hindustani **Theatre** (1958–1959). In 1959, Tanvir and his wife, actress-director Moneeka Misra, founded Delhi's New (Naya) Theatre. Here he wrote, directed, and adapted plays in English, Urdu, Chhattisgarhi, and Hindi.

In the 1970s, Tanvir, an advocate of the "theatre of roots" philosophy, focused on the tribal culture of Chhattisgharh, and its *nacha* • **folk theatre**, in his home state of Madhya Pradesh, producing his landmark parable play *Charandas the Thief* (Charandas chor, 1975), imbued with the spirit of the local folk, many of whom belonged to his collective-like **theatre company**. (They moved to Bhopal—to the Bharat Bhavan Cultural Center [Bharat Bhavan Rangmandal]—when Delhi bureaucrats forbade their shared quarters.)

His other plays similarly derived inspiration from folk culture, using **music** and **dance** and blending it with a modern sensibility, often Brecht-inspired. His major stagings (in which he always acted) comprised Western and Indian classics, as well as folk and **politically** leftwing plays, and were staged in various languages. They include **Sanskrit** classics like an operatic version of *The Little Clay Cart* (Mitti ki gadi, 1958) and *The Signet Ring of Rakshasa* (Mudrarakshasa, 1968), plays by Brecht and Lorca, and Shakespeare's *A Midsummer Night's Dream* (2000).

B. Ananthakrishnan

TAN XINPEI (1847–1917). Chinese • *jingju* • actor, specializing in the "older male" (*laosheng*) **role type**, but mastering several others as well. His voice was noted for its sweetness, his teacher **Cheng Changgeng** likening its quality to strong sweet wine.

Tan, son of an actor, came from Hubei Province. He entered a **training** school in Beijing at ten. Not long after graduation he entered Cheng's Three Celebrations (Sanqing) Company as his disciple. After a few years leading a traveling **theatre company**, he returned to Beijing in the early 1870s, joining the Three Celebrations Company again. On Cheng's death, he left the company, unable to realize his ambition to lead it, and successively joined several Beijing troupes. In 1890, he debuted at court, becoming the favorite of Empress Dowager Cixi (1835–1908). About then he founded the Same Celebration (Tongqing) Company (not to be confused with **Yu Shuyan**'s company of that name), with which his name is most closely linked. These achievements began his nearly three decades as "king of the acting world." When he traveled to Shanghai in 1913, he was greeted with unprecedented acclaim.

Tan was a devout Buddhist, an opium smoker, and had a reputation for being headstrong, even intolerant. As a star, he earned large sums, lifting actors' social status. His influence on *jingju* was in three main areas: (1) he established his own singing style, based on the work of predecessors like Cheng, but also adding his own distinctive, mellifluous style emphasizing Hubei dialect and **music** rather than Anhui's; (2) he mentored numerous following actors, notably *laosheng* specialists; and (3) he saw five of his eleven children become actors, one a famous *laosheng*. A grandson and great-grandson also excelled in this type.

Colin Mackerras

TARLING. Indonesian • **musical** theatre accompanied by *gamelan* instruments and guitars performed in Cirebon, Indramayu, Subang, and nearby parts of the north coast of western Java, since the 1950s. *Tarling* is formed by abbreviating *gitar* (guitar) and *suling* (side-blown bamboo flute), two principal instruments. (Others are bass guitar, drums, gongs, and *kecrek*—stacked metal plates struck with mallets.) Performances are on temporary, six-feet-tall **stages**, using handheld microphones.

Evening performances run from about 8 p.m. until 3 a.m. and have a four-part structure. (Daytime performances run from 12:30 p.m. until 3 p.m. and are less formally structured.) A musical overture (*gagalan*) is played by the core ensemble for the first hour. Then follows a concert lasting two or three hours by a pop band and singers. The *tarling* musicians remount the stage to accompany a comedy skit, lasting thirty minutes to an hour and featuring two or more "clowns" (*bodhor*). Then follows a drama with songs and extemporized dialogue lasting about two hours in which the clowns and *tarling* musicians also take part. **Costumes** are glamorized versions of everyday dress: **actresses** wear high heels and sequinned dresses, while leading males wear smart sport coats. Stories tend to be melodramatic tearjerkers dealing in domestic themes, such as thwarted love, abuse, cheating spouses, financial crises, and class differences. The most significant local precedent for *tarling* is *tonil*; telenovellas and Bollywood film are recent influences. Until the 1960s, *tarling* was commonly known as *melodi kota udang* ("Shrimp City Melody"); Cirebon is called Shrimp City after its delectable seafood.

Matthew Isaac Cohen

TATSUMATSU HACHIROBEI (?–1734). **Puppeteer** of **Japan**'s *bunraku* theatre, extremely important in the genre's early years. A female-puppet (*oyama* or *onnagata*) specialist, he was involved from the outset with **Takemoto Gidayû**'s revolutionary Takemoto **Theatre** (Takemoto-za, 1684). This was still when puppets were each handled by a single puppeteer rather than the three-man system introduced in 1734. Hachirobei handled Ohatsu in **Chikamatsu Monzaemon**'s *Love Suicides at Sonezaki* (Sonezaki shinjû, 1703), the first "domestic drama" (*sewa mono*) in *bunraku*; it reversed the theatre's failing fortune. He introduced the now standard "puppeteer's appearance" (*dezukai*) convention of the puppeteer being visible to the audience in *Emperor Yômei and the Mirror of Craftsmen* (Yômei tennô shokunin kagami, 1705). Two years later he joined **Toyotake Wakatayû** I as comanager of the new Toyotake Theatre (Toyotake-za), although he later returned to Gidayû's theatre where, following Gidayû's death in 1714, he was responsible for manipulating the major female puppets in such Chikamatsu blockbusters as *The Battles of Coxinga* (Kokusenya kassen, 1715).

In 1719, he ventured to Edo (Tokyo) where he practiced his art at Shinagawa, opening the Tatsumatsu Theatre (Tatsumatsu-za), inviting chanters (*tayû*) from Osaka and enjoying some success. Among his skills was the ability to remain steady no matter how active his puppets were.

Samuel L. Leiter

TENDULKAR, VIJAY (1928–). **Indian** Marathi-language **playwright**, television and screen writer, journalist, social activist, and fiction writer, born in Kolhapur, Maharashtra. At fifteen, he got a job in a bookshop, became a proofreader, and soon was manager of a printing press. He began a career as a journalist in 1948. In the 1950s, he turned to playwriting, quickly becoming a theatrical force. His first plays were aired on the radio before being produced in a **theatre**.

He came to notice with *The Wealthy* (Shrimant, 1955), a critique of middle-class values, with a vagabond as its unusual hero. It was followed by *An Island Called Man* (Manus navacha bait, 1956), about the plight of four middle-class but unemployed young men facing homelessness, but it was *Silence! The Court Is in Session* (Shantata! court chalu ahe, 1967) that brought him national attention. This play-within-a-play, the first such Marathi work, attacked male chauvinism and middle-class hypocrisy in its depiction of the cruelty that an adult unmarried woman is subjected to in society. Its huge success inspired a 1971 film version and translation into sixteen languages.

Among his other plays are *Vultures* (Gidhade, 1970) and *Sakharam the Book-Binder* (Sakharamam binder, 1972); in the first a family becomes vulture-like in its grasping for property; in the latter, seen as a slam at the holy institution of marriage, the title character uses poor **women** to serve him in return for providing them with basic needs. Many thought these plays obscene, which raised considerable controversy. *Ghashiram the Policeman* (Ghashiram kotwal, 1972), the first Marathi play to gain wide recognition abroad, was especially noteworthy. Its premiere at Pune took the **stage** by storm. A **political** allegory using an historical incident of the eighteenth-century Peshva rulers to allude to contemporary issues of party corruption as well as caste system problems, it is a **musical** combining Marathi **folk theatre** styles and contemporary techniques. One of its touches was a group of ten singers, acting like a human **curtain** to expose or conceal the action. It raised hackles because it was considered anti-Brahman and led to struggles with those who would **censor** it. While *Ghashiram*, filmed in 1976, now ranks among Marathi classics (it has been performed more than six thousand times and is India's most frequently revived post-independence play), it does not overshadow Tendulkar's other works, such as *Wanted from the Right Caste* (Pahiche jhatiche, 1976), *A Friend's Story* (Mitrachi gost, 1981), or *Giving Away the Daughter* (Kamala, kanya dan, 1983), also controversial because of its depiction of a Brahman girl whose Dalit husband beats her. Tendulkar was also likely to say things in public that spurred people to take legal action against him.

The prolific Tendulkar, considered by some India's most influential modern playwright, has penned over thirty full-length plays, as well as one-acts, children's plays, screenplays, essays, and short stories. His early works were produced by **Vijaya Mehta** and Bombay's (Mumbai) Rangayan troupe. In 1971, he joined the leadership of Awishkar. In 1992, this troupe offered a twenty-play retrospective of his work, each staged by a different **director**, during its fifth annual Arvind Deshpande Memorial Theatre **Festival**.

His plays comment on burning social issues and reflect society's frightening realities. They provided much needed relief to Marathi drama, which previously had been burdened by melodramatic, sentimentalist plays and artificial language. Tendulkar's plays drew praise for their finely tuned, understated dialogue and the provocative manner in which they express the relationships among sex, marriage, and the family.

Shashikant Barhanpurkar

TERAYAMA SHÛJI (1935–1983).

TERAYAMA SHÛJI (1935–1983). Japanese • **playwright, director**, filmmaker, *butô* collaborator, **theorist**, photographer, poet, novelist, memoirist, and essayist. As the iconoclastic founder of the **experimental** • **theatre company**, the Peanut Gallery (Tenjô Sajiki, 1967), Terayama dominated post-1960 avant-garde theatre, was much awarded, and achieved international renown. Since his death, his works have attained cult status, with revivals by many directors, including **Ninagawa Yukio** and **Kisaragi Koharu**. Fans have established nearly one thousand Web sites. A museum in Misawa, his hometown in northern Aomori Prefecture, is devoted to his life and art.

Influenced by Artaud and **Izumi Kyôka**, Terayama's work is invariably provocative, emphasizing lyrical poetry, nostalgic or terrifying childhood memories, surreal imagery, evocative or psychedelic **music**, and pop art. It often reflects Aomori's shamanistic traditions and his volatile, love-hate relationship with his seductive, demanding, widowed mother. Performances featured white-faced actors, sideshow freaks, bizarre machinery, disturbing sexuality, even violent confrontations with spectators. From the mid-1970s, Terayama favored large-scale spectacles, chance encounters, and alternative **theatre** spaces.

Early plays include the jazz-inspired *Blood Is Standing Asleep* (Chi wa tatta mama nette iru, 1960), the sideshow reworking of *Oedipus Rex*, *The Hunchback of Aomori* (Aomori-ken no semushi otoko, 1967), the folkloric Inugami: The Dog God, 1967, (*Inugami*) and the transvestite parody of Christianity and motherhood, *La Marie-Vison, a.k.a. Mink Marie* and *Maria in Furs* (Kegawa no Marii, 1967). In *Throw Away Your Books, Go Out onto the Streets* (Sho o suteyo machi e deyô, 1967; revised 1968; film 1971), non-**actor** students read their own deeply personal poems. Claustrophobia created by *Heretics* (Jashûmon, 1971) caused audience hysteria. The radio drama *Adult Hunting* (Otona-gari, 1960) and its film version, *The Emperor Tomato Ketchup* (Tomato kechappu kôtei, 1970), were condemned as **politically** dangerous and pornographic.

Terayama's "city dramas," like *Man-Powered Plane Solomon* (Jinriki hikôkisha Soromon, 1970) and *Knock* (Nokku, co-written with **Kishida Rio**, 1975), encompassed whole cities, transforming ordinary citizens into unsuspecting actors or spectators. Other plays plunged audiences into darkness, transported them to multiple locations, or prevented access to parts of the play. Examples include *We're All Riding on a Circus Elephant* (Jidai wa sakasu no zô ni notte, 1969), *The Crime of Dr. Galigari* (Garigari hakase no hanzai, 1969), *Opium War* (Ahen sensô, 1972), *Blindman's Letter* (Môjin shokan, 1973), *Journal of the Plague Year* (Ekibyô ryûkôki, 1975), and *Directions to Servants* (Nuhikun, 1979). These and other plays, including *Shintokumaru: Poison Boy*

Terayama Shûji's "city theatre" production of *The Hollow-Earth Theory*, produced by the Peanut Gallery, August 1–6, 1973, Minami Koenji, Suginami-ku, Tokyo. (Photo: Kujô Kyôko; courtesy of Terayama Eiko)

(Shintokumaru, co-written with Kishida Rio, 1978), *Bluebeard's Castle* (Aohigeko no shiro, 1979), and *Lemmings* (Remingu, 1979), often contain metatheatrical elements.

Although identifying with outcasts, Terayama desired the communal connections characteristic of Japanese society. He encouraged student rebellion not for specific political motives (such as opposition to the Vietnam War), but for individual and communal liberation. His politics were never overt, but his plays are often haunted by ambivalence to American cultural hegemony and postwar Japanese loss of identity. The quest for identity—personal and national—anchors Terayama's work.

FURTHER READING

Sorgenfrei, Carol Fisher. *Unspeakable Acts: The Avant-Garde Theatre of Terayama Shûji and Postwar Japan.*

Carol Fisher Sorgenfrei

TERUKKUTTU. South **Indian**, ritually based, Tamil-language form, practiced in many regions of Tamilnadu. It is most significantly represented in Tamilnadu's northeastern regions in the sacred contexts of temples and celebrations connected with a widespread **religious** tradition that developed around certain **Mahabharata** figures. *Terukkuttu* utilizes **music**, **dance**, chant, song, memorized formal prose, and improvised colloquial prose to reenact episodes from the epic.

Total Theatre. *Terukkuttu* is the most important form of epic reenactment in the Tamil region; when compared to most other genres, including ***kutiyattam***, it is the only one to manifest the full-blown concept of "theatre" (*natya*) as conceived in the ancient *Treatise on Drama* (Natyashastra; see Theory), wherein a dramatic reenactment is a multidimensional total theatre in which **actor**s and other performers use music, dance, chant, song, prose dialogue, and strongly stylized **makeup** and **costumes** in an aesthetic balance.

Most other traditional theatres favor one element over another. For example, *kutiyattam* puts a primary emphasis on **Sanskrit** chant with a minimal emphasis on dance, whereas ***yakshagana*** and ***kathakali*** make very significant use of dance but accord the actors little opportunity to sing or present prose dialogue. All songs and prose in these latter forms, that is, the lines/text of a performance, are presented by singers who sit offstage surrounded by a small group of accompanying instrumentalists, which always include a drummer or drummers. While *terukkuttu* also utilizes offstage singers and instrumentalists, its performers dance, sing, chant, and speak scripted and improvised prose dialogue in a manifestation of the *Natyashastra*'s concept of *natya* found nowhere else.

Meaning and Origins. *Terukkuttu* is a Tamil compound in which *teru* ("street") simply indicates that it is performed outdoors in the ritual contexts of temples with no enclosed or indoor **theatre**. It is by no means a form of "street theatre," as understood in **Western** theatre studies. *Kuttu* means more than just "dance" or "drama," as in modern dictionaries. *Kuttu*, at the most ancient levels of Tamil religion and culture, refers to rites of enactment and re-enactment involving sacred possession or entrancement by deities or sacred entities immanent in early Tamilnadu's ritual contexts.

Terukkuttu probably originated in these rituals, the earliest descriptions of which are in classical poetry from the second century AD. The core elements of these rites closely resemble *terukkuttu*'s in being rites of sacred impersonation involving sacred poetry and stories, music, dance, drumming, and ritual entrancement relating to specific deities. Through the centuries, as the *Mahabharata* and other mythic traditions became important in South India, these rituals coalesced with them to develop into religious traditions in which *terukkuttu* became a vital mode of re-enactment.

Some recent scholarship has attempted to substitute *kattaikkuttu* for the genre terms *terukkuttu* or *kuttu*. *Kattai* ("block of wood") refers to the painted wooden ornaments inlaid with glass worn by kingly characters. This term is controversial since it is unattested in Tamil literature and other written evidence over the last two millennia. It has been artificially inserted into the dialogue concerning *kuttu* in an attempt to eliminate negative connotations attached to the word *teru*. It is important to note, however, that since *kuttu* is performed and patronized primarily by lower-income communities at the lower end of the traditional caste hierarchy, the term *kuttu* itself, attested as a refined and elevated term in earlier literature, has in recent times in the region's complex and changing social climate also taken on an unjustified derogatory secondary connotation of "ludicrous public performance" or "commotion," as in "*Itu enna kuttu?*" ("What kind of commotion is this?").

Literature. *Terukkuttu*'s literary corpus comprises the scores on which all performances are based. At a minimum, between two hundred and three hundred *kuttu*s have been composed and performed. The manuscripts of many were preserved by **theatre companies** and, in the last two centuries, were printed by small presses focused on supplying devotional literature to everyday Hindus. These nonacademic presses proved invaluable in preserving *terukkuttu* scores.

The scores can be divided into four categories: (1) "goddess" (*amman*) *kuttu*, (2) "battle" (*cantai*) *kuttu*, (3) "marriage" (*kalyanam*) *kuttu*, and (4) "liberation of the soul" (*moksha*) *kuttu*. These categories indicate the dramatic and narrative foci of *terukkuttu* as a genre drawn from mythic and epic texts that put primary devotional and ritual emphasis on such episodes. If one looks specifically at the episodes connected with the *Mahabharata* cult of northeastern Tamilnadu, there is a cycle that is most frequently performed over a span of eight consecutive evenings as a central part of annual ritual **festivals**. Each all-night episode is performed from about 9 p.m. to about 5 a.m. The titles, all drawn from Tamil-language *Mahabharata* traditions, are: (1) "The Marriage of Draupadi," (2) "The Marriage of Subhadra," (3) "Arjuna's Penance," (4) "The Defeat of King Kichaka," (5) "Krishna's Peace Embassy," (6) "The Battle of Abhimanyu," (7) "The Liberation of the Soul of Karna," and (8) "The Battle of the Eighteenth Day."

Performance Structure. The score of an episode provides the performative and ritual framework and skeleton of a *kuttu* reenactment. Each begins with the texts of opening musical pieces with musical modes and meters indicated. These opening pieces are non-narrative, nondramatic, and purely ritualistic/devotional in nature; they provide the textual body and structure of a performance's initiatory rituals, called "drumming" (*kottu*), wherein all instruments, drums, cymbals, voices, and important musical modes and meters will be blessed.

Following these ritual pieces, the score moves into a new mode, characterized by a framework of chants and songs containing an episode's seminal dramatic and narrative material. The performance skeleton is musical or operatic in nature. Moreover, the ritual intensity of episodes involving sacred trance emerges from its music, rhythms, and dance. Interspersed with and dependent on this skeleton is another vital composed dramatic/narrative element, the formal, literarily elevated prose dialogue, placed at important transitional points to clarify the action and move it forward.

The fourth dramatic/narrative element is improvised, colloquial prose dialogue that further moves the story forward. This never appears in the published or written text, but is created at important points following the composed dialogue. It functions as a commentary on the action; compelling and entertaining, it provides a vital link between sacred time and space and the audience's contemporary world. The action, therefore, follows a continuous rhythm, moving from chant to song to explanatory prose, then back to chant to song to explanatory prose, until it reaches its concluding event.

However, a score does not end at this point. The concluding portion is one or several auspicious songs called "auspiciousness" (*mangalam*), which are shorter but homologous to a performance's ritual initiation. After the conclusion of an episode's action, the *mangalam* blesses the audience and performers in the transition from sacred time and space to everyday time and space. The scores' structure, therefore, is tripartite, with the predominating musical and prose dramatic/narrative material being framed by ritually auspicious initiatory and concluding materials.

Makeup and Costumes. Other vital elements are *terukkuttu*'s highly stylized and traditional makeup and costuming. *Terukkuttu*, like other traditional makeup systems, is color coded—mainly using red, green, and rose—to indicate dramatic and moral position. Interacting with this is an equally stylized costuming system. The most distinctive costumes are those of the numerous kingly and male royal characters that play predominant roles in most performances. These regal figures wear glittering glass-inlaid wooden crowns, shoulder ornaments, and breast plates, which go over stylized royal robes. The size and style of the crown and other ornaments indicate the degree or measure of the majesty and authority of each of these king/warrior/heroes or king/warrior/enemies.

***The* Kattiyankaran.** Of considerable importance is the "court herald" (*kattiyankaran*), who, in reality, is an omnipresent court jester-clown-companion figure. He initiates the action after the opening ceremonies, plays a catalyzing role in the **curtain** entrances bringing new figures into the action, and punctuates and propels a performance by singing humorous songs at important transitions; as a court jester, he tells jokes that infuriate his epic hosts but entertain the audience. He is the only figure continuously at the border or interface between the action's epic reality and the audience's contemporary reality. His makeup and costuming represent this liminality in being neither distinctly male or female nor distinctly stylized or realistic but reflecting both *terukkuttu* and reality without being situated in either one.

Festival Performances. The most important context for *terukkuttu* performances are festivals connected with the region's *Mahabharata* cult. Two major foci of this tradition are major epic figures who have transformed into important deities worshiped in temples. They are Draupadi, worshiped as the village goddess Tirupataiyamman, and Dharmaraja (king of morality/justice), eldest of the five heroic Pandava brothers who marry Draupadi as a spouse-in-common.

Scene from the *terukkuttu* play *The Dice Game and the Disrobing* in which Duhshanana attempts to tear off Draupadi's clothes as she prays to Krishna. (Photo: Richard Frasca; courtesy of *Asian Theatre Journal*)

Annually or periodically, a village with a temple will conduct an eighteen- to twenty-day Paratam (Mahabharata) festival, which ritually and dramatically reenacts the sacred narrative in a cycle of selected episodes spread over the celebration's entire span. It has three modes: musical recitation of the epic verses, formal rituals in the Draupadi/Dharmaraja temple, and, most important, the sacred, sometimes ecstatic reenactments that take place in a cycle of eight all-night performances. Vital episodes are "The Dice Game and the Disrobing," "Arjuna's Penance," and "The Battle of the Eighteenth Day."

The re-enactment of "The Dice Game and the Disrobing" exemplifies *terukkuttu*'s dramatic, sacred, and ecstatic aspects. Draupadi is wagered and lost in a dice game by Dharmaraja. During the game, Dharmaraja prays to Krishna, while his opponent, a scheming uncle named Shakuni, conjures a local demon in a frenzied dance. Both actions ritually charge the game into a confrontation between the divine and the demoniac. In the final scene, the disrobing, the Pandavas' archenemy, Duhshanana, attempts to dishonor Draupadi by undressing her in front of a large group of nobles. Draupadi prays to Krishna for protection. Just when Duhshanana is defeated by Krishna, who miraculously replaces every sari removed with another, both Draupadi and Duhshanana may lapse into ritual entrancement/possession.

FURTHER READING

Bruin, Hanne de. *Kattaikkuttu: The Flexibility of a South Indian Theatre Tradition*; Frasca, Richard A. *The Theater of the Mahabharata: Terukkuttu Performances in South India*.

Richard A. Frasca

TEYYAM. **Indian • religious** performances of North Kerala. A colloquial expression meaning "god," *teyyam* (also *theyyam*) refers to the spirits, deified heroes, lineage ancestors, and pan-Indian deities propitiated in these rituals. *Teyyam* is unique to this region, and is the primary form of popular Hinduism. It may date from as early as the first century, when heroes killed in battle were deified by erecting stones to be worshipped in their honor. Today, over three hundred different *teyyam*s are propitiated at specific **festivals** in community or lineage shrines on schedules that range from annual to once every twelve years. Each is unique and can serve quite different functions. Some are worshipped exclusively by a joint family or an individual household, while others are worshipped by a specific caste or entire community.

Performances in community shrines are on fixed dates set by astrological calculations. Some propitiate a single *teyyam* and are modest affairs, while others propitiate twelve to thirty-two gods in a single festival lasting seven or more days. Occasionally, an individual may commission a new *teyyam* as a "vow to god"—as did one householder who, cured of leprosy, built a shrine to Visnumurti for annual propitiation.

Performances are organized in a series of stages through which a low-caste dancer is eventually transformed into the deity, becoming the vehicle for visitation by the god/goddess, who interacts with his/her devotees. The performance sequence begins with preliminary rituals, progresses to chanting songs about the deity, may include a special dance representing the deity, and culminates in the full visitation of the fully **costumed** and made-up (see Makeup) performer who is the vehicle for the deity's visitation as he/she interacts with devotees by answering questions, offering prophecies, giving blessings, and receiving offerings.

FURTHER READING

Kurup, K. K. N. *Teyyam: A Ritual Dance of Kerala*; Richmond, Farley, Darius L. Swann, and Phillip B. Zarrilli, eds. *Indian Theatre: Traditions of Performance*; Varadpande, M. L. *History of Indian Theatre: Loka Ranga; Panorama of Indian Folk Theatre.*

Phillip Zarrilli

THAILAND. Officially known as Siam until 1948, **Thailand** (Prathet Thai, literally, "land of the free," signifying the fact that it has never been colonized by any **Western** country) is a Southeast Asian country with a population of 64.6 million (2006), 6 million of whom live in the capital city Bangkok. Ethnically, 80 percent are Thai, 10 percent Chinese, and 3 percent Malay; 95 percent are Buddhists and 4 percent Muslims; and the workforce is engaged predominantly in agriculture and fishing. Thai is the national and official language, while English is widely spoken and understood in major cities. In 1932, Thailand changed from an absolute monarchy to a democracy with a constitutional monarchy. In other words, while the king remains head of state, the prime minister—the leader of the party with the most votes in each general election—heads the government.

Geographically, Thailand is at the center of the Indochina peninsula. Not only is it between the two dominant ancient civilizations of **India** and **China**, but Thailand also borders **Burma** (Myanmar) to the west and north, **Laos** to the north and northeast, **Cambodia** to the east, and **Malaysia** to the south, with the Gulf of Thailand, part of the South China Sea, in the middle, and the Andaman Sea, part of the Indian Ocean, on the southwestern coast. Thus it is impossible for Thailand to close itself off from foreign relations. Foreign influences therefore have played a major role in the evolution of Thai arts and culture throughout her more than seven-century history.

Foreign Influences. From the beginning, foreign dramatic texts and theatrical forms have had strong influence on Thai theatre. For example, the *Ramakien*, Thailand's most significant literary influence on drama, derives from India's ***Ramayana***, and many Thai classical **dance** movements were based on India's ***bharata natyam***. As well, many dramatic works were adapted from Chinese and Javanese tales, such as the **Panji** cycle. However, theatrical practices have evolved over the centuries and developed distinctive characteristics. Contemporary practices of traditional genres are far different from their foreign sources, revealing that adaptations can lead to the creation of new traditions. For instance, the **masked** dance-drama ***khon*** bears a resemblance to its Cambodian counterpart ***lakhon khol***, yet scholars are unsure as to which was the original. The **puppetry** of *nang yai* cannot be found in the traditions of either Malay or Javanese theatre, in which shadow puppetry has been dominant. While Thailand's shadow theatre techniques reflected Malay and Javanese influences, the puppeteers were trained as *khon* performers and performed *in front* of the screen, a style not practiced in Malay and Javanese theatre. As King Prajadhipok (Rama VII, r. 1925–1935) said in a 1931 interview with the *New York Times*: "Our slogan is to adapt, not to adopt. The Siamese people are an adaptable people."

Major Genres. Since the establishment of Sukhothai as the first capital city in the early thirteenth century, various forms of theatre have been presented in formal ceremonies and as casual entertainment all over the country, from the royal court to rural villages. Scholars usually categorize traditional Thai theatre into four major genres: masked dance-drama (*khon*), classical dance theatre (***lakon***), rod and string puppetry (*hun*), and shadow puppetry (*nang*).

In addition, some scholars use the patronage system in separating the subgenres—of both live performers and puppets—into court and popular forms. The former includes, for example, *khon*, ***lakon nai***, and *hun luang*, and the latter ***lakon nok***, ***lakon chatri***, ***liké***, *hun lakon lek*, and *nang talung*. However, this categorization is problematic because, for example, such subgenres as ***lakon dukdamban*** and ***lakon phan thang*** were performed for the general public, despite royal sponsorship. Also, after the country's democratization in 1932, the establishment of the Department of Fine Arts in 1933, and that of School of Classical Dance and **Music** the next year, court forms were not restricted to the palace compounds, as the royal household was no longer traditional theatre's major patron.

Development of Modern Theatre. The golden ages of Thai theatre were in the reigns of King Nangklao (**Rama II**, r. 1809–1824) and King Vajiravudh (**Rama VI**, r. 1910–1925), both of whom were major **playwrights**, producers, and patrons. Under the former, traditional genres, especially *khon* and *lakon*, were fully developed. Under the latter, modern genres, mostly hybrids and adaptations of **Western** theatre, emerged amidst the threat of Western imperialism. This cultural development helped complete the full spectrum of Thailand's modernization. Rama VI's practices proved that Thailand, whose traditional theatre was also flourishing, was also willing to adopt European dramaturgy, not by carbon copying, but by adapting it to fit local audience's tastes. European imperialists were perhaps not aware that by the time their performing arts went beyond the palace grounds and reached the general public, they had already been appropriated and integrated into Thai theatre arts. For example, the new genre of "spoken drama" (*lakon phut*) has played significant roles socially, culturally, and **politically** ever since.

As elsewhere, movies replaced theatre as popular entertainment, and **theatres** were transformed into cinemas during the early twentieth century. In the century's second half, television similarly drew audiences from theatre. Nevertheless, audiences found a new alternative when *lakon phut* morphed into the more broadly inclusive "modern spoken theatre" (***lakon phut samai mhai***) after theatre departments were founded on two major campuses in the early 1970s and modern theatre rapidly developed and spread to the urban public.

Nowadays, traditional forms coexist with their modern counterparts, just as one can find a skyscraper next to a century-old temple in Bangkok. While the new genre of *lakon khanob niyom mhai* (literally, "new traditional dance-drama"), an amalgam of traditional and modern theatre, is slowly gaining recognition, *liké*, the most hybridized genre, is Thailand's most popular form. This is probably because its highly improvisational style allows for

Scene from Pornrat Damrhung's *lakon khanob niyom mhai* production of *Sita: Sri Rama?* at the Art Theatre, Chulalongkorn University, August 2005. (Photo: Supanit Riansrivilai)

the integration of many traditional and modern genres and stories. In contrast, other forms, especially *khon* and *lakon nai*, remain rigidly conservative and fail to reach contemporary audiences.

The Department of Fine Arts' National Theatre (Ronglakon Haeng Chat) and the Colleges of Dramatic Arts (Witayalai Natasilp) are, respectively, the main producers of *khon* and **lakon ram** and the major **training** grounds for their performers. While modern **theatre companies** were overlooked by the government, the newly founded state agency of the Office for Contemporary Art and Culture now supports Patravadi Theatre and Bangkok Theatre Network's annual showcases of modern and traditional theatre.

It is noteworthy that the number of traditional and modern theatre productions rose significantly in certain auspicious years, such as in 2006, when Thailand celebrated the sixtieth anniversary of the ascension to the throne of King Bhumibol Adulyadej (Rama IX, r. 1946–), the world's longest reigning monarch.

Unfortunately, while Thailand's thriving tourism industry brings in more than 10 million potential theatregoers every year, cultural tourism's management is so ineffective that only a small percentage attends traditional and modern productions or opts instead for "exotic tourist shows," comprising mainly cultural spectacles and transvestite cabaret performances.

FURTHER READING

Rutnin, Mattani Mojdara. *Dance, Drama, and Theatre in Thailand: The Process of Development and Modernization*; Yupho, Dhanit. *Classical Siamese Theatre.*

Pawit Mahasarinand

THANG-TA. "Sword and spear," **Indian** martial arts form of the Meitei people of Manipur, first documented in the sixteenth century or seventeenth century and formally known as "art of warfare" (*huyen-lallong*). A *thang-ta* warrior carried a pair of swords in one hand and a pair of swords in the other, with an additional spear and sword on his back. Forced to become a secret art when banned by the British colonizers following the Anglo-Manipuri war in 1891, it emerged following independence (1947) as a significant martial arts form and as a **training** method for Manipuri theatre arts. Major **directors** who have employed *thang-ta* include **Ratan Thiyam** and **Heisnam Kanhailal**.

Its movements can also be traced in the postures, leaps, and gestures of Manipuri ritual dances, such as *lai haroba* and *sankirtana*, performed solo or in duets, which is why dancers in these forms train in *thang-ta*. It is closely associated with certain deities, and its movement patterns can be seen in Manipuri snake-lore diagrams. The *thang-ta* exponent makes cutting, piercing, stamping, leaping, and turning movements on what is deemed the figurative head of a thousand-headed snake, while holding a sword or spear. The movements also display a clear identification with hunting for animals. The four chief components are spear-dancing, swordplay, unarmed combat, and, but only rarely, "touch and call" (*thengkourol*), magically imbued ritual behavior intended to ensure victory.

FURTHER READING

Awasthi, Suresh. *Drama, The Gift of Gods: Culture, Performance and Communication in India.*

Samuel L. Leiter

THEATRE COMPANIES

Theatre Companies: Bangladesh

Theatre parlance in **Bangladesh** refers to companies as "groups." Groups have dominated Bangladeshi theatre in developing, discovering, projecting, and disseminating the plays of at least three generations of **playwrights**. The groups retain an organizational continuity at a semiprofessional level, continually losing their performers to films and television; fortunately, replacements are always available. Groups are often identified with a **director**, **actor**, or **political** position.

The movement originated in Dhaka, when Habib Productions produced three Bengali plays in 1951–1952, also making waves with a mixed-gender company. A more important group emerged in 1956, when students at Dhaka University established the politically progressive Drama Circle, Bangladesh's first repertory company, which, until 1959, offered new ideas in play selection and staging. The first "group" theatre, it staged both Bengali and **Western** plays. Meanwhile, other troupes were being created, and there was even a playwriting prize established in 1960 by the Bangla Academy.

In 1968, Zia Hyder (1936–) and Ataur Rahman founded Citizen (Nagorik), although it became active only in 1973. Among its innovations was the first regular ticket system. Bengali and Western plays constituted its repertoire. Theatre was established in 1972; it focused on original work and published the country's first theatrical journal, *Theater* (1972). Wilderness (Aronyak, 1971), second only in repute to Citizen, was established by Mamunur Rashid (1948–) in 1971. Dhaka Theatre (1973), led by Nasiruddin Yusuf (1950–), added a new dimension by producing plays based on **folk** culture.

Companies also sprouted in various other cities, from Chittagong to Kushtia. In 1980, the Bangladesh Group Theatre Federation was established. It had 124 groups in 2002.

Bishnupriya Dutt

Theatre Companies: Cambodia

During the Angkor empire (ninth through fifteenth centuries), **dance** companies, the ancestors of *robam kbach boran* and *lakhon khol* troupes, belonged to temples and to the sacred king. Company members associated with these companies probably were their property. Additional troupes performing **dance**-drama or shadow **puppetry** may have existed, but no documentation survives.

When records of the performing arts resumed in the mid-nineteenth century, *robam kbach boran* and *lakhon khol* were sponsored by the palace. By the reign of King Norodom (r. 1860–1904), three all-female troupes were part of the sequestered harem. Norodom also hosted companies from all over Southeast Asia. Other **Cambodian** VIPs—including provincial governors and Norodom's brother and successor, Sisowath (r. 1904–1927)— had *robam kbach boran* and *lakhon khol* troupes, which were status symbols even if they lacked the **religious** dimensions of the king's troupe. By the 1930s, impresarios, often former royal dancers, ran *robam kbach boran* companies that performed for tourists in Phnom Penh and at Angkor. (Royal companies sometimes performed at Angkor as well.) Finally, lesser companies of ex-dancers and their trainees performed for ordinary people and were considered declassé if not morally suspect. Meanwhile, the royal troupe was repeatedly the object of unsuccessful takeover attempts by the French colonial authorities, but the premiere troupe retained royal sponsorship and control until the 1970 coup d'état.

The more popular forms, including *lakhon bassac*, **yiké**, *lakhon sbaek touch* (see Puppet Theatre), and *lakhon niyeay*, mainly have been performed by private troupes and companies of stars and lesser lights hired for individual productions. The Royal University of Fine Arts, founded under Prince Norodom Sihanouk (1922–), taught these popular forms and **folk** dances along with the "classical" genres, and the university-sponsored troupes. Today, the new Royal University of Fine Arts has companies made up of faculty and star students who perform *robam kbach boran, lakhon khol, lakhon sbaek, yiké*, and *lakhon bassac*. In addition, the national Department of Arts has several *robam kbach boran* and *lakhon khol* troupes as well as more popular genres. These play for tourists and on certain official or festive occasions. Private companies also perform the popular forms for locals and *robam kbach boran* for tourists at Phnom Penh and Siem Riep hotels as well as at Angkor Wat.

Eileen Blumenthal

Theatre Companies: China

Traditional Companies. Throughout the ages, there have been two main types of **Chinese** theatre company: professional or independent, and private. Amateur or **folk** companies also exist.

Troupes performing Yuan period (1280–1368) *zaju* were mainly family concerns, with husband, wife, children, and relations often being members. In the Ming (1368–1644) and Qing (1644–1911) dynasties, and for most of the Republican (1911–1949) period, mixed troupes were rare or nonexistent. However, **actors** still often encouraged their sons to follow their profession and company membership. The professional companies provided the backbone for the development of such major forms as *bangzi qiang*, *jingju*, and *chuanju*.

The most important is *jingju*, the early history of which is closely associated with companies from Anhui Province termed "Anhui companies" (*huiban*). By about 1820, the Beijing **stage** was dominated by the "four great famous companies" (*sida mingban*) or the "four great Anhui companies" (*sida huiban*): Spring Stage (Chuntai), Three Celebrations (Sanqing), Four Joys (Sixi), and Harmonious Spring (Hechun). Other than Harmonious Spring, which disbanded about 1850, these troupes controlled nineteenth-century *jingju*. Two are discussed here.

Spring Stage Company. Founded in the 1770s or 1780s by Jiang Chun (ca. 1725–1793), an eminent salt merchant of Yangzhou in Jiangsu Province, Spring Stage was exceptional among privately sponsored companies in performing not the aristocratic *kunqu* but the more popular regional theatre, including *bangzi qiang* and *erhuang*. Jiang invited famous stars to join him, among them **Wei Changsheng** (1788).

In the early 1790s, a Spring Stage company, probably this one, went to Beijing. It made a major contribution as a professional company, and had the longest life of the four great troupes, not disbanding until the Boxer disaster of 1900. Its most famous members included the "older male" (*laosheng*) specialists Mi Xizi (1780–1832) and **Yu Sansheng** (see Role Types).

Three Celebrations. Three Celebrations is first recorded in 1790, when it went to Beijing to celebrate Emperor Qianlong's (r. 1736–1796) eightieth birthday, an event sometimes regarded as the birth of *jingju* because it was the first time that its main **musical** styles, *erhuang* and *xipi*, were heard in combination in Beijing. It lasted through most of the nineteenth century, but disbanded in 1887, being re-established briefly in 1892 and again in 1896. Three Celebrations was led by such stars as **Cheng Changgeng**.

Historical Developments. Company leadership was much sought after among actors as a status symbol. However, from the 1890s, a few, like **Tan Xinpei**, started setting up their own companies rather than joining existing ones. This trend became more or less exclusive when, in 1900, the eight-power invasion against the Boxer Rebellion led to the burning of much of Beijing's **theatre** district and the destruction of the two remaining star companies, Spring Stage and Four Joys.

Throughout the centuries the work of many professional companies was seasonal. The height of activity was in the summer or at special **festivals**. In the slack seasons, these companies, or individual members, often created itinerant troupes. For example, in areas around the Yangzi River's lower reaches, urban company members often wandered around villages during the spring and autumn sacrifices to the harvest gods. Minor urban companies might disband altogether, while their members formed wandering companies.

Private companies focused mainly on *kunqu*, the style favored by educated patrons rich enough to run their own troupes. A famous patron was Ruan Dacheng (ca. 1587–1646), a corrupt **politician** and **playwright** who **trained** his own troupe to perform his plays, both inside his mansion and elsewhere. For most of late imperial history, the court had its own companies consisting of specially trained eunuchs.

Many regional styles being of folk origin, folk amateurs are a part of China's tradition, especially in the countryside where it was most difficult to access professionals. These were seasonal actors, working only during the slack agricultural seasons, and focusing especially on major festivals.

People's Republic of China. The People's Republic of China (PRC) radically changed the companies' structures. The state set up its own companies, taking over most of the privately run troupes. These new, much larger, companies were more integrated than their predecessors, containing not only actors, but also playwrights, designers, accountants, and others. Everyone received a state salary. Nonstate professional troupes were virtually nonexistent during the Cultural Revolution (1966–1976). For much of the Maoist period, especially the Cultural Revolution, authorities sent urban troupes to the countryside to perform for the peasants, both to give peasants access to professional theatre and to spread socialist ideology.

In the reform period, state-owned troupes continued but tended to lose public favor along with the general decline of traditional theatre. Members of more popular companies can earn more than others. Some companies are still partly itinerant, touring when invited or when home audiences dwindle.

Amateur folk companies persist. In the early days of the PRC and during the Cultural Revolution state units, like factories, educational institutions, and communes, strongly encouraged workers or members to join amateur companies, and used them for propaganda purposes. In the reform period, they have become more traditional in style, being used during festivals or for private occasions like weddings. Amateur performances are also frequently tourist attractions.

Colin Mackerras

Huaju *Companies.* The birth of modern Chinese drama was deeply indebted to the amateur societies that emerged and thrived in the early twentieth century. In 1906, inspired by the **Western**-style theatre in **Japan**, overseas students Zeng Xiaogu (1873–1936) and Li Shutong (1880–1942) cofounded the Spring Willow Society (Chunliu She) in Tokyo. Immediately after, in 1907, Wang Zhongsheng (1884?–1911) established Shanghai's Spring Sun Society (Chunyang She), China's first modern company.

In subsequent years, numerous modern "spoken drama" (*huaju*) companies emerged in major cities, including Shanghai, Beijing, and Tianjin; many used drama as a means to inseminate revolutionary ideas. The most influential included the Shanghai Drama Society (Shanghai Xiju Xieshe, 1921–1933), the China Traveling Company (Zhongguo Lüxing Jutuan, 1933–1947), and the Shanghai Amateur Dramatist Association (Shanghai Yeyu Juren Xiehui, 1935–1937), founded under the influence of the leftist theatre movement initiated by the Chinese Communist Party.

In 1949, after the foundation of the PRC, the government reorganized existing *huaju* troupes into state-subsidized companies. Almost every province and major city established its own. The most prestigious include the Beijing People's Art Theatre (Beijing Renmin Yishu Juyuan, 1952), the Shanghai Center for Dramatic Arts (Shanghai Huaju Yishu Zhongxin, 1995; formerly the Shanghai People's Art Theatre [Shanghai Renmin Yishu Juyuan] and Shanghai Youth Spoken Drama Company [Shanghai Qingnian Huajutuan]), the National Theatre Company of China (Zhongguo Guojia Huajuyuan, 2001; formerly the China Youth Art Theatre [Zhongguo Qingnian Yishu Juyuan] and the Central Experimental Theatre [Zhongyang Shiyan Huajuyuan]), the Guangzhou Repertory Theatre (Guangzhou Huajutuan, 1976), and the Liaoning Art Theatre (Liaoning Yishu Juyuan, 1951). In recent years, budgetary cuts have placed some companies in dire straits and led others to creative solutions. In 2004, the Beijing Children's Art Theatre (Beijing Ertong Yishu Juyuan) became the first incorporated company.

Most companies consist of administrative personnel and resident playwrights, designers, **directors**, and actors, who maintain some freedom to work elsewhere. Guest artists are often hired for particular projects.

Since the late 1980s, independent companies, such as the **Lin Zhaohua** Drama Studio (Lin Zhaohua Xiju Gongzuoshi) and Shanghai Modern People's Theatre (Shanghai Xiandairen Jushe), emerged to produce mostly **experimental theatre**. Many universities' amateur companies actively produce theatre on and off campus.

Nan Zhang

Theatre Companies: Hong Kong

The number of **Hong Kong** companies has been estimated at around five hundred. Despite the legal procedures a group has to go through to be established, the lack of formal action when groups become inactive (temporarily or permanently) makes it impossible to provide an accurate figure. However, it is probably reasonable to assert that around one hundred groups are active at any one time.

The largest professional company is the Hong Kong Repertory **Theatre** ([HKRT] Xianggang Huajutuan, 1977), administered by the government. Under the past artistic directorship of Chung King-fai (Zhong Jinghui, 1937–), Daniel S. P. Yang (Yang Shipeng, 1935–), and Joanna Chan (Chen Yinying), and the present leadership of Fredric Mao (Mao Junhui, 1947–), the company has grown to embrace a repertoire of more than two hundred plays. The HKRT, with twenty-three **actors** and nearly thirty front-of-house and backstage staff, is unquestionably Hong Kong's "national theatre company." It stages six to eight productions a year, most of them mainstream, totaling about 120 performances. Its incorporation in 2001 marked its alignment with the trend of community-led cultural development. It thus has become an independent operation and a duly recognized charitable institution supervised by a voluntary council, although it still receives annual subsidies of around 27 million Hong Kong dollars.

Before the birth of the HKRT, local theatre consisted of a number of amateur groups founded and led by experienced practitioners. Their enthusiastic members produced many quality plays, and laid the foundations of Hong Kong's modern theatre.

In 1966, the Hong Kong Federation of Student Associations, an organization aiming to unify college students, began organizing a yearly drama **festival**. This offered young **playwrights** a suitable platform for developing their skills. Against this background the HKRT was born.

A number of significant groups were founded prior and subsequent to the HKRT's establishment. Most important is the Sino-English (Chung Ying) Theatre Company (Zhongying Jutuan), which originated under the auspices of the British Council in 1979, became independent in 1982, and grew into Hong Kong's second largest company. Sino-English was first led by Glen Walford, Colin George, Bernard Goss (?– 1988), and Chris Johnson (1955–). Ko Tin-lung (Gu Tiannong, 1954–) became artistic **director** in 1993, the company's first Chinese in that role. Though small, Sino-English's image is that of an energetic ensemble. Because of its link with the British Council, Sino-English runs excellent theatre-in-education programs; its productions often focus on education issues. It held a three-year grant from the Hong Kong Arts Development Council; other companies have held similar or one-year grants.

The Academy of Performing Arts produced its first batch of theatre graduates in 1988. This, together with the return of certain dramatists from abroad, inspired the rapid growth of medium- and small-sized professional companies. Among them are Zuni Icosahedron (Jinnian Ershimianti) and Theatre Ensemble (Juchang Zuhe). These

Multimedia Architectural Music Theatre series: CORBU, directed and designed by Mathias Woo for Zuni Icosahedron, Hong Kong, 2005. (Photo: Courtesy of Zuni Icosahedron)

companies, together with the HKRT and CY, provide a colorful and diversified theatre spectrum. Their different foci include children's plays, educational theatre, community theatre, multimedia theatre, and physical theatre. For instance, the Prospects Theatre (Xinyu Jutuan) is appreciated for staging plays using lively, typical Hong Kong language; Theatre du Pif (Jin Juchang) has produced many successful bilingual (English/ **Chinese**) plays of literary value, and Edward Lam **Dance** Theatre (Feichang Lin Yihua) has created plays that challenge the local education system. Many other groups manage without subsidies to stage frequent performances; they are irreplaceable complements to the larger groups.

Some groups attend to the needs of marginal minorities. The Asian People's Theatre **Festival** Society organizes productions in Hong Kong and elsewhere to promote exchanges between races. It pays great attention to the empowerment of poor laborers, particularly migrants. Hong Kong Deaf Theatre (Xianggang Long Jutuan) and Theatre of the Silence (Wuyan Tiandi Jutuan) both employ deaf actors; their "silent" performances actually provide them with more opportunities to tour overseas than other troupes.

From the late 1980s onwards, commercial theatre has taken root but it has encountered rough sailing. Haocai (Haocai Zhizuo) and High Noon Production (Zhongtian Zhizuo) closed after struggling for about ten years. However, they paved the way for the more successful Springtime **Stage** Productions Limited (Chuntian Zhizuo, 1995). Springtime has offered a number of well-received productions; some have toured mainland China and elsewhere in Asia.

Amateur groups also remain active. Hong Kong districts have their own theatres, which can be seen as a trend to bring drama to the community, thereby making theatre much more popular among ordinary people.

Ping Kuen Cheung

Theatre Companies: India

In traditional **Indian** theatre, performance as a profession is associated with caste lineage. Almost all traditional genres are associated with a particular caste whose art is hereditary. Social institutions like temples and traditional village systems look after their livelihood and welfare. Despite the many socioeconomic transitions that have occurred over the years, this system has remained basically intact apart from the additional patronage and support extended by governmental agencies. On the other hand, certain forms, such as *jatra*, abandoned their lineage ties so that their members and companies became secular as a way of developing their commercial possibilities. *Jatra* companies across Orissa, Bihar, and West Bengal have grown into large-scale entertainment outfits with professional management structures, contract systems, and star **actors**.

Traditional troupes are typically known by the name of their leading performer or by the name of the best-known family member, which leads to troupe name changes over the years.

Beginning of Commercial Theatres. In modern India, theatre as a professional, commercial institution began with the emergence of **Parsi theatre** in the nineteenth century. Parsi theatre, whose main objective was to make money, was initiated by the

Parsi (Zoroastrian) business community in Bombay (Mumbai) and inspired by touring British companies that visited pre-independence India. Later, Parsi-style companies producing **musical** plays became popular throughout India.

Company Dramas and Parsi Theatre. A significant offshoot was the "company drama" or "company theatre" (*company nataka*) movement, which was both a commercial production system and the performance genre it exploited. The latter was born in Karnataka as a hybrid form combining elements of Parsi theatre, Marathi *sangeet natak*, and other local traditions, with performances given through the night in tents. The most celebrated company drama troupe was the Gubbi Theatre Company (Gubbi Channabasaveswara Nataka Sangha, 1884), which reached its apex under **actor**-manager **Gubbi Veeranna**. It toured South India, gaining popularity even in non-Kannada-speaking areas, like Andhra Pradesh and Tamilnadu. Its use of spectacular **scenography**, rapid scene changes, indigenous **music**, **folk** interludes, and **dance** created a new formula for popular entertainment. Company dramas influenced all of South India; in Tamilnadu many *sangeet natakam* companies emerged starring prominent performers such as S. G. Kittappa (1906–1933) of the Kanniah Company, his wife, K. B. Sundarambal (1906–1980), M. Krishnamurthy Thyagaraja Bhagavathar (1910–1959), and so on. These troupes influenced Kerala, where additional commercial companies were formed, among the best known being the Manomohanam Nataka (literally, "Theatre to Delight the Mind/Senses") Company, Rasika Ranjini (literally, "Pleasuring the Connoisseur"), and Paramasivavilasom (literally, "The Place of Lord Shiva").

The influence of Parsi companies in India was multifaceted. Many newborn companies during the last decades of the nineteenth century tried to follow Parsi production methods whereas companies like Maharashtra's **Kirloskar** Drama Company (Kirloskar Natak Mandali) were seeking to counter the influence of Parsi techniques through new appropriations with indigenous components. Still, Parsi theatre remained the principal model for professional, commercial theatre companies.

Theatre of a Changing Age and Annapurna Theatre. Two more significant pioneer companies were Theatre of a Changing Age (Natyamanwantar Ltd.) in Bombay, Maharashtra, and Annapurna Theatre in Orissa. Theatre of a Changing Age—devoted to European-style drama in the Ibsenian mold, operating outside the traditional actor-manager system, and instrumental in adding **women** to the professional **stage**—was created in 1933 but closed within two years because of financial problems.

Annapurna, founded under another name in 1933 and constituted as Annapurna in 1936, survived until the 1970s. Annapurna performed modern dramas in permanent **theatres**—an A-group was located in Puri and a B-group in Cuttack—and on tour. Later, a C-group was formed, but eventually the three groups had conflicts and became independent.

In the first half of the twentieth century, many other modern groups performing both in permanent playhouses and on tour were formed in Calcutta (Kolkata) and Bombay. However, they were not based on a commercial structure, so they disappeared after accomplishing their immediate mission or after the demise of whatever prominent figure was behind them seeking to forward some message or artistic approach.

Commercial and Noncommercial Companies. In a general sense, most Indian troupes are profit-oriented. Following the path laid down by the Parsi theatre, modern drama companies were established to produce new plays and explore new themes, but with the additional purpose of earning a livelihood. In addition, numerous groups whose productions reveal professional-quality artistry and techniques were founded on noncommercial activist foundations or as the result of philanthropic gifts. Such groups are supported either by grants from government or other funding agencies, or by selling enough tickets to keep the troupe alive, with everyone contributing for the company's sake. All earnings that exceed expenses are plowed back into the company for future work. Thus, the term "company" actually is not technically or even legally correct, since it signifies in India a profit-based entity, which is why most theatre institutions call themselves "groups," "societies," "associations," and the like. The truly commercial institutions alone have the authority to call themselves "companies."

Shakespeare Companies. One phenomenon has been the existence of successful English-language touring troupes performing Shakespeare, with casts made up of foreign-born actors and Indians. Among the famous British troupes traveling with Shakespeare and other English classics was Shakespeareana, founded by Geoffrey and Laura Kendal, whose work was a powerful impetus to native activists who started companies of their own. The Kendals arrived in 1944, during World War II, toured from 1947 to 1948, and were back again from 1953 to 1956, when they also toured all over Asia. They were especially influential in Calcutta's (Kolkata) Bengali-language theatre. Among **directors** they influenced was **Utpal Dutt**, who started Shakespeareana-like companies in Calcutta.

Kerala People's Arts Club. In Kerala, an offshoot of the Marxist-based Indian People's Theatre Association (founded 1942–1943) called themselves the Kerala People's Arts Club (KPAC), and performed their popular, propagandistic *You Made Me a Communist* (Ningalenne cammunistakki, 1952). This ideologically slanted commercial success was followed by less **political**, more universally oriented social dramas, thereby generating similar companies that evolved into commercial companies performing at temple **festivals** and for fine arts societies. Over two hundred such companies exist in Kerala in addition to KPAC.

National School of Drama Repertory Company. India's major theatre company directly supported by the central government is New Delhi's National School of Drama (NSD) Repertory Company. It was founded in 1964–1965 by **Ebrahim Alkazi**. During its forty-year history, it has performed in Hindi over 150 plays by more than ninety playwrights. These ranged from **Western** and Indian classics and modern plays to adaptations of literary works; some productions were **experimental** and some conventional. The NSD Repertory includes twenty actors and technicians. Actors earn a decent salary according to a ranking system for a period of six years. Directors and others are paid as well. Profits help to sustain the NSD's alumni, who make up its roster of artists. The company's mission is to disseminate theatrical culture among a discerning public and to generate theatre literacy through providing the highest quality productions.

Another NSD-based professional company with a paid staff is the Theater in Education Company, which produces children's theatre and has an educational mission. Groups of the NSD Repertory Theatre pattern, with actors hired on an annual contract, include the Bharat Bhavan Cultural Center (Bharat Bhavan Rangmandal) in Bhopal.

Other Companies. The only state-owned repertory company exclusively devoted to a regional language is Karanataka's Rangayan, which has produced Kannada-language plays since 1989. It was founded in Mysore by director **B. V. Karanth**. Rangayan has a permanent company and tours widely across Karnataka and other states.

There are many other companies concentrating on experimental productions in many Indian languages, but such companies do not really function with a professional structure. Professionalism is not widely practiced in Indian theatre, and is more likely to be seen in indigenous genres like *jatra* or ***tamasha*** than in the realm of modern theatre. Many of the best post-independence companies, such as a number of those listed below, are loosely called "amateur." Such an amateur company, says Aparna Bhargava Dharwadker, "was an artistically serious but nonprofessional organization managed by a prominent director and/or actor. It mounted major productions for paying customers but could not operate with any predictable regularity because it lacked a stable internal or external sources of support."

Despite its general lack of professional theatre organizations, India has nonetheless created numerous groups that have made important contributions. Some were short-lived, some survived for many years. In addition to those mentioned above, a representative list might include:

- Alfred Theatrical Company (1871): Parsi company in Bombay, begun as the Alfred Club (1858) and reorganized as the Alfred Theatrical Company. Under different guises, it lasted until 1937.

- Amateur Dramatic Association (1909): Influential Kannada-language, amateur troupe of Karnataka, founded in Bangalore, that produced Western and new native drama, and continued until the mid-twentieth century.

- Aryan Theatre (1935): Manipuri (Meitelon)–language amateur theatre of Imphal, Manipur. It produced mainly socially oriented new plays until its theatre burned down (1995).

- Mobile Theatre (Bhramyaman Mancha): Thirty large-scale (75- to 125- member) professional Assamese troupes that tour four-play repertories with eclectic themes on trucks fully equipped with technical equipment, stages, and up to two thousand seats for shows produced in tents.

- Bohurupee (literally, "Many, Many Forms,") (1949–1950): Still active, first-class Bengali troupe of Calcutta, and known for its "new drama" repertory of Indian (especially **Rabindranath Tagore**'s) and foreign plays and high-quality productions under **Sombhu Mitra**'s direction.

- D. J. Singh College Amateur Dramatic Society (1894): Important Sindhi-language organization founded at Karachi College; it ended in 1914.

- Elphinstone Dramatic Club (1861): Amateur Parsi-style group founded in Bombay and lasting until 1889. It was at the Victoria Theatre from 1870.

- Gorkha National Theatrical Party (1909): **Nepali**-language amateur group that lasted until 1912 in Darjiling, North Bengal, and dedicated to Nepali theatre.

- Group Theatres: Generic name for the many amateur troupes in post-independence India that provided urban audiences with socially oriented, serious drama when the professional companies faded away under the influence of movies in the second half of the twentieth century.

- Indian National Theatre (1944): Still active Mumbai-based multilingual commercial troupe, considered the finest Gujarati company of its time.

- Janata Theatre (1953): Commercial company located in Cuttack, Orissa, founded by actors from the Annapurna group. Internal dissension closed it down in 1965 despite considerable promise in its early stage.

- Theatre Space (Natmandal, 1950): Gujarati-language **training** school (1949) and troupe in Ahmadabad, which remained active for twenty years, producing modern and classic works, often with an experimental approach.

- New (Naya) Theatre (1959): Professional Hindi-language theatre of New Delhi, founded by **Habib Tanvir**, and known for its devotion to productions using folk narratives and tribal performers from central India's Chhattisgarh region.

- Ninasam (1949): Originally an amateur Kannada-language group founded by director-playwright-translator (of major Western dramas) **K. V. Subbanna** (1932–). Located in the remote, rural hamlet of Heggodu, Karnataka, it evolved into an important training center, the Ninasam Theatre Institute, by 1980, and established a professional touring repertory troupe in 1985, Ninasam Tirugata.

- Parsee Stage Players (1853): Parsi company founded in Bombay that lasted until 1861, and is considered a pioneer of the Parsi movement.

- Prithvi Theatres (1944): Important commercial company founded in Bombay by **Prithviraj Kapoor** and terminated in 1960. It was known for its outstandingly tasteful productions, most of them socially oriented. The Prithvi Theatre of 1978 was named after the original company.

- Rabindranath Literary and Dramatic Club (1923): Sindhi amateur organization founded at Hyderabad, and devoted to socially meaningful plays. It closed in 1931.

- Cultural Center (Rangmandal, 1937): Like Theatre Space (Natmandal), an amateur Gujarati training and performance organization in Ahmadabad.

- Rupmahal Theatre (1943): Professional Manipuri proscenium theatre company in Imphal, and subsequently very successful in creating its own memorable acting style, although ultimately devoted to box-office escapism.

- Community (Samudaya, 1975): Still active cultural organization in Karnataka, and devoted to enhancing the cultural life of the region, especially through leftist oriented plays and programs.

- Sopanam: Trivandrum (Thiruvananthapuram)–based company founded by **Kavalam Narayana Panikkar**, and known for its use of **Sanskrit theatre** techniques and traditional forms, such as *kutiyattam*, to create outstanding productions of classical and modern plays.

- Surabhi Theatres: Telugu-language theatre collective of rural touring companies that take their name from a village in Andhra Pradesh. Founded in the late nineteenth century, it had thirty-six units by 1960, but only four remain.
- T. K. S. Brothers (1925): Professional Tamil company founded by three actor sons of female impersonator T. S. Kannuswamy Pillai. It took the name T. K. S. Brothers in 1950, ending in 1972.
- Victoria Theatrical Company (1868): Parsi company of Bombay, that lasted until 1923, and was notable for building the Victoria Theatre (1870) and introducing **women** to the local stage.

FURTHER READING

Dharwadker, Aparna Bhargava. *Theatres of Independence: Drama, Theory, and Urban Performance in India since 1947*; Lal, Ananda. *The Oxford Companion to Indian Theatre.*

B. Ananthakrishnan and Samuel L. Leiter

Theatre Companies: Indonesia

Since the turn of the twentieth century, indigenous contemporary theatre in **Indonesia** has struggled to establish an authentic native identity while embracing **Western** dramatic constructs. Early itinerant **acting** troupes, dating from the 1890s to 1920s, performed at improvised local **theatres** throughout **Malaysia**, **Singapore**, and Indonesia (see *Bangsawan*; *Komedi stambul*). These imported troupes, consisting of primarily Eurasian actors, presented **musical** versions of European fairy tales, operas, Indian and Persian romances, true crime stories, and **political** allegories that incorporated **dance**, slapstick, and satire. One such company that achieved a level of notoriety in the 1920s was Dardanella.

Dardanella. Dardanella was a *tonil* company that toured Indonesia and elsewhere in Asia for a decade starting in 1926. Its founders were White Russians A. Piëdro and his mother, both former circus performers. Dardanella reached its apogee after **Andjar Asmara** joined as publicist in 1930, with "The Java Big Five," headlining **Devi Dja**, Miss Riboet II (a **Miss Riboet** imitator), Tan Tjeng Bok (the "Douglas Fairbanks of Java"), "heavy" actor Astaman, and choreographer Ferry Kok. Fifi Young and Ratna Asmara, who became film stars, joined later.

The repertory mingled Ibsenian problem plays and melodramatic spectacles. Extra numbers included ethnic **dances** of many nations, a Charlie Chaplin impersonator, chorus line dances, and Broadway show tunes. Dardanella advertised heavily and fielded a soccer team that engaged local teams wherever it toured. The company transformed into a dance troupe in 1936 that toured Europe and the United States.

Late Colonial and Postcolonial Developments. During the late colonial era the literary efforts of a handful of nationalist writers schooled in Western realism and naturalism greatly influenced the evolution of contemporary Indonesian theatre, including

Roestam Effendi (1903–1978), Utuy Tatang Sontani (1920–1979), Muhamid Yamin (1903–1962), and brothers **Armijn Pané** and Sanusi Pané (1905–1968). Plays were performed by amateurs in improvised theatres.

Following independence, professional companies combined Western themes with traditional styles. Usually founded around the leadership of a talented **director-playwright**, these companies found inspiration in Western **dramatic structure**, and combined it with indigenous styles in their own plays and in translations of Western texts. The Bandung Theatre Study Club (Studiklub Teater Bandung, 1958), founded by Suyatna Anirun (1936–2002), still produces mostly educationally oriented works, teaching the production process, including acting, directing, **scenography**, and management. Workshop Theatre (Bengkel Teater, 1967), established by **Rendra**, is noted for its innovative productions. Workshop Theatre blended traditional theatrical and musical forms, such as *wayang kulit* shadow **puppets** and *gamelan* orchestras, with Western forms and plays, including Shakespeare.

Politically Concerned Companies. Other celebrated companies are Popular Theatre (Teater Populer), founded by film director Teguh Karya (1937–2001), Comma Theatre (Teater Koma), founded by **Nano Riantiarno**, Independent Theatre (Teater Mandiri), founded by **Putu Wijaya**, and Little Theatre (Teater Kecil), founded by **Arifin C. Noer**. These were the five leading companies of the 1970s, producing innovative, politically oriented plays, usually written by the founders themselves or adapted from English and American contemporary and classic works.

The 1980s and 1990s witnessed an explosion in the number of new companies producing politically themed plays. Many Indonesian artists expressed their outrage at the human rights abuses and government corruption that sparked the collapse of the Suharto-led government (1998). Among notable regional companies that emerged during this period are Lenong S'mas (an acronym for Sandiwara Situasi Masyarakat, or the Community's Situational Drama), founded by Azuzan J. G. (1958–), based on the traditional Jakarta theatre form *lenong*, and Garage Theatre (Teater Garasi), founded in 1993 by a group of students at Gadjah Mada University in Yogyakarta.

Experimental groups gained notoriety in the 1980s and 1990s for presenting controversial issues using nonlinear, nontext-based performances featuring mood-enhancing imagery, sound, music, and lighting, reminiscent of Rendra. By doing so, they were able to avoid the disruptions of **censorship**. They include Black Umbrella Theatre (Teater Payung Hitam, Bandung), founded by Rachman Sabur, Open Space Theatre (Teater Ruang, Solo), and Lightning Theatre (Teater Gandrik, Yogyakarta, 1983), founded by Jujuk Prabowo.

Other companies have flourished as well since the early 1980s, among them Actors Limited from Bandung, founded by Fatul, and Earth and Water Theatre (Teater Tanah Air), founded by Yose Rizal Manua, whose works are mostly dedicated to children's theatre.

Theatre companies tend to be poorly funded, with the bulk of subsidies going toward the preservation of traditional forms. In recent years, some companies have enjoyed financial support from nongovernmental organizations, but often have found themselves at odds with the political agenda of their supporters.

James Hesla

Theatre Companies: Japan

While following **Western** artistic models, **Japan**'s modern theatre companies usually retain patterns typical of traditional genres: a single leader's dominance (recalling the traditional "headmaster" [*iemoto*] system), adherence to a distinctive style (often based on **political** or aesthetic ideology), loyalty to a single troupe (**actors** performing elsewhere retain company identification and sometimes perform in a "house style"), and the birth of new troupes from older ones, creating theatrical genealogies. Unlike traditional genres, actor recruitment and **training** are open (not confined within a family), both sexes may perform, and actors join as teenagers or adults. Hundreds of companies encompass various styles, including *shingeki*, children's theatre, **experimental theatre**, **puppetry**, mime, and movement/dance-based performance.

Early Companies. Theatre historian Ôzasa Yoshio argues that the first modern companies (forerunners of *shingeki*) were nonpolitical *shinpa* troupes specializing in melodrama, adaptations of Western plays, popular novels, newspaper serializations, and optimistic works about social equality. Such troupes (featuring both female actors and *onnagata*) eventually overshadowed the flamboyant, often political *shinpa* of **Kawakami Otojirô**. Actor Ii Yôhô (1871–1932), with financial backing from Yoda Gakkai (1833–1909), led one of the most significant nonpolitical troupes. Similarly, the Shôchiku entertainment conglomerate began in 1896 as an offshoot of actor Shizuma Kojirô's (1868–1938) *shinpa* troupe.

Shôchiku. Shôchiku was born when twin brothers Ôtani Takejirô (1877–1969) and Shirai Matsujirô (1877–1951) began independently investing in *kabuki* • theatres in Kyoto. In 1902, they formed the Matsutake Company, using the first character of their respective given names, and in 1906 expanded into Osaka by producing **Nakamura Ganjirô** I's company at the Central Theatre (Naka-za). In 1909, they took control of Osaka's ailing *bunraku* troupe, retaining it until 1964. In 1910, they entered Tokyo with the purchase of the Shintomi Theatre (Shintomi-za) and three years later took over the Kabuki Theatre (Kabuki-za).

In 1920, they established a Cinema Division and in 1936 changed their name to Shôchiku Joint Stock Company, with Ôtani as president. It later expanded into nontheatrical enterprises, ranging from bowling alleys to a symphony. Excepting brief periods in the 1930s and 1960s, Shôchiku has maintained control of nearly all *kabuki* and *shinpa* actors and theatres since the 1920s, and with rival Tôhô remains one of the two entertainment giants of Japan.

Early Shingeki Troupes. Despite varying approaches, early *shingeki* troupes supported modernization/Westernization. The Literary Arts Society (Bungei Kyôkai, 1906), founded by **Tsubouchi Shôyô**, emphasized academic analysis of Western classics. Soon, the desire for public performance demanded skilled actors. Tsubouchi believed *kabuki* actors would never master Western realistic performance. Lacking teachers or established methods, Tsubouchi **trained** amateurs (including **women**) in elocution, movement, and play reading. In 1911, **Matsui Sumako** performed Ophelia in *Hamlet* and created a sensation—and scandal—as Nora in Ibsen's *A Doll's House.*

Desiring more commercial success, Bungei Kyôkai members eventually rebelled against Tsubouchi's old-school, moralistic approach. When **director** • **Shimamura**

Hôgetsu and actors, including **Sawada Shôjirô** and Matsui Sumako, broke away to found the Art Theatre (Geijutsu-za) in 1913, the Literary Arts Society disbanded. Unlike its progenitor, the Art Theatre depended on box-office receipts, raising doubts about its seriousness. Following a twin-track policy, popular shows (often **critically** scorned) financed serious drama. The adaptation of Tolstoy's *Resurrection* (1914) included such merchandising tie-ins as the phonograph recording of Matsui singing "Katusha's Song," Japan's first pop hit. The Art Theatre toured extensively in Japan and East Asia. Its successful foray into Asakusa, Tokyo's popular-entertainment quarter, proved *shingeki*'s appeal to nonintellectuals. The company disbanded in 1919. Major *shingeki* artists through the 1930s reflected the legacy of these two companies.

In contrast, the Free Theatre (Jiyû Gekijô, 1909), cofounded by **Osanai Kaoru** and **Ichikawa Sadanji** II (who had visited the West), encouraged retraining *kabuki* actors, including Sadanji himself. Named after Antoine's Théâtre Libre, this company tried to emulate Europe's experimental "little theatres." Whereas Tsubouchi wanted to transform amateurs into professionals, Osanai wanted professionals to become amateurs. However, few *kabuki* actors had seen realistic plays or were familiar with European manners. Unlike *kabuki*, realism demands that actors move while speaking, use natural gestures, repeat dialogue as written, and be the same sex as their character. In directing Ibsen's *John Gabriel Borkman* (1909), Osanai tried unsuccessfully to duplicate European acting as described by a friend's letters. In 1912, he visited Europe, taking detailed notes at plays. Although *kabuki* actors failed to master realistic performance, the troupe's translations of modern European plays shaped emerging **playwrights**' ideas.

Transformation to Contemporary Practices. Osanai's disillusionment led him to Moscow to observe Stanislavski's methods. Osanai's aristocratic pupil **Hijikata Yoshi** immersed himself in German expressionism and Meyerhold's biomechanics. Using Hijikata's money and Osanai's professional credentials, they built a new theatre on European models. The Tsukiji Little Theatre (Tsukiji **Shôgekijô**) opened on June 13, 1924, marking a *shingeki* watershed; it existed four and a half years, but it molded *shingeki*'s future.

Osanai's announcement of two years devoted to modern European plays dismayed young playwrights. They remained frustrated when, in 1926, Tsubouchi's *En the Ascetic* (En no gyôja, 1916) became the Tsukiji's first Japanese-written production. Despite opposing artistic agendas, Hijikata and Osanai worked collaboratively, training and directing in realistic and experimental styles. With Osanai's 1928 death, ideological rifts escalated, and the company collapsed. Hijikata established the more political New Tsukiji Troupe (Shin Tsukiji Gekidan), while Aoyama Sugisaku (1889–1956) created the more aesthetically inclined Tsukiji Little Theatre Company (Gekidan Tsukiji Shôgekijô).

Proletarian troupes emerged as Marxist ideology thrived. The Left Theatre (Sayoku Gekijô, 1928) troupe first performed at the Tsukiji Little Theatre. By World War II, **censorship** was pervasive. All leftist companies were banned and their leaders, including Brechtian/Marxist **Senda Koreya**, imprisoned. In contrast, the Literary Theatre (Bungaku-za, 1937), founded by **Kishida Kunio**, **Kubota Mantarô**, and Iwata Toyoo (1893–1969), was the only *shingeki* company permitted to perform throughout the war. Consequently, postwar *shingeki* was wary of government support and interference.

***Orthodox Postwar* Shingeki.** Postwar *shingeki* boomed. Beginning with only twelve members in 1950, the leftist People's Art Theatre (Mingei) had 119 members by 1960 and 250 by 1970, annually producing ten plays. Other major companies included the apolitical Bungaku-za, among the oldest and largest troupes, employing over one hundred members, producing four to five main and four smaller productions yearly; and the socially conscious Actor's Theatre (Haiyû-za, 1944), founded by Senda Koreya.

Shingeki in the 1950s focused on dialogue and actor-based realism, such as the Actor's Theatre's *The Cherry Orchard* (1951) and the Literary Theatre's *A Streetcar Named Desire* (1953), and on social realism, such as People's Art Theatre's *Death of a Salesman* (1954). These "big three companies" and others benefited from the "theatre company" (*gekidan*) system. Members who performed outside were "taxed" up to 50 percent of their earnings. Film and television supported live performances, since actors received little or no payment for **stage** work; in effect, actors donated time and money to support the companies. Such loyalty yielded psychological benefits analogous to lifetime employment in business. Although actors remained nonunionized, the Marxist-oriented Workers' Theatre Councils subsidized the companies by discounting tickets for union members, especially outside Tokyo.

In 1954, the Actor's Theatre, financed by taxes on outside work, built its own, independently managed, playhouse. Despite Senda's Marxism, the Actor's Theatre today is apolitical, and produces Western-style, orthodox *shingeki*. It uses realism to "express the 'present' of the world we live in today" and "to learn from our predecessors while positively directing our attention to new trends." Its training institute (1949) evolved into Tôhô Gakuen Junior College.

In 1963, a mass defection from the Literary Theatre resulted in self-redefinition, including accepting **Mishima Yukio**'s three-part "new conception": productions of new plays, contemporary restagings of *kabuki*, and reappraisal of Western practices. Mishima withdrew in 1964 when his obsessive anti-communism created further rifts. The original defectors, led by **Fukuda Tsuneari**, established the Contemporary Theatre Association (Gendai Engeki Kyôkai) and the Cloud Troupe (Gekidan Kumo), today called the Pleiades (SUBARU), which is affiliated with the Institute of Dramatic Arts, an organization with training laboratories, research facilities, and a theatre library. SUBARU emphasizes text-based productions, tours internationally, and participates in exchanges with foreign groups, including London's Royal Academy of Dramatic Art (RADA). Recent successes include the international collaboration and tour of *Silence* (Chinmoku, 1995), based on Endo Shûsaku's (1923–1996) novel of Japanese Christianity.

The Four Seasons Company (Gekidan Shiki, 1953), founded by **Asari Keita**, rejected psychological realism and staged French playwrights Giraudoux and Anouilh. Shifting focus in 1969, it turned to producing commercial musicals including *Cats, Jesus Christ Superstar, Phantom of the Opera, The Lion King*, and *Mamma Mia!*, and original Japanese **musicals**. Owning theatres throughout Japan, it employs about eight hundred artists and staff. Gross box-office receipts in 2003 totaled around $209 million, for 2,660 performances seen by 2.55 million people.

Although Four Seasons is often disparaged for excessive commercialism, its transformation to big business typifies orthodox *shingeki* (and some "little theatre"). By the late 1980s, Japan's economic transformation ("the bubble economy") included a consumption tax, devastating small troupes. In 1989, the Agency for Cultural Affairs offered massive corporate funding and business promotions. State subsidies and/or corporate status became essential. As of 1997, most Association of Japanese Theatre Companies members (*shingeki* and alternative) had corporate status. The sixty-eight member troupes (Four Seasons is not a member) employed about four thousand artistic and business staff, producing over four hundred shows (nearly 12,500 performances) yearly—about half of Japan's nontraditional activity.

Alternative Companies. Widespread, unsuccessful demonstrations against the 1960 and 1970 renewals of the U.S.-Japan Mutual Security Treaty (Anpo) and against the Vietnam War combined with growing unease over lost national identity, rapid urbanization, excessive materialism, even (in some cases) Japan's colonialist/militarist past. Many young artists viewed *shingeki*—originally anti-traditional—as aesthetically, morally, and politically irrelevant, even corrupt; it had become the tradition to rebel against.

Such dissidents, unhampered by established practices and seniority systems, experimented with nonrealistic theatre in small, often borrowed spaces: cafés, warehouses, tents, vacant lots, even city streets. The "little theatre" (*shôgekijô*) movement, like Osanai's similarly titled experiment four decades previously, augured change and continuity. *Angura* dominated the 1960s–1970s *shôgekijô* movement.

In 1959, young People's Art Theatre members established the Youth Art Theatre (Seinen Geijiutsu Gekijô, or Seigei). It embraced leftist politics, like People's Art Theatre, but rejected Western-style dramaturgy and staging. Associated artists included **Betsuyaku Minoru**, **Kara Jûrô**, and **Satoh Makoto**. In 1962, Betsuyaku and **Suzuki Tadashi** launched their Free Stage (Jiyû Butai) troupe. Its initial production, considered *angura*'s origin, was Betsuyaku's *The Elephant* (Zô), a parable about atomic bomb victims. In 1966, with actor Ono Seki, the troupe reorganized as Waseda Little Theatre (Waseda Shôgekijô), initially performing above a café. Suzuki gradually developed his signature actor-training method, directing adaptations of classical Japanese and Western plays, often featuring the charismatic **Shiraishi Kayoko**. The emphasis on acting rather than playwriting caused Betsuyaku's 1968 departure. To avoid urban distractions, the troupe relocated in 1976 to rural Toga Village in Toyama Prefecture, where it performs in an outdoor theatre designed by Isozaki Arata (1931–). In 1982, Suzuki founded the Toga International Theatre **Festival**. His troupe, known since 1984 as Suzuki Company of Toga (SCOT), tours internationally, offers acting workshops, and is associated with American director Ann Bogart's company.

Kara Jûrô's Situation Theatre (Jôkyô Gekijô, 1963) set up its trademark Red Tent (Aka Tento, pioneered in 1967) in October 1968 at the place in Kyoto where **Izumo no Okuni** first performed *kabuki*. Claiming genealogical descent, Kara called his actors "riverbed beggars" (*kawara kojiki*), a pejorative term for *kabuki* actors. Kara's goal was to destroy *shingeki* complacency. Situation Theatre opposed text-based performance, emphasizing popular entertainment, total theatre, and nonlinear, often confusing narrative. Like Suzuki, Kara privileged the actor's body over text; unlike Suzuki, he avoided international festivals and Western tours. In 1989, the troupe became Kara Group (Karagumi), occasionally working in developing nations like **Bangladesh**.

The Free Theatre (Jiyû Gekijô), probably named after Osanai's 1909 venture, emerged in 1966. Organized by former Actor's Theatre students, it vilified orthodox *shingeki*, performing in a basement. Primarily associated with Satoh Makoto, it presented complex, mythical, multilayered, social/historical critiques such as Satoh's *Nezumi Kozô: The Rat* (Nezumi Kozô Jirôkichi, 1969). Merging with two other groups and performing in a huge, movable black tent, it metamorphosed into Black Tent Theatre 68/71 (Kokushoku Tento a.k.a. Kuro Tento and BTT 68/71). No longer using the tent, it remains politically progressive, often collaborating with other Asian theatres.

Like Suzuki, Satoh, and Kara, **Terayama Shûji** preferred alternative spaces and rejected *shingeki*. Not overtly political, his Peanut Gallery (Tenjô Sajiki, 1967) nevertheless attracted disaffected youth and outraged the establishment. Actors included circus entertainers, students, cabaret singers, and porn stars. Gradually, the company began to explore new actor-audience relationships. Plays were performed in total darkness, in multiple locales, in public baths, and on the street. The troupe often performed at European festivals but disbanded after Terayama's death (1983).

After Angura. As the 1960s–1970s political, aesthetic, and social protests waned, so did *angura*'s passionate experimentalism. By the 1980s–1990s, *angura*, like *shingeki* earlier, had become the tradition to rebel against. New companies reflected the times: fast-paced consumerism, science-fiction, and mindless parody in the 1980s; "quiet theatre" (*shizuka na engeki*) and "neo-*kabuki*" in the 1980s–1990s; social and political engagement from the late 1990s, responding perhaps to natural disasters and domestic terrorism. Troupes often embraced communal or group theatre, rejecting *shingeki*'s "company system."

Yume no Yûminsha (Dream Wanderers, 1976), founded by **Noda Hideki**, became *angura*'s antithesis. Huge, playful, pun-filled, pop-art spectacles, weaving frenetic action, music, and fractured mythology, entertained 26,000 people at the National Yoyogi Sports Stadium, and toured to the Edinburgh International Festival. Dissolving the troupe in 1992, Noda went to London to reconsider his approach, returned to Japan in 1993, and founded NODA MAP, interrogating serious issues, including the atomic bomb and the emperor's war responsibility.

The Youth Group (Seinen-dan, 1982), founded by **Hirata Oriza**, originally produced fast-paced spectacles like Noda's; by the late 1980s, Hirata changed course, developing "quiet theater," which attempted to grasp "contemporary colloquial life" and rejected everything theatrical.

The Phosphorescence Troupe (Rinko-gun, 1982), founded by **Sakate Yôji** as an "artists' center" rather than a theatre troupe, emphasizes collective creation, collaborations/exchanges with **Chinese** and German counterparts, and interactions among various arts.

The Shinjuku Go-Getters' Club (Shinjuku Ryôzanpaku, 1987), founded by Kim Sujin (1954–), continues *angura*'s legacy with its purple tent. Its theatrically arresting "new romantic" productions offer visibility and voice to minority ethnic **Koreans** and Chinese. The Flower Theatre (Hanagumi Shibai, 1987), founded by Kanô Yukikazu (1960–), deconstructs classics using parodic "neo-*kabuki*" style. Nylon 100° C (1993) presents Keralino Sandorovich [Kera]'s (1963–) comedic/absurdist plays. The collective dumb type (1984), founded in Kyoto, principally by **Furuhashi Teiji**, offers nonverbal, multimedia, avant-garde performance/installations. Notable women-led troupes include **Kisaragi Koharu**'s NOISE, **Watanabe Eriko**'s 300 (Sanjû-maru), and **Kishida Rio**'s Kishida Company + Optimists' Troupe (Kishida Jimusho + Rakuten-dan).

FURTHER READING

Leiter, Samuel L, ed. *Japanese Theater in the World.*

Carol Fisher Sorgenfrei and Julie A. Iezzi (Shôchiku section)

Theatre Companies: Korea

Theatre companies have been fomenters in the development of **Korean** theatre since the groundbreaking **Experimental Theatre** Company (Shilhŏm Kŭkchang, 1960). During the previous fifty years, the **Japanese** occupation and Korean War (1950–1953) saw the birth and brief life of many "dramatic arts study associations" and companies, one of the most notable being the New Association Theatre Company (Kŭkdan Shinhyŏp, 1951), whose productions literally saved theatre during the Korean War and afterward.

Prior to the early twentieth-century establishment of modern theatre, roving bands of performers were common, and villages everywhere had local groups of *t'alch'um* or **puppet theatre** performers. But such groups generally were identified with village or regional forms (such as *hahoe pyŏlshin-gŭt*), rather than by a company name. As for *p'ansori*, the solo performer and solo drummer team obviated any "company" designation. Companies thus are an aspect of modern Korean theatre.

More than one hundred companies operate in Korea today, mostly in Seoul, but some in Pusan and environs. Many companies remain small and impecunious, mounting few productions; some exist in name only. However, among active and influential companies in 2005 were: A-Com (**musical** theatre), Hakjŏn Theatre Company (Kŭkdan Hakjŏn, international dramas/musicals), the National Drama Company (Kungnip Kŭkdan), **Sohn Jin-Chaek**'s Beauty and Ugliness Theatre Company (Kŭkdan Michoo), **Oh T'ae-sŏk**'s Raw Cotton Repertory Theatre Company (Mokhwa), Kim A-ra's Muchŏn Theatre Company (Kŭkdan Muchŏn), **Lee Yun-t'aek**'s Yŏnhŭidan Theatre Group (Yŏnhŭidan Kŏrip'ae), Sanullim Theatre Company (Kŭkdan Sanullim), and Yŏnu Stage Company (Yŏnu Mudae, giving original works only).

FURTHER READING

Kim, Yun-Cheol, and Miy-Ye Kim, eds. *Contemporary Korean Theatre: Playwrights, Directors, Stage-Designers.*

Richard Nichols

Theatre Companies: Malaysia

Theatre companies can be found in every **Malaysian** state; most of the prominent companies are located in or near Kuala Lumpur. The majority are amateur. Previously, artists organized drama clubs or groups. Two are notably long-standing. The Selangor Philharmonic Society has staged **Western** musicals since its 1958 founding. It provides educational programs and contributes to charitable causes. LIDRA (the Literary and Dramatic Society) has, since 1960, staged plays in English at the University of Malaya.

Elite Theatre. Since the 1980s, many artists have opted to set themselves up as a business. Elite Theatre (Teater Elit) initiated this trend in the late 1970s, led by **Usman Awang**, poet Sutong R. S. (1948–), **experimental** • **playwright** Dinsman (1949–), and others. The name was intended satirically to demonstrate that Malaysians could produce their own commercial theatre rather than rely solely on foreign touring companies frequenting the major hotels. Therefore, Elite Theatre, which operated until the mid-1980s, arranged its dinner theatre, poetry readings, and business office in a hotel.

Theatre Companies in the 1980s. During the 1980s, new companies, some founded by established artists, helped to reinvigorate the Malaysian scene. Centrestage (1985), a private Malay company, operates under the team of Normah Nordin and Najib Nor, both **trained** in design. Centrestage produces Malay translations of international plays as well as its own creative work, poetry readings, and **musical** theatre.

The Five Arts Centre was founded in 1984 by **Krishen Jit**, choreographer Marion D'Cruz, **director** Chin San Sooi, artist Redza Piyadasa, and playwright K. S. Maniam (1942–). The Centre, which also supports nontheatrical arts, promotes English-language plays by Malaysian writers. Some productions are initially presented as workshops so they can elicit feedback before a final version is staged. The Centre is also known for producing novel multiethnic and multilingual productions reflective of Malaysian life. In addition, it collaborates closely with **Singapore** groups. Also under the company's auspices are a Directors' Workshop and a Young Theatre (Teater Muda). The latter, spearheaded by Janet Pillai (1955–), provides a training program.

The Actors' Studio (1989) was founded by Australian Joe Hasham (1948–) and his Malaysian spouse, Faridah Merican (1939–). It has staged North American, Australian, and British plays and adapted Irish ones to the Malaysian milieu. Initially known for English-language performances, both Western and locally written, the company began sponsoring Malay-language works in 2000. It managed two small **theatres** in Kuala Lumpur, along with a bookstore café, academy, and rehearsal space. Later, the Actors' Studio moved to a larger space in the Bangsar Shopping Centre, became a founding partner for the new Kuala Lumpur Performing Arts Centre, and opened an additional venue in Penang.

Instant Café Theatre (1989) was founded by Jo Kukathas, Andrew Leci, Jit Murad, and Zahim Albakri. It specializes in sophisticated **political** satire for urban, corporate audiences. It also stages local dramas as well as works by major international playwrights. Additionally, it has mounted three Shakespeare productions: *A Midsummer Night's Dream* (1992) and *Twelfth Night* (1995), both out of doors, and a localized version of *The Merchant of Venice* (2000).

Theatre Companies from the 1990s Onward. The trend in establishing new companies, often with specific purposes, has continued since the 1990s. Productions generally feature new plays by founding members or created in workshops, reflecting a range of generations. In 1994, Drama Lab was founded by Zahim Albakri, Jit Murad, and Pia Zain to promote Malaysian playwrights. Notable productions include Jit Murad's *Gold Rain and Hailstones* (1993), *Spilt Gravy on Rice* (1993), and *The **Storyteller*** (1996).

Kuali Works (1994) comprises five female members: Ann Lee, Karen Quah, Anita Zafina Mat Fadil, Goh Soon Siew, and Shahimah Idris. The company features plays dealing with interethnic relationships as well as feminist and gender issues. In 1999, the company produced Idris's solo piece, *From Table Mountain to Teluk Intan*, which draws upon the playwright's journeys from South Africa to Australia to Malaysia, as well as the injuries she suffered after being attacked in a Kuala Lumpur shopping center parking lot.

In 1996, the Straits Theatre Company was founded by Huzir Sulaiman (1973–). Its first effort was Sulaiman's *Lazy Hazy Crazy* (1997), which addresses in part the severe haze afflicting areas of Southeast Asia at the time, attributed to forest fires in **Indonesia**. As for other **politically** engaged companies, three have formed since 2000: the Alternative Stage established by Toe Moe, Nam Ron, and Faisal Tehrani; Ashken, under the Five Arts Centre; and Rep 21.

Chinese and Indian Companies. Theatre in Mandarin is facilitated by the Dramatic Arts Society, which works cooperatively with the Mandarin-based Malaysian Institute of Arts. Other **Chinese** organizations, such as the Malaysian Chinese Cultural Society, Chinese Assembly Halls, and the Chinese Opera Society, also promote theatre for the community. The Dan Dan Theatre (1992) stages experimental works in Mandarin.

The Temple of Fine Arts provides training in **India**'s performing arts. Its elaborate **dance**-dramas derive from a variety of source materials, including Indian, Malay, and Chinese stories and legends. It also produced *A Midsummer Night's Dream* (1992), transferred to sixteenth century Rajasthan. The proceeds support a health clinic and other charities. In addition, there are Indian groups that perform in different languages for local communities.

Theatre companies contribute to a stimulating performing arts scene although most operate in and near the capital. Companies often work together and help to mentor new artists. Productions of plays by Malaysian authors, sometimes in workshops, help to encourage and develop local talent; works by foreign authors, including those adapted to the Malaysian milieu, keep audiences in touch with theatre as an international art. While it is still difficult to make one's living doing theatre in Malaysia, there is a high degree of professionalism among those engaged.

FURTHER READING

Lo, Jacqueline. *Staging Nation: English Language Theatre in Malaysia and Singapore.*

Nancy Nanney

Theatre Companies: Nepal

There are approximately twenty companies in **Nepal**, although many perform rarely and few have the resources to travel to theatre **festivals** in Kathmandu. Representing Everyone (Sarwanam), founded in 1980 by Asesh Malla (1950–), is the most important street troupe; most **directors** around the country cut their teeth on Representing Everyone's agitprop **political** style developed during the pro-democracy movement of the 1980s and continued today. Former members of this troupe founded Reflected Images (Pratibimba) in the western city of Pokhara, which benefits from the combined leadership of **playwright** Saru Bhakta and director-**actor** Anup Baral. No longer interested solely in agitprop, the productions of Reflected Images are intellectually charged.

In 1982, **Sunil Pokharel**, who was with Representing Everyone at its formation, founded To Climb (Aarohan), Nepal's foremost theatre company. To Climb began as a street theatre troupe during the pro-democracy movement, but since then has worked with Nepal's disenfranchised, dabbled in film and television, and cultivated relationships with foreign institutions to translate **Western** masterpieces into Nepalese and bring world theatre to Kathmandu. Members of To Climb have trained in and taught the methods of Augusto Boal and toured productions to Denmark, Norway, and Russia. To Climb has nurtured Nepali playwrights, produced theatre festivals, and participated in South Asian festivals, traveling to Bangladesh in 2000. In 2002, it founded Practical Training Collective (Gurukul), Nepal's first theatre **training** school.

The Council of Mithila Dramatic Arts (Mithila Natya Kala Parishad) of Janakpur, southern Nepal, is one of the few companies without roots in Representing Everyone. Plays are performed in Maithili, Nepal's second-most spoken language, and focus on local figures and local concerns, such as corrupt priests and police, dowry, and child marriage.

Carol Davis

Theatre Companies: Pakistan

Many urban companies began forming in **Pakistan** in the 1950s. Producing English plays were Karachi's Clifton Players and Lahore's Alpha Players. In Peshawar, non-professional groups performed in Pashto, Urdu, and English. In Karachi, Khwaja Moe-nuddin founded Drama Guild to stage his own plays, and Ali Ahmed produced his plays with Avant-Garde Theatre (later, Natak). Most such groups ended by the 1980s.

The Arts Council (1948) in Lahore was most vibrant from 1964 to 1976. Taken over by the government in 1974, it planned new **theatres**, which opened during General Zia-ul-Haq's (1924–1988) government (1979–1988). Because state funding was cut, production diminished, and the buildings were leased out.

Many groups opposed to martial law arose in the 1980s. At first, most took an egali-tarian approach based on volunteerism and **political** commitment. In Lahore, Dawn of a New Day (Ajoka, 1984) split into People's Theatre (Lok Rehas, 1986) and Unity (Sanj, 1986–1988). In Karachi, there were Grips (1979), **Women's** Movement (Tehrik-e-Nis-wan, 1981), and the Knock (Dastak, 1983–1988), which later inspired Story (Katha, 1994). Since the fall of the Soviet Union (1989), most such companies continue to thrive as nongovernmental organizations (NGOs), funded mostly by foreign donors, placing emphasis on social developmental issues; countless NGO troupes have appeared, like Interactive Resource Centre (2000) and Human Drama (Insan Natik, 1994).

Rafi Peer Theatre Workshop (1974) works in direct mass communication across mediums, and has an annual international **festival**. New companies have formed funded by multinationals since the 2000s, performing adaptations of **Western** blockbuster films. Karachi's Black Fish (2002) performs comic improvisation solely funded by ticket revenue.

FURTHER READING

Afzal-Khan, Fawzia. *A Critical Stage: The Role of Secular Alternative Theatre in Pakistan.*

Claire Pamment

Theatre Companies: Philippines

The earliest theatre companies in the **Philippines** were formed during the Spanish colo-nial period (1521–1898) with the establishment of groups that specialized in particular theatre forms, such as the *sinakulo*, the *komedya*, and the *sarsuwela*. Starting out as informal organizations based in communities, these groups were usually headed by a **director**, a **playwright**, or someone who was both. Examples of these companies are the Grand Tagalog Zarzuela Company (Gran Compañia de la Sarsuwela Tagala), Gabri-el's Company (Samahang Gabriel), and Ilagan's Company (Samahang Ilagan), which produced *sarsuwela*s during the American colonial period (ca. 1900–1946); the San Dionisio Comedia Company (Komedya ni San Dionisio), recently organized formally and based in San Dionisio; Parañaque; and the Nazarene Company (Samahang Nazareno), which continues to perform *sinakulo* in Cainta, Rizal, during the Lenten season.

With the introduction of English and drama in the curriculum during the American colonial period, theatre groups started out by performing English-language plays and, later, original plays in both Filipino and English. Among them are the Ateneo Players Guild (later Ateneo Dramatic Society [1921–1950s]), founded by Henry Lee Irwin SJ (1892–1976) and later directed by James Reuter SJ (1916–); Arena Theatre (1953–), directed by Severino Montano at Philippine Normal College; Chamber Theatre (1964–1970), led by Nick Agudo (1924–) at Far Eastern University; and Aquiñas Theatre Guild (1952–1969), directed by Antonio Piñon OP and, later, Tomas Hernandez at the University of Santo Tomas.

The University of the Philippines has had the largest number of groups. They include the UP Dramatic Club (1930–1966) and the UP Mobile Theatre (1962–1981), directed by Wilfrido Ma. Guerrero (1917–); Dulaang UP (1976–) and the UP Playwrights' Theatre, founded by Antonio Mabesa; the UP Repertory Company (1968–), directed by **Behn Cervantes**; the UP Peryante (1980–1986), directed by Chris Millado (1961–); and the UP Tropa, founded by Aureus Solito (1969–).

Among professional and semiprofessional companies, most of them nonprofit, are Repertory Philippines (1967–), founded by Zenaida Amador (1933–2005), and known for its professional English-language productions; the Philippine Educational Theatre founded by Cecile Guidote-Alvarez (1943–); Filipino Theatre (Teatro Pilipino, 1976–1992), led by Rolando Tinio and Ella Luansing, which specialized in translations of the classics; Filipino Stage (Tanghalang Pilipino, 1987–), the company of the Cultural Center of the Philippines; Hall of Prize-winning Plays (Bulwagang Gantimpala, 1980–), which produces curriculum-oriented plays; **Actors**' Actors (1992–), led by Bart Guingona (1962–); Garage Theatre (Dulaang Talyer, 1983–), led by Paul Morales (1969–); Monique Wilson's innovative New Voice Company; and Dramatis Personae, headed by Lito Casaje (1957–).

There are also groups spawned by socio-**political** conditions, the need to assert an ethnic identity, or the mission to serve one's community. Among groups known for staging political plays are (Golden Rays) Gintong Silahis, Incense Players (Kamanyang Players) and Blacksmiths of Art (Panday Sining), active during the First Quarter Storm period (late 1960s and early 1970s); Palanyag Theatre (Dulaang Palanyag) of Parañaque; Riverbanks (Dalampasigan) of Pasig; and **Theatre** • **Stage** (Entablado) of Ateneo, during the years of the Marcos dictatorship (1972–1986). Known for their use of indigenous cultural forms to articulate contemporary issues are **Storytellers**' Art (Sining Kambayoka), the Integrated Performing Arts Group, and the Kaliwat Theatre Collective in Mindanao, and the Cordillera Cultural Centre (Dap-ayan ti Kultura iti Kordilyera) in the Cordillera region. In other parts of the country, the Negros Theatre League used to present plays on the plight of farm workers, while Barasoain Kalinangan, in Bulacan, mined history for its plays. Other sector-based groups include Workers' Theatre (Teatro Pabrika), May First Theatre (Teatro Mayo Uno), Gabriela Cultural Group, and Medical Theatre (Teatro Medikal).

Theatre companies in the Philippines have proven that theatre can survive on minimal budgets if driven by the passion to use drama as a tool of education, a weapon of protest, and an art that contributes to social change.

Joi Barrios

Theatre Companies: Singapore

The 1980s saw the birth of a number of companies devoted to creating and staging new **Singaporean** plays. Of these, TheatreWorks, Necessary Stage, and the Malay-language company One Vision (Teater Ekamatra) have made the most significant and lasting contributions. At TheatreWorks, **Ong Keng Sen** spearheaded the company's shift away from staging new Singaporean plays to developing original, pan-Asian intercultural work. The Necessary Stage, founded by **playwright** Haresh Sharma (1965–) and **director** Alvin Tan (1963–), continues to stage plays dealing with the concrete social problems affecting Singaporeans, extending its influence through a broad outreach program. While One Vision (Teater Ekamatra) has undergone numerous incarnations, it remains an important force, bridging cultural boundaries and tackling difficult subjects.

Practice Theatre Ensemble, created by **Kuo Pao Kun** in 1986 as a bilingual company devoted to new works, continues with a modest production program as The Theatre Practice. In addition, Action Theatre under the direction of Ekachai Uekrongtham (1962–), the Toy Factory Ensemble led by Goh Boon Teck (1971–), Dramaplus Arts under Roger Jenkins (1953–), the youth company Act 3 International, and William Teo's (1957–2001) Asia-in-Theatre Research Center, with its Ariane Mnouchkine–inspired intercultural practice, have all made important contributions.

Singapore Repertory Theatre follows the model of American regional **theatres** with relatively mainstream programming of plays popular in England and the United States. Under the leadership of American expatriate founder Tony Petito it was the first to cast **actors** from other Asian countries and to establish an ongoing practice of paying artists a professional wage.

FURTHER READING

Peterson, William. *Theater and the Politics of Culture in Contemporary Singapore.*

William Peterson

Theatre Companies: Taiwan

During the period of **Japanese** colonization (1895–1945), glove **puppets** (*budai xi*) and the Taiwanese *xiqu* form called "song opera" (*gezai xi*) were **Taiwan**'s most prevalent company types, though amateur "spoken drama"–style (*huaju*) troupes also existed. *Huaju* later became known as *wutai ju* locally, though *huaju* is used interchangeably with it. In the 1950s, following the "Speak Mandarin" campaign launched by the **Chinese** Nationalist Party, more *huaju* companies (then synonymous with Mandarin theatre) were created to further that goal. With **censorship** and anti-communist cultural **politics** in place, most companies were either affiliated with government units (such as the entertainment units of the armed forces) for propaganda purposes, or with universities for pedagogical purposes; the latter included the Ministry of Education's Chinese **Experimental Theatre** (Jiaoyu Bu Zhonghua Shiyan Jutuan, 1950; disbanded 1971) and College Drama Society (Dazhuan Jushe).

Independent, professional, commercial *wutai ju* companies that cater to larger audiences were not established until the late 1960s, when a group of diasporic Chinese and Taiwanese **playwrights** and **directors** returned, after studying abroad, to work together to establish new troupes. **Lee Man-kuei**, **Ma Sen**, and others applied their transnational **training** and experiences to their work. The most notable new company of this period was Gengxin Experimental Theatre (Gengxin Shiyan Jutuan, 1976). Wu Ching-chi (1939–) and Huang Mei-hsu (1930–) trained a group of **actors** who became leading figures; they included Chin Shi-chieh (Jin Shijie, 1951–), **Lee Kuo-hsiu**, and **Liu Ching-min**. Funded by the Tien Cultural Foundation (1963), and founded by Rev. Edward Murphy, the company has been training and performing in a well-equipped professional **theatre** in Taipei, the Tien Cultural Theatre (Gengxin Wenjiao Yuan).

There are three shared characteristics of post-1980s theatre companies. First, *wutai ju* companies continue to be shaped by artists with transnational experiences. Second, many companies are interested in a wide spectrum of plays, venues, and forms of representation. In 1988, Godot Theatre (Guotuo Juchang) was founded by Liang Chi-min (1965–) and his wife, Lin Chi-lou. They have staged experimental plays, classical plays, and American and Taiwanese musicals (*gewu ju*). The Green Light Theatre (Lüguang Jutuan, 1993), founded by Lo Pei-an, performed *Taipei Show! Show! Show!* (Taipei Hsiu Hsiu Hsiu, 1998), a *wutai ju*, in a disco pub. Third, many post-1980s companies demonstrate strong ties to their founders and core members, which in turn foster collaborative work.

The charisma of their founders has been crucial to these companies' success because most plays staged were written in-house. Many plays were created collaboratively, initiated by the founder-playwrights. The Performance Workshop (Biaoyan Gongzuo Fang, 1985), founded by Lai Sheng-chuan, his wife, Ding Nai-chu, and Lee Li-chun and Lee Kuo-hsiu, is a prominent example. Almost all of its works were created collaboratively by the actors and Lai (as playwright-director).

Repertory companies tend to concentrate in the larger cultural hubs and metropolises, such as Taipei, while there are many small groups outside Taipei, such as community theatres. Smaller companies tend to stage experimental works in alternative venues and in local dialects, like Taiwanese or Hakka. Especially since 1980, Taiwan's companies have evolved along a self-sustaining route of commercialization and internationalization.

Alexander C. Y. Huang

Theatre Companies: Thailand

Most modern **Thai** theatre professionals juggle jobs to make ends meet. Many companies remain active only briefly. It is common for artists to be concurrently affiliated with two or more groups. They may perform in one group's **political** satire while directing a **musical** for another.

Larger, well-established companies with a year-round performance schedule are Patravadi **Theatre** and Dream Box. The former **trains** an ensemble and stages *lakon khanob niyom mhai* (literally, "theatre of a new tradition"), and the latter hires television **actors** to perform in dramas and comedies.

Smaller yet equally prominent troupes are Maya and Grassroots Micromedia Project (Klum Lakon Makhampom), both of which work with underprivileged communities on social issues. Along with the politically oriented Crescent Moon Theatre (Prachan Siew

Karn Lakon), they were born out of the 1970s political crisis. Groups such as New Heritage (Moradok Mhai), Flower of Entertainment (Dokmai Karn Bunterng), Theatre 8×8, B-Floor Theatre, Dream Masks, Krajidrid, Sao Soong, and Life Work Company have been continually productive since the 1990s.

In 2002, these smaller groups formed the Bangkok Theatre Network and have since organized the Bangkok Theatre **Festival** under the artistic directorship of Grassroots Micromedia Project's Pradit Prasartthong (1960–). This festival, Thailand's largest showcase of contemporary theatre, held on November weekends, presents professional troupes and university drama clubs performing fringe-style in a park, bookstores, restaurants, bars, and cafes along the historic Phra Arthit Road. More than 50,000 local and foreign spectators annually attend. Nonetheless, most companies still have a problem filling the seats in their regular programs outside the festival.

Pawit Mahasarinand

Theatre Companies: Vietnam

The earliest permanent "spoken drama" (***kich noi***) companies were established in the 1930s: the Quintessence Troupe (Ban Kich Tinh Hoa, 1935) and The Lu's (1907–1989) Company (Doan Kich The Lu, 1937; renamed Anh Vu Drama Company [Doan kich Anh Vu] in the 1940s, when it began presenting anti-colonialist social-realist plays).

Influenced by Soviet practices, Ho Chi Minh's (1890–1969) government funded "nationalistic" companies beginning in the l950s to resist foreign occupation. After "reunification" (1975), the Ministry of Culture and Information assumed control of all companies. Among today's rare privatized *kich noi* groups are the Hanoi Drama Theatre (Nha hat Kich Ha Noi) and Hanoi's Youth Theatre (Nha hat Tuoi Tre); others include Saigon's most popular **experimental** companies: Small **Stage** Theatre (Nha hat Kich San Khau Nho, 1997) and Thai Duong Theatre Arts (San khau-Nghe thuat Thai Duong, 2000), an outgrowth of the French Cultural Exchange Institute, where **actors** experiment with French and Vietnamese influences.

Vietnam's twenty traditional *cheo* troupes include the Cheo Troupe of Thai Binh Province (Nha hat Cheo Thai Binh), where *cheo* was born. The municipally sponsored Hanoi Cheo Theatre (Nha hat Cheo Ha Noi) presents three weekly shows for locals and tourists, while Hanoi's nationally funded Vietnam Cheo Theatre (Nha hat Cheo Viet Nam, 1951) travels extensively within Vietnam and abroad.

Similarly, Hanoi's nationally funded Vietnam **Tuong** Troupe (Nha hat Tuong Viet Nam, 1951) tours frequently and **trains** young artists. In its Hong Ha **Theatre**, the company's performances include experiments like adaptations of *Othello* (2000), using *tuong* conventions and aesthetics. Other notable companies, like the Dao Tan Theatre (Nha hat Tuong Dao Tan), perform in Quang Nam, Quang Ngai, Phu Yen, and Bình Dinh Provinces—the cradle of *tuong*. In the south, where *tuong* is known as *hat boi*, it is performed by Ho Chi Minh City's Hat Boi Theatre (Doan Nghe thuat Hat Boi Thanh pho Ho Chi Minh, 1977). In Vietnam's central region, the Hue Royal Palace Arts Troupe (Doan Nghe thuat Cung Dinh Hue, 1985) performs *tuong* adaptations for tourists in the newly restored Royal Theatre (Duyet Thi Duong).

Lorelle Browning and Kathy Foley

THEATRES

Theatres: Bangladesh

Dhaka's two renowned troupes, Citizen (Nagarik) and Wilderness (Aryanak), use the British Council auditorium and the Engineer's Institute as venues. Subsequently the Mahila Samiti was transformed into an independent **experimental** space. The Guide House adjacent to the Mahila Samiti emerged as a second viable auditorium for theatre performances. Despite their limitations in terms of both space and facilities these theatres are sites for Dhaka's "group" **theatre companies**.

One of the dreams of postliberation Bangladeshi theatre people has been a state-of-the-art national theatre. Debates have centered on whether it should be a proscenium theatre or a flexible space to accommodate an alternative aesthetic.

The suburban centers also have a few theatres around which production activities have grown. In Chittagong, the Shilpa-Sahitya Parishad Mancha has been transformed into the Shilpakala Academy. The other area theatre is the Muslim Hall. In Barishal, the older theatre sites were the Town Hall, Dipali (Cinema) Theatre, and Jagdish Theatre. The Barishal Natyangan also has become popular over the years. In 1988, its management inaugurated a studio theatre. Rajshahi and Rangpur are other suburban locales with a few theatres.

Bishnupriya Dutt

Theatres: Cambodia

Cambodia's one-thousand-seat Bassac Theatre, constructed in the 1960s as the country's premiere public performing arts venue, was horribly damaged by fire in 1994. Home to the Ministry of Culture and Fine Arts' Department of Performing Arts (and all its troupes) since 1980, its destruction has left Phnom Penh–based artists without a reasonably-sized **stage** on which to rehearse, as well as leaving the capital without a professionally equipped proscenium house. Public performances take place at the Royal University of Fine Arts Theatre (rebuilt in 2006 as the university moved to a new campus), and the Chaktomuk Theatre (designed in the 1960s as a government conference hall and now in private hands). The French Cultural Center has monthly shows of Cambodian forms in an auditorium seating 130. The Royal Palace's Phocheny Pavilion, open on three sides, with a small raised stage, produces *robam kbach boran* for state guests on special occasions. The private Sovanna Phum Khmer Arts Association has a resident troupe of **dancers**, **musicians**, and **puppeteers** who open their intimate theatre in Phnom Penh to the public twice weekly for shows.

Most privately run small theatres formerly used by *lakhon bassac* companies no longer exist, though intermittent shows take place in outdoor theatres in different parts of the capital, one venue being run by the Phnom Penh municipality, as well as on privately owned lots. Theatres in provincial capitals once run by Ministry of Culture regional offices have, for the most part, been sold to private entities, and have, with few exceptions, stopped producing.

Toni Shapiro-Phim

Theatres: China

Early Examples. Although performance venues are very ancient in **China**, dating from at least the second century BC, the first large structures, including seating and **stage** in an enclosed building, date from the early twelfth century. In the highly commercialized capital of the Northern Song dynasty (960–1279), Kaifeng, there were large amusement centers, termed *wa* (literally, "tiles"), where various classes went to enjoy themselves. A large center could contain fifty or more theatres, called *goulan* (literally, "balustrades"); the biggest seated several thousand.

These flourished into the fourteenth century and were the major venues for ***zaju*** during their heyday, not only in national and provincial capitals but also in other towns. Shows were advertised through playbills hung up outside the theatre, or by men hired to shout the production's merits. Spectators paid to enter, but also threw money to favored **actors**. Theatres were probably flimsy, and a 1366 record notes an incident in Songjiang, Jiangsu Province, when one collapsed. However, they were intended to be permanent, not dismantled when no longer in use.

Ming through Nineteenth Century. During the Ming dynasty (1368–1644), there were few permanent theatres, performances for mass audiences being mainly outdoors in marketplaces, or on a temple or guild hall stages, or in temporary theatres. The imperial court had its own theatres, while wealthy private houses often used a red carpet in a banquet hall with the guests sitting beside or around the performers.

The seventeenth to nineteenth centuries saw the next great age of theatres, especially but not only in Beijing, largely because of the rise of ***jingju***. The Qing dynasty (1644–1911) issued many edicts in trying to control this, seeking especially to prevent or restrict attendance by groups such as officials, the military, and **women**.

Theatre types included "play establishments" (*xizhuang*) and "play gardens" (*xiyuan*) or "teahouse-theatres" (*chayuan*). At their height in the nineteenth century, there were about ten *xizhuang* and nearly forty *chayuan*, all in the Outer City. *Xizhuang* were small theatres for private parties featuring refined performances like **kunqu**. *Chayuan* were large and for mass audiences. Upstairs was the "tables" (*zhuozi*) section, where people chatted, drank tea, and ate refreshments around a table, while the masses sat or stood downstairs. From the late eighteenth century women could attend only exclusive family parties; thus they hardly ever went to *xizhuang* and never to *chayuan*. By the late 1800s, prostitutes and courtesans could enter Shanghai's theatre. The main center for these theatres was Beijing, but they existed also in Shanghai and Tianjin, at least from the mid-nineteenth century. In 1900, fire destroyed most of Beijing's Outer City theatres.

Twentieth Century. The twentieth century's first half saw major reforms. In 1908, Xia Yueheng and his brothers set up Shanghai's New Stage (Xin Wutai), which aimed to modernize the theatre's structure. The audience sat before the stage, not on three sides, and there was no class differentiation, although prices differed according to distance from the stage. Very importantly, the audience was supposed to concentrate on and remain silent during the performance. Women attended, although in Beijing they were segregated until about 1920. The Republican period (1912–1949) saw many such theatres constructed, with some old-style ones remaining.

Nowadays, it is only exceptional **theatre companies** that have their own theatres, rental houses being shared by modern "spoken drama" (*huaju*; see Playwrights and

Playwriting), regional *xiqu*, and others. The early years of the People's Republic of China (PRC) saw theatres built all over China; the number rose from 891 in 1949 to more than 2,800 in 1959. They were modern in style, but sometimes attempted a Chinese-style exterior. For example, Beijing's People's Theatre (Renmin Juchang) has a Chinese-looking roof with rising eaves. Ticket prices were extremely cheap. Titles and main performers were announced outside the theatre and in the press. The Cultural Revolution (1966–1976) put a stop to further construction.

By the early 1980s, there were about 1,700 theatres, rising to about two thousand in the early 1990s. The official figure for theatres and music halls in 2002 was 1,794. For traditional drama a notable 1990s development was the construction of several theatres specially designed as modernized versions of the old *chayuan*. Some old-style theatres have reopened. Beijing's seventeenth-century Zhengyi Temple, converted to a theatre that many *jingju* stars acted in, reopened in 1995 after decades of disuse. Such venues are designed mainly for tourists, with very high entry prices. Other traditional revivals include when a traditional troupe performs away from home and builds a temporary theatre in a large tent.

The Capital Theatre (Shoudu Juchang, 1955) is home to the prestigious Beijing People's Art Theatre (Beijing Renmin Yishu Juyuan: BPAT) and is the birthplace of many *huaju* classics. The 1,200-seat theatre was constructed refurbished with a proscenium stage (1995). Its exterior combines European and Russian influences with elements reminiscent of classical Chinese architecture. In 1995, the 252–seat BPAT Small Theatre was built. In 2004, the BPAT Experimental Theatre, an even smaller black box, was opened. The new additions reflect an increasing interest in more **experimental theatre** approaches.

The Shanghai Grand Theatre (Shanghai da Juyuan) opened in 1998 for 1999's fiftieth year celebration of the PRC's founding. The architecture and interior decoration, designed by Jean-Marie Charpentier and Associates, are modern and luxurious. Its three theatres seat, respectively, 1,800, 600, and 250. Beijing's National Grand Theatre of China (Zhongguo Guojia da Juyuan, 2005) was designed by French architect Paul Andreu and is situated next to Tiananmen Square.

FURTHER READING

Mackerras, Colin. *Chinese Drama, A Historical Survey*.

Colin Mackerras and Nan Zhang

Theatres: India

Popular **folk theatre** performances in **India** take place largely in the streets and on open ground, whereas classical performances take place in well-defined structures either attached to the temples or independently built. Most forms, like *terukkuttu*, *nautanki*, and *ramlila*, continue to be presented in conventional, open-air environments, making use of nearby structures within and around the village, including buildings and streets shared by performers and audiences.

Sanskrit Theatres. The playhouse as an interior space designated exclusively for performance is described in the ancient *Treatise on Drama* (Natyashastra; see Theory).

The *kuttampalam* inside the vast, walled compound of the Lord Vadakkunnathan (Siva) temple in Trissur, central Kerala. The main shrine housing Vadakkunnathan is to the right. (Photo: Phillip Zarrilli)

It describes nine different kinds of theatres based on measurement and shape, with specifically demarcated areas for different purposes related to performance. The oldest existing structures that follow the *Natyashastra*'s specifications are the *kuttampalam* (see Stages) in Kerala, where **kutiyattam**, the regional derivation of **Sanskrit theatre**, has been performed for several centuries. A *kuttampalam*'s space is basically divided into two, stage and auditorium, with the stage itself subdivided into two parts: performance space and greenroom.

There is no clear evidence about the ancient Sanskrit playhouse except the existing *kuttampalam*, some directions in the *Natyashastra* and its commentaries, hints in the extant plays, ancient ruins, and other such sources. Three theatre shapes are described: rectangular, square, and triangular, each being available in small, medium, and large sizes, with the rectangular, medium-sized (sixty-four by thirty-two cubits) considered ideal. It consisted of equally sized halves, one for the "stage pavilion" (*ranga mandapa*) and one for the "auditorium" (*prekshaka-nivesana*). The auditorium was tiered, and the different castes were delegated to their own sections.

Two ancient ruined structures have been excavated, one at the Sitabenga cave and the other at Nagarjunakonda. The Sitabenga cave is located in the Ramgarh hills near Ambikapur, Surguja District, Chhattisgarh State, while Nagarjunakonda is at Nalgonda District, Andhra Pradesh. The former, believed by some to date from the third century BC (making it India's oldest theatre structure), presents a small hall with tiered seats in a semicircular shape used to view a performance on a stage created on a hill outside. The material performed is disputed, and might have been for a picture story told with a scroll or even for boxing matches. The Nagarjunakonda structure, from the second or third century AD, presents a rectangular, open-air amphitheatre with tiered seating at its four sides and with exit and entry channels for **actors** and audience. Performances were held on the same floor level as the lowest seats.

Theatre spaces are seen in many temples' "dance pavilions" (*nritya mandapa*), earmarked for temple-related performances. They are rectangular (Brihadeswara Temple, Tanjavur, Tamilnadu), octagonal (certain temples in Gujarat), or square (Belur Temple, Hassan, Karnataka). Extant pre-modern spaces include amphitheatres constructed by King Mansingh Tomar (1486–1516) at Barai in Gwalior in Madhya Pradesh; the "music hall" (*sangeet mahal*) in Tanjavur Palace, believed to have been built by Accutappa Nayak (1560–1600); Madurai Palace theatre in Tamilnadu; and Padmanabhapuram Palace theatre in Nagerkoil, presently in Tamilnadu and earlier in Kerala.

Proscenium Theatres. Proscenium theatres came to India as early as 1753, when British colonizers built the Playhouse in Calcutta (Kolkata). In 1776, the Bombay Theatre was erected, supposedly based on London's Drury Lane. Later, many proscenium theatres went up, among them private playhouses such as those at Wajid Ali Shah's (1822–1877) Lucknow court, the mansions of Calcutta's *zamindar* officials, the estate of **Rabindranath Tagore**'s family, and so on. Major nineteenth-century public examples include Bombay's (Mumbai) Grant Road Theatre, Chennai's (Madras) Museum Theatre, and Calcutta's National Theatre, Great National Theatre, Star Theatre, and Minerva Theatre. The **Parsi theatre** was a major inspiration for the building of such venues, many of which later were converted into movie houses.

The twentieth century saw proscenium theatres erected in many cities. With the popularity of movies even villages could boast of permanent or temporary structures capable of being used for performances by removing the screen to make a proscenium opening. When temple **festivals** are given, many villages and towns erect a temporary proscenium stage in an open temple space, providing a roof and sides, as well as a greenroom. Professional companies arrive with sets using portable **curtains**, wings, and lights. Spectators sit on the ground in the open.

Other Theatres. Some *jatra* companies in Orissa, Bengal, and Bihar, as well as the Surabhi Theatres of Andhra Pradesh, the Bhramyaman Mancha companies of Assam, and the Ninasam Tirugata troupe of Karnataka, visit villages with mobile theatres on trucks, some of which can accommodate hundreds of spectators in temporary auditoria.

In 1961, during the celebration of Tagore's birth centenary, the national government provided grants to construct theatres in his name in major cities. This produced the Rabindrabharathi, the Tagore Theatre, the Rabindra Kalakshetra, the Rabindra Sadan, and so on. The emergence in each state of regional drama academies hastened the establishment of additional theatres. Both governmental and nongovernmental institutions involved with the performing arts constructed theatres. Important examples include New Delhi's Sri Ram Centre, Kamani Auditorium, and National School of Drama; Kolkata's Academy of Fine Arts Auditorium; Mumbai's Prithvi Theatre and National Centre for Performing Arts; and Chennai's **Music** Academy Theatre, Narada Gana Sabha Theatre, Krishna Gana Sabha Theatre, and Rani Seetha Hall.

A number of modern theatres have incorporated elements of traditional architecture. Prominent among them are those available in Kalakshtra and Sittarangam on island grounds at Chennai, the Mukta Angan in Kolkata, and the *kuttampalam*-style auditorium at the Kalamandalam, Cheruthuruthy, Kerala.

FURTHER READING

Panchal, Goverdhan. *Kuttampalam and Kutiyattam*; Panchal, Goverdhan. *The Theatres of Bharata and Some Aspects of Sanskrit Play-Production.*

B. Ananthakrishnan

Theatres: Japan

Nô *and* Kyôgen. Although the **stage** structures used in **Japan**'s *nô* and *kyôgen* were already highly developed by the Edo period (1603–1868), the concept of a theatre as a dedicated indoor space had not yet fully evolved. The *nô-kyôgen* theatre remained an outdoor venue, set up on the grounds of temples and shrines. The oldest extant example is at Kyoto's Nishi Hongan-ji Temple, moved there from another location in the late sixteenth century. During the Edo period, such stages also proliferated on the estates of powerful *daimyô*, with that built at Edo Castle, home of the Tokugawa shoguns, being considered an exemplar of the style.

The first indoor *nô-kyôgen* theatre (*nôgakudô*) was built in 1881, during the Meiji period (1868–1912), in Tokyo's Shiba Park. It established the form according to which all such theatres were later to be built, that is, the construction in a large, roofed, indoor space of precisely the kind of wooden stage and accoutrements that one would find out of doors, including the ornate, gabled roof over the **acting** platform supported by four thick pillars. The details of such configurations differ slightly from one *nôgakudô* to another, depending on the amount of space available, among other factors, but most do not have seating behind the chorus verandah (*jiutai-za*) at stage left. These theatres seat between five hundred to eight hundred, sometimes with balconies, and often include lobby space as well as shops and restaurants. They continue to be built throughout Japan, which has more than seventy of them.

The audience sits on two sides of the thrusting stage platform, part facing the area between the downstage stage left and right pillars, the other part facing the area between the downstage and upstage right pillars. To its left is the "bridgeway" (*hashigakari*) leading from the offstage "mirror room" (*kagami no ma*) to the stage proper. A wedge-shaped seating area is placed between the two main groups of spectators.

Nô and *kyôgen* may also be performed in nontraditional venues, including proscenium theatres, halls, and elsewhere. Platforming is set up in the available space, and the pillars are often suggested by small, symbolic ones set in the appropriate places. The 591–seat National Nô and Kyôgen Theatre (Kokuritsu Nôgakudô, 1983), in Tokyo's Shibuya Ward, is now the flagship theatre for these genres.

Kabuki *Theatres.* The idea of permanent, indoor theatres arose with *kabuki*, although it took over two centuries of evolution for such theatres to take shape. At first, *kabuki* performances were held, like *nô-kyôgen*, out of doors, and stages were directly based on those of the earlier genres. Performances were held in dry riverbeds (the first being in the bed of Kyoto's Kamo River, where **Izumo no Okuni** performed); a host of other entertainments—including **puppet** performances (see *Bunraku*; *Ko-jôruri*)—were being given nearby as well, so each venue separated itself from the others by erecting bamboo palisades. Audiences sat on the ground, which is how *kabuki* gained its alternative name, *shibai* (literally, "on the grass"). The spaces grew larger and more sophisticated during the seventeenth century, but it was not until the mid-1720s that theatres were authorized to build roofs, which, it was hoped, would help contain fires, a common occurrence. The frequent loss of theatres through fire was one reason for the ongoing progress made in developing theatre architecture.

From 1624, beginning with the Saruwaka Theatre (Saruwaka-za, later the Nakamura Theatre [Nakamura-za]), theatres had to be officially licensed, the sign of their approval being the large "drum tower" (*yagura*, literally, "arrow storehouse") above the entranceway. Such theatres came to be known as "grand theatres" (*ôshibai*) to differentiate them from the smaller, unlicensed theatres that sprang up to provide performances on a temporary basis. These were "shrine-ground theatres" (*miyaji shibai*), operating at shrines and temples, and the "small theatres" (*koshibai*) likely to arise at busy entertainment centers.

Edo (Tokyo) was famous for four *ôshibai* until 1714, when the Yamamura Theatre (Yamamura-za) was closed down in the wake of a scandalous event involving an unauthorized visit of the court lady Ejima to see her presumed lover, actor Ikushima Shingorô (1641–1743), perform. The remaining theatres—the Nakamura Theatre, Ichimura Theatre (Ichimura-za, 1634), and Morita Theatre (Morita-za, 1660), each named for the actor-manager (*zamoto*) dynasty that managed it—came to be known as "Edo's three theatres" (*edo sanza*). The number of theatres permitted was fixed by law, and it was not until the Meiji era that additional theatres were licensed.

Osaka's chief types were *ôshibai* and "middle-size theatres" (*chû shibai*). The major *ôshibai* were the Corner Theatre (Kado no Shibai; a.k.a. Kado-za, 1652), Middle Theatre (Naka no Shibai; a.k.a. Naka-za, 1652), and Great Western Theatre (Ônishi Shibai; a.k.a. Osaka Theatre [Naniwa-za], Chikugo Theatre [Chikugo Shibai], and Western Theatre [Nishi Shibai]). The Middle Theatre lasted until 2000, when it was replaced by the nearby Shôchiku Theatre (Shôchiku-za), named for the entertainment conglomerate. Corner, Middle, and Western noted their locations on the Dôtonbori entertainment strip.

Kyoto's most famous theatre was the still extant (but often rebuilt) Southern Theatre (Minami-za), although it, like other Kyoto theatres, was usually known by the name of whatever actor-manager happened to be running it at the time; although the word "southern" had been part of its name at various times, it received the name Southern Theatre only in 1909.

Nonlicensed theatres were not permitted to use certain *ôshibai* features, most particularly the traveler **curtain** (*hiki maku* or *jôshiki maku*), which meant they were restricted to drop curtains (*donchô*); second-class status was signified by the nickname "drop-curtain theatres" (*donchô shibai*). The restrictions were lifted during Meiji.

In Edo, a system of "alternative management" (*hikae yagura*) arose when one of the *ôshibai* went broke and had to shut down. Another management would move in and change the theatre's name to its own; thus theatres like the Kawarasaki Theatre (Kawarasaki-za), Capital City Theatre (Miyako-za), and Kiri Theatre (Kiri-za), among others, became famous venues. As a result, despite their long histories, dating to the end of the nineteenth century, and, in the case of the Ichimura Theatre, until 1932, none of the *edo sanza* had an unbroken performance record.

The *ôshibai* grew gradually larger, holding up to 1,500 by the end of the Edo era. The main audience area was the earth-floored "pit" (*doma*); more expensive seating was in the raised, railed-in "galleries" (*sajiki*) at the sides, which were on two levels, running straight alongside the outer walls of the rectangular space. This space, originally open, was eventually divided into discrete, boxed-in seating areas (*masu*) for groups of half a dozen or so (an eventual size decrease allowed only four), seated on the ground, and separated from each other at first by ropes and then by narrow, wooden beams. At the *doma*'s rear, facing the stage, were additional galleries, the "great beyond" (*ômukô*), generally occupied by aficionados. The *sajiki* were considered the best seats, not only because of their view of both the stage and auditorium runway (*hanamichi*), but because they adjoined the "theatre teahouses" (*shibai jaya*) built on either side of the theatre, which provided spectators with restaurants, toilets, changing rooms, and even ticketing services.

Other special audience areas included the cheap seats upstage right, on two levels, facing the audience proper (and the actors' backs). The upper level was *yoshino*, named for Mount Yoshino, because it faced the decorative cherry blossom border over the stage (reminiscent of Mount Yoshino's famed blossoms); the lower level was the "500 avatars platform" (*rakandai*), from the crowd's resemblance to Buddha's avatars (*rakan*).

With the construction of roofed-in theatres, the "backstage" (*gakuya*) architecture became more complex. A three-story arrangement was devised but, to circumvent fire-prevention regulations against the construction of three-story buildings, the "second floor" (where the "female impersonators" [*onnagata*] dressed) was dubbed the "mid-second floor" (*chû nikai*), although the third floor, where the "male-role actors" (*tachiyaku*) had their dressing rooms, was the "third floor" (*sankai*). A precise hierar-chy governing the distribution of dressing rooms developed, and space was also made available for **property** and **costume** storage and construction. As a result, *kabuki* had the most complex architectural configurations in Asian theatre.

The level of commercial organization could be gauged by a glance at the theatres' façade, which provided a platform on which "barkers" (*kido geisha*) could lure passer-sby into the theatre by imitating the stars inside; gorgeously arrayed gifts from big business firms, announcing their brand names; and a highly developed system of "billboards" (*kanban*) announcing cast lists, actors' names and specialties, titles of both full-length plays and their individual acts, and even paintings of scenes from the play.

Pre-Meiji theatres were restricted to specific parts of their cities, the so-called "theatre districts" (*shibai machi*). Osaka's theatres, as today, were mostly located in the Dôtonbori district. Kyoto's were (and are) mainly in the Gion district, while Edo's theatres were in Sakai-chô, Fukuya-chô, and Kobiki-chô, not far from today's Ginza. However, in the early 1840s, the *edo sanza* fell victim to the sumptuary restrictions of the Tenpô Reforms, which forced them (and the city's puppet theatres, the Satsuma Theatre [Satsuma-za] and Yuki Theatre [Yuki-za]) to move Saruwaka-chô in the city's then distant outskirts in Asakusa, near the Yoshiwara brothel quarters. Traveling there—largely by boat on the Sumida River—made theatregoing an arduous experi-ence. The theatres began to return to the central city in 1872, when **Morita Kanya** XII moved his Morita Theatre (later, the Shintomi Theatre [Shintomi-za]) to Shintomi-chô. During the Meiji period and the twentieth century, a number of other important *kabuki* playhouses opened, both in the major cities and elsewhere, among them the Kabuki Theatre (Kabuki-za, 1889; see below) and National Theatre of Japan (Kokuri-tsu Gekijô, 1966).

Alongside the big city theatres, venues were available throughout the countryside, as many towns and villages enjoyed performing amateur *kabuki*. Some provincial theatres also were intended for professional touring companies. Many old-time amateur venues,

Façade of Tokyo's Kabuki Theatre (Kabuki-za), Japan's most famous playhouse. (Photo: Samuel L. Leiter)

each with its idiosyncrasies, can be found, but there are only a handful of old theatres fully consonant with the needs of professionals, among them the Yachiyo Theatre (Yachiyo-za), in Yamaga City, Kyûshû, built in 1911. The oldest specimen is the Kanamaru Theatre (Kanamaru-za), built in 1836 in Kotohira, Shikoku, and renovated in the 1980s to resemble its original form. Visitors can experience here the features familiar to urban, nineteenth-century audiences.

Bunraku *Theatres*. The puppet theatre (*ningyô jôruri,* a.k.a. *bunraku*) followed an architectural trajectory not unlike that of *kabuki*, although on a smaller scale. In the late eighteenth century, it flourished in a number of Edo venues before being forced to move to Saruwaka-chô in the 1840s. However, puppet theatre's real base was Osaka, and its two chief theatres were the Takemoto Theatre (Takemoto-za, 1686) and Toyotake Theatre (Toyotake-za, 1703). These produced most of the classic plays that later became *kabuki* stalwarts. The Takemoto, which closed in 1767, was founded by chanter (*tayû*) **Takemoto Gidayû**, while its rival was founded by **Toyotake Wakatayû**; it closed in 1765. After their mutual demise, both the Toyotake and Takemoto made brief reappearances (including as *kabuki* theatres) in the following years.

The subsequent history of Osaka's puppet playhouses through the third quarter of the nineteenth century was associated with structures built on shrine grounds. The chief venue was the Inari Theatre (Inari no Shibai) at the Inari (or Nanba) Shrine in Osaka's Bakurô-machi, founded in 1811 by Uemura Bunrakuken II (a.k.a. Jôrakuô), son-in-law of Uemura Bunrakuken (1737–1810), who helped revive *bunraku* and who gave his name to the form. This theatre, which went under several names, while remaining under the management of Bunrakuken's descendents, sometimes was forced to move to other locales, including Dôtonbori, until 1856, when the manager, Bunrakuô, together with three leading performers, revived the Inari Theatre as the Bunraku

Theatre (Bunraku Shibai). It moved to the new Matsushima district in 1872 under a special rent-free agreement with the government, and was christened with another name also meaning Bunraku Theatre (Bunraku-za), under which it lasted until 1962.

Its principal competiton was the Hikoroku Theatre (Hikoroku-za, 1884), which opened at the Inari Shrine but was dissolved in 1893 (although returning under several names until merging with the Bunraku Theatre in 1914). Fighting back, the Bunraku Theatre, unhappy in Matsushima, moved to the Goryô Shrine in the Funaba district as the Goryô Bunraku Theatre (Goryô no Bunraku–za), remaining there until it burned (1926), with a disastrous loss of manuscripts and puppets. Meanwhile, its management had been taken over in 1909 by the rising Shôchiku Company (see Theatre Companies). Following the fire, the company played in several other locations. The Dôtonbori theatre it occupied in 1945 was bombed by American planes. It played in temporary arrangements until 1956, when the new, one-thousand-seat Bunraku Theatre opened. In 1963, it became the Asahi Theatre (Asahi-za). In 1984, the impressive National Bunraku Theatre (Kokuritsu Bunraku Gekijô), close by Dôtonbori, was built.

Holly A. Blumner and Samuel L. Leiter

Modern Theatres. Japan's principal traditional genres have retained the essential features of their respective performance spaces. Knowledge of **Western** practice in the late nineteenth century, however, wrought changes in *kabuki* theatres. When the Shintomi Theatre was rebuilt (1878), it featured three variations from tradition. The standard thrust stage was foreshortened, toilets were installed inside the theatre (instead of in adjoining teahouses), and some Western-style seating was provided, mainly for foreigners. This theatre's advances culminated in the magnificent Kabuki Theatre.

Kabuki Theatre. The Kabuki Theatre, located in Higashi Ginza, Tokyo, built in 1889 and managed from 1913 by Shôchiku, its owner since 1931, is *kabuki*'s primary venue. Burned down in 1922, it reopened in 1925. It was bombed in 1945 and rebuilt in 1951. It was initially constructed with a Western-style exterior, but in 1911 this was changed to Japanese palace style. The original Japanese-style interior had traditional seating arrangements. The 1925 version, with its late-sixteenth-century-style exterior, had Western-style seats except for the side galleries (and, for a time, the third floor); its seating capacity was between 1,100 and 1,200. The 1951 Kabuki Theatre seated 2,600 (reduced in the 1980s by about four hundred), all Western-style except for the traditional *tatami*-mat seating in the side galleries.

The original manager was **playwright** Fukuchi Ôchi (1841–1906), an advocate of the Meiji-period reform movement, among whose longest-lasting results were the construction of Western-influenced theatres. This led to an increase in stage size (approximately twice as big as earlier examples), the introduction of the proscenium (1911), a larger seating area, a greater separation between acting and audience spaces represented by the elimination of the thrust, the removal of onstage seating, and the widening of the "flower path" (*hanamichi)* runway. The result was a loss of intimacy in the audience-actor relationship.

Osaka also has had theatres of the same name, the present one being the 1,871-seat New Kabuki Theatre (Shin Kabuki-za, 1958), where *kabuki* is now staged infrequently.

Early Twentieth-Century Theatres. **Kawakami Otojirô** took a further step toward Western methods with his Kawakami Theatre (Kawakami-za, 1896), featuring a full proscenium arch, but the Yûraku Theatre (Yûraku-za, 1908), dispensing with the *hanamichi* and utilizing seats throughout, was the first to introduce Tokyo to a completely Western-style auditorium. The much larger—and still existing, if much renovated—Imperial Theatre (Teikoku Gekijô, 1911), Japan's first completely Western-style theatre, brought grand opera (among other large-scale entertainments, including *kabuki*) to Japan's new moneyed bourgeoisie.

Little Theatres, Big Theatres. Japan's first European-style "little theatre," the Tsukiji Little Theatre (Tsukiji **Shôgekijô**, 1924), greeted audiences with a Gothic-Romanesque exterior, a plain grey interior with bench seats giving uniform sight lines, and a stage backed by a German-originated *kuppelhorizont* (a solid, arched backdrop) that allowed use of the latest lighting. The Tsukiji was the only purpose-built ***shingeki*** theatre until it burned at the end of World War II. By contrast, commercial theatre building continued in the 1930s, including the Tokyo Theatre (Tôkyô Gekijô, a.k.a. Tôgeki, 1930) for *kabuki*, the Japan Theatre (Nihon Gekijô, popularly abbreviated to Nichigeki, 1934, known in the postwar period as the home of revue), and the massive International Theatre (Kokusai Gekijô, 1937) for extravaganzas, with its over 180-feet stage opening and seating for five thousand. Also built for huge-cast spectacles were the **Takarazuka** Grand Theatre in Takarazuka (1924) and its later (1934) Tokyo counterpart.

Postwar Theatres. Few theatres remained usable right after the war. *Kabuki* made do at the Tokyo Theatre, but *shingeki* had no home. In 1946, the Mitsukoshi Department Store made its in-store hall available for *kabuki*. The Kabuki Theatre was reopened in 1951, and commercial theatre had adequate performing spaces in the early 1950s, but *shingeki* had no purpose-built space until Tokyo's Actor's Theatre (Haiyûza, 1954) was built in Roppongi. It soon became a focal point for postwar *shingeki*. (During the economic boom years of the 1970s and early 1980s several theatres, including this one, were rebuilt inside office blocks.) In 1964, the Nissei Theatre (Nissei Gekijô) set a new trend with its ultramodern auditorium and stage designed both for commercial and *shingeki* productions.

National Theatres. During the early 1960s, most commercial theatre was concentrated in downtown Tokyo, with offshoots in Asakusa, the entertainment district. With the National Theatre (Kokuritsu Gekijô, 1966), a somber, modern-looking building inspired by ancient Japanese log-cabin (*azekura*) architecture designed primarily for *kabuki* and *bunraku*, large-scale theatre became more widely available. Important in signaling official recognition of the performing arts, it inspired other "National Theatres": Osaka's National Bunraku Theatre (Kokuritsu Bunraku Gekijô, 1983) and Tokyo's National Nô and Kyôgen Theatre (Kokuritsu Nôgakudô, 1984) and New National Theatre (Shinkokuritsu Gekijô, 1997) for opera, ballet, and modern drama.

Angura Theatres. Meanwhile, in the 1960s, cutting-edge theatre companies began a process of rejecting, then readopting, conventional spaces. The ***angura*** movement, gradually superseding *shingeki*, appropriated spaces such as cafés, basement rooms, tents, vacant lots, and even city streets (for example **Kara Jûrô**'s and **Satoh Makoto**'s tents and **Terayama Shûji**'s street theatre). Such work often altered the typical proscenium relationship between actors and audiences, using thrust, arena, and other variations. As less iconoclastic groups emerged in the 1970s, small theatres (*shôgekijô*) were again in demand, and Kinokuniya Hall (1964), a traditional proscenium stage, opened inside the Shinjuku district's large Kinokuniya bookstore. In 1982, a business-man built the first of three small theatres, Honda Theatre (Honda Gekijô), in Shimo-kitazawa, a residential area, instantly transforming it into a theatregoers' magnet. Subsequently, large numbers of little theatres, often producing **experimental theatre**, appeared around Tokyo, with the greatest concentration in Shinjuku (for example, Space Den), but with important spaces also in Shibuya (such as Theatre Cocoon and the iconic JeanJean, now defunct) and Meguro (the Komaba Agora Theatre [Komaba Agora Gekijô]). Here one can observe a clear symbiotic relationship between the agenda of the *shôgekijô* **playwrights** and the playing spaces they utilized.

Shakespearean Theatres. Shakespeare's plays began to appear on Japanese stages in the late nineteenth century, typically in proscenium theatres, but Waseda University—home of Shakespeare translator **Tsubouchi Shôyô**—built a passable replica of the Elizabethan-period Fortune Theatre's stage in 1928. In 1988, however, Tokyo's world-class Panasonic Globe Theatre, designed by Isozaki Arata (1931–), and based on Shake-speare's Globe Theatre, opened for native and international Shakespeare productions.

Theatres Everywhere. The national picture changed radically in the 1980s, when local authorities throughout Japan constructed theatres where none had existed before. From a country where in the mid-twentieth century good theatre spaces were confined to the big conurbations, Japan can now boast a theatre culture with comprehensive and well-distributed facilities.

FURTHER READING

Ernst, Earle. *The Kabuki Theatre*; Komparu, Kunio. *The Noh Theatre: Principles and Perspectives.* Leiter, Samuel. *New Kabuki Encyclopedia: A Revised Adaptation of Kabuki Jiten.*

Brian Powell and Katherine Saltzman-Li (Kabuki Theatre section)

Theatres: Korea

Seoul, South **Korea**'s theatre center, hosts a variety of theatres: large complexes, small aboveground theatres, belowground theatres, intimate spaces in university satellite buildings, and modern laboratory theatres on some university campuses. Among the large complexes are: National Theatre (Kuknip Kŭkchang, large hall: 1,518 seats; small hall: 454 seats), Munye Theatre (Munye Kŭkchang, large hall: 710 seats; flexible theatre: 200 seats), Sejong Cultural Center (Sejong Munwha Hoegwan, main hall: 3,895 seats; small hall: 522 seats), Seoul Arts Center (Seoul Yesul ŭi Chŏdang, opera house: 2,300 seats; small theatre: 700 seats; flexible space: 300–500 seats), and the 950-seat Ho-Am Art Hall, popular for opera, **musical**s, and *ch'anggŭk*. Two important, intimate, aboveground theatres are the Sanullim Theatre (Sanullim Kŭkchang) and Theatre Cecil (Seshil Kŭkchang), each seating 200–250.

Belowground theatres, including **Oh T'ae-sŏk**'s Theatre Arunggŭji (Kŭkchang Arunggŭji), are located in the Taehangno entertainment district. These fifty to sixty minimally equipped spaces seating less than 150 hold the majority of South Korean performances; they are insufficient to meet the demand. Sangmyŏng University and Dongdŏk **Women**'s University were innovators, incorporating miniature, well-equipped, comfortable theatres into new (2003–2004) satellite buildings in the entertainment district, renting space to **theatre companies**. The few modern campus theatres, such as Kookmin University's, do not address commercial demand, but provide long-needed, well-equipped, proscenium **stages** and **experimental** spaces for some of South Korea's approximately forty-two theatre departments.

Richard Nichols

Theatres: Malaysia

Although Kuala Lumpur does not have a theatre district, there are several well-equipped theatres with sophisticated lighting and sound systems. City Hall Auditorium can seat approximately one thousand. Close by is the Arts Theatre (Panggung Seni), which reopened in 2002 after having been gutted by a fire ten years earlier. It seats three hundred and has a small proscenium **stage**, best suited for intimate productions.

The Malaysian Tourist Information Center (MATIC) seats four hundred and has a proscenium stage and large apron. MATIC saw the launching of government-initiated one-act comedies in 1991 after the doldrums of the late 1970s and 1980s.

The Actors' Studio, in the Bangsar Shopping Center, is a testimony to the tenacity of Datuk Faridah Merican (1939–) and her husband, Joe Hasham (1948–), to ensure theatre's popularity. This new Actors' Studio was constructed after the original theatre, located beneath Merdeka Square in Plaza Putra, was destroyed by floods (2003). Merican and Hasham's devotion to theatre is also evidenced in the 2004 opening of the Kuala Lumpur Performing Arts Centre (a.k.a. KLPAC), a four-story building overlooking a lake, and formerly the Malayan Railway Warehouse. It includes a five-hundred-seat main theatre, a two-hundred-seat **experimental theatre**, ten studios, and a set construction shop.

The National Theatre (Istana Budaya or Palace of Culture, 1999) is touted as a "world-class performing arts" facility, and was built at a huge cost. Its main auditorium, the Panggung Sari, seats 1,412. It is a lavishly designed, cutting-edge venue with the most advanced technology, and offers concerts, films, opera, and theatre.

Away from the city center, in the satellite town of Petaling Jaya, is the Petaling Jaya Civic Center. **Noordin Hassan**'s famous *'Tis Not the Tall Grass Blown by the Wind* (Bukan lalang ditiup angin, 1970) was produced here.

Major towns have facilities such as town halls or school halls that can be used as theatre spaces. Universities also have large halls and/or their own theatre facilities. These include a number of experimental theatres. The National Arts Academy also has its own experimental theatre at its new campus situated in the former National Cultural Complex in Padang Merbuk, Kuala Lumpur.

Solehah Ishak

Theatres: Nepal

Nepal's first established theatres were raised platforms on palace grounds. During the Malla dynasty (1200–1768), theatre was a major pastime for the entire community, and royalty invited commoners into their walled compounds where together they watched **dances** and plays on open-air raised **stages** (*dabali*). The kings of the Shah dynasty (1769) were less interested in rubbing shoulders with commoners; the use of *dabali* declined as palace grounds entertainments were offered only for a select few. The hereditary Rana prime ministers (1846–1948) built **Western**-style theatres within their palaces where nobility sat according to rank to watch an eclectic mix of entertainment. In 1895, Dumbar Shumsher Rana (1858–1922) moved theatre out of the palace proper and into his antechamber, where upper-class citizens might view new plays, creating the first "open" theatre of the Rana regime.

King Mahendra Shah (r. 1955–1972), an arts patron, established the Royal Nepal Academy (1957) to support major artists. The Academy houses a Western-style proscenium theatre that hosts local and international dance, theatre, and **musical** performances. Nepal's most sophisticated theatre, with a manually operated light board and fly system, it is in high demand. King Mahendra also inaugurated the National Theatre (Rastriya Naach Ghar), in 1961. This more intimate house, despite its uncomfortable seats, poor sight lines, and limited backstage space, serves as an important venue for local **theatre companies** and student productions. Both theatres are in dire need of cleaning, maintenance, renovation, and modernization, although both are highly valued as sites of important theatre.

Today, the *dabali* are once again in use by socially oriented groups who perform plays aimed at reaching and influencing the largest possible audiences. Groups such as ABC Art Group stage their plays about girl trafficking on the *dabali* of old royal squares that are now at the centers of towns throughout the Kathmandu Valley. In 1999, Puskar Gurung (1965–) formed a new company named Dabali in honor of these open-air communal stages.

Carol Davis

Theatres: Pakistan

In the 1930s, many **Pakistani** theatres were converted into cinemas. *Lok* **folk theatre** had a roving existence, pitching temporary arrangements on rented grounds at fairs, circuses, and Sufic **festivals**. Despite college auditoriums and Lahore's open-air Baghe-Jinnah Theatre, there were no public, weatherproof, purpose-built theatres right after Partition (1947).

In Lahore, the Pakistan Arts Council (1948) created a small makeshift theatre with limited facilities, seating approximately 120, performing mostly English drawing-room comedies and adaptations. When it was declared unsafe in the 1970s, theatre activity was on the upswing. Its productions spread into venues such as the YMCA, Wapda Auditorium, the Falettis Hotel, and the Sheraaz Restaurant. In 1974, the Arts Council was taken over by the government; plans for a complex with a greenroom, auditorium, and workshop facilities were born. Hall 1 (750 seats) opened in 1981 with a later addition of two smaller theatres. Soon, a large open-air theatre (three thousand seats) with two smaller spaces opened at the Cultural Complex.

During General Zia-ul-Haq's (1924–1988) rule (1979–1988), state funding was cut, and the new auditoriums were leased to commercial producers. The "parallel" **political** theatre took to the streets, private houses, and foreign cultural centers, which closed after 9/11. The rise of Lahore's commercial theatre led to the first private theatre,

Tamaseel (1991), its up-to-date facilities including a revolving **stage**. There followed a 1990s trend of converting movie houses into privately run playhouses. Lahore examples include the Mehfil, Crown, Al Falah, Naaz, and Shama Theatres. Cinemas converted into theatres can be found in many cities.

Claire Pamment

Theatres: Philippines

Theatres in the **Philippines** include formal structures influenced by **Western** architecture, school auditoriums used for multiple purposes, open-air **stages** in town centers, and makeshift structures built by mobile troupes. According to Cristina Lacónico-Buenaventura, the earliest theatres were nipa and bamboo structures that showcased *komedya*s in Tondo and Arroceros, open-air stages (*teatros al aire libre*), and mobile theatres for roving pantomimes.

However, the first example built in the grand manner of old Spanish theatres was Teatro de Binondo (1846). Made of brick, stone, and wood, it had arches and columns, a lobby, and a balustraded balcony. Among other important nineteenth-century theatres were the Teatro del Principe Alfonso (a.k.a. Teatro Español, 1862), Teatro Circo de Bilibid (1851; first used for plays in the 1870s), Teatro de Sibacon (ca. late 1840s), Teatro de Variedades (1881), Teatro Filipino (ca. 1881), and Teatro Circo de Zorrilla (1893). They featured *komedya*s, **zarzuela**s, *dramas*, short plays (*sainetes*), monologues, dramatic spectacles, and variety shows.

By the early twentieth century, only Teatro Zorillo and Teatro Filipino still survived, but new theatres were also being built. Among them were the popular Manila Grand Opera House (1902); Teatro Libertad (1900), remembered for its nationalist plays; Teatro del Oriente (ca. 1905), which had a resident company, the Compania Zarzuela Comico-Lirica; and Teatro de la Comedia (1907), which featured **musical** dramas in Spanish.

The most magnificent twentieth-century playhouses were built through **political** patronage. Metropolitan Theatre (1931) was a project of Manila Mayor Tomas Earnshaw (1867–1954). Envisioned as a "national theatre," it was designed by Juan Arellano (1888–1960), who incorporated bas-reliefs of Philippine plants and Malay textile designs in the art nouveau architectural style. The Cultural Center of the Philippines (1969), built during the controversial years of the Marcos government (1972–1986), uses the sculptural approach, and houses several venues. Aside from the regular spaces of companies such as Repertory Philippines' Globe Theatre and PETA's Theatre Center, other popular venues include Philamlife Theatre, Meralco Theatre, Rajah Sulayman Theatre in Fort Santiago, the Carlos Romulo Theatre, and the Wilfrido Ma. Guerrero Theatre, at the University of the Philippines. Except for the T-shaped Rajah Sulayman Theatres and alternative venues (for example, building lobbies, convertible halls), most theatres are in the proscenium style.

FURTHER READING

Lacónico-Buenaventura, Cristina. *The Theatre in Manila 1846–1946*.

Joi Barrios

Theatres: Singapore

During the 1990s, **Singapore**'s National Arts Council (NAC) implemented an ambitious Arts Housing Scheme providing established **theatre companies** with permanent homes in one of three officially designated arts belts or other prime locations. Among the established companies benefiting from subsidy schemes are TheatreWorks, The Necessary Stage, Action Theatre, Singapore Repertory Theatre, One Vision (Teater Ekamatra), Toy Factory Theatre Ensemble, Dramaplus Arts, Wild Rice, and Spell #7, some of which have dedicated spaces as well. The Substation (1990), Singapore's first independent arts center, created by **Kuo Pao Kun**, provided the original model for a successful multiple-use facility with its popular gallery space, black-box theatre, and **dance** studio. The $363 million Esplanade-Theatres on the Bay, with its four spaces, attached shopping mall, and range of eating establishments, opened in 2002. The Esplanade features a concert hall accommodating 1,600, a theatre seating two thousand, a recital and theatre studio, as well as two outdoor venues, the largest seating six hundred.

Smaller proscenium houses include the 338–seat Jubilee Hall inside the historic Raffles Hotel complex, and the 615–seat Drama Center inside the new National Library. Larger proscenium houses include Victoria Theatre, seating nine hundred, the 1,744–seat Kallang Theatre, and the Singapore Indoor Stadium, which hosts the country's National Day **musicals** before an audience of up to twelve thousand. In addition, universities and junior colleges boast impressive facilities, with the cavernous University Cultural Center at the National University of Singapore accommodating 1,700 in the larger of two theatres.

William Peterson

Theatres: Thailand

Since its launch in 1992, Bangkok's Patravadi Theatre has been the only company with its own permanent venue of the same name. This complex now comprises two playhouses, namely Theatre in the Garden (four hundred seats) and Studio I (one hundred seats), plus indoor and outdoor rehearsal spaces, an art gallery, a library, a restaurant, and accommodation for international guest artists.

With Dream Box (formerly DASS Entertainment) as its resident company, Bangkok Playhouse (six hundred seats) was the most popular theatre from 1995 to 2004. From 2005, Dream Box co-leased the largest movie house in a downtown cineplex, and reconfigured it as Bangkok Theatre at Metropolis (six hundred seats).

Other Bangkok **theatre companies** depend on rental houses whose owners occasionally coproduce the play. Frequently used are **Thailand** Cultural Center's Main Hall (1,800 seats), Small Hall (450 seats), and Amphitheatre (eight hundred seats), Pridi Banomyong Institute Auditorium (three hundred seats); Sala Chalermkrung Royal Theatre (six hundred seats), Saeng Arun Cultural Center (150 seats), and Alliance Française Auditorium (250 seats). The largest venue is Grand Ratchada Theatre (two thousand seats), exclusively for the cultural show *Siam Niramit*. In 2006, Siam Opera (1,800 seats), the country's most lavish theatre, opened.

Major campus theatres are Chulalongkorn University's Auditorium (1,700 seats) and Art Theatre (150 seats), Thammasat University's Main Auditorium (2,500 seats), and

Sriburapha Auditorium (five hundred seats). Bangkok University's Black Box Theatre (two hundred seats) is the most flexible space.

Outside Bangkok, Kad Performing Arts Centre in Chiang Mai houses Kad Theatre (1,600 seats), Thailand's first playhouse designed to meet Broadway **musical** standards, and Kad Playhouse (five hundred seats).

Pawit Mahasarinand

THEATRE OF ROOTS. *See* Directors and Directing: India; India.

THEORY

Theory: China

Chinese theoretical writing emphasizes the social function of performance, not genre analyses. Followers of Confucius (551–479 BC), like Xun Kuang (ca. 313–238 BC), theorized that performance and **music** should accompany ritual and spread social harmony and happiness.

The ruling elite argued for theatre as **political** and moral propaganda and imposed severe restrictions (see Censorship) on it, especially from the Ming dynasty (1368–1644). **Tang Xianzu** stressed not only theatre's role in strengthening society's Confucian relationships, such as those between emperor and subjects, or fathers and sons, but also its ability to promote happiness and excellence. Tang was unusual in analyzing the relationship between theatre and life.

Dramatic literature was not highly regarded. With the rise of regional theatre in the Ming, *kunqu* assumed the highest social status among drama forms, the educated elite scorning more popular styles. An exception was philologist Jiao Xun (1763–1820), who wrote in praise of the local popular theatre. **Li Yu** and Hu Zhiyu were other major theorists.

Li Yu and Hu Zhiyu's Theories. Li's treatise on *chuanqi* makes up two of the eight chapters in *Casual Expressions of Idle Feeling* (Xianqing ouji, 1671). Fifty-four topics are arranged under eleven rubrics. Six—"structure" (*jiegou*), "language" (*cicai*), "prosody" (*yinlü*), "dialogue" (*binbai*), "comedy" (*kehun*), and "form" (*geju*)—concern play composition; five—"repertoire" (*xuanju*), "revision" (*biandiao*), "singing instruction" (*shouqu*), "dialogue coaching" (*jiaobai*), and "imitation" (*tuotao*)—relate to play production. Li argued for drama as literature but also wrote: "the only reason for writing a play is to have it performed onstage."

Hu Zhiyu (1227–1292), a scholar and official, developed a list of "nine beauties" (*jiumei*) in performance, including brilliant body movements, eloquent speech, clear singing, expressive gestures, vivid emotions, and innovativeness. Most striking is the integration of skills. Although most theorists prized transmission of traditions over innovativeness, the importance of the "nine beauties" persists.

Modern Theories. Modern theory has been heavily influenced by **Western** and Soviet ideas. Wang Guowei (1877–1927), who theorized on *xiqu*, believed that the

The Younger Generation, by Chen Yun, directed by Zhu Duanjun for the Shanghai Youth Spoken Drama Company, 1964. (Photo: Courtesy of Shanghai Theatre Academy)

lack of Western-style tragedy in Chinese drama, and the preference for happy endings, was due to the people's worldly and optimistic nature.

Modern theorists have been preoccupied with *xiqu* reform. Traditionalists have argued for little or no change. Probably the most radical theory was that of Mao Zedong's (1893–1976) wife, Jiang Qing (1913–1991). In a 1966 speech, she advocated a thoroughgoing *jingju* revolution (see *Yangban xi*). During the Cultural Revolution (1966–1976), character creation was based on the "three prominences," which she created along with Yu Huiyong (1925–1977) and Yao Wenyuan (1932–). This proclaims that positive characters must be given prominence over all others, heroic characters must be given prominence over positive ones, and, among the heroic figures, prominence must be given to the main hero. When she was overthrown (1976), her theories were discredited.

The theoretical implications of twentieth-century theatre can be best understood through the use of theatre for politics and propaganda and discourses on the Sinicization of modern "spoken drama" (*huaju*; see Playwrights and Playwriting).

Theatre as Political Propaganda. Communist theories of art as a political tool apply to all theatre forms. Although dating to the 1920s, their main expression was in Mao's "Talks at the Yan'an Forum on Literature and Art" (1942), when he proclaimed the supremacy of political criteria over artistic concerns in judging an artwork's value.

Ideological propaganda was most prominent after 1949, when leading communist theorists like Zhou Yang (1907–1989), Feng Xuefeng (1903–1976), and Yao Wenyuan dictated principles of artistic creation. Chief among their theories were the "socialist realism" of the early 1950s and its later variant of "the unity of revolutionary realism and revolutionary romanticism" and **criticism** of "neutral character theory" (1964).

For *huaju* in the 1950s, this meant an adherence to "socialist realism," a Soviet term meaning that writers should exaggerate and eulogize socialist society, negativity being forbidden. China officially adopted this in 1953 during the Second National Congress of Literature and Arts. As Sino-Soviet relations soured in the late 1950s, Mao proclaimed the adoption of "unity of revolutionary realism and revolutionary romanticism." In essence, these theories dictated the distortion of history to serve contemporary political needs, glorification of socialism, and falsification of the class struggle in accordance with Mao's teachings. Well-known plays created under these principles include *Red Storm* (Hongse fengbao, 1958), *Sentries under the Neon Lights* (Nihong deng xia de shaobing, 1962), and *The Younger Generation* (Nianqing de yidai, 1963).

Party doctrines were reinforced through political campaigns as during the 1964 movement against the so-called "neutral character theory" allegedly put forward by Shao Quanlin (1906–1971), a theorist and cultural official who advocated writing about not only positive or negative characters, but also those in the middle of the spectrum; they were the majority in any society, their existence providing a supporting background to the heroes. They were usually the most interesting and colorful ones. In the ever left-leaning pre–Cultural Revolution atmosphere, his views were criticized. The campaign against "neutral characters" led to the polarization of characters transposed into dry, ideological symbols.

***Sinicization of* Huaju.** Since the late 1920s, several debates have focused on the Sinicization of *huaju* as its practitioners attempted to bring this imported form closer to Chinese audiences. These debates include the "national theatre movement" of the 1920s, the "Sinicized style" debate of the late 1930s and early 1940s, the "*huaju* Sinicization" movement of the 1950s, and the *xieyi* and "dramatic outlook" debates of the 1980s.

In 1926, Yu Shangyuan and others envisioned a place for *xiqu* in *huaju* during the "national theatre movement." Yu was the first to describe *xiqu* as "depicting meaning" (*xieyi*), a concept used in traditional painting where it refers to a freer and more metaphorical style as opposed to more realistic and representational "depicting facts" (*xieshi*). Yu felt that Western theatre attempted to create a realistic illusion, ignoring both theatricality and the audience. By contrast, Chinese theatre strived to impress via the total performance (singing, reciting, **acting**, and **dance**/martial arts). By pointing out the shared roots of Chinese and Shakespeare's theatre, Yu advocated *xiqu* conventions in the service of modern content.

However, Yu's argument received widespread skepticism and found little resonance among practitioners. It was not until 1939 that an essay by scholar Zhang Geng (1911–2003) triggered another debate over the "Sinicized style" of *huaju*. The debate reached consensus on several issues. First, Sinicized forms should not equal **folk** art. Second, Sinicization of content took precedence over style. Third, *huaju* had served the demands of the time and reflected social realities, which should be considered part of Sinicization. Finally, learning from *xiqu* and folk art should not preclude learning from Western theatre. *Huaju*'s emphasis on content and its self-congratulatory tone resulted in little stylistic change.

It was not until the "*huaju* Sinicization" campaign of the late 1950s and early 1960s that practitioners began to focus on stylistic issues. Although a response to an ideology-based official demand, the debate was welcomed by many practitioners eager to extend *huaju*'s appeal through adopting *xiqu* techniques. For the playwright this meant learning from *xiqu*'s rhythmical and poetic language, its flexible tempo, and its **dramatic structure** unrestricted by spatial and temporal boundaries.

Directors could benefit from *xiqu*'s utilization of time and space as well as its emphasis on physical actions. Actors would be trained in *xiqu* conventions and in manipulation of body, voice, and facial expression. **Scenographers** would provide a stimulating atmosphere leaving much to the audience's imagination. Many practitioners, like Jiao Juyin, both debated and staged acclaimed productions, such as *The Tiger Tally* (Hufu, 1957), *Cai Wenji* (1959), and *Wu Zetian* (1962). At the same time, some **experiments** failed, as with Wu Xue's (1914–) *Subdue the Dragon and Tame the Tiger* (Xianglong fuhu, 1959), where the *xiqu* percussion appeared mechanical and monotonous.

Still, the Stanislavski System dominated most productions up until the 1980s, when the debate over "theatrical outlook" and *xieyi* once again stimulated Sinicization experiments. Spearheaded by practitioners like Gao Xingjian, this debate promoted a production's "theatricality" (*juchangxing*) and "conditionality" (*jiadingxing*), both terms derived from Russian ones, by envisioning the performance as a psychological space with a goal aimed at live communication between actors and audience with a mutual agreement on conventions.

The *xieyi* debate grew from a 1962 speech by **Huang Zuolin**. By comparing Stanislavski, Brecht, and **Mei Lanfang**, Huang concluded that *huaju* should learn from the *xieyi* essence of *xiqu* and not be limited by illusionism. In the 1980s, Huang revitalized the debate. He attributed four tenets to *xieyi* theatre, namely, "rhythmical smoothness and continuity" (*xianjiexing*), "temporal and spatial flexibility" (*linghuoxing*), "three-dimensional characterization unconfined by the proscenium" (*diaosuxing*), and "conventionality distilled from daily life" (*chengshixing*).

These debates helped *huaju* escape from Ibsenian-Stanislavskian realism, resulting in such landmark productions as *China Dream* (Zhongguo meng, 1987) and *Sangshuping Chronicles* (Sangshuping jishi, 1988).

FURTHER READING

Fei, Faye Chunfang, ed. and trans. *Chinese Theories of Theater and Performance from Confucius to the Present*; Hsu, Tao-ching. *The Chinese Conception of the Theatre*; Zhao, Henry Y. H. *Towards a Modern Zen Theatre: Gao Xingjian and Chinese Theatre Experimentalism.*

Siyuan Liu and Colin Mackerras

Theory: India

Natyashastra. India's earliest dramatic theory text is the **Sanskrit** *Treatise on Drama* (Natyashastra), seemingly compiled around the middle of the first millennium. It is ascribed to the (mythical) sage Bharata, but was likely not by a single author. This encyclopedic work deals with topics ranging from the mythical origins of drama and the proper ritual preliminaries for a dramatic performance to the theory of emotional response, the principles of **dramatic construction**, the typology of genres, and the details of gesture, vocal expression, and **costume**. Performance (*abhinaya* [see below]) is analyzed in four components: "gestural" (*angika*), "verbal" (*vacika*), "imposed" (*aharya*), that is, costume, **makeup**, and the like, and "bodily" (*sattvika*), that is, crying, sweating, fainting, and so on; each is elaborated in painstaking detail. The *Natyashastra* also provides an analysis of **role types**.

Rasa. The *Natyashastra* provides the first full articulation of the theory of *rasa* ("aestheticized emotion," literally, "flavor"). Some form of the theory was apparently known to **playwrights** at least as early as **Kalidasa**. According to the *Natyashastra*, *rasa* is a scene's overall emotional mood, created by the combination of all the elements of a performance, which the text compares to the flavor produced by the mixture of ingredients in food or drink. Eight such moods are listed: love, laughter, grief, fury, heroism, fear, disgust, and wonder. To these canonical *rasa*s the Kashmiri theorist Udbhata (ca. 800) added a ninth, peacefulness, adopted by later theorists (though some argued that it was not portrayable and could exist only in nondramatic poetry). Several authors tried to add further *rasa*s, such as (nonsexual) affection and **religious** devotion, but these did not gain acceptance. While *rasa* was originally conceived of specifically as a drama feature, the theory eventually was applied to nondramatic poetry as well.

According to the *Natyashastra*, *rasa*s are created through the presentation together of *bhava*s: "determinants" (*vibhava*s), "consequents" (*anubhava*s), and "transient emotional states" (*vyabhicaribhava*s) associated with the eight basic "emotional states" (*sthayibhava*s). Determinants are factors that would be expected to produce these emotions in real life, for example, in the case of fear, a dangerous animal. Consequents are the visible symptoms of emotion displayed, such as trembling in the case of fear. Transient emotional states are shifting emotions that arise in connection with the basic emotional states; in the case of love, these would be longing, anxiety, joy, and the like.

The *Natyashastra*'s claim that *rasa* is produced by a combination of these factors is accepted, but there have been heated arguments about the precise nature and locus of the *rasa* experience. Is the *rasa* of a drama the same as the real world emotion it is named after? Is it an imitation of such an emotion? Or is it an experience different in kind from any real-world emotion? Furthermore, is it something that occurs in a play's characters, in the **actors** portraying them, or in the audience? The respective positions of the commentators on these issue are summed up in the earliest surviving *Natyashastra* commentary, the *Abhinava Speaks* (Abhinavabharati) of Abhinavagupta.

Abhinavagupta and Bhattanayaka. Abhinavagupta (ca. 950–1025), an influential theorist and theologian, is noted for his analysis of *rasa*. He develops his understanding of *rasa* through a survey of earlier theorists. The first is Lollata (ca. 850), who held that *rasa* is simply an intensification of the emotions that occur in real life, existing in the character being portrayed. Lollata's contemporary, Shankuka, however, argues that the *rasa* of a play differs from the real-world emotion it is based on precisely in being a simulation. *Rasa* is not an emotion that actually exists in a character, but one that we infer to exist in an actor, because he presents an imitation of the behavior appropriate to that emotion. We do not actually mistake his emotion for a real one, believing that the one portraying a lover is actually in love, but we recognize that his situation and his response to it are appropriate for a person in love. Shankuka compares this to our experience upon seeing a picture of a horse we recognize as a horse, without forgetting that it is only a representation.

The greatest shift in *rasa* theory came with Bhattanayaka (ca. 900), who transferred the focus away from the character and actor and toward the audience. *Rasa* cannot be simply an intensified form of real-world emotion, or an imitation of it, because we as spectators do not respond as we would if this were so. When we witness a love scene, we do not feel what we would if we saw a real pair of lovers' embarrassment or jealousy or what we would if we saw people simply pretending to be in love, that is, indifference. As spectators, we participate emotionally in the scene in a manner that is neither that of a real participant nor of a disinterested third party. Bhattanayaka sees this as the result of a process he calls "generalization" (*sadharanikarana*): we partake of the emotions depicted not as if they were our own, nor as if they belonged to persons other than ourselves, but in a generalized form that eclipses distinctions of personal identity. For him, it is this generalized emotional experience, located in the audience, that Bharata calls *rasa*.

Abhinavagupta's theory is close to this—he too takes *rasa* to be a generalized emotional response located in the spectator. His only major disagreement concerns the source of this response. For Abhinavagupta, the drama we see does not produce in us an emotional response that did not exist previously. Rather, it revives in us traces of our own prior emotional experience in our current and previous lives.

After Abhinavagupta's time, interest in the *Natyashastra* waned. No further commentaries were produced, and the *Natyashastra* was largely supplanted as a textbook on theory by more user-friendly manuals, such as *The Ten Forms of Drama* (Dasharupaka) of Dhananjaya (ca. 1000) and *The Mirror of Drama* (Natya darpana) of Ramachandra (eleventh century).

FURTHER READING

Ahuja, R. H. *Theory of Drama in Ancient India*; Rangacharya, Adya. *The Nātyaśāstra.*

Lawrence McCrea

Background to Modern Theories. Indian theoretical approaches to theatre have focused on the following areas: performance semiotics; the physics and metaphysics of acting; self, role, **mask**; reception theory and aesthetics; and the ethics and **politics** of theatre practice. These have been addressed in terms of anthropology, phenomenology, history, feminism, postcolonialism, and poststructuralism by **critics** and practitioners in India and abroad. In other words, Indian theatre has given rise to a wide spectrum of debate, and the particular configurations of practice have enabled some key areas to be explored. The *Natyashastra* established a theoretical basis for acting and production and for the interpretation of the reception process, and its analysis of aesthetic experience has underpinned philosophical debate about all forms of literature ever since. It focused attention on all aspects of semiotic transfer in theatre—gesture, movement, facial expression, speech, makeup, and so on. It provided codification that served practice; **training**, in ways of communicating emotional mood (*bhava*) and inciting aesthetic pleasure (*rasa*); and theory (identifying categories, structures, and systems that can be applied to much performance).

Indian thought has always been rich in subtle and elaborate codification in all fields, and this complexity has given rise to a long tradition of post-*Natyashastra* commentary, much of it by nonpractitioners on aesthetic issues. It is only fairly recently that practitioners themselves have contributed to more wide-ranging debates, usually in the form of interviews, short articles, or prefaces to published plays rather than extended monographs. Among the few practitioner-theorists of post-independence India who have provided longer studies are **Badal Sircar**, **Vijay Tendulkar**, and **Utpal Dutt**. The twentieth century also saw extensive interest from **Western** critics and practitioners who continue to use Indian practice to develop their thinking on links between theatre and anthropology, theatre and politics, and theatre in postcolonial and intercultural modes.

The sorts of questions that have been opened up include Richard Schechner's interrogation of the social framing of performance events, particularly via an examination of traditional and ritual practice; Eugenio Barba's attempt to isolate and compare structural patterns of the body in performance and to speculate on degrees of acculturation and methods of engendering "presence"; intense debates about cultural politics, often stimulated by Peter Brook's "international" production of *The Mahabharata* (1989) and focused by Rustom Bharucha's critique of it; discussion of trance and masking with reference to theories of what state of mind actors can or must inhabit; and extended questioning of the possibilities of adapting or combining performance modes in order to articulate the increasingly fluid nature of realities in a multicultural world.

FURTHER READING

Dhanamjaya. *The Dasarupa: A Treatise on Hindu Dramaturgy*; Rangacharya, Adya. *The Natyasastra: English Translation with Critical Notes*; Schwartz, Susan. *Rasa: Performing the Divine in India*.

Ralph Yarrow

Theory: Japan

Nô. Japanese writings on **actor • training, playwriting**, and performance, which can fall under the rubric of "theory," began with **nô**. **Zeami Motokiyo** introduced the practice of recording ideals and customs of performance in secret writings, borrowing an earlier convention of poets and **religious** professionals, who had recorded esoteric knowledge to control its dissemination. Secret writings became common to nearly all performing arts by the sixteenth century, and these writings were recognized as authoritative even after some were printed for a general audience beginning around 1590, when they became "secret" in name alone. The generic name "transmitted texts" (*densho*), indicates that they were usually written with specific individuals in mind, and their readership was restricted to senior students if not just the author's heir; consequently, transmission was secret in practice if not also in name, hence the also used term "secret treatise" (*hidensho*). The most selective works were restricted to one student per generation. Most of Zeami's writings did not circulate outside of the Konparu and Kanze troupes until the twentieth century, although they are today's most cited works on *nô* theory; dissemination of the writings of **Konparu Zenchiku** was even more restricted.

Zeami and Zenchiku produced approximately twenty theoretical writings each, their contents ranging from legends about the origins of their art, to metaphysical speculations that set *nô* in a cosmological context, to notations on the appropriate **costumes** for specific plays. Two of the most approachable of Zeami's works are *Treatise on the Flower* (Kadensho, 1418) and *Zeami's Talks on Sarugaku* (Sarugaku dangi, compiled 1430), recorded by Zeami's son, Kanze Motoyoshi, but probably edited by Zeami. The former's first three chapters provide guidelines for training; how to enact different roles, such as women, old men, and deities, according to the concept of "role playing" (*monomane*), and a question and answer section with tips for successful performances.

Chapter four expands on the history of *nô* introduced in chapter one. Chapter five explains the secrets of "grace" or "mysterious beauty" (*yûgen*) and of the "flower" (*hana*) in a performance, and how an actor can achieve his full creative potential. Chapters six and seven offer observations on these two important concepts in terms of playwriting and performance respectively. *Talks on Sarugaku* is organized according to different headings, including the contributions of great performers, **music**, rhythm, composition, staging, costuming, and troupe organization.

The concepts of *monomane*, *yūgen*, and *hana* are key. Zeami claimed *monomane* as a specialty of his troupe in the Yamato *sarugaku* (*nô*'s early name) tradition. He defined *monomane* as imitation, and he required that a performer study the mannerisms of actual nobles with exactitude, but he warned that it was vulgar to impersonate people of lowly occupations too closely. *Yûgen* found earlier use in **Chinese** philosophy and discussions of Japanese poetry, where it absorbed nuances of mystery and profundity. Zeami associated *yûgen* with the style of Ômi *sarugaku*, but he contended that all actors must master it since it was *nô*'s highest principle. *Yûgen* is a key to a successful play, especially those about the imperial court **women** who particularly embodied that quality, but Zeami thought it should also be found in even the roughest characters. Zeami used the metaphor of *hana* to describe an actor's accomplishment. Young boys have a natural **stage** charm that constitutes their "flower of youthful beauty." By the time an actor reaches his thirties, those who through proper training and experience perform consistently well can be said to possess the true flower, which will maintain the quality of their art as they age. Besides *Style and the Flower*, many of Zeami's writings, such as *Finding Gems, Gaining Flower* (Shûgyoku tokka) and *Mirror of the Flower* (Kakyô, 1424), exhibit his attempts to guide actors to this elevated level of performance.

While Zenchiku touches on most of these themes in works such as *Record of the Essentials of Song and Dance* (Kabu zuinô ki) and his cycle of eight texts on the "Six Circles and One Dew Drop" (Rokurin ichiro), he demonstrates a great interest in poetry as the heart of performance and in metaphysics to chart the actor's development according to spiritual and cosmological stages. **Konparu Zenpô** advanced the theory of the five modes (*go'on*) of music—"celebratory" (*shûgen*), "elegant music" (*yûkyoku*), "romantic longing" (*renbô*), "mourning" (*aishô*), and "consummate music" (*rangkyoku*)—a categorization introduced by Zeami and continued by Zenchiku for classifying dominant dramatic themes. However, in contrast to Zenchiku, Zenpô preferred concreteness to abstraction, and his advice is more focused on specific plays than directed toward philosophical issues.

Sixteenth-century writings show several developments. First, they reveal a variety of texts that often are all or in part compilations of earlier writings. Second, these treatises are more specialized, especially regarding music. Works intended for hip and shoulder drum performers appeared first followed by texts for flute. Finally, sixteenth-century texts focus less on abstract theory and more on stage directions, costuming notations, and other practicalities. Late in the century, actors began creating "form-added" (*katazuke*) texts, which provided the exact music or **dance** form (*kata*) to be used in specific passages. Such writings demonstrate the role of sixteenth-century actors in refining their aesthetics. The *Eight Volume Treatise on the Flower* (Hachijô kadensho), an anonymous, post-1550 work, is representative in that it is a compilation of earlier texts of Zeami, Zenpô, Miyamasu Yazaemon (?–1566), and others; several chapters are devoted to instruments. This text was misattributed to Zeami around 1600, about the time it first found its way into print, and the so-called *Treatise on the Flower* (Kadensho, 1402–1418) became the most widely circulated *nô* text in the Edo period (1603–1868). Other authoritative writings published include the works of actor Shimotsuma Shôshin (?–1616).

Kyôgen. Okura Tora'akira authored the earliest text on **kyôgen**, known today as *Young Leaves* (Waranbe gusa); its first draft was a record of his father, Torakiyo's (?–1646), instructions, *Ancient Sayings* (Mukashi gatari, 1651). In 1660, Tora'akira fleshed out the text with his own commentary. Like contemporary *nô* treatises, this is not a unified narrative, but instead lists information on the minutiae of performance, including observations about specific plays, *kyôgen*'s history, and its close relationship to *nô*. Tora'akira observes that where *nô* makes fiction into reality, *kyôgen* turns reality into fiction, making the serious comical and the comical serious. (See Ōkura School)

Kabuki. The best-known **kabuki** theoretical work is *The Actors' Analects* (Yakusha rongo or Yakusha banashi), seven treatises on acting published in 1776 although written earlier in the century. It is largely practical advice rather than esoteric theorizing. The highlight is the "Words of Ayame" (*Ayame gusa*) by **Yoshizawa Ayame**, a "female impersonator" (*onnagata*), who advises aspiring specialists in that field to adopt a female persona off stage as well as on. "Dust in the Ears" (*Nijinshû*), "Sequel to Dust in the Ears" (*Zoku nijinshû*) by Kaneko Kichizaemon, and "Kengai Collection" (*Kengaishû*) by Somewaka Jûrobei, include instructions and anecdotes from **Sakata Tôjûrô**, innovator of *kabuki*'s "gentle style" (*wagoto*) of acting.

An important treatise on Osaka playwriting is *Valuable Notes on Playwriting* (Kezairoku, 1801), by Nyûgatei Ganyû, among its subjects a description of how dramatic "worlds" (*sekai*) and "plot devices" (*shukô*) are the dramaturgical warp and woof of plays. The book provides playwright biographies, differences between Edo (Tokyo) and Kamigata (Osaka/Kyoto) responses to **dramatic structure**, play titles, seasonal notions, and "billboard" (*kanban*) writing, among other things.

Although *bunraku* artists, like **Takemoto Gidayû**, often wrote explanations of their artistic approaches, the most famous statement about Japan's **puppet theatre** is found in the writings of Confucian scholar, Hozumi Ikan (?–1769), who quotes **Chikamatsu Monzaemon**'s views on the nature of dramatic art. Chikamatsu stated, "art is something that lies in the thin margin between truth and falsehood." In the same work, Chikamatsu defends puppet theatre against **critics** who faulted it for a lack of realism compared to *kabuki* acting, explaining that exact imitation of reality produces a failure dramatically. For Chikamatsu, the playwright and performer need to be truer to a character's inner life than to superficial details. He noted: "In recent plays female characters speak many things which real women could not possibly say. These belong to the domain of art; as they reveal what real women cannot say, one comes to know what their innermost feelings are."

Today, the most widely read works on traditional drama are the "artistic discourses" (*geidan*), written by modern performers of the traditional genres. While some are purely autobiographical, the more informative texts provide readers an understanding about how actors apply traditional knowledge to their work. They explicate the finer points of difficult plays and provide insights into the lore and history of the art.

FURTHER READING

Dunn, Charles J., and Torigoe Bunzô, trans. and eds. *The Actors' Analects*; Rimer, J. Thomas, and Yamazaki Masakazu, trans. and eds. *On the Art of the Nô Drama: The Major Treatises of Zeami*; Ueda, Makoto. *Literary and Art Theories in Japan*; Saltzman-Li, Katherine. *Creating Kabuki Plays: Context for Kezairoku*; Thornhill, Arthur, III. *Six Circles, One Dewdrop: The Religio-Aesthetic Theories of Komparu Zenchiku*.

Eric C. Rath

Meiji-Period Theory. Key moments when modern theatre theory became particularly prominent include *shingeki*'s rise, from the 1880s to 1920s; challenges to *shingeki* from the left in the 1920s and 1930s, and from the right in the late 1930s and 1940s, and from *angura* in the 1960s and 1970s.

The first such moment occurred in the Meiji period (1868–1912) when the Theatre Reform Society (1886) advanced goals to showcase Japan as a civilized nation: elevating theatre by eliminating old-fashioned elements like the *onnagata*, elevating the playwright's status, and constructing better **theatres**. Although these initiatives led to greater acceptance—the emperor witnessed *kabuki* in 1887 for the first time—and eventually to new playhouses, they elicited mixed responses from practitioners. *Kabuki* reformer **Morita Kan'ya** XII welcomed them, while authors **Mori Ôgai** and **Tsubouchi Shôyô** objected to the emphasis on outer trappings.

Further, Mori and Tsubouchi publicly debated the concept of ideals, Mori arguing for historical progression toward European ideals, countering Tsubouchi's more naïve formalism. Tsubouchi later advocated a new form of "historical drama" (*shigeki*) modeled on Shakespeare and opposed to the mechanical "living history plays" (*katsureki geki*) **experiments** then current. Tsubouchi also proposed a new national form to synthesize traditional theatrical aspects, poetry, music, and dance in a total art. His ideas encountered resistance even among his followers, who preferred performances of translated modern European dramas. In *shingeki*'s early years, **Osanai Kaoru** expressed several controversial ideas, advocating, for example, that actors be puppets subordinate to the script. He also advocated the "single road" (*ichigen no michi*) of art for art's sake, opposing **Shimamura Hôgetsu**, who advocated the "dual road" (*nigen no michi*) of using profits from popular performances to finance more experimental efforts.

Shôwa-Period Theory. Theory's next prominent moment occurred with the rise of proletarian theatre during the early Shôwa period (1926–1989). Numerous articles promoting theatre for **political** ends appeared, and several major plays, including Fujimori Seikichi's (1892–1977) *What Made Her Do It?* (Nani ga kanojo o sô saseta ka, 1927) and **Kubo Sakae**'s *Land of Volcanic Ash* (Kazanbaichi, 1938), advanced leftist agendas. **Murayama Tomoyoshi** wrote *Theory of Japanese Proletarian Theatre* (Nihon pururoretaria engeki-ron, 1930), calling for proletarian realism, as against *shingeki*'s bourgeois, psychological, and linguistic realism, exemplified by **Kishida Kunio**'s theories and plays, which Murayama saw as reactionary. Debates raged over the definition of socialist realism, recommended in 1932 by the Union of Soviet Writers. In the late 1930s, the ideal of a "national theatre" (*kokumin engeki*) serving the state's, rather than artistic, ends was debated. Authorities increasingly mobilized theatre for the war effort in the 1940s, just as leftists had for prewar proletarian causes.

Postwar Theory. After the war, leftwing *shingeki* was considered the heir to proletarian theatre. **Senda Koreya** wrote *Modern Acting* (Kindai haiyû-jutsu, 1949), the first such comprehensive treatise for modern Japanese theatre, and his *Introduction to Theatre* (Engeki nyûmon, 1966) synthesized his ideas, including the Brechtian theory of alienation. The Stanislavski System became widely known in the 1950s, and *shingeki* continued its preoccupation with realism.

Angura and ***shôgekijô*** in the 1960s challenged orthodox *shingeki*'s privileging written text and realistic staging. Instead, *angura* focused on the actor's body and the **director**'s role in orchestrating performance. **Terayama Shûji** challenged all conventional definitions of theatre. In his "theory of privileged bodies" (*tokken-teki nikutai-ron*, 1968), **Kara Jûrô** argued for the significance of the actor's physical presence, while paradoxically calling his actors "riverbed beggars" (*kawara kojiki*)—recalling their pre-modern denigration. **Suzuki Tadashi**, another practitioner opposed to orthodox *shingeki*, advanced his theory of physicality in articles propagating an emphasis on the body's lower half in training; he has enjoyed wide influence abroad, especially in Europe and the United States. In the 1990s, **Hirata Oriza**, discussing "quiet theatre" (*shizuka na engaki*), proposed that performances should reflect daily speech, even if it results in barely audible dialogue. Since the 1990s, the journal *Theatre Arts* (Shiatâ âtsu) has been an active locus of theorizing, bringing together practitioners, critics, and scholars to consider all aspects of theatre, including related socio-political issues such as feminism, sexuality, colonialism, and the emperor system.

FURTHER READING

Eckersall, Peter. *Theorizing the Angura Space;* Goodman, David G. *Japanese Drama and Culture in the 1960s: The Return of the Gods;* Rimer, J. Thomas. *Toward a Modern Japanese Theatre: Kishida Kunio;* Suzuki, Tadashi. *The Way of Acting: The Theatre Writings of Tadashi Suzuki.*

Ayako Kano

THIYAM, RATAN (1948–). Indian Manipuri-language **director, playwright, actor, theorist,** poet, and novelist. He was born in Nabhadwep, Nadia District, West Bengal, his father being **dance** teacher Tarunkumar Thiyam. He originally studied painting but turned to writing in the 1970s, when he became active in the literary movement searching for Manipuri identity. This led to his involvement with Manipuri theatre. Soon, he enrolled in the National School of Drama (NSD); after graduating in 1974, he spent the next two years acting in the NSD's Repertory **Theatre**.

He left to launch the Chorus Repertory Theatre (1976) in Imphal, Manipur. In recent years, he not only designed its beautiful three-hundred-seat **theatre**, but built it with his own hands along with the **theatre company**'s young artists. The company, whose motto is "Bread, if not butter!", lives together on a communal farm. All participants learn acting, dancing, martial arts, **music**, and other arts. He gave renewed expression to Hindu mythology, brilliantly using elements from the Manipuri **folk** and martial arts (***thang-ta***); these interests demonstrate his commitment to the "theatre of roots," based on respect for indigenous traditions. Nonverbal communication is fundamental to his work. Thiyam's actors are trained with rigorous discipline, enabling them to perform difficult vocal and physical actions (they also study stagecraft and design). An important role is played by acoustic effects—vocal, physical (such as stamping), and technologically enhanced. Lighting, symbolic **properties**, and richly colored, exquisite **costumes**—red is crucial—play an important role, with simple architectural platforms constituting the **scenographic** design.

Thiyam's work is often derived from the ***Mahabharata***, used to make analogies to contemporary strife in Manipur. Among his acclaimed productions, known for their spectacle, are **Bhasa**'s *The Broken Thighs* (Urubhanga, 1981), **Dharamvir Bharati**'s *Blind Age* (Andha yug, 1984), his own highly stylized *Battle Formation* (Chakravyuha, 1984), *Uttara Priyadarshi* (1996), based on Ajneya's poem about Emperor Ashoka (who spread Buddhism in India), and *Hiroshima* (1994), inspired by the writing of **Badal Sircar**. Most of Thiyam's plays bring out the futility of war and violence or trace the quest for peace and spirituality. From 1986 to 1988, he served as the NSD's director.

His productions have been seen at most of the major international **festivals**, making him one of the best-known Indian directors abroad, and helping him achieve many prestigious awards, including the National Academy of Music, Dance, and Drama (Sangeet Natak Akademi) award (1987), and the first **B. V. Karanth** Memorial award. In 2000, *Some Roots Grow Upward: The Theatre of Ratan Thiyam*, a documentary, was produced.

Shashikant Barhanpurkar

THOL PAVAIKKUTHU. *See* Puppet Theatre: India.

THOL PAVAKUTHU. *See* Puppet Theatre: India.

THOLU BOMMALATTA. *See* Puppet Theatre: India.

TIAN HAN (1898–1968). Chinese • **playwright** and **critic** who wrote sixty-three modern "spoken dramas" (*huaju*), twenty-seven *xiqu* scripts, two *geju*, and twelve film scripts. He also wrote over two thousand poems, including the lyrics of the national anthem. Regarded as a founder of China's modern theatre, Tian started writing plays at fourteen. As a student in Tokyo between 1916 and 1922, he came into contact with **Western** films and *shingeki* productions of both European classics and neoromantic, or modernist, plays. He published criticism of Western literature, and translated *Salomé* and *Hamlet*, the latter being the first Chinese literal translation of a Shakespeare play.

After returning to Shanghai in 1922, he published theatre journals, organized the Southern China Society (Nanguo She, 1926), became president of Shanghai Art University in 1927, and formed the Southern China Arts College in 1928.

Throughout the 1920s, he was deeply concerned with the neoromantic conflict between body and soul, as shown in his staging of *Salomé* and in his plays *Violin and Rose* (Fan'elin yu qiangwei, 1920), *The Night the Tiger Was Caught* (Huo hu zhi ye, 1925), and *Death of a Famous Actor* (Ming you zhi si, 1927). In addition to writing and producing *huaju*, he befriended well-known *xiqu* **actors** like **Zhou Xinfang** and

Yuan Xuefen (1922–). He refused to equate *xiqu* with "old" and *huaju* with "new," believing instead that a modern theatre should include both. He staged plays of each genre in the 1927 Fish and Dragon **Festival**.

In the 1930s, Tian renounced his neoromantic plays as "art for art's sake," became a leader of the leftwing dramatic movement, and joined the Communist Party. His works became more socially conscious, as in *Rainy Season* (Meiyu, 1931) and *Moonlight Sonata* (Yueguang qu, 1932) and in his film scripts. In 1935, he was arrested for his **political** activities. Upon his release half a year later, he was kept away from Shanghai, the leftist theatre center, and remained in Nanjing, until 1937.

During the Second Sino-Japanese War (1937–1945), Tian was in charge of wartime mobilization and organized tours to war zones. He also focused on *xiqu* reform, writing new and adapting old scripts and organizing forums, all aimed at instilling a modern soul into traditional theatre. In addition, he published a theatre magazine and helped organize the Southwestern Dramatic Exhibit (Xinan Xiju Zhanlanhui, 1944), a review of wartime theatre.

After the war, he returned to Shanghai where he wrote *The Charming Ladies* (Liren xing, 1947). Even after he became president of the All-China Dramatists Association, he kept writing influential plays, including the *jingju The White Snake* (Bai she zhuan, 1952) and *Xie Yaohuan* (1961) and the *huaju* **Guan Hanqing** (1958). Persecuted during the Cultural Revolution (1966–1976), he died in prison.

Siyuan Liu

TIBET. The Tibet Autonomous Region (established 1965), located in **China**'s southwest, has a population of 2.62 million, 92.2 percent of which is Tibetan. Including Tibet, the total Tibetan population in China is 5,416,021 (2000 census), with over 120,000 in other countries, especially **India** and **Nepal**. Since shortly after a major anti-Chinese rebellion was suppressed (1959), Tibet's spiritual leader, the Fourteenth Dalai Lama (1935–), has headed a Tibetan community in Dharamsala, India. Overwhelmingly, the people follow Tibetan Buddhism, which is crucial to their culture.

Traditional Musical Drama. Among China's minorities, the Tibetans are alone in producing a traditional **musical** drama form entirely independently of the Han Chinese. The most important is ***ache lhamo***, dating back to the mid-fifteenth century, and typically performed through the day at **festivals**, although the plays—while infused with Tibetan Buddhism—are basically secular. Its stories, which have happy endings, mostly concern Tibetan history and mythology, with a few set in India.

Another tradition is the sacred **dance** termed ʻcham. These are ceremonial dance-dramas performed in monasteries by monks who wear awesome **masks** representing divinities. Stories are narrated through the dances, which function as rituals designed to beg protection. Musical accompaniment features very long trumpets (*radong*), which produce one very deep note only, as well as cymbals, drums, and shawms.

The Tradition since 1959. No attempt at drama reform was undertaken until after the suppression of the 1959 rebellion. The community in exile immediately set up the Tibetan Performing Arts Institute, which has flourished in Dharamsala since 1960, aiming to preserve Tibet's performing arts. In China's Tibetan areas, authorities sponsored the establishment of professional troupes and the reform of some old dramas. The aim was to diminish the **religious** content and to emphasize the serf, peasant, or proletarian nature of the positive characters, and the serf-owner, aristocratic, or prelate character of the negative ones. The reformed dramas were much shorter than the traditional ones, lasting only two to three hours, and took place in a **theatre**, with elaborate **scenography**. Amateur **folk** troupes continued to perform some of the old dramas in traditional ways.

During the Cultural Revolution (1966–1976), traditional Tibetan drama was suppressed, but quickly revived in the 1980s. Though reformed versions of the old *ache lhamo* dramas and new ones based on the traditional style are sometimes performed, Tibetans much prefer the old items in unreformed versions. Folk troupes are still active all over the Tibetan areas, and the summer festivals in Lhasa, begun under the Fifth Dalai Lama (1617–1682), were revived in the mid-1980s. Traditional items performed in the old style under a tent are still frequent, including in the Dalai Lama's Summer Palace, the Norbu Lingka, in Lhasa. The ritual *'cham* dances are also still performed in some of the main Tibetan monasteries, both in China and outside. Although tourists attend traditional *ache lhamo* and *'cham*, traditional theatre is stronger among the ordinary people in the Tibetan areas than elsewhere in China.

Modern Spoken Drama. In the early 1960s, the government sent a group of Tibetans to Shanghai to learn modern spoken drama, resulting in the establishment of a bilingual (Tibetan and Chinese) professional **theatre company** (1962). Although the troupe was inactive during the Cultural Revolution, it was revived afterward.

Modern drama has never greatly appealed to Tibetans, even when in Tibetan, one reason being that modern dramas tend to follow the current **political** propaganda line more closely even than reformed traditional items. In the 1960s, some plays focused on contemporary times, including attacking the Tibetan serf system and welcoming

Stage at Drepung Monastery outside Lhasa, Tibet. Formerly, the Dalai Lama sat in his room above, looking down at the drama. Other spectators were in the square in front of or beside the stage. (Photo: Colin Mackerras)

liberation from China. Since the 1980s, such themes have fallen into disfavor. Themes focus instead on history and heroes, emphasizing Tibetan culture and identity, though certainly not advocating independence even indirectly. **Western** plays, such as *Romeo and Juliet*, have been performed in Tibetan. As in the rest of China, plays are performed mainly in modern-style theatres with elaborate **costuming** and décor.

FURTHER READING

Kohn, Richard J. *Lord of the Dance: The Mani Rimdu Festival in Tibet and Nepal*; Pearlman, Ellen. *Tibetan Sacred Dance, A Journey into the Religious and Folk Traditions*; Norbu, Thubten Jigme, and Robert B. Ekvall, trans. *The Younger Brother Don Yod: A Tibetan Play*.

Colin Mackerras

TOGALU GOMBEYATA. *See* Puppet Theatre: India.

TOLENTINO, AURELIO (1867–1915). Filipino **playwright**, poet, and fiction writer best known for his allegorical plays written during the American colonial period (ca. 1900–1946). Writing in Tagalog, Pampango, and Spanish, he produced sixty-nine works, mainly plays and novels. After earning a bachelor's degree and dropping out of law studies at the University of Santo Tomas, Tolentino taught and worked in the Court of First Instance in Manila and Rizal.

A militant nationalist, he was one of the founding members of the Katipunan (the organization founded to secure independence), and one of the signatories of the Declaration of Independence in Cavite (1898). He organized guerillas at the outbreak of the **Philippine**-American War and throughout the colonial period, and wrote articles for various nationalist newspapers. Tolentino was imprisoned nine times for his **political** activities.

Tolentino's most significant works include the symbolic dramas *Tagalog Tears* (Luhang Tagalog, ca. 1903), about the Philippines' occupation by a foreign power, and *Yesterday, Today, and Tomorrow* (Kahapon, ngayon, at bukas), whose allegorical characters are the hero Taga-ilog (the Tagalog Provinces), Ynang Bayan (Mother Country), and Bagongsibol (the United States). Two other works focus on workers' rights and conditions: *New Christ* (Bagong Cristo, 1907), in which he reinterpreted the Christ story; and the *sarsuwela* Germinal (Germinal, 1908), about tobacco factory workers. His involvement with the labor movement led to the founding of the workers' cooperative Katimawan (1910).

Although Tolentino wrote many *sarsuwela*s, such as *Oath* (Sumpaan, 1904), *drama*s, such as *Magdalena* (1913), and novels, such as *Ester's Strand of Hair* (Ang buhok ni Ester, 1914–1915), he made his greatest contribution through his discourses on colonialism and nationalism.

Joi Barrios

TONIL. Indonesian variety theatre that emerged after 1925, in which spoken, character-based drama was interspersed by song-and-**dance** numbers. *Tonil* emerged as a reaction against *komedi stambul*, which was seen as overly formulaic and unable to represent the sort of weighty psychological dramas displayed in films imported from the **West**. *Tonil* is derived from the Dutch *toneel*, meaning "theatre." By the appropriation of this Dutch word for an Indonesian-language genre, *tonil*'s creators intended to demonstrate parity with the colonizer's culture.

Two touring **theatre companies, Miss Riboet**'s ORION (1925) and Dardanella (1926), quickly established themselves at the forefront of this movement, attracting mass audiences from all races and classes. Both companies mined recent movie hits for plots and engaged **Chinese**, Javanese, and Sumatran **playwrights** to write for them. While songs and dances were downplayed in dramatic scenes, Broadway show tunes, syrupy ballads, and jazz were played alongside ethnic dances of Indonesia, Hawaii, **Malaysia**, **India**, and **Thailand** as "extra numbers" between acts of the main play. Many companies featured a Charlie Chaplin imitator, and **musicians** and dancers from the **Philippines** found employment. *Tonil* **directors**, **actors**, writers, and choreographers formed the creative core for Indonesia's early film industry. A ban on Dutch words during the **Japanese** occupation (1942–1945) resulted in the formal end of *tonil* and the full emergence of *sandiwara*.

Matthew Isaac Cohen

TOPENG. Western **Indonesian** • **masked** • **dance**-theatre. Masks to impersonate characters from Hindu mythology and local legends and chronicles go back over one thousand years in Java. As masks are danced for ritual purposes among indigenous peoples of Southeast Asia, Indonesian mask performance predates Hinduism and written history. *Topeng* genres are found today in Java, Bali, Madura, and southern Kalimantan. *Topeng* is both a solo art, in which either a single masked dancer impersonates one or more characters with *gamelan* **musical** accompaniment, or an ensemble features a group of masked **actors**. Masks, generally considered sacred, require offerings and incantations.

Cirebonese **Topeng.** *Topeng* in the Cirebon area, north coastal West Java, once involved an ensemble of ten to twenty performing all-night episodes of the *Ramayana*, *Mahabharata*, and local tales. It was sometimes called *wayang wong*. It vanished with the death of its last master (1989). Today *topeng* is a daytime entertainment, sometimes called "scene-by-scene *topeng*" (*topeng babakan*), in which a soloist dances a series of masks, interspersed with clowning, pop tunes, and social dance. Some masks, for example Klana, the covetous foe of **Panji**, are presented with narration and dialogue. *Topeng* shows in the Losari region, Cirebon, regularly conclude with an hour-long play-episode with four or five actors.

Banjarese **Topeng.** Intensive exchange between southern Borneo and northern Java going back more than four hundred years resulted in *topeng*'s export to the Banjar cultural area of Kalimantan. Banjarese *topeng* still closely resembles Cirebonese *topeng* in music, **costume**, and choreography. Prior to Indonesian independence, small Cirebonese *topeng* groups toured western Java during the off-season. They performed and taught at well-to-do homes and busked at street corners and marketplaces. Locals emulated Cirebonese *topeng*, and new genres—some maskless—emerged on the north coast west of Cirebon.

Jakarta **Topeng.** *Topeng* (*topeng betawi* to outsiders) in the greater Jakarta area begins with non-narrative singing and dancing by a female singer-dancer, the *kembang* *topeng* (literally, "flower of the *topeng*"), continues with clowning and sometimes further dancing, and ends with a play in Betawi Malay. Occasionally, an incidental comic piece featuring a half-masked clown concludes the performance. Plays set during the colonial era concern bandits, cruel landlords, imperiled virgins, and the oppressed poor. Horror plays are also performed. *Betawi topeng* is roughly similar to *topeng* in Karawang (*topeng banjet* or *topeng karawang* to outsiders) and Banten, located respectively east and west of Jakarta along Java's northern littoral. Sometimes **stages** and painted **scenographic** backdrops are used, but performances are commonly arena fashion, at ground level.

Central and East Javanese* Topeng.** In Central and East Java, *topeng* usually means a solo masked dance with *gamelan* music performed as part of a dance recital. In the nineteenth century, local elites supported *wayang topeng* troupes that performed masked versions of *wayang* plays in palaces and in public **theatres** in towns and cities. A related form, *topeng dalang*, was formerly patronized by Madura's royal houses and played public theatres in eastern Java. In *wayang topeng* and *topeng dalang*, a narrator (*dalang* or *dhalang*) speaks for masked characters, except for the half-masked clowns. Theatrical versions of *topeng* are now rare in Central and East Java, although there have been some noteworthy revival attempts in Malang, formerly a major *wayang topeng* center. Masks also figure in Central and East Java in a variety of ritual dramas used to ward off harmful spirits; some are ***barong while others are *topeng*. *Topeng dongkrek*, found in Madiun, Ngawi, and Wonosari, is essentially a processional whose performers dance demonic masks to prevent plague; sometimes there are "attractions" also found in ***reog*** and *kuda kepang* ("hobbyhorse dancing"), like fire breathing, glass eating, and snake handling.

***Balinese* Topeng.** Traditionally, Bali's *topeng* fell into two main forms: "arranged" *topeng* (*topeng pajegan*) and "five (person) *topeng*" (*topeng panca*). Balinese *wayang wong* also uses masks. *Topeng pajegan* features a soloist who changes masks and shifts among ten or so characters. It is performed in temple courtyards during "anniversary" (*odalan*) **festivals**; thus the term "sacred *topeng*" (*topeng wali*). Plays are extemporized mingling Balinese and Old Javanese, with many contemporary references. Entrances and exits are through a **curtained** doorway over a bamboo frame. Performances end with the dance of Sidha Karya ("Completer of the Ceremony"), a demonic white-faced mask with a gaping mouth and protruding teeth, who scatters coin offerings, picks up children, and bridges the worlds of the play, the gods, and the profane. *Topeng panca* is performed by around five actor-dancers. The form is considered more profane than *topeng pajegan*, and "clown-servants" (*penasar*) address the audience and connect the play to current events. Ad-hoc troupes often play without rehearsals; improvisation contributes to the fun.

Many new Balinese *topeng* genres emerged in recent decades. "Mixed *topeng*" (*topeng prembon*), a humor-filled mask genre developed in the 1940s and 1950s, combines the vocal style of ***arja*** with *topeng panca*. "Dance-drama *topeng*" (*dramatari topeng*) is a scripted form emphasizing dance over dialogue, catering to tourists and non**religious** festivals. *Topeng bondres* is a recent craze, a free-for-all version of *topeng panca* playing off the "zany" (*bondres*) *topeng* characters and their anarchic humor in a send-up of traditional *topeng* along the lines of ***kethoprak*** humor. It is popular at conventions, and on television and recordings.

Performance of Balinese *topeng*. The *manis* ("refined") mask represents a noble prince. (Photo: Kathy Foley)

Topeng *Influences*. Javanese and Balinese *topeng* have inspired many performers. For example, **Rendra** used tradition-based masks and Javanese mask **training** techniques in his ritualistic *Oedipus Rex* (Oedipus sang raja, 1969). **Ikranagara** studied with Balinese *topeng* artist Tempo and, from 1972, created a series of abstract, tradition-based plays titled *Rites of the Mask* (Ritus topeng). American professor John Emigh has applied his *topeng pajegan* studies to create **politically** pointed solo works. Among others furthering *topeng* on the international scene, transgender performer Didik Nini Thowok (1954–) combines Javanese, Balinese, **Japanese**, and other traditions to create unique solo mask dances that he performs nationally and internationally.

FURTHER READING

de Zoete, Beryl, and Walter Spies. *Dance and Drama in Bali*; Dibia, I Wayan, and Rucina Ballinger. *Balinese Dance, Drama and Music: A Guide to the Performing Arts of Bali*; Emigh, John. *Masked Performance: The Play of Self and Other in Ritual and Theatre*; Yousof, Ghulam Sarwar. *Dictionary of Traditional South-East Asian Theatre*.

Matthew Isaac Cohen

TOYOTAKE WAKATAYÛ. Ten generations of chanters (*tayû*) in **Japan**'s *bunraku*. Wakatayû I (1681–1764), the most important, was also a **playwright** (as Ryô Jinken) and manager. Using the name Takemoto Uneme, he began as a disciple of **Takemoto Gidayû** I at the latter's Takemoto **Theatre** (Takemoto-za) in Osaka. When an attempt to start his own **puppet theatre** turned sour, he went on tour, returning to Osaka in 1703 to found the Toyotake Theater (Toyotake-za), using the name Toyotake Wakatayû. This established what eventually would be a rivalry with the Takemoto Theatre that would dominate eighteenth-century *bunraku* through the 1760s.

Unfortunately, business was poor so, after two years, he closed the theatre down and toured to Bitchû and elsewhere, after which he rejoined Gidayû before reopening the Toyotake at the end of 1707; his partners included the puppeteer **Tatsumatsu Hachirobei** and playwright **Ki no Kaion**; they put on one new work after the other in competition with the Takemoto Theatre. In 1718, he was given the honorary name Fujiwara Shigekatsu Kôzuke no shôjô. In 1724, when fire destroyed both puppet theatres, he performed at the Arashi Theatre (Arashi no Shibai)—calling it the New Toyotake Theatre (Shin Toyotake-za)—and serving as landlord, producer, and chief chanter. Business was slackening in 1726 when he produced *Chronicles of Hôjô Jirai* (Hôjô jirai-ki), which ran for two years and put the theatre back on its feet. In 1731, he received yet another honorary name, Fujiwara Shigeyasu Echizen no shôjô. He retired in 1745, devoting himself to management. A year after his death, the Toyotake Theatre was forced by financial problems to shut down.

He and Gidayû I had a similar style, but Wakatayû, renowned for his exquisite voice and brilliant **musicality**, developed his own approach, considered more complex and theatrically colorful than the drier, more psychologically oriented *gidayû* style. His was called the "eastern style" (*higashi fû*) in contrast to the Takemoto's "western style" (*nishi fû*).

Scholars question whether the chanter known as Wakatayû III was actually a member of the line, thereby casting doubt on the number of artists who should be counted in the genealogy.

Samuel L. Leiter

TOYOTAKE YAMASHIRO NO SHÔJÔ (1878–1967).
Chanter (*tayû*) of **Japan**'s *bunraku* **puppet theatre**. Born in Tokyo, unlike most chanters, who are from Osaka, he nevertheless was recognized as the leading chanter of his time. When he was three, he became a pupil of *kabuki* • actor Kataoka Gadô III (later, **Kataoka Nizaemon** X), debuting as Kataoka Itchô. At seven, he began to study puppet theatre chanting with a Tokyo chanter and *shamisen* player, and in 1887 became a disciple of Takemoto Tsukadayû V (?–1899), becoming Kotsukadayû and performing at a variety house (*yose*).

He moved to Osaka in 1889 and studied with Takemoto Tsudayû II (later, Takemoto Tsunatayû VII, 1839–1912), being called Takemoto Tsubamedayû and making his debut at the Goryô Bunraku **Theatre** (Goryô Bunraku-za). He briefly performed at the Inari Theatre (Inari-za), where he received **training** from the *shamisen* great **Toyozawa Danpei** II. In 1899, he became Toyotake Kôtsubodayû. Following the Shôchiku Company's acquisition of *bunraku* (1909), he became Toyotake Kôtsubodayû II; that year he teamed up with *shamisen* virtuoso Tsuruzawa Seiroku III (1868–1922), who provided severe but influential training. From 1912, he was given the privilege of chanting the major dramatic scenes (*kiriba*). In 1923, he teamed up with *shamisen* player Tsuruzawa Seiroku IV (1889–1960). His fame was such that, around this time, he and the chanters Takemoto Tsudayû III (1869–1941) and Toyotake Tosadayû VI (1863–1941) were known as *bunraku*'s "three greats" (*san kyotô*).

In 1942, after Tsudayû's death, he became "company leader" (*monshita*) of the Bunraku Theatre. His honors include being made a member of the Japan Arts Academy in

1946 and his being granted the honorary name of Yamashiro no shojô by Prince Chichibu in 1947. He retired in 1959.

Samuel L. Leiter

TRAINING

Training: Cambodia

Many artists in **Cambodia**'s traditional genres continue to come from artistic families. In the countryside they inherit and learn specific roles from family members (most of whom work the land by day), and have been involved in village and temple celebrations—even if only as onlookers—since they were very young. Training tends to be concentrated in the months just prior to a certain **festival** or rite. At the Royal University of Fine Arts in Phnom Penh, the Faculty of Choreographic Arts includes departments of theatre (*lakhon niyeay*, *lakhon bassac*, *yiké*), **dance** (*robam kbach boran*, *lakhon khol*, *robam propeiny* [**folk** dance]), **puppetry** (*lakhon sbaek*), and circus arts.

Theatre students begin at about twelve, after completing primary school. Students enter the dance program by audition at around eight. The girls are typecast as potential male, female, or ogre characters; the boys as monkeys in court dance or as monkeys or giants in *lakhon khol*. After a few years, some students are selected to concentrate on folk dance. Even though the academy has been called a university once again since 1989, only in 1999 was a bachelor's degree reinstated, as before the war. From 1980 until that time, performance students could study only through the high school level. Upon graduating, they continue at the university as teachers and performers, move to the Ministry of Culture and Fine Arts' Department of Performing Arts as professional performers, or leave to work in schools, private troupes, or elsewhere.

Toni Shapiro-Phim

Training: China

Historical Background. Throughout most of **Chinese** history, training has taken place within the **theatre company** where **actors** worked, or at attached schools. Tang (618–907) Emperor Xuanzong (Minghuang; r. 712–756) had a **musical** school built in the Pear Garden (Liyuan) in his capital of Chang'an (Xi'an). His aim was more to teach Buddhist songs than theatrical, but so famous did the school become that even today actors are called "children of the Pear Garden." In the Yuan dynasty (1280–1368) and later, acting families passed their skills down generation to generation, and troupes added to the skills of those brought in from outside. This system was still prevalent after single-gender troupes became the norm in the Ming dynasty (1368–1644). Individuals could train their own staff or have them trained. When author-bibliophile He Liangjun (1506–1573) became ill, to amuse himself he personally taught his houseboys to perform, but he also hired a famous musician to teach his mansion's slave girls.

Master-Disciple System. By the eighteenth century it had become common for actors or managers to buy small boys on contract. Each boy would then attend a "training school" (*keban*) attached to the troupe and/or become disciple to a master. Existence was miserable, despite recorded exceptions. These schools and the master-disciple system existed throughout China.

As China's economy worsened in the late eighteenth century, an indenture system became prevalent, feeding demand from Beijing's rising ***jingju***. Small boys, from about seven to thirteen, were purchased on contract from their fathers. Although the contract allowed release, the price was exorbitant. The boys came from Suzhou and Yangzhou in Jiangsu Province and Anqing in Anhui Province and were taken north along the Grand Canal; training sometimes began during the journey.

In Beijing, they were delivered to schools attached to troupes, where they were taught. Most enjoyed a good standard of living, but were totally subordinate to their masters, not unlike male courtesans. The Taiping Rebellion (1851–1866) saw devastation in Jiangsu and Anhui and cut off the supply of recruits from there, but actors could still buy boys from the Beijing area.

The turn of the twentieth century and later saw major changes. Though the norm was still to attach schools to particular companies, a few independents were established. In Chengdu, Sichuan Province, ***chuanju*** star Kang Zilin (1870–1930) ran a school attached to his troupe, where he banned beatings. The indenture system did not die out until after 1949.

Beiping Private Advanced Xiqu School. Founded in Beijing (then Beiping) in 1930, the Beiping Private Advanced Xiqu School was a pioneering jingju school aimed at reforming theatre through a more rounded education than was then standard. Its motto was "Respect our profession and entertain our people."

The first two principals were **Jiao Juyin** and Jin Zhongsun, a disillusioned **politician** who devoted himself to **playwriting** and theatre education. In 1941, the school closed to prevent its takeover by pro-**Japanese** collaborationists. It had trained over three hundred students, including stars like **Li Yuru**.

Unusually, the curriculum included nontheatrical subjects: Chinese, mathematics, English, French, geography, history, and citizenship. It ran a six-year program, plus a two-year foundation course, admitting students of both sexes at about ten and training them together. Students studied six days per week and had to remain on premises; parents could visit on Sundays. There was no tuition, and the school supplied accommodation, food, and uniforms. Discipline was harsh: there were beatings for misbehavior. From Level 2, students started touring. The repertoire included traditional *jingju*, adaptations from other *xiqu* genres, and newly written items. A "Reforming Committee" oversaw all textual matters. Many stars, including **Chang Yanqiu**, "spoken drama" (*huaju*; see Playwrights and Playwriting) actors, and famous scholars were invited to teach.

Fuliancheng Training Company. The Fuliancheng (1904) was the longest-lived early jingju training company, gaining fame from the large number of actors it produced. **Mei Lanfang** and **Zhou Xinfang** performed there during their early years. The company (first named Xiliancheng) was founded by *jingju* actor Ye Chunshan (1875–1935), who began by training six students himself, but when the school flourished more tutors were employed. From 1906, public performances commenced. It became

Fuliancheng in 1912. In 1935, Ye Longzhang succeeded his father as headmaster and undertook reforms—including literacy classes and a contract with a hospital—spurred by the challenge of the Beiping Private Advanced Xiqu School. However, later that year Fuliancheng faced closure because of its sponsor's bankruptcy. Ye raised the money to run the company as his family business. Fuliancheng continued to train and perform until 1948, when civil war erupted between the communists and Nationalists.

The People's Republic of China (PRC). The PRC has established its own system of state-run training institutions. In 1950, the China Xiqu School was set up in Beijing, adding a college program in 1958 and becoming the China Xiqu Academy. Other institutions are mostly provincial-level secondary schools, teaching the main local style(s). For decades these schools allocated graduates where needed. However, the allocation system is disappearing, and the trend is for graduates to find work where they can.

Contemporary Conditions. Entry to all training institutions remains highly competitive, students undergoing auditions, health checks, and sometimes written examination. Students typically enter secondary schools at about twelve, though children who show special promise might begin training earlier. Students receive a general education as well as acting training, which has been reduced from eight to five or six years. Most college-level training includes both short-term and full degree programs. Into the 1980s, tuition was free, but fees are now in place. Students live on campus and receive much individual attention. Beatings are prohibited. Institutions are coeducational, though boys generally outnumber girls. The once crucial female impersonators are dying out, with only a few being trained.

Schools attached to particular companies are widespread; for many regional styles these are the only route to training. Some attached to larger troupes offer general education as well as actor training. However, trainees in smaller towns may be able to attend only in their spare time because compulsory general education is not available at the schools. Graduates of company schools enter the companies themselves.

Methods and Curriculum. *Xiqu* training is rigorous and progressive, involving the gradual and carefully sequential mastery of extensive techniques. Despite the growing availability of textbooks, training remains imitative, following the principle of "learning oral instructions by heart" (*kouchuan xinshou*). Major aspects include physical and vocal "basic skills" (*jiben gong*); "repertory" (*jumu*), involving learning particular roles as performed by specific actors; and ongoing experience.

"Leg skill" (*tuigong*) involves making the legs strong and flexible by exercising them through a wide variety of stretches, lifts, and straight-leg kicks. "Waist skill" (*yaogong*) focuses on the *yao*, the area from the lowest rib to the top of the pelvis, and is considered the body's "central joint" and the source and controlling factor for all movement.

Some basic physical skills are taught differently to boys and girls, with "older male" (*laosheng*) and "martial male" (*wusheng*) **role types** being standard for boys, and young, high-status women (*qingyi*, literally, "blue garments") and "sword and horse" (*daoma dan*) for girls. Students learn standing, walking, hand gestures, arm positions, weapon use, and conventional movements intended to convey specific meanings.

Particular role types are studied for their use of fans, "water sleeves" (*shuixiu*), beards, headdress feathers, and so forth. Numerous other physical techniques, including acrobatics, are part of the intense training.

Vocal skills are equally arduous, beginning with exercises to build vocal strength and explore placement, resonating areas, and pitch control, and progressing to singing skills.

The training is carefully calibrated, year by year, with students gradually being assigned role types, learning the leading role in one to three plays per semester, and performing them in full **costume** and **makeup** with live orchestra, as dress rehearsals or "report performances" (*huibao yanchu*). The roles get progressively more difficult over time. The goal is for actors to internalize performance skills so that they can later instinctively apply them to new plays.

Training of Other Artists. Training schools are designed primarily to train actors. As training progresses, however, a number of students "change profession" as strengths and weaknesses become apparent. Classes for musicians and costume, makeup, and designers are therefore offered at most institutions; college-level academies also offer programs for **directors**, **playwrights**, teachers, and researchers. Most changes in profession occur during the second and third years of secondary training. Because their voices change and may no longer be suitable for acting, more boys switch than girls, and some even switch after graduating.

Kunqu ***Training since 1949.*** In 1921, a *kunqu* school was established in Suzhou, halting *kunqu*'s demise by training sixty boys from poor families. In 1954, twelve members of this generation made up the core faculty of a *kunqu* training class, which became part of the Shanghai Xiqu School (1955). In 1954, sixty students aged ten to twelve selected from two thousand applicants began training. The Shanghai school combined traditional training with a middle school curriculum that concluded each day's formal training. Fifty-four graduates formed the Shanghai Kunqu Troupe (1961).

The rigorous training system remains the same now as then, lasting four or five years. At graduation, a student may know as many as twenty plays.

Colin Mackerras, Elizabeth Wichmann-Walczak, Ruru Li, and Catherine Swatek

Modern Training. Modern training began at the same time as the introduction of **Western** theatre. The first school that trained "civilized drama" (*wenming xi*, a form leading to modern "spoken drama" [*huaju*]) performers was the Tongjian School (1907), founded in Shanghai by Ma Xiangbo and Wang Zhongsheng (1884?–1911). It emphasized teaching drama through practical experience. In September 1907, the school, now called the Spring Sun Society (Chunyang She), staged an adaptation of *Uncle Tom's Cabin* at the Lyceum Theatre. The school survived for only six months, but produced the first generation of modern talents, including actor Wang Youyou (1888–1937).

The Beijing Renyi Theatre School (1922) is considered the first professional modern training institution. It promoted mixed-gender casting and offered a three-year professional program modeled after Western methods, with courses in acting, movement, theatre history, dramaturgy, **scenography**, and music theory. The National Theatre School (1935), founded in Nanjing, was headed by **Yu Shangyuan**. It combined acting training and education in literature and art. Major theatrical figures lectured there.

The Nankai New Drama Company (Nankai Xinjutuan, NNDC, 1914) at the Nankai School, was one of the earliest amateur **theatre companies** within an academic institution that trained theatre artists. Against a prevalence of casual improvisations at the time, the NNDC stressed the importance of playwriting. During its forty years, the company established a renowned repertoire, including *A Momentary Lapse* (Yi nian cha, 1916) and *The New Village Head* (Xin cunzheng, 1918). Among those emerging from the school was **Cao Yu**, *huaju* pioneer.

In 1950, the Central Academy of Drama (CAD) was founded by the Ministry of Culture in Beijing. In 1952, CAD's Eastern China campus was established in Shanghai. The school became the Shanghai Theatre Academy (STA, 1956).

Both CAD and STA hosted Soviet experts, invited by the government in the 1950s, who taught the Stanislavski System and helped build curricula based on the Russian programs, which influenced modern theatre over the next few decades. Today, CAD offers undergraduate and graduate programs in acting, **directing**, dramatic literature, theatre studies, design, broadcasting, and arts administration. In 2003, CAD became a nationally accredited postdoctoral institution. STA is currently divided into departments of acting, directing, dramatic literature, design, television, *xiqu*, **dance**, public education, and continuing education. Both schools offer continuing education programs for professionals and acting classes for ethnic minorities. Many commencement performances of STA and CAD have played significant roles in *huaju*'s development.

Although the emergence of provincial arts colleges and theatre programs in universities in recent years has diversified theatre training, CAD and STA remain the most distinguished and influential training institutions.

FURTHER READING

Mackerras, Colin, ed. *Chinese Theatre from Its Origins to the Present Day.*

Nan Zhang

Training: Hong Kong

Professional training in **Hong Kong** is provided by the School of Drama of the Hong Kong Academy for Performing Arts (APA), established in 1985. The programs include **acting**, **directing**, and **playwriting**. After two successful rounds of competitive auditions and an interview, in addition to satisfactory secondary school results, candidates are accepted into the two-year diploma course, after which they either pursue the advanced diploma by spending an extra two years (followed by an optional one-year professional diploma), or enter straight into three-year bachelor's of fine arts programs.

In addition to classes and workshops, the training emphasizes productions in Cantonese. The School of Drama produces around seven shows per academic year for the general public, including both local and Chinese plays and world drama. As the APA is a multidiscipline institution that includes the School of Dance, Music and Technical Arts, its productions are platforms where the schools collaborate.

The total number of students in drama and technical arts is approximately 220; about fifty graduate yearly. Graduates generally find work in the local theatre, the media, and films; some continue their training overseas. Recent years have seen both the musical theatre and Cantonese opera introduced into the curriculum as electives. From 2001, the school and local theatres have collaborated further, including drama-in-education courses in response to the growing need in the primary and secondary sectors.

Some local professional **theatre companies** offer training sporadically but on a much lesser scale.

Hardy Tsoi

Training: India

Traditional Theatre. In traditional **Indian** theatre, training starts at a very young age and the student **actor** becomes part of the chain of the unique "teacher-student relationship" (*guru-sishya-parampara*) where the student undergoes a period of apprenticeship, ideally residing with the guru. Perseverance and perfectionism are traditional theatre's two cornerstones. Repetition is its breath and devotion its guiding light. Mastering the techniques requires time and patience, since these generally involve a high degree of sophistication and extra-daily balance.

Bharata's ancient *Treatise on Drama* (Natyashastra; see Theory) spends several chapters on movement and body postures, but about training all it says is that one has to perform exercises on the floor and in the air and that the body should be massaged with oil or barley gruel. It also emphasizes the importance of nourishing and medicating the body to maintain its vitality and health, leaving the methodology to the teacher's wisdom. However, a close observation of Bharata's verses reveals that Ayurvedic and Yogic understandings of the body have crept into training.

The training's stringency also depends on the extent of stylization that each form requires in its acting or **dancing**. In this sense, *kutiyattam* and *kathakali* training involve long years of pain, patience, and devotion, as compared to, for example, *tamasha*. The main object of *kathakali*, *chhau*, *bharata natyam*, or *kutiyattam* training is to create a "codified" body and sophisticated movement patterns that become second nature. However, the training is principally intended to cultivate a state of constant readiness for action, in order to achieve extra-daily levels of consciousness during performance. Unlike **Western** training, almost all Indian aspects, such as eye training or physical movements, are employed on **stage**. In this sense, training in traditional theatre should not be related to or equated with warm-up processes in Western theatre.

Students of *kutiyattam* or *kathakali* start their day at 3:30 or 4 a.m. They begin with eye and face exercises and slowly move on to movement exercises. *Kutiyattam* students also undergo voice training. Both *kutiyattam* and *kathakali* students normally have an oil massage to add flexibility to their movements. The movement patterns of *chhau*, *kathakali*, and *kutiyattam* are based largely on martial art techniques, particularly **kalarippayattu**. Certain other forms employ **thang-ta**.

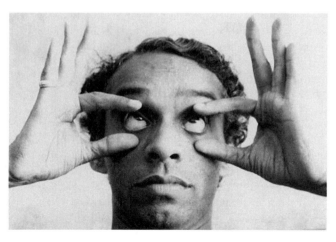

M. P. Sankaran Namboodiri of the Kerala Kalamandalam demonstrates preliminary eye exercises. (Photo: Phillip Zarrilli)

If learning the skill is the basic tenet of the forms mentioned above, learning the role is central to *raslila*, while voice training is important to **nautanki**. A *nautanki* student is instructed to sing into a large earthen jar or inside a temple with a domed ceiling so that he can hear his own voice and train it to attain perfection. Learning songs and rhythms from a close family relative forms the major training that students of ritual forms like **teyyam** must receive. The central tenets of dance training are rhythm and movement.

Arya Madhavan

Training Overview. Actor training institutions in India are relatively scarce. The important training establishments are either (1) mainly state or national government funded; (2) partly private funded with state government support; or (3) mainly private funded. There are also **theatre companies** and **directors** that train actors during the regular course of company development. In addition, an assortment of other training providers are workshop or event related. Occasionally, foreign artists arrive to offer their special approaches.

Training, in general, is related to desired outcomes, which means that while the educational institutions offer a cross-section of Indian and non-Indian methodology and practice, other academies are focused on specific forms (the Kerala Kalamandalam trains performers only in *kathakali* and *mohiniattam* ["dance of the enchantress," a Keralese dance form], Margi in *kutiyattam*, and Udupi in **yakshagana**); companies also tend to have a dominant—often regionally inspired—style, although since they are often led by experienced directors, this is not necessarily exclusive. In many cases across the board, training is inspired, founded by, or led by, a major director or writer; since Indian forms rely heavily on physical, rhythmic, and **musical** skills, this is often in conjunction with other key figures who provide particular input. The ethos of the teacher-disciple tradition and of a devotional degree of commitment still usually applies, even where company training takes place after or alongside other occupations, which is frequent. In the training establishments themselves, dedication is expected, although in the relative sophistication of New Delhi and with the main focus of many of its students oriented toward television and film work, the National School of Drama is a good deal less "monastic" than more rural institutions.

FURTHER READING

Zarrilli, Phillip B. *When the Body Becomes All Eyes: Paradigms, Practices, and Discourses of Power in Kalarippayattu*; Zarrilli, Phillip B. *The Psychophysical Actor at Work—Acting "... at the nerve ends."*

Ralph Yarrow

Training: Indonesia

Indonesia has six highly influential government-run arts training institutions founded by the Department of Education and Culture beginning in the 1960s in order to preserve the traditional arts. While critics have argued that their establishment has led to unwanted standardization of forms, they have also resulted in the preservation and popularization of forms that would otherwise have disappeared.

Of the six schools, only three provide training specifically in theatre. Jakarta Institute of the Arts, established in 1977, provides the most intensive professional-level training in contemporary **acting** and **directing** for approximately forty students. The school offers a three-year diploma course, with an optional four-year BA in theatre. Graduates generally find work in local **theatre companies**, television, film, or in cultural centers around the country; almost none go overseas to further their training.

Other arts academies tend to concentrate on training for traditional **dance** and theatre. For example, Bandung's Indonesia College of the Arts concentrates on the preservation and innovation of the Sundanese performing arts, offering programs in traditional dance, **music**, and theatre. This school, a former high-school level conservatory, became the Academy of Traditional Dance (1970), and, in 1995, was promoted to its current college level. Similarly, academies in Denpasar (Bali), Surakarta, Yogyakarta (Central Java), and Padangpanjang (West Sumatra) focus on teaching the traditional performing arts of their respective regions. Private training in traditional dance and music is also widely available; moreover, Jakarta is home to a private acting studio, the Sakti Actors' Studio.

Eka D. Sitorus

Training: Japan

Traditional Forms. **Zeami Motokiyo** wrote in *Treatise on the Flower* (Kadensho, 1418) that **actor** training usually began at seven, but most traditional performers start at a much younger age, debuting sometimes at three or four. These actors are born into acting families where they are instructed by their fathers or other relatives; most traditional performing arts remain hereditary professions. Training is generally restricted to boys for ***kabuki*** (there have been several exceptions), but some ***nô*** actors also train their daughters, **women** having been allowed to perform *nô* professionally since 1949, although this remains uncommon. Training is broad but with a particular attention to the family's specialty. Thus a *nô* actor whose family specializes in *shite* roles (see Role Types) would also study *nô*'s **musical** instruments, but most training would prepare them to take *shite* roles and to sing in the chorus.

Instead of learning exercises, traditional performers study actual pieces or parts of plays before mastering an entire work. **Dance** and musical passages can be learned by studying their discrete "patterns" (*kata*), the building blocks for these. Each dance or musical *kata*, composed of a series of movements or musical phrases, has a name; by mastering a *kata*, students develop a vocabulary that serves as the basis for learning more advanced pieces. The essential method is "seeing and learning" (*minarai*), followed in all traditional forms. Thus growing up in the world of a traditional art is the best way to learn.

Actors study works of increasing difficulty appropriate to their age, passing through one or more "graduation pieces." For ***kyôgen*** performers, the first such piece is *The Monkey Quiver* (Utsubozaru) in which the child wears a monkey **mask** and **costume** and acts in unison with another performer. For *nô*, *Dôjô-ji Temple* (Dôjô-ji), in which the actor must leap inside a falling temple bell suspended over the **stage**, serves as a similar test of mettle. Successful completion of such pieces marks entry into professional standing, and actors continue to challenge themselves by other works throughout their life. Middle-aged *kyôgen* actors can aspire to play the fox in *Catching the Fox* (Tsurigitsune), while senior *nô* performers may act in difficult old women roles like *Komachi at the Gravesite* (Sotoba Komachi).

Training of amateurs provides a major source of income for professional *nô* and *kyôgen* performers. Like professionals, amateurs start by learning portions of plays such as the dances and eventually work up to an entire piece. Some talented amateurs who begin their studies early can become professionals, although they may never be able to perform parts restricted to influential dynasties.

The traditional way aspiring professionals (from actors to **puppeteers** to musicians) in all genres gained training was to become a live-in disciple of a teacher, even if that sometimes meant being adopted by an artist who had no son (or none either talented or interested enough to pursue his father's art). Many artists—especially *bunraku* puppeteers and musicians—have recounted the harsh treatment they received under these circumstances, while acknowledging the value of such training. Today, performing arts universities provide training for students who lack a familial connection to the traditional arts but desire to become professionals. After graduation, students continue their studies with professionals. The National **Theatre**s (Kokuritsu Gekijô) in Tokyo and Osaka provide similar training in *kabuki* and *bunraku*, respectively. In contrast to other arts, nearly all professional *bunraku* artists train in the National Theatre program since, unlike *nô*, *kyôgen*, and *kabuki*, it is not a hereditary occupation.

Eric C. Rath

Modern Theatre. As noted above, in traditional Japanese theatre, the fundamental method of actor training was "seeing and learning." ***Shinpa*** and ***shinkokugeki*** also generally followed traditional patterns.

Female parts in *kabuki* had been played by men for over two centuries when women were first allowed on **stage** (1890). The consequent necessity for actress-training was first addressed by **Kawakami Sadayakko**, who, with her spouse, **Kawakami Otojirô**, founded Japan's first acting school, the Imperial Actress Training School (1908), to prepare women for the modern commercial theatre, including **Western**-style singing and dancing. The most thorough, long-lasting women's training program has been that of the musical revue form, **Takarazuka**.

The first comprehensive facility to provide mixed training for *shingeki* was **Tsubouchi Shôyô**'s Literary Arts Society (Bungei Kyôkai, 1909), offering, beyond theatre history and **theory**, practice in a declamatory delivery style retaining elements of *kabuki* diction. The Tsukiji Little Theatre (Tsukiji **Shôgekijô**, 1924) founders focused attention on training the body, initially utilizing Dalcroze eurhythmics, a popular European body-control method, but the acting school they envisioned never materialized. The proletarian Vanguard Theatre (Zen'ei-za) founded its own Drama Study Center (1927), emphasizing Marxist theory. In the early 1930s, Iwata Toyoo (1893–1969) found running a *shingeki* acting school frustrating because teachers of practical techniques were rare. Contemporary *shingeki* actors depended mainly on **directors'** instructions during rehearsal.

The Actors' Theatre (Haiyû-za), acknowledging the acute need for postwar training, established its own Actor's School in 1949. It produced a generation of *shingeki* actors, heavily influenced by **Senda Koreya**'s commitment to a modified Stanislavski System.

Other *shingeki* companies relied on regular studio performances to give their new members, called "research students" (*kenkyûsei*), experience. By the mid-1960s, several schools were operating in Tokyo. The ***angura***/*shôgekijô* movement, however, required more intense physicality; accordingly, several directors instituted tough physical training programs de-emphasizing theoretical knowledge. Most famous is **Suzuki Tadashi**, whose Suzuki Method emphasizes complete control of legs and feet. This is the principal modern Japanese training system with an international influence; it is taught in many countries, and is especially widespread in the United States.

Although since the 1960s many acting schools have operated in Tokyo, they have prepared actors not only for the stage but also for film and television. Most *shôgekijô* groups have relied on personal training by their director-playwright leaders, such as the prerehearsal warm-ups conducted by **Noda Hideki**, but in some cases this has been very limited. Recently, **Hirata Oriza** has attracted attention with his workshops (also given internationally), where a central objective is freeing the participants' imagination.

Brian Powell

Training: Korea

Traditional Theatre. Training in **Korean** traditional performing arts, ***p'ansori*** and **dance**, for example, still relies on the one-on-one, master-pupil system common throughout Asia. However, traditional performance curricula at performing arts high schools and select universities, such as the Korean National University of the Arts, offer training, as do university traditional dance and **masked • dance** clubs, regional schools teaching local forms, such as *hahoe pyŏlshin-gut*, and contemporary **theatre companies**, such as the Beauty and Ugliness Company (Kŭkdan Michoo), where traditional dance, **music** and masked-dance techniques anchor contemporary training.

Modern Theatre. As for the modern theatre, **Western** training methods were introduced to Korea decades ago (mostly interpretations of Stanislavski), but, as **experimental** or presentational methods developed alongside realism in the 1960s, small theatre companies began "in-house" training to inculcate the desired approach. Training at the National Drama Company (Kungnip Kŭkdan), for example, has favored a realistic style, while **Oh T'ae-sŏk**'s Raw Cotton (Mokhwa) Repertory Theatre Company style is demandingly psycho-physical, and **Lee Yun-t'aek** promulgates an approach based on what he deems unique qualities of Korean breathing and movement.

University Training Programs. Many university programs are rather new, and most have not yet developed training methods matched to the varying demands of the live theatre and electronic media. There is more general theatre education than **actor**-specific training. With few exceptions (the School of Drama, Korean National University of the Arts, among them), university programs rely mostly on part-time teachers, piecing together elements from traditional forms and unassimilated techniques from Asia and the West as they seek a philosophy of training. The role of voice/speech and movement in training generally is vague, and classes in new programs often are taught by **directors** unfamiliar with or disdainful of acting pedagogy. Despite the obstacles, exciting work *is* evident in university programs, but the popularity of television dramas diminishes student interest in live theatre; university training will be challenged to adjust. Some emerging private studios, such as the Kim Dong-su Actors' Studio in Seoul, directly reflect market demand, offering scene study and film/television technique taught by a recognized actor.

Musical Theatre Training. Universities do not offer the intensive, in-depth training needed to best stage Western **musicals** and Western-style Korean musicals; the Seoul Performing Arts Company (Seoul Yesultan), however, offers ongoing musical theatre training to its company and in its feeder school. Still, Korean singers and dancers generally need much more training in acting, dance, and musical theatre vocal techniques if the form is to mature.

Design and Technical Training. As for designers and technicians, quality training in **scenography** has been available for decades in select schools, such as the Seoul Institute of the Arts, and graduates of such programs usually seem better trained than actors of the same age. However, training lags in technical production, lighting, and related areas, hampered by incommodious theatres, few appropriate construction shops, and a paucity of trained technical production mentors.

Richard Nichols

Training: Malaysia

Formal training in the performing arts is a fairly recent phenomenon in **Malaysia**. While dramatists such as **Syed Alwi** and **Noordin Hassan** were educated or exposed to theatre in the United Kingdom or United States, and theatre scholars received their education either locally or abroad, academic training in the performing arts began in 1970 when Universiti Sains Malaysia established the Arts Centre. The Centre offers theatre, **music**, and **dance** programs at undergraduate and graduate levels. Now, almost all local universities offer a performing arts program, or, at the least, basic drama courses.

Through its School of Malay Language, Literature, and Culture Studies, the National University of Malaysia offers theatre courses. The University of Malaya has a Faculty of Culture, offering dance, theatre, and music programs. University Sarawak Malaysia has a Performing Arts Faculty aimed at professionalism in theatre, film, and television. MARA University of Technology also has a Performing Arts Faculty, currently offering courses in theatre, dance, film, and music at a diploma level, but soon to be elevated to the bachelor's level. In 1994, the then Ministry of Culture, Arts, and Tourism established the National Arts Academy, aimed at formally training students in theatre (traditional and modern), dance, and music. Training is also provided by **theatre companies** such as the Actors' Studio, Five Arts Centre, Suasana Dance Company, Sutra Dance Company, and Temple of Fine Arts.

Some universities offer courses in traditional theatre, sometimes employing traditional practitioners, especially in ***bangsawan***, ***mak yong***, and *wayang* (see Puppet Theatre). Still, traditional theatre does not have its own training institution. The norm for slowly dying forms continues to be master artists teaching new artists through the arduous and uncertain apprentice system.

Solehah Ishak

Training: Philippines

There are three types of theatre training in the **Philippines**: formal training undertaken in schools; informal training, through workshops and seminars; and apprenticeships.

Three universities, the University of the Philippines (UP), the Ateneo de Manila University, and Mindanao State University offer a bachelor's degree in theatre arts. In addition, UP, the first university to offer a theatre program (spearheaded by Antonio Mabesa), offers a two-year certificate course and a master's degree. De La Salle University-College of St. Benilde, Manila, differs from other universities because instead of offering a bachelor's in theatre, it offers degree programs in arts management, production design, and technical theatre. The only high school offering theatre courses is the Philippine High School for the Arts.

Short-term training through workshops, especially during the summer (April and May), is offered mainly by **theatre companies**. Among those regularly offering workshops on children's theatre, teen theatre, **musical** theatre, **playwriting**, **acting**, and **directing** are Filipino Stage (Tanghalang Pilipino), the resident company of the Cultural Center of the Philippines; Repertory Philippines; the Philippine Educational Theater Association (PETA); and New Voice Theatre Company. In the 1970s and 1980s, PETA was also instrumental in giving workshops to communities, thus enabling them to use theatre in articulating their conditions, needs, and issues. Similarly, theatre and film directors such as Ishmael Bernal, Joel Lamangan, and Joonee Gamboa also have worked extensively with poor, urban community groups, workers' groups, and regional groups.

The oldest form of training, however, is apprenticeship. The epic chanter (*binukot*), for example, learns styles and techniques from other *binukot*s. Ritual **dancers** in indigenous communities learn by observation and participation. Performers of **religious** dramas such as ***sinakulo*** and "Easter Vigil" (*salubong*) in communities learn either through their directors or through those who have earlier played the roles. Today, the most respected apprenticeship program is provided by Filipino Stage, whose salaried members undergo intensive training. Other large troupes provide similar training to members.

Joi Barrios

Training: Taiwan

Modern Methods. Modern **actors** come from a wide range of institutions and methods, ranging from universities to workshops run by individual **theatre companies**. Training employs both realistic and nonrealistic methods including **experimental** and improvisational approaches. During the **Japanese** colonization period (1895–1945), a performing style called "new drama" (*xinju*) appeared. *Xinju*'s illusionist and mimetic skills were passed on orally from master to disciple, imitating realistic **Western** theatre (filtered through Japan) dealing with topics of immediate relevance. After the Nationalists took over (1949), most actors and their masters were affiliated with the entertainment and **political** propaganda sections of the armed forces. Institutionalized formal actor training did not start until 1962, when **Lee Man-kuei** founded the first major producing agency and actor-training organization, the Spoken Drama Committee.

A large number of **directors** and scholars (such as **Ma Sen** and **Lai Sheng-chuan**) returned to Taiwan from the West in the 1970s and 1980s. Their experimentalist tendencies, emphasizing improvisation and audience participation, influenced the training of the next generations.

Taipei National University of Arts offers bachelor's of fine arts, master's of fine arts, and PhD programs in theatre. National Taiwan University and Chinese Cultural University also offer undergraduate and graduate programs. In addition, troupes such as Creative Society (Chuangzuo She, 1997), U Theatre (You Juchang, 1988), and Pingfeng Performance Troupe (Pingfeng Biaoyan Ban) also hold regular workshops or year-long training programs according to their own distinct styles.

Alexander C. Y. Huang

Training: Thailand

With the inspiration of **Sodsai Pantoomkomol** and **Mattani Rutnin Mojdara**, Chulalongkorn University and Thammasat University began offering bachelor's degrees in modern theatre in 1970 and 1978, respectively. Nowadays, their counterparts include Silpakorn University, Bangkok University, and Srinakharinwirot University. Generally modeled after those of American universities, their curricula include introductory, intermediate, and advanced classes in **acting**, **directing**, **playwriting**, and **scenographic** design; students concentrate on one for their senior projects. Courses are also offered in children's theatre, world drama, Asian theatre, **criticism**, and **stage** management.

Drama departments' annual main stage productions are mostly translations of **Western** plays. Directed and designed by instructors with casts combining students and professionals, these productions are frequently covered in national media and reviewed by professionals. However, as modern **Thai** theatre careers are scarce, most graduates apply their training to television, movies, advertising, and publishing.

Off campus, **theatre companies**, such as Dream Box (formerly DASS Entertainment), Patravadi Theatre, Theatre 8×8, B-Floor Theatre, Dream Masks, and Life Work Company, occasionally offer workshops for the general public. Some participants become company members. In addition, university instructors teach acting and writing in private schools affiliated with television companies. For example, Bangkok Drama Academy for Performing Arts, a station subsidiary, was founded by Pantoomkomol, who applied stage techniques in training actors for television dramas.

Pawit Mahasarinand

TROT. *See* Folk Theatre: Cambodia.

TSAM. *See* Mongolia.

TSUBOUCHI SHÔYÔ (1858–1935). **Japanese** novelist, **critic**, translator, **playwright**, and scholar. Tsubouchi was a reformer of fiction and *kabuki*, pioneer (with **Osanai Kaoru**) in creating *shingeki*, and founder of theatre history as a discipline in Japan. He studied English literature at Tokyo University, where he became acquainted with European fiction and drama. He started translating Shakespeare in 1884, completing his work forty-four years later. He influenced many young writers who went on to change the character of Japanese fiction.

Tsubouchi's impact on Japanese theatre was extensive. While he loved *kabuki* and was the first to recognize affinities between **Chikamatsu Monzaemon** and Shakespeare, he nevertheless believed that *kabuki* needed to broaden and modernize to maintain its vibrancy and exalted status in contemporary Japan. Recognizing that plays of the early *kabuki* reform movement in the late nineteenth century lacked psychologically realistic and compelling characters, Tsubouchi wrote his own modern *kabuki* drama, *A Paulownia Leaf* (Kiri hitoha, 1885), subtly structuring it on aspects of *Hamlet*. Finally staged in 1904, it is considered the first example of *shin kabuki*. Tsubouchi's second *shin kabuki* drama, *En the Ascetic* (En no gyôja, 1916), is his masterpiece; influenced by *The Tempest*, it is a psychological re-examination of a Buddhist saint's life.

Tsubouchi also advocated reforming classical Japanese **dance** (*nihon buyô*), the basis of *kabuki* movement. His essay, "New Theories of **Music** Drama" (Shin gakugeki-ron, 1914), and his dance-drama, *The New Urashima* (Shinkyoku Urashima, 1914), were central to this effort.

Tsubouchi's work with *kabuki* **actors** in his Shakespeare adaptations convinced him that for Japan to develop a modern, psychological, realist drama, actors would have to **train** in methods completely different from *kabuki*'s. In 1906, he founded the Literary Arts Society (Bungei Kyôkai) at Waseda University, where he taught. This is considered *shingeki*'s starting point. The group's membership included students who practiced Tsubouchi's interpretation of modern acting and elocution styles. Although teacher and students proved unable to entirely avoid *kabuki* influences, their efforts constituted the necessary first steps away from that tradition, and some of Tsubouchi's students later became leading *shingeki* actors and dramatists. Early Literary Art Society productions included *The Merchant of Venice* (1906) and *Hamlet* (1907, 1910). Ibsen's *A Doll's House* (1911), starring **Matsui Sumako** and directed by **Shimamura Hôgetsu**, was so successful that the company performed it at the Imperial Theatre (Teikoku Gekijô), the era's grandest venue.

Laurence Richard Kominz

TSUKA KÔHEI (1948–). Japanese • **playwright** and **director** who attracted **critical** attention with *The Atami Murder Case* (Atami satsujin jiken, 1974), winning the **Kishida [Kunio]** Prize. Performances sparked a "Tsuka Boom"—young people subsequently flocked to plays such as *A Stripper's Tale* (Sutorippaa monogatari, 1980) and *Fall Guy* (Kamata kôshinkyoku, 1981), seeking answers about themselves and their **political** disillusionment.

Faced with the challenge of maintaining the artistic and political energies of the 1960s' iconoclastic, often nonliterary playwrights, Tsuka carved his niche by reviving words as a legitimate theatrical vehicle, and the individual—as opposed to mere types—as a theme for drama.

A second-generation resident-**Korean** without Japanese citizenship, Tsuka uses a Japanese pen name. His plays do not directly address the socio-political issues surrounding resident-Koreans' marginalization, but his experiences of discrimination and passing as a Japanese nonetheless led Tsuka to create characters who enact life with bitter laughter, reflecting the empty spiritual and political existence of 1970s youth. *The Atami Murder Case* centers on police officers concerned only with performing to maintain their images and reputations rather than serving justice.

For My Father, Who Failed to Die in the War (Sensô de shinenakatta otôsan no tame ni, 1971) satirizes how common people identified with World War II leadership. *Revolution 101: Legend of the Hero* (Shokyû kakumei kôza hiryûden, 1972) is a scathing look at hypocrisy in 1960s leftwing politics—the characters attempt to give meaning to empty memories of their socio-political situations by playing a class-struggle game.

John D. Swain

TSURUYA NANBOKU IV (1755–1829). One of the two greatest *kabuki* • **playwrights**, the other being **Kawatake Mokuami**. The Edo (Tokyo)–born son of a dyer, Nanboku wrote more than 120 plays and also published a number of fictional tales. In his early twenties he began apprenticing to "head playwright" (*tate sakusha*) Sakurada Jisuke I (1734–1806). Applying himself steadily, Nanboku rose in his profession. In 1801, the year he became a head playwright, he took the name Nanboku IV, having previously been called Sakurada Heizô and Sawa Heizô. His father-in-law was **actor** Tsuruya Nanboku III. His grandson was playwright Nanboku V (1796–1852).

Nanboku is renowned for inventive plots and brilliant dialogue frequently delivered in the poetic rhythm of alternating lines of seven and five syllables (*shichigochô*). He is famous for a sharply realistic style that contrasts with earlier *kabuki* practice. Nanboku's realism produced a genre known as "raw" or "pure domestic plays" (*kizewa mono*). His signature work, *The Ghost Stories at Yotsuya on the Tôkaidô* (Tôkaidô Yotsuya kaidan, 1825), is representative of pieces that depict the dark side of Edo society and its population of disturbing—and fascinating—murderers, extortionists, thieves, and other such figures who came to prominence in his plays. Acutely conscious of the gulf between the ideals of an increasingly ineffective samurai ruling class and the everyday problems of poverty and crime affecting ordinary people, Nanboku and his colleagues boldly linked the premier of *The Ghost Stories* with the high-toned revenge masterpiece *Treasury of Loyal Retainers* (Kanadehon chûshingura, 1748) and its cast of model-samurai characters by presenting parts of these together on alternate days.

Spirits of the departed take the **stage** in a number of works, in addition to *The Ghost Stories*. His first "ghost play" (*kaidan mono*) was also a first great success, *The Tale of Tokubei from India* (Tenjiku Tokubei ikoku-banashi, 1804). The popularity of *Tokubei*, a fresh treatment of a story dramatized numerous times before, set the pattern for presenting ghost plays during the summer, the season of the Buddhist Obon **festival** when the souls of the dead are believed to return temporarily to the world of the living.

Ghost plays, typically about a deceased character aiming to exact revenge for past wrongs, were both the product of and the stimulus for the development of increasingly complex technical devices and performance techniques, some of them developed in collaboration with actor Onoe Matsusuke I (later, Shôroku I; 1744–1815), a master of the quick-change (*hayagawari*). As Tokubei, he made stage history when he sank into a vat of water on stage, shortly after appearing at the entrance to the "flower path" runway (*hanamichi*) as a different, and utterly dry, character. Nanboku collaborated with **scenographer** Hasegawa Kanbei XI (1777–1841), whose inventions, including the double revolving stage (*janome mawashi*), allowed for unusual stage effects.

Suggestively sexual and violent scenes—including murder and suicide—run through Nanboku's work. In *The Scarlet Princess of Edo* (Sakura-hime azuma bunshô, 1817), which Nanboku wrote for "female impersonator" (*onnagata*) Iwai Hanshirô V (1776–1847), a priest and his acolyte lover set out to commit double suicide by drowning themselves. Only the acolyte, however, dies, but he is reborn as a princess. She is reunited with the priest, who has become a leading **religious** figure. The characters take the audience with them on a fascinating and gruesome downward spiral, pushed along by lust and despair.

Even Nanboku's **dance** plays capture elements of madness, sexuality, and violence. *Yasuna* (1818) portrays a handsome youth driven crazy by despair over his lover's suicide. *Kasane* (1823) is a horrific ghost story sunk in a morass of sexual jealousy. It exemplifies the "aesthetic of cruelty" (*zankoku no bi*), the elegant portrayal of shocking behavior identified with Nanboku's work.

Some *kabuki* actors are virtuosos at playing multiple roles within a single work. Nanboku provided a major vehicle in *The Scandalous Love of Osome and Hisamatsu* (Osome Hisamatsu ukina no yomiuri, 1813) in which the star plays seven different characters, using up to thirty changes. Borrowing a story already dramatized by others, he transplanted to Edo the story of Osome, daughter of a merchant family, and Hisamatsu, son of a samurai family who has become one of her father's apprentices in an effort to find his family's lost sword. Nanboku replaced the story's conventional double-suicide ending with an upbeat conclusion in which Hisamatsu kills his enemy, gets back the sword, and begins a new life with Osome.

FURTHER READING

Brandon, James R., and Samuel L. Leiter, eds. *Kabuki Plays on Stage: Darkness and Desire;* Keene, Donald. *World within Walls.*

Barbara E. Thornbury

TUONG. **Vietnamese** "operatic" genre, a.k.a. *hat boi* in the southern regions. It probably has its roots in **Chinese** • *jingju*, but has developed its own distinctive conventions since the tenth century, when the Vietnamese successfully repelled a thousand years of Chinese domination.

Historical Background. Records documenting court performances date back to the Ly dynasty (1010–1225), when **actors** were first acknowledged as court functionaries. These simple comic performances gradually evolved into more sophisticated productions, depicting heroic battles, foolish mandarins, and stories of great kings.

Legend suggests that *jingju* was informally introduced in 1285, when captured Mongolian soldier-actor Li Yuanji **trained** court actors in its conventions. Despite official discrimination against theatre—and a ban on court performances—for its corrupting influence, *tuong*'s synthesis of stylized acting, singing, **dancing**, acrobatics, **music**, and pageantry allowed the form to survive.

Tuong advocate Dao Duy Tu (1572–1634) used his **political** leverage to build support for royal performances. Prohibited from taking examinations for public office, Dao moved south, where he assisted the Nguyen viceroys and encouraged them to support *tuong* for its values as a medium of recreation and traditional morality. Yet it was not until the nineteenth century that *tuong* became respected and institutionalized under the Nguyen kings. In the mid-1800s, the Nguyen lords encouraged the development of royal performance art and supported **playwrights** such as Dao Tan (1845–1926), poet, **director**, and **critic**, who wrote or revised more than forty plays.

Themes. Common themes depicted feudal life and extolled Confucian virtues, stressing the importance of righteousness, justice, filial piety, and loyalty to one's superiors, while exposing corruption, greed, and cruelty among the powerful. Most plays tended to be of epic scope, emphasizing conflicts between love and hate, will and duty; heroes managed to triumph through amazing deeds and extraordinary courage, all expressed through a fusion of heroic language and song, accompanied by traditional musical instruments.

Under French colonialism (1884–1954), themes became more **Westernized**, emphasizing romantic love and idealized historic scenes. During the early 1900s, adaptations of French classics, such as Corneille's *Le Cid* and translations of Molière, were enormously popular with the colonists and the Vietnamese bourgeoisie.

Postcolonial Developments. After 1954, once the French had been expelled, the Ho Chi Minh (1890–1969) government began supporting *tuong* as part of its efforts to restore and preserve Vietnamese cultural identity. Many historical pieces were adapted

The *tuong* play *The Female General Dao Tam Xuan*, produced by the National Tuong Company at the Hong Ha Theatre, Hanoi, Vietnam, December 2002. (Photo: Gerry Herman)

to focus on patriotic struggles in plays such as *The Call of the Country* (Tieng goi non song), *The Way Back to Lam Son* (Duong ve Lam Son), and *De Tham*, named for a hero of anti-French resistance and performed over five hundred times.

Despite its efforts to revive and preserve traditional *tuong* by focusing on more contemporary themes, stories, and characters, even today Vietnam's National Tuong Company (Nha Hat Tuong Trung Uong, 1959) struggles to attract audiences and to develop more contemporary libretti in competition with the mass media market.

Conventions. Ironically, *tuong*'s struggle for audiences is perhaps also limited by its greatest aesthetic value—its distinctive symbolic staging, which integrates sophisticated acrobatic and operatic conventions that seem foreign and archaic to most young Vietnamese. Elaborately painted **makeup** gives clues to a character's personality, motives, and social class, as do various beard designs, **costumes**, and gestures. **Properties** are also highly symbolic; for example, a specially colored whip can signify a horse's type as well as its rider's status. Movement is complex and technically rigorous; actors combine stylized gesture, dance, and acrobatics to convey motives, social status, and emotions. These elements, accompanied by traditional wind, string, and percussion music, convey mood and setting, while also punctuating the action and songs. The onstage orchestra emphasizes gestures with cymbals and tambourines, and reaches its crescendo during acrobatic duels of great warriors.

FURTHER READING

Brandon, James R. *Theatre in Southeast Asia*; Dinh Quang et al. *Vietnamese Theater*.

Lorelle Browning

U KYIN U (1819?–?). Burmese (Myanmar) **playwright** active during the reign of King Bagyidaw (r. 1819–1837). The Burmese "dramatist's dramatist," he was familiar with drama as both performance and literature. His dialogue and songs were rhymed. Although not highborn, he was learned, famous for his elegant language. Nevertheless, he wrote in a way that anyone could understand; his works remain popular, partly because they deal with still-interesting issues of human relationships. These were written as scenarios, their words added in the course of production, which he probably **directed**; they were meant for performance, not publication, although they were widely read. Some believe he was made a nobleman for his services.

U Kyin U wrote many plays of fantasy and myth, although only three appear to survive. Two dramatized Buddha's birth stories (*jataka*), *Mahaw* (Ma-haw-thada zat), in which the Buddha-to-be is a wise minister, and *Wey-than-daya* (Wey-than-daya zat), where the Buddha-to-be is a charitable king. His plays were performed only at court. He is said to have written the non-*jataka*-derived *Deva-kon-bon* (Deva-kon-ban zat), with a somewhat ambivalent hero, at the urging of Crown Prince Tharyarwaddy, Bagyidaw's younger brother, to reveal the **political** intrigues of Bagyidaw's queen, Mai Nu, and her brother, U Oh. Its dialogue and story are well constructed, precise, and eloquent. In his non-*jataka* masterpiece, *Parpahein* (Parpahein zat), he offered the unusual device of its hero—supposedly based on U Oh—possessing villainous tendencies. Among U Kyin U's drawbacks is the absence of memorable females and comic characters in his work.

Ma Thanegi

UMEWAKA MINORU. Two Japanese • *nô* • actors. A year after the fall of the Tokugawa military government (1868), the head of the Kanze school (*ryû*) left Tokyo with the ex-shogun for Shizuoka Prefecture, leaving Minoru I (1828–1909) in charge of the school's affairs. Lacking the old regime's patronage, Minoru I struggled to preserve *nô* by performing first on a practice **stage** in his home and later for the imperial family and greater public. Although he predicted the art's demise, Minoru I, along with **Hôshô Kurô XVI** and **Sakurama Banma,** was recognized as one of *nô*'s three Meiji period (1868–1912) stars. One of the first to teach *nô* to **Westerners,** his students included Japan scholars Edward Morse (1838–1925) and Ernest Fenollosa (1855–1908).

After Minoru I's death, the Umewaka came into conflict with the head of the Kanze school over the authority to issue licenses to amateurs and to receive payments for doing so. In 1921, Minoru II (1878–1959), Minoru I's son, and several prominent actors broke away from the Kanze to create the Umewaka school, which published its own "*nô* libretti" (*utaibon*) and issued its own licenses. However, the new school encountered difficulties, since other performers refused to appear with them. The Umewaka school persisted until 1954, when Minoru II recognized the authority of the Kanze "family head" (*iemoto*) and returned to the Kanze fold.

Eric C. Rath

UNO NOBUO (1904–1991). Japanese • playwright, critic, *rakugo* (see Storytelling) artist, screenwriter, opera librettist, essayist, and novelist. A Tokyo native, Uno began writing *shingeki* plays while attending Keio University. His first successful *shin kabuki* effort was *Blizzard Pass* (Fubuki tôge, 1933), written for *kabuki* • actor • **Ichikawa Sadanji** II. The same year, Uno wrote a successful piece for **Onoe Kikugorô** VI.

Uno's *shin kabuki* plays, characterized by sentimental love themes, humor, and careful attention to social context, season, and locale, include *Grandpa, Grandma* (Jiisan baasan, 1951), *A Blind Man's Tale* (Mômoku monogatari, 1957), and *The Tale of Lady Ochikubo* (Ochikubo monogatari, 1959). Like many of his plays, they were inspired by important works of fiction, the first two by, respectively, **Mori Ôgai** and **Tanizaki Jun'ichirô** short stories, the last by a Heian-period (794–1185) tale. *Grandpa, Grandma,* frequently performed, presents the reunion after twenty-eight years of a faithful old samurai couple following the husband's release from prison. *A Blind Man's Tale* describes the unrequited love of a blind masseur for the wife of the late-sixteenth-century warlord Toyotomi Hideyoshi. Uno converted *Lady Ochikubo,* Japan's Cinderella story, into a ribald comedy.

Uno also reworked Edo-period (1603–1868) classics. Best known is his 1953 adaptation of **Chikamatsu Monzaemon**'s 1703 **puppet** play, *The Love Suicides at Sonezaki* (Sonezaki shinjû).

Laurence Richard Kominz

U PONNYA (1807–1866). Burmese (Myanmar) **playwright,** also known as Sa-le U Ponnya because his hometown was Sa-le. He entered the Buddhist Sangha order at eight and made a name in both writing and astrology. Astrology is forbidden for members of the Sangha so he returned to secular life in his late twenties, serving as a composer to Crown Prince Kanaung (1819–1866), younger brother to King Mindon (r. 1853–1878). His most famous plays are *Pa-du-ma* (Pa-du-ma zat, 1855), the story of an adulterous **woman;** *Wi-za-ya* (Wi-za-ya zat, ca. 1865), the story of a rebellious son; and *The Water Seller* (Yay-the zat, 1856). Prince Kanaung had asked him to write *Pa-du-ma* to warn the king of the behavior of some queens, but when others protested U Ponnya wrote *Wey-than-daya* (ca. 1857), about Madhi, the virtuous wife of the eponymous Buddha-to-be king. He also wrote stories and many verses and songs. His signature talent was his wit.

The highly popular *Wi-za-ya,* one of Burma's first important **political** plays, is said to have had a strong impact on public attitudes. Because it dealt with the sensitive issue of usurpation, the author set it in Ceylon (**Sri Lanka**). It had been written by order of King Mindon to warn two of his sons, whom he suspected of treason, to be loyal, but the point was not taken. In an 1866 coup attempt by these princes during which Prince Kanaung was killed, U Ponnya was found guilty of prophesizing the best time to rebel; he was summarily executed without the knowledge of the king.

Ma Thanegi

U PO SEIN (1882–1952). **Burmese** (Myanmar) **actor-dancer,** known as the Great Po Sein, who radically changed native theatre traditions by introducing plays based on Budda's birth stories (*jataka*, previously performed only by **puppets**), an enclosed hall with a raised **stage** (instead of a circle on the ground), ticket sales, and additional choreography for the male lead. He invented foot movements based on **Indian** classical and American tap dancing, and introduced the *anyein* dance form to the repertoire. He excelled in all four talents of a *zat pwe* performer: dance, dialogue, song, and the specialized "weeping song" (*ngo chin*). Po Sein was well read, highly articulate, memorized the classics, and excelled at improvisation.

Born to a famous dancer father, he was a professional at fifteen. One of his earliest and best-known partners was Aung Bala (1882–1917), a youth who danced the female role so successfully that he too became famous. Before Po Sein's time, plays for the masses were mostly based on myths and legends; his introduction of *jataka* plays was welcomed even by the monks as a way to spread Buddhism (see Religion in Theatre). He recorded nearly forty plays on LP.

Po Sein lived well and made sure his younger brothers and his children were educated in missionary schools and abroad, thereby helping to raise the social status of theatre artists.

FURTHER READING

Sein, Maung Khe, and Joseph A. Withey. *The Great Po Sein.*

Ma Thanegi

USMAN AWANG (1928–2001). **Malaysian** novelist, essayist, **playwright, critic,** and romantic poet, born in Kuala Sedili, Johor. He was most renowned as a poet although he wrote more than twenty plays in the 1960s and 1970s. Best known by one of his many pen names, Tongkat Warrant, he was **politically** active in the anti-colonialist movement. A self-taught dramatist, Usman first worked as a policeman under British rule (a job whose potential for violence appalled him) before moving to **Singapore,** where he became involved in the Malay community's efforts to end British domination at home. Back in Malaysia, he joined Kuala Lumpur's Institute of Language and Literature and earned an honorary doctorate (1981). In 1983, he became the third recipient of Malaysia's highest literary award, the Anugerah Sastera (1983), making him the national laureate.

Usman's plays deal with socio-political issues, such as precolonial feudalism, the rights of farmers, and contemporary relationships between urban **women** and poor, rural men. They often show a movement from towns—despite their well-developed infrastructure—to poverty-stricken villages (*kampung*), when the characters ultimately return to the *kampung* to bring education and progress. This theme can be found in plays such as *Flute of the Night* (Serunai malam) and *On the Eve of Id* (Menjelang takbir). His frequently revived *Visitors* (Tamu di bukit kenney, 1968) is a realistic work dealing with a perfect, idealistic civil servant. "Death of a Warrior (Jebat)" (Matinya seorang pahlawan [Jebat], 1961) is a one-act verse drama about the legendary fifteenth-century warrior friends Hang Jebat and Hang Tuah. Another noteworthy play is *A Woman Surrenders* (Menyerahnya seorang perempuan, 1969), which serves as an interesting counterpoint to feminist ideology.

Usman's *Uda and Dara: A Musical* (Musika Uda dan Dara, 1976) influenced modern Malay drama's development. Inspired by one of his own poems, its trenchant social criticism calls for a revolt by the impoverished farmers who must rise and fight for their rights, a realization they make only after the death of the beloved village son, Uda.

Solehah Ishak

VARMA, RAM KUMAR (1904–1990). Indian • playwright, critic, theorist, poet, and scholar, the "father of Hindi-language one-acts." He was born in Sagur, Madhya Pradesh, and began playwriting at twelve. A professor of literary history and a world traveler, he was knowledgeable in Marathi and English, in addition to his native Hindi. Varma was prolific, producing 125 one-acts and twenty-eight full-length plays, in addition to five books of criticism and many collections of poetry. He was also an authority on the theory of aesthetic emotions first explained in the ancient *Treatise on Drama* (Natyashastra). To Bharata's nine "aesthetic flavors" (*rasa*s), he added a tenth, *udveg* (literally, "being fed up with every kind of feeling").

Although Varma's characters were influenced by **Western** dramatists—mainly Shaw, but also Ibsen, Maeterlinck, and Chekhov—his achievement was to incorporate an Indian point of view into his characterizations and themes. His major one-act collections, which incorporate social and historical subjects, include *Eyes of Prithviraj* (Prithviraj ki ankhen, 1938), *Silk Tie* (Reshmi tie, 1941), *Seven Rays* (Saptakiran, 1947), *Four Historical One-Acts* (Char aitihasik ekanki, 1950), *Form and Color* (Ruprang, 1951), and *My Best Literary One-Act Plays* (Sahityik tatha meri sarveshreshth ekanki, 1958).

His full-length dramas include *Era of Victory* (Vijay parva, 1954), *Art and Weapons* (Kala aur kripan, 1958), *Full Moon Festival* (Kaumudi mahotsav, 1961), *Ashoka's Sorrow* (Ashok ka shok, 1967), *Johar's Flame* (Johar ki jyoti, 1967), *Lord Buddha* (Bhagwan Bhudha, 1978), *Era of Discipline* (Anushasan parva, 1980), *Emperor **Kalidasa*** (Samrat Kalidas, 1982), and *Kunti's Great Deed* (Kunti ka paritap, 1983).

Varma is generally credited with the advent of amateur theatre at school and college campuses. Although he touched upon various issues and themes, he was most successful at period and social plays. He firmly believed in Indian moral values and principles, which provide the backbone of his writings. He beautifully brings out both subtle and stark differences between Western and Eastern ways of life as he juxtaposes their effect on the emerging middle class.

Kumar received several important honors, including the Kalidas Samman (1960), and the Padma Bhushan (1963).

Shashikant Barhanpurkar

VEERANNA, GUBBI (1890–1972). Indian Kannada-language **actor**-manager, **playwright,** and film actor and producer. Born in Gubbi, Tumkur District, South Karnataka, he began his career as a child stagehand with the local Gubbi Theatre Company (Gubbi Channabasaveswara Nataka Sangha), then became an actor in it, rose to a partnership position, and, by 1917, was the owner. The Gubbi Theatre Company consolidated its leading reputation by hiring top actors (including Subbaiya Naidu [1895–1962]) and dramatists (such as Bellave Narahari Sastri [1882–1951]) and providing advanced methods emphasizing spectacular and technically advanced **scenography** (famous for quick changes), flashy **costumes,** and electric lighting. The company is now Karnataka's oldest.

Veeranna's eye-catching mythological productions, like *Kurukshetra* (1934), *Krishna's Play* (Krishnalila, 1944), and *Ten Avatars* (Dashavatatara, 1958), were widely popular. The company toured through Andhra Pradesh, Karnataka, and Tamilnadu, with three branches employing a staff of around three hundred.

Veeranna was renowned for developing minor roles into principal ones; he was closely associated with the role of a thief in *Sadarame*. His productions made comedy a central element. He was honored by the King of Mysore with the title "Versatile Comedian."

Samuel L. Leiter

VEERESALINGAM, KANDKURI (1848–1919).

Indian Telegu-language **playwright,** poet, novelist, editor, and social activist, born into poverty in Rajamundry, Andhra Pradesh. He managed to attain a fine education and became a teacher and then a Senior Telugu Pundit whose reformist concerns included the education of **women,** child marriages, concubine-keeping, groom dowries, and Hindu widows' remarrying; he was, in fact, responsible for the first such widow remarriage (1881). Even violence did not stop his pursuits. Renowned for sparking the Telugu cultural renaissance, he was responsible for many literary firsts. His books total nearly one hundred. He also edited various journals that fought for social reform. His accomplishments earned him the government title of Rao Bahadur (1893).

His playwriting career began by translating two acts of *The Merchant of Venice* (1875), moved on to satirize the custom of old men marrying girls in *Brahman Marriage* (Brahma Vivaham, 1879), and was followed by his writing and directing the first Telegu modern play to be produced, *Manual on Legal Practice* (Vyavahara dharmabodhini, 1880), a satirical attack on lawyers. The student association he formed for the purpose became the first modern Telugu **theatre company**. He subsequently wrote original plays, such as *Prahlada* (1885), *True Harishchandra* (Satya Harishchandra, 1886), *Wisdom Revealed* (Viveka dipika, 1880), and *Assembly of Learned Crooks* (Tiryag-vidvan mahasabha, 1889), the latter two concerning widow remarriage and greedy Brahman priests, respectively. He adapted **Sanskrit** dramatists Harsha and **Kalidasa,** as well as England's Shakespeare and Sheridan. He also wrote socially biting pieces based on English farces.

Samuel L. Leiter

VIETNAM.

Vietnam's population is over 86 million (2006), nearly half of which is younger than thirty-five. The elders are understandably concerned about cultivating traditional Vietnamese cultural values in young people inundated with global media and free market prosperity—especially in urban areas but now in rural areas as well.

People of Viet/Kinh ethnicity constitute 87 percent of the population, and the balance comprises fifty-four different ethno-linguistic groups, all of which have their unique customs, language, and **folk** rituals.

Vietnam shares borders with **China** to the north and with **Laos** and **Cambodia** to the east. Although three-quarters of Vietnam consists of mountains and hills, its spectacular yet extensive coastline has contributed to the country's vulnerability to outside invasion, as well as to its interaction with other cultures, particularly China and **India**. China dominated northern Vietnam for over one thousand years, until 938 AD. Thereafter, for nearly five hundred years, the first Vietnamese dynasties— the Early Le, Ly, and Tran—attempted to unite the north, as well as to defend against periodic Chinese attacks (which were successfully repelled), from the Cham civilization of the central region, and from the Khmer of the south. Yet during that period, the Vietnamese also synthesized and adapted many Chinese neo-Confucian ideals stressing studies of the classics and scholarly preparation for government service.

The Vietnamese did not fully regain control of the north until 1428, after the Lam Son Uprising, organized by Le Loi (a.k.a. Emperor Ly Thai To). Under his leadership, the Later Le Dynasty was established; for the first time, scholars were encouraged to use Vietnamese (previously considered primitive in contrast to Han Chinese), and legal reforms afforded **women** equal rights in most domestic issues. Two classes remained excluded from full civil rights: slaves and **actors,** which reflects neo-Confucian prejudice against theatre activities, considered as detrimental to the ideals of social and **political** morality.

The millennium of Chinese control brought Confucianism and Taoism to Vietnam, as well as Mahayana ("Greater Vehicle") Buddhism, still prominent. Catholicism eventually had more impact on Vietnam than any other Asian country, except the **Philippines**. Northern Vietnamese were particularly receptive to the Catholic **religion,** despite the church's opposition to ancestor worship, polygamy, and Confucianism. Paradoxically, the imperial court retained Jesuit scholars, astronomers, mathematicians, and physicians, and Confucianist Mandarin teachings. Thus Vietnam's unique location has contributed to its cultural identity and fierce determination for independence, while also cultivating its flexibility and adaptability to eclectic foreign influences. This paradoxical theme of independence and preserving "Vietnamese" cultural identity versus the people's willingness to incorporate diverse influences—particularly from China, India and, later, France—created a profoundly rich cultural foundation for Vietnam's traditional performing arts.

The traditional theatre forms of *cheo* and *tuong* (a.k.a. *hat boi*), date back over one thousand years; both reached their peak of popularity at the end of the nineteenth century, under the patronage of the Nguyen Dynasty (1802–1945). In the early twentieth century, *cai luong* began evolving as a separate and distinctive style that incorporated many of the conventions found in *tuong* and *cheo*; this "reformed" **musical** theatre became immensely popular in the south, and *cai luong* companies began struggling to appeal to and attract young contemporary audiences. Today, this "renovated theatre" is most popular with the older generations, who see it as a vital aspect of Vietnam's theatrical legacy.

In the northern regions, beginning in the early 1920s, *kich noi* was developed by artists and intellectuals who sought to combine some the influences of French "spoken drama" with the elements of traditional theatre; this still-performed "hybrid" form incorporates **Western** techniques to recount Vietnamese historical and contemporary narratives. *Kich noi* also developed into a powerful propaganda form, which was used to resist the French and, later, the American occupation of Vietnam.

FURTHER READING

Brandon, James R. *Theatre in Southeast Asia*; Dinh Quang et al. *Vietnamese Theater*.

Lorelle Browning

WATANABE ERIKO (1955–). Japanese • **playwright, director**, and **actress** who founded the 200 (Nijû-maru) **theatre company** (1978), changing it to 300 (Sanjû-maru, 1980). The pronunciations of the company's names mean "twenty circle" and "thirty circle," respectively, reflecting Watanabe's notion of drama as layered circles transcending conventional, earthbound concepts. Watanabe disbanded 300 in 1997 for the flexibility of periodic open-call productions through her current company, Universe Hall (Uchûdô).

Watanabe's works typically shift between memories of past and present, fantasy and reality, her characters moving back and forth. Reflecting the characters' confused search for meaning in their ordinary lives, her actors sometimes play dual characters. Their confusion is expressed through doggerel songs and over-the-top spectacle, recalling her mentor, **Kara Jûrô**.

In Watanabe's **Kishida** [**Kunio**] Prize–winning play *Kitarô the Ghost Buster* (Gegege no ge, 1982), a young boy, Makio, bullied in school and haunted by his still-born twin sister, calls on the popular comic-hero Kitarô and is transported into the comic world, where he struggles against his tormentors. Watanabe herself played three characters, a school bully, the twin sister, and a bed-ridden old woman. *A Girl with Eyelids* (Mabuta no me, 1987), awarded the Kinokuniya Prize, features a young girl connecting with the spirit of her older brother through a magical letter from the ocean. In *TEMPO—Goodbye, Night!* (TEMPO—yoru yo sayonara, 1995), a young man, caught between the known and unknown, confronts his brothers' deaths, and furniture comes to life in a Disneyesque fantasy/dreamscape.

John D. Swain

WAYAN WIJA, I (1952–). Balinese (see Indonesia) shadow **puppeteer** (*dalang*), one of the island's most prominent and innovative. Born in Sukawati, Gianyar regency—a village famed for its many talented puppeteers—Wija began **training** under his father, I Wayan Gombloh, at eleven. He went on to teach *wayang* and traditional Balinese **music** at the High School of Performing Arts (1981–1987).

In 1980, Wija created a new set of puppets to perform stories from the Tantri cycle, an *Arabian Nights*–like epic of **Indian** origin, including tales reminiscent of *Aesop's Fables*. His innovative *wayang tantri* was widely recognized as a significant break from tradition, featuring a new, nonclassical range of puppets (including a set of giant dinosaurs), narratives derived from outside the *Mahabharata* repertoire, and new **musical** instruments supplementing the traditional *gender wayang* ensemble. Nonetheless, Wija has always remained faithful to the classical spirit of *wayang kulit*. He has performed *wayang tantri* and more traditional interpretations of **Ramayana** stories around the world.

In 1998, Wija collaborated with American puppet artist Larry Reed to create *Electric Shadows* (Wayang listrik), which used electric lights instead of naked flame to illuminate the screen, for New York's Henson International Festival of Puppet Theatre. Wija is currently working on another innovation, *wayang kaca*, with puppets created from plastic sheeting. He remains one of the world's most active ambassadors of Indonesian shadow puppetry.

Laura Noszlopy

WAYANG. *See* Puppet Theatre: Indonesia.

WAYANG BEBER. *See* Puppet Theatre: Indonesia.

WAYANG GOLEK. *See* Puppet Theatre: Indonesia.

WAYANG GUNG. *See* Puppet Theatre: Indonesia.

WAYANG KRUCIL. *See* Puppet Theatre: Indonesia.

WAYANG KULIT. *See* Puppet Theatre: Indonesia.

WAYANG WONG. **Indonesian** Central and East Javanese *wayang* genre (a.k.a. *ringgit tiyang* in High Javanese), using human (*wong*) **actor-dancers** in thick **makeup** performing like *wayang kulit* **puppets**. Dialogue is recited by the actors, while narration and "mood songs" (*sulukan*) derived from classical literature are articulated by a "narrator" (*dalang*) seated with the *gamelan* **musicians**. References to this sort of dance-drama go back to the thirteenth century.

The current Javanese practice seems to have developed in eighteenth-century Central Java's royal courts. Courtiers and sultans lavished time and money to create massive *wayang wong* spectacles through the end of the colonial period. Performances occurred in the main pavilions of princely houses, using minimal **scenography**, but **costumes** fashioned from hide and embroidered cloth could be sumptuous. Scripts were inscribed in gold letters in massive tomes, and casts of hundreds were drilled daily for a year preceding performances. Most leads were played by royalty. These one-off performances were attended by Javanese and Dutch elites and could last for a week at a time. Smaller-scale shows were commonly produced in colonial Java by arts clubs, largely for self-entertainment. Economic limitations of the hereditary nobility have meant that this sort of *wayang wong*, sometimes called "pavilion *wayang wong*" (*wayang wong pendapa*), is rarely performed.

Wayang wong's court tradition was popularized in the 1880s in a form occasionally called "**stage** *wayang wong*" (*wayang wong panggung*). Plays lasting three to four hours were performed on commercial stages by itinerant troupes, sometimes trained by moonlighting court masters. Commercial *wayang wong* kept pace with technical developments, incorporating modern scenography and sound effects. A number of films were made in the 1960s, but in the 1970s commercial *wayang wong* lost public favor. Government-subsidized troupes in Jakarta and Solo perform to small audiences. More excitement is generated at annual competitions that attract groups from all over Java.

Wayang wong is not exclusively Javanese. It is also found in Bali, where it was considered until recently a **religious** form limited to temple ceremonies. When performing **Ramayana** plays, actors are all **masked**, but in plays based on the **Mahabharata** (so-called *wayang wong parwa*), only the clowns wear masks. The extinct *wayang wong* of the Cirebon area of West Java, likewise, used masks.

FURTHER READING

Soedarsono. *Wayang Wong: The State Ritual Drama of the Court of Yogyakarta.*

Matthew Isaac Cohen

WEI CHANGSHENG (1744–1802).

Chinese • actor of the "female" (*dan*) **role type**, whose 1779 entry into Beijing made the city China's theatre capital for the first time in centuries and marked an early stage in *jingju*'s development. Wei came from Chengdu, Sichuan Province, and performed *qinqiang*, a form of **bangzi qiang** from Shaanxi Province, already popular in Sichuan (see also *Chuanju*).

His bawdy acting led the authorities to issue bans against him (see Censorship) in 1782 and 1785. He was able to flout the first, possibly through a love affair with the scurrilous but powerful minister Manchu Heshen (1750–1799), but the second made him flee Beijing. In 1788, he acted in Yangzhou in the Spring **Stage** (Chuntai) Company and shortly afterward in Suzhou, both well-known theatre cities at the time. In 1792, he returned to Sichuan. In 1800, he was again in Beijing, but died following a fainting fit.

Wei retained his popularity to the end, but was unable to handle the money he earned. As the first great star, he had been able to accumulate immense wealth and property during his first visit to Beijing. However, when he died, his possessions would not cover a decent funeral.

Some of Wei's **music** has survived in *jingju* items. During his last visit to Beijing, he excelled in military pieces involving spectacular acrobatics. His most important innovation was "false feet" (*caiqiao*), stilted shoes tied to the feet with cotton bandages, enabling the actor to imitate the gait of a **woman**'s bound feet. This art survived until 1954, when it was suppressed as "feudal."

Colin Mackerras

WEI LIANGFU (CA. 1502–CA. 1588). Founding ancestor of **China**'s Kunshan style of southern *qu* (see *Kunqu*), known as the "Sage of Song." Wei was from Taicang District, a textile-producing center within the municipality of Suzhou, and was an itinerant singing master who also practiced medicine. His travels brought him into contact with singers and **musicians** from neighboring districts, including Kunshan, and he participated in public performances of *qu*, such as those held every autumn at Tiger Hill, Suzhou. He had expertise in northern *qu* and was friendly with masters of *haiyan qiang*, the musical style for southern *qu* most popular among early 1500s literati. Wei played a key role in recreating Kunshan music from a local style to the pre-eminent form of southern music (*zhengsheng*), which supplanted *haiyan qiang* in popularity by the mid-1560s.

Scholars differ on Wei's contribution to *kunqu*'s transformation, but agree that his role was large and his methods collaborative. It was said that he spent some ten years in the 1530s investigating the fine points of singing technique and musical accompaniment with associates such as Zhang Yetang, an expert on northern *qu* and master of the three-stringed lute (*sanxian*). By 1547, a treatise attributed to him was circulating in manuscript, titled *Adducing Correct [Forms] for Southern Lyrics* (Nanci yinzheng) and consisting of twenty prescriptions, in plain language, intended to elevate the aesthetic level of the new Kunshan music and enhance its prestige.

Wei and his associates built on rustic Kunshan songs used primarily for nondramatic *qu*, incorporating elements from *haiyan qiang* and assembling a rich accompaniment for them by adding stringed instruments used for northern *qu* to the ensemble of percussion instruments, woodwinds, and pear-shaped plucked lute (*pipa*) hitherto favored for southern *qu*. Sometimes referred to as "water-polished" (*shuimo*) because of its melismatic singing technique, *kunqu* was poised to develop from a style purely sung to one performed on **stage**, a step taken when Wei's disciple Liang Chenyu (1520–ca. 1593) wrote the first dramatic text for *kunqu*, *Washing Silk* (Huansha ji).

Catherine Swatek

WEI MINGLUN (1940–). Chinese • *chuanju* • **playwright**. Born in Neijiang, Sichuan Province, the son of a *chuanju* drummer and dramatist, he learned *chuanju* very young and at ten joined the Zigong City Chuanju Troupe as an **actor**, playing the "young male" (*xiaosheng*) and "young clown" (*xiaochou*) **role types**. Losing his voice at thirteen, he decided to learn playwriting and **directing**.

Wei won his first national awards in 1980 and 1981 for *Bold Yi* (Yi danda) and *Fourth Daughter* (Si guniang). *The Scholar of Bashan* (Bashan xiucai, 1983), a **xinbian lishi ju**, brought him national fame. His most successful play, the controversial *Pan Jinlian* (1985), offered Wei's unorthodox interpretation of the archetypal "bad **woman**" in traditional literature. Wei's experimentation with **Western** theatre elements, designed to modify *chuanju* into what he described as "*chuanju* of the absurd," sparked **criticism**, but also tagged him as the "modernizer" of traditional drama.

After adapting Puccini's opera *Turandot* into *jingju* (1993), Wei turned it into a *chuanju* as well. This adaptation, with an altered storyline, won him thirteen awards at the 1994 Chengdu National Drama Festival. In 1995, Wei successfully adapted his acclaimed screenplay *Changing Face* (Bianlian) to *chuanju*.

Wei is resident playwright at the Zigong City Chuanju Troupe. His work continues to be performed nationally and internationally. His *Good Woman, Bad Woman* (Hao nü, huai nü, 2001) was inspired by Brecht's *The Good Person of Setzuan*, and demonstrates Wei's continuing pursuit of novelty, even after more than fifty years in *chuanju*, a pursuit that has brought him the nickname "genius from Sichuan."

Ursula Dauth

WESTERN INFLUENCE

Western Influence: China

The modern "spoken drama" (*huaju*) of **Chinese** theatre was established under the influence of mainstream Western drama at the turn of the twentieth century; the same can be seen in all aspects of theatre: **playwriting**, **directing**, **acting**, **scenographic** and **costume** design, and **theatre** architecture. Several sources were instrumental in its formation. Among them were dramatic activities at missionary schools in coastal cities like Shanghai and Tianjin, where students read original plays and performed them on special occasions, such as Easter or Christmas. A more significant source was students returning from **Japan** and the West.

Because of its geographical and cultural proximity and early success in modernization, Japan served as a bridge for Western theatre, out of which emerged the first Western-style production, the most influential "civilized drama" (*wenming xi*, precursor of *huaju*) troupe, Spring Willow Society (Chunliu She), and key *huaju* practitioners, such as **Ouyang Yuqian**, **Tian Han**, Xia Yan (1900–1995), and Guo Moruo (1892–1978). Graduates from the United States provided the earliest direct link to Western theatre.

In 1916, Zhang Pengchun (1892–1957) returned to Tianjin's Nankai High School to direct the Nankai New Drama Company (Nankai Xinjutuan), which, although amateur, played an essential role in transforming *wenming xi* to *huaju*. In the 1920s and 1930s, graduates from American theatre departments, including **Hong Shen**, **Yu Shangyuan**, and **Xiong Foxi**, contributed to establishing a modern system of production, organization, and education. Europe not only provided China with playwrights and translators steeped in classical and modern theatre, like Ding Xilin (1893–1974) and Li Jianwu (1906–1982), but also two master directors, **Huang Zuolin** and **Jiao Juyin**.

Although various Western movements exerted their impact during the past century, China's socio-historic conditions eventually chose European realism as the dominant *huaju* mode. Ibsen's realism became a tool for both social enlightenment in the early decades and for social criticism in the 1930s and beyond. Playwrights also learned character and plot creation from Ibsen, as exemplified in **Cao Yu**'s *Thunderstorm* (Leiyu, 1933), an often revived and adapted classic. Also deemed a realist, Chekhov helped *huaju* move beyond Ibsen's well-made plays and inspired plays like Cao Yu's *Beijing Men* (Beijing ren, 1940) and Xia Yan's *Under Shanghai Eaves* (Shanghai wuyan xia, 1937). Shaw, with his biting satire on social issues, was another favorite. Popular during his 1933 China trip as a Nobel laureate, Shaw proved equally appealing in 1991 when *Major Barbara* (Babala shangxiao) reinvigorated the post–Tiananmen Square theatre scene.

Complementary to these realists was the Stanislavski System of acting, which was systematically translated and studied in the 1930s. It became the dominant approach and, between the 1950s and early 1980s, the sole government-sanctioned **training** method. It also served as the guideline for establishing China's only two drama academies in the 1950s, when Soviet experts were invited to teach there.

In contrast to realism, the impact of other styles was felt only occasionally. In the 1920s, playwrights like Tian Han sought inspiration from aestheticism, symbolism, and expressionism. In the 1980s, existentialist and absurdist plays contributed to a revolt against social-realist theatre and inspired considerable **experimental** activity. Another inspiration for the anti-illusionism rebellion was Brecht, whose epic theatre gave Chinese practitioners an alternative way of presenting their works. Along with Wilde, Maeterlinck, Beckett, Dario Fo, and many others, O'Neill has cast a long shadow, as evidenced by Hong Shen's *Yama Zhao* (Zhao Yanwang, 1922) and Cao Yu's *The Wilderness* (Yuanye, 1937), both inspired by *The Emperor Jones*. In 1988, both Nanjing and Shanghai hosted O'Neill Centennial **Festivals**. The **theories** and practices of Artaud, Schechner, and Grotowski also have influenced a generation of directors.

China has had a century-long experience with Shakespeare. He has often been called into service in attempts either to create new theatrical forms or to extend existing genres with new methods. Two Shakespearean festivals were held in 1986 and 1994.

FURTHER READING

Eide, Elisabeth. *China's Ibsen: from Ibsen to Ibsenism;* Li, Ruru. *Shashibiya: Staging Shakespeare in China;* Tam, Kwok-kan. *Ibsen in China 1908–1997: A Critical-Annotated Bibliography of Criticism, Translation and Performance;* Zhang, Xiaoyang. *Shakespeare in China: A Comparative Study of Two Traditions and Culture.*

Siyuan Liu

Western Influence: India

Stages of Development. The reception in **India** of "Western" practice has, over the last one hundred years or so, provided a number of modes and sites of influence, prescription, resistance, stimulus, challenge, and contention. In urban and **Parsi theatre** using the proscenium, influence has been expressed in terms of architecture, economics, class and audience composition, and the "drawing room" and "well-made play" style. Some **critics** have lamented this, but here as elsewhere the situation has moved through stages, from relatively passive acceptance, through analysis and negotiation, and ultimately toward integration and development; the recent middle-class theatre of, for example, **Vijay Tendulkar**, **Mahesh Elkunchwar**, and **Mahesh Dattani** demonstrates that Western modes can be adapted to Indian contexts.

School, college, and touring productions of Shakespeare and other Western figures, especially Eliot, Wilde, Brecht, Ibsen, Beckett, and Ionesco, have figured prominently in the development of India's theatrical consciousness, though they have also been balanced against indigenous forms. Touring companies have included the National Theatre, the Royal Shakespeare Company, the Actors' Touring Company, and Théâtre de Complicité. French **theatre companies**, including the Comédie Française, have also toured, as has the Berliner Ensemble. There also have been celebrated joint English/ Indian companies like those operated in the 1940s by Grant and Laura Kendal (immortalized in the 1964 film *Shakespeare Wallah*) or Grant Anderson, whose company included the young **Prithviraj Kapoor**. Here too the story is not one of simple acceptance, but of negotiation, adaptation, and development; Mumbai's (Bombay) **Prithvi Theatre** has become a leading center for major Indian and **experimental** productions of all kinds.

Foreign Directors. Encounters with leading **directors** have included the Indian People's Theatre Association–led adoption of aspects of Brecht; **Badal Sircar** saw work by Grotowski, Littlewood, and Lyubimov, and met with Beck, Malina, and Schechner. He suggests that the taste for Western styles was due to a degree of city snobbery, and his "Third Theatre" (*anganmancha*, literally, "open-air theatre") both draws on the work cited above and attempts to challenge it. The ***Mahabharata*** debate around Peter Brook's visit to India and subsequent adaptation of the epic focused around cultural **politics** in a particularly controversial way, but there have been many ways of managing influence.

Jana Sanskriti, a theatre company in rural West Bengal, has worked with and adapted Augusto Boal's methodology with great success; several other significant ventures are using similar methods to engage with social, political, and environmental issues.

Theatre workers have made use (as resistance, adaptation, reinforcement of indigenous features) of Western texts, theories, practices, finance, and personnel in the service of an elaboration, interrogation, and expression of successive stages and forms of "Indian" identity. In no case has this taken the form of a simple acceptance of the discourse of the (neo)colonizer. Just as Indian English is not what the Queen speaks, neither is Shakespeare nor Boal in India the same as they might be in their original country.

Interculturalism. There has been an increasing level of East-West traffic, of debate and exchange among practitioners and theoreticians, much of it mentioned in other entries. Indian forms have been venerated and/or raided, depending on one's position, for the following qualities: the profound symbolic insights they offer into the nature of art and reality, and on links between the human/individual and the cosmic/universal; the employment of a rich semiotic spectrum, including a wide range of forms; the thoroughness of **training** methodologies, particularly in the context of mind-body relationships; extreme flexibility and expressivity of the body; the importance of archetypal examples of cultural signifiers; and, finally, the commercial possibilities of marketing the exotic. One example in recent practice, apart from that of Brook, might be that of Mnouchkine: her productions of *Les Indiades* and *Les Atrides* contain significant Indian material in the form of content, **costume**, and **musical** elements. Her base outside Paris at the Cartoucherie and her company Le Théatre du Soleil consciously reflect aspirations to a multicultural aesthetic spirituality and performance style.

This demonstrates that Indian practice has been part of the ongoing international interrogation of theatre and performance, and of the latter's insertion in both the cultural and political spectrum. For their part, Indian artists have amended, adapted, argued with, and developed Western models and practices: Shakespeare is performed in ***kathakali***, and Beckett is a standard reference. Within universities, dialogue with aspects of Western **theory** has been intense, particularly with reference to aesthetics and politics. Although much of this has been carried out by academics who are not especially linked to practice, there have been significant exceptions: director, cultural critic, and dramaturg Rustom Bharucha is a good example, but so are editors of literature and theatre journals, organizers of seminars and conferences, founders of new ventures that aim to bring together theory and practice and to draw on insights from many cultures, as well as those engaged in traditional forms who have consistently invited foreign academics to attend performances and discuss nuances with Indian experts, such as G. Venu and **Kavalam Narayana Panikkar**.

The result has been considerable movement in and as praxis. This seems to have produced an increasing degree of interdependence or interpenetration alongside, and as a part of, increasing awareness of other cultural forms: what could be described as globalization and/or multiculturalism. The respective Indian and Western positions have been a spectrum of kinds of hybridization, exchange, and development of ideas, models, practices, aims, and achievements, which have materialized some of the notions of important cultural critics.

FURTHER READING

Trivedi, Poonam, and Dennis Bartholomeusz, eds. *India's Shakespeare: Translation, Interpretation, and Performance*; Yajnik, R. K. *The Indian Theatre: Its Origin and Its Later Developments under European Influence, with Special Reference to Western India*.

Ralph Yarrow

Western Influence: Indonesia

Formative interactions between indigenous traditions of **Indonesia** and Europe go back to the mid-nineteenth century. **Dance-**dramas associated with Java's royal courts, including *wayang wong* and *langendriya*, developed with a mixed audience of Javanese and European elites in mind, and catered to European expectations for spectacle. These same royal courts sponsored brass bands, often with European conductors. Notation for *gamelan* **music**, **theoretical** treatises on aesthetics, and play scripts for *wayang kulit* (see Puppet Theatre) were inscribed after Western models by elites associated with the Surakarta and Yogyakarta courts. The standardization of *wayang kulit*'s repertoire under Mangkunagara VII (r. 1916–1944) was influenced by the monarch's association with European philologists, theosophists, and Orientalists.

The Dutch who colonized Indonesia were not avid theatre makers, and the nineteenth-century public **theatres** (*schouwburgs*) they built in Batavia (Jakarta), Semarang, and Surabaya, were continually in financial disarray. Few Indonesians attended. It is likely that the first Indonesians to enact theatre based on Western models were military men who performed farces, comedies, and **costume** drama in Malay (the armed forces' lingua franca), primarily for their own entertainment. At the end of the nineteenth century, a number of hybrid Malay-language genres—*abdul muluk, komedi stambul, bangsawan*—became popular among urban audiences. All of these mixed Western dramaturgy with Indonesian **acting**, musical, and narrative features. These genres in turn influenced **folk theatres** such as *ludruk* and *lenong*, yielding hybrid theatres in local languages (see also *Drama gong*; *Kethoprak*; *Longser*; *Opera batak*; *Randai*). *Tonil* took Western films as a story source, and included European dance (tango, foxtrot, jazz) as "extra numbers" between acts.

Malay-language plays for actors written by **Chinese** and Eurasian authors began to be published in the 1890s. Scripts were intended for amateur or semiprofessional production, and were often adapted from European sources. Javanese-language social drama (*tunil jawa*) was briefly popular among enthusiasts in the 1910s and 1920s. Dedicated Javanese and Sumatran **playwrights** emerged alongside the nationalist movement in the late 1920s. Their Indonesian-language plays were not only modeled after Western dramaturgy, however: the symbolic dramas of **India**'s **Rabindranath Tagore** were also influential.

The first theatre academy was formed during the **Japanese** occupation (1942–1945). This incorporated both Western and Japanese pedagogical principles. Drama academies formed in Yogyakarta (1952), Jakarta (1955), and Bandung (1963) became major centers for translating Western acting treatises and plays into Indonesian-language productions.

Cold war cultural politics brought funding for Indonesian **directors**, playwrights, **scenographers**, and other artists to study in the United States, the Soviet Union, Czechoslovakia, Poland, and elsewhere starting around 1960. Many returned to share the fruits of their training. Intercultural exchanges between Indonesia and Western countries have been common since the 1980s.

Matthew Isaac Cohen

Western Influence: Japan

Without substantial outside influence during the long Edo period (1603–1868), Japanese culture turned inward, becoming somewhat ossified. **Traditional** Japanese theatre in the Meiji period (1868–1912) was so entrenched, though not universally esteemed—*nô* • **actors** could barely make a living and *kabuki* was regarded as lowclass entertainment—and Western theatre's initial presence so different that any such phenomenon as a new kind of Japanese theatre almost inevitably would have to break with its classical past and accommodate to Western forms.

The process began with five key events. First, Iwakura Tomomi (1825–1883), leading the Iwakura Mission (1871–1873) to study Western institutions, observed Western leaders using theatre to entertain prominent guests—unthinkable in Japan; he nevertheless staged *nô* for the imperial family in 1876. Then, Iwakura Mission member and future prime minister Itô Hirobumi (1841–1909) met in 1878 with *kabuki* stars **Ichikawa Danjûrô** IX and **Onoe Kikugorô** V, and manager **Morita Kan'ya** XII, encouraging them to realize a high-class theatre. Third, Iwakura entertained visiting American ex-president Ulysses Grant in 1879 with a *nô* play; the rough-hewn Grant earnestly urged the form's preservation, giving *nô* a new cachet. Fourth, the Theatre Reform Society (1886) was established to elevate theatre's respectability. Finally, the emperor, empress, and courtiers, visiting foreign minister Inoue Kaoru's (1836–1915) home in 1887, saw *kabuki* for the first time. These events helped promote theatre as respect-worthy and attending performances as appropriately high-class entertainment.

Perhaps inevitably, however, given the enormous divide between traditional Japanese presentationalism and Western representationalism, initial efforts at creating a new theatre by reforming *kabuki* were confused, even ludicrous. A play in 1881 showcased a character sporting such Western accoutrements as a straw hat, leather boots, an umbrella, a briefcase, and a pocket watch. Another featured foreign actors untrained in *kabuki*. Lest anyone miss the point, the **director** touted his modern lifestyle, preferring beer to *sake* and cooked to raw fish. In pandering to such Western-inspired "innovations," *kabuki*, hardly reformed or elevated, merely compromised its traditions, confirming its lower-class status. *Shin kabuki*, however, was marginally more successful at reform, as with **Tsubouchi Shôyô**'s *A Paulownia Leaf* (Kiri hitoha, publ. 1894, prod. 1904) subtly incorporating aspects of *Hamlet*.

Efforts at presenting Western theatre fared better. Two pioneering **theatre companies**, Tsubouchi's Literary Arts Society (Bungei Kyôkai, 1906–1913) and **Osanai Kaoru**'s Free Theatre (Jiyû Gekijô, 1909–1919, named after Antoine's Théâtre Libre and Brahm's Freie Bühne), produced mostly translated Western plays, including Tsubouchi's Shakespeare translations and Osanai's staging of Ibsen's *John Gabriel Borkman* (1909)—the first *shingeki* production. In 1912–1913, Osanai witnessed Reinhardt's work in Berlin and Stanislavski's in Moscow; he saw in Ibsen's social implications—especially those exposing bourgeois hypocrisies—the ideal modern theatre. Both companies virtually enshrined Ibsen as the god of modern Japanese theatre, with Chekhov and Shakespeare completing the trinity. Establishing the Tsukiji Little Theatre (Tsukiji **Shôgekijô**) in 1924, Osanai staged only translated Western plays for two years. His famous slogan, "Ignore tradition," reflected his conviction that new Japanese theatre could emerge only in breaking completely with traditional forms and mastering Western models.

This atmosphere, of course, alienated Japanese **playwrights**, affording their work few outlets. Osanai finally staged an original Japanese play in 1926, Tsubouchi's *Tempest*-influenced *En the Ascetic* (En no gyôja, 1916). While dense and redolent of *kabuki*, it incorporated psychological elements and signaled that plays by Japanese playwrights could be relevant and performable. By emphasizing Shakespeare's grand human dilemmas and social and psychological realism in Ibsen, Chekhov, Hauptmann, Wedekind, and Gorky, among others, and by gradually inculcating Western methods for actor **training**, Tsubouchi and Osanai paved the way for *shingeki* (Osanai coined the term), which would be expressive of the new age.

In the late 1920s, *shingeki* split into proletarian and aesthetic branches. The proletarian branch germinated in Taishô-period (1912–1926) liberalism, enhanced by the increasing appeal of Christian and socialist ideals. **Murayama Tomoyoshi** and **Senda Koreya**, studying in Germany in the 1920s, returned to Japan armed with Piscator's and Brecht's Marxist activism. Osanai associate **Hijikata Yoshi**, visiting Moscow in 1922, sought to replicate Meyerhold's way of folding **politics** into performance. While most Japanese proletarian plays were blatantly didactic and **critically** unsustainable—exceptions were by **Kubo Sakae** and **Miyoshi Jûrô**—their Western-inspired realism in plot, dialogue, and acting demonstrated applicable alternatives to traditional Japanese stagecraft. Another Osanai associate, **Kishida Kunio**, tended the aesthetic branch. After working with Copeau in Paris in the early 1920s, he purveyed Western stagecraft as the *shingeki* standard, determined to develop Japanese playwrights and actors capable of shirking *kabuki* modes. He envisioned plays about real life with actors speaking and moving naturally and identifying psychologically with their characters. Disagreeing with Osanai's predilection for translated Western plays, he vigorously encouraged younger playwrights, like **Morimoto Kaoru**, to create original work. He crystallized his vision by founding the influential Literary Theatre (Bungaku-za, 1937).

Given this Western-influenced itinerary, modern Japanese theatre remained derivative. Originality was foreshadowed in the 1950s by *butô*'s progenitors, **Hijikata**

Tatsumi and **Ôno Kazuo**, who, influenced by Artaud, Genêt, and German Neue Tanz, developed their inchoate, pre-verbal movements, consciously reacting against ubiquitous Western realism, attempting to recover traditional Japanese patterns of stylization and evoke mythic forces and shamanistic practices. Such roundabout Western influence persisted into the 1960s and after: when the playwrights emerging with the *angura* and *shôgekijô* movements, equally disaffected with *shingeki* and their traditional theatre, gradually learned that certain Western figures they revered—Brecht, Barrault, Béjart, Brook, Robbins, Grotowski, Kantor, Mnouchkine, and Wilson—had appropriated aspects of traditional Japanese theatre, and they began to reconsider their own tradition. That confirmed their pendulum swing away from *shingeki*'s hard-won quotidian realism, resulting in completely open **experimentation**, testing the very limits of theatre.

While Western influence has remained significant—**Abe Kôbô** frankly acknowledged greater common ground in his often absurdist plays with modern Western drama than with his own tradition—plays are no longer merely epigonic but have galvanized multifaceted influences—Japanese and Western, traditional and modern—into a uniquely Japanese idiom. **Suzuki Tadashi** and **Ninagawa Yukio** compellingly adapt Shakespearean and Greek tragedy, often with acting ideas and choreography drawn from *nô* and *kabuki*. **Kara Jûrô**'s work has been called *kabuki* brought-up-to-date, even as he explores Japanese youth culture and identity through the Western rogue John Silver. **Ôta Shôgo** employs a lyrical quiescence recalling *nô* to expose contemporary existential malaise. **Betsuyaku Minoru**'s absurdist *Water-bloated Corpse* (Umi yukaba mizuku kabane, 1978) freely adapts Beckett's *Endgame* to explore Japan's war-skewed sense of identity. **Terayama Shûji**'s *The Hunchback of Aomori* (Aomori-ken no semushi otoko, 1967) relocates the Oedipus story to Taishô Japan. **Shimizu Kunio**'s nuance-filled dialogue borrows from Tennessee Williams. Meanwhile, Western-style realism remains strong, as in the commercially successful *shingeki* of **Asari Keita** and his Four Seasons Theatre (Gekidan Shiki).

FURTHER READING

Kishi, Tetsuo, and Graham Bradshaw. *Shakespeare in Japan;* Sasayama, Takashi, J. R. Mulryne, and Margaret Shewring, eds. *Shakespeare and the Japanese Stage;* Sorgenfrei, Carol Fisher. *Unspeakable Acts: The Avant-Garde Theatre of Terayama Shûji and Postwar Japan.*

John K. Gillespie

Western Influence: Korea

Korean theatre during the past century developed out of responses to Western cultural challenges and artistic models. Information about Western practice was available in the late nineteenth century, but conscious attempts at Western-style dramas, using everyday language and logical **dramatic structures**, were not made until the 1910s.

During the following decades, translations of Shakespeare, Ibsen, Strindberg, Chekhov, Gogol, Tolstoy, Maeterlinck, Shaw, and others were staged. Shakespeare's works remain influential; however, among modern Western styles, realism was the most avidly studied model for *shinguk* • **playwrights**.

The first Korean production of Ibsen's *A Doll's House* was in 1925. From 1921 until 1936, nearly seventy scholars contributed articles and translations of Ibsen's plays to magazines and newspapers. In roughly the same period, the Stanislavski System for **actor • training** was introduced, and Ireland's struggle against British domination struck a cord deep in the hearts of writers whose native land had been usurped by **Japan**. Nationalism and the spirit of resistance advocated by Yeats, Synge, and O'Casey inspired realists such as **Yu Ch'i-jin** and Ham Se-dŏk (1915–1950).

Western dramas constituted roughly one-fifth of the modern repertoire in the 1930s, but no significant influence was evident in the 1940s because of harsh **censorship** imposed by the Japanese during World War II. In the 1950s, especially immediately after the Korean War (1950–1953), American influence was significant. O'Neill, Williams, Miller, and others were represented in *shingŭk*'s growing repertoire, joined by Europeans like Pirandello and Ionesco.

The post–Korean War generation's enthusiastic response to Osborne's *Look Back in Anger* (1960) and productions of works by absurdists such as Albee and Beckett foretold the resistance to establishment culture and politics in the 1970s. Young artists rejected the earlier *shingŭk* in favor of nonrealistic **experimental theatre**. While, on one hand, an intense yearning for cultural identity generated an atavistic movement to revive traditional forms, on the other, theories by Artaud, Brecht, and Grotowski were closely studied, providing alternatives for the post-*shingŭk* avant-garde.

Under military dictatorships in the 1980s (see Politics in the Theatre), a desire to diversify contemporary theatre intensified; plays by Pinter, Shepard, and Mamet were introduced, and, in 1988, plays by Brecht were at last permitted to be staged.

In the 1990s, feminist theatre represented by Caryl Churchill, Marsha Norman, and others captivated audiences. Greek tragedies and Shakespeare continued as singularly important artistic resources; however, since the 1990s, the ratio of Western to Korean works has dropped to about one-third from its longtime ratio of about half. Nevertheless, large-scale Broadway and West End **musicals** now dominate commercial theatre.

FURTHER READING

Korean International Theatre Institute, ed. *Korean Performing Arts*.

Ah-Jeong Kim

Western Influence: Philippines

There are two kinds of Western influence on **Philippine** theatre: the colonial influence during the Spanish (1521–1898), American (1900–1946), and **Japanese** (1942–1945) occupations, respectively; and the influence of new plays and trends in the West.

The Spanish period introduced not only Western forms that became *komedya*, *sinakulo*, *sarsuwela*, and *drama*, but also the point of view that only these forms, and not indigenous ritual forms, **dances**, and songs, should be considered drama. Theatre, through **religious** plays, also asserted the supremacy of both Western civilization and Catholicism, thus justifying colonization. With the establishment of formal **theatres**, dramatic art became less accessible to community members who could not afford tickets, and seating arrangements became reflective of economic and social status.

New Western forms introduced during the American period included *bodabil* (from vaudeville) and modern plays. Influenced by **playwrights** whose works they studied in university English classes, Filipinos soon wrote their own plays, first in English, and then in native languages. **Experimenting** with, adapting, and even combining realism, expressionism, epic theatre, and black comedy, playwrights and **theatre companies** articulated issues of language, gender, colonialism, class, and power relations. Similarly, **criticism** was influenced by Western **theories** on literature, theatre, and culture.

Western theatre continues to be a strong influence in various forms: copies of Broadway and West End musicals with matching wigs and perfect accents; the translation of Western classics, especially in universities; the adaptation of plays such as *The Vagina Monologues* to the Philippine setting; and the use of realist and expressionist techniques in Filipino-language plays.

Joi Barrios

Western Influence: Singapore

Education and language policies were twin factors behind the rapid emergence of a significant audience for **Singapore**'s English-language theatre in the 1980s. Prior to that time, relatively few adult Singaporeans had the benefits of a university education, and of that group even fewer would have been interested in seeing theatre in English. Apart from the works of university-educated **playwrights** Lim Chor Pee (1936–) and Goh Poh Seng (1936–) in the 1960s, the history of English-language theatre prior to the early 1980s was largely that of British and expatriate groups.

After theatre became a subject at the junior college (college preparatory) and university level in the late 1980s and early 1990s, the curriculum retained strong Western influences, and many English-educated Singaporeans still possess greater knowledge of Brecht's theories than of Asians like **Zeami**. Similarly, younger Singaporeans are more likely to have seen a Western-style **musical** than **Chinese • *xiqu*:** for many young people the musical is their idea of theatre. Touring Western musicals routinely include Singapore on their schedule, and the Esplanade arts complex provides a suitable venue for such large-scale works. Many Singaporean practitioners have received **training** in the West, and much Singaporean theatre borrows freely from techniques introduced by avant-garde **directors** such as Schechner, Grotowski, and Mnouchkine.

While there is an ostensible concern with Asian content in new Singaporean theatre, the cool, elegant staging that has come to characterize many new productions owes as much to the postmodern aesthetics of intercultural practice increasingly popular on the international **festival** circuit than to anything that is uniquely and specifically Singaporean.

William Peterson

Western Influence: Taiwan

Western influence on **Taiwan**'s theatre, felt in both styles and repertoire, did not start until the 1960s, when artists and scholars began returning from the West, and when **censorship** became less strict. Theatre artists not only appropriated Western idioms (such as illusionist and environmental theatres) but also adapted plays by Western **playwrights**, including Brecht, Maeterlinck, and Pirandello. Shakespeare in translation—the majority directed by Wang Sheng-shan (Wang Shengshan, 1921–2003)—played an important role in popularizing Western classics and stagecraft, which laid the groundwork for more innovative adaptations. **Lee Man-kuei**, the first serious Western-conscious playwright and **director**, pioneered the introduction of Ibsenian realism. She founded the Huaju ("spoken drama") Promotion Committee in 1962, starting a local tradition of adapting Western plays. It organized and sponsored annual World Drama **Festivals** that produced as many as 236 performances of Western plays (in English or **Chinese**) between 1962 and 1974. Moreover, new ones were written under the influence of Western **theory**. **Yao I-wei**'s *Jade Bodhisattva* (Nian yu guanyin, 1967) used nonillusionist modes inspired by Brecht's epic theatre and *xiqu*. **Ma Sen**'s *Flies and Mosquitoes* (Cangying yu wenzi, 1967) was influenced by Theatre of the Absurd.

In the 1980s, Lee's successors, notably Yao I-wei, extended her project to create hybrid idioms by bringing Western and Chinese (both *xiqu* and *huaju*) theatres together. Yao launched five annual **Experimental Theatre** Festivals between 1980 and 1984, where a wide range of Western methods, such as Artaud's Theatre of Cruelty, were tested. At the first festival, Lanling Theatre Workshop (Lanling Jufang, 1976–1990) staged a romantic comedy, *Hezhu's New Match* (Hezhu xin pei, 1980), to **critical** success. Using a hybrid style taken from both realism and *jingju*, the play reframes the *jingju Hezhu's Match* (Hezhu pei) in Mandarin and context (Taipei). While Lee Man-kuei believed that playwriting, not performing, is the key to developing a proficient theatre culture, Yao and his followers emphasized performance.

The 1990s saw more varied and successful intercultural engagements. Godot Theatre (Guoduo Juchang, 1988), a major musical **theatre company** (*gewu ju*), staged retitled adaptations of classics, such as *Kiss Me, Nana* (Wenwo ba Nana, 1995) and *Oriental Rock Midsummer Night's Dream* (Dongfang yaogun zhongxiaye, 1999). The Contemporary Legend Theatre (Dangdai Chuanqi, 1986), a Westernized *jingju* company, has innovatively staged a series of *jingju* adaptations of Greek tragedies and Shakespearean plays since it was founded. These productions are not confined to small audiences, like many experimental works, but are popular both at the local and global levels. They have created new local traditions of engaging Western theatre cultures.

Alexander C. Y. Huang

Western Influence: Thailand

The adaptation of Western plays together with the hybridization of Western forms has been evident throughout the history of modern **Thai** theatre. In the reign of King Chulalongkorn (Rama V, r. 1868–1910), three new forms—*lakon rong*, *lakon phan thang*, and *lakon dukdamban*—were created from the blending of Thai and Western forms by two princes and two noblemen, all of whom had lived in Europe. Likewise, in the subsequent reign, the beginning of *lakon phut* owes a great deal to **Rama VI**'s translations of Shakespeare, Sheridan, Labiche, and Molière. The king not only adopted European **theories** and practices but also altered them significantly so as to better communicate with his audience.

In the 1970s, translations of Western plays greatly contributed to the emergence of *lakon phut samai mhai* ("modern spoken drama"). Also, university theatre departments hired British and American lecturers to help develop their curricula. Afterward, artists and scholars continued their graduate studies and advanced **training** abroad. Many are supported by grants from the Fulbright Foundation, the Asian Cultural Council, the University of

Hawaii's East-West Center, and the British Council, among others. Returning home to work for either university or professional theatre, they stage translations of Western dramas, most with modified contexts, or write original plays utilizing Western dramaturgy.

In addition, cultural agencies, such as the Alliance Française, support the participation of foreign companies in local programs, and also organize their own **festivals**, to which Thai troupes are invited.

Pawit Mahasarinand

WICHITWATHAKARN, LUANG (1898–1962). Thai **playwright**, lyricist, composer, novelist, diplomat, **politician**, and scholar. Major General Luang Wichitwathakarn, most commonly known as Luang Wichit, served in the Ministry of Foreign Affairs for decades, with various levels of appointment from clerk to minister and ambassador.

In 1934, as director-general of the Fine Arts Department, Ministry of Education, Luang Wichit, an admirer of French culture, founded the School of Classical Music and Dance, later the College of Dramatic Art, after French models. In 1936, he composed the **music** for his historical play *The Blood of Suphan* (Luad Suphan). Loosely based on a Siam-**Burma** war, it shows the values of freedom while depicting the misery of prisoners of war. Its profits made a significant contribution toward the construction of Thailand's first National **Theatre**, and its title song is still widely performed.

In addition to his many novels and textbooks (on politics and history), he wrote twenty plays and composed 204 musical numbers, 120 of them theatrical. Thai scholars refer to them collectively as *lakon luang wichit* and, because of their distinctive style, do not categorize them in any dramatic genre. Written mostly after World War II, when the Thai government was promoting patriotism, these plays are known for their witty dialogue and unique sense of humor. Inspired by historical events, they are filled with romantic and politically motivated musical numbers in both traditional and modern styles, and with corresponding **dance** movements. They show unified community spirit with the use of large casts. A typical *lakon luang wichit* commences with a prologue presenting the main theme, and concludes with an epilogue summarizing it. Another notable work is *The Might of King Ramkhamhaeng* (Anupap Pokhun Ramkhamhaeng, 1954).

Pawit Mahasarinand

WOMEN IN ASIAN THEATRE

Women in Asian Theatre: Burma (Myanmar). *See* Women in Asian Theatre: Southeast Asia

Women in Asian Theatre: Cambodia. *See* Women in Asian Theatre: Southeast Asia

Women in Asian Theatre: China

Until the twentieth century, women were generally barred from **Chinese** theatre, with women's roles mostly played by men. Throughout the ages, entertainers were very low in social status, **actresses**, in particular, being associated with prostitution.

The twentieth century, especially within the People's Republic of China (PRC), has seen major policy changes and concerted efforts to involve women in traditional theatre. Women now play almost all female roles, and have equal rights in *xiqu* attendance. Women *xiqu* **playwrights** and producers are encouraged, but in practice remain rare.

Pre-modern Conditions. Actresses may have dominated **canjun xi**, sometimes even playing males. In thirteenth- and fourteenth-century *zaju*, troupes often consisted of families, with the troupe leader's wife and daughters-in-law acting or performing other functions. A wall painting (1324) in a temple in Hongdeng County, Shanxi Province, praises and displays an actor called Elegance of Zhongdu, who is dressed as a man but whose face and name suggest a woman. Material about *zaju* actresses largely extols them both as performers and courtesans.

From the Ming dynasty (1368–1644) on, mixed troupes were rare, and women spectators were forbidden. Confucian ideology demanded the public separation of the sexes and looked askance at behavior that could lead to sexual immorality. Foot-binding for women was not new to the Ming but spread within society then, making acting difficult. Actresses in mixed troupes were mostly prostitutes, the exceptions being girls in private mansions **trained** in theatre. Men played "females" (*dan*), and the skill of the male *dan* developed to a high degree. Poet and minister Lu Rong (1436–1494) wrote of his shock at how realistic were the actors of a style called *haiyan qiang*, and admonished all educated men and their families to abjure such immoral people. Until the twentieth century, all principal actors of **kunqu**, **jingju**, and other styles were male.

In general women attended only private performances. The Qianlong emperor (r. 1736–1796) even banned women from Beijing's **theatres** altogether, which lasted through the nineteenth century. In the south, Shanghai, for example, rules against women attending performances were less rigid.

Republican and People's Republic Periods. The Republican period (1912–1949) saw a gradual relaxation against women in the theatre. In Beijing, females were allowed to attend, at first sitting in separate sections, but from 1924 they sat together with males. The great male *dan* **Mei Lanfang** was a front-runner in taking on female disciples, and it became possible for women to train as actors. All-female Shaoxing *yueju* troupes first appeared in the early 1920s, later becoming the norm.

From the beginning, in 1949, the PRC declared gender equality. Although evading reality, social attitudes toward women have changed drastically since then. Actresses are no longer automatically associated with prostitution, and most parents happily allow their daughters to go perform.

Training schools accept girls as well as boys, though in fact boys still predominate, the number of male *xiqu* roles outnumbering female. Virtually all companies are mixed. Female instrumentalists, once nonexistent or rare, have become common.

In the 1950s, the government strongly denounced the training of any new male *dan* as feudal and discriminatory against women, Premier Zhou Enlai (1898–1976) telling male *dan* Zhang Junqiu (1920–1997), "up to you the male *dan* and that's it." This proscription has generally remained in force. Although there is a dwindling number of male *dan* remaining from the old days, notably Mei Lanfang's son, Mei Baojiu (1934–), the best known of those trained since the 1980s is Beijing-based Wen Ruhua (1947–). However, since the 1980s, there have been more actresses performing males. In Shaoxing *yueju*, women still play positive males, such as the traditional scholar-lover, although men can play negative males. There are many female military roles, and women have shown themselves capable of their gymnastics.

No rules exist regarding women attending theatre. Men tend to outnumber women *jingju* spectators, although not necessarily in other styles. Among children, girls go more readily to *xiqu* than boys.

The most famous theatre woman since 1949 is Jiang Qing (1914–1991), Mao Zedong's (1893–1976) wife. She took a lead in *jingju* reform from 1963 until her political fall (1976). Her role was extensive, ranging from supervising content to singing styles and characterization. She banned most items as insufficiently revolutionary, allowing only a very few *jingju*, and her rigidity has made her generally excoriated since her fall.

FURTHER READING

Li, Siu Leung. *Cross-Dressing in Chinese Opera*; Ma, Qian. *Women in Traditional Chinese Theater: The Heroine's Play.*

Colin Mackerras

Women in Asian Theatre: India

Prior to the 1930s, only four traditional South Asian theatres—all **Indian**—included females in their troupes: Kerala's **kutiyattam** and *nangyar kuttu*, north Karnataka's **sannata**, and Maharashtra's **tamasha**. Many traditional forms still maintain all-male troupes.

The earliest record of women in Indian theatre is the ancient *Treatise on Drama* (Natyashastra; see Theory). It includes minutely detailed descriptions of how females should portray various women in different moods, emotions, and situations, and instructions for **costumes** and **makeup**. Women also played delicate gods and men.

Women *kutiyattam* performers are *nangyar*s and have their own separate solo form of theatre, *nangyar kuttu*. In addition to being **Sanskrit** scholars and actresses, they also play small cymbals and chant Sanskrit verses to which their male counterparts act. *Sannata*, which arose in the late 1800s, also included women from the start.

The origins of the highly popular **tamasha** probably include remnants from the ancient Sanskrit and Prakrit theatre described in the *Natyashastra* and elements of the entertainments procured for Moghul troops in the late 1600s, including *nautch*, a degenerate form of *kathak* **dance**. Female singers and dancers came from North India, and locals joined them, adding songs composed in Marathi, the local language. After the Moghul emperor's death (1707), the Marathas gained power and patronized the artistic yet bawdy *tamasha* until the kingdom was lost to the British in the 1800s. Under the Marathas, women still danced, but young boys played women. Women regained their place when the actress Pawala was brought to the limelight by her actor husband, Patthe Bapu Rao, in the 1900s. She solidified *tamasha*'s female performer tradition.

Women did not directly imitate male performances of female role, but they also did not go beyond the established conventions. Most female performers are from the Dalit ("untouchable") communities and are still being sold into *tamasha* and into prostitution. Attempting to free themselves from exploitation, some have established their own troupes. In addition, performers have a union. Some cooperative foundations have established contests to upgrade performances, as well as the conditions for female performers. Offering money on **stage** to female performers has been outlawed, but money is still commonly given to stage managers to pass on, thus curbing the previously demeaning behavior exhibited in this custom.

During the twentieth century, women had some success breaking into all-male forms. These genres, which emerged between the twelfth and seventeenth centuries, incorporated many of the practices in the *Natyashastra*, but each substituted its own local language for Sanskrit and did not include women. Many still have all-male troupes.

Kuchipudi is a traditionally all-male style originating in Kuchipudi Village, Andhra Pradesh, India, sometime between the twelfth and early fifteenth centuries. It was not until the 1930s that teachers ventured to Madras and Hyderabad and taught their dance to females as a solo form. Two of earliest female students were the famed *bharata natyam* dancer Balasaraswati (1918–1984) and Esther Sherman (1893–1981), an American who performed as Ragini Devi. Today, *kuchipudi* is a major Indian solo dance form and a modern dance-theatre using traditional techniques, but it remains in its traditional form of an all-male dance-theatre in the villages.

Among formerly all-male forms that introduced women in the twentieth century are *doddata* and *jatra*. The latter, seen in Bengal and **Bangladesh**, began the practice in the late 1950s and 1960s. Bangladesh is the only South Asian country other than India in which women perform in traditional theatre. In *jatra*, males and females—Hindus and Muslims—perform females. Some women manage troupes.

After the 1959 Suppression of Immoral Traffic Act, courtesans and dancing girls joined the *nautanki* troupes of Uttar Pradesh, Punjab, and Rajasthan. Beginning in the 1970s, there occasionally have been all-women amateur *kathakali* and *yakshagana* troupes. The first all-night, all-female performance of *terukkuttu* took place in 1996.

South Asian women have excelled in traditional dance forms but, with the exceptions mentioned above, women, for the most part, still remain excluded from traditional **theatre companies**. What happened along the way that caused forms emerging from the twelfth to seventeenth centuries to abandon the *Natyashastra*'s tradition of women in the theatre? Muslim invasions? Stricter adherence to the Laws of Manu, the ancient Hindu code governing morality? More research is needed to answer this question.

FURTHER READING

Subramanyam, Lakshmi, ed. *Muffled Voices: Women in Modern Indian Theatre.*

Martha Ashton-Sikora (Syed Jamil Ahmed, Nicholas C. M. Hill,
Kathryn Hansen, and Eleanor Zelliot assisted)

Women in Asian Theatre: Indonesia. *See* Women in Asian Theatre: Southeast Asia

Women in Asian Theatre: Japan

Early Forms. From prehistoric to pre-modern times, women have played integral roles in the development of **Japanese** theatre. Clay figurines from the Kofun period (ca. 300–710) depict female shamans and nude dancing girls, illustrating early shamanic trance and **dance**. The first indigenous written records, the *Records of Ancient Matters* (Kojiki, 712) and *Chronicles of Japan* (Nihongi, 720), tell of goddess Ame no Uzume no Mikoto adorning herself with sacred vines and dancing on an upturned tub before the cave in which sun goddess Amaterasu no Omikami had hidden herself. Becoming possessed, Uzume exposed her breasts and genitals, causing laughter among the deities, drawing out the sun goddess, and bringing light back to the world. This myth establishes the lineage of female shamans (*miko*), who delivered oracles and conjured souls via their erotic trance dances. "Wandering *miko*" traveled the countryside serving as mediums for numerous villages, and often as prostitutes. *Miko* dances eventually lost their shamanic nature, becoming the graceful choreographed dances of the *miko kagura* seen at Shinto shrines (see Religion in Theatre).

Many traveling medieval female performers may have originated from *miko*. The *asobime* ("entertaining women") lived on boats and performed a type of song called *imayo*, consisting of eight or twelve phrases of twelve syllables each. Other itinerant *imayo* performers were the *shirabyôshi* (literally "white rhythm"), who were primarily women. Dressed in white clothing resembling men's hunting garb and a tall black hat (*eboshi*), accompanied by a drum, they sang *imayo*, followed by solo dances. Though considered outcasts, some became powerful men's wives or mistresses. The *shirabyôshi* Gio was consort to Regent Taira no Kiyomori (1118–1181) before being replaced by another *shirabyôshi*, Hotoke Gozen, also later cast aside. General Minamoto no Yoshitsune (1159–1189) also supposedly had a *shirabyôshi* lover, Shizuka Gozen, a relationship dramatized in **nô**, *bunraku* (see Puppet Theatre), and **kabuki**.

Women's contributions to several pre-*nô* forms are also significant. In a diary, courtier Fujiwara no Akihira (989–1066) describes a *sarugaku* performance involving a man, his wife, and sons. Records from 1349 tell of *miko* performing *Okina*, the "old man" dance, and two *sarugaku* plays at Kasuga Shrine in Nara. One performer, Otozuru Gozen, could possibly be the same as *kusemai* dancer Otozuru of Nara, who taught *kusemai* to **Kan'ami Kiyotsugu**. *Kusemai*, a song and dance type rhythmically different from what was then used in *sarugaku*, was later incorporated into *sarugaku* by Kan'ami, a major step in *nô*'s development. Other diaries mention "female" (*onna*) *sarugaku* troupes, consisting of five to six women accompanied by male **musicians**, coming from Shikoku in 1432 and Echizen in 1456 to perform in Kyoto. Female troupes are also known to have appeared before General Toyotomi Hideyoshi (1536–1598) in 1593. Records mention others in the late sixteenth and early seventeenth centuries, but there is no evidence of women in the four Yamato troupes, which became the five current *nô* schools.

Kabuki. A legendary female performer is **Izumi no Okuni**, a supposed *miko* from Izumo Shrine, credited with establishing *kabuki* on the banks of Kyoto's Kamo River. An itinerant performer, Okuni is believed to have begun in *yayako odori*, a dance of young girls, performed in the homes of aristocrats by itinerant troupes from the 1580s. The term *kabuki odori* ("*kabuki* dance") first appears in 1603. Okuni's dances and cross-gender portrayals of samurai buying prostitutes in "teahouse visiting" (*chaya asobi*) scenes were a raging success. Other troupes of women, including prostitutes, imitated Okuni, leading to "women's" (*onna*) *kabuki* and "prostitutes'" (*yûjo*) *kabuki*, which were widespread phenomena. Alongside *kabuki* women were those in the *ko-jôruri* theatre (later *bunraku*), providing *shamisen* music and sung narrative. A major turning point came in 1629, when the Tokugawa shogunate banned women from public performance. The ban is thought to have been promulgated to maintain social order, as classes were mixing in **theatre** audiences, and brawls erupted over the women. The ban may have also been an attempt to prevent unlicensed prostitutes from interfering with the licensed industry, well established by the 1620s. Though the edict was reissued several times before 1647, it nevertheless removed women from public performance until the late nineteenth century.

Thereafter, women took positions in samurai households giving private performances and teaching music and dance. Some Edo-era (1603–1868) courtesans may have received *nô* **training** and performed for patrons in teahouses. A Kyoto widow named Chisei (?–1759) ran a school for *nô* chant unaccompanied by dance (*su utai*) for thirty years. In *kabuki*, troupes of female **actors** (*okyôgen-shi*) performed privately in the female quarters of large samurai estates and imperial households. Female performers of *gidayû*, *bunraku*'s narrative music, performed in private salons and brothel quarter teahouses.

Post-Meiji Period. In the 1870s, the ban on female performers was lifted, and women who performed *gidayû* concerts in music halls became extremely popular. This "girls'" (*musume*) *gidayû* was popular into the 1920s and may have contributed to the survival of both *gidayû* and *bunraku*. Regular programs of women's *gidayû* were run at Tokyo's Honmokutei from 1950 to 1990, and monthly at the National Theatre (Kokuritsu Gekijô) in Tokyo since 1990. In 1980, "women's" (*joryû*) *gidayû* was designated a National Cultural Property, authenticating and elevating the status of these female performers. In 1982, Takemoto Tosahirô (1897–1992) was designated a Living National Treasure.

The Meiji era (1868–1912) saw great debate about whether women should return to *kabuki*, in which "female impersonators" (*onnagata*) had made tremendous artistic contributions to the depiction of females. **Ichikawa Danjûrô** IX, a dedicated reformist, appeared in dances with his two daughters, whom he trained for professional careers that were unfulfilled. More important, he raised the former *okyôgen-shi* Ichikawa Kumehachi (1846?–1913) to professional status as modern *kabuki*'s first actress, but her career floundered after his death, and she migrated to the new forms of **shinpa** and **shingeki**. When Tokyo's Imperial Theatre (Teikoku Gekijô, 1911), Japan's first fully **Western**-style theatre, opened, it instituted a training program designed to introduce actresses into *kabuki*, but they were unable to sustain interest; the program was abandoned, and women did not return to professional *kabuki*. In the late 1940s, an all-women's *kabuki* **theatre company**, Ichikawa Girls' Kabuki (Ichikawa Shôjo Kabuki), was created in Toyokawa City, Aichi Prefecture, and, in 1952, received approval from the head of the Ichikawa family line, but after more than a decade of popularity, their star waned and the company dissolved. Many women participate in regional "**folk**" *kabuki*, and in 1983, the all-female Nagoya Girls' Kabuki (Nagoya Musume Kabuki) was founded. Though amateurs, they give highly polished performances and toured internationally (2002).

In *nô*, the Meiji era marked the end of samurai patronage, sparking a period of **experimentation**, including the short-lived *azuma nô*, performed with *shamisen* accompaniment and including women. In the early twentieth century, *nô* study was advocated for young women's physical and cultural education. One product of this was Tsumura Kimiko (1902–1974), who, with her sister, studied under a Kanze schoolmaster. For years her petitions to turn professional were refused. She taught shoulder drum in

Hyogo Prefecture and **Korea**, where she mounted full-length plays with her students, resulting in her banishment from *nô* (1921). The Nôgaku Association, established that year, affirmed its prohibition of women in 1922; this continued until 1948. Tsumura authored an original *nô* play, *The Love Letter* (Fumigara), translated by Ogamo Rebecca Teele, herself a professional performer and the first Western woman admitted to the Nôgaku Association. Today, although women constitute 10 percent of *nô* professionals, and July 2004 saw twenty-two female *nô* performers designated as Important Intangible Cultural Properties, performance opportunities are limited, and women are relegated to the subgenre of "women's" (*joryû*) *nô*.

Kyôgen has no formal policy forbidding females, but has been even more resistant to admitting them. Daughters of *kyôgen* families are often trained to perform animal roles, such as the monkey in *The Monkey Quiver* (Utsubozaru), but from adolescence professional training is limited to males. Two exceptions are the Izumi sisters, Junko and Yôko, later Miyake Tôkurô XIII, history's first professional female *kyôgen* actors (see Izumo School). However, professionals of other families will not perform with them; they therefore appear with each other or with their younger brother. In 1999, they published *I Am a Female Kyôgen Actor* (Josei kyôgen-shi de gozaru). Even the National Nô Academy, which permits women in its training courses, has produced some *nô* professionals but none yet in *kyôgen*.

Julie A. Iezzi

Modern Theatre. As noted, in 1629, Japanese women were barred from appearing on the public **stage**, though some continued performing privately. The ban was lifted in 1890, and women started performing, for several reasons: Western theatre allowed actresses, increasing numbers of Japanese perceived male impersonation of females as perverse and outdated, realism had been introduced, and feminist consciousness was growing.

The first male and female joint performance in Tokyo occurred in 1891 (but earlier in other cities before the ban was lifted), with six women participating, including former geisha Chitose Beiha (1855–1918). Many initial female performers were either geisha, *kabuki* daughters, or "female actors" (*onna yakusha*), like the above-mentioned Ichikawa Kumehachi, who shifted from *kabuki* to **shinpa** and **shingeki** under the stage name Morizumi Gekka; still, she was not really an "actress" (*joyû*) trained for modern theatre.

Modern Japan's first professional actress is considered to be **Kawakami Sadayakko**, who started performing when touring abroad with her husband **Kawakami Otojirô**. She established the Imperial Actress School (1908), and trained actresses like Mori Ritsuko (1890–1961) in both traditional and modern styles. Given actors' traditionally loose reputation, many prospective actresses, especially those from bourgeois backgrounds, faced considerable opposition from their families and schools to entering this profession.

The Theatre Institute of the Literary Arts Society (Bungei Kyôkai, 1909), one of the first modern **theatre companies**, was among the first attempts to train men and women in *shingeki*, based on modern Western drama. **Matsui Sumako**, an early trainee, became the troupe's star, later forming her own troupe, Art Theatre (Geijutsu-za), with **Shimamura Hôgetsu**. Matsui premiered plays with memorable female characters, such as the title role in Wilde's *Salomé* (1913), and Katusha in Tolstoy's *Resurrection* (1914). The premiere of Ibsen's *A Doll's House* (1911) coincided with the founding of the feminist literary journal *Blue Stockings* (Seitô); actresses and the roles of "new women" they performed came to be identified with the incipient feminist movement. Still, women on stage continued to be regarded as sexual commodities, and this perception dogged the first actresses, like Yamakawa Uraji (1885–1947), Izawa Ranja (1889–1928), and Hanayagi Harumi (1896–1962). Women also continued performing as geisha, as practitioners of traditional dance (*nihon buyô*), and traditional music.

Except for **Mitzutani Yaeko**, who became a star, *shinpa* continued to be dominated by men, especially "female impersonators" (*onnagata*). Yet many memorable *shinpa* roles were female, like those in plays based on **Izumi Kyôka**'s novels. One-time actress and novelist Tamura Toshiko (1884–1945) explained that *onnagata* were able to portray the kinds of women popular in *kabuki* and *shinpa* because these characters accentuated women's weakness; only real women, she maintained, could portray women's strength.

Given the challenges facing actresses, the advent of all-female troupes is hardly surprising. The all-female **Takarazuka** theatre (1913), founded to attract families to a hot-spring resort, had become by the 1920s a full-fledged troupe known for French-style musical revues. To compete with Takarazuka, the Shôchiku Company created its own all-female troupe. Unlike its rival, Takarazuka continued to stress its mission as a finishing school preparing students for eventual marriage. Nonetheless, many graduates became professionals in various genres. The postwar appearance of all-female *kabuki* troupes is noted above.

The 1920s and 1930s in Japan saw other venues emerge, like Casino Folies (1929) and Moulin Rouge (1931), capitalizing on women's sexual appeal. Meanwhile, serious actresses, especially those in *shingeki*, worked diligently to establish their credentials, resulting in stellar acting by, among others, Tamura Akiko (1905–1983), **Yamamoto Yasue**, and **Sugimura Haruko**. Some, like Okada Yoshiko (1902–1992), distinguished themselves in **politically** oriented proletarian theatre. (Okada created a sensation in 1938 by emigrating with a lover to Soviet Russia.) Many actresses also began appearing in movies and television, including, before the war, Mizutani Yaeko, and, postwar, Kishida Kyôko (1930–), Watanabe Misako (1932–), and Ôtake Shinobu (1957–). While remarkable actresses like **Shiraishi Kayoko** and Ri Reisen (1942–) emerged from avant-garde *angura* and *shôgekijô* in the 1960s and 1970s, charismatic, even authoritarian, male **directors** dominated the forms; their portrayals of women tended to focus on the darker side, such as sexually exploited women and madwomen.

Some modern plays, written by men but with female protagonists, are noteworthy. *What Made Her Do It?* (Nani ga kanojo o sô sasetaka?, 1927) by Fujimori Seikichi (1892–1977), a typical proletarian play, focuses on a girl who, exploited in capitalist society, ends up committing arson. **Morimoto Kaoru**'s *A Woman's Life* (Onna no isshô, 1945) uses realism to portray the vicissitudes of a remarkable woman whose long life links the Meiji, Taishô (1912–1926), and Shôwa (1926–1989) eras. This play, performed over half a century by Sugimura Haruko, defined her career. Other plays closely associated with particular actresses include **Kinoshita Junji**'s *Twilight Crane* (Yûzuru, 1949), performed over one thousand times by Yamamoto Yasue, and the record-holder, *Diary of a Vagabond* (Hôrôki, 1930), based on Hayashi Fumiko's (1903–1951) autobiographical work, performed over 1,700 times by Mori Mitsuko (1920–).

Female Playwrights. Some prewar plays by female **playwrights** were performed, such as the prizewinning *kabuki* play *Haômaru* (meaning "triumphant king," 1908) by Hasegawa Shigure (1879–1941), who started the left-leaning journal *Women and the Arts* (Nyonin Geijutsu, 1928), and the leftwing *shingeki* play *Restless Night in Late Spring* (Banshun sôya, 1928) by Enchi Fumiko (1905–1986). Okada Yachiyo (1883–1962), sister of **Osanai Kaoru**, established the Association of Japanese Women Playwrights (1948), yet female playwrights remained rare well into the postwar era. Tanaka Sumie (1908–2000), **Tanaka Chikao**'s wife, was among the few women whose plays were performed in the 1940s and 1950s. **Akimoto Matsuyo** began writing in the 1940s, receiving wide acclaim in the 1960s and 1970s for folklore-based plays, such as *Kaison the Priest of Hitachi* (Hitachibô Kaison, 1960).

Many female playwrights emerged in the 1980s and 1990s, some with specifically feminist sensibilities, including **Kishida Rio**, **Kisaragi Koharu**, and **Nagai Ai**. Women also attained prominence as **scenographers** (**Asakura Setsu**) and directors (Miyata Keiko, 1957–). Kisaragi, with NOISE, and **Watanabe Eriko**, with 300 (Sanjû-maru) and her current Universe Hall (Uchûdô), led their own troupes. The all-female Bluebird Troupe (Aoitori) was established in 1974, its productions written and directed into the 1990s under the troupe's collective *nom de plume* Ichidô Rei, meaning "all together, bow."

Reflecting the rise in awareness about women's issues in theatre, the first Conference for Asian Women and Theatre was held in Tokyo and Kyoto (1992). Playwrights Kisaragi and Kishida and female scholars like Ikeuchi Yasuko (1947–) and Tonooka Naomi (1960–) were among the organizers.

FURTHER READING

Kano, Ayako. *Acting Like a Woman in Modern Japan: Theater, Gender, and Nationalism;* Brown, Steven T., and Sara Jensen, eds. *Performing Japanese Women;* Downer, Lesley. *Madame Sadayakko: The Geisha Who Bewitched the West.*

Ayako Kano

Women in Asian Theatre: Korea

Theatre was a man's world in pre-modern **Korea**, as the old Confucian social system prohibited women from participating in public activities. Traditional forms such as the **puppet theatre** (*kkoktu kakshi*) and *t'alch'um* were performed entirely by men, the exception being *p'ansori*, which allowed women by the mid-nineteenth century. Thus the notion of "women in theatre" largely belongs to the modern period, and it was not until the 1990s that "women's theatre" (*yŏsŏng yŏngŭk*) became firmly established.

The first woman performer was Chin Ch'ae-son (1847–?), a *p'ansori* singer trained by Shin Chae-hyo (1812–1884) in the mid-nineteenth century. Chin is said to have performed for the royal court. In the 1910s, *shinp'agŭk* served as a **training** ground for professional **actresses**, but the first modern actress did not appear until 1917. Most women shunned theatre careers, and the early *shinp'agŭk* frequently employed female impersonators, following **Japan**'s *kabuki* tradition. By the 1920s and 1930s, *shinp'agŭk* produced professional actresses who also performed in *shingŭk*.

The 1930s witnessed the emergence of a few amateur women **playwrights**, but the first professional woman playwright was Kim Cha-rim (1926–), who won a literary award with *Gusty Wind* (Tolgae param, 1959). A handful of women playwrights have followed in her footsteps.

During the war-ravaged 1950s, *yŏsŏng kukgŭk* overshadowed the male-dominant *ch'anggŭk* and conquered the commercial theatre world for a time. However, *yŏsŏng kukgŭk* declined in the late 1950s, never regaining its former glory. In the 1960s and 1970s, the "little theatre movement" (*sokŭkjang yongŭk undong*) was initiated by a woman, **Lee Byŏng-bok**, founder of the Café Theatre (Kkap'e Tteattŭrŭ, 1969).

The women's theatre movement gained momentum in 1986 with a "monodrama," *Woman in Crisis* (Wigi ŭi yŏja), adapted from a Simone de Beauvoir novel. An unprecedented success, it was performed five hundred times by three different actresses between 1986 and 1990. In 1999, it was restaged with a new title, *That Woman* (Kŭ yŏja), starring leading actress Son Suk (1944–), former minister of the Department of Environment.

The 1990s is considered when the ideology of feminism or feminist theatre entered the consciousness of modern Koreans. Reflecting the advancement of their social status, women challenged male authority in all areas of theatre. A number of Western plays, such as Fo and Rame's *Female Parts*, Norman's *'Night Mother*, Wesker's *Letters to a Daughter*, Churchill's *Top Girls*, and Dunn's *Steaming*, served as important vehicles in advancing feminist ideals.

Today, many talented women work in theatre, further developing the trend of the 1990s. Although Korean women still suffer from gender inequality at home and society at large, their tireless efforts are moving the theatre forward into a promising future.

Ah-Jeong Kim

Women in Asian Theatre: Laos. *See* Women in Asian Theatre: Southeast Asia

Women in Asian Theatre: Malaysia. *See* Women in Asian Theatre: Southeast Asia

Women in Asian Theatre: Philippines. *See* Women in Asian Theatre: Southeast Asia

Women in Asian Theatre: Singapore. *See* Women in Asian Theatre: Southeast Asia

Women in Asian Theatre: Southeast Asia

Women have an important role in Southeast Asian performance as animist spirit mediums, village **festival** performers, courtesan entertainers, royal **dancers**, and contemporary theatre artists.

Burma (Myanmar). "Mediums" (*nat kadaw*) are female trance-dance mediums for **Burmese** • **religious** festivals of the tutelary spirits. The "votaress" (*apodaw*) dancer who opens a traditional performance is a theatrical extension of the *nat kadaw*. *Yein*, the female court group-dance, is a high-class variant of women as channels of power. The largely female variety show *anyein pwe*, with its dancer-singer-comedians, is a secular permutation. In the early twentieth century, women began replacing the female impersonators in *zat pwe*, and now both genders share the **stage**.

Cambodia. The importance of female dance to Southeast Asian royal and fertility cults has its roots in tantric Hindu-Buddhism. Seventh-century **Cambodian** female dancers were dedicated to Angkor temples, and by the thirteenth century a temple could have three thousand dancers on its rolls. As the Thai sacked Angkor (1431), court traditions lapsed. Village forms persisted, including spirit mediumship and young women's singing jousts (*ajay*) with potential suitors. Female court performance, *lakhon kbach boran*, was reintroduced from nineteenth-century **Thailand**. The all-female royal consorts performed for cremations, rain rituals (*buong suong*), and state visitors. Queen **Sisowath Kossamak** modernized court dance, refining the "celestial being" (*apsara*) image and introducing male dancers for monkey roles. **Chea Samy** was a recent master teacher, and Norodom Buppha Devi (1943–), Kossamak's grand-daughter, continues her dance legacy as minister of culture.

Indonesia. Women are important ritual specialists in **Indonesian** rice ceremonies: in *pantun* traditions female groups improvised song-dance jousts with male suitors. Small girls participating as trance dancers in Javanese *sintren* and Balinese *sang hyang dedari* bring luck. The dancer-courtesan (*ronggeng*) forms developed from harvest **festivals** where a village girl represented the rice goddess. These dances relate to **India**'s *devadasi* genres. Sixteenth-century Sufi mystics reinterpreted *ronggeng*, often replacing women with transvestite males. *Tayuban*, aristocratic dance parties, are higher-class variants of *ronggeng*. The singer-dancers perform while men drink and dance.

Palace arts included *bedhaya*, for royal consorts, and *srimpi*, a dance for aristocratic daughters. Sultan Agung (1616–1645) spiritually "wed" the goddess of the south ocean via the *bedhha ketawang* dance, which continues in the Solonese court. The dance articulated tantric power, so monarchs would take dancers to battles to ensure success. By 1800, Balinese kings developed a related female palace dance, *legong*. In the Mankunegaran palace in Solo, an all-female dance opera, *langendriya*, was born, performing stories of the grass cutter prince, Damar Wulan. Such forms promoted women's impersonation of refined males, a practice that persists. Balinese *arja* is an all-female dance-opera, developed in the early twentieth century.

Women from traditional Javanese performing art families appeared as **masked** dancers or **puppeteers**, but some had to give up performing if they married. Cirebon artists Ibu Sawitri (1924–1999) and Ibu Rahsinah (1930–) are important twentieth-century masters.

Under the influence of **Malaysian •** *bangsawan* and other **Chinese** and local forms women mounted urban stages by the early twentieth century. With the development of academic theatre **training** after independence (1945), women have flourished as major choreographers, dancers, and **actors**. Top dancers include Irawati Durban Arjo (1943–), Tatih Saleh (1944–), Maruti (1944–), and Ni Ketut Arini (1943–). Notable actresses include Yayang Nur (1952–) and Ratna Riantiarno (1950–). **Ratna Srumpaet** has emerged as the first major contemporary woman **playwright**.

Laos. Women of **Laos** perform in *mawlam*, the sung debates between female and male voices in villages. *Mawlam* was professionalized in the twentieth century, and many mixed-gender forms have evolved from it.

Malaysia. **Malay** traditions relate to Indonesian patterns. In *ulek bandel*, a female dancer communes with the rice spirit. In the trance genre *main puteri*, a male medium cures female patients of psychic disorders. *Ronggeng* dances are found throughout the country. *Asik* is the graceful female dance of the Patani court. A theatrically developed early-twentieth-century female court form is Kelantan's **mak yong**, in which the female troupe was augmented by two male clowns. Urban *bangsawan* developed in the late nineteenth century, introducing mixed-gender performance.

Modern drama including actresses blossomed from the 1970s; an important woman playwright emerging in the 1990s was Leow Puay Tin (1957–). Choreographer Marion D'Cruz (1953–) and children's theatre **director** Janet Pillai (1955–) are among significant artists of the 1980s and 1990s.

Philippines. Early European visitors to the **Philippines** reported female shaman dancers and epic singers, and female court dance was found in Islamic courts. The Spanish introduced **Western** theatre, and Spanish touring **theatre companies** became popular. Elisea Raguer was important in establishing *sarsuwela* in the 1880s. Singer-actress Atang de la Rama (1902–1991) became the queen of *sarsuwela* in the 1920s and 1930s. After World War II, actresses became prominent in the American-influenced realist theatre, as exemplified by Daisy Avellana (1917–). The politically energized Philippine Educational Theatre Association (PETA), founded by Cecile Guidote (1943–) in the 1960s, developed playwrights like Malou Jacob (1948–). Amelia Lapena-Bonifacio (1930–) is another important female playwright-director and head of the puppet-oriented Awakening Theatre (Teatrong Mulat).

Singapore. The overseas Chinese community of colonial **Singapore** supported Chinese female entertainers in popular street operas. Indians in twentieth-century Singapore supported **bharata natyam**, and Malays watched *ronggeng*. The 1980s, however, brought a flowering of modern drama as the affluent city-state invested in culture. *Emily of Emerald Hill* (1982) by Stella Kon (1944–) is a central work.

Thailand. **Thailand**'s monarchs built on Khmer traditions to create the **lakon nai** female court dance. Consorts of the monarch formed the royal troupe, managed by the senior queen. On the ruler's death his group dissolved, but some ladies were selected by the next ruler to train his wives. Non-narrative choreographies in which women might do female group dances, or refined male (*phra*) and female (*nang*) couples and dramas where women danced all roles, were presented. Refined female singing and intricate poetry marked the genre. Khun Suwan was the nineteenth-century female dramatist of *Unarut*, based on the Javanese **Panji** story.

With the dissolution of palace dance in the 1930s, performances continued in urban **theatres**, but soon men took on monkey and demon roles; female dance melded with the male **khon** dance. State-supported programs continue training in the female style. Meanwhile, Thai "spoken theatre" (**lakon phut samai mhai**) and contemporary dance has developed. Strong female artists active in contemporary genres during the 1990s include playwright **Daraka Wongsiri** and director-actress **Patravadi Mejudhon**.

Vietnam. Women increasingly emerged as significant performers in the last century. Village performances in the north included **cheo**, a song and dance drama featuring performers of both genders, while **cai luong** became popular in the south beginning in the 1930s. Contemporary women are trained and perform in all the arts, including "water puppetry" (*mua roi nuoc*), "spoken drama" (**kich noi**), and traditional theatre.

Kathy Foley

Women in Asian Theatre: Vietnam. *See* Women in Asian Theatre: Southeast Asia

WONGSIRI, DARAKA (1954–). Thai • *lakon phut samai mhai* • **playwright**, producer, and television writer. A graduate of Chulalongkorn University, where she studied with **Sodsai Pantoomkomol**, Wongsiri cofounded a commercial **theatre company**, DASS Entertainment (1990), and has since worked as its resident dramatist.

Having written more than twenty plays known for well-rounded characters, up-to-date situations, and social commentary, she is inarguably Thailand's most prolific modern playwright. Representative dramas include *The Crimson Rose* (Kularb seeh luad, 1988), *Where the Rainbow Ends* (Sudsai plai rung, 1991), and *A Madwoman's Will* (Pinaikam khong ying vikoncharit, 1994). Noteworthy satirical comedies include *Old Maids* (Tuen tuek, 1992), *Doc! But That's Not . . .* (Khun mor kha, tae wa . . . man maichai, 1995), and *Three Misbehaving Women* (Sam sao sarm sarm, 1996). She has written **stage** adaptations of Andersen's fairy tale *The Snow Queen* (Nang phaya hima, 1991) and the **Chinese** folktale *The White Snake* (Nang phaya ngoo khao, 1999). She also penned book and lyrics for the **musicals** *The Happy Farm* (Rai saen suk, 1986) and *The Doomed Duo* (Koo karma, 2003). Her latest work is an adaptation of *La Cage aux Folles* (2006). Most of her works are staged by resident **director** Suwandee Jakravoravudh.

Her most popular work, and the company's most commercially successful production to date, is *Mayhem behind the Golden Sand Mansion* (Onla-mhan lhang Baan Sai Thong, 1999). A hybridization of Frayn's *Noises Off* and Ko Surangkhanang's (1911–1999) best-selling novel *Baan Sai Thong*, this farce was revived in 2000, 2003, and 2005, and toured to Chiang Mai (1999) and Khon Kaen (2000) for a nationwide total of one hundred performances in six years, a *lakon phut* record.

Pawit Mahasarinand

WUJU. Chinese • **dance**-drama incorporating the choreography and techniques of **Western** ballet, Chinese **folk** dance, and *xiqu*. Its **music** typically follows Western harmonic rules while its melodies are characteristically Chinese. It uses both Western and Chinese instruments. *Wuju* has followed two distinct visions: "ethnic dance-drama" (*minzu wuju*) and "Chinese ballet" (*zhongguo balei*).

Minzu wuju aims at establishing a choreographic vocabulary rooted in classical and folk dances. *The Precious Lotus Lamp* (Baoliandeng, 1956), adapted from a *jingju* play about love between a goddess and a mortal, is considered the first large-scale example. *The Small Sword Society* (Xiaodao hui, 1959), praising the eponymous nineteenth-century anti-Manchu court secret society, incorporated *xiqu* and local folk dance movement. *Tales of the Silk Road* (Silu huayu, 1979) featured movements and **costumes** derived from the paintings in Gansu Province's Dunhuang Buddhist caves.

Other *minzu wuju* featured music, movements, and costumes of China's ethnic minorities. They often are adapted from folklore or myths. The best-known company is the National Song and Dance-Drama Ensemble (Zhongguo Geju Wuju Yuan).

Chinese ballet has ventured to blend Western classical style with Chinese traditional. Notable productions include *The Red Detachment of Women* (Hongse niangzijun, 1964) and *The White-haired Girl* (Baimaonü, 1965), adapted from a 1945 *geju*. Both were among the eight revolutionary "model plays" (*yangban xi*) of the Cultural Revolution (1966–1976). The 1980s saw adaptations of contemporary literary masterpieces, such as *Blessing* (Zhufu, 1981), *The Thunderstorm* (Leiyu, 1982; see Cao Yu), and *Home* (Jia, 1983); they attempt to explore character psychology through choreography. Recently heralded was *Raise the Red Lanterns* (Dahong denglong gaogao gua, 2001) staged by film **director** Zhang Yimou (1951–). Major companies, which also produce Western ballet, include the National Ballet of China (Zhongyang Baleiwu Tuan) and the Shanghai Ballet (Shanghai Baleiwu Tuan).

FURTHER READING

Mackerras, Colin, ed. *Chinese Theatre from Its Origins to the Present Day.*

Nan Zhang

XINBIAN LISHI JU. A form of *xiqu* in the People's Republic of **China**. Its name means "newly written historical drama" and its themes reflect past figures and events. "Historical" almost always refers to pre-twentieth-century China and includes both real and mythical and legendary people and events. These plays are in any of China's regional styles. In techniques, **costumes**, and **role types** they are similar or identical to "traditional dramas" (*chuantong xi*) but contrast in several ways:

- The script is new or recent and not anonymous but attributed to one or more authors.
- The **music**, mainly traditional, is especially composed, and the orchestra often adds **Western** instruments.
- The drama usually takes a full afternoon or evening, with the plot rising to a climax and dénouement, different from the episodic style and much shorter duration of traditional items.
- The **scenography** and **properties** are usually much more complex.

Early *xinbian lishi ju* included items theatre scholar Qi Rushan (1877–1962) wrote for **actor • Mei Lanfang**. However, it was the Chinese Communist Party (CCP) that took up the genre and promoted it for **political** purposes. Late in 1943, a group of amateurs in CCP headquarters in Yan'an, northern Shaanxi Province, premiered *Forced up Mount Liang* (Bishang Liangshan) by Yang Shaoxuan, Qi Yanming, and others. It is based on the classic novel about rebels, *Water Margin* (Shuihu zhuan), and shows how ruling-class oppression forced protagonist Lin Chong to go up Mount Liang to join the rebels there. CCP Chairman Mao Zedong (1893–1976) saw it (1944), and praised it for "restoring history's true face" because it showed positively not "lords and ladies" but rebels and the masses.

From 1949 to 1964, *xinbian lishi ju* continued to promote the CCP's ideology or to extol past rebels or other marginalized people, like **women**. Representative is *Women Generals of the Yang Family* (Yangmen nüjiang, 1960). Set in the eleventh century, it shows China under attack from the north with a court faction prepared to compromise with the enemy. Infuriated, the Yang clan's centenarian dowager encourages the family's women to defend the nation; imperial policy changes, and the enemy suffers military defeat. The message is clear: women can contribute patriotically to the nation even as military leaders.

Despite Mao's earlier approval, the genre was banned during the Cultural Revolution (1966–1976), along with all items having pre-twentieth-century Chinese themes.

The 1980s saw revivals of pre-1964 *xinbian lishi ju* as well as a new flowering. Although ideology remained important, the range of heroic characters was broader, even including emperors, and social commentary was far subtler and more wide-ranging than before, an excellent representative being *chuanju* • playwright • **Wei Minglun**. However, this genre has suffered the flagging of interest that accelerating modernization has brought to traditional drama.

FURTHER READING

Mackerras, Colin, ed. *Chinese Theater from Its Origins to the Present Day.*

Colin Mackerras

XIN YANQIU (1911–). Chinese *jingju* • **actress** of the "female" (*dan*) **role type**. Born in Beijing, she started learning *bangzi* at nine. Two years later, she switched to *jingju*, debuting at fifteen. Around 1930, she took the **stage** name Xin ("New") Yanqiu, which expressed her admiration for **Chang Yanqiu** and her determination to be included in the Chang school (*chang pai*). However, Chang refused to take female disciples. Therefore Xin Yanqiu studied Chang's technique, particularly his singing, by observing his performances, listening to his records, and learning from Wang Yaoqing (1882–1954), a great male *dan* who had performed for the Manchu court and had taught generations of performers, including all the "four great *dan*" (among them **Mei Lanfang**). Wang had given Chang enormous help in establishing the Chang school, particularly in the creation of new melodies and arias. Xin Yanqiu was just seven years younger than Chang and witnessed the full development of his school, but she remained most interested in his early style whereas others inclined toward his more mature repertoire.

In 1928, Xin Yanqiu became the first actress to perform with a male actor in Beijing, three years before the ban on mixed-sex casts was lifted. By special permission, **Yang Xiaolou**, a master of *jingju*'s warrior type, and the seventeen-year-old Xin performed a sensational *Farewell My Concubine* (Bawang bieji), which contributed to Beijing's permanent adoption of mixed-gender casts.

From 1956, Xin Yanqiu taught in the Jiangsu **Xiqu** School in Nanjing, Jiangsu Province, and **trained** many actresses in the Chang school.

Ruru Li

XIONG FOXI (1900–1965). Chinese "spoken drama" (*huaju*) **playwright, director**, and educator known for his achievements in popularizing *huaju* in rural areas. While attending university in Beijing (1920–1923), Xiong wrote several plays and participated in the creation of the People's Drama Society (Minzhong Xiju She), a prominent "amateur drama" (*aimeide xiju*) group. After receiving a master's from Columbia University (1926), Xiong chaired the theatre departments of Beijing National School for the Arts and National Beiping University (1928–1933), the first college-level drama department. Apart from playwriting, he published two essay anthologies.

In 1932, he was invited to direct the drama division of the Council for the Promotion of Education for the Ordinary People, where he carried out one of the most significant experiments of *huaju* popularization. In the villages of Ding County, Hebei

Province, he trained amateurs and put on popular productions of both original plays written for his target audience and adaptations of traditional, **folk**, and **Western** plays. His landmark production, *The Bridge* (Guodu, 1935), was staged in a four-thousand-seat outdoor **theatre** with a large amateur cast performing both onstage and around and within the audience, aided with songs, fluid movement, and effective lighting. It won wide acclaim for popularizing *huaju*, but its efforts were thwarted by the ensuing Second Sino-Japanese War (1937–1945).

After 1937, apart from playwriting and directing, Xiong's major contribution to *huaju* was linked to theatre education as he headed drama schools in Sichuan (1938–1941) and Shanghai (1946). The latter eventually evolved into Shanghai Theatre Academy in 1956, where Xiong remained president until his death.

Siyuan Liu

XIQU. Literally, "theatre [of] sung-verse," Mandarin for the indigenous **Chinese** conception of theatre. Variously known as "Chinese traditional theatre," "Chinese **music**-drama," and "Chinese opera" in English, *xiqu* actually represents a complex, multifaceted conception that defies the use of a simple translation. It dates from the twelfth century but acquired its present meaning in the modern era. The concept encompasses Song (960–1279) and Yuan (1280–1368) *nanxi*, Yuan and Ming (1368–1644) *zaju*, Ming and Qing (1644–1911) *chuanqi*, and *jingju*, and the more than three hundred forms of regional theatre; it distinguishes these forms from **folk theatre** and modern **Western**-inspired forms, including "spoken drama" (*huaju*; see Playwrights and Playwriting) and *geju*.

Xiqu is conceived of as theatrically comprehensive, including both prose and rhymed verse, with comic and serious elements in most plays. Moreover, performance involves the main elements of the performing arts—story, dialogue, music, song, acting, **dance**, and, often, combat and acrobatics—presented not in sequence, but rather in synthesis. Performers execute dance and dance-like movement while speaking and singing; dance and other movement without vocalization occur in an orchestral fabric of sound that extends the physical precision and expressivity into the aural dimension. Synthesis makes *xiqu* a rich performing art, and an exacting one for performers, who receive years of rigorous **training** in basic skills: song (*chang*); speech, literally, "recitation" (*nian*); dance-acting, literally, "do[ing]" (*zuo*), encompassing dance and the visibly detectable results of acting in the Western sense; and combat and/or acrobatics, literally, "fight[ing]" (*da*). The well-trained performer combines the skills of an opera singer, a ballet dancer, and a classically trained Western actor; many also attain skills equivalent to those of a martial artist or gymnast.

Other defining characteristics are stylization and conventions. In most forms, stylization involves what is termed the raising and refining of daily life behaviors in order to present their essential nature and fundamental beauty. This often includes using curved, circular gestures and movement patterns; it also usually requires the appearance of effortlessness, both physically and vocally. The conventions provide comprehensive, presentational means for establishing certain aspects of character, handling time and space in highly mutable fashion, and communicating both direct and implied meaning nonverbally. For example, movement conventions indicate locale, circumstance, and activity; **makeup** conventions denote psychological and moral character and gender;

and **costume** conventions convey gender, social status, and circumstance. *Xiqu* **role types** offer complex conventions for indicating gender, age, and level of dignity. The music conventions are complete languages of structure and emotion involving instrumentation, vocal technique, and compositional practices. Together with the use of regional language, the unique musical practices of each form create the primary means for distinguishing among them.

FURTHER READING

Wang-Ngai, Siu, and Peter Lovrick. *Chinese Opera: Images and Stories*; Wichmann, Elizabeth. *Listening to Theatre: The Aural Dimension of Beijing Opera.*

Elizabeth Wichmann-Walczak and Trevor Hay

XUE YANQIN (1906–1989). Chinese • **actress**, one of the first **women** to perform the *jingju* "female" (*dan*) **role type**, previously played only by men. Born to a Hui ethnic family, she began **training** in both *bangzi* and *erhuang* at seven. After training in *qingyi* (literally, "blue garments"), a female role subtype specializing in singing, Xue extended her range to the vivacious young "flower female" (*huadan*), where the performer concentrates on acting and speaking. From about fifteen, she started performing in female troupes in Beijing and, in 1931, when the municipal government lifted the prohibition on mixed-gender casts, Xue led such a troupe. In the 1930s, she and Tan Fuying (1906–1977), grandson of the famous **Tan Xinpei,** costarred in *Young Master No. 4 Visits His Mother* (Silang tanmu), the first full-length, sound *jingju* film produced by a Chinese studio, causing a sensation.

Xue Yanqin's voice was sweet, and her repertoire mainly followed that of **Mei Lanfang** but with infusions from **Shang Xiaoyun** and **Xun Huisheng,** plus plays newly written especially for her. For a time during the 1920s and 1930s, her fame surpassed even the "four great *dan*," but Xue left the stage after she married Puguang, the brother of the last emperor, Puyi (1906–1967). After 1949, recommended by Mei, she joined the China Jingju **Theatre** (Zhongguo Jingju Yuan) and later devoted herself to *jingju* teaching.

Ruru Li

XUN HUISHENG (1900–1968). Chinese • *jingju* • **actor**, born in poverty in Hebei Province and, with his brother, sold into service to a *xiqu* school, performing for the master and his wife in funeral retinues and at temple fairs. He endured a harsh **training** and was enrolled at eight in the Yishun Hebei **Bangzi Qiang** Company. He excelled in the **role type** of vivacious young "flower female" (*huadan*) and, as a "female" (*dan*) specialist, became one of the "four great *dan*" (with **Mei Lanfang, Chang Yanqiu,** and **Shang Xiaoyun**). He eventually founded the famous Xun school (*xun pai*) of *jingju*. After his apprenticeship period in *bangzi qiang*, Xun began training in *jingju* at fifteen, and perfected a distinctive style in which he integrated singing and acting derived from Hebei *bangzi qiang* with male, and especially female, *jingju* roles.

Xun had a sweet voice, and was renowned for roles of artful young **women** of humble circumstances, such as servant girls and maids. These enabled him to develop characters with a distinctive charm, wit, and initiative, and to portray a sense of the dignity and courage of ordinary working folk turning the tables on feudal landlords and tyrants. He was also famous among *jingju* aficionados for roles in which he conveyed subtle sexual expressions and gestures. He adopted the **stage** name of Bai Mudan (White Peony).

Xun performed with many of *jingju*'s greatest names, including Yang Xiaolou, **Zhou Xinfang**, and Mei Lanfang. He was famous for his performances in *The Red Maiden* (Hong niang), *Tenth Girl Du* (Du shiniang), based on the much-loved story *The Courtesan's Jewel Box*, and *Two Sisters of the Red Mansion* (Honglou er). Like others among the "four great *dan*," Xun supported innovation, and was among Republican-period (1912–1949) actors who played a leading role in popularizing new works, or new arrangements.

After 1949, Xun became principal of the Beijing Municipality Xiqu Research Institute and the Hebei Provincial Hebei Bangzi Company (Hebei Bangzi Juyuan). He also wrote books about his art. Despite his support for reform, Xun was condemned as a supporter of feudal and bourgeois culture during the Cultural Revolution (1966–1976). After abuse in 1966 by the Red Guards during the "smash the four olds" phase (a campaign in which Red Guards sought to destroy remnants of "feudal" culture), he died tragically, having been neglected in the hospital. He has since been honored by commemorative and rehabilitative ceremonies attended by famous artists, calligraphers, performers, and **political** leaders. In 1990, the Beijing Municipal Antiquities Bureau declared his home in Xuanwumen District, Beijing (near the old **theatre** quarter), a special site.

Trevor Hay

XU WEI (1521–1593).
Chinese calligrapher, poet, essayist, painter, **playwright**, and **theorist**, who rated the first four accomplishments most highly but is remembered chiefly for the last two. Born of a concubine into a military family, Xu achieved early fame as one of "Ten Talents" from his native Shaoxing but could not advance beyond the preliminary government examination, despite eight tries. He had to settle for work as a teacher and later as a secretary to an official. Sensitive and suspicious, Xu became unstable in his forties, attempted suicide several times, then killed his wife in a jealous fit. Released from prison at fifty-three, he likely wrote all but one of his plays late in life.

His *Account of the Southern Drama* (Nanci xulu, ca. 1557) is China's earliest theoretical treatise on drama and is devoted to *nanxi*, the indigenous southern form neglected in Xu's day. It consists of: (1) an account of the origins and development of *nanxi*, its **music**, regional styles, notable plays, and compositional techniques; (2) a glossary of **stage** terms; and (3) a catalogue of sixty-three Song (960–1279), Yuan (1280–1368), and Ming dynasty (1368–1644) titles. Soon forgotten, it is now considered an invaluable source for the pre-Ming theatre of Zhejiang and Jiangsu.

Four Cries of the Gibbon (Sizheng yuan, 1588) collects four *zaju* that experiment formally and feature unconventional heroines. In *A Dream of Chan Master Yu Tong and Li Cui* (Yu Chanshi cuixiang yimeng, two acts, ca. 1552), a prostitute who has seduced a monk exposes hypocrisy when he blames her for his broken vows. *The Heroine Mulan Joins the Army for her Father* (Ci Mulan daifu congjun, two acts, ca. 1577–1580) reinterprets a popular story by having its martial heroine fight

Japanese bandits rather than Xiongnu invaders (Xu also excelled at bandit suppression). *A Female Prize Candidate Takes on the Man's Role* (Nü zhuangyuan ci huang de feng, five acts, ca. 1577–1580) features a civil heroine who solves several court cases before abandoning her male disguise and marrying. Only "The Mad Drummer Plays Thrice in Yuyang" (Kuang guli Yuyang sannong, one act, ca. 1577–1580) features a hero, Mi Heng, who castigates Cao Cao's ghost in the underworld. Laced with satire and humor, *Four Cries of the Gibbon* has been described as a sustained shriek of rage by a self-described "man out of tune with his times" and reflects a Ming trend of using *zaju* to express personal concerns. *Singing Instead of Whistling* (Ge dai xiao)—four blackly comic one-acts—is included in modern editions of Xu's collected works despite some doubts about its authorship.

Xu prized *nanxi*'s unaffected, even vulgar, directness as an antidote for the phoniness of official culture, which he felt had infected the drama of his day. He advocated "down-to-earth" language for the stage that uneducated people could understand.

Catherine Swatek

XU XIAOZHONG (1928–). Chinese • **director** and **theorist** of "spoken drama" (*huaju*; see Playwrights and Playwriting). He achieved fame through productions of *Macbeth*, *Peer Gynt*, and *Sangshuping Chronicles* (Sangshuping ji shi, 1988), staged after the Cultural Revolution (1966–1976).

Xu became interested in theatre through listening to the few ***jingju*** records his family had collected. During the Second Sino-Japanese War (1937–1945), the "living newspaper" (*huobaoju*), acted in the streets to encourage the people's patriotism, made Xu recognize theatre's potential social function. In 1948, Xu joined the Communist Party while studying at the National Drama School. Having studied directing at Moscow's A. V. Lunacharsky Institute of Theatrical Arts (1955–1960), Xu, who later became president of the Central Academy of Drama, belongs to the first generation of "New China" directors.

Xu was trained in the Stanislavski System though he aspired to integrate traditional conventions in order to create a "new vocabulary" for *huaju* with a strong national awareness. A prominent example of his new **stage** vocabulary is *Sangshuping Chronicles*. The play, which has no central story line, offers three intertwined narratives of the daily existence of peasants on China's remote northwest yellow-earth plateau. Presented as "living fossils," the characters' lives are viewed as tragedies caused by the direst poverty, suffocating traditions, and ultra-leftism. Scenes where a peasant's wife is publicly stripped, an ox slaughtered, and adulterers caught, were conveyed with rich imagery; Xu's production featured a chorus, tableaux, and **dances**, rarely seen *huaju* techniques. To experience authentic conditions, Xu twice took his company to live and work in the region.

Ruru Li

YAKSHAGANA. **Folk theatre** of the Kannada-speaking state of Karnataka in south-western **India**. *Yakshagana* literally means "songs of the *yakshas*" (*gana*, vocal **music**; *yaksha*, a demigod serving Kubera, the Hindu god of wealth). In the past, this singing style was prevalent in South India. Today, *yakshagana* refers both to this style and to several forms of the Kanara coast of Karnataka that include it.

Attending *yakshagana* is a sensual experience. There are the highly pitched sounds of vocal music, piercing and mellow sounds of the drums, and stylized speech patterns. The **costumes** and **makeup** are spectacular in color and design. The **dance** is fast-moving and the demonstrative hand language easily understood. The clown performs risqué antics and folk songs. There also is the variety of aromas coming from the food and beverage vendors and the exquisite pleasure of being entertained while sitting in the countryside under the stars.

Costumes and Makeup. Ancient India unfolds as enactment of the stories—taken from the *Mahabharata* and *Ramayana,* and other ancient legends—recount the human dilemmas and emotions involved in love and war. Several different styles of *yakshagana* exist. Though they differ in costume, makeup, music, and the relative importance of dance and dialogue, all troupes include a headdress that makes *yakshagana* unique. In 1979, this headdress, the *kedage mundale*, made it to the fashion runways of Paris when it inspired a hat designed by Ungaro. All styles have wooden crowns, neck, arm, chest, and waist ornaments covered with gold-leaf. In all forms, saris for female characters vary, from the traditional black one with red border to variety in design and any color in the rainbow.

The northern style of South Kanara is mainly known for its vigorous and elaborate dance steps and patterns, the red and yellow checked *dhoti* and skirt, and the tear drop–shaped *kedage mundale* in several larger varieties—the regular *mundasu*, the slanted *mundasu*, and the double *mundasu*. All are wrapped anew by the **actor** for each performance, piece by piece, to

The character of Karthavirya Arjuna (Madhava Shetty), in southern style (*tenku*) *yakshagana*, South Kanara, Karnataka, India. (Photo: Robert P. Sikora)

fit his face and character, a process that can take hours. The basic makeup color scheme is a pinkish-yellow base, red and white patterns on the temples, and a red, white, and black symbol of a deity, Vishnu or Shiva, or a symbol representing Shiva and the goddess Parvati together on the forehead. Costume colors include red, yellow, green, black, and white.

The styles of North Kanara, the main ones being those of the Hegde family and those of the Hasyagar family, are famous for their powerful bravado in dance, facial expressions, and dialogue. Costumes and dance are similar to those of the northern style of South Kanara, yet each family has specialties of its own.

In South Kanara's southern style, performers wear colorfully banded skirts and are famous for their whirling dance, intellectual and philosophical dialogue, and variety of characters and makeup, especially demons. In addition to epic stories, the southern troupes also present the origin stories of the temples with which they are affiliated and the origin stories of local spirits and heroes. New makeup and costumes have been created for the origin stories, but their basic makeup colors are similar to the northern style of South Kanara. The costumes have a variety of colors—deep pink, peacock blue and several other shades of blue, red, yellow, black, and white.

Venues and Performance Conventions. The season for outdoor performances begins after the monsoon (end of November) and continues until the first rains (end of May–beginning of June). Currently there are several venues in which *yakshagana* is performed. For a traditional field performance, with free admission, the patron, usually an agricultural landowner, provides the space—a twenty-feet square demarcated by four bamboo poles secured in the ground and with a rope around the upper part decorated with flowers, areca palm nuts, coconuts, and mango leaves. The dressing room is a long rectangular structure, also simple—bamboo poles with palm-leaf mat walls and flooring.

Traditional performances take all night. They are heralded by drummers playing in the afternoon. One drummer plays a barrel-shaped drum (*maddale*), beaten with the hands, and another plays a cylindrical drum (*chande*), beaten with sticks. A singer keeps the rhythm with a small pair of thick cymbals. Together, they perform a sequence familiar to enthusiasts as the invitation to attend a performance. These sounds can be heard for miles.

Later in the afternoon, performers, all males, go to the dressing room and worship Lord Ganesha, the elephant-headed god, and other deities through song and the circular moving of a sacred flame. Near sunset, another drumming sequence occurs announcing the preliminary rituals (see Religion in Theatre). By this time the audience has begun to gather, some sitting on three sides of the **stage** area, others observing in the dressing room. Vendors set up stalls to sell tea, coffee, puffed rice, and other snacks throughout the night.

From the dressing room, two drummers, a junior singer, two young boys, and two staff members, the latter each carrying a shovel-shaped oil lamp, come, in procession, to the stage area where the staff affixes the lamps to posts on either side. The singer and the *maddale* player sit on a table at the rear of the performance area, and the *chande* player stands at the stage left corner or keeps his drum on a flat wooden box while he sits on a higher wooden box at stage right. Each wears the traditional local dress—a white *dhoti* and long white shirt—and a red silk turban. The singer begins the rituals with songs, to which the young boys dance, in praise of various Hindu deities. Included are poems chanted and recited in Sanskrit and Kannada meters without dance or drumming. After the exit of these boys, two more, a few years older, enter and dance to songs in praise of deities, especially Krishna and Ganesha. They are followed by two young men dressed as females, who dance to songs mostly in praise of Krishna but sometimes in praise of Shiva.

Around 10 p.m., drumming announces the beginning of the night's story. Staff members hold a colorful **curtain,** often containing the names of the **theatre company** and the deity of the troupe's affiliated temple. Behind it are the major characters. Over the curtain we can see the tops of their gilt-covered wooden crowns and festooned headdresses. In time, as they dance, the handheld curtain is lowered halfway and finally removed and they do an elaborate half-hour dance termed *oddolaga* to introduce themselves. Afterwards, the senior singer asks them who they are and why they have come. The group leader asks the singer in a roundabout way if he knows who lives in the palace located at a certain place, who the king is, and other questions. When the singer has properly answered, they agree that he is correct and then tell their mission.

This done, the singer sings the first song of the story accompanied by dancing by the characters mentioned. The songs are in Kannada. After the first song, the characters speak extemporaneously, dramatically creating the contents of that song. The oldest traditional song scripts (beginning ca. fifteenth century), on palm leaves, do not include dialogue. Students studied the epics with Kannada scholars who drilled them in the text's minutiae so that they could quickly create dialogue and concisely and accurately debate points with their opponents. Today, some publications include dialogue, but the old tradition of improvising remains.

The sequence of dancing to a song, then creating dialogue, moves the story along throughout the night and is broken only when another major character enters the plot. Other major and/or unusual characters, such as the warrior queen, the hunter, Hanuman (the monkey god), Varaha (the boar incarnation of Vishnu), and Mahishasura (the bull demon), also perform *oddolaga*s to introduce themselves. Some are quite spectacular, especially those of the demon and demoness, who traditionally come, lighted by fiery torches, from the surrounding forest, accompanied by frenzied drumming and making menacing sounds. Like other characters, most demons hide themselves behind a curtain and, upon entering the performance area, first show only the tops of their crowns; as the curtain lowers bit by bit to drum sounds, they gradually reveal their frightening makeup. They perform their introductory dance behind a half-curtain, and, finally, the curtain is whisked away. The audience sits in awe, especially the children.

The story must end by sunrise and the patron must pay. The final dance is one of gratitude to the deities for a successful performance and a request to the deities to bless everyone, including the audience. The staff packs the costumes, breakfast is served, and the troupe moves on to the next venue, where the routine begins again.

Changes in Tradition. If performing in the field, most of the troupes approximate the above sequence. In the past seventy years many changes have taken place in all elements. Some have been made to keep up with the times, others to maintain competition with mass media. The first change was the introduction of kerosene lamps to supplement the firelight. Then came electric lights and microphones.

A new venue was a tent with a raised stage. Here audience members pay a basic entrance price and more for chairs. In both tent and field performances some traditional costumes were completely abandoned or replaced in part with costumes similar to those seen in proscenium **theatre** productions and movies. Troupes, formerly managed internally, came under an outside manager, not necessarily knowledgeable in *yakshagana*, but the highest bidder when the troupe was auctioned by its affiliated temple.

By the time *yakshagana* troupes began performing in auditoriums, many potential theatregoers were no longer hearing these old stories in the lamplight after a day's work in the fields or small shops. They were working in offices and in other professions that dissuaded them from staying up all night. As auditorium performances last only a few hours, much of the story has to be deleted, and, most often, the elaborate dances, costumes, and makeup also are omitted. Firelight is generally out of the question. A major advantage for artists is that they can perform year-round.

Yakshagana artists now appear on television. Performance time is shortened, but *yakshagana* is exposed beyond its traditional territory and it provides a way to supplement artists' income. In the late 1970s, *yakshagana* began being performed on international stages through sponsored tours. From its roots as a rural theatre that still performs at village temples and in fields after the harvest, *yakshagana* has come a long way. In spite of many changes, some of its treasured traditions can still be seen.

FURTHER READING

Ashton, Martha B., and Bruce Christie. *Yakshagana*; Karanth, K. Shivarama. *Yaksagana*.

Martha Ashton-Sikora

YAMAMOTO YASUE (1902–1993). Japanese • *shingeki* • actress. Yearning to go act when theatre was still dominated by male *kabuki* actors, she was admitted in 1921 to the training school of **Ichikawa Sadanji** II. Here she studied with **Osanai Kaoru** and **Hijikata Yoshi** and was accepted into the Tsukiji Little Theatre (Tsukiji Shôgekijô), appearing in its initially all-foreign repertory, playing roles such as Natasha in Gorky's *Lower Depths*.

When the Tsukiji Little Theatre ended in 1928, Yamamoto joined the **politically** more radical of its two successors, the New Tsukiji Company (Shin-Tsukiji Gekidan). There she played Sumiko in Fujimori Seikichi's (1892–1977) *What Made Her Do It?* (Nani ga kanojo o sô saseta ka?, 1927), among the era's most celebrated proletarian productions. Illness interrupted her career after she played Ophelia in *Hamlet* (1938), and she soon became a famous radio actress. After World War II, she was closely associated with **Kinoshita Junji,** starring in all his plays. She performed the crane-wife, Tsû, in *Twilight Crane* (Yûzuru, 1949) more than one thousand times in the course of four decades. Her last role was the enigmatic Kagemi in Kinoshita's epic *Requiem on the Great Meridian* (Shigosen no matsuri, 1978). Yamamoto's small frame belied the emotional power that came through in her delivery of the simplest lines; she was precise but always intense in her acting style.

Brian Powell

YAMAMOTO YÛZÔ (1887–1974). Japanese • playwright and novelist. Writing mostly for *kabuki* and *shinpa,* Yamamoto secured his reputation with *The Crown of Life* (Seimei no kanmuri, 1920). So-called problem plays followed, notably *Infanticide* (Eiji-goroshi, 1920), about how dire poverty drives a woman to kill her child, and *Band of Brothers* (Dôshi no hitobito, 1923), about samurai ordered to execute their own comrades. In such plays, Yamamoto demonstrated his mastery of dramatic tension. He was also essentially a realist, like his friend **Kikuchi Kan,** using realism in his early plays to challenge the status quo.

The historically based *Sakazaki, Lord of Dewa* (Sakazaki Dewa no kami, 1923), perhaps Yamamoto's best play, concerns the fall of Osaka Castle (1615), but here the problem has shifted from a social ill to a tragic flaw. Sakazaki's heroism is inspired by love of a **woman**; his face is burned in the act of saving her, and she falls in love with a rival. *The Man of the Sea, the Man of the Mountain* (Umihiko yamahiko, 1923), a deft psychological study of two brothers, based on an ancient legend, featured a lyricism owing more to Maeterlinck and **Mori Ôgai** than to Ibsen's social drama.

Like Kikuchi, Yamamoto abandoned drama from the late 1920s—as with many contemporary playwrights, his work was preempted by **Osanai Kaoru**'s preference for staging translated **Western** plays—but he pursued a distinguished career into the postwar period as a novelist and **politician**.

M. Cody Poulton

YAMAZAKI MASAKAZU (1934–). Japanese • *shingeki* • playwright and critic.

Born in Kyoto and raised mostly in Manchuria during World War II, Yamazaki studied philosophy at Kyoto and Yale Universities. He began writing plays in the early 1960s when many playwrights used theatre for socio-**political** commentary. Yamazaki, by contrast, appropriates contemporary philosophical trends to reexamine historical figures. In the **Kishida [Kunio]** Prize–winning *Zeami* (1963), he utilizes current discourse on the relationships among politics, art, and the individual to reconsider the life of the eponymous fifteenth-century *nô* artist.

Yamazaki's work is often historically based, exploring questions of human interactions and personal and national identity. He turned to **Western** medieval history with *Oh, Heloise* (Ô, Eroizu, 1972), based on Abelard's ill-fated romance with his pupil Heloise, to explore the concept of pure love. In *Sanetomo Sets Sail* (Sanetomo shuppan, 1973), he examines conflicts between personal and public history. This play, produced by the Hands Company (Te no Kai, 1972), which he launched with **Betsuyaku Minoru,** exemplifies Yamazaki's indebtedness to Shakespeare and Pirandello in its metatheatrical portrayal of the young, thirteenth-century shogun's struggle to assert his identity amidst his uncle's and mother's political machinations. More recent plays include *The Ascension of Oedipus* (Oedipus shôten, 1984), *The Twentieth Century* (Nijusseiki, 2000), and *Words: The Man Who Captured Eichmann* (Kotoba—Aihiman o toraeta otoko, 2002), exploring the importance of language to notions of evil and justice through the relationship of Nazi fugitive Adolf Eichmann and his captor, Peter Malkin.

Michael W. Cassidy

YAMAZAKI TETSU (1946–). Japanese • playwright, director, critic, and

social commentator. Dropping out of Hiroshima University in 1970, Yamazaki joined **Kara Jûrô**'s Situation Theatre (Jôkyô Gekijô) as assistant director. The same year, he joined the itinerant **theatre company** Deaf Gallery (Tsunbo Sajiki) and became its head, aiming to cultivate new audiences by promoting theatre as a socio-cultural movement.

Disbanding Deaf Gallery in 1979, Yamazaki launched Transposition 21 (Ten'i 21, 1980), later renamed New Transposition 21 (Shinten'I, 2001). He posited the binaries "larger-than-life" (myth/fantasy) and "life-size" (social life), striving to deconstruct *angura*'s multidimensional, romantic aspects and to develop plays stringently focused on human possibilities. This entailed changing his charged poetic dialogue to colloquial speech and illustrating how the seemingly extra-daily was after all part of daily life. Performances were presentational, featuring simultaneous action, rapid, monotone speech, and **actors** looking into space to discourage actor identification with character.

His approach culminated in the "field notes on crime" drama series, sourced in bizarre yet actual criminal cases, probing relations between crime, family, and personal identity, and revealing a devastating sense of alienation. *The Family Adrift: The Jesus Ark Incident* (Hyôryû kazoku: Iesu no hakobune, 1981) exposes the collective delusion of cults led by self-designated visionaries and the failure of the nuclear family. For it and *The Legend of Pisces: The Murder Case of an Associate Professor's Student at St. Paul's University* (Uo densetsu: rikkyô daigaku jokyôju oshiego satsujin jiken) Yamazaki won the 1982 **Kishida [Kunio]** Prize.

Mari Boyd

YANGBAN XI. Chinese revolutionary "model plays" prominent just before and during the Cultural Revolution (1966–1976), under the principal stewardship of Chairman Mao Zedong's (1893–1976) wife Jiang Qing (1913–1991). These works represent both a thoroughgoing reform of traditional theatre and a concerted attack on aspects of traditional culture associated with leaders opposed to Mao's "revolutionary" faction. The plays represent not only an attempt to modernize and reform Chinese theatre, but to dramatize the factional struggle inherent in the Cultural Revolution itself. Aspects of the reforms, including theme and characterization, went beyond literature and art, becoming part of a revolutionary **political** campaign aimed at the eradication of "feudal" and "revisionist" thinking.

In the plays, contemporary revolutionary themes and heroes replaced the themes and protagonists of traditional theatre. A creative method, or aesthetic, was devised in which "revolutionary realism" combined with "revolutionary romanticism," and characterization was built around the exaltation of revolutionary heroes to the most positive roles, with class or national enemies presented negatively.

Some works came into existence as early as 1963, Jiang Qing extolling them as an embodiment of Mao's thinking on literature and art, especially the view that all the arts are a reflection of class struggle and must serve the masses of workers, peasants, and soldiers. Although the plays are sometimes called Cultural Revolution's "eight great model dramas" (*bada yangban xi*), there were eventually over fifteen, most being *jingju,* with two ballets. Although these "models" are termed "plays," they include representatives of nondramatic forms like piano concertos, symphonies, and sculptured tableaux.

By late 1967, the core group consisted of five *jingju*, two ballets, and a symphony. The *jingju* were *The Red Lantern* (Hongdeng ji), *Taking Tiger Mountain by Strategy* (Zhiqu Weihu shan), *Shajiabang*, *Raid on White Tiger Regiment* (Qixi Baihu tuan), and *On the Docks* (Haigang). Their final versions, including published libretti and picture books, appeared between late 1969 and 1971. Other *jingju* developed over the

Cultural Revolution decade include *Azalea Mountain* (Dujuan shan, 1972), *Ode to Dragon River* (Longjiang song, 1972), and *Boulder Bay* (Panshi wan, 1976). All plots show the Chinese Communist Party (CCP) as the dominant force and are set in the period of revolutionary wars from the late 1920s to the early 1950s, including the Korean War (1950–1953), or in the People's Republic of China.

Although the model plays were the product of a revolutionary ideology, they were a blend of key aspects of traditional theatre and radical reforms to **costumes, properties, role types,** singing and speaking styles, and orchestration, including the use of **Western • musical instruments**.

The model theory was largely negated soon after Mao's death and Jiang Qing's fall (1976). In recent years, the CCP has tried to isolate the genre of revolutionary modern plays as a stage in the historical development of *jingju* from the factional politics of the Cultural Revolution. The works have been reproduced in a variety of genres, including commemorative videos, compilations, and books.

FURTHER READING

Hay, Trevor. "China's Proletarian Myth: The Revolutionary Narrative and Model Theatre of the Cultural Revolution"; Mowry, Hua-yuan Li. *Yang-pan Hsi. New Theater in China.*

Trevor Hay

YANG XIAOLOU (1878–1938). Chinese • *jingju* • **actor** of the "martial male" (*wusheng*) **role type.** Born in Beijing, he was the son of "older male" (*laosheng*) specialist Yang Yuelou (1844–1890). At ten, he started *wusheng* **training,** and made his first major performance at eleven. He graduated at seventeen and started performing in Beijing and Tianjin as an understudy and in minor roles. He also studied under masters like **Tan Xinpei,** and became famous in Tianjin for his role in *Sunshine Mansion* (Yanyang lou). In his twenties, he performed in Beijing's Summer Palace, and in 1906 he performed and rehearsed at Beijing's Imperial Palace in a number of celebrated performances, including favorites of the Empress Dowager Cixi (1835–1908), who called him "the little monkey." In his thirties, he performed in plays featuring the Monkey King and learned the southern martial arts style, eventually combining three *wusheng* styles into his own unique one, termed the Yang school (*yang pai*).

In the early Republican era (1912–1949), he performed in Shanghai and became famous in *The Golden Coin Leopard* (Jinqian bao). In 1913, he began a collaboration with **Mei Lanfang** and established the Chonglin Society (Chonglin She), performing in *Farewell My Concubine* (Bawang bieji). In 1918, he also collaborated with **Shang Xiaoyun** in *The Struggle between Chu and Han* (Chu Han zheng), and with **Ma Lianliang**.

In 1919, Yang also performed in the contemporary play *The Brotherhood of Five* (Wu renyi), about a patriotic group. He collaborated with Mei again in 1921 and 1922. Also in 1922, he performed at the wedding of the last Manchu emperor, Puyi (1906–1967), a performance regarded as a highpoint in the development of *jingju* roles. In 1936, he refused to perform for the **Japanese** at a collaborating official's birthday party.

A *jingu* luminary, Yang had a pure voice and was sensitive to characterization. In battle scenes he was renowned not only for his physical skills, but for the way he blurred the boundaries between "literary" roles (*wenwu*) and "martial" ones (*wushu*), his strong, clear diction setting new standards in these roles. His most famous plays include *Eight Great Hammer Blows* (Bada chui), *Jia Family Mansion* (Jia jia lou), *Water Curtain Cave* (Shuilian dong), and *Wild Boar Forest* (Yezhu lin).

Trevor Hay and Ping Sun

YAO I-WEI [YAO YIWEI] (1922–1997). Taiwanese • playwright, theorist, **director,** translator of Aristotle's *Poetics*, and an **experimental theatre** pioneer. A native of Jiangxi Province, Yao moved from the mainland in 1946 and started a thirty-six-year career with the Bank of Taiwan. This did not stop him from finding outlets for his passion for theatre. He produced fourteen plays, seven monographs on dramatic theory, and six essay collections. Yao states that he follows the famous **Chinese** writer Lu Xun's (1881–1936) advice "not to become a writer without a goal." Yao aimed to prioritize creativity and artistic subjectivity.

Yao chaired the Chinese Huaju ("spoken drama") Performance Committee (1978) and initiated the first Experimental Theatre **Festival** (1979). He urged practitioners to challenge the established expressive modes and conventions. His ideas influenced an entire generation of writers and dramatists, including Huang Chun-ming (Huang Chunming, 1939–), Pai Hsien-yung (Bai Xianyong, 1937–), and **Lai Sheng-chuan**.

Yao argued that experimental theatre is not revenue generating; it challenges tastes and habits because it is a space in which practitioners can freely express their ideas and develop new methods. Ironically, this seemingly elitist, anti-popular culture attitude led to a renewed interest in live theatre that partly appropriated **Western** examples. A significant number of **actors** and directors currently active in Taiwanese theatre made their debut in Yao's festivals.

Alexander C. Y. Huang

YARYU. Southeastern **Korean** • **masked** • **dance**-drama established in the eighteenth century in Suyong by a naval commander who invited a masked dance group from another town, from which the Suyong form developed. It was soon adapted by the town of Tongnae, among others.

Traditionally presented on the fifteenth day of the first month as part of **religious** observances for the local mountain god, *yaryu* (literally, "field play") had two parts: a procession and a masked dance-drama. To finance performances, the Yaryu Guild solicited contributions by playing **music** to bless different households. On performance day, players and villagers held a rite to the mountain deity and paraded, playing music, singing, and dancing, which became louder and more ecstatic as they reached the performing area.

Typically, *yaryu* is short, having four acts with minor variances between versions. The Suyong version requires thirteen masks, including animals; nine are required for the Tongnae version. Most prominent is the servant (*malttugi*) mask, characterized by eye-catching boils, an upwardly skewed mouth, and long ears with two long openings. Lion masks are huge, manipulated by three or four men. All the *yaryu* forms are characterized by themes of power struggles, in particular, common men against powerful and pretentious upper-class men. Suyong and Tongae *yaryu* are Intangible Cultural Properties.

FURTHER READING

Cho, Oh-Kon, trans. *Traditional Korean Theatre.*

Oh-Kon Cho

YASHIRO SEIICHI (1927–1998). Japanese • *shingeki* • playwright, novelist, and essayist. Best known for confessional-style works, often expressions of his Catholicism, Yashiro was influenced both in his **religious** faith and writing by novelist Endô Shûsaku (1923–1996), his godfather. Yashiro enrolled in Waseda University to study French but began writing plays for **Senda Koreya**'s Actor's **Theatre** (Haiyû-za) in 1946 and for **Kishida Kunio**'s Literary Theatre (Bungaku-za) in 1949. He also translated new-wave French plays for the latter in the 1950s.

Demonstrating versatility in subject matter and approach, Yashiro quickly rose to prominence. He received the **Kishida [Kunio]** Prize for *The Mural* (Hekiga, 1953), followed by *The Castle* (Shiro, 1954), a play combining his signature themes: faith and morality and the role of the artist. These themes, in addition to those of sin, self-sacrifice, love, and redemption, structure his best plays, including *They Vanished at Dawn* (Yoake ni kieta, 1968), a play about first-century martyrs in Palestine, his "wood block print" (*ukiyo-e*) trilogy, *Sharaku* (Sharaku-ko, 1971), which won the Kinokuniya Drama Award, *Hokusai Sketchbooks* (Hokusai manga, 1973), and *Lewd Eisen* (Inransai Eisen, 1975); each concerns a famous artist. Yashiro's style is distinctive for its sparkling dialogue, highlighted by his ability to capture the Tokyo and Edo dialects.

Kevin J. Wetmore, Jr.

YATRA. See Jatra.

YIKÉ. Cambodian • **folk** opera. Native sources attribute the development of *yiké* predominantly to influences from **religious** drumming rituals of the Cham, a Cambodian Muslim minority. *Yiké*'s history, however, most likely includes a host of additional influences, including nineteenth-century tours by Malay **bangsawan** troupes. Itinerant *yiké* **theatre companies** were popular in the nineteenth and twentieth centuries. Performances—for temple fairs or for a paying indoor audience—might last all night. When the Royal University of Fine Arts started teaching and performing *yiké* in the 1960s, shows were shortened to about two hours.

Jataka tales (stories of the lives of the Buddha), Khmer legends, and contemporary stories are all in the repertoire. Staging and **scenographic** elements are formulaic and often symbolic: a low table might represent a palace, mountain, or forest; a doorway might signal a particular home. Though sometimes more than one painted backdrop is used, and changed as needed, one might hang as a general background for the entire play, even with action taking place in various locales. **Actors**' movements are highly stylized, referring in some ways to gestural patterns in the classical **dance**. (Indeed, university *yiké* students must receive **training** in the core movements of classical dance as a base for *yiké*.) In addition to special *yiké* drums (*skor yiké*), **musicians** play two-stringed fiddles (*tro ou* and *tro sau*) and an oboe (*sralai*) or bamboo or wooden flute (*khloy*). Traditionally, a narrator would sing from offstage, guiding both the action and the music. Toward the second half of the twentieth century, actors took on more of the singing themselves.

Toni Shapiro-Phim

YOKOUCHI KENSUKE (1961–). Japanese • **playwright** and **director,** born in Tokyo. In 1977, whenYokouchi saw his first play, by **Tsuka Kôhei,** he was so inspired he wrote *It's a Salamander!* (Sanshô-uo dazo!, 1978), achieving national notice at sixteen. He attended Waseda University, where he formed a small **theatre company,** imitating the flashy, poetic grotesqueries of **Kara Jûrô** and **Terayama Shûji.** Uncomfortable with that style, he founded the Baby Face Theatre Company (Gekidan Zennin-kaigi, 1982), changing its name in 1994 to Theatre of Doorways (Tobira-za), building his reputation on logical, narrative-based, socially critical plays that nevertheless stimulate fantasy with characters deformed or impossible in contemporary Japan. *Nocturne* (Yakyoku, 1986) features a samurai in a burnt-out kindergarten; *Gypsies* (Jipushii, 1989) presents gypsies (who do not exist in Japan); and *Fortinbras* (1990) borrows its title from *Hamlet.*

Similarly, Yokouchi's **Kishida [Kunio]** Prize–winning masterwork, *The King of La Mancha's Clothes* (Gusha niwa mienai Ra Mancha no ôsama no hadaka, 1991), is a brilliant postmodern tapestry of interwoven narratives, including Andersen's *The Emperor's New Clothes*, Cervantes's *Don Quixote*, Shakespeare's *King Lear*, references to Japan's 1980s' school violence, and elements of the popular television drama *Mr. Kinpachi, Third Year, Class B* (San-nen bii-gumi Kinpachi sensei). Yokouchi critiques the failure of public education, among other unsettling social issues, and with the very monstrosity or impossibility of certain characters, expresses frustration with society.

Yokouchi also has written scripts for *kabuki* • actors • **Nakamura Kanzaburô** XVIII and **Ichikawa Ennosuke** III and for **musicals.**

Hamilton Armstrong

YOKTHE PWE. *See* Puppet Theatre: Burma (Myanmar)

YOSHIDA BUNGORÔ (1869–1962). Puppeteer of **Japan**'s *bunraku*, born in Osaka, the son of a front man at the Bunraku **Theatre** (Bunraku-za). He was apprenticed to the puppeteer Yoshida Tamagorô I (?–1921), but curtailed his **training.** In 1883, he became a pupil of Yoshida Tamasuke I (1853–1886) and performed at the new Bunraku Theatre in Matsushima. He called himself Yoshida Tamanosuke, changing later to Yoshida Minosuke. In 1886, he appeared at the Goryô Bunraku Theatre (Goryô Bunraku-za), but moved soon after to the rival Hikoroku Theatre (Hikoroku-za), remaining with it and its successors until 1899, after which he wandered Japan, returning to Osaka in 1901. Less than half a year later, his wanderlust again took hold. In Tokyo, with the help of puppeteer Yoshida Kohyôkichi III, he performed at the Puppet Theatre (Ningyô Shibai). In 1905, he was back in Osaka, and became Kiritake Kamematsu III in 1907, but returned to Yoshida Minosuke a year later. In 1909, he became Yoshida Bungorô III.

Following the demise of Osaka's Chikamatsu Theatre (Chikamatsu-za)—an offshoot of the Hikoroku Theatre—in 1914, Bungorô worked at the Goryô Bunraku Theatre from 1915, eventually being recognized as the greatest specialist at handling female puppets (*oyama* or *onnagata*). His colorful style was a perfect complement to the intellectual approach of Yoshida Eiza I (1872–1945), with whom he often appeared. In 1956, he was honored with the esteemed name Yoshida Naniwa no jô. He performed into his nineties, despite having lost his sight.

Samuel L. Leiter

YOSHIDA BUNZABURÔ. Three generations of **puppeteers** in **Japan**'s *bunraku*. The most famous was Bunzaburô I (?–1760), born in Osaka, who was also a **playwright** called Yoshida Kanshi. He was the son of a Takemoto **Theatre** (Takemoto-za) puppeteer, Yoshida Saburobei (?–1747). He began as Yoshida Hachinosuke, debuting (1717) in *The Battles of Coxinga* (Kokusenya kassen). At the time, puppets were still handled by one operator each, in contrast to the three-man system (*sannin zukai*) created in 1734.

For three decades, from 1724 to 1754, he was the leading puppeteer at the Takemoto Theatre, appearing in all the great plays of the time. He manipulated both "leading males" (*tachiyaku*) and "females" (*oyama* or *onnagata*), gaining renown for his versatility. In *A Beginner's Version of the Rise and Fall of the Heike and Genji Clans* (Hirakana seisuiki, 1739), he performed the female roles of Tomoe Gozen and Umegae, as well as the hero Matsuemon. He created the now famous brown and white checkerboard pattern of Danshichi's summer kimono in *Summer Festival: Mirror of Osaka* (Natsu matsuri Naniwa kagami, 1745), as well as various other **costumes** now associated with major characters in *bunraku* and *kabuki*.

When, in 1748, he made a suggestion to Takemoto Konotayû, the chanter (*tayû*) of act IX of *The Treasury of Loyal Retainers* (Kanadehon chûshingura), Konotayû felt so insulted to be thus addressed by a lowly puppeteer that he resigned from the Takemoto and joined the rival Toyotake Theatre (Toyotake-za). This muddied the tradition of each theatre's unique **musical** style and led to a mixture of styles at each house that soon became standard.

Over the years, he tried on multiple occasions to set himself up as an independent artist, but failed each time. In 1759, he left the Takemoto and moved to Kyoto, but died a year later.

Samuel L. Leiter

YOSHIDA TAMAZÔ. Four generations of **puppeteers** in **Japan**'s *bunraku*. Tamazô I (1828–1905) was the most important. He was born in Osaka, the son of puppeteer Yoshida Tokuzô, and debuted (1839) as Yoshida Kameyoshi at the Inari Shrine Eastern Theatre (Inari Shanai Higashi Shibai); a year later he became Tamazô. The Tenpô period (1830–1844) reforms forced shrine **theatres** to close down, so he accompanied his father to various other venues as he acquired additional experience. During the 1850s, he rose to the top because of his versatility in handling both "leading male" (*tachiyaku*) and "female" (*oyama* or *onnagata*); ultimately, he was honored as a "versatile puppeteer" (*kaneru zukai*). Edo (Tokyo) **kabuki** • **actors** Ichikawa Kodanji IV (1812–1866) and Onoe Tamizô II (1799–1886) taught him the trick effects (*keren*) of "quick changes" (*hayagawari*) and "flying through the air" (*chûnori*), which he introduced to *bunraku* to great popular appeal. When the new Bunraku Theatre (Bunraku-za) opened at Matsushima (1872), he shared the position of troupe leader (*monshita*) with chanter (*tayû*) Takemoto Harutayû V (1808–1877), an unprecedented honor for a puppeteer. He enjoyed great success making seven quick changes in the **dance**-play *Eight Views of Matsushima* (Matsushima hakkei). Other productions saw him fly over the auditorium with his puppets, or be immersed in a tank of "real water" (*honmizu*). In 1885, he played in Tokyo. Thereafter, he was generally known as "Boss" (Oyadama), and was considered the best puppeteer since **Yoshida Bunzaburô** I. His greatest role was fox-Tadanobu in *Yoshitsune and the Thousand Cherry Trees* (Yoshitsune senbon zakura).

Tamazô retired in 1903 but was *monshita* until his death. He, chanter Takemoto Nagatodayû III (1800–1864), and *shamisen* player **Toyozawa Danpei** II (1828–1898) were acclaimed as the three greatest *bunraku* artists of their time.

Samuel L. Leiter

YOSHIZAWA AYAME. Five generations of **Japanese** • *kabuki* • **actors,** the most famous being Ayame I (1673–1729). Born in Kishû, he was *kabuki*'s foundational "female impersonator" (*onnagata*). In his boyhood he served as a male prostitute (*iroko*) in Osaka's Dotonbôri district, where a patron helped him receive **training** as an actor from Arashi San'emon I (1635–1690).

Most of his career was localized in Osaka and Kyoto. His early **stage** names were Yoshizawa Kikunojô and Yoshizawa Ayame (spelled with different Chinese characters). He achieved the highest rankings in the contemporary "actors' critiques" (*yakusha hyôbanki*), forcing **critics** to come up with ever more hyperbolic rankings to describe his greatness. Ayame, known for his beauty and diction, was at his peak in realistic roles more than in those requiring **dance**.

In 1712, he became an actor-manager (*zamoto*) in Kyoto. In 1713, he moved to Edo (Tokyo) for a year. In 1721, he changed his name to Yoshizawa Gonshichi in order to take up "leading male" (*tachiyaku*) acting, but this was unsuccessful, and he resumed *onnagata* parts a year later. His most successful role, which he played often, was Miura in *The Courtesan of Asamagatake* (Keisei Asamagatake, 1698). Today, his greatest fame comes from his commentary on the *onnagata*'s art, transcribed in the "Words of Ayame" (*Ayame gusa*) by **actor-playwright** Fukuoka Yagoshirô and published in 1779. The "Words of Ayame" advises *onnagata* that they must live their lives offstage as **women** in order to be fully believable when playing female roles. He had four sons, all of them talented: Yoshizawa Ayame II (1702–1754), Yamashita Matatarô I (1712–1762), Nakamura Tomijûrô I (1719–1786), and Yoshizawa Ayame III (1720–1774).

Samuel L. Leiter

YŎSŎNG KUKKŬK. Variant of **Korean** • *ch'anggŭk* performed by an all-female cast. *Yŏsŏng kukkŭk* ("**women**'s national drama") can be traced back to professional female entertainers who performed scenes from *ch'anggŭk* soon after that genre's advent in the 1910s. *P'ansori* singing, once an all-male art, increasingly became the province of women, who took male roles in *ch'anggŭk,* too.

In 1948, the Women's Traditional Music Society (Yŏsŏng Kugak Tonghohoe) performed a complete all-female dramatization of the *p'ansori* story of Ch'unhyang, possibly inspired by **Japan**'s **Takarazuka,** and the name *yŏsŏng kukkŭk* was introduced. The genre quickly became a sensation, particularly among women, and new **theatre companies** proliferated. Losing popularity through competition from films in the late 1950s, *yŏsŏng kukkŭk* did not attract the government funding that has sustained mixed-cast *ch'anggŭk* since 1962.

In 1983, after a fifteen-year hiatus, *yŏsŏng kukkŭk* was revived in a new incarnation appealing to nostalgia for the genre's heyday and featuring many of its original stars. Performances are still occasionally given, and although the aging stars cannot continue for long, efforts are being made to **train** a new generation. While *yŏsŏng kukkŭk* is often blamed for a lowering of artistic standards that brought *ch'anggŭk* into disrepute, its aesthetics generally resemble those of *ch'anggŭk* in the 1940s (when it, too, was known as *kukkŭk*), differing from today's form in a greater stress on spectacle and melodrama and less concern for fidelity to *p'ansori* originals.

Andrew Killick

YU CH'I-JIN (1905–1974). **Korean** • **playwright, director,** and producer, credited with generally modernizing and setting a path for the Korean theatre, including contributions to dramaturgy, directing, **criticism,** and management. Educated at **Japan**'s Rikkyû University, he wrote his thesis on Sean O'Casey. Returning to Korea, he was a founder of the Society for the Study of Dramatic Arts (1931), which heralded the *shingŭk* movement. Perhaps Korea's most influential playwright over the next twenty years, and author of some thirty plays, he also was the first president of the National Theater of Korea (Kuknip Kŭkchang, 1950) and the first artistic director of the Drama Center (Dŭrama Senta), built in 1962.

His early works of socio-**political** criticism, *Mud Hut* (Tomak, 1932) and *Cow* (So, 1934), portray destitute rural life under colonialism, reflecting his desire to strengthen national consciousness. Similarly, he strived to rediscover the form and value of traditional **folk theatre.** However, some of his colonial-era pro-Japanese writings and plays, such as *Amur River* (Hŭk Ryong-kang, 1941) and *Jujube Tree* (Taech'u namu, 1942), made him controversial. In the post–World War II period, he wrote historical and anti-communist plays such as *Mythical Alarm Drum* (Ja myŏng go, 1947), *Wŏn Sul-rang, an Elite Youth* (Wŏn Sul-rang, 1950), and *I, Too, Would Rather Want to Be a Human Being* (Na do inkan i doe-ryŏnda, 1953). Other major plays are *Motherland* (Cho kuk, 1946) and *The Han River Flows* (Han-gang ŭn hŭrŭnda, 1958).

Hyung-jin Lee

YUEJU. Chinese • *xiqu* genre with two distinct styles. The characters used to write *yue* also differ, though their pronunciation in modern standard Chinese is identical, including tone. One means Guangdong, hence Cantonese *yueju*, the other eastern Zhejiang or the Shaoxing area, hence Shaoxing *yueju*.

Cantonese **Yueju.** This is considered the most important form in southern China, and is widespread in Guangdong and Guangxi, **Hong Kong,** and **Macau**. Emigrants from Guangdong have made it the most popular *xiqu* style outside China, with **theatre companies** in Southeast Asia, Australia, North America, and elsewhere.

Yueju belongs to the *pihuang xiqu* **musical** system, but contains elements of other styles like *kunqu* and Guangdong **folk** music. Musical accompaniment includes string, wind, and percussion instruments.

Although Guangdong's drama performances go back at least to the sixteenth century, it was probably Hubei **actor** Zhang Wu who introduced the *pihuang* combination early in the eighteenth century. Over time, troupes from Hunan and Anhui, where *pihuang* music was already established, brought their *xiqu* forms to Guangdong.

In 1854, to support the Taiping Rebellion (1851–1866), well-known *yueju* actor Li Wenmao (?–1858) led an actors' group against the government, attempting to take Guangdong capital Guangzhou (Canton). In 1855, he entered Guangxi, setting up the Kingdom of Great Perfection. Because of the rebellion, the government imposed a ban on *yueju* in 1854 that lasted until 1868.

The revived *yueju* saw the beginnings of reform: a few plays using local stories or contemporary life were performed, and local Cantonese partly replaced the original official language. Some troupes later began to adopt directly **political** and antigovernment themes, using language easily accessible to ordinary people.

The Republican era (1912–1949), and especially the 1920s, saw further major reform and significant influence from outside, especially Hong Kong. *Yueju* took themes and performance elements from modern "spoken drama" (*huaju*; see Playwrights and Playwriting) and movies. **Scenographic** elements and special effects replaced the bare **stage**. The transition to using Cantonese was completed. The natural (nonfalsetto) male singing voice came more into vogue. Major actor-reformers, like Xue Juexian (1904–1956) and Ma Shizeng (1904–1964), added **Western** instruments, including the violin, saxophone, and even the electric guitar. Both actors traveled abroad to places like **Vietnam** and **Singapore**.

Under the People's Republic of China, *yueju* at first did well, the major Guangdong Yueju Company (Guangdong Yueju Yuan) being set up in 1958. Although the Cultural Revolution (1966–1976) saw severe restrictions imposed, *yueju* revived in the late 1970s.

Role types, costumes, and **makeup** are similar to other major *xiqu* styles like *jingju,* but are not identical. Themes are also similar, with a contrast between "civilian plays" (*wenxi*) and "military plays" (*wuxi*); many items are based on classical novels, such as *The Romance of the Three Kingdoms* (Sanguo zhi yanyi) and the stories of the third-century civil wars it relates. However, there are also major differences. A compendium of *yueju* items from the late nineteenth to the late twentieth century lists some ten thousand items, including many written specifically for *yueju*.

FURTHER READING

Yung, Bell. *Cantonese Opera: Performance as Creative Process.*

Colin Mackerras

***Shaoxing* Yueju.** Originally called *didu xi* because of its distinctive clapper (*didu*) accompaniment, *yueju* takes its modern name, first used in 1925, from Yue, the ancient name of its birthplace (near Shaoxing, Zhejiang Province). A simple form of **storytelling** originating in the late nineteenth century and performed by peasants in the off-season, it became a stage form in 1906 and by the 1920s had entered Shanghai together with the migrants it served (from Ningbo and Shaoxing). By the early 1940s, *yueju* had become an all-female theatre. In its heyday from the late 1930s to the mid-1960s, *yueju*'s popularity rivaled that of *jingju*, the latter appealing primarily to men while the core audience for the former was **women**. Even after it came to epitomize the glamour and sophistication of Shanghai, *yueju* did not sever its ties to rural Zhejiang, which continues to supply much of its talent.

Yueju's emergence paralleled that of women in Shanghai (as both workers and consumers) and of women's issues in Republican China's public rhetoric. Its success in distinguishing itself from other *xiqu* styles owed much to the initiative of a cohort of stars from the 1940s who transformed *yueju,* enhancing its appeal to their fans and making shrewd use of modern media to reach ever larger audiences.

Top stars were Yuan Xuefen (1922–), a specialist in "female roles" (*dan*) who set out to purge *yueju* of what she thought was vulgar and demeaning to women. Building on earlier reforms, Yuan pioneered changes whereby *yueju*'s music was softened (no gongs and drums, a lower musical register, slower tempos), its staging updated, and production methods (modeled on *huaju*'s) modernized.

Directors and **playwrights,** largely male, created scripts and ran rehearsals intended to curtail improvisation. While sentimental romances such as *Liang Shanbo and Zhu Yingtai* predominated, *yueju*'s subjects expanded to include exotica (*Desert Prince* [Shamo wangzi, 1943]), social critique (*The Widow Xianglin* [Xianglin sao, 1946], based on a story by Lu Xun [1881–1936]), and contemporary Shanghai life (*Prodigal Son* [Langdang zi, 1947]).

Despite this division of labor between male producers and female actors, *yueju*'s stars retained artistic control and promoted their own schools (*liupai*) into the 1960s. They created a distinctly feminine theatre whose appeal derives from the pairing of ultra-feminine *dan* and cross-dressed "male role" (*sheng*) actors, the latter portraying elegant men who are capable, caring, and loyal, *yueju*'s answer to the idealized women impersonated by male *jingju* actors. For this reason mixed-gender troupes, reintroduced in the 1940s by the Communist Party, have not garnered many fans.

FURTHER READING

Chan, Sau Y. *Improvisation in a Ritual Context: The Music of Cantonese Opera*; Wang-Ngai, Siu, and Peter Lovrick. *Chinese Opera: Images and Stories*; Yung, Bell, *Cantonese Opera: Performance as Creative Process,*

Catherine Swatek

YU SANSHENG (1802–1866). Chinese • **actor** and (along with **Cheng Changgeng** and **Zhang Erkui**) one of the three great "older male" (*laosheng*) **role-type** specialists of the early period of *jingju.* Yu was the most notable actor of the Spring Stage (Chuntai) Company during the 1840s and 1850s.

Yu came from Hubei Province and promoted its singing and acting style in Beijing, founding a school of acting called Hubei school (*han pai*) or Yu school (*yu pai*). He sang with a pronounced Hubei accent his whole career and followed the **music** and performance style introduced into Beijing by Hubei actors in the late 1820s. In contrast to Anhui actor Cheng Changgeng, Yu tended to emphasize the *xipi* side of the *erhuang-xipi* duality that forms the basis of *jingju* music.

Yu was notable for his prodigious knowledge of the classical novel *The Romance of the Three Kingdoms* (Sanguo zhi yanyi)—a source of many *jingju* plays. Yu played several of the novel's heroes, including the old general Huang Zhong in *Mt. Dingjun* (Dingjun shan). Compared with Cheng Changgeng, Yu's voice was higher in pitch and his acting included more acrobatics. He was also much better at improvisation. He had a lively sense of humor and was known for inserting amusing improvisational interludes.

Yu had no sons, but adopted Yu Ziyun (1855–1899), later a famous player of "female roles" (*dan*), and lived with him as father and son. Yu Ziyun was the disciple of Mei Qiaoling (1842–1882), grandfather of the great **Mei Lanfang,** and had four sons, the third being famous *laosheng* **Yu Shuyan.**

Colin Mackerras

YU SHANGYUAN (1897–1970). Chinese • theorist, educator, and **playwright.** After graduating from Peking University (1922), Yu studied theatre at the Carnegie Institute of Technology and Columbia University. Upon returning to China (1925), Yu joined the new Beijing National School of Art and established the nation's first academic theatre department.

In 1927, with others, including **Xiong Foxi,** Yu cofounded the *Theatre Journal* (Jukan). As editor-in-chief, Yu helped initiate a year-long debate over Chinese theatre's identity. He advocated creating a new genre, "national theatre" (*guoju*), which, in the preface to his edited volume *The National Theatre Movement* (Guoju yundong, 1927), he defined as "Chinese people performing Chinese material for a Chinese audience." Yu criticized both unquestioning preservation of traditional theatre and superficial denunciation of the traditional in favor of imported **Western** forms. He envisioned the national theatre to be a reincarnation of traditional theatre in a modern society, favoring the symbolic expressions that characterize the traditional theatre and replacing outdated clichés therein with realistic examinations of modern humanity.

In 1935, Yu founded Nanjing's National School of Theatre and served as president for fourteen years. Its affiliation with the Nationalist government, as well as certain **politically** suspect relationships, made Yu subject to a series of investigations after 1949. Around this time, Yu's scholarship was challenged because of his reactionary ideas of literature and theatre.

In 1959, Yu became a drama professor at the Shanghai Theatre Academy, teaching, translating, and writing on Western theatre theory. Yu's published plays include *Mutiny* (Bingbian, 1925) and *Statue* (Suxiang, 1928).

Nan Zhang

YU SHIZHI (1928–). Chinese • **actor** of "spoken drama" (*huaju*; see Playwrights and Playwriting) and film who had worked in the Beijing People's Art **Theatre** (Beijing Renmin Yishu Juyuan) where he was deputy artistic director from 1983 until his retirement. He is closely associated with many classic productions, including **Cao Yu**'s *Thunderstorm* (Leiyu) and **Lao She**'s *The Teahouse* (Chaguan) and *Dragon Beard Ditch* (Longxugou).

Born in Tangshan, Hebei Province, he was forced by poverty to leave school at fifteen and work as a clerk. His acting career started when former classmates invited him to take part in a student club. This activity, together with a French course at a free evening school, helped him find some slight happiness. He was also influenced by actor **Shi Hui**, a relative. In 1945, he turned professional with the Ancestral Land Drama Company (Zuguo Jutuan). In 1950, when Yu was cast as Mad Man Chen in *Dragon Beard Ditch*, he started his "student-master" relationship with **Jiao Juyin**.

A devout believer in Jiao's "**Theory** of Mental Images," Yu always paid attention to the specific personality of the characters he created. Yu stressed that character creation started by nurturing the image of that character in his mind. He not only explored the characters' inner world but always tried to evince feelings and emotions through specific gestures, body movements, steps, and ways of speaking that he designed for them.

Ruru Li

YU SHUYAN (1890–1943). Chinese • *jingju* • **actor,** especially of the "older male" (*laosheng*) **role type**. The son of a well-known acting family from Hubei, Yu's father was Yu Ziyun (1855–1899), himself the adopted son of **Yu Sansheng**. His most important teacher was **Tan Xinpei,** of whose style he was the main transmitter. It was largely from developing this style that he was credited with his own style, *yu pai*.

Yu was noted for his voice, loud, clear, and strong, but also melodious and smooth. He made thirty-seven gramophone records issued through 1940. His movements and gestures were regarded as meticulous and beautifully crafted.

Early in his career, Yu made his name in Tianjin, near Beijing, moving to the capital in 1918. One reason, perhaps, was his unrequited love for an actress in the same **theatre company,** mixed troupes being still unusual then and banned in Beijing. Her fate was concubinage with warlord Zhang Xun (1854–1923), famous for his short-lived restoration of the monarchy (1917).

The main phase of Yu's career was from 1918 to 1928, most of it in Beijing, despite several tours, especially to Shanghai and Hankou. At first he joined **Mei Lanfang**'s company, but in 1923 founded his own, Same Celebration (Tongqing; not to be confused with **Tan Xinpei**'s company of that name). He often performed jointly with other stars, such as Mei and **Yang Xiaolou.**

After falling seriously ill in 1928, his *jingju* contributions were via recordings, establishing the National Drama Society (1931), and performing at invited private functions. His first of two wives was the daughter of famous actor Chen Delin (1862–1930).

Colin Mackerras

YU ZHENFEI (1902–1993). Chinese • *kunqu* and *jingju* • **actor, musician,** calligrapher, and writer. Born in Suzhou, Jiangsu Province, the son of a famous *kunqu* master, he started in *kunqu* at six and by fourteen had begun a career as a "young male" (*xiaosheng*) **role-type** specialist. He studied under *kunqu* master Shen Yuequan. In 1931, he resigned a university position and accepted an invitation from **Chang Yanqiu** to make a special study of *jingju*. He also began a long collaboration with Chang, **Mei Lanfang, Ma Lianliang,** and Zhang Junqiu (1920–1997). In the late 1940s, he performed in **Hong Kong,** returning to Beijing in the mid-1950s. By 1957, he was principal of the Shanghai Municipal School of Chinese Traditional Drama, where he **trained** many performers. In 1959, he joined the Chinese Communist Party, performing overseas.

Yu developed his own style, combining *jingju* and *kunqu* with a unique rhythm. His major items include *A Rude Awakening from a Garden Stroll* (Youyuan jingmeng), *Broken Bridge* (Duanqiao), *Li Bai Writes Drunk* (Taibai zuixie), *Burying Jade* (Jingbian maiyu), and *Jade Hall Spring* (Yutang chun). Several were made into films.

Yu Zhenfei published many works on *jingju*, *kunqu*, and Chinese performing arts. He was a member of the Fifth National Congress of the Chinese People's **Political** Consultative Conference.

Trevor Hay and Ping Sun

ZAJU. Chinese traditional genre of short theatrical forms, literally meaning "miscellaneous acts" and sometimes translated as "variety drama" or "comedy," but usually left untranslated. *Zaju*'s precise meaning varied over its long career from the Song dynasty (960–1279) through modern times. Such changes were partly due to its migration through different social milieus, with the principal setting shifting from the entertainment quarters and temples in the Song and Yuan (1280–1368) dynasties to the court in the early and mid-Ming dynasty (1368–1644) to literati circles in the late Ming and Qing (1644–1911). During its Yuan heyday, *zaju* created numerous precedents in the performative, textual, and **critical** domains, which would be taken up and developed by subsequent *xiqu* forms.

Dramatic Structure. In its textualized form, *zaju* dramatic structure consists of a sequence of four song-suites or acts set to **music** now lost. Such song-suites are derived from a Song-dynasty **storytelling** genre, *zhugongdiao* (literally, "all keys and modes"). Occasionally, the four acts are enlarged with short melodic prologues or interludes known as "wedges" (*xiezi*); in rare cases, such as *The Orphan of the House of Zhao* (Zhaoshi gu'er), *zaju* are comprised of five acts. A singular case straddling the conventions of *zaju* and **chuanqi**, *The Story of the Western Wing* (Xixiang ji), has five books consisting of four acts each.

Each song-suite accommodates different sets of melodies, which may have held different emotive connotations. All songs are sung by a single **role type,** which usually means that one character will refract the story's emotional import. The singing role's aria sequences are interspersed with dialogue and **stage** movements. In Yuan-printed texts, dialogue is alluded to rather than fully elaborated. By contrast, extant Ming versions from court or literati venues not only greatly expand the dialogue, but admix other rhymed forms in order to flesh out secondary characters. In *zaju* written after the mid-Ming, many formal conventions were ignored; instead, *zaju* was applied to distinguish short theatrical pieces from the much longer *chuanqi* that came to dominate theatrical output.

Performance. Zaju performance changed significantly over time. Under the Song, *zaju* (a.k.a. *yuanben* in North China) was a form of variety show, with the dominant element being a farce or comic skit featuring a small number of recurring types, such as the "leading man" (*moni*), "clowns" (*fujing* and *fumo*), and "official" (*zhuanggu*). Such shows were performed in large commercial **theatres** in the entertainment districts and at court. At the same time, **theatre companies** would also perform ritual plays in temples, a practice to which the many temple stages dating to that period attest. From the depiction of theatricals in Song paintings, coffins, and tomb tiles, it would appear that distinctive **makeup, costumes,** and **properties** were already featured. In mature Yuan *zaju*, the roles were expanded to include a variety of "female roles" (*dan*), "male roles" (*mo*), "clowns" or "villains" (*jing*), "supporting male roles" (*wai*), and a host of minor designations tied to age, profession, or social status. Troupes tended to be relatively small family-based entities, where a single player would assume multiple roles in a play. Cross-gender performance, particularly of **women** as males, was common. Given that most of our textual and visual evidence showcases females, it may well be that they, rather than, say, the all-male casts of *jingju,* were Yuan *zaju*'s stars.

With the fall of the Yuan, the Ming court took an active role in consuming and regulating *zaju*. Expanding on the practices of their Song and Yuan counterparts, the Ming court created troupes within the palace itself; thus, a performance could involve hundreds of extras. Ming princes, notably Zhu Quan (1378–1448) and Zhu Youdun (1379–1439), wrote *zaju* for various social occasions, giving rise to an unprecedented display of **scenographic** spectacle, special effects, and sheer pageantry. By the early sixteenth century, Yuan *zaju* music appeared headed toward demise, with new southern forms beginning to crowd out Yuan-inspired *zaju*. Nevertheless, in conjunction with the burgeoning literati interest in colloquial literary forms, mid- and late-Ming literati such as Wang Jiusi (1468–1551), Kang Hai (1475–1541), and **Xu Wei** (1521–1593) began to write their own *zaju*, albeit without adhering to the Yuan form's strict constraints. As late as the nineteenth century, such informal *zaju* were still written and, possibly, performed.

Texts. *Zaju* supply the earliest body of Chinese theatrical texts. The earliest extant *zaju*, numbering thirty in all, date to the first half of the fourteenth century. Printed in one of the northern (Dadu/Beijing) and one of the southern centers (Hangzhou) of Yuan *zaju*, these rather shoddy and individually distinct texts may have served either as actors' scripts and/or audience libretto "supertitles." With the inclusion of Yuan *zaju* in the imperial encyclopedia *Great Canon of the Yongle Emperor* (Yongle dadian), *zaju* began to be transformed into a literary medium in the Ming dynasty. Thus some of the one thousand or so plays in circulation were preserved, albeit in substantially altered form. The Ming court not only collected texts, but functionaries revised and expanded them in conformity with imperial edicts that forbade, among other things, the representation of emperors on stage. Further, Zhu Quan and Zhu Youdun produced carefully printed editions of their art songs and *zaju*, creating an important precedent for subsequent song- and drama-related publishing ventures.

Court, commercial, and literati *zaju* anthologizing efforts culminated in Zang Maoxun's (1550–1620) *Selections of Yuan Plays* (Yuanqu xuan, a.k.a. *One Hundred Yuan Plays* [Yuanren baizhong qu], 1615–1616). Catering to an emergent circle of connoisseurs, Zang's edition brought drama-related publishing to new heights. Cleverly claiming that the Yuan palace graduates were selected on account of their aria writing, Zang provided a new sheen of literary respectability for *zaju* in particular and *xiqu* in general. Not only did this landmark edition pave the way for other refined collections, but it firmly enshrined Yuan *zaju* as a literary genre in the late imperial corpus. When literary **critic** Jin Shengtan (1608–1661) created a new canon of six works called "books of genius," he included his idiosyncratic but successful version of *The Story of the West Wing* as the "Sixth Book of Genius." Together with Zang's anthology, the many successive reprints and versions of Jin's "Sixth Book of Genius" ensured the continued dissemination of Yuan *zaju* long after its music had ceased being performed. In the twentieth century, accidental discoveries enlarged the number of extant Yuan *zaju* to around 162 plays, although only thirty represent Yuan-dynasty originals.

Playwrights. In contrast to the anonymous Song variety show *zaju* and the occasionally pseudonymous *zaju* of Ming and Qing court and literati authors, Yuan *zaju* originated mainly with a social stratum of respectable professional writers. The evidence for such professionalism is largely circumstantial, but nevertheless suggestive. Except for a handful, the best-known authors, such as **Guan Hanqing,** Gao Wenxiu, Zheng Guangzu (?–ca. 1320), Wang Shifu (fl. late thirteenth century), and Ma Zhiyuan (?–ca. 1325), were said to have been obscure functionaries; such official assignations may have been largely nominal or even rhetorical, especially since no corroborating information has surfaced. Even if they held such appointments, it did not prevent their being extraordinarily prolific. Furthermore, in the wake of Guan's success, other playwrights were dubbed "Little Hanqing" and "Southern Hanqing," indicating that playwriting was not only a primary pursuit, but that such designations may also have had a stage name's promotional value. Research suggests that the entertainment quarters provided a social forum where scholar-officials, songwriter-cum-playwrights, and courtesans mingled in the shared pursuit of a staged form of narrative lyricism.

Plots. *Zaju* evolved out of the mainstream of the popular storytelling traditions that flourished in the Song capital's entertainment districts. The earliest variety show *zaju* portrayed emperors, officials, scholars, courtesans, military heroes, immortals, and ghosts, most likely in a humorous vein. Full-fledged Yuan *zaju* also ran the gamut of all genres, covering love, reclusion, history, martial heroes, **religion,** crime, and manners. Its characters ranged across all social strata, and no one, including imperial figures, was exempt from the sting of light mockery. However, despite the existence of thirty Yuan-printed *zaju*, most understandings *of zaju*'s thematic concerns are defined by Zang Maoxun's anthology, which privileges romance, particularly that between scholars and courtesans, but also prominently features dramas about the Confucian values of filial piety, chastity, and loyalty, courtroom dramas exalting wise judges, Daoist and Buddhist plays emphasizing deliverance and enlightenment, plays about characters who reject fame and fortune for reclusion, and those about the exploits of generals and outlaws alike.

Language. Mature Yuan *zaju* share a profound affinity with the poetic tradition, particularly the *sanqu* art song. Most important, their arias are intensely lyrical, owing a debt to earlier poetic forms in terms of imagery and allusion. The lyrical focus is underscored by most plays having a single character as their expressive vehicle. At the same time, the linguistic register departed from traditional poetry. Thanks to a certain metrical elasticity, both *zaju* and *sanqu* could more readily accommodate spoken language's patterns. Termed "neither vulgar nor elegant" by later critics, the hybrid aesthetic of such arias would be emulated by later *chuanqi* playwrights, such as **Tang Xianzu**.

Criticism. *Zaju* became the occasion for the first works of literary criticism regarding *xiqu*. Written by men fully knowledgeable about theatre and art song, such works in turn became models for similar efforts in subsequent traditions, such as **kunqu** and *jingju*. In terms of composition, Zhou Deqing (1277–1365) compiled new and simplified rhyme schemes for *sanqu* and *zaju*. In terms of performers, Xia Tingzhi (ca. 1300–post-1368) wrote a work appraising female performers. In terms of play-wrights, Zhong Sicheng (ca. 1277–post-1345) compiled a series of biographical appraisals of playwrights together with listings of their respective song-dramas. In terms of arias, Zhu Quan produced a formulary designed to simultaneously provide a template, a history, and a critical taxonomy for both song-drama and art song.

Impact. Although the musical form gradually died out in the sixteenth century, many of the stories from the Yuan corpus found their way into the regional operas of the Qing period. Moreover, since Yuan *zaju* were the earliest Chinese plays to be introduced into Europe, they provided an early inspiration for the development of intercultural theatre, a tradition continued by Broadway adaptations of Yuan drama in the early twentieth century. Moreover, due to modern scholars' rediscovery of Yuan drama, many important playwrights, such as Guo Moruo (1892–1978) and **Tian Han,** seized upon Yuan *zaju*, or rather their modified Ming counterparts, to address pressing cultural concerns. More recently, other playwrights have staged Chinese and **Western** versions of *Orphan of the House of Zhao* (Zhaoshi gu'er) side-by-side. Thus the legacy of *zaju* continues to evolve at the crossroads of Chinese and world theatre.

FURTHER READING

Jing, Anning. *The Water God's Temple of the Guangsheng Monastery: Cosmic Function of Art, Ritual, and Theater;* Shih, Chung-wen. *The Golden Age of Chinese Drama: Yuan Tsa-chu;* Sieber, Patricia. *Theaters of Desire. Authors, Readers, and the Reproduction of Early Chinese Song-Drama, 1300–2000.*

Patricia Sieber

ZARZUELA. *See* Sarsuwela.

ZAT PWE. **Burmese** (Myanmar) classical theatre, which has flourished since the eighteenth century, when court dramas such as *Manikhet* (1733) were produced. The plays, which mingle drama with comedy, are mostly based on romantic fiction, histori-cal anecdotes, pagoda or spirits' (*nat*) legends, folktales, and myths. Moralistic Buddha birth stories (*jataka*) were an important source. Court intrigues are common. Perfor-mances include **acting,** singing, **dancing,** and clowning. The greatest **playwrights** were **U Ponnya** and **U Kyin U.** Court support was lost following Britain's annexation of Burma (1886). The most innovative modern actors were **Po Sein** and **Shwe Man Tin Maung.** After 1948, modern dramas (*pya zat*) were added to the classical repertory.

Zat pwe troupes are always led by a "male actor-dancer" (*zat mintha*); often, the sec-ondary leads are his brothers or sons. In earlier times, the male dancer was not allowed to touch his female partner or come closer than an arm's length. By the 1920s, he could touch her, but more intimacy was symbolized by gestures such as placing a flower in her hair. Cross-gender performance is acceptable but rare.

A traditional all-night program begins around 9 p.m. and ends at dawn. First is the *a-pyo-daw*, a solo handmaiden dance to appease the spirits. Then comes a *pya zat*, with the second leads often taking the main roles. In the 1940s, the *aw-pai-ya* ("opera"), a **musical** drama, was added. The *thit-sa-hta* dance of the male lead, originally accompanied by one female dancer but, since the twentieth century, several, is performed before the intermission. After the intermission comes the classical play with its set structure, which inevitably ends with a moral message of good triumphing over evil with the help of the savior King of the Celestials, Thagyar Min. The leading man converses directly with the audience even during a classical drama. Costumes are elaborate for all characters, rich and poor. Most pieces are accompanied by the traditional *saing waing* orchestra, but **Western** instruments are used as well.

An integral item of such performances is the "weeping song" (*ngo chin*), essential during scenes of torment and in pleading for the help of the King of the Celestials. A dancer's effortless blend of singing, weeping, and talking during the *ngo chin* mark his talent.

In April, after the Myanmar New Year, troupes perform at the Shwe Mawdaw Pagoda Festival in Bago. Booking agents attend to judge the new shows planned for the next off-Lenten and dry season, beginning in October after the monsoon. The troupe, living on the advance money received, rehearses throughout the monsoon. Beginners who do not get bookings perform free in open spaces. Booked shows perform in bamboo halls with spectators seated on floor mats.

FURTHER READING

Aung, Maung Htin. *Burmese Drama: A Study, with Translations, of Burmese Plays*; Brandon, James R. *Theatre in Southeast Asia*.

Ma Thanegi

ZEAMI MOTOKIYO (1363?–1443?). Japanese • nô • playwright, actor, and writer of twenty-one **theoretical** works that are the earliest such essays on Japanese theatre. Zeami received his **training** under his father, **Kan'ami,** the second leader of the Kanze troupe, which grew out of the older Yûzaki troupe, one of four Yamato *sarugaku* troupes that served **religious** institutions in Nara. At around twelve, Zeami won the patronage for his troupe of the shogun, Ashikaga Yoshimitsu (1358–1408). Yoshimitsu's patronage opened the door for Zeami to study elite culture, including courtly manners and poetry such as linked verse (*renga*), which he learned under the tutelage of Nijô Yoshimoto (1320–1388), who may also have introduced him to secret writings on poetry that inspired Zeami to create similar treatises for *nô*.

When his father died (1384), Zeami became head of the Kanze, but he continued to recall his father's legacy, which he recorded in *Treatise on the Flower* (Kadensho, 1418). Zeami's art also owed a debt to ***dengaku*** performer Kiami and Inuô (?–1413), a *nô* performer from Ômi Province known for the gracefulness of his **dancing** and singing and whose fame eclipsed Zeami's own in the early 1400s. In 1422, at sixty, Zeami passed the Kanze leadership to his son Motomasa (?–1432), although he continued to perform. In the early 1420s, he also devoted himself to recording his ideas on *nô* performance, play composition, and actor **training** in *The Way to the Attainment of the Flower* (Shikadô, 1420), *The Three Ways* (Sandô, 1423), and *The Mirror of the Flower* (Kakyô, 1424).

Zeami's career and personal fortunes began to decline when Ashikaga Yoshinori (1394–1441) became shogun (1428). Yoshinori favored Zeami's nephew, **Kanze**

Motoshige (a.k.a. On'ami), who, by 1429, had established a rival Kanze troupe that assumed privileges once enjoyed by Zeami and Motomasa. Zeami responded by attempting to consolidate control of his troupe through writing *Learning the Way* (Shûdôsho, 1430), a text directed to the Kanze that emphasized the authority of the troupe's "master" (*tayû*). He also conveyed his teachings to **Konparu Zenchiku,** a rival troupe member who developed a close personal relationship with Zeami as evidenced by Zeami's dedication of the treatise *Finding Gems, Gaining the Flower* (Shügyoku tokka, 1428) to him. Zeami's second son, Motoyoshi, recorded his own collection of Zeami's instructions, *Zeami's Talks on Sarugaku* (Sarugaku dangi), before he retired (1430). Motomasa, likely escaping shogunal persecution, fled Kyoto for Ise Province where he died in 1432, leaving Zeami without an heir to his tradition. Zeami's failure to recognize On'ami as his successor may explain why he was exiled to Sado Island in 1434, but the exact circumstances are unknown as is whether Zeami died in exile or returned.

After his death, portions of his writings, including *Style and the Flower* and some works on **music,** were disseminated outside of the Kanze and Konparu troupes as part of the work titled *Treatise on the Flower* (Kadensho, 1402–1418, now called the *Eight Volume Treatise on the Flower*, Hachijô kadensho), but most of his theoretical corpus did not become fully known until the twentieth century, when his writings were edited and published by scholar Yoshida Tôgo (1864–1918), beginning with *Talks on Sarugaku* (1908) and other writings a year later. *Nô* scholars and actors, particularly **Kanze Hisao,** helped to popularize Zeami's theories after World War II when the full Zeami corpus was published, and his ideas are widely referenced today. *Nô*'s aesthetic vocabulary is imbued with his terminology, in particular the concept of "mysterious beauty" (*yûgen*); his metaphor of the "flower" (*hana*) for expressing a performer's stage accomplishment; "introduction-break-fast" (*jo-ha-kyû*), a pacing concept; and his perception of the "three modes" (*santai*) of aged, female, and martial characterization.

Dozens of plays have been attributed to Zeami in light of his recognition as *nô*'s greatest playwright; at least thirty can firmly be attributed to him, but he may have authored or revised scores of others. In his comments on playwriting, Zeami explained the importance of finding a "seed" of inspiration in earlier literary traditions; many of his works, most of which are "dream" (*mugen*) *nô*, were inspired by classical literature.

FURTHER READING

Hare, Thomas Blenman. *Zeami's Style: The Noh Plays of Zeami Motokiyo*; Ortolani, Benito, and Samuel L. Leiter, eds. *Zeami and the Nô Theatre in the World*; Rimer, J. Thomas, and Yamazaki Masakazu, trans. *On the Art of the Nô Drama: The Major Treatises of Zeami;* Quinn, Shelley Fenno. *Developing Zeami: The Noh Actor's Attunement in Practice.*

Eric C. Rath

ZHANG ERKUI (1814–1864).

Chinese • actor and (along with **Cheng Changgeng** and **Yu Sansheng**) one of the three great "older male" (*laosheng*) **role-type** specialists of early *jingju*. He probably came from a family of officials in Beijing. Zhang initially performed as an amateur, his brother trying to prevent him because of actors' low social status.

Zhang gave some successful performances as a guest actor in the Harmonious Spring (Hechun) Company, one of the "four great Anhui **theatre companies.**" This led him to take up acting as a full-time profession, though his brother lost his job for his theatre connections. By 1845, he was the most notable member of the Four Joys (Sixi) Company. By 1851, he headed the Double Stride (Shuangkui) Company, less renowned than the four Anhui companies, but still a leading troupe.

Zhang had a powerful build and a loud, clear voice. He founded the Kui school (*kui pai*) of *jingju*. Its main feature was probably the blending of Anhui and Hubei dialects with that of Beijing, the basis of Mandarin. Since so many *jingju* actors were from Anhui and Hubei, or had close associations with them, this was a significant contribution.

Zhang excelled in the parts of ancient emperors. Though it was then actually forbidden to enact emperors, the rule was frequently ignored. Another famous role was Chen Gong in *Capturing and Releasing Cao Cao* (Zhuofang Cao), a story from *The Romance of the Three Kingdoms* (Sanguo zhi yanyi).

Colin Mackerras

ZHOU XINFANG (1895–1975).

Chinese *jingju* • **actor, playwright,** educator, and scholar, born in Zhejiang Province. After beginning his **training** at six, he began performing the "older male" (*laosheng*) **role type** at seven. He adopted the **stage** name Qiling Tong (Seven-year-old Star), which he later changed to the homonym Qilin Tong (Unicorn Boy), after which his own special style was eventually named "unicorn school" (*qi pai*). At thirteen, he became a soloist in his **theatre company,** performing in Tianjin and Beijing.

Around the time of the May Fourth Movement (1919), Zhou absorbed the prevailing spirit of innovation and opposed *jingju*'s conservatism. In particular, he introduced realism into his performances and a style based on "seven parts spoken, three parts sung." His most famous roles include Song Shijie in *The Four Top Graduates* (Si jinshi), Xu Ce in *Xu Ce Goes to the City* (Xu Ce pao cheng), Xiao He in *Xiao He Chases Han Xin in the Moonlight* (Xiao He yuexia zhu Han Xin), and Zhang Yuanxiu in *Breezy Pagoda* (Qingfeng ting). The first two were filmed in the 1950s. After the **Japanese** bombing of Shanghai (1937), Zhou joined a patriotic group called Restless Wind Society (Yi Feng She) and collaborated with **Ouyang Yuqian** in the production of contemporary plays, such as *Wen Tianxiang* and *The Hatred of the Fragrant Concubine* (Xiang fei hen).

Zhou was greatly influenced by leftist writers like **Tian Han** and Ouyang Yuqian, and collaborated with Ouyang in the coproduction of *Pan Jinlian*. He also performed major roles in modern "spoken drama" (*huaju*), performing Zhou Puyuan in **Cao Yu**'s *Thunderstorm* (Leiyu).

In the 1950s, Zhou was appointed **director** of the Huadong Theatre Research Institute and principal of the Shanghai Drama Society. In 1959, he wrote and produced a *xinbian lishi ju* called *Hai Rui Petitions the Emperor* (Hai Rui shangshu). It later was associated with "revisionism" and formed a key element in the first struggles of the Cultural Revolution (1966–1976); thus Zhou later became embroiled with **political** figures, especially Lin Biao (1907–1971) and Mao Zedong's (1893–1976) wife, Jiang Qing (1913–1991). He also wrote a number of books on Chinese theatre.

Trevor Hay and Ping Sun

SELECTED BIBLIOGRAPHY

The bibliography is restricted to English-language books, chapters in books mentioned in the Further Readings given in the text, and a representative number of doctoral dissertations.

For China, India, Japan, and Korea, books are listed under two subheadings: General: Historical and Critical Works and Plays in Translation (both single plays and collections). Selected plays published in anthologies—not journals or similar sources—are included even when such anthologies do not specifically focus on drama. Such plays are listed by title except where they are included in drama anthologies, whose titles are given instead.

English-language journals with an extensive focus on Asian theatre include:

Asian Theatre Journal
Contemporary Theatre Japan
The Drama Review
Enact
National Centre for the Performing Arts: Quarterly Journal
Natya: Theatre Arts Journal
Sangeet Natak
Seagull Theatre Quarterly

WORKS COVERING MULTIPLE NATIONS

Arnold, Alison, ed. *South Asia, the Indian Subcontinent.* Vol. 5. *Garland Encyclopedia of World Music.* New York: Garland, 2000.

Blumenthal, Eileen. *Puppetry: A World History.* New York: Harry N. Abrams, 2005.

Boon, Richard, and Jane Plastow, eds. *Theatre and Empowerment: Community Drama on the World Stage.* Cambridge: Cambridge University Press, 2004.

Bowers, Faubion. *Theatre in the East: A Survey of Asian Dance and Drama.* New York: Grove Press, 1956.

Brandon, James R. *Theatre in Southeast Asia.* Cambridge: Harvard University Press, 1967.

———. *The Performing Arts of Asia.* Paris: UNESCO, 1971.

———, ed. *Traditional Asian Plays.* New York: Hill and Wang, 1972.

———. *Brandon's Guide to Theatre in Asia.* Honolulu: University of Hawaii Press, 1976.

———, ed. *The Cambridge Guide to Asian Theatre.* Cambridge: Cambridge University Press, 1993.

Brandon, James R., and Elizabeth Wichmann, eds. *Asian Theatre: A Study Guide and Annotated Bibliography.* Theatre Perspectives no. 1. Washington, DC: American Theatre Association, 1980.

Chua Soo Pong, ed. *Traditional Theatre in Southeast Asia.* Singapore: UniPress for SPAFA [and] the Centre for the Arts, National University of Singapore, 1995.

Cohen, Selma Jeanne, ed. *International Encyclopedia of Dance*. New York: Oxford University Press, 1998.

Coldiron, Margaret. *Trance and Transformation of the Actor in Japanese Noh and Balinese Masked Dance-Drama*. Lewiston, NY: Mellen, 2004.

Crosscurrents in the Drama: East and West. Special issue of *Theatre Symposium* 6 (1998).

Crump, J. I., and William P. Malm, eds. *Chinese and Japanese Music-Dramas*. Ann Arbor: Center for Chinese Studies, University of Michigan, 1981.

Davis, Carol, ed. *Theatre East and West Revisited*. Special issue of *Mime Journal* (2002–2003).

Emmert, Richard, ed. *Dance and Music in South Asian Drama*. Tokyo: Japan Foundation, 1983.

Erven, Eugène van. *The Playful Revolution: Theatre and Liberation in Asia*. Bloomington: Indiana University Press, 1992.

Foley, Kathy, ed. *Essays on Southeast Asian Performing Arts: Local Manifestations and Cross-Cultural Implications*. Berkeley: International and Area Studies, Center for Southeast Asia Studies, University of California at Berkeley, 1992.

Ghulam-Sarwar, Yousof. *Dictionary of Traditional South-East Asian Theatre*. Kuala Lumpur: Oxford University Press, 1994.

Irwin, Vera, ed. *Classical Asian Plays in Modern Translation*. Baltimore, MD: Penguin, 1972.

Kennedy, Dennis, ed. *The Oxford Encyclopedia of Theatre and Performance*. 2 vols. London: Oxford University Press, 2003.

Kohn, Richard J. *Lord of the Dance: The Mani Rimdu Festival in Tibet and Nepal*. Albany: State University of New York Press, 2000.

Lo, Jacqueline. *Staging Nation: English Language Theatre in Malaysia and Singapore*. Hong Kong: Hong Kong University Press, 2004.

McGreal, Ian P., ed. *Great Literature of the Eastern World*. New York: HarperCollins, 1996.

Miettenen, Jukka O. *Classical Dance and Theatre in South-East Asia*. Singapore: Oxford University Press, 1992.

Miller, Terry E., and Sean Williams, eds. *Southeast Asia*. Vol. 4. *Garland Encyclopedia of World Music*. New York: Garland, 1998.

Mitchell, John. *Theatre: The Search for Style*. Midland, MI: Northwood Institute Press, 1982.

Napier, David A. *Masks, Transformation, and Paradox*. Berkeley: University of California Press, 1986.

Osman, Mohammed Taib, ed. *Traditional Drama and Music of Southeast Asia*. Kuala Lumpur: Dewan Bahasa dan Pustaka, 1974.

Plowright, Poh Sim. *Mediums, Puppets, and the Human Actor in the Theatres of the East*. Lewiston, NY: Edwin Mellen, 2002.

Pronko, Leonard. *Theater East and West: Perspectives Toward a Total Theatre*, Rev. ed. Berkeley: University of California Press, 1974.

Provine, Robert C., Yoshihiko Tokumaru, and J. Lawrence Witzleben, eds. *East Asia: China, Japan, and Korea*. Vol. 7. *Garland Encyclopedia of World Music*. New York: Routledge, 2002.

Ridgeway, William. *Dramas and Dramatic Dances of Non-European Races, in Special Reference to the Origin of Greek Tragedy*. New York: Benjamin Blom, 1964 [1915].

Rubin, Don, ed. *The World Encyclopedia of Contemporary Theatre*. Vol. 5. *Asia/Pacific*. London: Routledge, 1998.

Scott, A. C. *Theatre in Asia*. New York: Macmillan, 1973.

Tenggara 23. Special issue on Southeast Asian theatre (1989).

Tilakasiri, J. *The Puppet Theatre of Asia*. Ceylon: Department of Public Affairs, 1968.

Wells, H. W. *The Classical Drama in the Orient*. New York: Asia Publishing House, 1965.

Zarina, Xenia. *Classic Dances of the Orient*. New York: Crown, 1967.

BURMA (MYANMAR)

Aung, Maung Htin. *Burmese Drama: A Study, with Translations, of Burmese Plays*. Oxford: Oxford University Press, 1956 [1937].

Ni, U Pok. *Konmara Pya Zat: An Example of Popular Burmese Drama in the XIX Century*. London: Luzac, 1952.

Sein, Maung Khe, and Joseph A. Withey. *The Great Po Sein*. Bloomington: Indiana University Press, 1965.

Singer, Noel F. *Burmese Puppets*. Singapore: Oxford University Press, 1992.

———. *Burmese Dance and Theatre*. Singapore: Oxford University Press, 1995.

Thanegi, Ma. *The Illusion of Life: Burmese Marionettes*. Bangkok: White Orchid Press, 1994.

BALI (See Indonesia)

CAMBODIA

Davaruth, Ly, and Ingrid Muan. *Cultures of Independence: An Introduction to Cambodian Arts and Culture in the 1950s and 1960s*. Phnom Penh: Reyum, 2001.

Kravath, Paul. "'Earn in Flower': An Historical and Descriptive Study of the Classical Dance Drama of Cambodia." PhD diss., University of Hawaii, 1974.

Kravel, Pech Tum. *Sbek Thom: Khmer Shadow Theater*. Trans. Sos Kem; Abr., adapt., and ed. by Martin Hatch. Ithaca, NY: Southeast Asia Program, Cornell University, 1995.

Phim, Toni Samantha, and Ashley Thompson. *Dance in Cambodia*. Singapore: Oxford University Press, 2000.

Shapiro, Toni. "Dance and the Spirit of Cambodia." PhD diss., Cornell University, 1974.

CHINA (INCLUDING HONG KONG, MONGOLIA, TAIWAN, AND TIBET)

General: Historical and Critical Works

Bender, Mark. *Plum and Bamboo: China's Suzhou Chantefable Tradition*. Urbana: University of Illinois Press, 2003.

Birch, Cyril. *Scenes for Mandarins: The Elite Theater of the Ming*. New York: Columbia University Press, 1995.

Bordahl, Vibeke. *The Oral Tradition of Yangzhou Storytelling*. Richmond, UK: Curzon, 1996.

———, and Jette Ross. *Chinese Storytellers: Life and Art in the Yangzhou Tradition*. Boston: Cheng and Tsui, 2002.

Brown, William A., and Urgunge Onon, trans. and annot. *History of the Mongolian People's Republic*. Cambridge: East Asian Research Center, Harvard University, 1976.

Buss, Kate. *Studies in the Chinese Drama*. London: J. Cape and H. Smith, 1930.

Chan, Sau Y. *Improvisation in a Ritual Context: The Music of Cantonese Opera*. Hong Kong: Chinese University Press, 1991.

Chen, Fan Pen Li. *Visions for the Masses: Chinese Shadow Plays from Shaanxi and Shanxi*. Ithaca, NY: Cornell East Asia Series, 2004.

Chen, Jack. *The Chinese Theatre*. London: Dennis Dobson, 1949.

Chen, Xiaomei. *Acting the Right Part: Political Theater and Popular Drama in Contemporary China, 1966–1996*. Honolulu: University of Hawaii Press, 2002.

Conceison, Claire. *Significant Other: Staging the American in China*. Honolulu: University of Hawaii Press, 2004.

Crump, James I. *Chinese Theater in the Days of Kublai Khan*. Tucson: University of Arizona Press, 1980.

Dauth, Ursula. "Strategies of Reform in Sichuan Opera Since 1982: Confronting the Challenge of Rejuvenating a Regional Opera Style." PhD diss., Griffith University, Australia, 1997.

Dolby, William. *A History of Chinese Drama*. New York: Barnes and Noble, 1976.

Eide, Elisabeth. *China's Ibsen: From Ibsen to Ibsenism.* London: Curzon, 1987.

Entell, Bettina S. "Post-Tian'anmen: A New Era in Chinese Theatre—Experimentation during the 1990s at China National Experimental Theatre/CNET." PhD diss., University of Hawaii, 2002.

Evans, Anne Megan. "The Evolving Role of the Director in *Xiqu* Innovation." PhD diss., University of Hawaii, 2003.

Fei, Faye Chunfang, ed. and trans. *Chinese Theories of Theater and Performance from Confucius to the Present.* Ann Arbor: University of Michigan Press, 1999.

Gerasimovich, Ludmilla. *History of Modern Mongolian Literature (1921–1964).* Bloomington, IN: Mongolia Society, 1970.

Goldman, Andrea S. "Opera in the City: Theatrical Performance and Urbanite Aesthetics in Beijing, 1770–1900." PhD diss., University of California at Berkeley, 2005.

Guo, Qitao. *Ritual Opera and Mercantile Lineage: The Confucian Transformation of Popular Culture in Late Imperial Huizhou.* Stanford, CA: Stanford University Press, 2005.

Guy, Nancy. *Peking Opera and Politics in Taiwan.* Urbana: University of Illinois Press, 2005.

Hanan, Patrick. *The Invention of Li Yu.* Cambridge: Harvard University Press, 1988.

Hay, Trevor. "China's Proletarian Myth: The Revolutionary Narrative and Model Theatre of the Cultural Revolution." PhD diss., Griffith University, Australia, 2000.

Henry, Eric. *Chinese Amusement: The Lively Plays of Li Yü.* Hamden, CT: Archon Books, 1980.

Howard, Roger. *Contemporary Chinese Theatre.* London: Heinemann, 1978.

Hsu, Tao-ching. *The Chinese Conception of the Theatre.* Seattle: University of Washington Press, 1985.

Hu, John Y. H. *Ts'ao Yu.* New York: Twayne, 1972.

Hu, Xuehua Sherwood. "Exploration Theatre in Chinese *Huaju* of the 1980s." PhD diss., University of Hawaii, 2000.

Hung, Josephine Huang. *Ming Drama.* Taipei: Heritage Press, 1966.

Idema, Wilt L. *The Dramatic Oeuvre of Chu Yu-tun (1379–1439).* Leiden: E. J. Brill, 1985.

———, and Stephen West. *Chinese Theater, 1100–1450: A Source Book.* Wiesbaden: Steiner, 1982.

Ingham, Mike, and Xu Xi, eds. *City Stage: Hong Kong Playwriting in English.* Hong Kong: Hong Kong University Press, Eurospan, 2005.

Jain, Susan Pertel. "'Helping, Striking, and Singing': The Role of *Qupai* in Structuring Sichuan Opera *Gaoqiang* Performance." PhD diss., University of Hawaii, 1994.

Jin Jiang. "Women and Public Culture: Poetics and Politics of Women's Yue Opera in Republican Shanghai, 1930s–1940s." PhD diss., Stanford University, 1998.

Jing, Anning. *The Water God's Temple of the Guangsheng Monastery: Cosmic Function of Art, Ritual, and Theater.* Leiden: E. J. Brill, 2002.

Johnson, David, ed. *Ritual Opera, Operatic Ritual: "Mu-lien Rescues His Mother" in Chinese Popular Culture.* Berkeley: University of California Press, 1989.

Kalvodova-Sis-Vanis. *Chinese Theatre.* London: Spring Books, 1950.

Kuoshu, Harry. *Lightness of Being in China: Adaptation and Discursive Figuration in Cinema and Theater.* New York: Peter Lang, 1999.

Lau, Joseph S. M. *Ts'ao Yu: The Reluctant Disciple of Chekhov and O'Neill: A Study in Literary Influence.* Hong Kong: Hong Kong University Press, 1970.

Law, Kar, and Frank Bren. *From Artform to Platform: Hong Kong Plays and Performances 1900–1941.* Hong Kong: International Association of Theatre Critics, 1999.

Leung, K. C. *Hsü Wei as Drama Critic: An Annotated Translation of the Nan-tz'u hsü-lü.* Eugene: University of Oregon, 1988.

Li, Ruru. *Shashibiya: Staging Shakespeare in China.* Hong Kong: Hong Kong University Press, 2003.

Li, Siu Leung. *Cross-Dressing in Chinese Opera.* Hong Kong: Hong Kong University Press, 2003.

Liley, Rozanna. *Staging Hong Kong: Gender and Performance in Transition.* Honolulu: University of Hawaii Press, 1999.

Lin, Wei-yu. "Lin Zhaohua and the Sinicization of *Huaju.*" PhD diss., University of Hawaii, 2006.

Lopez, Manuel D. *Chinese Drama: An Annotated Bibliography of Commentary, Criticism, and Plays in English Translation.* Metuchen, NJ: Scarecrow Press, 1991.

Lu, Tina. *Persons, Roles, and Minds: Identity in Peony Pavilion and Peach Blossom Fan.* Stanford, CA: Stanford University Press, 2001.

Ma, Qian. *Women in Traditional Chinese Theater: The Heroine's Play.* Lanham, MD: University Press of America, 2005.

Mackerras, Colin. *The Rise of the Peking Opera, Social Aspects of the Theatre in Manchu China.* Oxford: Clarendon Press, 1972.

———. *The Chinese Theatre in Modern Times: From 1840 to the Present Day.* Amherst: University of Massachusetts Press, 1975.

———. *The Performing Arts in Contemporary China.* London: Routledge, 1981.

———, ed. *Chinese Theater from Its Origins to the Present Day.* Honolulu: University of Hawaii Press, 1983.

———. *Chinese Drama, A Historical Survey.* Beijing: New World Press, 1990.

———. *Peking Opera.* Hong Kong: Oxford University Press, 1997.

Malmqvist, Goran, ed. *A Selective Guide to Chinese Literature, 1900–1949.* Vol. 4: Drama. Leiden: E. J. Brill, 1997.

McDougall, Bonnie, and Kam Louie. *The Literature of China in the Twentieth Century.* New York: Columbia University Press, 1997.

McLaren, Anne E. *Chinese Popular Culture and Ming Chantefables.* Boston: E. J. Brill, 1998.

Miller, Arthur. *Salesman in Beijing.* New York: Viking, 1984.

Mowry, Hua-yuan Li. *Yang-pan Hsi. New Theater in China.* Berkeley: University of California, 1973.

Obrotsov, Sergei V. *The Chinese Puppet Theatre.* London: Faber, 1961.

Pan, Xiafeng. *The Stagecraft of Peking Opera.* Beijing: New World Press, 1995.

Pearlman, Ellen. *Tibetan Sacred Dance, A Journey into the Religious and Folk Traditions.* Rochester, VT: Inner Traditions, 2002.

Perng, Ching-Hsi. *Double Jeopardy: A Critique of Seven Yüan Courtroom Dramas.* Ann Arbor: Center for Chinese Studies, University of Michigan, 1978.

Quah, Sy Ren. *Gao Xingjian and Transcultural Chinese Theater.* Honolulu: University of Hawaii Press, 2004.

Riley, Jo. *Chinese Theatre and the Actor in Performance.* Cambridge: Cambridge University Press, 1997.

Ruisendaal, Robin. *Marionette Theatre in Quanxhou.* Leiden: E. J. Brill, 2006.

Scott, A. C. *The Classical Theatre of China.* London: George Allen and Unwin, 1957.

———. *An Introduction to the Chinese Theatre.* Singapore: Donald Moore, 1958.

———. *Mei Lan-fang: Leader of the Pear Garden.* Hong Kong: Hong Kong University Press, 1959.

———. *Chinese Costume in Transition.* New York: Theatre Arts Books, 1960.

———. *Actors Are Madmen: Notebook of a Theatregoer in China.* Madison: University of Wisconsin Press, 1982.

Shen, Grant Guangren. *Elite Theatre in Ming China, 1368–1644.* London: Routledge, 2005.

Shih, Chung-wen. *The Golden Age of Chinese Drama: Yuan Tsa-chu.* Princeton, NJ: Princeton University Press, 1976.

Sieber, Patricia. *Theaters of Desire. Authors, Readers, and the Reproduction of Early Chinese Song-Drama, 1300–2000.* New York: Palgrave, 2003.

Siu, Wang-Ngai, with Peter Lovrick. *Chinese Opera: Images and Stories.* Vancouver: University of British Columbia Press, 1997.

Snow, Lois Wheeler. *China On Stage: An American Actress in the People's Republic.* New York: Random House, 1972.

Stalberg, Roberta Helmer. *China's Puppets.* San Francisco: China Books, 1984.

Stock, Jonathan P. J. *Huju: Traditional Opera in Modern Shanghai.* Oxford: Oxford University Press, 2003.

Strassberg, Richard E. *The World of K'ung Shang-jen, A Man of Letters in Early Ch'ing China.* New York: Columbia University Press, 1983.

Sun, Mei. "*Nanxi*: The Earliest form of *Xiqu* (Traditional Chinese Theatre)." PhD diss., University of Hawaii, 1995.

Swatek, Catherine C. *Peony Pavilion Onstage: Four Centuries in the Career of a Chinese Drama.* Ann Arbor, MI: Center for Chinese Studies, 2002.

Tam, Kwok-kan, ed. *Soul of Chaos: Critical Perspectives on Gao Xingjian.* Hong Kong: Chinese University Press, 2001.

———. *Ibsen in China, 1908–1997: A Critical-Annotated Bibliography of Criticism, Translation and Performance.* Hong Kong: Chinese University Press, 2001.

Tung, Konstantine, and Colin Mackerras, eds. *Drama in the People's Republic of China.* Albany: State University of New York Press, 1987.

van der Loon, Piet. *Classical Theatre and Art Song of South Fukien: A Study of Three Ming Anthologies.* Taipei: SMC Publishing, 1982.

Wagner, Rudolf. *The Contemporary Chinese Historical Drama: Four Studies.* Berkeley: University of California Press, 1991.

Wang, Aixue. *A Comparison of the Dramatic Work of Cao Yu and J. M. Synge.* Lewiston, NY: Edwin Mellen Press, 1999.

West, Stephen H. *Vaudeville and Narrative: Aspects of Chin Theater.* Wiesbaden: Steiner, 1977.

Wichmann, Elizabeth. *Listening to Theatre: The Aural Dimension of Beijing Opera.* Honolulu: University of Hawaii Press, 1991.

Wu, Zuguang, Huang Zuolin, and Mei Shaowu. *Peking Opera and Mei Lanfang.* Beijing: New World Press, 1981.

Xu Chengbei. *Peking Opera.* Trans. Chen Gengtao. Beijing: China Intercontinental Press, 2003.

Yang, Daniel S. P. *Yan Xijiao: Chinese and English Scripts and Production Materials.* Hong Kong: Cosmos Books, 2000.

Yu Dexiang and Liao Pin (text); Zhou Daguang (design and ed.). *Peking Opera Facial Designs.* Beijing: Foreign Language Press, 2000.

Yung, Bell. *Cantonese Opera: Performance as Creative Process.* Cambridge: Cambridge University Press, 1989.

Żbikowski, Tadeusz. *Early Nan-hsi Plays of the Southern Sung Period.* Warsaw: Wydawnictwa Uniwersytetu Warszaskiego, 1974.

Zhang, Xiaoyang. *Shakespeare in China: A Comparative Study of Two Traditions and Culture.* Newark: University of Delaware Press, 1996.

Zhao, Henry Y. H. *Towards a Modern Zen Theatre: Gao Xingjian and Chinese Theatre Experimentalism.* London: School of Oriental and African Studies, University of London, 2000.

Zhao Shaohua, ed. *Costumes of Peking Opera.* Beijing: Intercontinental Press, 1999.

Zung, Cecilia S. *Secrets of the Chinese Drama. A Complete Explanatory Guide to Actions and Symbols as Seen in the Performance of Chinese Dramas.* New York: Benjamin Blom, 1964 [1937].

Plays in Translation (China, Hong Kong, Taiwan, Tibet)

Arlington, Lewis Charles, and Harold Acton, trans. and ed. *Famous Chinese Plays.* New York: Russell and Russell, 1963 [1937].

Cao Yu. *Bright Skies.* Trans. Pei-chi Chang. Beijing: Foreign Language Press, 1960.

———. *Sunrise.* Trans. A. C. Barnes. Beijing: Foreign Language Press, 1978.

———. *Thunderstorm*. Trans. Wang Tso-liang and A. C. Barnes. Beijing: Foreign Language Press, 1978.

———. *The Consort of Peace*. Trans. Monica Lai. Hong Kong: Kelly/Walsh, 1980.

———. *The Wilderness*. Trans. Christopher Rand and Joseph Lau. Hong Kong: Hong Kong University Press, 1980.

———. *Peking Man*. Trans. Leslie Nai-kwai Lo et al. New York: Columbia University Press, 1986.

Chen, Xiaomei, ed. *Reading the Right Text: An Anthology of Contemporary Chinese Drama*. Honolulu: University of Hawaii Press, 2003.

Cheung, Martha, and Jane Lai, eds. *An Oxford Anthology of Contemporary Chinese Drama*. Hong Kong: Oxford University Press, 1997.

Dolby, William. *Eight Chinese Plays from the Thirteenth Century to the Present*. New York: Columbia University Press, 1978.

Ebon, Martin, ed. *Five Chinese Communist Plays*. New York: John Day, 1975.

Gamble, Sidney D., ed. *Chinese Village Plays from the Ting Hsien Region (Yang Ke Hsuan): A Collection of Forty-eight Chinese Rural Plays as Staged by Villagers from Ting Hsien in Northern China*. Amsterdam: Philo Press, 1970.

Gao Xingjian. *The Other Shore: Plays by Gao Xingjian*. Trans. Gilbert C. F. Fong. Hong Kong: Chinese University Press, 1999.

———. *Snow in August: Play by Gao Xingjian*. Trans. Gilbert C. F. Fong. Hong Kong: Chinese University Press, 2003.

———. *Cold Literature: Selected Works by Gao Xingjian*. Trans. Gilbert C. F. Fong and Mabel Lee. Hong Kong: Chinese University Press, 2005.

Guan Hanqing. *Selected Plays of Guan Hanqing*. Trans. Yang Xianyi and Gladys Yang. Beijing: Foreign Language Press, 1979 [1958 as *Selected Plays of Kuan Han-ching*].

Gunn, Edward M., ed. *Twentieth-Century Chinese Drama: An Anthology*. Bloomington: Indiana University Press, 1983.

Han, Wu. *Hai Jui Dismissed from Office*. Trans. C. C. Huang. Honolulu: University of Hawaii, 1972.

Hung, Josephine Huang, ed. and trans. *Children of the Pear Garden: Five Plays from the Chinese Opera*. Taipei: Mei Ya Publications, 1968.

———, ed. and trans. *Classical Chinese Plays*. 2nd ed. New York: Drama Book Specialist Publisher, 1971.

———, ed. and trans. *A Handful of Snow: A Traditional Chinese Play*. n.pl.: n.p., 1993.

Hung Sheng [Hong Sheng]. *The Palace of Eternal Youth*. Trans. Yang Xian-yi and Gladys Yang. Peking: Foreign Language Press, 1955.

Kao Ming [Gao Ming]. *The Lute: Kao Ming's P'i-p'a chi*. Trans. Jean Mulligan. New York: Columbia University Press, 1980.

K'ung Shang-jen [Kong Shangren]. *The Peach Blossom Fan, T'ao-hua-shan by K'ung Shang-jen*. Trans. Chen Shih-hsiang and Harold Acton, with the collaboration of Cyril Birch. Berkeley: University of California Press, 1976.

Lao She. *Dragon Beard Ditch: A Play in Three Acts*. Beijing: Foreign Language Press, 1956.

———. *Teahouse: A Play in Three Acts*. Trans. John Howard-Gibbon. Beijing: Foreign Language Press, 1984.

Liu Jung-en, trans. *Six Yuan Plays*. Harmondsworth, UK: Penguin, 1972.

Mei, Lanfang. *The Phoenix Returns to Its Nest: A Beijing Opera Created by Mei Lanfang*. Trans. Elizabeth Wichmann. Beijing: New World Press, 1986.

Meserve, Walter J., and Ruth I. Meserve, eds. and comp. *Modern Drama from Communist China*. New York: New York University Press, 1970.

Mitchell, John Dietrich, ed. *The Red Pear Garden: Three Great Dramas of Revolutionary China*. Boston: David R. Godine, 1973.

Norbu, Thubten Jigme, and Robert B. Ekvall, trans. *The Younger Brother Don Yod: A Tibetan Play*. Bloomington: Indiana University Press, 1969.

Scott, A. C., trans. and ed. *Traditional Chinese Plays*. 3 vols. Madison: University of Wisconsin Press, 1967, 1969, 1975.

Shih, Chung-wen. *Injustice to Tou O* (Tou O Yüan): *A Study and Translation*. Cambridge: Cambridge University Press, 1972.

Tang Xianzu. *The Peony Pavilion*. Trans. Cyril Birch. Bloomington: Indiana University Press, 1980.

Tung, Chieh-yü 'en. *Master Tung's Western Chamber Romance: A Chinese Chantefable*. Trans. Li-li Ch'en. Cambridge: Cambridge University Press, 1989 [1976].

Wang Shifu. *The Moon and the Zither: The Story of the Western Wing*. Trans. Wilt Idema and Stephen West. Berkeley: University of California Press, 1991.

———. *Xixiang ji Romance of the Western Bower*. Trans. Xu Yuanchong. Beijing: Foreign Language Press, 2000.

Williams, Dave. *The Chinese Other, 1850–1925: An Anthology of Plays*. Lanham, MD: University Press of America, 1997.

Yan, Haiping, ed. *Theater and Society: An Anthology of Contemporary Chinese Drama*. Armonk, NY: M. E. Sharpe, 1998.

Yang, Richard F. S., trans. and ed. *Four Plays of the Yuan Drama*. Taipei: The China Post, 1972.

Yihe, Zhang, ed. *Chinese Theatre*. Beijing: Culture and Arts Publishing House, 1999.

Yu, Shiao-ling, ed. *Chinese Drama after the Cultural Revolution, 1979–1989: An Anthology*. London: Edwin Mellen, 1996.

HONG KONG (See China)

INDIA AND SOUTH ASIA (BANGLADESH, NEPAL, PAKISTAN, AND SRI LANKA)

General: Historical and Critical Works

Abrams, Tevia. "Tamasha: People's Theatre of Maharashtra State, India." PhD diss., Michigan State University, 1975.

Afzal-Khan, Fawzia. *A Critical Stage: The Role of Secular Alternative Theatre in Pakistan*. Calcutta: Seagull, 2005.

Ahluwalia, Kailash. *Karyala: An Impromptu Theatre of Himachal Pradesh*. New Delhi: Reliance Publishing House, 1995.

Ahmed, Syed Jamil. *Acin Pakhi Infinity: Indigenous Theatre of Bangladesh*. Dhaka: University Press, 2000.

Alkazi, Roshen. *Ancient Indian Costume*. New Delhi: Art Heritage, 1983.

Ambrose, Kay. *Classical Dances and Costumes of India*. London: Adam and Charles Black, 1950.

Anand, Mulk Raj. *The Indian Theatre*. London: Dennis Dobson, 1950.

Ashton, Martha B., and Bruce Christie. *Yakshagana*. New Delhi: Abhinav Publications, 1977.

———, and Robert P. Sikora. *Krishnattam*. New Delhi: Oxford and IBH Publishing, 1993.

Aspects of Theatre in India Today. New Delhi: Ministry of Scientific Research and Cultural Affairs, 1960.

Awasthi, Suresh. *Drama, The Gift of Gods: Culture, Performance and Communication in India*. Tokyo: Tokyo University Institute for the Study of Languages and Cultures of Asia and Africa, 1983.

———. *Performance Tradition in India*. New Delhi: National Book Trust, 2001.

Baradi, Hasmukh. *History of Gujurati Theatre*. Trans. Vinod Meghani. New Delhi: National Book Trust, 2003.

Baskaran, S. Theodore. *The Message Bearers: Nationalist Politics and the Entertainment Media in South India 1880–1945*. Madras: Cre-A, 1981.

Baumer, Rachel Van M., and James R. Brandon, eds. *Sanskrit Drama in Performance*. Honolulu: University of Hawaii Press, 1981.

Benegal, Som. *A Panorama View of Theatre in India*. Bombay: Popular Prakashan, 1968.

Bharata. *Natyashastra*. Trans. and ed. Manmohan Ghosh. 2nd rev. ed. Vol. 1. Calcutta: Manisha Granthalaya, 1967; Vol. 2. Calcutta: Asiatic Society, 1961.

Bharucha, Rustom. *Rehearsals of Revolution: The Political Theater of Bengal*. Honolulu: University of Hawaii Press, 1984.

———. *Theatre of Kanhailal*. Calcutta: Seagull, 1998.

Bhat, G. K. *The Vidushaka*. Ahmedabad: New Order Book, 1959.

Bhattacharyya, Asutosh. *Chhau Dance of Purulia*. Calcutta: Rabindra Bharati University, 1972.

Blackburn, Stuart. *Inside the Drama House: Rama Stories and Shadow Puppets in South India*. Berkeley: University of California Press, 1996.

Blank, Judith. "The History, Cultural Context and Religious Meaning of the Chhau Dance." PhD diss., University of Chicago, 1972.

Bolland, David. *A Guide to Kathakali*. New Delhi: National Book Trust, 1980.

Bowers, Faubion. *The Dance of India*. New York: AMS Press, 1967.

Bruin, Hanne de. *Kattaikkuttu: The Flexibility of a South Indian Theatre Tradition*. Gonda Indological Series 7. Groningen: Egbert Forsten, 1999.

Byrski, Christopher. *Concept of Ancient Indian Theatre*. New Delhi: Munshiram Manoharlal Publishers, 1974.

Chattopadhyaya, Kamaladevi. *Towards a National Theatre*. Bombay: All India Women's Conference, 1945.

Choondal, Chummar. *Christian Theatre in India*. Trichur: Kerala Folklore Academy, 1984.

Chopra, P. N., ed. *Folk Entertainment in India*. New Delhi: Ministry of Education and Culture, 1981.

Contemporary Playwriting and Play Production. Delhi: Bharatiya Natya Sangh, 1961.

Contractor, Meher R. *Puppets of India*. Bombay: Marg, 1968.

Cousins, James H. *The Plays of Brahma: An Essay on the Drama in National Revival*. Bangalore: Amateur Dramatic Association, 1921.

Dalmia, Vasudha. *Poetics, Plays, and Performances: The Politics of Modern Indian Theatre*. New York: Oxford University Press, 2006.

Das Gupta, Hemendranath. *The Indian Stage*. 4 vols. Calcutta: Metropolitan and M. K. Das Gupta, 1934–1944. [Rpt. as *The Indian Theatre*, 1988.]

Das, Pulin. *Persecution of Drama and Stage: Chronicles and Documents*. Calcutta: M. C. Sarkar, 1986.

Das, Varsha. *Traditional Performing Arts: Potentials for Scientific Temper*. New Delhi: Wiley Eastern, 1992.

Dash, Dhiren. *Danda Nata of Orissa*. Bhubaneswar: Orissa Sangeet Natak Akademi, 1982.

Dass, Veena Noble. *Modern Indian Drama in English Translation*. Hyderabad: V. N. Dass, 1988.

de Zoete, Beryl. *Other Mind: A Study of Dance in South India*. London: Victor Gollancz, 1953.

———. *Dance and Magic Drama in Ceylon*. New York: Theatre Arts Books, 1958.

Desai, Sudha R. *Bhavai: A Medieval Form of Ancient Indian Dramatic Art (Natya) Prevalent in Gujarat*. Ahmedabad: Gujarat University, 1972.

Deshpande, G. P., ed. *Modern Indian Drama*. New Delhi: Sahitya Akademi, 2000.

Dhanamjaya. *The Dasarupa: A Treatise on Hindu Dramaturgy*. Trans. George C. O. Haas. Delhi: Motilal Banarsidass, 1962.

Dharwadker, Aparna Bhargava. *Theatres of Independence: Drama, Theory, and Urban Performance in India since 1947*. Iowa City: University of Iowa Press, 2005.

Dhingra, Baldoon. *A National Theatre for India.* Bombay: Padma, 1944.

Durga, S. A. K. *The Opera in South India.* Delhi: B. R. Publishing, 1979.

Farber, Carole Marie. "Prolegomenon to an Understanding of the Jatra of India: The Traveling Popular Theatre of the State of West Bengal." PhD diss., University of British Columbia, 1979.

Frasca, Richard A. *The Theater of the Mahabharata: Terukkuttu Performances in South India.* Honolulu: University of Hawaii Press, 1990.

Gargi, Balwant. *Theatre in India.* New York: Theatre Arts, 1962.

———. *Folk Theater of India.* Seattle: University of Washington Press, 1966.

George, K. M., trans. *Masterpieces of Indian Literature.* New Delhi: National Book Trust, 1997.

Ghosh, Manomohan. *Contributions to the History of the Hindu Drama: Its Origin, Development and Diffusion.* Calcutta: Firma K. L. Mukhopadhyay, 1958.

Ghurye, G. S. *Indian Costume.* Bombay: Popular Prakashan, 1966.

Gokhale, Shanta. *Playwright at the Centre.* Calcutta: Seagull Books, 2000.

Goonatilleka, M. H. *Masks of Sri Lanka.* Sri Lanka: Department of Cultural Affairs, 1976.

Gowda, H. H. Anniah, ed. *Indian Drama.* Mysore: University of Mysore, 1974.

Gupt, Somnath. *The Parsi Theatre: Its Origins and Development.* Trans. and ed. Kathryn Hansen. Calcutta: Seagull, 2005.

Gupta, Chandra Bhan. *The Indian Theatre.* New Delhi: Munshiram Manoharlal, 1991.

Haberman, David. *Acting as a Way of Salvation: A Study of Raganuga Bhakti Sadhana.* New York: Oxford University Press, 1988.

Hansen, Kathryn. *Grounds for Play: The Nautankî Theatre of North India.* Berkeley: University of California Press, 1992.

Hawley, John Stratton, and Shrivatsa Goswami. *At Play with Krishna: Pilgrimage Dramas from Vrindaban.* Delhi: Motilal Banarsidass, 1992.

Hein, Norvin. *The Miracle Plays of Mathura.* New York: Yale University Press, 1972.

Indian Drama. New Delhi: Publications Division, Ministry of Information and Broadcasting, 1956. [2nd ed., 1981.]

Iyengar, K. R. Srinivasa, ed. *Drama in Modern India and the Writer's Responsibility in a Rapidly Changing World.* Bombay: P. E. N. All-India Centre, 1961.

Iyer, K. Bharata. *Kathakali.* London: Luzac, 1955.

Iyer, S. Subramania. *Sanskrit Drama.* Delhi: Sundeep Prakashan, 1984.

Jacob, Paul, ed. *Contemporary Indian Theatre: Interviews with Playwrights and Directors.* New Delhi: Sangeet Natak Akademi, 1989.

Jain, Nemichandra. *Indian Theatre: Tradition, Continuity and Change.* New Delhi: Vikas, 1992.

———. *Asides: Themes in Contemporary Indian Theatre.* New Delhi: National School of Drama, 2003.

Jerstad, Luther G. *Mani-Rimdu: Sherpa Dance-Drama.* Seattle: University of Washington Press, 1969.

Jones, Clifford R., ed. *The Wonderful Crest-Jewel in Performance.* Delhi: Oxford University Press, 1984.

———, and Betty True Jones. *Kathakali: An Introduction to the Dance Drama of Kerala.* New York: American Society for Eastern Arts and Theatre Arts Books, 1970.

Kale, Pramod. *The Theatric Universe.* Bombay: Popular Prakashan, 1974.

Kapur, Anuradha. *Actors, Pilgrims, Kings and Gods: The Ramlila at Ramnagar.* Calcutta: Seagull, 1990.

Karanth, K. Shivarama. *Yaksagana.* Mysore: Institute of Kannada Studies, University of Mysore, 1974.

Keith, A. Berriedale. *The Sanskrit Drama.* London: Oxford University Press, 1971.

Khiangte, L. *Mizo Drama.* New Delhi: Cosmo, 1993.

Khokar, Mohan. *Traditions of Indian Classical Dance.* London: Peter Owen, 1980.

Kinsley, David R. *The Divine Player: A Study of Krishna Lila.* Delhi: Motilal Banarsidass, 1979.

Konow, Sten. *The Indian Drama*. Trans. S. N. Ghosal. Calcutta: General Printers and Publishers, 1969.

Kuiper, F. B. J. *Varuna and Vidushaka: On the Origin of Sanskrit Drama*. Amsterdam: North-Holland, 1979.

Lal, Ananda. *The Oxford Companion to Indian Theatre*. New York: Oxford University Press, 2004.

———, and Chidananda Dasgupta, eds. *Rasa: The Indian Performing Arts in the Last Twenty-Five Years; Theatre and Cinema*. Calcutta: Anamika Kala Sangam, 1995.

———, and Sukanta Chaudhuri, eds. *Shakespeare on the Calcutta Stage: A Checklist*. Calcutta: Papyrus, 2001.

Levy, Sylvain. *The Theatre of India*. Vols. 1 and 2. Trans. Narayan Mukherji. Calcutta: Writers Workshop, 1978.

Lidova Natalia. *Drama and Ritual of Early Hinduism*. New Delhi: Motilal Banarsidass, 1996.

Lutze, Lothar, ed. *Drama in Contemporary South Asia*. Heidelberg: Heidelberg University, 1981.

Marathi Natya Prishad. *The Marathi Theatre: 1843–1960*. Bombay: Popular Prakashar, 1961.

Mathur, Jagdish Chandra. *Drama in Rural India*. New York: Asia, 1964.

McGregor, R. S. *The Round Dance of Krishna and Uddhav's Message*. London: Luzac, 1973.

Mehta, C. C., ed. *Bibliography of Stageable Plays in Indian Languages*. Baroda: M. S. University, 1963.

Mehta, Tarla. *Sanskrit Play Production in Ancient India*. New Delhi: Motilal Banarsidass, 1999.

Meyer, Kurt, and Pamela Deuel. *Mahabharata: The Tharu Barka Naach*. Lalitpur, Nepal: Himal Books, 1998.

Mukherjee, Sushil Kumar. *The Story of the Calcutta Theatres 1753–1980*. Calcutta, New Delhi: K. P. Bagchi, 1982.

Mukhopadhyay, Durgadas. *Lesser-Known Forms of Performing Arts in India*. New Delhi: Sterling, 1975.

Nadkarni, Dnyaneshwar. *Balgandharva and the Marathi Theatre*. Bombay: Roopak, 1988.

———. *The Indian Theatre*. New Delhi: Shri Ram Centre for the Performing Arts, 1999.

Nadkarni, Mohan. *Bal Gandharva: The Nonpareil Thespian*. New Delhi: National Book Trust, 1988.

Naidu, M. A. *Kuchipudi Classical Dance*. Hyderabad: Andhra Pradesh Sangeeta Nataka Akademi, 1975.

Narasimhaiah, C. D., and C. N. Srinath, eds. *Drama as Form of Art and Theatre*. Mysore: Dhvanyaloka, 1993.

Narayan, Kirin. *Storytellers, Saints, and Scoundrels: Folk Narrative in Hindu Religious Teaching*. Philadelphia: University of Philadelphia Press, 1989.

Nayak, D. G. *Rise and Decline of Dashawatar*. Bombay: Konkan Marathi Dialects Research Institute, 1962.

Nopani, Nandini, and P. Lal. *The Bhagavata Purana: Book X*. 2 vols. Calcutta: Writers Workshop, 1997.

Obeyesekere, Ranjini, and C. Fernando, eds. *An Anthology of Modern Writing from Sri Lanka*. Phoenix: University of Arizona Press, 1981.

———. *Sri Lanka Theatre in a Time of Terror: Political Satire in a Permitted Space*. Thousand Oaks, CA: Sage, 1999.

Panchal, Goverdhan. *Kuttampalam and Kutiyattam*. New Delhi: Sangeet Natak, 1984.

———. *The Theatres of Bharata and Some Aspects of Sanskrit Play-production*. New Delhi: Munshiram Manoharial Publishers, 1996.

Pandey, Sudhakar, and Freya Taraporewala, eds. *Studies in Contemporary Indian Drama*. New Delhi: Prestige, 1990.

Pandeya, Avinash C. *Art of Kathakali*. New Delhi: Munshiram Manoharlal Publishers, 1999.

Paniker, Nirmal. *Nangiar Koothu: The Classical Dance-Theatre of the Nangiars*. Kerala: Natala Kairali, 1992.

Parmar, Shyam. *Traditional Folk Media in India*. New Delhi: Research Press, 1994.

Paulose, K. G., ed. *Natankusa: A Critique on Dramaturgy*. Tripunithura: Government Sanskrit College Committee, 1993.

———. *Kudiyattam a Historical Study*. A Trippunithura: Ravivarma Samskrta Grandhavali, 1998.

———. *Introduction to Kudiyattam*. Trippunithura: International Centre for Kudiyattam, 1998.

Perumal, A. N. *Tamil Drama, Origin and Development*. Adaiyarum Madras: International Institute of Tamil Studies, 1981.

Qureshi, M. Aslam. *Wajid Ali Shah's Theatrical Genius*. Lahore: Vanguard, 1987.

Rahu, Kironmoy. *Bengali Theatre*. New Delhi: National Book Trust, 1978.

Raja, K. Kunjunni. *Kutiyattam: An Introduction*. New Delhi: Sangeet Natak, 1964.

Rajagopalan, L. S. *Women's Role in Kudiyattam*. Chennai: Kuppuswami Sastri Research Institute, 1997.

———. *Kudiyattam: Preliminaries and Performance*. Chennai: Kuppuswami Sastri Research Institute, 2000.

Ranade, Ashok D. *Stage Music of Maharashtra*. New Delhi: Sangeet Natak Akademi, 1986.

Rangacharya, Adya. *Drama in Sanskrit Literature*. 2nd rev. ed. Bombay: Popular Prakashan, 1967.

———. *Indian Theatre*. New Delhi: National Book Trust, 1984.

———. *The Natyasastra: English Translation with Critical Notes*. New Delhi: Munshiram Manoharial, 1996.

Reynolds, Christopher. *An Anthology of Sinhalese Literature of the Twentieth Century*. Ashford, Kent: Paul Norbury, 1987.

Richmond, Farley, Darius L. Swann, and Phillip B. Zarrilli, eds. *Indian Theatre: Traditions of Performance*. Honolulu: University of Hawaii Press, 1990.

Samson, Leela. *Rhythm in Joy: Classical Indian Dance Traditions*. New Delhi: Lustre Press, 1987.

Sarachchandra, E. R. *The Folk Drama of Ceylon*. 2nd ed. Ceylon: Department of Cultural Affairs, 1966.

Sarat Babu, M. *Indian Drama Today: A Study in the Theme of Cultural Deformity*. New Delhi: Prestige, 1997.

Sarkar, Sushanta, and Nazmul Ahsan, eds. *Origin and Development of Jatra*. Khulna: Lokenatya o Sangskritik Unnayan Kendro, 1994.

Sathyanarayana, R. *Bharatanatya: A Critical Study*. Mysore: Varalakshmi Academies of Fine Arts, 1969.

Sax, William S., ed. *The Gods at Play: Lila in South Asia*. New York: Oxford University Press, 1995.

———. *Dancing the Self: Personhood and Performance in the Pandav Lila of Garhwal*. New York: Oxford University Press, 2002.

Schwartz, Susan. *Rasa: Performing the Divine in India*. New York: Columbia University Press, 2004.

Seizer, Susan. *Stigmas of the Tamil Stage: An Ethnography of Special Drama Artists in South India*. Durham, NC: Duke University Press, 2005.

Shah, Anupama, and Uma Joshi. *Puppetry and Folk Dramas for Non-formal Education*. New Delhi: Sterling, 1992.

Sharma, H. V. *The Theatres of the Buddhists*. Delhi: Rajalakshmi, 1987.

Sinha, Biswajit. *Encyclopaedia of Indian Theatre*. 3 vols. Delhi: Raj, 2000 and continuing.

Sircar, Badal. *The Third Theatre*. Calcutta: Badal Sircar, 1978.

Srampickal, Jacob. *Voice to the Voiceless: The Power of People's Theatre in India*. London: Palgrave Macmillan, 1994.

Stoler Miller, Barbara, ed. *Theater of Memory: The Plays of Kalidasa*. New York: Columbia University, 1984.

Subramanyam, Lakshmi, ed. *Muffled Voices: Women in Modern Indian Theatre*. New Delhi: Shakti, 2002.

Swann, Darius L. "Three Forms of Traditional Theatre of Uttar Pradesh, North India." PhD diss., University of Hawaii, 1974.

Tilakasiri, J. *Puppetry in Sri Lanka*. Sri Lanka: Department of Cultural Affairs, 1971.

Trivedi, Poonam, and Dennis Bartholomeusz, eds. *India's Shakespeare: Translation, Interpretation, and Performance*. Newark: University of Delaware Press, 2005.

Unni, N. P., and Bruce M. Sullivan. *The Wedding of Arjuna and Subhadra: The Kudiyattam Drama Subhadra Dhananjaya*. New Delhi: Nag Publications, 2001.

Valmiki. *The Ramayana*. Adapt. P. Lal. New Delhi: Vikas, 1981.

Van Zile, Judy. *Dance in India: An Annotated Guide to Source Materials*. Providence: Asian Music Publications, 1973.

Varadpande, M. L. *Traditions of Indian Theatre*. New Delhi: Abhinav, 1978.

———. *Ancient Indian and Indo-Greek Theatre*. New Delhi: Abhinav, 1981.

———. *Krishna Theatre in India*. New Delhi: Abhinav, 1982.

———. *Religion and Theatre*. New Delhi: Abhinav, 1983.

———. *Invitation to Indian Theatre*. New Delhi: Arnold Heinemann, 1987.

———. *The Mahabharata in Performance*. New Delhi: Clarion, 1990.

———. *History of Indian Theatre: Loka Ranga; Panorama of Indian Folk Theatre*. New Delhi: Abhinav, 1992.

———, and Sunil Subhedar, eds. *The Critique of Indian Theatre*. Delhi: Unique, 1981.

Vatsyayan, Kapila. *Classical Indian Dance in Literature and the Arts*. Delhi: Sangeet Natak Akademi, 1968.

———. *Traditional Indian Theatre: Multiple Streams*. New Delhi: National Book Trust, 1980.

Venu, G. *Production of a Play in Kutiyattam*. Trichur: Natanakaital Publication, 1989.

Vyasa. *The Mahabharata*. Adapt. P. Lal. New Delhi: Vikas, 1980.

Wade, Bonnie. *Performing Arts in India: Essays on Music, Dance and Drama*. Berkeley: University of California, 1983.

Wells, Henry W. *The Classical Drama of India: Studies in Its Value for the Literature and Theatre of the World*. New York: Asia Publishing House, 1963.

Wilson, H. H., trans. *Select Specimens of the Theatre of the Hindus*. London: Trubner, 1871.

Yajnik, R. K. *The Indian Theatre: Its Origin and Its Later Developments under European Influence, with Special Reference to Western India*. London: Alien and Unwin, 1933.

Yarrow, Ralph. *Indian Theatre: Theatre of Origin, Theatre of Freedom*. Richmond, UK: Curzon, 2001.

Zarrilli, Phillip B. *When the Body Becomes All Eyes: Paradigms, Practices, and Discourses of Power in Kalarippayattu*. New Delhi: Oxford University Press, 1998/2000.

———. *Kathakali Dance-Drama: Where Gods and Demons Come to Play*. London: Routledge, 2000. With videotapes.

———. *The Psychophysical Actor at Work—Acting "... at the nerve ends."* London: Routledge, forthcoming. With DVD-ROM.

Plays in Translation (India)

Body Blows: Women, Violence and Surviva: Three Plays. Calcutta: Seagull, 2000.

Coulson, Michael, trans. *Three Sanskrit Plays*. Harmondsworth, UK: Penguin, 1981.

Deshpande, G. P., ed. *Modern Indian Drama*. New Delhi: Sahitya Akademi, 2000.

Kambar, Chandrasekhar, ed. *Modern Indian Plays*. 2 vols. New Delhi: National School of Drama, 2000–2001.

Karnad, Girish et al., trans. *Three Modern Indian Plays*. Delhi: Oxford University Press, 1989.

Katyul, Anjum. *Indian Plays*. London: Nick Hern, 2002.

Lal, P., trans. *Great Sanskrit Plays*. New York: New Directions, 1964.

Mee, Erin B., ed. *Drama Contemporary: India*. Baltimore: Johns Hopkins University, 2001.

Tagore, Rabindranath. *Three Plays*. Trans. Marjorie Sykes. Oxford: Oxford University Press, 1950.

Van Buitenen, J. A. B., trans. *Two Plays of Ancient India*. New York: Columbia University Press, 1968.

Wells, Henry, ed. *Six Sanskrit Plays*. New York: Asia, 1964.

INDONESIA (INCLUDING BALI)

Anderson, Benedict R. O'G. *Mythology and the Tolerance of the Javanese*. Ithaca, NY: Cornell Modern Indonesia Project, Southeast Asia Program, Cornell University, 1996 [1965].

Arps, Bernard, ed. *Performance in Java and Bali: Studies of Narrative, Theatre, Music, and Dance*. London: School of Oriental and African Studies, University of London, 1993.

Aveling, Harry. *Man and Society in the Works of the Indonesian Playwright Utuy Tatang Sontani*. Honolulu: University of Hawaii Southeast Asian Studies Program, 1979.

Bandem, I Made, and Fredrik Eugene de Boer. *Balinese Dance in Transition*. Kuala Lumpur: Oxford University Press, 1995 [1981].

Basari. *Demon Abduction: A Wayang Ritual Drama from West Java*. Trans. and introd. Matthew Isaac Cohen. Jakarta: Lontar Foundation, 1999.

Brakel-Papenhuyzen, Clara. *Classical Javanese Dance*. Leiden: KLTIV Press, 1995.

Brandon, James R., ed. *On Thrones of Gold: Three Javanese Shadow Plays*. Honolulu: University of Hawaii Press, 1993.

Buurman, Peter. *Wayang Golek: The Entrancing World of Classical Javanese Puppet Theatre*. New York: Oxford University Press, 1988.

Coast, John. *Dancing out of Bali*. London: Faber, 1954.

Cohen, Matthew Isaac. "An Inheritance from the Friends of God: The Southern Shadow Puppet Theater of West Java, Indonesia." PhD diss., Yale University. Ann Arbor: UMI, 1997.

———. *The Komedie Stamboel: Popular Theater in Colonial Indonesia, 1891–1903*. Athens: Ohio University Press, 2006.

———, ed. *The Lontar Anthology of Indonesia Drama, 1*. Jakarta: Lontar, 2006.

Covarrubias, Miguel. *Island of Bali*. Singapore: Periplus, 1999 [1946].

de Zoete, Beryl, and Walter Spies. *Dance and Drama in Bali*. Boston: Tuttle, 2002 [1938].

Dibia, I Wayan, and Rucina Ballinger. *Balinese Dance, Drama and Music*. Singapore: Periplus, 2004.

Djajasoebrata, Alit. *Shadow Theatre in Java: The Puppets, Performance and Repertoire*. Amsterdam: Pepin, 1999.

Emigh, John. *Masked Performance: The Play of Self and Other in Ritual and Theatre*. Philadelphia: University of Pennsylvania Press, 1996.

Foley, Mary Kathleen [Kathy]. "The Sundanese Wayang Golek: The Rod Puppet Theatre of West Java." PhD diss., University of Hawaii, 1979.

George, David E. R. *Balinese Ritual Theatre*. Cambridge and Alexandria, VA: Chadwyck-Healey, 1991.

Groenendael, Victoria M. Clara van. *The Dalang Behind the Wayang: The Role of the Surakarta and the Yogyakarta Dalang in Indonesian-Javanese Society*. Cinnaminson, NJ: Foris, 1985.

———. *Wayang Theatre in Indonesia: An Annotated Bibliography*. Cinnaminson, NJ: Foris, 1987.

Hatley, Barbara. "*Ketoprak*: Performance and Social Meaning in a Javanese Popular Theatre Form." PhD diss., University of Sydney, 1985.

Heimarck, Brita Renée. *Balinese Discourses on Music and Modernization: Village Voices and Urban Views*. New York: Routledge, 2003.

Hellman, Jörgen. *Performing the Nation: Cultural Politics in New Order Indonesia*. Copenhagen: NIAS Press, 2003.

Herbert, Mimi, with Nur S. Rahardjo. *Voices of the Puppet Masters*. Jakarta: Lontar Foundation; Honolulu: University of Hawaii Press, 2002.

Herbst, Edward. *Voices in Bali: Energies and Perceptions in Vocal Music and Dance Theater*. Hanover, NH: University Press of New England, 1997.

Hinzler, H. I. R. *Bima Swarga in Balinese Wayang*. The Hague: Martinus Nijhoff, 1981.

Hobart, Angela. *Dancing Shadows of Bali: Theatre and Myth*. New York: KPI, 1987.

———. *Healing Performances of Bali: Between Darkness and Light*. New York: Berghahn Books, 2004.

Holt, Claire. *Art in Indonesia: Continuities and Change*. Ithaca, NY: Cornell University Press, 1967.

Hooykaas, Christiaan. *Kama and Kala: Materials for the Study of Shadow Theatre in Bali*. London: North-Holland Publishing, 1973.

Hough, Brett, and Barbara Hatley, eds. *Intercultural Exchange between Australia and Indonesia*. Clayton, Victoria: Monash Asia Institute, Monash University, 1995.

Irvine, David. *Leather Gods and Wooden Heroes: Java's Classical Wayang*. Singapore: Times Edition, 1996.

Jotaryono, Sindu. *The Traitor Jobin: A Wayang Golek Performance from Central Java*. Trans. Daniel McGuire and Lukman Aris. Jakarta: Lontar, 1999.

Kartomi-Thomas, Karen Sri. "Tradition and Modern Indonesian Theatre." PhD diss., University of California, 1994.

Keeler, Ward. *Javanese Shadow Plays, Javanese Selves*. Princeton, NJ: Princeton University Press, 1987.

———. *Javanese Shadow Puppets*. Singapore: Oxford University Press, 1992.

Koesasi, B. *Lenong and Si Pitung*. Clayton, Australia: Centre of Southeast Asian Studies, Monash University, Working Paper 73, 1992.

Long, Roger. *Javanese Shadow Theatre: Movement and Characterization in Ngayogyakarta Wayang Kulit*. Ann Arbor: University of Michigan Press, 1982.

Mangkunagara VII. *On the Wayang Kulit (Purwa) and Its Symbolic and Mystical Elements*. Trans. Claire Holt. Ithaca, NY: Southeast Asia Program, Cornell University, 1957 [1933].

Mellema, R. L. *Wayang Puppets: Carving, Colouring, Symbolism*. Trans. Mantle Hood. Amsterdam: Koninklijk Instituut voor de Tropen, 1954.

Merrin, Leona Mayer. *Devi Dja: Woman of Java*. Santa Monica, CA: Lee and Lee, 1989.

Moerdowo, R. M. *Wayang: Its Significance in Indonesian Society*. Jakarta: Balai Pustaka, 1982.

Mohamad, Goenawan. *Modern Drama of Indonesia*. New York: Festival of Indonesia Foundation, 1991.

Morgan, Stephanie, and Laurie Jo Sears, eds. *Aesthetic Tradition and Cultural Transition in Java and Bali*. Madison: Center for Southeast Asian Studies, University of Wisconsin, 1984.

Mrázek, Jan. *Puppet Theater in Contemporary Indonesia: New Approaches to Performance Events*. Ann Arbor: Centers for South and Southeast Asian Studies, University of Michigan, 2002.

———. *Phenomenology of a Puppet Theatre: Contemplations on the Art of Javanese Wayang Kulit*. Leiden: KITLV Press, 2005.

Mulyono. *Human Character in the Wayang*. Trans. M. M. Medeiros. Jakarta: Gunung Agung, 1981.

Ness, Edward C. van, and Shita Prawirohardjo. *Javanese Wayang Kulit: An Introduction*. Kuala Lumpur: Oxford University Press, 1980.

Noer, Arifin C. *Moths*. Trans. Harry Aveling. Kuala Lumpur: Dewan Bahasa dan Pustaka, 1974.

———. *The Bottomless Well*. Trans. Karin Johnson and Bernard Sellato. Jakarta: Lontar, 1992.

Nor, M. A. *Randai Dance of Minangkabau Sumatra with Labanotation Scores.* Kuala Lumpur: Department of Publications, University of Malaysia, 1986.

Pauka, Kirstin. *Theater and Martial Arts in West Sumatra: Randai and Silek of the Minangkabau.* Athens: Ohio University Press, 1998.

Pausacker, Helen. *Behind the Shadows: Understanding a Wayang Performance.* Melbourne: Indonesian Art Society, 1996.

Peacock, James L. *Rites of Modernization: Symbols and Social Aspects of Indonesian Proletarian Drama.* Chicago: University of Chicago Press, 1987 [1968].

Picard, Michel. *Bali: Cultural Tourism and Touristic Culture.* Trans. Diana Darling. Singapore: Archipelago Press, 1996 [1992].

Purwacarita, Sarib. *Released from Kala's Grip: A Wayang Exorcism Performance from East Java.* Trans. and introd. Victoria M. Clara van Groenendael. Jakarta: Lontar, 1999.

Rafferty, Ellen, ed. *Putu Wijaya in Performance: A Script and Study of Indonesian Theatre.* Madison: Center for Southeast Asian Studies, University of Wisconsin, 1989.

Rassers, W. H. *Panji, the Culture Hero: A Structural Study of Religion in Java.* The Hague: Nijhoff, 1959.

Rendra, W. S. *The Struggle of the Naga Tribe: A Play.* Trans. Maxwell Ronald Lane. St. Lucia: University of Queensland Press, 1979.

———. *The Mastodon and the Condors.* Calcutta: P. Lal, 1981.

Riantiarno, N. *Time Bomb and Cockroach Opera.* Trans. Barbara Hatley and John H. McGlynn. Jakarta: Lontar, 1992.

Scott-Kemball, Jeune. *Javanese Shadow Puppets: The Raffles Collection in the British Museum.* London: Trustees of the British Museum, 1970.

Sears, Laurie Jo. *Shadows of Empire: Colonial Discourse and Javanese Tales.* Durham, NC: Duke University Press, 1996.

Sedyawati, Edi, ed. *Performing Arts.* Singapore: Archipelago Press, 1998.

Simatupang, Iwan. *Square Moon and Three Other Short Plays.* Trans. John H. McGlynn. Jakarta: Lontar, 1997.

Simatupang, R. O. *Dances in Indonesia.* Jakarta: Yayasan Prapanca, n.d.

Slattum, Judy. *Masks of Bali: Spirits of an Ancient Drama.* San Francisco: Chronicle, 1992.

Soedarsono. *Dances in Indonesia.* Jakarta: Gunung Agung, 1974.

———. *Living Traditional Theaters in Indonesia: Nine Selected Papers.* Yogyakarta: Akademi Seni Tari Indonesia, 1974.

———. *Wayang Wong: The State Ritual Drama of the Court of Yogyakarta.* Yogyakarta: Gadjah Mada University Press, 1984.

Sontani, Utuy Tatang, Usman Awang, and Joo For Lee. *Three South East Asian Plays: Si Kabayan by Utuy Sontani.* Kuala Lumpur: Tenggara, 1970.

Spies, Walter, and Beryl de Zoete. *Dance and Drama in Bali.* Hong Kong: Periplus, 2002 [1938].

Sunarya, Asep Sunandar. *The Birth of Gatotkaca: A Sundanese Wayang Golek Purwa Performance from West Java.* Trans. and introd. Andrew N. Weintraub. Jakarta: Lontar, 1999.

Susanto, Budi. *Ketoprak: The Politics of the Past in the Present-Day Java.* Yogyakarta: Kanisius, 1997.

Sweeney, Amin. *Malay Shadow Puppets: The Wayang Siam of Kelantan.* London: Trustees of the British Museum, 1972.

Vickers, Adrian. *Journeys of Desire: A Study of the Balinese Text Malat.* Leiden: KITLV Press, 2005.

Weintraub, Andrew. *Power Plays: Wayang Golek Puppet Theater of West Java.* Athens: Ohio University Press, 2002.

Widapandaya, Gaib. *Gatutkaca on Trial: A New Creation in the Shadow Theater of Central Java.* Trans. Gloria Soepomo Poedjosoedarmo. Jakarta: Lontar, 1999.

Winet, Evan. "Facing Indonesia: Character, Actor and Nation in Jakarta's Modern Theatre." PhD diss., Stanford University, 2001.

Zurbuchen, Mary Sabina. *The Language of Balinese Shadow Theater*. Princeton, NJ: Princeton University Press, 1987.

JAPAN

General: Historical and Critical Works

Adachi, Barbara. *The Voices and Hands of Bunraku*. Tokyo: Kôdansha, 1978; rpt. as *Backstage at Bunraku*. Tokyo: Weatherhill, 1985.

Addiss, Stephen, ed. *Japanese Ghosts and Demons: Art of the Supernatural*. New York: George Braziller, 1985.

Albery, Nobuko. *The House of Kanze*. New York: Simon and Schuster, 1985.

Allain, Paul. *The Art of Stillness: The Theater Practice of Tadashi Suzuki*. London: Palgrave Macmillan, 2003.

Allyn, John. "The Tsukiji Little Theatre and the Beginning of Modern Theatre in Japan." PhD diss., UCLA, 1970.

Ando, Tsuruo. *Bunraku: The Puppet Theatre*. New York: Walker/Weatherhill, 1970.

Araki, James. *The Ballad Drama of Medieval Japan*. Berkeley: University of California Press, 1964.

Ariyoshi, Sawako. *Kabuki Dancer: A Novel of the Woman Who Founded Kabuki*. Trans. James R. Brandon. Tokyo: Kôdansha, 1994.

Arnott, Peter D. *The Theatres of Japan*. London: Macmillan, 1969.

Asai, Susan Miyo. "Music and Drama in *Nômai* of Northern Japan." PhD diss., UCLA, 1988.

———. *Nômai Dance Drama: A Surviving Spirit of Medieval Japan*. Westport, CT: Greenwood Press, 1999.

Atkins, Paul. *Revealed Identity: The Noh Plays of Komparu Zenchiku*. Ann Arbor: Center for Japanese Studies, University of Michigan, 2006.

Avitabile, Gunhild. *Early Masters: Ukiyo-e Prints and Paintings from 1680 to 1750*. Trans. Celia Brown. New York: Japan Society, 1991.

Bach, Faith. "The Contributions of the *Omodakaya* to *Kabuki*." PhD diss., St. Antony's College, Oxford University, 1990.

Beck, L. Adams. *The Ghost Plays of Japan*. New York: Japan Society, 1933.

Berlin, Zeke. "Takarazuka: A History and Descriptive Analysis of the All-Female Performance Company." PhD diss., New York University, 1988.

Bethe, Monica. "The Use of Costumes in *Nô* Drama." In *Five Centuries of Japanese Kimono: On the Sleeve of Fondest Dreams*. Art Institute of Chicago Museum Studies 18:1 (1992).

———, and Karen Brazell. *Nô as Performance: An Analysis of the Kuse Scene of Yamanba*. Ithaca, NY: Cornell East Asia Papers, 1978.

———, and Karen Brazell. *Dance in the Nô Theater*. 3 vols. Ithaca, NY: Cornell East Asia Papers, 1982.

Blacker, Carmen. *The Catalpa Bow: A Study of Shamanism Practices in Japan*. London: Allen and Unwin, 1986.

Blumner, Holly, et al., eds. *101 Years of Kabuki in Hawaii*. Honolulu: Department of Theatre and Dance, University of Hawaii, 1995.

Board of Tourist Industry. *Japanese Drama*. Tokyo: Board of Tourist Industry, 1935.

Bowers, Faubion. *Japanese Theatre*. New York: Hermitage House, 1952.

Boyd, Mari. *The Aesthetics of Quietude: Ôta Shôgo and the Theatre of Divestiture*. Tokyo: Sophia University Press, 2006.

Boyd, Julianne K. "The *Bunraku* Puppet Theatre from 1945 to 1964." PhD diss., City University of New York, 1986.

Brandon, James R., William P. Malm, and Donald H. Shively, eds. *Studies in Kabuki: Its Acting, Music, and Historical Context*. Honolulu: University of Hawaii Press, 1978.

————, ed. *Chûshingura: Studies in Kabuki and the Puppet Theatre*. Honolulu: University of Hawaii Press, 1982.

————, ed. *Nô and Kyôgen in the Contemporary World*. Honolulu: University of Hawaii Press, 1997.

Brown, Steven T. *Theatricalities of Power: The Cultural Politics of Noh*. Stanford: Stanford University Press, 2001.

————, and Sara Jensen, eds. *Performing Japanese Women*. Special edition of *Women and Performance* 12:1 (2001).

Carruthers, Ian, and Takahashi Yasunari. *The Theatre of Suzuki Tadashi*. Cambridge: Cambridge University Press, 2004.

Cavaye, Ronald. *Kabuki: A Pocket Guide*. Rutland, VT: Tuttle, 1993.

————, Paul Griffith, and Akihiko Senda. *A Guide to the Japanese Stage: From Traditional to Cutting Edge*. Tokyo: Kôdansha, 2004.

Clark, Timothy T., Osamu Ueda, with Donald Jenkins. *The Actor's Image: Print Makers of the Katsukawa School*. Ed. Naomi Noble Richard. Chicago: The Art Institute of Chicago, in association with Princeton University Press, 1994.

Coaldrake, A. Kimi. *Women's Gidayû and the Japanese Theatre Tradition*. London: Routledge, 1997.

Colbath, James A. "The Japanese Drama and its Relation to Zen Buddhism." PhD diss., Western Reserve University, 1963.

de Poorter, Erika. *Zeami's Talks on Sarugaku: An Annotated Translation of the Sarugaku Dangi*. Amsterdam: Hotei, 2002.

Downer, Lesley. *Madame Sadayakko: The Geisha Who Bewitched the West*. New York: Gotham Books, 2003.

Dunn, Charles J. *The Early Japanese Puppet Drama*. London: Luzac, 1966.

————. "Religion and Japanese Drama." In James Redmond, ed., *Themes in Drama*. "Drama and Religion" vol. 5. Cambridge: Cambridge University Press, 1983.

————, and Bunzô Torigoe, trans. and eds. *The Actors' Analects*. New York: Columbia University Press, 1969.

Eckersall, Peter. *Theorizing the Angura Space*. Leiden: Brill Academic Publishers, 2006.

Edelson, Loren. "Danjûrô's Girls." PhD diss., City University of New York, 2006.

Edwards, Osman. *Japanese Plays and Playfellows*. London: Heinemann, 1901.

Ernst, Earle. *The Kabuki Theatre*. Rev. ed. Honolulu: University of Hawaii Press, 1974.

Fraleigh, Sondra Horton. *Butoh, Zen, and Japan*. Pittsburgh: University of Pittsburgh, 1999.

————. *Hijikata Tatsumi and Ohno Kazuo*. London: Routledge, 2006.

Fujii, Takeo. *Humor and Satire in Early English Comedy and Japanese Kyôgen Drama: A Cross-Cultural Study in Dramatic Arts*. Hirakata: KUFS Publication, 1983.

Fujiwara-Skrobak, Makiko. "Social Consciousness and Madness in Zeami's Life and Work: Or the Ritualistic-Shamanistic-Divine Aspects of *Sarugaku* for an Ideal Society." PhD diss., UCLA, 1996.

Garfias, Robert. *Gagaku: The Music and Dances of the Imperial Household*. New York: Theatre Arts Books, 1959.

Gerstle, Andrew C. *Circles of Fantasy: Convention in the Plays of Chikamatsu*. Cambridge: Council on East Asian Studies, 1986.

————, Kiyoshi Inobe, and William P. Malm. *Theater as Music: The Bunraku Play "Mt. Imo and Mt. Se: An Exemplary Tale of Womanly Virtue."* Ann Arbor: University of Michigan Press, 1990.

————, Timothy Clark, and Akiko Yano. *Kabuki Heroes on the Osaka Stage 1780–1830*. Honolulu: University of Hawaii Press, 2005.

Goff, Janet. *Noh Drama and The Tale of Genji: The Art of Allusion in Fifteen Classical Plays*. Princeton, NJ: Princeton University Press, 1991.

Goodman, David G. *Angura: Posters of the Japanese Avant-Garde*. New York: Princeton Architectural Press, 1999.

Goto, Yukihiro. "Suzuki Tadashi: Innovator of Contemporary Japanese Theatre." PhD diss., University of Hawaii, 1988.

Grand Kabuki Overseas Tours: 1928–1993. Tokyo: Shôchiku, 1994.

Griffiths, David. *The Training of Noh Actors and the Dove (Mask: A Release of Acting Resources*, Vol. 2). Amsterdam: Overseas Publishers' Association, 1998.

Gunji, Masakatsu. *Buyo: The Classical Dance*. Trans. Don Kenny. New York: Walker/Weatherhill, 1970.

———. *Kabuki*. Trans. John Bester. 2nd ed. New York: Kôdansha, 1985.

———. *The Kabuki Guide*. Trans. Christopher Holmes. Tokyo: Kôdansha, 1987.

Haar, Francis. *Japanese Theatre in Highlight: A Pictorial Commentary*. Text by Earle Ernst. Tokyo: Tuttle, 1952.

Halford, Aubrey S., and M. Giovanna. *The Kabuki Handbook*. Tokyo: Tuttle, 1961.

Hamamura, Yonezo et al. *Kabuki*. Trans. Fumi Takano. Tokyo: Kenkyûsha, 1956.

Hare, Thomas Blenman. *Zeami's Style: The Noh Plays of Zeami Motokiyo*. Stanford, CA: Stanford University Press, 1986.

Harich-Schneider, Eta. *A History of Japanese Music*. Oxford: Oxford University Press, 1973.

Harris, A. J. "This Radical *Nô*." PhD diss., Ohio State University, 1973.

Hata, Michio. *Tradition and Creativity in Japanese Dance*. Tokyo: Weatherhill, 2001.

Havens, Thomas. *Artist and Patron in Postwar Japan: Dance, Music, Theatre and the Visual Arts, 1955–1980*. Princeton, NJ: Princeton University Press, 1982.

Haynes, Carolyn. "Parody in the *Maikyôgen* and the *Monogurui Kyôgen*." PhD diss., Cornell University, 1988.

Hempel, Rose. *Gems of the Floating World: Ukiyo-e Prints from the Dresden Kupferstich-Kabinett*. Ed. Erica Hamilton Weeder. New York: Japan Society, 1995.

Herwig, Arendia, and Henk Herwig. *Heroes of the Kabuki Stage. An Introduction to Kabuki with Retellings of Famous Plays Illustrated by Woodblock Prints*. Amsterdam: Hotei Publishing, 2004.

Hibbett, Howard. *The Floating World in Japanese Fiction*. New York: Oxford University Press, 1959.

Hironaga, Shuzaburô. *Bunraku: Japan's Unique Puppet Theatre*. Tokyo: Tokyo News Service, 1964.

Hoff, Frank. *Song, Dance, Storytelling: Aspects of the Performing Arts in Japan*. Ithaca, NY: Cornell East Asia Papers, 1978.

Horie-Webber, Akemi. "The Essence of *Kabuki*: A Study of Folk Religious Ritual Elements in the Early *Kabuki* Theatre." PhD diss., University of California, Berkeley, 1982.

———, ed. *Japanese Theatre and the West*. Special edition of *Contemporary Theatre Review: An International Journal* 1:2 (1994).

Iezzi, Julie. "The Art of *Kabuki* Speech: Rules and Rhythms." PhD diss., University of Hawaii, 2000.

Ikenouchi, Nobuyoshi. *Explanation of No Plays: A Vade Mecum for Spectators of No Plays*. Trans. Y. Negishi. Tokyo: Nôgaku-kai, 1925.

Inoura, Yoshinobu, and Toshio Kawatake. *The Traditional Theatre of Japan*. Tokyo: Japan Foundation, 1981.

International Symposium on the Conservation and Restoration of Cultural Property, ed. *Kabuki: Changes and Prospects*. Tokyo: Tokyo National Research Institute of Cultural Properties, 1996.

International Theatre Institute. *Theatre Yearbook*. Published annually. Tokyo: ITI Japan Centre, 1972–.

Ishibashi, Hiro. *Yeats and the Noh: Types of Japanese Beauty and Their Reflection in Yeats's Plays*. Dublin: Dolmen Press, 1966.

Izumi, Motohide, ed. *Kyôgen: Traditional and Shakespearean of Izumi School*. Tokyo: Izumi Souke, 1993.

Izutsu, Toshihiko, and Toyo Izutsu. *The Theory of Beauty in the Classical Aesthetics of Japan*. The Hague: Martinus-Nijhoff, 1981.

Izzard, Sebastian. *Kunisada's World*. Ed. M. E. D. Laing. New York: Japan Society, 1993.

Jortner, David, Keiko McDonald, and Kevin J. Wetmore, Jr., eds. *Modern Japanese Theatre and Performance*. Lanham, MD: Lexington Books, 2006.

Kabuki through Theater Prints: Collection of the Honolulu Academy of Arts, James A. Michener Collection. Tokyo: Azabu Museum of Arts and Crafts, 1990.

Kamimura, Iwao, and Shunji Ohkura. *Kabuki Today: The Art and Tradition*. Tokyo: Kodansha International, 2001.

Kano, Ayako. *Acting Like a Woman in Modern Japan: Theater, Gender, and Nationalism*. New York: Palgrave, 2001.

Kawatake, Shigetoshi. *Development of the Japanese Theatre Arts*. Tokyo: Kokusai Bunka Shinkôkai, 1936.

———. *Kabuki: Japanese Drama*. Tokyo: Foreign Affairs Association of Japan, 1958.

———, and Kubota Mantarô. *Theatre in Japan*. Tokyo: Japanese National Commission for UNESCO, 1963.

Kawatake, Toshio. *Kabuki: Eighteen Traditional Dramas*. Trans. Helen Kay. San Francisco: Chronicle, 1985.

———. *Japan on Stage: Japanese Concepts of Beauty as Shown in the Traditional Theatre*. Trans. P. G. O'Neill. Tokyo: 3A Corporation, 1990.

———. *Kabuki: Baroque Fusion of the Arts*. Trans. Frank and Jean Connell Hoff. Tokyo: LTCB Library Trust/International House of Japan, 2003.

Keene, Donald. *Bunraku: The Art of the Japanese Puppet Theatre*. Tokyo: Kodansha, 1965.

———. *Nô: The Classical Theater of Japan*. Tokyo: Kôdansha, 1966.

———. *World within Walls: Japanese Literature of the Pre-Modern Era, 1600–1867*. New York: Henry Holt, 1976.

———. *Dawn to the West: Japanese Literature in the Modern Era: Poetry, Drama, Criticism*. New York: Holt, Rinehart and Winston, 1984.

———. *Seeds in the Heart: Japanese Literature from Earliest Times to the Late Sixteenth Century*. New York: Henry Holt, 1984.

Kenny, Don. *On Stage in Japan: An Invitation to Traditional Japanese Theatres*. Tokyo: Shufunotomo, 1974.

———. *A Guide to Kyôgen*. 4th ed. rev. Tokyo: Hinoki Shoten, 1990.

Keyes, Roger S., and Keiko Mizushima. *The Theatrical World of Osaka Prints*. Philadelphia: Philadelphia Museum of Art, 1973.

Kincaid, Zoë. *Kabuki: The Popular Stage of Japan*. London: Macmillan, 1925.

Kirihata, Ken. *Kyôgen Costumes: Suô (Jackets) and Kataginu (Shoulder-Wings)*. London: Thames and Hudson, 1990.

———. *Kabuki Costumes*. Trans. Shimoyama Ai and Judith Clancy. Tokyo: Shikosha, 1994.

Kishi, Tetsuo, and Graham Bradshaw. *Shakespeare in Japan*. London: Continuum, 2005.

Klein, Susan Blakely. *Ankoku Butô: The Premodern and Postmodern Influences on the Dance of Utter Darkness*. Ithaca, NY: Cornell East Asia Papers, 1988.

———. "Allegories of Desire: Kamakura Commentaries on the *Noh*." PhD diss., Cornell University, 1994.

Kokusai Bunka Shinkôkai, ed. *K.B.S. Bibliography of Standard Reference Books for Japanese Studies with Descriptive Notes*. Vol. 7 (B) *Theatre, Dance and Music*. Tokyo: Kokusai Bunka Shinkôkai, 1960.

Kominz, Laurence R. *Avatars of Vengeance: Japanese Drama and the Soga Literary Tradition*. Ann Arbor: Center for Japanese Studies, University of Michigan, 1995.

———. *The Stars Who Created Kabuki: Their Lives, Loves and Legacy*. Tokyo: Kôdansha, 1997.

————, ed. *Mishima on Stage: The Black Lizard and Other Plays*. Ann Arbor: Center for Japanese Studies, University of Michigan, 2007.

Komiya, Toyotaka, comp. and ed. *Japanese Music and Drama in the Meiji Era*. Trans. Edward G. Seidensticker and Donald Keene. Tokyo: Obunsha, 1956.

Komparu, Kunio. *The Noh Theater: Principles and Perspectives*. Trans. Jane Corddry (text) and Stephen Comee (plays). New York: Weatherhill/Tankosha, 1983.

Kongô, Iwao. *Nô Costumes*. Trans. Chitose Kuroha. Kyoto: Kôrinsha Co., 1949.

Konparu, Nobutaka, and Katsumi Tanaka. *Takigi Noh*. Tokyo: Graphic-sha, 1987.

Kusano, Eisaburo. *Stories behind Noh and Kabuki Plays*. Tokyo: Tokyo News Service, 1962.

LaFleur, William. *The Karma of Words: Buddhism and the Literary Arts in Medieval Japan*. Berkeley: University of California Press, 1983.

Law, Jane Marie. *Puppets of Nostalgia: The Life, Death, and Rebirth of the Japanese Awaji Ningyô Tradition*. Princeton, NJ: Princeton University Press, 1997.

Leabo, Karl, ed. *Kabuki*. New York: Theatre Arts Books, 1982.

Leiter, Samuel L. *Tachimawari: Stage Fighting in the Kabuki Theatre*. Monographs on Music, Dance, and Theatre in Asia. Vol. 3. New York: Performing Arts Program of the Asia Society, 1976.

————. *New Kabuki Encyclopedia: A Revised Adaptation of "Kabuki Jiten."* Westport, CT: Greenwood Press, 1997.

————, ed. *Japanese Theater in the World*. New York: Japan Society, 1997.

————, ed. *A Kabuki Reader*. Armonk, NY: M. E. Sharpe, 2001.

————. *Frozen Moments: Writings on Kabuki, 1966–2001*. Ithaca, NY: Cornell East Asia Series, 2002.

————. *Historical Dictionary of Japanese Traditional Theatre*. Lanham, MD: Scarecrow Press, 2006.

Link, Howard. *The Theatrical Prints of the Torii Masters: A Selection of 17th- and 18th-Century Ukiyo-e*. Honolulu: Honolulu Academy of Arts, Riccar Museum, 1977.

Lombard, Frank Alanson. *An Outline History of Japanese Drama*. London, 1928; rpt. Surrey: Curzon Press, 1994.

Malm, William P. *Japanese Music and Musical Instruments*. Rutland, VT: Tuttle, 1959.

————. *Nagauta: The Heart of Kabuki Music*. Tokyo: Tuttle, 1963.

————. *Six Hidden Views of Japanese Music*. Berkeley: University of California Press, 1986.

Maruoka, Daiji, and Tatsuo Yoshikoshi. *Noh*. Trans. Don Kenny. Tokyo: Hoikusha, 1969.

Matisoff, Susan. *The Legend of Semimaru, Blind Musician of Japan*. New York: Columbia University Press, 1978.

McKinnon, Richard N. "Zeami on the *Nô*: A Study of 15th-Century Japanese Dramatic Criticism." PhD diss., Harvard University, 1951.

Mezur, Katherine. *Beautiful Boys/Outlaw Bodies: Devising Kabuki Female-Likeness*. Hampshire, UK: Palgrave-Macmillan, 2005.

Miner, Earl, Hiroko Odagiri, and Robert E. Morrell, eds. *The Princeton Companion to Classical Japanese Literature*. Princeton, NJ: Princeton University Press, 1985.

Mitchell, John, and Miyoko Watanabe. *Noh and Kabuki: Staging Japanese Theatre*. Key West: Institute for Advanced Studies in the Theatre Arts Press in association with Florida Keys Educational Foundation, 1994.

Miyake, Shûtarô. *Kabuki Drama*. Tokyo: Japan Travel Bureau, 1961.

Morioka, Heinz, and Miyoko Sasaki. *Rakugo: The Popular Narrative Art of Japan*. Cambridge: Harvard University Press, 1990.

Murakami, Upton. *A Spectator's Handbook of Noh*. Tokyo: Wanya Shoten, 1963.

Nakamura, Matazo. *Kabuki: Backstage, Onstage, An Actor's Life*. Trans. Mark Oshima. New York: Kôdansha, 1988.

Nakamura, Yasuo. *Noh: The Classical Theatre*. Trans. Don Kenny. Tokyo: Walker/Weatherhill, in collaboration with Tankosha, Kyoto, 1971.

Nathan, John. *Mishima: A Biography*. Rutland, VT: Tuttle, 1974.

Nishikawa, Kyôtarô. *Bugaku Masks*. Trans. Monica Bethe. Tokyo: Kôdansha, 1977.

Nishiyama, Matsunosuke. *Edo Culture: Daily Life and Diversion in Urban Japan, 1600–1868*. Trans. Gerald Groemer. Honolulu: University of Hawaii Press, 1997.

Nogami, Toyoichiro. *Masks of Japan: The Gigaku, Bugaku and Noh Masks*. Tokyo: Kokusai Bunka Shinkokai, 1935.

———. *Noh: Japanese Noh Plays—How to See Them*. Rev. ed. Tokyo: Nôgaku-Shorin, 1954.

———. *Zeami and His Theories on Nô*. Trans. Ryozo Matsumoto. Tokyo: Hinoki Shoten, 1955.

Noma, Shôji. *Japanese Theater: From the Origin to the Present*. Osaka: Osaka Kyôiku Tosho, 1996.

O'Neill, P. G. *Early Nô Drama: Its Background, Character and Development 1300–1450*. London: Lund Humphries, 1958.

———. *A Guide to Nô*. Kyoto, 1953; rpt. Westport, CT: Greenwood, 1974.

Ôchi, Reiko. "Buddhism and Poetic Theory: An Analysis of Zeami's *Higaki* and *Takasago*." PhD diss., Cornell University, 1984.

Okamoto, Shiro. *The Man Who Saved Kabuki: Faubion Bowers and Theatre Censorship in Occupied Japan*. Trans. Samuel L. Leiter. Honolulu: University of Hawaii Press, 2001.

Ortolani, Benito. *Zenchiku's Aesthetics of the Nô Theater*. No. 3 (monograph). Bronx, NY: Riverdale Studies for Religious Research, 1976.

———. *Bugaku: The Traditional Dance of Japanese Imperial Court*. Monographs on Asian Music, Dance, and Theatre in Asia. Vol. 5. New York: Performing Arts Program of the Asia Society, 1978.

———. *Japanese Theatre: From Shamanistic Ritual to Contemporary Pluralism*. Rev. ed. Princeton, NJ: Princeton University Press, 1995.

———, and Samuel L. Leiter, eds. *Zeami and the Nô Theatre in the World*. New York: CASTA, 1998.

Parker, H. S. E. *Progressive Traditions: An Illustrated History of Plot Repetition in Traditional Japanese Theatre*. Leiden: E. J. Brill, 2002.

Poulton, Cody. *Spirits of Another Sort: The Plays of Izumi Kyôka*. Ann Arbor: Center for Japanese Studies, University of Michigan, 2001.

Powell, Brian. "Left-wing Theatre in Japan, Its Development and Activity to 1934." PhD diss., Oxford University, 1971.

———. *Kabuki in Modern Japan: Mayama Seika and His Plays*. New York: St. Martin's, 1990.

———. *Japan's Modern Theatre: A Century of Continuity and Change*. London: Taylor and Francis, 2002.

Pringle, Patricia. *An Interpretive Guide to Bunraku*. Honolulu: Community Service Division, University of Hawaii, 1992.

———. "Patronage of *Gidayû* Narrative Performers of Japanese *Bunraku* Puppet Theatre 1868–1945." PhD diss., University of Hawaii, 1999.

Pronko, Leonard. *Guide to Japanese Drama*. Boston: G. K. Hall, 1973.

———. *Theater East and West: Perspectives toward a Total Theater*. Rev. ed. Berkeley: University of California Press, 1974.

Qamber, Akhtar. *Yeats and the Noh: With Two Plays for Dancers by Yeats and Two Noh Plays*. New York: Weatherhill, 1974.

Quinn, Shelley Fenno. *Developing Zeami: The Noh Actor's Attunement in Practice*. Honolulu: University of Hawaii Press, 2005.

Rath, Eric C. *The Ethos of Noh: Actors and Their Art*. Cambridge: Harvard University Asia Center, 2004.

Raz, Jacob. *Audiences and Actors: A Study of Their Interaction in the Japanese Traditional Theatre*. Leiden: E. J. Brill, 1983.

Rimer, J. Thomas. *Toward a Modern Japanese Theatre: Kishida Kunio*. Princeton, NJ: Princeton University Press, 1974.

————, and Yamazaki Masakazu, trans. *On the Art of the Nô Drama: The Major Treatises of Zeami*. Princeton, NJ: Princeton University Press, 1984.

Robertson, Jennifer. *Takarazuka: Sexual Politics and Popular Culture in Modern Japan*. Berkeley: University of California Press, 1998.

Saito, Seijiro et al. *Masterpieces of Japanese Puppetry: Sculptured Heads of the Bunraku Theatre*. Tokyo: Tuttle, 1958.

Sakanishi, Shio. *A List of Translations of Japanese Drama into English, French, and German*. Washington, DC: American Council of Learned Societies, 1935.

Saltzman-Li, Katherine. *Creating Kabuki Plays: Context for Kezairoku, "Valuable Notes on Playwriting."* Leiden: E. J. Brill, forthcoming.

Sasayama, Takashi, J. R. Mulryne, and Margaret Shewring, eds. *Shakespeare and the Japanese Stage*. Cambridge: Cambridge University Press, 1998.

Scholz-Cionca, Stanca, and Samuel L. Leiter, eds. *Japanese Theatre and the International Stage*. Leiden: E. J. Brill, 2001.

Scott, A. C. *The Kabuki Theatre of Japan*. London: 1955; rpt. Mineola, NY: Dover, 1999.

————. *The Puppet Theatre of Japan*. Tokyo: Tuttle, 1963.

Scott, Joseph Wright. "The Japanese Noh Plays: The Essential Elements in Its Theatre Art Form." PhD diss., Ohio State University, 1949.

Scott-Stokes, Henry. *The Life and Death of Yukio Mishima*. New York: Farrar, Straus and Giroux, 1974.

Secor, James Leo. "*Kabuki* and Morals: The *Onnagata* Heroine as Ethical Example in the Late 18th Century." PhD diss., University of Kansas, 1987.

Sekine, Masaru. *Ze-ami and His Theories of Nô Drama*. Gerrards Cross, UK: Colin Smythe, 1985.

————, and Christopher Murray. *Yeats and the Noh: A Comparative Study*. Savage, MD: Barnes and Noble, 1990.

Senda, Akihiko. *The Voyage of Contemporary Japanese Theatre*. Trans. J. Thomas Rimer. Honolulu: University of Hawaii Press, 1997.

Sesar, Carl G. "*Nô* Drama and Chinese Literature." PhD diss., Columbia University, 1971.

Shaver, Ruth. *Kabuki Costume*. Rutland, VT: Tuttle, 1966.

Shibano, Dorothy T. "Kyôgen: The Comic as Drama." PhD diss., University of Washington, 1973.

Shields, Nancy. *Fake Fish: The Theatre of Kôbô Abe*. New York: Weatherhill, 1996.

Shillony, Ben-ami. *Politics and Culture in Wartime Japan*. Oxford: Oxford University Press, 1981.

Shimanouchi, Toshirô, and William Aker. *The Noh Drama*. Tokyo: Kokusai Bunka Shinkôkai, 1937.

Shioya, Sakae. *Chûshingura: An Exposition*. Tokyo: Hokuseidô, 1956.

Smethurst, Mae J. *The Artistry of Aeschylus and Zeami: A Comparative Study of Greek Tragedy and Nô*. Princeton, NJ: Princeton University Press, 1989.

Sorgenfrei, Carol Fisher. *Unspeakable Acts: The Avant-Garde Theatre of Terayama Shûji and Postwar Japan*. Honolulu: University of Hawaii Press, 2005.

Suetsugu, Ryôko. *The Influence of Japanese Noh Plays upon the Symbolist Plays of W. B. Yeats*. N.p.: Bryn Mawr College, 1957.

Susilo, Judith Mitoma, ed. *Japanese Tradition: Search and Research*. Los Angeles: University of California at Los Angeles, 1981.

Suzuki, Tadashi. *The Way of Acting: The Theatre Writings of Tadashi Suzuki*. Trans. J. Thomas Rimer. New York: Theatre Communications Group, 1986.

Takaya, Ted Terujiro. "An Inquiry into the Role of the Traditional *Kabuki* Playwright." PhD diss., Columbia University, 1969.

Tamba, Akira. *The Musical Structure of Noh*. Trans. Patricia Matoréas. Tokyo: Tôkai University Press, 1981.

Taylor, Richard. *The Drama of W. B. Yeats: Irish Myth and Japanese Nô*. New Haven: Yale University Press, 1977.

Teele, Rebecca, ed. *Nô/Kyôgen Mask and Performance*. Special issue of *Mime Journal* (1984).

Terasaki, Etsuko. "A Study of *Genzai* Plays in *Nô* Drama." PhD diss., Columbia University, 1969.

———. *Figures of Desire: Wordplay, Spirit Possession, Fantasy, Madness, and Mourning in Japanese Noh Plays*. Ann Arbor: Center for Japanese Studies, University of Michigan, 2002.

Thornbury, Barbara E. *Sukeroku's Double Identity: The Dramatic Structure of Edo Kabuki*. Ann Arbor: Center for Japanese Studies, University of Michigan, 1982.

———. *The Folk Performing Arts: Traditional Culture in Contemporary Japan*. Albany: SUNY Press, 1997.

Thornhill, Arthur, III. *Six Circles, One Dewdrop: The Religio-Aesthetic World of Komparu Zenchiku*. Princeton, NJ: Princeton University Press, 1993.

Togi, Masataro. *Gagaku: Court Music and Dance*. Trans. Don Kenny. Tokyo: Walker/Weatherhill, 1971.

Toita, Yasuji. *Kabuki: The Popular Theatre*. Trans. Don Kenny. New York: Walker/Weatherhill, 1970.

———, and Chiaki Yoshida. *Kabuki*. Trans. Fred Dunbar. Osaka: Hoikusha, 1967.

Toki, Zenmaro. *Japanese Nô Plays*. Tokyo: Japan Travel Bureau, 1954.

Tsubaki, Andrew T. "An Analysis and Interpretation of Zeami's Concept of *Yûgen*." PhD diss., University of Illinois, 1967.

Tsuboike, Eiko, ed. *Theater Japan 1989. A Companion to the Japanese Theater: Companies and People*. Tokyo: Pia Institute for the Arts, 1989.

Tsubouchi, Shôyô, and Yamamoto Jirô. *History and Characteristics of Kabuki, the Japanese Classical Drama*. Trans. Ryozo Matsumoto. Yokohama: Heiji Yamagata, 1960.

Tsuge, Genichi. *Japanese Music: An Annotated Bibliography*. New York: Garland, 1986.

Tsukui, Nobuko. *Ezra Pound and the Japanese Noh Plays*. Washington, DC: University Press of America, 1983.

Ueda, Makoto. *Zeami, Bashô, Yeats, Pound*. The Hague: Mouton, 1965.

———. *Literary and Art Theories in Japan*. Ann Arbor: Center for Japanese Studies, University of Michigan, 2000 [1967].

Unno, Mitsuko. *The Challenge of Kabuki*. Trans. Ann B. Cary. Tokyo: The Japan Times, 1979.

Wolz, Carl. *Bugaku, Japanese Court Dance, with the Notation of Basic Movements of Nasori*. Providence: Asian Music Publications, 1971.

Yokomichi, Mario. *The Life Structure of Noh*. Trans. Frank Hoff. Tokyo: Hinoki Shoten, 1973.

Yokota-Murakami, Gerry. *The Formation of the Canon of Nô: The Literary Tradition of Divine Authority*. Osaka: Osaka University Press, 1997.

Yoshida, Chiaki. *Kabuki: The Resplendent Japanese Theater*. Tokyo: Japan Times, 1977.

Young, Margaret H. *Kabuki: Japanese Drama*. Bloomington, IN: Eastern Press, 1985.

Zeami Motokiyo. *Ze-ami, Kadensho*. Trans. Sakurai Chûichi et al. Kyoto: Sumiya-Shinobe Publishing Institute, 1968.

———. *The Fûshikaden*. Trans. Shimada Shôhei. Nara: Nara-ken, 1975.

Plays in Translation (Japan)

Abe, Kôbô. *Friends*. Trans. Donald Keene. New York: Grove Press, 1969.

———. *The Man Who Turned into a Stick*. Trans. Donald Keene. Tokyo: University of Tokyo Press, 1975.

Bethe, Monica, and Richard Emmert, trans. *Noh Performance Guides*. Tokyo: National *Noh* Theatre (*Matsukaze* and *Fujito*, 1992, with Royall Tyler; *Atsumori* and *Miidera*, 1993, and *Tenko*, 1994, with Karen Brazell; *Ema*, 1996; *Aoi no Ue*, 1997).

Betsuyaku, Minoru. *The Story of Two Knights Travelling Around the Country—After Don Quixote*. Trans. Masako Yuasa. Leeds: Alumnus, 1990.

Brandon, James R., trans. and ed. *Kabuki: Five Classic Plays*. Cambridge: Harvard University Press, 1975.

———, and Samuel L. Leiter, eds. *Kabuki Plays on Stage: Brilliance and Bravado, 1697–1766*. Vol. 1. Honolulu: University of Hawaii Press, 2002.

———, and Samuel L. Leiter, eds. *Kabuki Plays on Stage: Darkness and Desire, 1804–1864*. Honolulu: University of Hawaii Press, 2002.

———, and Samuel L. Leiter, eds. *Kabuki Plays on Stage: Villainy and Vengeance, 1773–1799*. Vol. 2. Honolulu: University of Hawaii Press, 2002.

———, and Samuel L. Leiter, eds. *Kabuki Plays on Stage: Restoration and Reform, 1872–1905*. Honolulu: University of Hawaii Press, 2003.

———, and Samuel L. Leiter, eds. *Masterpieces of Kabuki: Eighteen Plays on Stage*. Honolulu: University of Hawaii Press, 2004.

Brazell, Karen, ed.; asst. by J. Philip Gabriel. *Twelve Plays of the Noh and Kyôgen Theaters*. Rev. ed. Ithaca, NY: Cornell East Asia Papers, 1990.

———, ed. *Traditional Japanese Theatre: An Anthology of Plays*. New York: Columbia University Press, 1997.

Brinkley, Frank, trans. "The Three Cripples" (*Sannin Katawa*). In *Japan, Its History, Arts and Literature*. Boston: J. B. Millet, 1901.

Dickins, F. V., trans. *Chiushingura or the Loyal League: A Japanese Romance*. London: Gowans and Gray, 1912.

Endô, Shûsaku. *The Golden Country*. Trans. Francis Mathy. Rutland, VT: Tuttle, 1970.

Ernst, Earle, ed. *Three Japanese Plays from the Traditional Theatre*. New York: Grove Press, 1960.

Gerstle, Andrew C., ed. and trans. *Chikamatsu: 5 Late Plays*. New York: Columbia University Press, 2002.

Goodman, David G., trans. *After Apocalypse: Four Japanese Plays of Hiroshima and Nagasaki*. New York: Columbia University Press, 1986.

———, ed. *Five Plays by Kishida Kunio*. Ithaca, NY: Cornell East Asia Papers, 1995.

———. *Japanese Drama and Culture in the 1960s: The Return of the Gods*. Armonk, NY: M. E. Sharpe, 1988.

Hasegawa, Kôji. *Kôji Hasegawa's Plays: The Two Worlds of Hirosaki Theatre*. Trans. Mari Boyd, Don Kenny, and John D. Swain. Tokyo: Ohta, 2002.

Hikata, Noboru. *The Passion by Mushakôji Saneatsu and Three Other Plays*. Honolulu: University of Hawaii Press, 1933.

Hirano, Umeyo. *Buddhist Plays from Japanese Literature*. Tokyo: CIIB Press, 1962.

Inoue, Hisashi. *The Face of Jizô*. Trans. Roger Pulvers. Tokyo: Komsatsuza, 1998.

Inoue, Jukichi, trans. *Chûshingura*. Tokyo: Nakanishiya, 1910.

Iwamatsu, Ryô. *Futon and Daruma*. Trans. Masako Yuasa. Leeds: Alumnus, 1992.

Iwasaki, Yozan T., and Glenn Hughes, trans. *Three Modern Japanese Plays*. Cincinnati: Steward Kidd Co., 1923.

———. *New Plays from Japan*. London: Ernest Benn, 1930.

Japan Playwrights Association, ed. *Half A Century of Japanese Theater*. Vols. 1–8. Tokyo: Kinokuniya Shoten Shuppanbu, 2000–2006.

Jones, Stanleigh H., Jr., trans. *Sugawara and the Secrets of Calligraphy*. New York: Columbia University Press, 1985.

———, trans. *Yoshitsune and the Thousand Cherry Trees*. New York: Columbia University Press, 1993.

Keene, Donald, trans. *The Battles of Coxinga*. London: Taylor's Foreign Press, 1951.

———, ed. *Anthology of Japanese Literature, From the Earliest Era to the Mid-Nineteenth Century*. New York: Grove Press, 1955.

————, trans. *Major Plays of Chikamatsu*. New York: Columbia University Press, 1961.

————, ed. *Twenty Plays of the Nô Theatre*. New York: Columbia University Press, 1970.

————, trans. *Chûshingura: The Treasury of the Loyal Retainers, A Puppet Play by Takeda Izumo, Miyoshi Shôraku, and Namiki Senryû*. New York: Columbia University Press, 1971.

————, trans. *Three Plays by Kôbô Abe*. New York: Columbia University Press, 1993.

Kenny, Don. *The Book of Kyôgen in English*. Tokyo: Gekishobo, 1986.

————, trans. *The Kyôgen Book: An Anthology of Japanese Classical Comedies*. Tokyo: Japan Times, 1989.

Kikuchi, Kwan. *Tôjûrô's Love and Four Other Plays*. Trans. Glenn W. Shaw. Tokyo: Hokuseidô, 1956.

Kinoshita, Junji. *Between God and Man: A Judgment on War Crimes*. Trans. Eric J. Gangloff. Tokyo: University of Tokyo Press, 1979.

————. *Requiem on the Great Meridian and Selected Essays*. Trans. Brian Powell and Jason Daniel. Tokyo: Nan'un-dô, 2000.

Kishida, Kunio. *Three Plays: Paper Balloon, New Cherry Leaves, Love Phobia*. Trans. Masako Yuasa. Leeds: Alumnus, 1994.

Kitani, Shigeo. *A Volcanic Island: The Sound of Night*. Trans. Andrew T. Tsubaki. Tokyo: Teatoro, 1970.

Kôkami, Shôji. *The Angels with Closed Eyes*. Trans. A to Z Network. Tokyo: Hakusuisha, 1991.

Kubo, Sakae. *Land of Volcanic Ash*. Trans. David G. Goodman. Ithaca, NY: Cornell East Asia Papers, 1986.

Kurata, Hyakuzô. *The Priest and His Disciples*. Trans. Glenn W. Shaw. Tokyo: Hokuseido, 1922.

————. *Shunkan*. Trans. K. Andô. Tokyo: Kenkyûsha, 1925.

Leiter, Samuel L., trans and comm. *The Art of Kabuki: Five Famous Plays*. Rev. ed. Mineola, NY: Dover, 2000 [1979].

Masakazu, Yamazaki. *Mask and Sword: Two Plays for the Contemporary Japanese Theater by Yamazaki Masakazu*. Trans. J. Thomas Rimer. New York: Columbia University Press, 1980.

McKinnon, Richard, trans. *Selected Plays of Kyôgen*. Tokyo: Uniprint, 1968.

Mishima, Yukio. *Twilight Sunflower*. Trans. Shinozaki Shigeo and Virgil A. Warren. Tokyo: Hokuseidô, 1958.

————. *Madame de Sade*. Trans. Donald Keene. New York: Grove Press, 1967.

————. *Five Modern Nô Plays*. Trans. Donald Keene. New York: Vintage Books, 1973.

————. *My Friend Hitler and Other Plays of Yukio Mishima*. Trans. Hiroaki Sato. New York: Columbia University Press, 2002.

Miyamori, Asatarô. *Tales from Old Japanese Dramas*. New York and London: Putnam's Sons, 1915.

————, trans. *Masterpieces of Chikamatsu, the Japanese Shakespeare*. London: K. Paul, Trench, Trübner, 1926.

Morley, Carolyn Anne, trans. *Transformations, Miracles, and Mischief: The Mountain Priest Plays of Kyôgen*. Ithaca, NY: Cornell East Asia Papers, 1993.

Motofuji, Frank T., trans. *The Love of Izayoi and Seishin, A Kabuki Play by Kawatake Mokuami*. Rutland, VT: Tuttle, 1966.

Mushakôji, Saneatsu. *The Sister*. Trans. Nishi Kiichi. Tokyo: Kairyûdô, 1935.

————. *Two Fables of Japan*. Trans. Jun'ichi Natori. Tokyo: Hokuseido, 1957.

Nakamura, Matagorô II, et al., trans. "The Forty-Seven Samurai: A Kabuki Version of Chûshingura." In James R. Brandon, ed. *Chûshingura: Studies in Kabuki and the Puppet Theatre*. Honolulu: University of Hawaii Press, 1982.

Nippon Gakujutsu Shinkôkai, trans. *Japanese Noh Drama*. 3 vols. Tokyo: Nippon Gakujutsu Shinkôkai, 1955, 1959, 1960 [Vol. 1 rpt. as *The Noh Drama*, 1973].

Noguchi, Yone, trans. *Ten Kiogen in English*. Tokyo: Tôzaisha, 1907.

Obata, Shigeyoshi, trans. *The Melon Thief, From a Medieval Japanese Farce*. New York: Samuel French, 1923.

Okamoto, Kidô. *The Human Pillar*. Trans. Zoe Kincaid and Hanso Tarao. New York: Samuel French, 1928.

———. *The Mask-Maker*. Trans. Zoe Kincaid and Hanso Tarao. New York: Samuel French, 1928.

———. *The American Envoy*. Trans. Masanao Inoue. Kobe: J. L. Thompson, 1931.

Pound, Ezra, and Ernest Fenollosa, trans. *The Classical Noh Theatre of Japan*. New York: New Directions, 1959 [1916 as *"Noh" or Accomplishment: A Study of the Classical Stage of Japan*].

Richie, Donald, and Miyoko Watanabe, trans. *Six Kabuki Plays*. Tokyo: Hokuseidô, 1963.

Rolf, Robert T., and John K. Gillespie, eds. *Alternative Japanese Drama: Ten Plays*. Honolulu: University of Hawaii Press, 1992.

Sadler, Arthur. *Japanese Plays: Nô Kyôgen Kabuki*. Sydney: Angus, 1934.

Sakanishi, Shio, trans. *Japanese Folk-Plays: The Ink-Stained Lady and Other Kyôgen*. Rutland, VT: Tuttle, 1960.

Scott, A. C., trans. *Genyadana*. Tokyo: Hokuseidô, 1953.

———, trans. *Kanjinchô*. Tokyo: Hokuseidô, 1953.

Shimazaki, Chifumi, trans. *The Noh*. Vol. 1. *Kami(god)-Noh*. Tokyo: Hinoki Shoten, 1972.

———, trans. *The Noh: Sambamme Mono*. 3 vols. Tokyo: Hinoki Shoten, 1976, 1977, 1981.

———, trans. *The Noh*. Vol. 2. *Battle Noh*. Tokyo: Hinoki Shoten, 1987.

———, trans. *Warrior Ghost Plays from the Japanese Noh Theater*. Ithaca, NY: Cornell East Asia Papers, 1993.

———. *Restless Spirits from Japanese Noh Plays of the Fourth-Group*. Ithaca, NY: Cornell East Asia Papers, 1995.

Shively, Donald, trans. *The Love Suicide at Amijima: A Study of a Japanese Domestic Tragedy by Chikamatsu Monzaemon*. Cambridge: Harvard University Press, 1953; rpt. Ann Arbor: University of Michigan Press, 1991.

Smethurst, Mae J., trans. *Dramatic Representations of Filial Piety: Five Noh in Translation*. Ithaca, NY: Cornell East Asia Papers, 1998.

———, and Christina Laffin, eds. *The Noh Ominaeshi: A Flower Viewed from Many Directions*. Ithaca, NY: Cornell East Asia Papers, 2003.

Stopes, Marie C., and Jôji Sakurai, trans. *Plays of Old Japan: The Noh*. London: William Heinemann, 1913.

Suzuki, Beatrice Lane, trans. *Nôgaku: Japanese Nô Plays*. New York: E. P. Dutton, 1932.

Takaya, Ted T., trans. *Modern Japanese Drama: An Anthology*. New York: Columbia University Press, 1979.

Takeda, Izumo, *The Pine-Tree*. Trans. M. C. Marcus. New York: Duffield and Company, 1916.

Tyler, Royall, ed. and trans. *Granny Mountains: A Second Cycle of Nô Plays*. Ithaca, NY: Cornell East Asia Papers, 1978.

———, ed. and trans. *Pining Wind: A Cycle of Nô Plays*. Ithaca, NY: Cornell East Asia Papers, 1978.

———, ed. and trans. *Japanese Nô Dramas*. London: Penguin, 1992.

Ueda, Makoto, trans. *The Old Pine Tree and Other Noh Plays*. Lincoln: University of Nebraska Press, 1962.

Unno, Mitsuko, ed. *You Mean to Say You Still Don't Know Who We Are?* Ashiya, Japan: Personally Oriented, 1976.

Waley, Arthur, trans. *The Nô Plays of Japan*. London, 1921; rpt. New York: Grove Press, 1957.

Yamamoto, Yûzô. *Three Plays*. Trans. Glenn W. Shaw. Tokyo: Hokuseidô, 1957.

Yasuda, Kenneth, trans. *Masterworks of the Nô Theatre*. Bloomington: Indiana University Press, 1989.

Zeami, Motokiyo. *Birds of Sorrow*. Trans. Meredith Weatherby and Bruce Rogers. Tokyo: Obunsha, 1947.

KOREA

General: Historical and Critical Works

Cho, Dong-il. *Korean Mask Dance*. Seoul: Ewha Woman's University Press, 2005.

Cho, Oh-kon. *Korean Puppet Theatre: Kkoktu Kakshi*. East Lansing: Asian Studies Center, Michigan State University, 1979.

———, trans. *Traditional Korean Theatre*. Fremont, CA: Asian Humanities Press, 1988.

Cultural Properties Administration. *Traditional Music and Dance*. Elizabeth, NJ: Hollym International, 2000.

———. *Korean Intangible Cultural Properties: Folk Dramas, Games and Rites*. Elizabeth, NJ: Hollym International, 2001.

Han, Sang-chul. "Trends in Postwar Theatre." In *Korean Cultural Heritage*. Vol. 3, *Performing Arts*. Ed. Korea Foundation. Seoul: Samsung Moonwha Printing, 1997. 1962–06.

Howard, Keith. *Korean Musical Instruments*. Hong Kong: Oxford University Press, 1995.

———, ed. *Korean Shamanism*. Seoul: Seoul Press, 1998.

Jang, Won-Jae. *Irish Influences on Korean Theatre during the 1920s and 1930s*. Buckinghamshire, UK: Colin Smythe, 2003.

Kim, Ah-Jeong. "The Modern Uses of Tradition in Contemporary Korean Theatre—A Critical Analysis from an Intercultural Perspective." PhD diss., University of Illinois, 1995.

Kim, Ho-Soon. "The Development of Modern Korean Theatre in South Korea." PhD diss., University of Kansas, 1974.

Kim, Hyunggyu. *Understanding Korean Literature*. Trans. Robert J. Fouser. Armonk, NY: M. E. Sharpe, 1997.

Kim, Jinhee. "Disembodying the Other: East-West Relations and Modern Korean Drama." PhD diss., Indiana University, 1996.

Kim, Malborg. *Korean Dance*. Seoul: Ewha Woman's University Press, 2005.

Kim, Yun-Cheol, and Miy-Ye Kim, eds. *Contemporary Korean Theatre: Playwrights, Directors, Stage-Designers*. Seoul: Theatre and Man Press, 2000.

Koo, John H., and Andrew C. Nahm, eds. *An Introduction to Korean Culture*. Elizabeth, NJ: Hollym International Corp., 1997.

Korea Foundation, ed. *Korean Cultural Heritage*. Vol. 3, *Performing Arts*. Seoul: Samsung Moonwha Printing, 1997.

Korean International Theatre Institute, ed. *Korean Performing Arts: Drama, Dance and Music Theatre*. Seoul: Jipmoondang Publishing, 1997.

Korean National Commission for UNESCO, ed. *Traditional Performing Arts of Korea*. Seoul: Seoul Computer Press, 1986.

Lee, Byong Won. *Styles and Esthetics in Korean Traditional Music*. Seoul: National Center for Korean Traditional Performing Arts, 1997.

Lee, Hyekyoung. "The Transplantation of Western Drama in Korea: Basis of Modern Theatre." PhD diss., University of Michigan, 1989.

National Academy of the Korean Language. *An Illustrated Guide to Korean Culture*. Seoul: Hakgojae Publishing, 2002.

Park, Chan E. *Voices from the Straw Mat: Toward an Ethnography of P'ansori Singing*. Honolulu: University of Hawaii Press, 2003.

Pihl, Marshall R. *The Korean Singer of Tales*. Cambridge: Harvard University Press, 1994.

Pratt, Keith, and Richard Rutt. *Korea: A Historical and Cultural Dictionary*. Richmond, UK: Curzon, 1999.

Soh, Yon-Ho. "Ritual Reborn in Modern Theatre." In *Korean Cultural Heritage*. Vol. 3, *Performing Arts*. Ed. Korea Foundation. Seoul: Samsung Moonwha Printing.

Van Zile, Judy. *Perspectives on Korean Dance*. Middleton, CT: Wesleyan University Press, 2001.

Plays in Translation (Korea)

Kim, Ah-jeong, and R. B. Graves, trans. *The Metacultural Theatre of Oh T'ae-sŏk: Five Plays from the Korean Avant-Garde*. Honolulu: University of Hawaii Press, 1999.
Korean National Commission for UNESCO, ed. *Wedding Day and Other Korean Plays*. Seoul: Si-sa-yong-o-sa Publishers, 1983.

MALAYSIA

Ariffin, Zakaria. *Modern Theatre of Malaysia*. Kuala Lumpur: Dewan Bahasa dan Pustaka, Institute of Language and Literature Malaysia, 2002.
Bujang, Rahmah. *Boria: A Form of Malay Theatre*. Singapore: Institute of Southeast Asian Studies, 1987.
Ghulam-Sarwar, Yousof. *Panggung Semar: Aspects of Traditional Malay Theatre*. Petaling Jaya: Tempo Publishing, 1992.
———. *The Malay Shadow Play: An Introduction*. Penang: Asian Centre, 1997.
Ishak, Solehah. *Histrionics of Development: A Study of Three Contemporary Malay Playwrights*. Kuala Lumpur: Dewan Bahasa dan Pustaka and Kementerian Pendidikan Malaysia, 1987.
———, and Nur Nina Zuhra (Nancy Nanney). "Malaysia." In Don Rubin, ed., *The World Encyclopedia of Contemporary Drama* (see above).
Jit, Krishen. *Krishen Jit, an Uncommon Position: Selected Writings*. Ed. Kathy Rowland. Singapore: Contemporary Asian Arts Centre, 2003.
Matusky, Patricia. *Malaysian Shadow Play and Music: Continuity of an Oral Tradition*. Kuala Lumpur: Oxford University Press, 1993.
Nur Nina Zuhra (Nancy Nanney). *An Analysis of Modern Malay Drama*. Shah Alam: MARA Institute of Technology, 1992.
Sulaiman, Huzir. *Eight Plays*. Kuala Lumpur: Silverfishbooks, 2002.
Sweeney, Amin. *Malay Shadow Puppets: The Wayang Siam of Kelantan*. London: British Museum, 1972.
———. *The Ramayana and the Malay Shadow-Play*. Kuala Lumpur: Penerbit Universiti Kebangsaan Malaysia, 1972.
Tan Sooi Beng. *Bangsawan: A Social and Stylistic History of Popular Malay Opera*. Singapore: Oxford University Press, 1993.

PHILIPPINES

Bañas, Raymundo C. *Pilipino Music and Theater*. Quezon City: Manlapaz Publishing, 1969.
Carpio, Rustica C. *Hermogenes Ilagan: Father of Tagalog Zarzuela*. Manila: University of Santo Tomas, 2000.
Enriquez, Mig Alvarez. *Three Philippine Epic Plays*. Quezon City: New Day Publishers, 1983.
Erven, Eugène van. *Stages of People Power: The Philippines Educational Theatre Association*. The Hague: Centre for the Study of Education in Developing Countries (CESO), 1989.
Fernández, Doreen G. *The Iloilo Zarzuela, 1903–1930*. Quezon City: Ateneo de Manila University Press, 1978
———. *Palabas: Essays on Philippine Theater History*. Quezon City: Ateneo de Manila University Press, 1996.
Hernandez, Tomas C. *The Emergence of Modern Drama in the Philippines, 1898–1912*. Honolulu: Asian Studies Program, University of Hawaii, 1976.

Lacónico-Buenaventura, Cristina. *The Theater in Manila, 1846–1946*. Manila: De La Salle University Press, 1998 [1994].

Tiongson, Nicanor G. *Dulaan: An Essay on Philippine Theater*. Manila: Sentrong Pangkultura ng Pilipinas, 1989.

———. *Dulaan: An Essay on Philippine Ethnic Theater*. Manila: Sentrong Pangkultura ng Pilipinas, 1992.

———. *Dulaan: An Essay on the Spanish Influence on Philippine Theater*. Manila: Sentrong Pangkultura ng Pilipinas, 1992.

———. *Komedya*. Diliman, Quezon City: University of the Philippines Press, 1999.

———. *Sinakulo*. Diliman, Quezon City: University of the Philippines Press, 1999.

MONGOLIA (See China)

MYANMAR (See Burma)

SINGAPORE

Krishnan, Sanjay, ed. *9 Lives: 10 Years of Singapore Theatre, 1987–1997: Essays Commissioned by The Necessary Stage*. Singapore: Necessary Stage, 1997.

Oon, Clarissa. *Theatre Life! A History of English-Language Theatre in Singapore through the Straits Times, 1958–2000*. Singapore: Singapore Press Holdings, 2001.

Peterson, William. *Theater and the Politics of Culture in Contemporary Singapore*. Middletown, CT: Wesleyan University Press, 2001.

Tan Chong Kee, and Tisa Ng, eds. *Ask Not: The Necessary Stage in Singapore Theatre*. Singapore: Times Editions, 2004.

Vente, Ines, and Lim Geok Eng. *Wayang: Chinese Street Opera in Singapore*. Singapore: MPH, 1984.

THAILAND

Broman, Sven. *Shadows of Life: Nang Talung, Thai Popular Shadow Theatre*. Bangkok: White Orchid Press, 1996.

Chandavij, Natthapatra, and Promporn Pramualratana. *Thai Puppets and Khon Masks*. London: Thames and Hudson, 1998.

Gunatilaka, Kamron. *The 1932 Revolution*. Trans. S. J. Bangkok. Committees on the Project for the National Celebration on the Occasion of the Centennial Anniversary of Pridi Banomyong, 1999.

Hemmet, Christine. *Nang Talung: The Shadow Theatre of South Thailand*. Amsterdam: Royal Tropical Institute, 1996.

Ingersoll, Fern S., ed. *Sang-Thong: A Dance Drama from Thailand*. Tokyo: Charles E. Tuttle, 1973.

Miller, Terry E. *Traditional Music of the Lao: Kaen Playing and Mawlum Singing in Northeast Thailand*. Westport, CT: Greenwood Press, 1985.

Rutnin, Mattani Mojdara. *The Siamese Theatre: A Collection of Reprints from the Journals of the Siam Society*. Bangkok: Sompong Press, 1975.

———. *Dance, Drama, and Theatre in Thailand: The Process of Development and Modernization*. Chiang Mai: Silkworm, 1993.

Yupho, Dhanit. *Classical Siamese Theatre*. Trans. P. S. Sastri. Bangkok: Hatha Dhip, 1952.

TAIWAN (See China)

TIBET (See China)

VIETNAM

Durand, M., and Tran Huan Nguyen. *An Introduction to Vietnamese Literature*. New York: Columbia University Press, 1985.

Nguyen, Huy Hong, and Tran Trung Chinh. *Vietnamese Traditional Water Puppetry*. Hanoi: GIOI Foreign Language Publishing House, 1992.

Quang, Dinh et al. *Vietnamese Theater*. Hanoi: Gioi Publishers, 1999.

Song, Ban. *The Vietnamese Theatre*. Hanoi: Foreign Languages Publishing House, 1960.

INDEX

ABOUT THE EDITOR
AND CONTRIBUTORS

EDITOR

Samuel L. Leiter (Japan, traditional), Distinguished Professor Emeritus of Theatre, Brooklyn College, and the Graduate Center, CUNY, is a specialist in Japanese theatre. Former editor of *Asian Theatre Journal* (1992–1994), he has published twenty-three previous books, including the co-edited, four-volume *Kabuki Plays on Stage* series (2002–2004, with James R. Brandon), and *Historical Dictionary of Japanese Traditional Theatre* (2006).

ADVISORY BOARD

Matthew Isaac Cohen (Southeast Asia, traditional), Senior Lecturer, Department of Drama and Theatre, Royal Holloway, University of London, has published extensively on Indonesian theatre and performance, including *The Komedie Stamboel: Popular Theater in Colonial Indonesia, 1891–1903* (2006). He is a practicing shadow puppeteer and has taught and performed in Europe, North America, and Asia.

Richard A. Frasca (India, traditional) teaches Tamil in the Department of Sanskrit and Indian Studies at Harvard University. He is a specialist in the traditional theatre forms of India and has written extensively on *kuttu*, the ritual theatre genre of Tamil-speaking South India. He is the author of the book *Theatre of the Mahabharata* and numerous articles and translations.

John K. Gillespie (Japan, modern) is president of Gillespie Global Group, a cross-cultural consultancy, in New York City. He focuses on mutual influences between modern Japanese and Western theatre, has translated several contemporary plays, and is co-editor of the anthology, *Alternative Japanese Drama: Ten Plays* (1992).

Craig Latrell (Southeast Asia, modern) is Associate Professor and chair of the Department of Theatre at Hamilton College. He has published articles in many journals, including *TDR* and *Asian Theatre Journal*, and is president emeritus of the Association for Asian Performance.

Ruru Li (Chinese-language theatre, modern), Senior Lecturer in East Asian Studies at the University of Leeds, UK, is a specialist in Chinese theatre. Her publications include *Shashibiya: Staging Shakespeare in China* (2003), "Mao's Chair: Revolutionizing

Chinese Theatre" (*Theatre Research International*, 2002), and "Sino the Times: Three Spoken Drama Productions on the Beijing Stage" (*The Drama Review*, 2001).

Colin Mackerras (Chinese-language theatre, traditional), Professor Emeritus, Griffith University, and Fellow of the Australian Academy of the Humanities, is a specialist in Chinese theatre and ethnic minorities in China. Among his eleven single-authored books, five are on Chinese theatre, most notably *The Rise of the Peking Opera* (1972).

Sreenath K. Nair is a Lecturer in Drama at the University of Lincoln, United Kingdom. He teaches critical and cultural theories, performance theory, intercultural theatre, and post-colonial drama. He is an editorial board member of *Consciousness, Literature and the Arts* and has published plays and essays on aesthetics and theatre.

Richard Nichols (Korea) is Professor of Theatre at Penn State University and a former Fulbright Senior Research Scholar in Korea, now engaged in cotranslating modern Korean dramas.

CONTRIBUTORS

B. Ananthakrishnan, Professor of Theatre, Sarojini Naidu School of Performing Arts, University of Hyderabad, is a scholar-practitioner specializing in Indian performance studies. He has published articles on Indian theatre in English and Malayalam journals and anthologies. He is currently general secretary of the Indian Society for Theatre Research (ISTR).

Hamilton Armstrong, Lecturer in Theatre and Social Justice at Aoyama Gakuin University, Tokyo, has specialized in cross-gendered representations on the Japanese contemporary stage. He has presented papers on several heretofore little-known actors and is writing a book, *On the Trail of the Black Lizard: Edogawa Rampo's Kurotokage on Stage and Screen*.

Martha Ashton-Sikora, independent scholar, is a specialist in Indian theatre and a performer of *yakshagana* dance. She has taught Indian theatre and dance at the University of Chicago and the University of California, Berkeley, and is senior author of *Yakshagana: A Dance Drama of India* (1977) and *Krishnattam* (1993).

Weihong Bao is assistant professor at the Department of East Asian Languages and Literatures at The Ohio State University. She specializes in early Chinese cinema and modern drama and has published in a number of journals such as *Camera Obscura, Nineteenth Century Theatre and Film*, and *Journal of Modern Chinese Literature*.

Shashikant Barhanpurkar heads the Department of Dramatics at Dr. Babasaheb Ambedkar University, Aurangabad, Maharashtra. He practices theatre in rural India using Augusto Boal's techniques. The director of over fifty plays in Marathi and Hindi, he also is the founder-chairman of the Marathwada Lokotsav festival.

Joi Barrios is Associate Professor at the University of the Philippines and author of *From the Theater Wings* (2005), about Filipino women's theatre. She has also published volumes of poetry and has received the TOWNS (Ten Outstanding Women in the Nation's Service) Award. She is literary manager of Ma-yi Theatre Company.

Eileen Blumenthal, Professor of Theater, Rutgers University, specializes in Cambodian theatre, experimental performance, and puppetry. In addition to over three hundred essays and reviews, she has written *Puppetry: A World History* (2005), *Les danseuses sacrées d'Angkor* (2002, contributing author), *Julie Taymor: Playing With Fire* (1995, with Taymor), and *Joseph Chaikin* (1984).

Holly A. Blumner, Assistant Professor of Theatre, Film, and Media Studies, St. Mary's College of Maryland, is a specialist in traditional Japanese theatre. Her work has been published in *Kabuki Plays on Stage: Brilliance and Bravado* (2002) and *A Kabuki Reader* (2002).

Mari Boyd teaches theatre at Sophia University, Tokyo. She is the head translation editor of *Half a Century of Japanese Theatre*, Vols. 1–8, and is the author of *The Aesthetics of Quietude: Ôta Shôgo and the Theatre of Divestiture* (2006).

Bonnie Brereton, independent scholar, specializes in northeast Thailand's shadow theatre, religious art, and Buddhist rituals. She has taught courses in Southeast Asian culture at Payap University in Chiang Mai, and is the author of *Thai Tellings of Phra Malai: Texts and Rituals Concerning a Popular Buddhist Saint* (1995).

Lorelle Browning, Professor of English and Peace Studies, Pacific University, Oregon, is founder-director of Vietnam-America Theatre Exchange, through which she organizes collaborations between Vietnamese and American stage artists. Her work on a joint Vietnamese and American production of *A Midsummer Night's Dream* is documented in the film *A Dream in Hanoi* (2001).

Michael W. Cassidy is a doctoral student at the University of Pittsburgh specializing in modern Japanese theatre. He is currently at work on his dissertation, "The Propaganda Picture Show: Nationalism and Nation-building in the History of *Kamishibai*."

Pak Tim Chan earned his master's degree in theatre studies in England, then returned to Macao, where he was active in theatre circles for years. He is now studying for his doctorate.

Sau Yan Chan, Professor at the Chinese University of Hong Kong, has written numerous works on Cantonese *yueju*, including the two-volume Chinese-language *Research on Hong Kong's Guangdong Yueju* (1988, 1990) and *Improvisation in a Ritual Context: The Music of Cantonese Opera* (in English, 1991).

Ping Kuen Cheung is head of Liberal Arts Studies at the Hong Kong Academy for Performing Arts. He is a playwright, director, dramaturg, critic, drama educator, and journal editor and has been an elected member of the Hong Kong Arts Development Council since 1996.

Oh-Kon Cho is Professor of Theatre and Arts for Children, State University of New York–Brockport. A specialist in Korean theatre, he has published books (including *Traditional Korean Theatre* [1988]), articles, translations of plays, and coauthored an opera libretto.

Margaret Coldiron teaches Eastern Dance Drama at Reading University and lectures on Asian performance at the British Museum. She performs with Lila Cita *gamelan* and Lila Bhawa Balinese Dance Troupe and is the author of *Trance and Transformation of the Masked Actor in Japanese Noh and Balinese Dance Drama* (2004).

Pornrat Damrhung is Associate Professor of Dramatic Arts, Chulalongkorn University, Bangkok. A producer of several performing arts troupes, her main interests are promoting new versions of traditional Thai performing arts for young people. She also creates dance-theatre based on her knowledge of traditional Thai (and Southeast Asian) stories and art forms.

Ursula Dauth holds a PhD from Griffith University, Australia, for a thesis on reform in *chuanju* since 1982. She has worked for the Queensland State Theatre Company and published several articles on Chinese theatre in various countries, as well as part of a CD-ROM.

Carol Davis is Associate Professor of Theatre at Franklin and Marshall College. She specializes in Nepali theatre and Shakespeare. She is the founding artistic director of Nepal Health Project educational street theatre. Her articles have appeared in *Asian Theatre Journal, Theatre Symposium, Education about Asia*, and elsewhere.

Aparna Dharwadker, Associate Professor of Theatre and Drama and English at the University of Wisconsin–Madison, is the author of *Theatres of Independence: Drama, Theory, and Urban Performance in India since 1947* (2005). She has published widely on early modern, postcolonial, and Indian theatre, and is completing an edited collection of modern Indian theatre theory.

Bishnupriya Dutt is Associate Professor, School of Arts and Aesthetics, Jawaharlal Nehru University, New Delhi. Her specializations include modern and contemporary Indian theatre (colonial and postcolonial perspectives), research methodology, dramatic literature, and popular performances and comic traditions.

Peter Eckersall, Senior Lecturer in Theatre Studies, University of Melbourne, is co-editor of *Alternatives: Debating Theatre Culture in an Age of Confusion* (2004) and of the online journal *Performance Paradigm*. He is the author of *Theorizing the Angura Space: Avant-garde Performance and Politics in Japan, 1960–2000* (2006).

Richard Emmert, Professor of Asian Performance, Musashino University, Tokyo. A licensed Kita *nô* school instructor, he heads the Noh Training Project and is founder of Theatre Nohgaku, which pioneers *nô* performances in English. He has coauthored a series of *nô* performance guides for the National Nô Theatre.

Catherine Filloux is an award-winning, internationally produced playwright, with many plays about Cambodia, including *Eyes Of The Heart, Silence Of God*, and

Photographs From S-21, and the operas, *Where Elephants Weep* (composer Him Sophy) and *The Floating Box* (composer Jason Kao Hwang).

Kathy Foley, Professor of Theatre at the University of California, Santa Cruz, authored the Southeast Asia section of *The Cambridge Guide to World Theatre* (1993) and is editor of *Asian Theatre Journal*. She has published widely on various Asian theatre subjects. A professional *dalang*, she performs Indonesian *wayang golek* puppetry.

Yoshiko Fukushima is Assistant Professor of Japanese Theatre, Department of Modern Languages, University of Oklahoma. Her publications include *Manga Discourse in Japanese Theater: The Location of Noda Hideki* (2003).

Cobina Gillitt is a specialist in Indonesian contemporary and Western avant-garde theatre. She is on the adjunct faculty of the undergraduate Department of Drama, New York University, and is a member of Teater Mandiri, based in Jakarta.

David G. Goodman is Professor of Japanese Literature, University of Illinois. His books on Japanese theatre include *After Apocalypse: Four Japanese Plays of Hiroshima and Nagasaki* (1986) and *The Return of the Gods: Japanese Drama and Culture in the 1960s* (1988). He edited *Concerned Theatre Japan* from 1969 to 1973.

Yukihiro Goto is Professor of Theatre Arts at San Francisco State University. An actor and director, he is a specialist in staging Western plays with Asian techniques. He has received several major grants, including the Lilly Endowment Teaching Fellowship, Japan Foundation Fellowship, and U.S. Department of Education National Graduate Fellowship.

Trevor Hay, Senior Lecturer of Artistic and Creative Education, Faculty of Education, University of Melbourne, is a specialist in the theatre and literature of China's Cultural Revolution. He has written several books on China, including biography and fiction, and is a reviewer of contemporary works employing Chinese themes in international theatre and literature.

Dana Healy, Lecturer in Vietnamese at SOAS, University of London, is the author of *Teach Yourself Vietnamese* (1997) and coauthor of *Aspects of Vietnamese Culture* (2002).

James Hesla is a freelance writer and educator, with a scholarly interest in contemporary Indonesian theatre. His plays have been produced in Seattle, Washington, D.C., and Arizona.

Alexander C. Y. Huang, Assistant Professor of Comparative Literature and Coordinator of the Chinese Program, Pennsylvania State University, is a specialist in critical theory, Chinese-language theatre, and Shakespeare. He has published in *Asian Theatre Journal*, *Comparative Literature Studies*, and other journals.

Julie A. Iezzi, Associate Professor of Theatre, University of Hawaii at Manoa, is a Japanese theatre specialist with a particular interest in voice and music. She has translated *kabuki* and *kyôgen* for both page and stage, and three of her *kabuki* translations appear in the *Kabuki Plays on Stage* series (2002–2004).

Solehah Ishak is Professor of Malay theatre, National University of Malaysia. Among her publications are *Histrionics of Development* (1987), *Siddhartha* (2004), and *Staging Eastern Voices* (2005). A former editor of *Malay Literature*, she has translated numerous Malay plays into English, and presented papers on Malay theatre locally and internationally.

David Jortner, Visiting Assistant Professor of Theatre, Allegheny College, is a specialist in modern Japanese and American theatre. He has written several articles on the Japanese stage and is the co-editor, with Keiko McDonald and Kevin Wetmore, of *Modern Japanese Theater* (2006).

Ayako Kano is Associate Professor in the Department of East Asian Languages and Civilizations at the University of Pennsylvania. She specializes in modern Japanese theatre and gender studies. Her publications include *Acting Like a Woman in Modern Japan: Theater, Gender, and Nationalism* (2001).

Andrew Killick, Senior Lecturer in Ethnomusicology at the University of Sheffield, is a specialist in Korean music and theatre. He has written a forthcoming book on *ch'anggŭk* and published articles in *Asian Theatre Journal*, *Asian Music*, *Ethnomusicology*, *Korean Studies*, and *Garland Encyclopedia of World Music*.

Ah-Jeong Kim, Professor of Theatre, California State University, Northridge, is a specialist in Korean theatre. She has published articles in both Korea and the West. She coauthored *The Metacultural Theater of Oh T'ae-sok* (1999) and wrote *Shamans in Contemporary Korean Theatre* (2006).

Alyssa S. Kim, Lecturer of English, Hongik University, works as a translator of Korean plays and is the cotranslator of *Allegory of Survival: The Theater of Kang-Baek Lee* (2006). She also has translated into Korean Ariel Dorfman's *The Other Side* and *Widows*, and Ronald Harwood's *The Dresser*.

Yun-Cheol Kim is Professor of Theatre at the Korean National University of the Arts, past president of the Korean Association of Theatre Critics, and current vice president of the International Association of Theatre Critics. He has authored hundreds of theatre reviews and numerous articles and books in Korean and English.

Laurence Richard Kominz is Professor of Japanese, Portland State University. A performer of *kyôgen* and Japanese dance, he also published *The Stars Who Created Kabuki: Their Lives, Loves, and Legacy* (1997), *Avatars of Vengeance: Japanese Drama and the Soga Literary Tradition* (1995), and *Mishima on Stage: The Black Lizard and Other Plays* (2007).

Hyung-Jin Lee, Assistant Professor of English and Translation Studies at Sookmyung Women's University, Seoul, Korea, has translated the plays of Tae-Sok Oh and Kang-Baek Lee and written scholarly articles about translating contemporary Korean plays. He is the author of *Theatre of Kang-Baek Lee* (2006).

Siyuan Liu, PhD candidate of Theatre Arts at the University of Pittsburgh, is a researcher on modern Chinese theatre. He has contributed entries to *The Oxford Encyclopedia of*

Theatre and Performance (2003), published papers in *Asian Theatre Journal* and *Text and Presentation*, and staged productions in China and the United States.

Lawrence McCrea is Preceptor in Sanskrit, Department of Sanskrit and Indian Studies, Harvard University. He specializes in the study of Sanskrit poetry, poetics, and language theory and is the author of *The Teleology of Poetics in Medieval Kashmir* (forthcoming).

Arya Madhavan is a PhD candidate studying the training and acting techniques of *kutiyattam* at the University of Wales, Aberystwyth. She is also a Research Fellow of the AHRB Centre for Cross-cultural Music and Dance, University of Surrey.

Pawit Mahasarinand, Lecturer of Dramatic Arts, Chulalongkorn University, has translated ten European and American plays for production. A Fulbrighter and an Asian Cultural Council fellow, he finished his graduate studies in the United States. His theatre and dance reviews are published in *The Nation* and *Bizweek* newspapers, and *DDT* and *Lips* magazines.

David V. Mason, Assistant Professor of Theatre, Rhodes College, is a specialist in traditional Indian theatre. He has undertaken several research projects in India, most recently as a Fulbright-Hays fellow. He has published on classical Sanskrit drama and *raslila*.

Terry E. Miller, Professor Emeritus of Ethnomusicology at Kent State University, is a specialist in the music and theatre of mainland Southeast Asia. Among his publications are two books on Thailand's music as well as major contributions to *The Garland Encyclopedia of World Music*, Vol. 4, *Southeast Asia*, which he also co-edited.

Debjani Ray Moulik, Guest Lecturer of English, Vijaygarh Jyotish Ray College, Kolkata (Calcutta), recently completed her M.Phil on nineteenth-century Bengali theatre from the University of Calcutta.

Nancy Nanney, chair of the Humanities Division, West Virginia University at Parkersburg, is the author of *An Analysis of Modern Malay Drama* (1992). She has written and spoken widely on Malaysian theatre and taught in Malaysia from 1987 to 1998.

Jonathan Noble, Visiting Assistant Professor, University of Notre Dame, specializes in Chinese modern theatre and film. He has published numerous scholarly writings on contemporary Chinese culture, translated over twenty plays and film screenplays into English, and is a member of the National Committee on U.S.-China Relations' Public Intellectual Program.

Judith Nordby is head of Mongolian Studies, Department of East Asian Studies, University of Leeds, England, where she teaches Mongolian language, history, and contemporary affairs. She writes regularly on the contemporary politics, economy, and culture of Mongolia. She compiled the *Mongolia* (1993) volume in the World Bibliographical Series.

Laura Noszlopy, independent scholar, writer, and editor, is a specialist in the anthropology of modern Indonesia. She has a PhD in sociocultural anthropology and has written on cultural politics, socioreligious change, performance, and urban youth culture.

Claire Pamment, a freelance dramaturg and director, is currently writing a PhD thesis on Pakistani theatre. She was artistic director of *The Sunay'ha Festival* in London (2005) and has been associated with The British Council, Escape Artists, Menagerie Theatre, Kali Theatre Company, Soho Theatre, Birmingham Rep, Context Theatre, and RADA.

Kirstin Pauka is Professor of Asian Theatre at the University of Hawaii. She served as editor for Southeast Asia for the *Oxford Encyclopedia of Theatre and Performance*, authored *Theater and Martial Arts in West Sumatra: Randai and Silek of the Minangkabau* (1998), and directed the first English-language *randai* productions in the United States.

Robert Petersen is Assistant Professor of Theatre and Art, Eastern Illinois University. He has received a Fulbright scholarship and has published on traditional and modern theatre in India and Southeast Asia.

William Peterson, Senior Lecturer in Drama and Theatre Studies at Monash University, Melbourne, Australia, has written extensively on theatre and politics in Singapore, New Zealand, and the Philippines. He is the author of *Theatre and the Politics of Culture in Contemporary Singapore* (2001).

M. Cody Poulton is chair of Pacific and Asian Studies, University of Victoria, Canada. Publications include *Spirits of Another Sort: The Plays of Izumi Kyôka* (2001), twenty entries for *The Oxford Encyclopedia of Theatre and Performance* (2003), and numerous translations of both *kabuki* and modern Japanese drama.

Brian Powell, Emeritus Professor of Oxford University, focuses on Japanese theatre since the late nineteenth century. He is the author of *Japan's Modern Theatre: A Century of Continuity and Change* (2002) and *Kabuki in Modern Japan: Mayama Seika and His Plays* (1990). His translations include plays by Mayama Seika and Kinoshita Junji.

Eric C. Rath, Associate Professor of History, University of Kansas, is a specialist in premodern Japanese history, the performing arts, especially *nô*, and food ways. His publications include *The Ethos of Noh: Actors and Their Art* (2004).

Jerry C. Respeto, Assistant Professor, Department of Filipino, School of Humanities, Ateneo de Manila University, specializes in Philippine theatre and the translation of foreign plays into Filipino. He has translated/adapted ten full-length plays, which have been produced by major Filipino theatre companies.

Katherine Saltzman-Li is Associate Professor of Japanese Literature and Comparative Literature, University of California, Santa Barbara. She has published articles on and translations of *kabuki* and is the author of *Creating Kabuki Plays: Context for Kezairoku* (Forthcoming).

Jonah Salz teaches theatre at Ryukoku University, Kyoto. He has translated *kyôgen* and plays by Yukio Mishima and Issey Ogata, and written on Samuel Beckett, intercultural theatre, and translating comedy. He directs the Noho Theatre Group, and has co-edited a *kyôgen* issue of *Asian Theatre Journal*.

William S. Sax, Professor and head of Ethnology, South Asia Institute, University of Heidelberg, is a specialist in South Asian theatre, ritual, and healing. He has published numerous books and articles on the topic, including *Dancing the Self: Personhood and Performance in the Pandav Lila of Garhwal* (2002).

Toni Shapiro-Phim is a cultural anthropologist with a specialization in Cambodian performing arts. Coauthor of *Dance in Cambodia* (1999) and author of numerous articles, she has taught dance ethnology and documentation at Cambodia's Royal University of Fine Arts and elsewhere.

Vibha Sharma is a Lecturer in English, Department of English, Aligarh Muslim University Aligarh, India. She specializes in literary theory (psychoanalysis) and modern drama and has published several papers on theatre, Indian literature, and literary theory. She runs a Hindi theatre working group based at Aligarh.

Patricia Sieber is Associate Professor of East Asian Languages and Literatures, Ohio State University. She is the author of *Theaters of Desire: Authors, Readers, and the Reproduction of Early Chinese Song-Drama, 1300–2000* (2003) as well as articles on various aspects of the reception history of Chinese performance-related genres.

Neluka Silva is Senior Lecturer and former head of the Department of English, University of Colombo, Sri Lanka. She has published on theatre and cultural production in South Asia, and has been involved as an actress and director in Sri Lanka's English theatre for the past twenty years.

Eka D. Sitorus is the founder and head of Sakti Acting Studio in Jakarta, Indonesia. Formerly, he was head of the Theatre Department at Jakarta School of the Arts (Institute Kesenian Jakarta), and has worked extensively as a director and acting teacher for film and theatre in Indonesia.

Carol Fisher Sorgenfrei is Professor of Theatre at the University of California at Los Angeles. An authority on postwar Japanese theatre, playwright, translator, and director, she authored *Unspeakable Acts: The Avant-Garde Theatre of Terayama Shûji and Postwar Japan* (2006) and is one of four coauthors of *Theatre Histories: An Introduction* (2006).

Yeon-Ho Suh, Emeritus Professor of Korean Literature, Korea University, is a scholar of traditional as well as contemporary Korean theatre. He co-edited *Korean Modern Playwrights* (1998) and published around thirty critical works including *Korean Mask Dance Theatre* (2002) and *Korean Theatre-Modern* (2003).

Bruce M. Sullivan, Professor of Religious Studies at Northern Arizona University, is a specialist in Hinduism, Indian drama, and Sanskrit literature. He has published four books, including two on *kutiyattam* with N. P. Unni: *The Sun God's Daughter and King Samvarana* (1995) and *The Wedding of Arjuna and Subhadra* (2001).

Ping Sun, choreographer and dance teacher, is on the faculty of Melbourne Girl's College and has taught at the Victorian College of the Arts, Australia. Winner of the prestigious Yangcheng International Dance Championship (1988), he wrote, directed, produced, and performed in such groundbreaking pieces as *Journey of the Northern Tiger* (1998).

John D. Swain, independent scholar and translator, received his PhD from UCLA in 2004. His research interests are in theatre by marginalized groups in Japan, especially the Korean diaspora in Japan, and theatre interactions among Japan, Korea, and Pacific Rim nations. His translations appear in the *Half Century of Japanese Theater* series and elsewhere.

Catherine Swatek, Associate Professor in the Department of Asian Studies, University of British Columbia, is the author of *Peony Pavilion Onstage: Four Centuries in the Career of a Chinese Drama* (2002). Her interests are focused on vernacular literature of the Ming and Qing dynasties, especially *xiqu*.

Ma Thanegi, freelance writer, has written many articles on Burmese (Myanmar) culture and arts. Among her eight books is *The Illusion of Life: Burmese Marionettes* (1994). She is contributing editor of the *Myanmar Times*, an English-language weekly, and *Enchanting Myanmar*, a cultural magazine.

Maung Maung Thein is a poet (under the name Nyein Way), performance artist, translator, and the principal of the Q.E.L.C. Language Center, Yangon. He has published a book on education and a volume of poetry, and has engaged in collaborative performances with artists from different countries, both inside and outside Burma (Myanmar).

Barbara E. Thornbury is Professor of Japanese in the Department of Critical Languages at Temple University. She has published widely on Japanese theatre, including *The Folk Performing Arts: Traditional Theatre in Contemporary Japan* (1997).

Nicanor G. Tiongson, Professor at the University of the Philippines Film Institute, specializes in Philippine theatre and cinema. He has published twenty-four books, including *Sinakulo* (1999) and *Komedya* (1999). He also edited the ten-volume CCP *Encyclopedia of Philippine Art* and the twenty-eight Tuklas Sining monographs and videos on Philippine arts.

Hardy Tsoi is arts administrator and manager of Sir Run Run Shaw Hall at the Chinese University of Hong Kong, where he is also coordinator of the Hong Kong Drama Program. A director, playwright, teacher, and artistic director of the TNT Theatre, he was a member of the Hong Kong Arts Development Council (2000–2004).

Ena Herni Wasli is a tutor in the Department of Malay Literature, University of Brunei Darussalam. She teaches Malay drama and scriptwriting and is studying for her master's in theatre in Australia. She is a practicing director, writer, and designer.

Kevin J. Wetmore, Jr., Assistant Professor of Theatre, Loyola Marymount University, Los Angeles, is a specialist in modern Japanese theatre. He co-edited *Modern Japanese Theatre and Performance* (2006) and has authored numerous articles on Japanese performance and drama.

Elizabeth Wichmann-Walczak, Professor and director of Asian Theatre, University of Hawaii, has published on *jingju* aesthetics, creative authority, and innovation, and has translated and directed *jingju* plays performed in Hawaii and China. The author of *Listening to Theatre: The Aural Dimension of Beijing Opera* (1991), she has won national Chinese awards for research, creation, and performance.

Evan Winet, Assistant Professor of Theatre, Macalester College, is a scholar, director, and mask-maker. He has published articles and book chapters on modern Indonesian theatre, and translated several Indonesian plays. He is writing a book, *This Play Is Not Set in Indonesia: Masks of Postcolonial Theater*.

Ralph Yarrow, Professor of Drama, UEA, Norwich, UK, teaches, directs, performs, and leads workshops across many forms of theatre including Indian, South African, European, and community/development practice. Publications include *Improvisation in Drama* (1990), *Consciousness, Literature and Theatre* (1997), and *Indian Theatre: Theatre of Origin, Theatre of Freedom* (2001).

Phillip Zarrilli, Professor of Performance Practice at the University of Exeter, UK, is a specialist in South Asian performance, theories, and practices of acting and embodiment, and performance studies. His books include *Kathakali Dance-Drama* (2000), *When the Body Becomes All Eyes* (1998), and *The Psychophysical Actor at Work* (forthcoming).

Nan Zhang, lighting designer and lecturer, teaches lighting design as well as thematic seminars at Smith College. She has designed numerous educational and professional productions in both the United States and China, including *Orpheus Descending* (Ohio State University, 2000) and *Hong Haitan* (Liaoning Opera, 2004).

Guohe Zheng is Associate Professor of Japanese at Ball State University. His publications include *A Study of Shiba Shirô and His Political Novel* Kajin no kigû (in Chinese, 2000) and an article on the *shingeki* classic *A Woman's Life* (Onna no isshô).